Everyday Finance: Economics, Personal Money Management, and Entrepreneurship

Everyday Finance: Economics, Personal Money Management, and Entrepreneurship

VOLUME 1

GALE
CENGAGE Learning™

Detroit • New York • San Francisco • New Haven, Conn • Waterville, Maine • London

GALE
CENGAGE Learning™

Everyday Finance: Economics, Personal Money Management, and Entrepreneurship
Thomas Riggs, Editor

Product Manager: Carol Nagel

Project Editor: Mary Rose Bonk

Rights Acquisition and Management: Margaret Chamberlain-Gaston, Jacqueline Key, and Kelly A. Quin

Composition: Evi Abou-El-Seoud

Manufacturing: Rita Wimberley

Imaging: Lezlie Light

Product Design: Jennifer Wahi

For product information and technology assistance, contact us at **Gale Customer Support, 1-800-877-4253.**
For permission to use material from this text or product, submit all requests online at **www.cengage.com/permissions.**
Further permissions questions can be emailed to **permissionrequest@cengage.com**

While every effort has been made to ensure the reliability of the information presented in this publication, Gale, a part of Cengage Learning, does not guarantee the accuracy of the data contained herein. Gale accepts no payment for listing; and inclusion in the publication of any organization, agency, institution, publication, service, or individual does not imply endorsement of the editors or publisher. Errors brought to the attention of the publisher and verified to the satisfaction of the publisher will be corrected in future editions.

Library of Congress Cataloging-in-Publication Data

Everyday finance : economics, personal money management, and entrepreneurship / editor, Thomas Riggs; project editor, Mary Rose Bonk.
    p. cm.
    Includes bibliographical references and index.
    ISBN 978-1-4144-1049-4 (set) – ISBN 978-1-4144-1123-1 (vol. 1) – ISBN 978-1-4144-1124-8 (vol. 2)
    1. Economics. 2. Finance, Personal. 3. Entrepreneurship. 4. Riggs, Thomas, 1963- 5. Bonk, Mary, 1960-

HB171.E86 2008
332.024–dc22   2007035070

Gale
27500 Drake Rd.
Farmington Hills, MI, 48331-3535

ISBN-13: 978-1-4144-1049-4 (set)   ISBN-10: 1-4144-1049-2 (set)
ISBN-13: 978-1-4144-1123-1 (vol. 1)   ISBN-10: 1-4144-1123-5 (vol. 1)
ISBN-13: 978-1-4144-1124-8 (vol. 2)   ISBN-10: 1-4144-1124-3 (vol. 2)

This title is also available as an e-book.
ISBN-13: 978-1-4144-2929-8 ISBN-10: 1-4144-2929-0
Contact your Gale sales representative for ordering information.

Printed in the United States of America
2 3 4 5 6 7 11 10 09

Contents

Supply and Demand: The Relationship between Businesses and Consumers

Competition between Businesses

What Motivates Businesses

Labor: The People Working in the Economy

How Governments Raise Money

Who Oversees the Economy: Government Organizations

VOLUME 2

Personal Money Management: Buying, Borrowing, Saving, and Insuring

Entrepreneurship: The World of Business

Reader's Guide

Economics has suffered a dismal and dry reputation. Supply and demand, production possibility curve, marginal utility, income and substitution effects. These are not the most alluring terms, which is unfortunate, because they describe a curious and important topic: how people behave in a world of possibilities. As such, economics helps to explain a significant part of our lives, how we make choices and manage our daily affairs with the aid of two everyday notions, money and prices.

The purpose of this book—*Everyday Finance: Economics, Personal Money Management, and Entrepreneurship*—is to introduce the field of economics, as well as its related topics personal money management and entrepreneurship, in a simple, meaningful way. It is to show that even obscure topics are based on easy-to-understand ideas and that economics, personal money management, and entrepreneurship are related to our ordinary, everyday lives. It is for this reason we chose the title *Everyday Finance*. The word *finance*, which has several meanings, is used here to describe anything related to money and the economy. *Everyday Finance* was motivated by the growing awareness in the United States that economic literacy is essential for functioning in the modern world.

To explain the world of money, *Everyday Finance* features 300 articles, organized by subject into three major sections. The first, How the Economy Works, contains essays within several broad areas: macroeconomics, describing the economy as a whole; microeconomics, focusing on individual parts or forces in the economy; international trade, or buying and selling between countries; and the government's role in the economy. Some essays relate to more than one area and were placed where they would be most useful to a person not familiar with economics.

After the first section introduces the basic ideas of economics, the second and third sections explain how people are personally involved in the economy, either as consumers or business owners. The second section, Personal Money Management, is broken down into four typical consumer roles: buying, borrowing, saving, and insuring. The third section, Entrepreneurship, discusses running a business, attracting customers, managing money, working with employees, and business ethics and the law.

Every essay in *Everyday Finance* has five parts:

1. **What It Means,** introducing the essay topic and defining any unfamiliar terms.

2. **When Did It Begin,** giving historical information helpful in understanding the subject and its significance.

3. **More Detailed Information,** explaining the topic more fully and discussing related issues.

4. **Recent Trends,** providing a glimpse into the role of the subject in the present-day economy.

5. Sidebar box, often illustrating the topic with an example or anecdote.

Everyday Finance also includes biographies on seven influential economists throughout history. The book has over 220 images, as well as nearly 50 tables, charts, and graphs; a glossary of financial terms; a further reading section; and a subject index, listing all the topics featured in the book.

Acknowledgments

This project was a collaboration between the editorial staff, writers experienced in producing educational materials, and professionals involved in teaching economics and in the development of economics curriculum. The essays topics were selected with the help of our three distinguished advisers: Robert F. Duvall, president and chief executive officer, National Council on Economic Education; Peter F. Bell, executive director, New York State Council on Economic Education; and Sue Weaver, mentor teacher, Foundation for Teaching Economics. We are grateful for their advice and support. We would also like to express our appreciation to Jeff Bookwalter, professor of economics, University of Montana, for his suggestions on the book's organization, for reviewing the essays for accuracy, and for answering our many questions big and small.

Essential to the project were the essay writers: Mark Lane, Joseph Campana, Erin Brown, Stephen Meyer, Jonathan Kolstad, and Martha Sutro. Experienced teachers and writers of educational text, they deserve praise for their hard work in accomplishing the project's main goal: presenting abstract subjects in simple, accessible prose. The editing of the text was overseen by Anne Healey; assisting her in the editing were Lee Esbenshade, Laura Gabler, Chuck Cegielski, and Catherine Okelman-Anderson. Mariko Fujinaka was involved from the very beginning of the project, working with the advisers and organizing day-to-day tasks. Anne Healey, Lee Esbenshade, and Mariko Fujinaka also contributed text. Erin Brown, as well as Stephen Meyer and Anne Healey, helped with the auxiliary parts of the book, such as the photo selection, the captions, sources for further reading, and the glossary. Martin White wrote the index.

Finally, many thanks must be given to Mary Bonk, the in-house editor at Gale, who oversaw the book's production and kept the project on schedule; Carol Nagel, involved in the development of the book's idea; and Ellen McGeagh, who was responsible for other in-house tasks.

Thomas Riggs
Editor

Comments

Although great effort has gone into this project, we would appreciate any suggestions for future editions of *Everyday Finance*. Please send comments to the following address.

Editor, *Everyday Finance: Economics, Personal Money Management, and Entrepreneurship*
Cengage Gale
27500 Drake Road
Farmington Hills, Michigan 48331

CETERIS PARIBUS. A Latin phrase that translates as "all other things being equal"; economists often use it to indicate that their analysis of a certain situation is based on the assumption that all other things besides the factors under consideration will remain constant.

CHANNEL OF DISTRIBUTION. The path a product takes as it moves from producer to end user (the consumer).

CHAPTER 11. A type of bankruptcy defined by the U.S. Bankruptcy Code; it allows a company to remain in business while the court decides how best to reorganize its debts.

CHARACTER LOAN. A loan based on the personal reputation, as well as credit rating, of the borrower.

CHARGE CARD. A kind of electronic-payment card that enables its holder to make purchases on short-term credit granted by the issuer of the card. Unlike a credit card, a charge card offers nonrevolving credit, meaning that the balance must be paid off in full each month.

CHARITY. An organization or fund that is established with the sole purpose of providing help or relief to people in need.

CHARTER. In business, a formal document legally establishing a company or organization as a corporation. Also called articles of incorporation.

CHECK. A paper form used to transfer money out of a bank account.

CHECK-CASHING ORGANIZATION. *see* check-cashing store.

CHECK-CASHING STORE. A business that cashes personal, payroll, and government checks for a fee. Also called a check-cashing organization.

CHECKING ACCOUNT. An account that an individual establishes at a financial institution that enables him or her to use forms called checks to transfer a specified amount of money to designated individuals or organizations.

CIRCULAR FLOW OF ECONOMIC ACTIVITY. An economic model illustrating the interaction between businesses and households in an economy, showing money and products moving in a circular fashion between the two.

CLAIM. A customer's formal request for reimbursement from an insurance company.

CLASS-ACTION LAWSUIT. A lawsuit that represents a large number of plaintiffs.

CLASSICAL ECONOMICS. The ideas of the first wave of modern economists, whose work spanned the late eighteenth century and much of the nineteenth century.

CLOSING COSTS. Fees for the various transactions that occur when a person buying a house has the property legally transferred to his or her name.

COBRA (CONSOLIDATED OMNIBUS BUDGET RECONCILIATION ACT). A U.S. federal law requiring group health-insurance plans sponsored by employers with 20 or more employees to offer continued health-insurance coverage to workers after they leave their jobs.

COLA. *see* Cost-of-Living Adjustment.

COLLATERAL. Any item or items of value that someone offers as proof of his ability to repay a loan, with the understanding that it will be forfeited to the lender if the loan cannot be repaid.

COLLECTION AGENCY. A business that specializes in collecting money owed to other companies.

COLLECTIVE BARGAINING AGREEMENT. An official agreement between a labor union and management regarding the specific terms of employment.

COLLISION INSURANCE. A form of car insurance that covers the policyholder's vehicle in the event of an accident in which he or she is determined to be at fault.

COLONIALISM. The practice by which nations create settlements, or colonies, in poorer countries for the purpose of exploiting their natural resources and labor force.

COMMAND ECONOMY. *see* planned economy.

COMMERCIAL BANK. A type of bank that has traditionally focused on short-term accounts and issuing business loans; can also mean a normal bank (as opposed to an investment bank).

COMMODITIES. Large amounts of bulk goods, such as crude oil, metals, sugar, coffee, and wheat, that investors buy and sell through agencies such as the New York Mercantile Exchange.

COMMON STOCK. The most common form of ownership in a company; its holders have the right to vote directly on matters related to the functioning of the company and receive dividends (shares in the company's profits) after the holders of preferred stock are paid.

COMMUNISM. A system in which the government controls the economy.

COMPARATIVE ADVANTAGE. An economic theory stating that two countries will maximize their profits by specializing and trading with each other, even if one

BUREAU OF COMPETITION (BOC). The antitrust division of the Federal Trade Commission; its mission is to protect healthy competition in the marketplace.

BUREAU OF CONSUMER PROTECTION (BCP). A division of the Federal Trade Commission dedicated to protecting consumers against unfair or deceptive business practices.

BUREAU OF ECONOMIC ANALYSIS (BEA). A division of the U.S. Department of Commerce that collects, analyzes, and publishes statistics about the American economy.

BUREAU OF LABOR STATISTICS (BLS). A division of the U.S. Department of Labor that collects and analyzes information about the American workforce and economy.

BUSINESS CONTRACT. Written agreements concerning specific aspects of a commercial transaction.

BUSINESS CYCLE. A cyclical pattern, common to all capitalist economies, of periods of economic expansion followed by periods of economic contraction.

BUSINESS ETHICS. The application of moral considerations to business practices.

BUSINESS FINANCING. The activity of funding the many aspects of a business, including starting a business, running it, or expanding it.

BUSINESS PLAN. A document that describes what a business is, what strategies it will use to accomplish its financial goals, and how it expects to do business as it grows, usually planning for several years into the future.

BUSINESS TAX. A tax that the government requires a business to pay.

C

CORPORATION. A traditional for-profit corporation, so called because it is taxed under Subchapter C of the United States tax code. The corporation, as a single entity, pays taxes on its profits, and then its individual stockholders are taxed on the dividends (portions of profit) they receive.

CAPITAL. Money, buildings, equipment, and other items needed to start, maintain, or expand a business.

CAPITAL ACCOUNT. *see* financial account.

CAPITAL ASSETS. A financial term that refers to everything a person owns for both personal use and investment, such as homes, cars, jewelry, computers, household furnishings, and stocks and bonds (investments).

CAPITAL GAIN. A term used in the filing of income taxes, referring to the profit made when the value of a capital asset increases from its original purchase price; such gains are taxed at a different rate from regular income.

CAPITAL LOSS. A term used in assessing income taxes that refers to the amount of money lost when the value of a capital asset decreases from its original purchase price.

CAPITALISM. An economic system in which businesses are owned by private individuals who are allowed to compete freely in the pursuit of profits.

CAR INSURANCE. A contract between an insurance company and the owner of a vehicle that protects the vehicle's owner (or the person who leases the vehicle) from financial losses that result from car accidents.

CARTEL. An association of companies or nations that collaborate to control the market for a product by fixing prices, setting production quotas, and regulating market share.

CASH. The banknotes (bills) and coins used as money and accepted as legal tender (currency) in a society.

CASH A CHECK. To receive the funds specified on a check.

CASH COST. An amount of money that a business pays out to someone.

CASH FLOW. The movement of ready money, or cash, into and out of a company over a specified period of time.

CASHIER'S CHECK. A type of prepaid check issued by a bank that a customer may purchase in a specific amount in order to make a payment to a third party. Also referred to as a bank check, bank draft, or treasurer's check.

CD. *see* certificate of deposit.

CENTRAL BANK. A government entity responsible for setting a country's monetary policy.

CERTIFICATE OF DEPOSIT (CD). An investment offered by banks, savings and loan associations, and credit unions. The customer deposits money with the institution and agrees not to make any withdrawals on the money for a fixed amount of time; in exchange the customer earns interest on the deposit, called the maturity period.

CERTIFIED PUBLIC ACCOUNTANT (CPA). A public accountant (that is, one who provides information to members of the public rather than working within a single company) licensed by a U.S. state to practice there.

BAIT AND SWITCH. A deceptive marketing tactic in which a retail business advertises a bargain to lure a customer into its store and then attempts to convince the customer to buy a more expensive product instead.

BALANCE. An amount of money remaining in a checking account; or an outstanding amount owed on a bill.

BALANCE OF PAYMENTS (BOP). A financial statement that summarizes a country's international economic purchases and sales. It shows all of the international money movements, called flows, in and out of the country in a certain time period.

BALANCE OF TRADE. The difference in value, over a period of time, between a country's imports and exports.

BALANCE SHEET. A document that details a company's assets (possessions) and liabilities (debts).

BANK. An institution that holds people's money for safekeeping and lends money to individuals and businesses for a variety of reasons.

BANK RESERVES. The money that a bank keeps on hand, either in its own vaults or in an account with a central bank.

BANKRUPT. The state of being unable to pay debts, which can lead to the seizure of property and other valuable resources.

BANKRUPTCY. A process by which a debtor who is deemed unable to pay off all his or her debts seeks legal protection from his or her creditors.

BARRIERS TO ENTRY. The obstacles that discourage and sometimes prevent new companies from entering an area of business.

BARTER. To exchange goods and services directly for other goods and services.

BBB. *see* Better Business Bureau.

BEA. *see* Bureau of Economic Analysis.

BEAR MARKET. A period during which stock prices generally decrease.

BENEFICIARY. A person or entity who receives benefits under the terms of a contract (such as an insurance policy or a will).

BENEFIT PACKAGE. The terms of an employment contract, including insurance coverage and other benefits.

BENEFITS. *see* employee benefits.

BETTER BUSINESS BUREAU (BBB). A national organization that protects consumers from unethical business practices.

BILL. A printed request for money that is owed for a particular product or service.

BLACK MARKET. The illegal buying and selling of goods and services.

BLACKLIST. To add someone to a list of people whom employers agree not to hire.

BLS. *see* Bureau of Labor Statistics.

BLUE CHIP. A stock that is expensive because it represents ownership in the world's largest and most stable corporations; also, a term used to refer to such companies; so named because of the color of high-value poker chips.

BLUE-COLLAR WORKERS. People who perform manual or physical labor, often for an hourly wage.

BOARD OF DIRECTORS. A group of people who the shareholders of a public company have elected to represent them in decisions regarding the operation of the company.

BOND. A type of investment that represents money loaned to a government or corporation, in exchange for which the borrowing government or company makes periodic payments of interest to the bond holder.

BOUNCED CHECK. A check that the recipient cannot cash because the person who wrote the check does not have sufficient funds in his or her bank account.

BRAND. A symbol (such as an image, a logo, or a name) that represents a product or service and that distinguishes the product or service from others in the marketplace.

BRAND RECOGNITION. The extent to which consumers recognize a company's brand among its competitors.

BROKER. A person who is authorized to make trades on a given stock exchange.

BROKERAGE FIRM. A company that facilitates trades between buyers and sellers on the stock market.

BUBBLE. A period of unsustainable economic growth (usually in the stock market or in real estate) fueled by excess optimism on the part of companies and investors.

BUDGET DEFICIT. The imbalance created when a country spends more money than it takes in.

BUDGETING. The practice of identifying income and desired expenditures and then creating a plan for spending.

BULL MARKET. A period of sustained stock-price increases during which investors make money rapidly.

Glossary

This glossary provides brief definitions of terms commonly used in economics, personal money management, and entrepreneurship.

A

ABSOLUTE ADVANTAGE. A term used in economics to describe the ability of one country to produce a specific good more efficiently than a second country can.

ACCOUNTANT. A person whose job is to manage the financial records of an organization and to prepare various kinds of financial reports.

ACCOUNTING. The recording and disclosure of a company's financial dealings.

ACQUISITION. The process of one company overtaking or absorbing another company.

ADVERTISING. All the methods that organizations use to communicate a message to potential customers. In most cases the message informs people about an organization's product or service and urges those people to purchase it.

AGGREGATE BEHAVIOR. The total results of individual actions in an economy.

AGGREGATE DEMAND. The amount of final products that all buyers in an economy demand (are willing and able to buy) at a given average price.

AGGREGATE EXPENDITURES. The total amount spent on goods and services in a nation's economy.

AGGREGATE SUPPLY. The total quantity of all final products an economy's sellers are willing to supply at a given price level.

AMERICAN STOCK EXCHANGE (AMEX). The third-largest U.S. stock exchange; it is located in New York City.

AMERICANS WITH DISABILITIES ACT. A U.S. federal law that prohibits workplace discrimination against people with disabilities.

AMEX. *see* American Stock Exchange.

ANNUAL PERCENTAGE RATE (APR). The interest rate on a loan, expressed as the percentage charged by the lender each year on the amount of a loan.

ANNUAL REPORT. A report issued by a company and covering the company's activities for the entire year, including financial statements and other documents.

ANTITRUST LEGISLATION. A set of laws that protect consumers and society by ensuring that businesses do not unfairly dominate their individual industries (a trust is a group of companies that attempts to do this).

APPRECIATION. An increase in value.

APR. *see* annual percentage rate.

ASSETS. All items of value (including investments) owned by a person or organization.

ATM. Automated teller machine; an electronic machine at which a bank customer can withdraw cash and make deposits by inserting a plastic card.

B

BACK TAXES. Taxes from a past taxation period that have not been paid.

has the ability to produce all goods more efficiently than the other.

COMPLEMENTARY GOOD. A product that is often bought in combination with, or consumed at the same time as, another good.

COMPREHENSIVE INSURANCE. A type of car insurance that covers damages to the policyholder's vehicle caused by incidents that are not considered to be collisions.

CONSOLIDATE. To combine a number of debts into one larger loan.

CONSUMER BILL OF RIGHTS. A set of U.S. regulations that protect consumers from hazards in the products they purchase and from misleading information about products. These regulations also provide support for consumers in instances when a product fails, breaks, or is faulty.

CONSUMER CREDIT PROTECTION ACT (CCPA). A consumer-protection law in the United States aimed at regulating the consumer credit industry.

CONSUMER PRICE INDEX (CPI). An index compiled by the Bureau of Labor Statistics that tracks the changing price of basic goods and services in the United States.

CONSUMER PRODUCT SAFETY COMMISSION (CPSC). An independent agency of the U.S. government whose mission is to protect the American public from unreasonable or significant risks of injury or death associated with consumer products.

CONSUMER SOVEREIGNTY. A term used by economists who argue that consumers dictate what goods and services are available in the market because producers respond to consumer buying patterns.

CONSUMER SURPLUS. The amount of money left over when a consumer is charged less for a good than he or she is willing to pay.

CONSUMPTION. In economics, a term that refers to how much money all consumers are spending on goods and services.

CO-PAYMENT. A portion of each medical or dental expense for which an insured patient is responsible.

COPYRIGHT. The legal right of an artist or writer to control the reproduction, distribution, display, performance, or circulation of his or her work.

CORE COMPETENCE. The centering of a business around the strengths that could give it an advantage over its competitors.

CORPORATE TAX REPORTING. The process by which corporations report their financial information to state and federal tax agencies.

CORPORATION. A kind of company that sells stocks (certificates that represent shares of ownership in the business) and that has a legal identity independent from the people who own or manage it.

COST OF LIVING. The amount of money required to maintain a certain basic level of material comfort from one year to the next.

COST-BENEFIT ANALYSIS. A method of comparing the positive and negative effects of a project, a decision, or another business venture that an organization is considering.

COST-OF-LIVING ADJUSTMENT (COLA). An annual adjustment of wage contracts, retirement benefits, and other payments; it is intended to offset increases in the cost of living.

COSTS OF PRODUCTION. The expenses to which a company is subject as it goes through the process of generating, selling, and delivering goods and services to consumers.

COUPON. The detachable portion of a bond (a type of investment) that the bond holder presents to receive the interest payment; can also mean a bond's interest rate.

CPA. *see* certified public accountant.

CPI. *see* Consumer Price Index.

CPSC. *see* Consumer Product Safety Commission.

CREDIT. In general terms, the capacity to borrow money; also, the maximum amount of money a lender is willing to lend to a customer.

CREDIT BUREAU. A for-profit company that evaluates and ranks the credit, or financial reputation, of individuals. Also called a credit-reporting agency.

CREDIT CARD. An electronic-payment card that allows the cardholder to make purchases on credit and pay for them at a later date.

CREDIT COUNSELING. A process in which a credit-counseling agency helps a debtor (a person in debt) make payments to his creditors (institutions, such as credit card companies and banks, to which a debtor owes money). Credit counseling is aimed at helping people avoid bankruptcy.

CREDIT HISTORY. A person's past borrowing and repayment behavior.

CREDIT INSURANCE. Protects businesses against loss when customers fail to pay the amounts they owe.

CREDIT LIMIT. The maximum amount a cardholder is allowed to charge to his or her card.

CREDIT REPORT. A detailed outline of a person's credit history (produced by a credit bureau) that lenders review to assess how financially responsible he or she is.

CREDIT SCORE. A numerical figure, calculated by a credit bureau based on a person's credit history, that is used to predict the likelihood that the individual will not adhere to the terms of a loan agreement.

CREDIT UNION. A nonprofit, member-owned financial institution that provides some of the same financial services as a bank.

CREDIT-COUNSELING AGENCY. An agency that helps people who owe money make a plan to pay off their debts.

CREDITOR. A person or institution to whom borrowed money is owed.

CREDIT-REPAIR COMPANY. A company that helps consumers get out of debt and restore their financial reputations.

CURRENCY. Bills and coins issued by a government.

CURRENCY EXCHANGE. The conversion of one country's currency to another's.

CURRENT ACCOUNT. The section of a balance-of-payments account that shows the financial transactions of imported and exported goods and services.

CUSTOMER SATISFACTION. A measure of how well a customer's expectations have been met by the product or service provided by a particular company.

CUSTOMER SERVICE. The term for building a relationship with customers and making this relationship a high priority for the business.

D

DAY TRADING. The buying and selling of high-risk stock in the same day.

DEBIT CARD. An electronic-payment card that withdraws funds directly from a personal bank account.

DEBT. Money owed by one person, company, or institution to another person, company, or institution.

DEBT CONSOLIDATION LOAN. One big loan that a borrower takes out in order to pay off a number of smaller debts.

DEBTOR. Anyone who borrows money and agrees to pay it back.

DEBT-TO-INCOME RATIO. The percentage of a consumer's monthly income that goes toward paying off credit card debt, student loans, and other debts.

DEDUCTIBLE. An agreed-upon amount of money that an insured person has to pay before the insurance company makes its contribution.

DEDUCTION. A sum that is deducted from a taxpayer's total, or gross, annual income, thereby reducing the amount of their income that can be taxed.

DEEDS OF PROPERTY. Documents showing proof of ownership of property.

DEFAULT. To fail to repay a loan or to keep to the terms of the loan agreement.

DEFICIT. The amount by which a government or business's expenditures exceed its income.

DEFICIT SPENDING. Government spending using borrowed money.

DEFLATION. A general fall in the prices of goods and services in an economy over an extended period of time; the opposite of inflation.

DEMAND. The amount of a particular good or service that buyers are willing or able to buy over a range of prices.

DENTAL INSURANCE. A plan designed to make dental care more affordable.

DEPARTMENT OF COMMERCE. *see* United States Department of Commerce.

DEPARTMENT OF LABOR. *see* United States Department of Labor.

DEPENDENT. A spouse, children, elderly parent, or other person whom a taxpayer financially supports.

DEPRECIATION. The decline in value of an asset over time.

DEPRECIATION TAX LAWS. Provisions that allow a business to count the depreciation of its aging assets (usually equipment) as a business loss. It subtracts from its taxable income certain amounts that represent the decrease in the value of its equipment, or assets.

DEPRESSION. A particularly long and severe recession (economic crisis).

DEPRESSION. *see* Great Depression.

DEREGULATION. The removal of government restrictions.

DERIVATIVE. A financial product whose value is based on (derived from) the performance of other financial products (one example would be a contract to buy a certain number of shares of a particular stock at a specific future date).

DEVELOPED COUNTRY. A fully modernized country with a high average income per citizen, high quality of life, and skilled labor force. Also referred to as an industrialized country or a First World country.

DEVELOPING COUNTRY. A country characterized by low per capita income, widespread poverty, and an undeveloped economic infrastructure; it typically has an economy based not on industry but on agriculture or extracting natural resources such as metals or coal. Sometimes referred to as a Third World country.

DIRECT DEPOSIT. A method of payment by which an employer deposits paychecks into employees' bank accounts electronically.

DIRECT MAILING. Marketing messages sent directly to consumers via the mail system.

DIRECT MARKETING. A specialized form of marketing in which promotional messages are delivered to a target population of people who have been identified as potential customers.

DISABILITY INSURANCE. An insurance plan that replaces a portion of a person's income when he or she cannot work because of an accident or illness.

DISCOUNT RATE. The interest rate that the Federal Reserve charges member banks to borrow money.

DISINFLATION. A slowdown in the rate of inflation.

DISPOSABLE INCOME. The amount of a person's income remaining after the deduction of taxes.

DISTRIBUTION. The movement of products from manufacturers to sales outlets to customers.

DISTRIBUTION OF INCOME. The way all the money earned in a nation is divided among people of various income levels.

DIVIDENDS. Portions of a company's profit that are distributed to its stockholders on a regular basis; the size of the dividend is calculated by taking the accumulated earnings the company chooses to distribute and dividing that amount by the number of shares held by the shareholder.

DIVISION OF LABOR. A method of producing goods or providing services whereby a job is split into separate, distinct tasks or roles, each of which is performed by one person or group of people. Also called specialization.

DOMESTIC. Based in the home country.

DOT-COM. A business that sells goods and services exclusively on the Internet.

DOUBLE-ENTRY ACCOUNTING. An accounting method in which each transaction is shown as a transfer from a source account (as a debit) to a destination account (as a credit).

DOW JONES INDUSTRIAL AVERAGE. A statistic that conveys the combined stock prices of the 30 top companies in the country; it is the figure most frequently used to measure the performance of the U.S. stock market.

DOWN PAYMENT. A portion of a product's price that is paid at the time of purchase, with the rest to be paid later.

DOWNSIZING. A strategy by which a company reduces its workforce and simplifies its business model in order to run its business more efficiently.

DUOPOLY. A situation in which two companies control a market for a particular good or service.

DURABLE GOODS. Goods that may be used repeatedly for a year or more (for example, wood products and computers).

DUTY. A tax on imports.

E

EARNED INCOME TAX CREDIT (EITC). A tax provision that reduces and in some cases eliminates the income taxes that the working poor pay in the United States, allowing people with low incomes to keep more of their earnings.

E-COMMERCE. The buying and selling of goods over the Internet.

ECONOMIC CONTRACTION. A period during which the economy slows down and fewer goods and services are sold.

ECONOMIC DEVELOPMENT. The transformation of a simple, stagnant national economy into a complex, dynamic one.

ECONOMIC GROWTH. An increase in the total value of goods and services produced by a country's economic system.

ECONOMIC INDICATOR. A statistic that reflects the health of the economy.

ECONOMIC INPUTS. The resources, such as land, raw materials, equipment, and labor, that are used to produce goods and services.

ECONOMIC LEGISLATION. Laws that regulate the affairs of private businesses with the intent of protecting consumers, small businesses, and the overall health of the economy.

ECONOMIC RENT. In modern economics, a term referring to the income generated by an asset over and above its "next best use."

ECONOMIC SHORTAGE. A situation in which sellers do not make enough of a product to satisfy those who want to buy it at a given price.

ECONOMIC SURPLUS. A general term for the monetary gain enjoyed by both producers and consumers in an economic transaction. For producers a surplus occurs when a product is sold for more than the cost of producing it; for consumers a surplus exists when they are able to purchase a product for less money than they would have been willing to pay for it.

ECONOMIES OF SCALE. An economic principle stating that when a company increases its output, its cost per unit will decrease.

EFFICIENCY. In economics, the ratio of the value of the output (goods produced or services performed) to the input (costs of production). A business is considered to be operating at optimal efficiency if it produces the greatest number of goods possible at the lowest possible cost.

ELASTICITY OF DEMAND. The degree to which price changes affect consumers' demand for a particular product; when the consumer reaction is strong, the demand for the product is said to be elastic (flexible), and when it is small, the demand is said to be inelastic (fixed).

ELECTRONIC BANKING. A form of banking in which funds are transferred through an exchange of electronic signals rather than through an exchange of cash, checks, or other types of paper documents.

ELECTRONIC BENEFIT TRANSFER (EBT) CARD. An electronic-payment card used in place of traditional paper food stamps.

ELECTRONIC FUNDS TRANSFER (EFT). Any financial transaction that originates from a telephone, electronic terminal, computer, or magnetic tape.

EMPLOYEE BENEFITS. The compensation an employee receives in addition to an hourly wage or annual salary. Common benefits include health insurance and vacation pay. Also called fringe benefits.

EMPLOYEE TURNOVER. The rate at which workers leave a company and are replaced.

EMPLOYMENT. In economics, the number of people in a country who are employed versus the country's entire labor force.

EMPLOYMENT AGENCY. A company that helps employers find employees in exchange for a fee.

ENTREPRENEUR. An individual who founds, owns, and manages his or her own businesses.

ENTREPRENEURSHIP. The practice of forming a new business or commercial enterprise, often in an industry or sector of the economy with a large capacity for growth.

EQUAL CREDIT OPPORTUNITY ACT. A U.S. law that prohibits credit lenders from discriminating against applicants on the basis of sex, race, age, marital status, religion, or national origin.

EQUAL EMPLOYMENT OPPORTUNITY COMMISSION (EEOC). The U.S. federal agency that investigates situations in which individuals claim they have been subject to discriminatory treatment in matters of employment.

EQUAL OPPORTUNITY. Providing every citizen with an equal chance of obtaining an education and a job and of being treated fairly on the job and in life generally. Most commonly used to refer to a company or organization's hiring and business practices.

EQUITY. The value of a mortgaged property minus the outstanding balance, or what the borrower still owes on the loan.

ERGONOMICS. The science of designing tools, machines, and work environments that allow people to perform tasks comfortably, safely, productively, and efficiently.

ESCROW. Money or property that will be transferred from one party to another but is held by a third party until the conditions of the transfer have been met.

ESTATE. The assets in a person's possession at the time of his or her death.

ESTATE TAX. In the United States, a tax on the right to transfer a deceased person's property to descendents. It is charged as a percentage of the total value of all the property owned by the deceased person.

EXCESS RESERVES. Any money in a bank beyond the amount that it is legally required to have on hand; this money can be used to make loans.

EXCHANGE RATE. The value of one country's currency expressed in terms of another country's currency.

EXCISE TAX. A fee charged by the government on specific goods or services that are purchased by some, but not all, consumers.

EXECUTIVE OFFICERS. The individuals who oversee the operational management of a company.

EXECUTOR. The person assigned the duty of carrying out the instructions contained in a will.

EXPECTED FAMILY CONTRIBUTION (EFC). The dollar amount the government determines that a family can contribute toward its child's expenses for college that year.

EXPENDITURE. An amount of money spent.

EXPENSE ACCOUNT. An allowance of funds allotted to an employee for business-related travel, dining, and entertainment.

EXPENSES. The money that a company spends in the course of doing business.

EXPLICIT COST. A measurement of the money sacrificed through actual payments for a particular economic choice. Compare with implicit cost.

EXPORTS. Goods and services that are produced or manufactured in one country and sent legally across borders for sale in another country.

EXTENDED WARRANTY. A plan that continues the manufacturer's warranty for a longer time period.

EXTERNALITY. A side effect of any market activity (an activity related to the buying and selling of goods and services) that either harms or benefits a third party not involved in that particular activity.

F

FACTORS OF PRODUCTION. In economics, all the resources required to produce goods and services. The three primary factors of production are land (including physical land and any natural resources such as oil or lumber needed in their operations), labor, and capital (money and equipment).

FAFSA. *see* Free Application for Federal Student Aid.

FAIR AND ACCURATE CREDIT TRANSACTIONS ACT. A U.S. law aimed at protecting consumers against identity theft; it stipulates that individuals must be able to obtain a free copy of their credit report from each of the major credit bureaus annually. The act also makes it possible for an individual to place a fraud alert on his or her credit history if he or she suspects that someone has stolen his or her identity.

FAIR CREDIT REPORTING ACT. A U.S. law that ensures the accuracy, privacy, and fairness of consumer credit files by imposing regulations on the credit-reporting industry.

FAIR DEBT COLLECTION PRACTICES ACT. A U.S. law that prohibits abusive, deceptive, and unfair debt-collection tactics.

FDA. *see* Food and Drug Administration.

FDIC. *see* Federal Deposit Insurance Corporation.

FEDERAL DEPOSIT INSURANCE CORPORATION (FDIC). An independent agency of the U.S. government whose mission is to maintain and strengthen public confidence in the American financial system. It does this by insuring (guaranteeing) deposits in banks and thrift institutions (which include savings banks, savings and loan associations, and credit unions) for up to $100,000 per depositor.

FEDERAL FUNDS RATE. The interest rate (fee expressed as a percentage of the loan amount) that banks charge one another to borrow money.

FEDERAL INSURANCE CONTRIBUTIONS ACT (FICA) TAX. *see* Social Security tax.

FEDERAL OPEN MARKET COMMITTEE (FOMC). A committee within the Federal Reserve System that is responsible for deciding whether the U.S. money supply should be increased, decreased, or kept constant, depending on economic conditions at the time.

FEDERAL RESERVE BOARD. The seven-member committee that oversees the Federal Reserve, the central banking system of the United States.

FEDERAL RESERVE SYSTEM. The central bank of the United States, an independent agency of the U.S. government. Often called "the Fed."

FEDERAL TRADE COMMISSION (FTC). An independent agency of the U.S. government that guards against business practices that interfere with competition in the marketplace and that protects American consumers from various kinds of fraud and deception.

FICA TAX. *see* Social Security tax.

FICO. The most widely used credit-scoring system, named after the company that developed the score, the Fair Isaac Corporation.

FINAL PRODUCTS. Products sold to their final buyer, rather than products sold in raw or intermediate forms and made into other products.

FINANCE CHARGE. The amount a customer is charged for the use of credit (interest fees plus any additional fees).

FINANCE COMPANY. An organization that makes loans to individuals and businesses. Unlike a bank, it does not receive cash deposits from clients, nor does it provide some other services common to banks, such as checking accounts.

FINANCIAL ACCOUNT. In balance-of-payment accounting, the financial account shows the transactions involving the purchase or sale of assets (including investments, loans, and currencies). Also called a capital account.

FINANCIAL AID. Monetary assistance for students pursuing a higher education; it includes loans, scholarships, and grants.

FINANCIAL MARKETS. Places, some real and some computerized, where people can buy and sell stocks (shares of ownership in a company) and bonds (shares of governmental and other types of debt).

FINANCIAL STATEMENTS. Documents that provide details about a company's performance and well-being over a given period of time.

FISCAL POLICY. The government strategy of influencing the nation's economy through alterations to tax rates and spending programs.

FIXED ASSETS. Tangible pieces of property, such as buildings or equipment, that a business keeps for long-term use. Also known as long-term assets.

FIXED COST. A production cost that does not change as the level of production activity varies. Examples include rent paid for office or factory space and the costs paid for insurance.

FIXED INCOME. Income payments that are set at a certain amount.

FOMC. *see* Federal Open Market Committee.

FOOD AND DRUG ADMINISTRATION (FDA). An agency within the U.S. Department of Health and Human Services that is responsible for protecting public health by guaranteeing the safety and effectiveness of foods, drugs, biological products (such as vaccines), cosmetics, and products that emit radiation.

FOOD STAMP. A coupon, issued by the U.S. government to low-income families, that can be redeemed for food.

FORECLOSURE. A legal process by which a bank takes possession of a property because the buyer of the property is no longer able to make payments on the loan he or she took out to purchase it.

FOREIGN AID. Money and other assistance that one nation gives to another.

FOREIGN DIRECT INVESTMENT (FDI). A company's investment of money or other resources in business activities outside its home country.

FOREIGN EXCHANGE. The exchange of one nation's currency for the currency of another nation.

FOREIGN EXCHANGE MARKET. A financial market for the buying and selling of currency, consisting of a worldwide network of brokers (agents who arrange purchases and sales) and banks. Also called the FX market.

FOREIGN WORKER. A person who travels to another country looking for work, usually in agriculture, and returns home or moves on to another country or region when the job is done. Also known as a migrant worker.

FRACTIONAL-RESERVE BANKING. A system in which banks keep cash on hand equal to only a fraction of the deposits they take in.

FRANCHISE. A license allowing one party, the franchisee, to use the brand name and business processes already developed by a parent company, the franchisor.

FREE APPLICATION FOR FEDERAL STUDENT AID (FAFSA). An application that a college student (or incoming student) in the United States uses to request financial aid from the federal government.

FREE MARKET. An economic system in which goods and services are bought and sold, with competition determining the prices.

FREE TRADE. The reduction or elimination of restrictions on goods traded across national borders or countries.

FREE TRADE ZONE. An area of a country where goods from foreign nations are not subject to normal export and import laws. Products may be shipped to free trade zones in a country without being subject to tariffs, quotas, or other restrictions. Products may be assembled, repackaged, refinished, or even manufactured there but not sold to consumers.

FREE-RIDER. A person who chooses not to contribute to or pay for a public good because he will benefit from that product or service whether or not he pays for it.

FRINGE BENEFITS. *see* employee benefits.

FTC. *see* Federal Trade Commission.

FULL-TIME EMPLOYEES. Those employees who work at least a standard number of hours per week (usually 40).

G

G8. *see* Group of Eight.

GAME THEORY. A branch of mathematics used to study real-world situations (especially economic decisions) in which two or more people make choices that affect one another. In such situations, each participant must take the other participant's potential decisions into account in order to make his or her own decisions.

GDP. *see* gross domestic product.

GENERAL PARTNERSHIP. A business partnership in which all the owners (partners) share in the financial profits and losses and share the liability for all debts.

GIFT CARD. A plastic, electronic version of the old paper gift certificate. It contains a computer microchip that stores a set value according to how much the giver spent to purchase the card.

GIFT CERTIFICATE. A voucher worth a certain amount of money that can be spent on products or services at the commercial establishment that issued it.

GLOBALIZATION. A process involving the merging of economies, governmental policies, political movements, and cultures around the world.

GNP. *see* gross national product.

GOVERNMENT FAILURE. A term used by economists to describe a situation in which a government's interventions in an economy make the economy less efficient or create new problems.

GOVERNMENT-GRANTED MONOPOLY. A legal form of monopoly in which the government grants one individual or corporation the right to be the sole provider of a good or service.

GRANT. Sum of money given for a specific purpose with no requirement that it be repaid.

GREAT DEPRESSION. A period of severe financial decline in North America and Europe that began in 1929 and lasted until about 1939.

GROSS DOMESTIC PRODUCT (GDP). The total value of all finished goods and services produced in a country in a given time period. More simply, it is a measure of the total size of an economy.

GROSS INCOME. The amount of a person's income before taxes are calculated.

GROSS NATIONAL PRODUCT (GNP). The total value of all the goods and services produced in a country during a specific period of time. GNP is similar to gross domestic product (GDP), except that it includes income the country's citizens make from foreign investments.

GROUP OF EIGHT (G8). An alliance of eight of the world's largest industrialized democratic nations that is dedicated to discussing major political and economic issues.

GUARANTOR. A person who agrees to assume responsibility for someone else's debts in the event that he or she fails to repay them.

GUILD. An association of workers involved with the same trade.

H

HEALTH INSURANCE. *see* medical insurance.

HEALTH MAINTENANCE ORGANIZATION. *see* HMO.

HEDGE FUND. A business that pools money together, typically from very wealthy people with experience in the financial world, and invests it in a wider variety of ways than more traditional investment firms do.

HEIR. A person who inherits property from a deceased person.

HMO (HEALTH MAINTENANCE ORGANIZATION). An organization in the United States that provides a specialized form of health insurance for a prepaid monthly fee. To receive reimbursement, subscribers to such plans must use doctors, hospitals, clinics, and other facilities and providers affiliated with the HMO.

HOME EQUITY LOAN. A form of loan in which the borrower uses his or her house as collateral to secure the loan. Also referred to as a second mortgage.

HOME INSURANCE. A contract between an insurance company and a homeowner that protects the homeowner from financial losses that can result from damages to his dwelling and to the possessions stored in it.

HOME LOAN. A loan that a person receives from a financial institution (such as a bank) to buy a house or apartment, with the house serving as security in the event that the homeowner fails to repay the loan. Often referred to as a mortgage.

HUMAN RESOURCES. The department in a company that is responsible for hiring and managing employees.

HYPERINFLATION. A drastic rise in prices across an economy.

I

IDENTITY THEFT. The act of stealing a person's identifying information and carrying out financial transactions in the victim's name.

IMF. *see* International Monetary Fund.

IMPLICIT COST. The value of anything (other than direct payment, which is the explicit cost) that is sacrificed in making an economic decision.

IMPORT QUOTA. A government-imposed limit on the quantity of a particular good or services that may be imported over a specified period of time.

IMPORTS. Foreign-manufactured goods and services that are brought into a country for sale.

INCOME. The money that an individual or businesses takes in during a given period as a result of work or investments.

INCOME EFFECT. An economic principle, used in the study of consumer behavior, stating that if a person has more money to spend, that person will purchase more goods.

INCOME STATEMENT. A report detailing a company's earnings and expenses.

INCOME TAXES. Taxes levied on the earnings that individuals and businesses make each year.

INCORPORATION. The process of forming a legal corporation.

INDEPENDENT CONTRACTOR. A person or company that works for another person or company without being a regular employee.

INDEX FUND. A bundle of investments composed of the same list of companies that make up a major stock market index (such as the S&P 500) and that will therefore mirror the financial performance of that index.

INDEX OF LEADING ECONOMIC INDICATORS. A system of evaluating the strength of the economy by monitoring statistics about the performance levels of 10 sectors of the economy and then combining the statistics into a single composite figure, or index, which is announced monthly.

INDIVIDUAL RETIREMENT ACCOUNT (IRA). An investment savings account that allows an individual to set aside money each year until he or she retires, when the individual can begin withdrawing money from the account. The account's gains are not taxed until that time.

INDUSTRIAL. Related to large-scale manufacturing.

INDUSTRIALIZED COUNTRY. *see* developed country.

INDUSTRIALIZED ECONOMY. An economy based on technology and manufacturing.

INELASTIC. Less sensitive to price changes; when a price change of a product does not have a strong effect on the demand for it, the demand is said to be inelastic (fixed).

INFLATION. The rising of prices across the economy, which can cause currency to lose value.

INFLATION RATE. The average percentage increase in the price of all goods and services in the economy.

INHERITANCE TAX. A tax on the portion of an estate an individual receives from a deceased person. It is calculated as a percentage of the amount that the heir receives.

INITIAL PUBLIC OFFERING (IPO). A process by which the public is given its first opportunity to purchase ownership in a previously private company.

INPUT. Any resource used to make a good or service.

INSIDER TRADING. The purchase or sale of a company's stocks, bonds, or mutual funds by a company insider; it is illegal if the insider is using information unavailable to the general public.

INSOLVENT. Unable to pay debts.

INSURANCE. An agreement that guarantees an individual, company, or other entity against the loss of money; it is provided to customers by an insurance company in exchange for regular payments.

INTELLECTUAL PROPERTY. Ideas or creative works that can be legally protected by copyrights, patents, or trademarks so that only the creator of the idea or work has the right to profit from it.

INTEREST. Fees paid to a lender by a borrower; its rate is usually a percentage of the loan amount.

INTEREST INCOME. Money earned on savings accounts.

INTERNAL REVENUE SERVICE (IRS). A bureau within the U.S. Department of the Treasury that is responsible for assessing and collecting most types of taxes owed by individual citizens and businesses.

INTERNATIONAL BANK FOR RECONSTRUCTION AND DEVELOPMENT (IBRD). The agency of the World Bank that offers loans to middle-income countries that have the means to repay such loans.

INTERNATIONAL DEVELOPMENT ASSOCIATION (IDA). The agency of the World Bank that is responsible for providing economic assistance and supervision to the world's poorest countries, which would not otherwise qualify for loans.

INTERNATIONAL LABOR ISSUES. A term used to refer to violations of workers' rights that recur consistently throughout the world.

INTERNATIONAL LABOR ORGANIZATION (ILO). The agency within the United Nations that seeks to secure rights for all workers.

INTERNATIONAL MONETARY FUND (IMF). A specialized agency of the United Nations that helps shape economic policies related to international trade, debt, and the exchange of money among participating countries.

INTERNATIONAL TRADE. Any legal exchange of goods and services between countries.

INTRA-INDUSTRY TRADE. The exchange of goods within the same industry.

INTRASTATE COMMERCE. Business transactions that occur between two or more U.S. states.

INVENTORY CONTROL. The tasks and activities related to the maintenance of a company's inventory (raw materials, unfinished products, and finished products that it still has on hand).

INVESTMENT. The spending of money by individuals, companies, and governments in order to make an economy grow.

INVESTMENT BANK. A bank that focuses on the buying and selling of stocks, bonds, and other securities in the financial markets.

INVESTMENT MANAGEMENT. The activity of overseeing and making decisions regarding the investments of an individual, company, or other institution.

IPO. *see* initial public offering.

IRA. *see* Individual Retirement Account.

IRS. *see* Internal Revenue Service.

ITEMIZE DEDUCTIONS. To list on a tax return (a report of one's annual income) each expense that will be exempt from taxation.

J

JOB APPLICATION. A questionnaire provided by an employer to every applicant for a given position; it creates a basic profile of a job candidate, including his or her contact information, level of education, previous employment history, and relevant skills.

JUMBO CD. *see* negotiable CD.

JUNK BOND. A bond issued by an unproven company or a company experiencing financial problems. In exchange for accepting the high risk of not being paid, purchasers of junk bonds are offered high interest rates. Also called a high-yield bond.

K

KEYNESIAN ECONOMICS. A school of thought based on the ideas of the twentieth-century British economist John Maynard Keynes. It emphasizes a balance between the private sector's freedom to conduct business and the government's role as a stabilizing force in the economy.

L

LABOR. In terms of the factors of production, labor refers to the supply of workers needed to produce goods and services as well as the abilities and skills that they are required to have.

LABOR FORCE. All the people in a country who are economically active during a given time period.

LABOR LAWS. Laws regulating employer-employee relationships.

LABOR MANAGEMENT. The process of planning which workers will take on which tasks, how workers will be organized, and who will supervise and direct them.

LABOR THEORY OF VALUE. The idea, upheld by the classical economists of the eighteenth and nineteenth centuries, that the value of a good or service results from the sum of the labor that went into producing it.

LABOR UNION. A group of workers who have joined together to negotiate with employers in order to bargain for better wages, benefits, and working conditions.

LAISSEZ-FAIRE ECONOMICS. The idea that society is best served when government has only minimal involvement in the economy.

LAW OF DEMAND. An economic principle holding that, all other factors being constant, buyers will purchase less and less of a particular product as prices for that product rise.

LAW OF DIMINISHING RETURNS. An economic idea that when one input in the production process is increased while the others are held steady, there will eventually be a point at which the increases in output per worker will begin to diminish.

LAW OF SUPPLY. An economic principle stating that, all other factors being constant, sellers will be willing to sell more and more of a particular product as prices for that product rise.

LEASE. A contract that grants someone the right to use a certain piece of property for a specific duration in exchange for a regular fee.

LEASING A CAR. A process by which a consumer pays for the right to drive a new car for a set length of time without actually purchasing it.

LEGAL TENDER. The currency (units of exchange) that by law cannot be refused in the settlement of a debt.

LEVY. To charge or collect a tax.

LIABILITIES. Debts that a company takes on as it conducts business.

LIABILITY. The responsibility that a company takes for damage or harm caused by its product.

LIABILITY INSURANCE. A type of insurance that covers bodily injury to others and damages to other people's property.

LIFE INSURANCE. A legal agreement between an insurance agency and the policyholder, according to which the agency agrees to pay a predetermined amount of money to a person or to a group of people, such as the insured's family, upon the death of the policyholder.

LIMITED LIABILITY COMPANY (LLC). A category of company that combines aspects of partnerships and corporations. As with a partnership, the owners have the freedom to choose how to split their profits among themselves. Unlike a partnership, however, an LLC is a legally separate entity, meaning its owners cannot be held personally liable (responsible) for the company's debts.

LIMITED PARTNERSHIP. A business partnership in which one or more of the owners (called the general partners) run the business and have unlimited liability, or are held entirely responsible for the business's debts. The limited partners, by contrast, invest in the business and have only limited personal liability for the debts.

LINE OF CREDIT. A form of loan, according to which a bank or other financial institution grants a consumer permission to spend up to a preapproved limit of money, with the understanding that he or she will pay it back over time.

LIQUID. Able to be converted into cash easily.

LIQUIDATE. To convert assets into cash.

LLC. *see* limited liability company.

LOAN. A sum of money borrowed by a corporation, individual consumer, or other entity.

LOBBY. To try to influence politicians to support, oppose, or modify certain legislation, according to the interests of the lobbying party (such as a particular industry or an organization).

LONG-TERM CAPITAL ASSETS. Assets that an investor has owned for more than a year (a distinction made in calculating capital-gains tax in the United States; gains on long-term assets are taxed at a lower rate than regular income).

M

M1. One of a variety of definitions of the U.S. money supply. It is the narrowest definition, including only those forms of money that can be used to purchase goods and services immediately without any substantial restrictions: currency (bills and coins issued by the government), traveler's checks, and checking-account balances.

M2. A definition of the U.S. money supply that includes M1 plus the money in most savings accounts, money market accounts, and CDs (certificates of deposit, a form of interest-bearing account that has time restrictions regarding when it can be cashed in) worth less than $100,000.

M3. One of a variety of ways to define the U.S. money supply. M3 is the broadest definition, including all the forms of money measured in M2 as well as some larger forms of assets and CDs valued at more than $100,000.

MACROECONOMICS. The branch of economics that examines the economy as a whole, concerning itself with the aggregate behavior (the total result of individual actions) of consumers and producers in various parts of the economy.

MANUAL LABOR. Work that involves a person's physical exertion.

MARGINAL UTILITY. The amount of satisfaction (or utility) a consumer receives from each additional unit of a good that he or she acquires.

MARKET. In economics, a place or system that allows buyers and sellers of goods and services to interact with one another.

MARKET ECONOMY. A system in which people voluntarily exchange goods and services for a price. Businesses and consumers, not the government, decide how much of a good or service is produced and purchased and how much it will cost.

MARKET FAILURE. A term used by economists to describe situations in which markets fail to serve, or are incapable of serving, the best interests of society.

MARKET FORCES. The interaction of supply and demand that drives a market economy.

MARKET RESEARCH. The gathering and analyzing of data about the best ways to advertise, sell, or distribute a particular product or service.

MARKET SHARE. The percentage of the total sales of a product that is sold by one company.

MARKETING. The process of promoting, selling, and distributing a product or service.

MARKETING STRATEGY. A plan describing how a company intends to build consumer awareness about its product or service.

MARXIST ECONOMICS. A branch of economic study based on the writings of the nineteenth-century German philosopher Karl Marx, who is best known for providing the intellectual foundation for the various socialist ideologies (beliefs in redistributing wealth and property so that individuals share the fruits of the economy more equally than under other political systems) that rose to prominence in Russia, China, and Eastern Europe in the early twentieth century.

MASS MARKETING. A form of marketing that attempts to create the largest possible market for a good or service. It includes print, radio, and television advertising; mail-order catalogs; catchy slogans and songs; and flyers.

MASS PRODUCTION. The manufacture, usually by machines, of products in large quantities.

MATURITY. The agreed-upon length of time that an investor will hold a security.

MECHANIZED LABOR. Work that is carried out by machines rather than people.

MEDICAID. A government-assistance program in the United States that provides health-care benefits to individuals and families with low income and limited resources.

MEDICAL INSURANCE. A contract under which a private medical insurance company or a government agency promises to pay for or provide health-care services to an individual or family. Also called health insurance.

MEDICARE. A national health-insurance program for Americans age 65 and older and disabled people.

MERGER. The joining of two separate companies into one larger company.

MICROECONOMICS. An approach to the study of economics that focuses on the decisions of individuals or groups and that involves attempts to understand particular sectors of an economy.

MICROLENDING. The practice of extending small loans to poor entrepreneurs who live in developing countries.

MIGRANT WORKER. *see* foreign worker.

MINIMUM WAGE. The lowest amount of money that employers are legally permitted to pay their workers per hour.

MIXED ECONOMIC SYSTEM. An economy that combines some amount of government planning with elements of a free-market economy.

MNC. *see* multinational corporation.

MONETARISM. *see* monetarist theory.

MONETARIST THEORY. An approach to economics that centers on the belief that the size of the money supply is more important than any other factor affecting the economy. Also called monetarism.

MONETARY POLICY. The government practice of adjusting the money supply in order to bring about a change in the economy.

MONEY. Anything to which people assign value in order to make it easier to exchange goods and services.

MONEY MARKET. The buying and selling of short-term, low-risk securities.

MONEY MARKET ACCOUNT. A type of savings account that usually requires larger minimum balances and places other restrictions on withdrawal of money in exchange for a higher interest rate (a fee paid to the customer for the use of his or her borrowed money) than standard savings accounts offer.

MONEY ORDER. A prepaid voucher for a specific amount of money that is used in lieu of cash or personal checks to make payments; it may be purchased at a bank, post office, and other qualified institution.

MONEY SUPPLY. The amount of money in circulation in an economy at any given time, including not just coins and bills but also bank-account balances.

MONOPOLISTIC COMPETITION. A market structure that combines the features of two opposing concepts, monopoly and perfect competition. In such a market numerous relatively small businesses sell similar but not identical products. Each firm has some amount of control over prices and market conditions even though there is a high level of competition among them.

MONOPOLY. A situation in which a single company or group of companies enjoys complete control over a certain business sector.

MORTGAGE. *see* home loan.

MORTGAGE BROKER. A person working at a bank or mortgage company who arranges home loans.

MORTGAGE PAYMENT. A monthly fee that goes toward paying off a loan used to buy a home.

MULTINATIONAL CORPORATION (MNC). Any business that has bases of activity in more than one country.

MULTIPLIER EFFECT. The idea that government spending has the power to promote further spending by businesses and consumers, thereby helping an economy grow.

MUNICIPAL BOND. A bond (a type of investment) issued by a government or a government agency below the state level.

MUTUAL FUND. A bundle of investments (including stocks, bonds, and other securities) that is managed for clients by an investment company.

N

NASDAQ. The largest electronic (meaning that all trading is done by computer) stock exchange in the United States.

NATIONAL CREDIT UNION ADMINISTRATION. An independent U.S. government agency that insures the deposits of its member credit unions.

NATIONAL DEBT. The amount of borrowed money a country's government owes.

NATURAL MONOPOLY. A situation in which a single company can produce a good more efficiently than two or more competing firms would be able to produce it.

NCD. *see* negotiable certificate of deposit.

NEGOTIABLE CERTIFICATE OF DEPOSIT (NCD). A CD with a face value of at least $100,000 that may be sold in secondary markets (from one investor to another). They are usually purchased by insurance companies, corporations, or other institutional investors.

NEGOTIABLE INSTRUMENT. A written order to pay an amount of money (such as a security) that can be sold by one party to another.

NEOCLASSICAL ECONOMICS. A school of economic thought, developed in the late nineteenth century, that accepts and builds upon the basic tenets of classical economics. Its basic principle is that the interaction of supply and demand is the most important element of a market economy. It is the dominant theoretical framework in modern economics.

NET EARNINGS. The amount of personal income an employee keeps after paying income taxes.

NET EXPORTS. The value of a country's exports minus the value of its total imports.

NET INCOME. The profit or loss that a company shows after all its costs, taxes, and other expenses are subtracted from the total receipts, or revenue.

NEW YORK STOCK EXCHANGE (NYSE). A stock exchange specializing in the stock of large companies. Located in New York City, it is the largest stock exchange in the world, in terms of the value of stocks that are bought and sold there.

NEWLY INDUSTRIALIZED COUNTRIES (NICS). Nations that have not quite attained the status of a developed country but are experiencing rapid economic and technological growth and are shifting from an agricultural economy into an industrialized economy (one based on technology and manufacturing).

NICHE MARKETING. Marketing that is focused entirely on one small segment of the population.

NO-FAULT INSURANCE. A type of car insurance policy that covers the insured person regardless of who is at fault in an accident.

NONDURABLE GOODS. Goods that cannot be reused or that are not expected to retain their value for more than a year (for example, food, clothing, and gas).

NONPROFIT ORGANIZATION. A business whose goal is to support an issue of public or private concern rather than achieve financial gain.

NORTH AMERICAN FREE TRADE AGREEMENT (NAFTA). A treaty between Canada, the United States, and Mexico that eased regulations for doing business across the borders of these three countries.

NYSE. *see* New York Stock Exchange.

O

OCCUPATIONAL SAFETY AND HEALTH ADMINISTRATION (OSHA). A division of the U.S. Department of Labor that regulates issues of safety and health in the workplace.

OFFSHORING. The practice of relocating businesses to parts of the world where production costs are lower.

OLIGOPOLY. A situation in which a small number of companies dominate the market for a particular good or service.

OPEN-MARKET OPERATIONS. A technique used in implementing monetary policy whereby the country's central bank (the Fed in the United States) buys and sells securities on the open market in order to make the nation's money supply larger or smaller (when it buys, it injects money into circulation, and when it sells, it takes money out of general circulation).

OPERATING COSTS. Expenses associated with running a business.

OPPORTUNITY COST. The cost of an economic decision expressed in terms of the next-best opportunity that is given up.

OUTPUT. The quantity of goods and services produced by an economy; also, in the context of production, the goods or services that a business produces.

OUTSOURCING. One business firm's hiring of another business firm to perform one or more jobs on its behalf.

OVERDRAFT. A situation in which a bank account holder does not have sufficient funds to cover checks and other withdrawals from the account.

OVERTIME. Time spent working above the agreed-upon number of hours per day, week, or month; also, the payment for overtime hours worked, usually calculated at an increased hourly rate.

P

PARTNERSHIP. A company in which two or more people, or partners, manage a business together and are personally responsible for the company's debts.

PATENT. The governmentally granted right to be the exclusive manufacturer or seller of an invention.

PAWNBROKER. A business that issues small, short-term loans in exchange for some piece of valuable property, which is held as collateral.

PAY STUB. The portion of a paycheck that includes information about an employee's earnings, which an employee keeps for his or her records.

PAYDAY. A specified date on which an employee receives his or her paycheck.

PAYDAY LOAN. A small, short-term loan that is intended to be repaid after the borrower's next payday.

PAYROLL. The record a company uses to keep track of the money it pays to its employees over a specific period of time; also, the total amount of money a company pays out to its employees during a given period.

PENSION. Regular payments an employee receives after he or she retires.

PER CAPITA INCOME. The average income per person in a country.

PERFECT COMPETITION. A theoretical concept describing a market composed of numerous sellers all offering an identical product, so that none of the sellers has the ability to control prices.

PERSONAL LOAN. Money lent by a financial institution to an individual for personal rather than commercial purposes.

PHILANTHROPIC INSTITUTION. An organization dedicated to helping people instead of making money.

PLANNED ECONOMY. An economic system in which government planners make all or most important economic decisions. Also referred to as a command economy.

POLICY. An insurance contract.

PORTFOLIO. The collection of investments held by an investor.

POSTDATE. To label something, usually a check, with a future date when it can be cashed.

POVERTY LEVEL. The level of household income beneath which an individual is determined to be living in poverty. The level is based on the amount of income that the government says is required to purchase the most basic necessities.

PPI. *see* Producer Price Index.

PPO (PREFERRED PROVIDER ORGANIZATION). A network of health-care providers that contracts with an insurer (usually an insurance company) to offer medical care at discounted rates in exchange for an increased volume of patients.

PREFERRED PROVIDER ORGANIZATION. *see* PPO.

PREFERRED STOCK. Stock that guarantees the shareholder the first right to receive a dividend. Unlike holders of common stock, preferred stockholders cannot vote on company matters.

PREMIUM. The fee for insurance coverage.

PRICE CEILING. A government-imposed maximum price that the seller of a particular good or service may charge.

PRICE FIXING. An illegal activity in which two or more competing businesses make agreements to keep their prices at levels that will ensure profitability.

PRICE FLOOR. A government-imposed minimum price that can be charged for a good or service.

PRICE GOUGING. The practice of setting unfairly high prices during a supply shortage.

PRICING. The process of determining and applying prices to goods and services.

PRIMARY CARE PHYSICIAN. A doctor who manages the health care of a patient with HMO insurance, referring the patient to specialists and authorizing procedures.

PRIME RATE. The standard interest rate set by major banks. It serves as a baseline to which individual banks add percentage points.

PRINCIPAL. The amount of a loan, not including interest (the fee for borrowing money).

PRIVATE SECTOR. That part of the economy that is not controlled by the government and that is run for profit.

PRIVATIZATION. Putting formerly state-run businesses into the hands of individuals and corporations.

PRODUCER PRICE INDEX (PPI). An index published monthly by the Bureau of Labor Statistics that measures the change in cost of materials used to make the products Americans consume.

PRODUCER SURPLUS. The difference between the minimum amount a producer can charge for a good or service without losing money and the price that the producer actually charges.

PRODUCT DEVELOPMENT. The process of bringing a new good or service to market. It includes generating ideas for a new product, gathering information about the needs and wants of the target market, and designing, engineering, and testing the product.

PRODUCT LIABILITY. The notion that anyone involved in the manufacturing or sale of a defective product may be held legally responsible for paying damages to anyone injured because of that product.

PRODUCTION COSTS. The money required to make and distribute a product.

PRODUCTION POSSIBILITIES CURVE. A graph used to show the different quantities of two goods that an economy can produce while using resources most efficiently. Also called the production possibilities frontier.

PRODUCTION POSSIBILITIES FRONTIER. *see* production possibilities curve.

PRODUCTIVITY. The ratio of output (goods created or services performed) to input (all costs of production, including workers' wages and costs required to run business equipment).

PROFIT. The money left over from a business's sales after all costs of production have been paid.

PROFIT SHARING. A plan that provides employees of a company with a percentage of the company's profits.

PROFIT-AND-LOSS STATEMENT. *see* income statement.

PROGRESSIVE TAX. A type of tax that imposes a larger percentage of tax on high-income earners than it does on low-income earners.

PROMISSORY NOTE. A written document that represents a debt and promises repayment at a later date.

PROMOTION. An employee's elevation to a more prestigious position, typically accompanied by a raise and additional responsibility.

PROPERTY. In financial terms, anything that can be owned; it can be tangible (for instance, land, a house, or shoes) or intangible (for instance, a bank-account balance or the patent on an invention).

PROPERTY TAX. A fee charged by the government on the value of privately owned property such as land, houses and other buildings, and machinery.

PROPORTIONAL TAX. A tax that takes the same percentage of income from everyone, regardless of how much or how little an individual earns. Sometimes known as a flat tax or flat-rate tax.

PROTECTIONISM. Any action taken by a government to protect domestic (its own country's) industries from foreign competition.

PUBLIC COMPANY. A company owned by investors or stockholders (people who have purchased shares in the company's ownership).

PUBLIC RELATIONS. The practice of building and maintaining an organization or individual's relationship with the public.

PUBLIC SECTOR. The part of a nation's economy that is controlled by the government.

PURCHASING POWER. The value of money measured by the items it can buy.

PYRAMID SCHEME. A fraudulent business practice that involves building a network, or "pyramid," of investors who pay money into the scheme with the hope of earning a high return on their investment. An investor pays to participate in the scheme and then recruits other investors, who subsequently pay money to the investor who recruited them.

Q

QUALITY CONTROL. A system by which products or services are inspected and evaluated to determine whether they meet expected levels of overall quality.

QUARTER. A period of three months, a unit of time commonly used in financial activity.

R

RAISE. An increase in a person's salary or wages.

RATE OF INFLATION. The percentage by which prices in general have gone up.

RATE OF RETURN. The gain or loss generated by an investment over a specific time period.

RATION. To place limits on the amount of a good that any individual can buy, usually in order to ensure that basic goods in short supply are distributed fairly.

RATIONAL EXPECTATION THEORY. An idea in economics that says that people use rationality, past experiences, and all available information to guide their financial decision-making. When considered as a factor in the overall economy, rational expectation theory leads to the conclusion that people's current expectations about the economy will influence the future course of the economy.

RECALL. A public request for consumers to return a product that has been found to be contaminated, defective, or otherwise unsafe.

RECESSION. A period of slow economic growth typically accompanied by increased unemployment.

REDISTRIBUTION OF WEALTH. The process of taxing the wealthy and using that money to pay for social benefits that will improve the living conditions of poorer people.

REFINANCE. To pay off a loan using another loan that has better terms (such as lower interest rates).

REGRESSIVE TAX. A type of tax that does not take income levels into account and in effect requires people with lower incomes to pay a larger proportion of their income than people with higher incomes.

REINSURANCE. Insurance for insurance companies.

REINVEST. To put a company's profits back into the company to help it grow.

RENT. The monthly fee paid by a person or business leasing an apartment, building, or other property.

RENTER'S INSURANCE. A form of property insurance for people who rent, rather than own, their homes; it covers the contents of the home in the case of theft or damage.

RENT-TO-OWN STORE. A business that allows customers to rent consumer goods, such as furniture and appliances, and that gives the customer the option of taking ownership of the item after a certain number of payments have been made.

RESERVE REQUIREMENT. The amount of money that the federal government requires banks to keep on hand (usually defined as a percentage of the amount of money that the bank takes in through customer deposits).

RESOURCES. The ingredients of production (including land and natural resources, the size and characteristics of the labor force, and the amount and variety of equipment available for production).

RÉSUMÉ. A document providing a detailed description of a person's previous work experience, educational background, and relevant job skills.

RETAIL BANK. A type of bank whose main business is handling the deposits and loans of individual consumers and businesses.

RETAIL PRICE. The price charged to a consumer.

RETAILING. The activity of selling goods directly to consumers who will use or consume the products (not resell them).

RETIREMENT PLAN. A financial arrangement that provides a person with income when he or she retires.

REVENUE. The total quantity of money that a business or organization brings in during a set period of time.

REVOLVING CREDIT. A credit agreement that allows a cardholder to carry a running balance on his or her credit card and requires that regular payments be made.

RIDER. A feature added to an insurance policy that offers a substantial benefit to customers for a small to moderate increase in price.

RISK MANAGEMENT. The process of identifying and analyzing risks (the possibility of loss, injury, disadvantage, or destruction) and creating plans to reduce the losses that an organization faces as it conducts business.

RISK PYRAMID. A diagram used to demonstrate the relationship between risk and reward in investing; the safest investments are located at the base of the pyramid, and the riskiest are grouped at the top. Both risks and rewards increase with each ascending tier.

RISK-BASED ASSETS. Investments that have value or generate money, or both, but that are not as secure as money in hand.

S

S CORPORATION. A type of corporation that is taxed under Subchapter S of the U.S. tax code. An S Corporation is taxed as if it were a partnership; all profit is passed directly to each of the company's owners, who in turn pays taxes as an individual.

S&P 500. An index used to gauge the performance of the U.S. stock market. It tracks the fluctuating stock values of 500 representative companies and combines them into one numerical figure. In full, Standard and Poor's 500.

SAFE-DEPOSIT BOX. A private, locked box inside a bank vault that an individual can rent to store valuables.

SALARY. An employee's pay, calculated on an annual basis.

SALES TAX. A fee charged by the government on the sale of a good or service and paid by the customer at the time of the sale.

SAVINGS ACCOUNT. A kind of bank account that pays the customer interest on the balance of the account.

SAVINGS AND LOAN ASSOCIATION. A type of financial institution that is member-owned and focuses on providing home loans.

SAVINGS BOND. A type of security (interest-paying investment) sold by the U.S. Treasury to individual investors and registered to the original purchaser.

SAY'S LAW. An economic theory developed in 1803 by French journalist, businessman, and economist Jean-Baptiste Say. It states that supply creates its own demand (and thus, an economic crisis will never be caused by supply outpacing demand). Also known as Say's Law of Markets.

SCARCITY. In economics, an imbalance between people's virtually unlimited desires and the limited resources available to satisfy those desires.

SCRIP. Any substitute for money or currency; it carries a monetary value without being legal tender.

SEC. *see* Securities and Exchange Commission.

SECOND MORTGAGE. *see* home equity loan.

SECURED LOAN. A loan in which the borrower is required to offer some form of collateral to the lender; if the borrower fails to repay the loan or to keep to the terms of the loan agreement, then the lender is legally entitled to take possession of the collateral.

SECURITIES AND EXCHANGE COMMISSION (SEC). A U.S. government agency that protects investors and maintains fair, orderly, and efficient financial markets.

SECURITY. A document, such as a stock certificate or a bond, that can be assigned value and bought and sold among investors.

SERVICE. The providing of intangible products such as health care, legal assistance, and insurance.

SERVICE INDUSTRIES. Forms of business activity dealing with human services rather than physical goods.

SEZ. *see* Special Economic Zone.

SHARE DRAFT ACCOUNT. A checking account at a credit union.

SHAREHOLDERS. People who own shares (portions) of a company.

SHORT-TERM CAPITAL ASSETS. Assets that an investor has held for less than a year; in the United States gains on such assets are taxed as ordinary income.

SMALL BUSINESS ADMINISTRATION (SBA). An independent agency of the U.S. government devoted to advancing the interests of American small businesses.

SMALL BUSINESS INVESTMENT COMPANY (SBIC). A government-sponsored private firm in the United States that assists entrepreneurs with the financing and management of their emerging companies. SBICs are licensed and financed by the Small Business Administration.

SOCIAL SECURITY. A U.S. government program that provides monthly financial benefits to senior citizens, veterans, the disabled, and surviving family members of deceased breadwinners; it is funded by a tax paid by all individuals who earn income.

SOCIAL SECURITY TAX. A tax paid by all working citizens to fund Social Security. Also known as the Federal Insurance Contributions Act tax (or FICA tax).

SOLE PROPRIETORSHIP. A business with a single owner (proprietor).

SOLVENT. Having enough money to pay back debts.

SPECIAL ECONOMIC ZONE (SEZ). A geographically separate area of a country that has fewer economic regulations than the rest of the country; its main purpose is to attract foreign investors.

SPECIAL SUPPLEMENTAL NUTRITION PROGRAM FOR WOMEN, INFANTS, AND CHILDREN. A government program in the United States whose mission is to improve the nutrition of low-income women, infants, and children under the age of five who are deemed to be at nutritional risk. Often referred to as the WIC Program.

SPECIALIZATION. *see* division of labor.

STAGFLATION. A term coined in the 1960s to describe the unusual economic phenomenon of inflation (the general rising of prices, usually a sign of economic growth) and economic stagnation occurring simultaneously.

STANDARD OF LIVING. The level of material comfort, or quality of life, enjoyed by an individual or group; in economics it is usually used to evaluate a nation's population.

START-UP COSTS. The money required to open a business.

STOCK. Portions of company ownership that can be bought and sold and that gain or lose value as the company prospers or struggles.

STOCK EXCHANGE. *see* stock market.

STOCK MARKET. A place where buyers and sellers of stocks come together to make trades. The term is also used to refer collectively to all the places in the world, some of which are real buildings and some of which exist mainly in computer networks, where stocks are bought and sold.

STOCK MARKET CRASH. A dramatic drop in the overall value of stocks on a stock exchange, causing widespread financial distress.

STOCK OPTIONS. Agreements providing employees of a company with the right to purchase shares in the company at a discounted price.

STOCKBROKER. A person who negotiates and executes the purchase and sale of stocks for clients.

STRESS MANAGEMENT. A set of strategies or responses used in the workplace to reduce the causes and effects of stress on workers and the organization.

STRIKE. A collective refusal of employees to report for work until their demands are met.

STUDENT AID REPORT (SAR). A report that the federal government issues after a college student (or incoming college student) applies for federal financial aid; the schools and state agencies use the report to determine the student's eligibility for additional aid.

STUDENT LOAN. A sum of money lent to a student who is pursuing higher education, such as college or university study.

SUBSIDIARY. A company that is controlled by a larger company.

SUBSIDY. Money that the government grants a company or organization to help it cover its operating expenses.

SUBSISTENCE FARMERS. Farmers who grow only enough to feed their own families.

SUBSTITUTE GOODS. Goods that can be used in place of other goods, in the way that margarine can be used in place of butter.

SUBSTITUTION EFFECT. An economic principle used in the study of consumer buying patterns, stating that if the price of the product a consumer usually buys goes up while the price of a similar item remains the same, the consumer will be more likely to substitute the second item for the first.

SUNK COST. A cost of production that has been incurred by a company in the past, that does not affect future costs, and that cannot be changed by any current or future actions or decisions.

SUPPLY. The amount of any good or service that a seller is willing or able to sell at a given price.

SUPPLY CHAIN. All of the elements in a process of providing a good or service to a customer, beginning with the raw material and ending with the sale of a finished product or service.

SUPPLY SIDE THEORY. An approach to economics based on the idea that the best way to make the economy grow is to encourage businesses to supply more goods and services for purchase.

SURPLUS. A situation in which there is more supply of a good than demand for it.

SUSTAINABLE DEVELOPMENT. Economic growth that minimizes pollution and the depletion of natural resources.

T

TARGET MARKET. The segment of consumers to whom a product is intended to appeal.

TARIFF. A tax on goods imported from other countries.

TAX. A fee that a government imposes on a type of economic activity.

TAX ASSESSOR. A public official who establishes the value of property for the purpose of determining the amount of tax the owner must pay.

TAX BRACKET. In the payment of U.S. income taxes, the category that determines what percentage of a person's income that he or she must pay as tax; the percentage increases as income increases.

TAX CREDIT. An amount of money that is subtracted from a person or business's total income-tax payment.

TAX EVASION. Hiding or failing to disclose earnings in order to avoid paying taxes on it.

TAX HAVEN. A country or other politically independent area with low or no income tax that attracts foreign businesses and individuals who want to avoid paying income taxes in their home country.

TAX LIABILITY. The amount of tax owed by an individual or business.

TAX REFUND. The money that the government returns to a person when he or she has overpaid on his or her income taxes.

TAX RETURN. A set of forms that individuals and businesses use to report the details of their earnings when paying income taxes to the federal and state governments.

TAX REVENUES. The amounts of money collected by the government through taxation.

TAX SHELTER. Any one of various tactics for reducing one's tax liability.

T-BILL. *see* Treasury bill.

TEMPORARY ASSISTANCE TO NEEDY FAMILIES (TANF). A government program administered by the Office of Family Assistance (a division of the U.S. Department of Health and Human Services) designed to create employment opportunities for needy families with dependent children.

TIME VALUE OF MONEY. An economic principle stating that cash received now is worth more than the same amount of cash received at a later date because money has the capacity to earn interest (fees paid to those who loan money).

TIPS. *see* Treasury Inflation-Protected Securities.

TITLE. A document showing proof of ownership of a piece of property.

TOTAL QUALITY MANAGEMENT (TQM). A philosophy of business management that seeks excellence and maximum efficiency in all areas of the production of goods and services.

TRADE. To buy and sell.

TRADE BARRIERS. Fees or limits on the goods and services that can move across borders.

TRADE BLOC. A group of nations that has reached a set of agreements regarding their economic relationships with each other. The agreements generally focus on the relaxation or elimination of trade barriers.

TRADE CREDIT. A contractual agreement in which one business receives goods or services from another business without having to pay immediately for those goods and services. The business that has received the goods or services will pay the lending business at a later date, which is specified in the agreement.

TRADE DEFICIT. The difference between the value of a country's imports and its exports, when the country imports more than it exports.

TRADE SURPLUS. The difference between the value of a country's imports and its exports, when the country exports more than it imports.

TRADEMARK. A legally registered name or symbol used to identify a brand or organization in the marketplace; registration gives the organization the right to be the sole user of the trademark.

TRANSFER PAYMENT. Money or other aid that a government gives to an individual or organization with no expectation that a good or service will be provided in return.

TRANSITION ECONOMY. An economy that is in the process of shifting from a planned-economy model to a free-market model.

TRANSNATIONAL COMPANY. A company that operates and invests in many countries around the world.

TRAVELER'S CHECK. A kind of check, typically used by people traveling in foreign countries, that may be purchased from a bank or other financial institution or at a travel service office in preset denominations ($10, $20, $50, $100, and higher). Unlike cash, they are protected against loss or theft.

TREASURY BILL. A government security that guarantees the investor a fixed return (usually about 3 percent of the invested amount) after a short period of time. Also called a T-bill.

TREASURY BOND. A long-term security sold by the U.S. Treasury that matures in 10 to 30 years and pays the investor interest every six months. Also called a T-bond.

TREASURY INFLATION-PROTECTED SECURITY. A type of security sold by the U.S. Treasury that takes inflation (the general rising of prices) into account; the face value of the security increases with inflation and decreases with deflation (a general decline in prices). Abbreviated as TIPS.

TREASURY NOTE. A security sold by the U.S. Treasury that has a maturity of 2, 3, 5, or 10 years and pays

the investor interest every six months. Also called a T-note.

TREASURY SECURITIES. Investments offered by the U.S. government (specifically the Treasury) to individuals, institutions (both inside and outside of the United States), and foreign governments; in effect, these investors are loaning money to the government, and in exchange, they receive interest payments.

TRUST. A combination of companies, the intent of which is to reduce competition and control prices; also, property or money held by one party (the trustee) for the benefit of another (the beneficiary).

TRUTH IN LENDING ACT (TILA). A U.S. federal law requiring all lending institutions to state fully, in writing and in plain language, the terms of the loans they offer to customers.

TUITION. The basic cost of attending school, not including supplies and room and board.

U

UN. *see* United Nations.

UNEMPLOYMENT. The state of being unemployed; can also mean the rate of unemployment (the percentage of a nation's workforce that cannot find jobs).

UNEMPLOYMENT INSURANCE. A government system by which regular payments are made to qualified unemployed individuals (usually those who have been laid off).

UNION. *see* labor union.

UNION DUES. A portion of a worker's wages that pays for costs associated with the organization and governing of the labor union.

UNITED NATIONS (UN). An international organization dedicated to fostering legal, political, and economic cooperation among various nations.

UNITED STATES DEPARTMENT OF AGRICULTURE (USDA). The department of the federal government that develops policies regarding agriculture and food.

UNITED STATES DEPARTMENT OF COMMERCE. The department of the federal government that deals with issues of economic growth.

UNITED STATES DEPARTMENT OF LABOR. The federal agency responsible for regulating issues pertaining to the U.S. workforce, including occupational safety, wage and work-hours standards, and unemployment-insurance benefits.

UNITED STATES DEPARTMENT OF THE TREASURY. The department of the federal government that manages the country's revenue.

UNIVERSAL HEALTH CARE. A national system in which all residents have access to health care regardless of their ability to pay or their medical condition.

UNLIMITED LIABILITY. A situation in which those obligated to pay a debt have unlimited responsibility to do so.

UNSECURED LOAN. A type of loan that does not require the borrower to put up collateral.

USDA. *see* United States Department of Agriculture.

USURY. The practice of charging a borrower more interest than the law allows.

UTILITIES. Everyday services that are typically purchased by homeowners, such as electricity, gas, water, and waste disposal.

UTILITY. In economics, the amount of satisfaction consumers receive from the goods and services they purchase.

V

VALUE-ADDED TAX. A type of sales tax charged to businesses based on the value, or price, the business adds to the product it makes.

VARIABLE COSTS. The costs of production that vary according to the number of units of a product made or with the scale of the company's operation. Examples include the cost of raw materials and the wages paid to workers who are hired specifically for the production of that good.

VELOCITY OF MONEY. The speed with which the average dollar changes hands.

VENTURE CAPITAL. Money that serves as financial backing for new, generally unproven business enterprises, typically known as start-ups.

VENTURE CAPITALIST. An individual or group that provides start-up funding to new businesses.

VOLATILITY. The frequency and amount of price fluctuation of an investment.

W

WAGES. The payment that a worker or employee receives for his or her labor, usually paid for a specified quantity of labor, which most often is measured as a unit of time.

WARRANTY. A guarantee offered by the seller or manufacturer of a product, promising repair if the product breaks within a certain time after purchase.

WEB MANAGEMENT. All of the activities included in the process of posting and maintaining a website.

WELFARE. Government programs that provide aid to the poor.

WHITE-COLLAR WORKERS. Employees whose jobs do not involve manual labor and who generally receive a salary rather than an hourly wage.

WHOLESALE. The selling of goods that are intended to be resold (as when a distributor sells to a retailer), typically in large quantities and at lower prices than an individual customer would be charged.

WIC PROGRAM. *see* Special Supplemental Nutrition Program for Women, Infants, and Children.

WIRE TRANSFER. The electronic transfer of funds across a network controlled and maintained by hundreds of banks around the world, allowing people in different geographic locations to transfer money easily.

WORKER'S COMPENSATION. A type of insurance that employers must have to provide monetary compensation to employees who experience work-related illnesses or injuries.

WORK-STUDY. A program in which college students are paid to do a job at the school.

WORLD BANK. An international organization (consisting of member nations) that helps poor and developing countries build their economies by making loans to these countries and providing them with financial assistance and supervision.

WORLD TRADE ORGANIZATION (WTO). An institution composed of more than 150 countries, the purpose of which is to monitor international trade and promote increasingly free (unregulated) trade between countries.

WTO. *see* World Trade Organization.

Z

ZERO-COUPON BOND. A form of bond that does not conform to the basic model of paying a face value and then collecting interest until maturity. Instead of paying interest, it is sold at a discount off its face value; when it matures, the investor is paid the bond's face value. They allow people to make long-term investments at a low initial cost.

How the Economy Works

Introduction: What Is Economics?

$ What It Means

Economics is a social science devoted to the study of how people and societies get what they need and want. Or, in more formal language, economics is the study of how societies divide and use their resources to produce goods and services and of how those goods and services are then distributed and consumed.

Resources are the basic ingredients that are needed to produce the goods and services that people buy. These ingredients can be physical things such as land and factory equipment, and they can be intangible things such as the intellectual and emotional capacities of people, whose work is necessary for the production of goods and services. Whether a society is rich or poor, large or small, resources are, from the viewpoint of economics, scarce. This means that almost everyone in every country would like more goods and services than can ever be produced. Given a limited supply of resources and an unlimited desire on the part of individual consumers and nations, choices must be made about what goods and services to produce, how to produce them, and for whom.

Economists study these often-difficult choices and their significance. They come up with theories about how such choices are made on both individual and collective levels, and they try to make predictions and find solutions to a wide range of societal problems.

Although thinkers in earlier societies sometimes addressed topics that today concern economists, economics as a field did not emerge until after the Middle Ages (a period that lasted from about 500 to 1500), when capitalism became a firmly established economic system. (In capitalism the economy is controlled by private individuals rather than the government.) Much of economic theory grew out of the ideas of Scottish philosopher Adam Smith, whose book *An Inquiry into the Nature and Causes of the Wealth of Nations* (1776) is generally considered the founding text of the field of economics. Later, as a result of the writings of English economist John Maynard Keynes in the 1930s, eco-

nomics came to be subdivided into two main branches, microeconomics and macroeconomics. These branches focus, respectively, on individual and collective economic behavior. Since Keynes's time many economists have worked on unifying these two branches of theory.

$ When Did It Begin

Throughout history many philosophers and religious thinkers have dealt with economic questions. In ancient Greece, for instance, the philosophers Plato and Aristotle addressed the issue of whether private property was a legitimate concept. Likewise, in the thirteenth century the Italian Christian philosopher Thomas Aquinas discussed the moral aspects of buying and selling goods and services. For much of history, religions such as Christianity and Islam opposed, on moral grounds, such economic trends as the charging of interest (fees paid to those who lend money). But the study of economics did not become systematic until after the Middle Ages.

In the sixteenth through eighteenth centuries, the nation-states of Europe (such as England, France, Spain, and Portugal) wanted to build up power partly by amassing wealth. Out of this desire grew economic theories that dictated the development of capitalism during that time. These theories, later grouped together under the label of mercantilism, generally held that a nation's wealth was equivalent to its store of gold, silver, and other precious metals. This belief led nations to pursue wealth by maintaining an imbalance in foreign trade. If a nation sold more goods abroad than it imported, then that nation would bring in more gold than it would send outside of its borders through trade. In this way, the developing European nations competed with each other by trying to stockpile gold.

In the eighteenth century Adam Smith (1723–90) conceived of his book *An Inquiry into the Nature and Causes of the Wealth of Nations* as a rebuttal to the mercantilist viewpoint, but it was much more than that.

ADAM SMITH

"It is not from the benevolence of the butcher, the brewer, or the baker that we expect our dinner, but from their regard for their own interest."

ADAM SMITH, *AN INQUIRY INTO THE NATURE AND CAUSES OF THE WEALTH OF NATIONS*, 1776.

Why He Is Important

Adam Smith (1723–90), Scottish economist and moral philosopher, is widely regarded as the father of modern economic thought. His groundbreaking work *An Inquiry into the Nature and Causes of the Wealth of Nations,* promoted laissez-faire capitalism, the idea that with a minimum of government interference, the economy will be guided by an invisible hand that operates for the good of the entire society. *The Wealth of Nations* was written in a style intended to be accessible to average readers. First published in 1776, just a few years before the Industrial Revolution was launched by the use of steam engines to power spinning machinery, it remains at the foundation of academic, philosophical, and practical debate about the role of government in the economy, the value of free trade, and the nature of rational economic self-interest.

Life

Adam Smith was born in the village of Kirkcaldy, just north of Edinburgh, Scotland, on June 5, 1723. His father had died shortly before his birth, and he was raised by his widowed mother, with whom he maintained a close bond until her death in 1784. At the age of fourteen Smith was sent to the University of Glasgow, where he was much influenced by the teachings of Francis Hutcheson (1694–1796), an esteemed moral philosopher who believed, among other things, that human beings were guided by innate moral instincts about right and wrong, more so than by a sense of self interest. In 1740 Smith went on to Balliol College at Oxford University, where he received his bachelor's degree in 1744. During his studies at Oxford, Smith discovered the work of David Hume (1711–76), a Scottish philosopher 12 years his senior. Smith was significantly influenced by Hume's essays about money and international trade, and the two later became close friends.

Smith returned to his home in Kircaldy in the late 1740s and then lived in Edinburgh until 1751, when he was appointed professor of logic at the University of Glasgow. The following year, at the age of 29, he became chair of moral philosophy at Glasgow, inheriting the position that had been held by his former teacher, Hutcheson, until 1746. In this capacity he lectured on such diverse topics as natural theology, ethics, jurisprudence, and economics. In 1759 he gained widespread attention with his *Theory of Moral Sentiments,* an examination of ethics, human nature, and the feelings that lead people to act virtuously. Although the work was later eclipsed by the *Wealth of Nations,* Smith still considered it his most important philosophical endeavor, revising it continually until the end of his life.

Moreover, it was based on the extraordinary merit of Smith's debut publication that he was hired as a tutor to the young Duke of Buccleuch, stepson of the prominent English politician Charles Townshend, who contracted to pay Smith a salary of 300 pounds per year for the rest of his life. Unable to refuse such a handsome offer, Smith abandoned his academic post in 1764 to live and travel in France and Switzerland with his pupil. During this period he came into contact with some of the foremost political-economic thinkers of the age, including Voltaire (1694–1778), Jean-Jacques Rousseau (1712–78), François Quesnay (1694–74), Anne-Robert-Jacques Turgot (1727–81), and Jacques Necker (1732–1804). Smith's sojourn on the European continent lasted about two years. Thereafter, having secured a life pension, he returned to Kirkcaldy to live with his mother and work on *Wealth of Nations.* When the lengthy masterpiece appeared in 1776, it was immediately recognized as the most systematic, comprehensive, and incisive study of economics ever written. Curiously, two years later Smith was made commissioner of customs in Scotland, which put him in the uncomfortable predicament of having to curtail smuggling, an activity he had defended in the *Wealth of Nations* as a natural consequence of the government's unreasonable import taxes.

Smith argued that a nation's wealth should be measured not just by its horde of gold but also by all of the goods and services that it produces. He also examined the nature of that enormously sophisticated production of goods and services. One of his guiding insights was the notion of the "invisible hand." This was the concept that, in a situation where buyers and sellers compete freely in the marketplace for what is in their own self-interest, the greatest good for all is consistently achieved, as if by the prodding of an invisible hand. The marketplace, in Smith's view, was a self-regulating system in which market prices were determined by the forces of supply (what the sellers want) and demand (what the buyers want).

This, together with Smith's many other crucial insights into the ways that societies use their resources, served as the foundation for much of the economic thought of the nineteenth century. Even in the twentieth and twenty-first centuries, economists continued to refine and reconsider Smith's ideas in new ways.

$ More Detailed Information

Nineteenth-century thinkers, foremost among them the English economists David Ricardo (1772–1823) and Thomas Malthus (1766–1834), followed Smith's lead, fleshing out the details of the self-regulating processes he had described and addressing some of the problems or omissions they saw in his analysis. Ricardo argued against barriers to foreign trade, as had Smith, but Ricardo focused on the ways in which the wages of workers, rent

Socially awkward and consumed by his ideas, Smith remained a bachelor throughout his life. Although he was quiet, reclusive, and incorrigibly absentminded, he was still known to be a brilliant lecturer who could expound his complex thoughts in an a fluid, animated, and thoroughly engaging style. Smith died in Edinburgh on July 17, 1790, having demanded from his deathbed that the bulk of his manuscript writings be destroyed.

Work

The Wealth of Nations marked a radical departure from the principles of the mercantilist economic system, which had been established in Europe since the sixteenth century. Under mercantilism, the government played a protectionist role in the economy by promoting the export of its goods and restricting the import of foreign goods, especially through the use of import taxes, called tariffs. The government also interfered with competition and technological innovation by granting unfair advantages to certain merchants, farmers, and manufacturers over others and by prohibiting the use of new laborsaving machinery.

In the *Wealth of Nations* Smith issues a stringent critique of mercantilism, arguing that free trade and competition, with a *minimum* of government regulation, are the key to national prosperity. The wealth of a nation, he suggested, should be judged not by the amount of gold in the government coffers but by the quantity and variety of goods available to its consumers. Not only will free trade expand the realm of consumer choice and spur economic growth, Smith asserts, but it will also foster the general welfare of the society. Indeed, central to Smith's economic model is the idea that people acting in their own self-interest—"the uniform, constant, and uninterrupted effort of every [person] to better [his or her] condition"—will lead to the creation of high quality goods that meet the needs of, and therefore benefit, the society.

Legacy

It would be difficult to overstate the importance of Smith's contributions to the study of economics. *The Wealth of Nations* established a new paradigm for understanding the process of creating wealth and paved the way for the tremendous economic expansion of the nineteenth century. The text is regarded as the cornerstone of what came to be called classical economics, as well as the definitive vision of free market capitalism. Most prominent economists in the history of the discipline—including David Ricardo and Karl Marx in the nineteenth century and John Maynard Keynes and Milton Friedman in the twentieth—have responded to his work.

Adam Smith founded the modern field of economics with the publication of *The Wealth of Nations* in 1776. In exchange for a spending a few years tutoring the young stepson of a prominent British politician, Smith secured a lifetime pension, which enabled him to devote nearly all of his time to developing his ideas. © *Bettmann/Corbis.*

levels, and business profits interacted. Because of the complex effects each of these factors had on one another, Ricardo argued, laws that protected British farmers from outside competition were actually harmful to the wider economy. Malthus, meanwhile, examined the questions of overpopulation and the prospect of a general glut, in which an excess of production might lead to economic stagnation.

Karl Marx (1818–83), the German economist and philosopher best known as the author of the highly influential pamphlet *The Communist Manifesto* (1848), built on the ideas of Smith and Ricardo to critique capitalism in his lengthier work *Das Kapital* (1867). Among Marx's wide-ranging conclusions was the influential idea that business owners essentially derived their profits by paying workers less than they deserved (given the value their labor added to the products). The English philosopher and economist John Stuart Mill (1806–73), meanwhile, also saw flaws in capitalism, but he used Ricardo's ideas to suggest ways of correcting rather than abolishing the system, as Marx wanted to do.

The theories of these and other thinkers are now commonly grouped together under the heading classical economics. Most economists throughout the late nineteenth and early twentieth centuries continued to accept the basic ideas of the classical economists. The leading figures in the field during this time often focused less on wide-ranging theories than on supporting preexisting theories with sophisticated mathematical principles. During this time economics moved away from its origins

---

Important Economists in History

- **Adam Smith** Scottish, 1723–1791

Known as the father of economics, Smith believed that when buyers and sellers competed freely for what was in their own self-interest, the greatest economic good for all was consistently achieved. His book *An Inquiry into the Nature and Causes of the Wealth of Nations* (1776) is considered the founding text in the field of economics.

- **David Ricardo** English, 1772–1823

Ricardo, also a supporter of the free exchange between buyers and sellers, argued against barriers to trade between countries, believing that laws that protected English farmers from foreign competition were actually harmful to the wider English economy.

- **Thomas Malthus** English, 1776–1834

Known for his grim predictions of the future, Malthus believed that the world's population would grow much more quickly than the economy's ability to produce food, leading one day to mass starvation.

- **John Stuart Mill** English, 1806–1873

Although a strong believer in individual and economic freedom, Mill was concerned about the risks of economic competition. He wrote, "I am not charmed with the ideal of life held out by those who think that the normal state of human beings is that of struggling to get on; that the trampling, crushing, elbowing, and treading on each other's heels . . . are the most desirable lot of human kind."

- **Karl Marx** German, 1818–1883

Marx, author of the *Communist Manifesto* and the economic text *Das Kapital*, inspired the worldwide movement of Communism in the late nineteenth and twentieth centuries. He believed that business owners made money, or profit, by paying workers less than they deserved.

- **Alfred Marshall** English, 1842–1924

Marshall reexamined and elaborated on the ideas of his predecessors, developing influential new concepts about prices and the value of products and services. He is credited with transforming economics into a more mathematical, scientific profession and encouraging people to apply economic principles to real world problems.

- **John Maynard Keynes** English, 1883–1946

Keynes believed that a struggling economy could be revived with increased government spending, which would create a demand for goods and services and thereby more jobs for people who produced them. His ideas became popular during the worldwide economic downturn known as the Great Depression (1929–1939).

Economics studies how a society uses its resources to produce goods and services. These seven thinkers were among the most influential in shaping the ideas of modern economics. *Illustration by GGS Information Services. Cengage Learning, Gale.*

in pure theory and observation and became dependent on highly sophisticated mathematical analysis.

Ideas such as the invisible hand (which guided the marketplace, ensuring the greatest good for all) continued to dictate the study and implementation of economic theory. The United States, for instance, had no cohesive economic policy prior to the Great Depression (the severe worldwide economic decline that lasted from 1929 to about 1939). Instead it largely trusted the self-regulating market to take care of itself. But the Great Depression presented economists with problems that their existing theories could not answer.

During the Depression roughly one-third of the U.S. labor force was out of work, which meant that people did not have the money to buy many of the basic necessities of life. Thus, it did not matter that new, enlarged factories with the latest technology were capable of producing goods in previously unimaginable quantities; there was no demand for those goods. The marketplace offered no solution to problems such as this.

It was in this climate that the British economist John Maynard Keynes (1883–1946) offered insights that revolutionized the field. His book *The General Theory of Employment, Interest, and Money* (1936) proposed that the economy, in certain conditions, might not have the capacity to correct itself. In such a situation, he argued, only a national government had the ability to provide solutions. The government could address the lack of demand created by high unemployment (joblessness) by spending money in a variety of ways. He reasoned that when a government spends money, that money goes into the hands of private citizens, who use it to buy what they want and need. This spurs the growth of business.

Keynes's ideas, which overturned many of the classical economists' assumptions, provided an intellectual foundation for many government programs aimed at reducing poverty and regulating the economy. His ideas also led to the creation of a new approach to the study of economics.

Before Keynes introduced his ideas, most economic theory concerned the choices of individual consumers and businesses; in other words, such theories built a picture of the larger economy from the bottom up. After Keynes this way of studying the economy came to be known as microeconomics.

Keynes's arguments showed the necessity of looking at the economy in another way as well: from the top down. He believed that by analyzing trends at the national level (especially factors such as the economy's growth, employment, prices, and the money supply), economists might be able to make discoveries that they were unable to see at the microeconomic level. This top-down view of the economy came to be known as macroeconomics. The field of economics today remains subdivided into these two basic ways of looking at economic activity.

$ Recent Trends

Keynesian economics dominated the academic world and government policymaking through the 1960s, but thinkers such as the American economist Milton Friedman (1912–2006) began to point out flaws in the idea that a government could fine-tune a national economy. Friedman and others brought back classical economic notions of the self-regulating market, arguing that an economy worked best in the absence of government interference. One of the only spheres in which Friedman believed a government should have a role in managing the economy was the money supply (the amount of money in circulation). Friedman's ideas continued to have influence at the close of the twentieth and the beginning of the twenty-first century, but they were never followed to their full extent.

Today many mainstream economists are engaged in uniting macroeconomic and microeconomic concepts. Whereas Keynesian economists had taken a macro view of the economy that was largely independent of the well-established principles of microeconomics, in the 1970s and beyond economists began finding microeconomic explanations for phenomena that are apparent at the macro level. There are also numerous alternative approaches to economics today, many of which are built on the ideas of nineteenth-century thinkers such as Marx, whose ideas other economists have since left behind.

The Big Picture: Macroeconomics

$ Overview: Macroeconomics

What It Means

The field of economics is divided into two main branches: microeconomics and macroeconomics. Microeconomics deals with the choices of individual people or groups (consumers, business firms, government agencies) and involves attempts to understand particular economic sectors. For instance, in microeconomics we might analyze the behavior of consumers and producers of chocolate candy during a period of time when chocolate prices were rising. Macroeconomics, by contrast, examines the overall health and growth of the economy. It focuses on the economy as a whole, concerning itself with the aggregate behavior (the total result of individual actions) of consumers and producers in various parts of the economy. In macroeconomics we would not pay attention to individuals or specific groups in the chocolate-candy market or even to the chocolate-candy market as a whole. Instead, we might consider such variables as aggregate demand (the collective demand in the entire economy) and inflation (the degree to which prices are rising) in the nondurable goods sector, a portion of the economy that includes all goods that cannot be reused or will not retain their value for more than a year.

Economists examine various large-scale factors to determine the health of an economy. Six of the most important are national income, prices, employment, fiscal and monetary policy, consumption and investment, and balance of payments.

National income is the total value of all goods and services produced in a country. There are different ways of measuring national income. In the United States the most common measurement is gross domestic product, or GDP.

When studying prices, economists analyze pricing trends among different categories of goods and services, and they ask questions such as "How much do goods and services cost, relative to incomes and other economic indicators?" and "How fast are prices rising?" Inflation (the general rising of prices) is perhaps the single greatest danger to any economy, outside of extraordinary conditions such as war and global upheaval.

Employment is another chief factor affecting the economy on a large scale. Economists attempt to determine how many people are out of work at a given moment and what this means for the economy. An economy's health is strongly tied to the proportion of the population that both wants to find work and can find work.

The government's approach to spending and taxation is called its fiscal policy, while its approach to the money supply (the amount of money in circulation) is called its monetary policy. Both types of policy have the ability to affect the overall economy in dramatic fashion.

Consumption is the purchase of goods and services by individuals and households; investment is the purchase of goods and services by businesses to buy things that will allow the production of other goods and services. These two forms of spending drive much of economic activity and together account for nearly 80 percent of GDP.

Balance of payments refers to the relationship between a country's imports and exports (the amount of money paid to foreign countries or institutions for their goods and services and the amount of money accepted as payment from foreign countries or institutions for our goods and services) in a given time period. The degree to which a country is in debt and the amount of money owed to it by other countries have an influence on overall economic health.

Macroeconomics revolves around these six topics. Economists pay close attention to these indicators, tracking their past and current fluctuations; they use the information they gather to help guide government policy. They also analyze such fluctuations in the context of national and global affairs in order to refine old theories and develop new ones. Macroeconomics as a field has been shaped by varying philosophical approaches to these six and other large-scale economic phenomena.

When Did It Begin

Modern economic theory dates from the book *An Inquiry into the Nature and Causes of the Wealth of Nations* (1776) by the Scottish philosopher Adam Smith (1723–90). Smith argued (among other things) that the market system (a market is any place where buyers and sellers come together) ensured the most efficient distribution of money, resources, and well-being. Applied on a national and international scale and refined by succeeding theorists, this view of a world kept in balance by the individual actions of buyers and sellers dominated economic thought for much of the following century and came to be known as the classical school of economics. There was no distinction between microeconomics and macroeconomics until well into the twentieth century.

But the Great Depression (a worldwide economic decline that started in 1929 and lasted through most of the 1930s) upset classical notions such as the idea that the balancing desires of buyers (demand) and sellers (supply) kept prices in line and ultimately ensured that, in a free market, healthy levels of employment would be maintained. Enormous numbers of people lost their jobs, and business activity ground to a halt across the developed world, but classical theory could not explain why this had happened.

In 1936 the British economist John Maynard Keynes (1883–1946) published *The General Theory of Employment, Interest, and Money*, a book that satisfactorily explained the causes of the Great Depression and offered what came to be known as macroeconomic solutions to the crisis. Keynes argued that an imbalance between savings and investment (the portion of income that households were saving was not getting back into the economy through business investment) had led to economic instability and the eventual collapse of the economy. In the vacuum created by that collapse, Keynes proposed, government should step in to make up for the lack of private investment. Governments could do so by changing their approach to fiscal and monetary policy, most notably by engaging in what is called deficit spending (spending using borrowed money that a nation does not have the means to pay back in the short term).

In the succeeding decades Keynes's ideas had an enormous influence on governments and revolutionized the study of economics. He was largely responsible for pointing out that large-scale factors (such as those listed in his book's title) should be studied as indicators of economic health without focusing on the individual behavior of economic decision makers. That is, theories about supply, demand, and prices as they applied to individual businesses and consumers (today these theories form the basis of what we call microeconomics) might not always tell the whole story about an economy. It was necessary, according to Keynes, to study an economy from the top down as well, using aggregate factors like those that are studied in macroeconomics today. Thus, it

is largely because of Keynes that macroeconomics was established as a discipline and the field of economics split in two.

More Detailed Information

Whereas microeconomic theory is based on simple, long-established ideas such as the laws of supply and demand, the basic principles of macroeconomic theory have been subject to debate and refinement in the years since Keynes outlined his views on the topics that would define the discipline.

Before Keynes had convincingly demonstrated his theories in *The General Theory of Employment, Interest, and Money*, most economists and political leaders believed that the government should stay largely on the margins of a national economy. They argued that, when governments involved themselves in public-works projects (such as dams and roads), they took business away from private companies and were less efficient at the projects than private companies were. Moreover, it was widely believed that a balanced national budget was a firm requirement: a government, like a household, should not spend more than it takes in; debt was irresponsible and dangerous.

While Keynes agreed with many principles of classical economics, he also argued that governments could apply their power directly to the macroeconomic factors that affected an economy. Governments, in Keynes's view, could at times regulate the balance between savings and investment (too much savings and too little investment had been a major cause of the Great Depression, in his view) through monetary policy (adjusting the money supply). In a deep recession or depression, however, monetary policy would have little effect; in those cases governments could borrow money to be used on spending programs. This would allow them to funnel money into the national economy without taking it out of citizens' pockets through higher taxes, which would in turn allow for the favorable macroeconomic effects of increased employment and increased purchasing power.

These ideas drove what was known as the Keynesian revolution in economics, and Keynesian economics became the successor to the classical economics school. In the 1930s government intervention such as President Franklin D. Roosevelt's large-scale public-works projects (including the Works Progress Administration, which provided jobs for the unemployed, mostly in construction) steered U.S. and European recovery from the Depression. The soundness of these policies reinforced Keynes's theories. Keynesian economics and its offshoots, neo-Keynesianism and neoclassical economics, dominated macroeconomics until the 1960s, both in academia and in the realm of government policy.

In the 1960s, however, the American economist Milton Friedman (1912–2006) began challenging Keynesian economics. Friedman believed, first, that

SAVINGS, INVESTMENT, AND THE GREAT DEPRESSION

The British economist John Maynard Keynes (1883–1946) virtually invented macroeconomics when he offered an explanation for the Great Depression (1929–39) that showed how the interaction of savings and investment on a large scale might not behave according to basic economic laws such as supply and demand.

When people save money, they usually put it in bank accounts or invest it in the stock market. Both approaches help businesses to grow; banks lend people's savings to businesses that want to expand their operations, and when investors buy stock (shares in a company), they likewise furnish companies with the money they need to grow. When businesses across the economy expand, they create jobs and cause the national income to rise. When the national income rises, individual people have more money, and they spend more and save more, making possible yet more business investment.

But during the severe economic decline known as the Great Depression, as financial conditions worsened, businesses became unwilling to invest in future expansion, regardless of the amount of accumulated savings at their disposal. The national income dropped, individual incomes dropped, and people had to use their savings to buy food and necessities. The pool of savings decreased, business investment stalled, and the market forces of supply and demand offered no solution to this standoff. For example, people with no money demanded no cars; therefore no cars were supplied.

There were, as Keynes pointed out, no market mechanisms for pulling the economy out of depression. In the absence of these market mechanisms, the only solution was for governments to begin spending money, employing people, and otherwise trying to create demand and restore the balance of savings and investment. Once people began earning money, they could begin saving money, buying things such as cars, and paving the way for further investment in the machinery and labor necessary for the nation's businesses to expand.

Adam Smith had been right to suggest that the market was by far the most effective means of promoting efficiency and well-being, and second, that government spending did indeed crowd out private businesses. His knowledge of macroeconomic forces, however, allowed him to go beyond the classical theory that Smith had used. Friedman argued that government could, in fact, contribute to the well-being of the economy, but only in one way: by controlling the money supply. This would allow the government to guard against inflation. In all other respects, government should refrain from interfering with the economy. Friedman's way of thinking about the economy was called monetarism because of his belief that inflation was tied strictly to the money supply.

Just as classical theory could not explain the Great Depression, Keynesian theory could not explain economic conditions in the United States in the 1970s, when something unprecedented happened: unemployment rose at the same time as inflation (a phenomenon that was dubbed "stagflation"). Friedman had been predicting that Keynesian economic policy would create just such a result, and his theories accordingly began to hold sway in macroeconomics.

Recent Trends

Friedman's views had a great deal of influence in the 1980s, especially with U.S. president Ronald Reagan and British prime minister Margaret Thatcher. Economists in academia were split between those who roughly agreed with Friedman and gravitated around the university where he had both studied and taught (the University of Chicago) and those who opposed many of his views about strict monetarism and government nonintervention and who were often associated with the Massachusetts Institute of Technology and Harvard University. Changing economic conditions in the mid-1980s seemed to contradict some of Friedman's predictions, however, and monetarism fell out of fashion. Although Friedman's approach to macroeconomic issues remained a major influence on conservative thought in the United States, monetarism was supplanted by the doctrines of what came to be known as "new classical economics."

New classical economics is similar to monetarism in that it represents a revival of classical economics, especially in its view that government intervention should be avoided. A key difference between new classical economics and monetarism is that the theoretical structure of the former is based on microeconomic theory. It uses the highly logical framework of microeconomics to derive macroeconomic theories and policies.

BASIC ECONOMIC CONCEPTS

$ Scarcity

What It Means

The world is not like the Garden of Eden, where all desires are always fulfilled. Instead, the earth's supply of resources is limited. Our desires as individuals and societies always exceed the world's ability to satisfy those desires. This central truth of life is what economists call *scarcity*.

As used in the field of economics, the term *scarcity* refers to the fact that no matter how much a society produces, people will always desire more. In this densely populated, highly developed area of Arizona, one of the scarcest resources is open space.   *Rich Reidl National Geographic/Getty Images.*

The problem of scarcity is plainly visible in poor societies. In drought-prone parts of Africa, for instance, there often is not enough food to go around. But increases in wealth at the individual or the societal level do not solve the problem of scarcity. Middle-class people in the United States may not be in danger of starving, but this does not mean that their desires are fully satisfied. A construction worker might want a nicer car and a larger house than he is currently able to obtain, but if he came into possession of those things, he would likely still have unsatisfied desires. We are all familiar with the phenomenon of celebrities who feel that they need houses the size of palaces equipped with private movie theaters, bowling alleys, and garages capable of housing dozens of luxury vehicles. Rare is the celebrity who, having acquired such things, stops wanting any more possessions. Because the supply of goods and services in the world is limited, even billionaires find it impossible to satisfy every single desire they have.

The problems faced by someone who wants but cannot obtain a private jet clearly pale in comparison with the problems faced by someone who is starving. Economists do not contend that all individuals and societies are equally affected by the problem of scarcity. They do, however, maintain that all individuals and societies are subject to the problem of scarcity and that this causes them to act in particular ways. Economics is the study of the ways in which people and societies respond to the problem of scarcity.

When Did It Begin

Scarcity as defined by economists has always been a fact of life. The ways in which societies have dealt with scarcity, however, have changed a great deal throughout history. Today capitalist systems are the chief means of determining how societies allocate scarce resources. In a capitalist economy businesses are largely owned by private individuals rather than the government, and prices are determined through the unrestricted dealings between buyers and sellers. Up through the Middle Ages (about 500 to about 1500), however, societies responded very differently to the problem of scarcity.

Prior to the rise of capitalism (which developed in Europe after the Middle Ages, during the sixteenth through eighteenth centuries), tradition and central authority figures determined how society's scarce resources were allocated. In most precapitalist systems only an elite group of people could own land and possess wealth, and these elites (along with the traditions that allowed them to remain in a privileged societal position) limited the production and distribution of goods and services. Farmers, bakers, cobblers, and blacksmiths may have existed in a medieval English village, but they did not own their land or the property they used to produce their goods, and they made only as much as tradition or a nobleman told them to produce. In general, only products left over after these conditions were met found their way to markets (places where buyers and sellers of goods and services come together).

Capitalist systems, by contrast, rely on markets to set the terms for the production and distribution of scarce goods and services. Once capitalism began to take hold in Europe, individuals such as farmers, bakers, cobblers, and blacksmiths could pursue their own self-interest with relative freedom from the dictates of tradition and authority figures. The competition among such tradesmen worked to the benefit of buyers. Because buyers were free to choose one baker's bread over another's, for instance, bakers had to produce high-quality bread at reasonable prices. Likewise, competition among buyers for a limited amount of bread meant that the price of bread could not fall too low. Demand (the amount of bread people were willing to buy over a range of prices) affected supply (the amount of bread a baker was willing to produce over a range of prices), and vice versa. Resources were thus more efficiently allocated than in previous systems, but this did not solve the problem of scarcity. According to economists, scarcity is the motor that propels market-based capitalism, and it will always be a fact of life.

More Detailed Information

Although scarcity is a central issue in any economic theory, economists over the years have viewed it in different ways. In his book *The Wealth of Nations,* considered the foundational text in the field of economists, Adam Smith (1723–90) discussed the relationship between scarcity and value. The value of precious metals, such as gold, Smith wrote, "is greatly enhanced by their scarcity." He noted, "With the greater part of rich people, the chief enjoyment of riches consists in the parade of riches, which in their eye is never so complete as when they appear to possess those decisive marks of opulence which nobody can possess but themselves."

Writing not long after Smith, Thomas Malthus (1766-1834) concentrated on a decidedly more grim view of scarcity, one in which even basic needs could not be met. He believed that population would always grow faster than the supply of food, leading to food shortages. Because, Malthus believed, humans had little ability to solve this problem, population would be kept in check by war, famine, disease, abortion, and infanticide.

A more positive approach to scarcity was taken by John Maynard Keynes (1883–1946), whose ideas during the Great Depression (a worldwide economic downturn that lasted from about 1929 to 1939) revolutionized economic thought. In discussing scarcity, Keynes proposed two types of human needs: absolute needs, such as food and shelter, which are independent of what other people have; and relative needs, those that exist "only if their satisfaction lifts us above, makes us feel superior to, our fellows."

In modern economic thought, scarcity is viewed more simply as an imbalance between people's virtually unlimited desires and the limited resources available to satisfy those desires. We can understand unlimited human desire by contemplating our own desires and the impossibility of completely satisfying them. But what, exactly, do we mean by *resources*? Economists divide resources into three categories: land, labor, and capital. These three kinds of resources are also commonly referred to as the factors of production.

Land In economic terms, land is not simply the plots of earth upon which people undertake economic activity; it also includes all of the natural resources connected to those plots of earth. A farmer's fields are land, but so are the trees on his or her property, the wildlife that populates his or her fields and forests, any gold or oil that may be underneath the ground, the rivers and lakes on the property, and even the air above that property. The natural resources included in the definition of land can be divided into two types: nonrenewable resources and renewable resources. Nonrenewable resources are those that, once used, are gone forever. For example, once all of the world's gold and oil has been extracted from the earth, there will never be any more. Renewable resources are those that, left alone, will naturally replenish themselves; examples include soil, forests, and rivers. But the fact that a resource is renewable does not mean that it is unlimited. For instance, there is a limited amount of forested land in the world. Likewise, even though a river's waters can eventually be renewed after being polluted, there is a finite amount of clean water on the planet at any given time.

Labor Labor refers to both the total number of available workers and the mental and physical capacities of those workers. The number of people willing and able to work is always limited, as are the skills that those workers must possess in order to produce various goods and services. The nature of the workforce within a given country greatly affects the kinds of goods and services that can be produced there.

Capital Capital is all of the man-made items used to produce goods and services. Examples of capital are factories, machines, computers, trucks, warehouses, and office space. Such items are distinguished from those that are meant to satisfy human desires directly. There is always a limited supply of capital in the world, and various types of capital are scarcer in some countries than in others. Capital everywhere is also subject to limitations imposed by technology. Computers and trucks, for instance, are only as productive as current technologies can make them.

Together, the factors of production dictate the amount of various goods and services that can be produced. Because each factor is subject to its own limitations, there can never be a situation in which production could be as unlimited as consumer desire. Given this gap between production and desire (which is the problem of scarcity), choices must be made in any society about what will be produced, how it will be produced, and for whom it will be produced.

In modern-day capitalist countries most of these choices are made through the interaction of buyers and sellers in market settings. Governments, however, also have the power to influence these choices through fiscal policy (which involves raising and lowering taxes and making laws relating to the economy) and monetary policy (which involves increasing and decreasing the amount of money in circulation).

Recent Trends

According to economists, every society must determine how best to allocate its scarce resources. This entails answering the questions of what will be produced, how it will be produced, and for whom. In a perfectly

THOMAS MALTHUS

"The germs of existence contained in this spot of earth, with ample food, and ample room to expand in, would fill millions of worlds in the course of a few thousand years. Necessity, that imperious all pervading law of nature, restrains them within the prescribed bounds. The race of plants, and the race of animals shrink under this great restrictive law. And the race of man cannot, by any efforts of reason, escape from it. Among plants and animals its effects are waste of seed, sickness, and premature death. Among mankind, misery and vice."

THOMAS MALTHUS, *AN ESSAY ON THE PRINCIPLE OF POPULATION*, 1798.

Why He Is Important

Thomas Malthus (1766–1834) was an English economist who is considered part of the classical school, a group of eighteenth- and nineteenth-century theorists who pioneered the field of study that we now call economics. He became famous for arguing that over-population would always outpace the growth of the food supply. He did not believe that humans themselves had significant power to control their rates of reproduction, maintaining that the only effective checks against overpopulation were phenomena such as war, famine, disease, abortion, and infanticide. By showing that nature would, through the tendency toward overpopulation, always thwart human progress, Malthus intended to disprove the utopian political and economic theories of his time (theories which argued that human beings and societies could be perfected).

Life

Malthus, who went by his middle name Robert, was born on February 14, 1766, at the Rookery, his father's country estate near Guildford, Surrey, England. The elder Malthus, Daniel, was a country gentleman and a thinker in his own right, a follower and friend of the Enlightenment philosopher Jean-Jacques Rousseau (whose ideas about individual freedom helped pave the way for the democratic revolutions in France and the United States) and an admirer of utopian theorists such as William Godwin and the Marquis de Condorcet. Malthus was educated by private tutors according to his father's progressive beliefs, and he enrolled in Jesus College, Cambridge, in 1784. In 1788 he became a minister in the Church of England, and in 1797 he accepted a ministerial position at a church near his father's home in Surrey.

Malthus and his father had always discussed philosophical matters together, and though they often disagreed, they remained close correspondents while the younger Malthus was away at school. Once Malthus returned to Surrey, he and his father had regular debates about the perfectibility of society. After one particular debate in which the younger Malthus laid out his case against the utopian theories of William Godwin, the elder Malthus suggested that his son put his argument into writing. The result was a short pamphlet called *An Essay on the Principle of Population*. Published in 1798, the essay was an immediate sensation, and Malthus became a controversial intellectual celebrity.

Widely ridiculed by many contemporary journalists and pamphleteers as an excessively pessimistic monster, Malthus was nevertheless recognized as a brilliant theorist who considered the well-being of society's lower classes. Incidentally, those who knew him claimed that his personality was far from monstrous. His economic theories may have been dark, but as a person he was said to be kind, thoughtful, and generous.

Malthus began to study money in 1800, and he wrote pamphlets about economics and revised his essay on population, bringing it out in 1803 as a book-length study supported by empirical evidence he had gathered on trips to Germany, Russia, and Scandinavia. He married in 1804 and became the father of five children, an ironic fact, as many scholars have observed, considering his deep concern for the perils of overpopulation. Malthus also became the first economist in England to hold a position in academia when, in 1805, he was offered a job as professor of modern history and political economy at the East India College in Haileybury.

In 1810 Malthus initiated a correspondence with the foremost economist of his time, David Ricardo, and the two became friends, though they disagreed vehemently on many economic questions. In response to their frequent debates about economics, Malthus continued to refine his theories, and he wrote a number of pamphlets presenting his ideas. His most important later work was *Principles of Political Economy Considered with a View to their Practical Application* (1820), in which he offered a comprehensive view of economic theories as he saw them. Malthus held his professorship in Haileybury until his death on December 29, 1834.

competitive economy, economic theory tells us, these questions would be answered in a way that maximized efficiency and provided for the greatest good. In other words, market mechanisms and competition would ensure that the goods and services that people most want and need would be produced at the lowest prices according to the most efficient methods.

But today there are people (even some who believe that the free market has the potential to allocate scarce resources efficiently) who wonder whether the global

economy is competitive enough to make this possible. Many industries in the global marketplace are dominated by a few multinational corporations that are not subject to unfettered competition or national laws and limitations, and the world's wealth has become increasingly concentrated in the hands of a few rich nations and, within those nations, ever-smaller circles of extremely rich individuals. Thus, substantial numbers of ordinary citizens, government officials, and economists around the world wonder how global capitalism might be altered to

Work

Malthus's most important contributions to economic theory were his theory of population, as presented in *An Essay on the Principle of Population*, and his theory of general gluts, as presented in *Principles of Political Economy*.

The basis of his theory of population was a set of two truths: that food is necessary for existence, and that sexual passion is a necessary and enduring fact of life. Humans, Malthus argued, would inevitably multiply geometrically (1, 2, 4, 8, 16, 32), while

Thomas Malthus was among the founders of classical economics. He is best known for his bleak view that human population would grow faster than the world's food supply. *Pictorial Parade/Hulton Archive/Getty Images.*

the food supply could only be increased arithmetically (1, 2, 3, 4, 5, 6). Extending his theory into the realm of public policy, Malthus argued that giving aid to the poor was self-defeating, since additional money merely encouraged the poor to reproduce. Once a poor couple had additional mouths to feed, they would be right back in the miserable conditions that the aid had been intended to alleviate.

Malthus's theory of general gluts did not excite the public imagination to the degree that his population theory did, but it was nevertheless a radical departure from existing economic theory. Other classical economists, such as Adam Smith and Malthus's friend David Ricardo, believed that supply creates its own demand; in other words, the production of greater quantities of goods stimulates the economy sufficiently to make people willing and able to buy those goods. Malthus believed, however, that businesses could grow too rapidly and produce quantities of goods out of proportion to consumers' willingness to buy them, resulting in a general glut, or surplus, of goods that could not be sold. He argued that such a situation could be catastrophic for the economy.

Legacy

Malthus's theory of population, though it revolted many of his contemporaries, was nevertheless enormously influential during his lifetime and for decades after his death. The 1834 reform of England's Poor Laws, which cut off all aid to able-bodied poor men, was largely based on the logic Malthus had presented in his work. Charles Darwin's theory of evolution is said to have been influenced by Malthus's ideas, which also had an impact on social policymakers for much of the nineteenth century. Malthus's population theory waned in influence in the late nineteenth century as increases in living standards were accompanied by falling birth rates, at least in industrialized Western countries. The theory continues to crop up in discussions about less-developed countries today, where overpopulation remains a concern.

Dismissed at the time by Ricardo and other economists, Malthus's theory of general gluts seemed to come true roughly a century after his death with the onset of the Great Depression, the severe economic crisis that afflicted the world economy in the 1930s. In the United States and Western Europe, enormous leaps in technology and production techniques over the preceding decades meant that the industrialized world was packed with modern, efficient factories capable of pumping out endless supplies of goods for sale. For the better part of the 1930s, however, few people had the money to buy any such goods, and the economy collapsed.

allow for a more sustainable allocation of scarce resources and, by extension, a more equitable distribution of income.

Meanwhile, some critics of modern capitalism question whether scarcity truly exists. In economic terms, scarcity implies that the humans desire for goods and services is virtually unlimited. These critics have suggested that the supposedly unlimited desire for goods and services might be cultural rather than innate, artificially created by such phenomena as advertising and status seeking.

$ Three Economic Questions: What, How, For Whom?

What It Means

In order to meet the needs of its people, every society must answer three basic economic questions:

- What should we produce?

- How should we produce it?

- For whom should we produce it?

Every nation must ask itself the three economic questions of what to produce, how to produce it, and for whom. In the United States issues relating to these questions are debated by Congress in the Capitol Building. *AP Images.*

A society (or country) might decide to produce candy or cars, computers or combat boots. The goods might be produced by unskilled workers in privately owned factories or by technical experts in government-funded laboratories. Once they are made, the goods might be given out for free to the poor or sold at high prices that only the rich can afford. The possibilities are endless.

Although every society answers the three basic economic questions differently, in doing so, each confronts the same fundamental problems: resource allocation and scarcity.

Resources are all of the ingredients needed for production, including physical materials (such as land, coal, or timber), labor (workers), technology (not just computers but, in a broader sense, all the technical ability and knowledge that is necessary to produce a given commodity), and capital (the machinery and tools of production). *Scarcity* refers to the essential fact that people's wants or desires are always going to be greater than the resources available to fulfill those wants.

Simply put, scarcity means that resources are limited. No country can produce everything, no matter how rich its mines, how massive its forests, or how advanced its technology. Because of the constraints of scarcity, then, decisions must be made about resource allocation (that is, how best to allocate, or distribute, resources for the maximum benefit of the society).

When Did It Begin

Questions of scarcity and resource allocation are as old as human civilization. Throughout history every society—whether society is defined as a nation, a tribe, or a single family—has had to determine what to produce, how, and for whom. While indirect attempts to answer these questions can be found in the writings of the ancient Greek philosophers Plato (c. 427–c. 347 BC) and Aristotle (384–322 BC), the questions were not articulated in their current form until economics was introduced as a discipline of study more than a thousand years later.

Modern economic theory as we know it today is founded on the writings of the Scottish philosopher Adam Smith (1723–90), especially his best-known work, a five-book treatise called *An Inquiry into the Nature and Causes of the Wealth of Nations.* Ever since this groundbreaking work was published in 1776, many competing economic theories have been presented, but all of them have been organized around the attempt to answer the three basic questions.

More Detailed Information

For every society the answers to the three basic questions depend on what kind of economic system it uses. The term *economic system* refers to the way in which a society organizes the production and distribution of good and services. The system that a society chooses reflects the philosophical and political ideas on which that society is founded. Historically, there have been three basic types of economic system: traditional, command, and market.

Traditional Economic System: A traditional economy is rooted in long-standing cultural customs. Resources (especially land) are allocated through inheritance or by decisions of cultural leaders, and the new generation performs the same economic roles as their parents and grandparents before them. Traditional economies are founded on a strong philosophy of social interdependence and community. They usually revolve around subsistence farming, in which food is grown to feed the members of the community, not to sell or trade in markets. Although most traditional economies have been replaced by more ·modern economic systems, they can still be found in the agricultural areas of developing countries in Asia, Africa, and South America.

Command Economic System: A command economy (also called a planned economy or centrally planned economy) is one in which economic decisions are controlled by a central authority, usually the state (government). The state controls the society's capital (means of production) and decides how resources should be allocated (including what should be produced, how prices should be set, and how much people should be paid for their work). Command economies go hand in hand with socialist or communist political philosophies, which emphasize the equal distribution of wealth but do not support individual entrepreneurship or the acquisition of private property. The Soviet Union was the most prominent planned economy of the twentieth century.

Market Economic System: A market (also called capitalist) economy is one in which answers to the three basic questions are the cumulative result of many individual decisions about what to buy and what to sell in the public marketplace. Buyers express their preference for certain goods and services, thereby influencing what is produced. The means of production are privately owned by sellers, who try to produce things as cheaply and efficiently as possible in order to make a profit (meaning that they sell an item for more than it cost to produce). In its purest form a market economy should function without any government intervention. Market economies are founded on the idea that the good of the whole society depends upon freedom of choice, competition, and the right of every individual to pursue private wealth. The United States is the largest market economy in the world.

In reality, most countries employ some mix of economic systems. For example, although the United States identifies itself as a market economy, the government controls public education, the postal service, and a number of other enterprises that are integral to the functioning of the economy. The U.S. government also imposes various business regulations that supersede market forces, such as a minimum wage that all businesses must pay their workers, emissions standards that limit pollution, and excise taxes designed to offset the negative social impact of certain goods, such as cigarettes. Implicit in such regulations is the idea that freedom to profit (in a pure, unregulated market) is not the only measure of public good. In the United States there is constant debate about how much or how little the government should intervene in the market.

Recent Trends

In the 1980s most of the world's command economies began to embrace elements of the market system. In 1985, for example, President Mikhail Gorbachev (b. 1931) introduced in the Soviet Union an economic-reform program called perestroika (the Russian word for "restructuring"). The reforms led to economic upheaval, however, and the Soviet Union collapsed in 1991. Since then Russia and other former Soviet countries have continued to gravitate toward a market economic system, but the process has been fraught with difficulties.

In the late twentieth century the country that had transitioned most successfully from a command to a market economy was China. Beginning in the late 1970s, reforms in China were carried out as the government began to relinquish its control over the means of production and allow market forces to exert an increasing influence over the three basic economic questions: what gets produced, how it gets produced, and for whom it gets produced. Despite these changes, in the early years of

NO COUNTRY CAN PRODUCE EVERYTHING

While one nation may concentrate on producing consumer goods and services, another may find it more beneficial to focus on building the machinery and equipment that other nations use to produce goods and services. A country with rich soil and a moderate climate might become a leader in agricultural production, while a country with a strong educational system might find that its most valuable product is an educated populace. Every country produces an assortment of different things, but while there are millions of combinations to choose from, no single country has infinite resources (ingredients of production); therefore, no single country can produce everything.

According to this premise, every country must make economic choices that will maximize the usefulness of its resources in order to foster the growth and stability of its society in the present and for future generations. These economic choices revolve around three basic questions: What should we produce? How should we produce it? For whom should we produce it?

the twenty-first century China still described itself as a "socialist market economy."

$ Factors of Production: Land, Labor, Capital

What It Means

In economics the term *factors of production* refers to all the resources required to produce goods and services. A paper company might need, among many other things, trees, water, a large factory full of heavy machinery, a warehouse, an office building, and delivery trucks. It might require a thousand workers to run the factory, take orders, market (or sell) the paper, and deliver it to wholesalers or retail stores. It might need thousands more resources of varying size and cost. Some of these items, such as workers' skills, might be intangible. Together, these resources constitute the factors of production necessary for the paper company to do business.

Though the number and variety of the different resources businesses require is limitless, economists divide the factors of production into three basic categories: land, labor, and capital. Land refers to all of the natural resources that businesses need to make and distribute goods and services. Among the resources that the paper company requires, the trees and water used to make paper would be classified as land, as would the ground on which the factory, warehouse, and office buildings are located. In economics, terms as various as gold, soil, forests, oil, coal, air, lakes, rivers, wildlife, fish, the sun, and even outer space fall under the heading of land. All of these

Factors of production are the land, labor, and capital necessary to produce goods and services. For example, capital expenses, such as this farm equipment in Zimbabwe, play a major role in maximizing agricultural production. © *Hulton-Deutsch Collection/Corbis.*

things are alike in that they are provided by nature rather than made by humans.

Labor refers to the workers needed to produce goods and services. The factory workers, office workers, marketing staff, and sales staff of the paper company would all be considered labor. Labor includes not just the number of employees but also the various abilities called for from workers. The labor needs of a paper company would probably differ substantially from the labor needs of a computer company, even if both needed the same number of employees.

Capital refers to the human-made equipment required to produce goods and services. The paper company's factory, machinery, office building, and delivery trucks would be examples of capital. Sometimes capital is also defined to include the money used to buy such equipment and to start and maintain business operations.

Some economists include a fourth category among the factors of production: entrepreneurship. Others consider entrepreneurship a form of labor or capital. An entrepreneur is someone with the creative ability required to organize the other factors of production in ways that produce profits. The profitability of the paper company depends not simply on the presence and quality of its

land, labor, and capital but also on the decisions made about how to employ these resources.

On a national scale the study of economics looks at problems related to the scarcity of resources, among other things. Since no economy has an unlimited supply of the factors of production, it is not possible to satisfy all of a population's wants and needs. All societies must make choices about how to use resources. In a market economy these choices emerge from the interactions of countless individual buyers and sellers competing with one another for profit and economic well-being. Economists study how these choices are made and how they might be made differently.

When Did It Begin

Capitalism, the economic system in which individuals own property and can compete freely for profits, could not exist without the factors of production. In fact the factors of production probably did not exist in any arrangement that could sustain capitalism before the sixteenth century. Though the ancient and medieval worlds had land, workers, and tools for producing goods and services, these things were controlled by central authority figures, such as kings and the elite classes of society, so that they could not be mobilized in the pursuit of wealth. Those who controlled the land controlled not just the natural resources but also the very people who lived on the land, and those in control had the authority to regulate the work these people did. Since workers were subject to the command of rulers, their tools did not function to create wealth in the same way that capital does.

A variety of historical and economic circumstances converged to bring the factors of production into being in Europe beginning in the sixteenth century. These changes took different forms in different countries, but they combined to pave the way for capitalism. In England peasants were evicted from rural areas so that nobles could use the land to pasture their sheep, whose wool had become a profitable commodity. This resulted in an influx of workers into cities, where they were able to (or were forced to) sell their labor to employers. Thus a market for labor developed. In France an influx of gold from the New World caused the prices of many goods and services to rise, and yet the landowning nobility had no way of increasing their wealth because it was based on collecting fixed amounts of money and farm produce from the tenants who farmed their land. These newly impoverished nobles thus began selling off their land to increasingly wealthy merchants. The result was the emergence of a market for land. In these and other ways land, labor, and capital were freed from their traditional restrictions and made available to anyone who could pay for them. Those who could buy the factors of production could combine them in the pursuit of profits.

More Detailed Information

The availability of the factors of production for use as economic resources was not an inherent feature of the world, then, but the result of specific historical changes. In particular, the freeing of land, labor, and capital from the control of rulers and other authority figures was necessary for these entities to function in a market economy. Released from traditional restrictions, the factors of production are now subject to the control of such market forces as supply and demand. Supply is the quantity of a good or service that sellers are willing to sell at a particular price, and demand is the quantity of a good or service that buyers are willing to buy at a particular price. Since both buyers and sellers want to maximize their economic well-being, sellers want to sell at the highest possible price, and buyers want to buy at the lowest possible price. The compromise between these opposing forces will set the terms for the production of any particular good or service.

While we may normally think of supply and demand as functioning in markets for consumer products, they are also components of markets for the factors of production (the factor, or resource, markets). The factor markets reverse the flow of the consumer markets: business owners are the buyers of land, labor, and capital, and individuals and households are the sellers. The owners of land receive payments (called rent) from businesses in return for the use of the land. In return for the use of their labor, workers receive payments (called wages) from businesses.

The payments that households receive in return for the third factor of production, capital, are called interest payments. Capital markets work according to slightly more complicated processes than do the land and labor markets. In general, businesses must borrow money to make the large investments in the equipment that they need to increase their profitability. Companies often borrow money from banks, but banks are really nothing more than intermediaries. Banks take in money from individuals and households in the form of deposits, then they lend it out to borrowers. The bank pays depositors interest (a fee for the use of their money), and borrowers pay the bank a higher rate of interest. The bank makes a profit on the difference between the two interest rates, but it is ultimately the savings of individuals and households, rather than the bank's money, that businesses are using to purchase capital. The interest payments that those individuals and households receive are the payments for capital in the factor markets.

The resource or factor markets, together with the markets for products, have a profound effect on all production and distribution decisions. The paper company above, for example, might find that at a certain price, its paper products sell rapidly and ensure it a comfortable rate of profit. If, however, the price of wood (a natural resource it depends on) rises drastically as a result of government regulation of the logging industry or some other event, the company might have to choose to either cut costs (by modifying the way it uses the factors of production) or raise the prices it charges consumers.

One way the company might cut costs is by laying off workers and increasing the workload required of its remaining employees. But those employees might, in response, demand higher wages, which would again force the company to find new ways of balancing its production and pricing decisions. Yet another way in which the paper company might juggle the factors of production in order to maintain or increase profits is to upgrade some of its machinery. To do this, it might need to borrow money. Interest rates fluctuate, however, and if the rates happen to be high when the company is thinking about making this investment in capital, the company may decide against the investment. From the point of view of a single business, then, the factor markets and the factors themselves are of supreme importance. Accordingly, there is a large body of economic theory devoted to investigating the best ways of combining the factors of production.

From the point of view of a nation or of the world as a whole, too, the factors of production represent one of the most important variables in the overall economic

IDEOLOGY AND THE FACTORS OF PRODUCTION

Market economies, in which individuals own property and compete with one another in the pursuit of profit, are possible only when there are markets (places and systems for buyers and sellers to come together) for the factors of production. The factors of production are usually divided into three categories: land (along with all natural resources), labor (the number and skills of workers), and capital (money and equipment that enables businesses to increase profits). When individual citizens of a nation are able to buy and sell land, labor, and capital, these basic resources of economic activity can be organized and combined in the pursuit of profit.

Since the factors of production are so crucial to the economic lives of individual citizens and the nations they live in, these factors figure prominently in any political ideology that takes the economy into consideration. Communism is an ideology based on the notion that the public should share ownership of the factors of production so that the proceeds of the economy may be divided equally among all citizens. At the other end of the political spectrum, those who believe in laissez-faire economic doctrines (which suggest that society is best served by a government that never interferes in the economy) argue that there should be absolutely no government participation in the markets for the factors of production.

Most governments today lean more heavily toward laissez-faire economic policies than toward communism, but there has probably never been a government that purely practiced one or the other of these extreme approaches. Political debate in many countries often continues to focus on the relationship between government and the factors of production.

an innovative, creative force capable of combining the other factors in visionary ways. Since these qualities seemed to distinguish entrepreneurship from other forms of labor or capital, many people have come to view entrepreneurship as a factor of production in its own right.

In the late twentieth century, moreover, agreement about the definition of the term *capital* began to dissolve. Capital had traditionally been defined as the investments in equipment that businesses make with a view toward future increases in profits, but the term increasingly came to include the financial resources a business has at its disposal.

Another form of capital has also taken on an increased prominence in economic thought: human capital. Human capital is the set of skills that any worker has as a result of his or her background, education, and experience. Some economists draw a distinction between human capital and traditional conceptions of labor, because investments in human capital yield future returns much in the same way that investments in physical capital (equipment) do. For example, a marketing manager at an insurance company might take time off of work and spend a great deal of money to pursue an M.B.A. degree. This investment would be likely to increase the manager's future income dramatically, as well as the future profits of the company that hired him or her. Sometimes employers support their workers in such endeavors.

equation. If we think of a nation's economic output as a river, the factors of production might be represented as the river's headwaters. Changes in the cost of land (or natural resources; for example, rising oil prices), labor (rising wages), or capital (rising interest rates) can profoundly affect the economy as a whole. Similarly, manipulation of the factors of production (for example, by raising or lowering taxes on imports, changing minimum wage laws, or raising or lowering interest rates) is one of the most direct and comprehensive ways a government has of altering its economy's shape. Any adjustments made at the headwaters of the economic river will affect nearly everything that happens downstream.

Recent Trends

Prior to the twentieth century economists often thought of a business owner primarily as an organizer of the existing factors of production. Increasingly, however, economists began to emphasize the role of the entrepreneur, who was not simply an organizing force but also

$ Circular Flow of Economic Activity

What It Means

All market economies are characterized by a circular flow of economic activity. This means that money and products (including the products businesses need to operate) move in a circular fashion between businesses and households. This situation is often illustrated using a diagram that allows us to visualize the basic workings of the overall economy.

A market is any place or system allowing buyers and sellers to come together. A market economy is one in which the free interaction of buyers and sellers determines most of the important features of economic life. Most economic decisions in a market economy are based on the forces of supply (the amount of any good or service that a seller is willing to sell at a given price), demand (the amount of any good or service that buyers are willing to buy at a given price), and prices. Sellers tend to supply more and more of their products as prices rise (because they want to maximize their profits), while buyers tend to buy less and less of a product as prices rise (because they want to maximize their own economic well-being). When buyers decide to purchase or not purchase certain goods

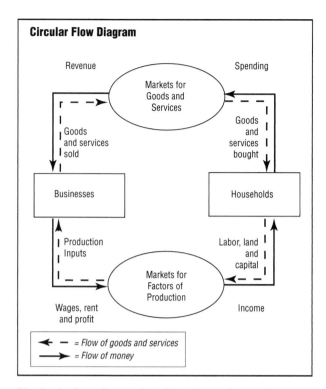

Circular Flow Diagram

Revenue   Spending

Markets for Goods and Services

Goods and services sold   Goods and services bought

Businesses   Households

Production Inputs   Labor, land and capital

Markets for Factors of Production

Wages, rent and profit   Income

◄ – – = Flow of goods and services
⟶ = Flow of money

The circular flow of economic activity refers to the way that money circulates continuously between businesses and households in the economy. Often represented by a diagram such as this one, the circular flow model shows the interdependence between these two groups of economic actors, both of whom act as sellers and buyers, or earners and spenders, at different times. *Illustration by GGS Information Services. Cengage Learning, Gale.*

in certain quantities, sellers make corresponding decisions about what to supply and in what quantities.

The circular flow model illustrates how market forces determine the overall shape of the economy. Businesses and households act as both buyers and sellers in the economy. Businesses sell products to households in exchange for money, and households sell products called the factors of production (land, labor, and capital [money and equipment], the resources required to do business) to businesses. The inner circle of the model shows products and services moving clockwise between businesses and households. The outer circle of the model shows income (money) moving counterclockwise between businesses and households.

This model is a simplification of economic activity, but it allows us to understand some central facts about market economies. Businesses and households are dependent on one another. They are bound to one another by supply and demand relationships that, in being played out, dictate the working of the economy. The money that households use to satisfy their needs and wants comes from businesses, and the money that businesses need in order to operate comes from households. Likewise, the products that households need and want come from

businesses, and the factors of production that businesses need in order to operate come from households.

When Did It Begin

The idea that income and goods flow in a circular fashion between businesses and households dates to the earliest economic theorists. An obscure Irish banker named Richard Cantillon (1680–1734) may have been the first to use the concept. Cantillon probably wrote his only surviving work, *Essai sur la Nature du Commerce en Général* (*An Essay on Commerce in General*), in the year 1732 or thereabouts, but it was not published until 1755 in France. Cantillon presented the economy as a unified system, comparable to the cosmos, in which the individual elements were interdependent on one another. The *Essai* directly influenced the Physiocrats, a group of French thinkers led by Francois Quesnay (1694–1774) who further laid the groundwork for the field that would become political economy (the original term for the discipline we now call economics). The Physiocrats' name was derived from Quesnay's occupation as the physician for King Louis XIV of France. Quesnay compared the economy to the human body, with money and goods functioning as the blood. In 1758 he drew an early version of the circular flow diagram to explain to the king how resources, money, and goods moved between farmers, landlords, and merchants.

The development of today's circular flow model is attributed to the American economist Frank Knight (1885–1972). Knight called the diagram "the wheel of wealth," and he used it as a teaching aide in his classes at the University of Iowa as early as the 1920s. Knight first published his diagram in some essays that he wrote in the early 1930s. Since that time it has become a fixture in economics textbooks worldwide.

More Detailed Information

The circular flow model concentrates on the relationship between the two primary groups of actors in the economy: households and businesses. Both households and businesses take in money, and both of them spend money on goods and services. Businesses and households interact with one another in two kinds of markets: the product markets and the factor markets.

The idea that businesses make money by selling products to households is probably familiar. Whether the products are tangible goods, such as lamps and automobiles, or intangible services, such as medical care or accounting work, businesses make money by exchanging these products for money with members of households. The exchanges are regulated by the forces of supply and demand. At the top half of the circular flow model, products move in one direction, from businesses to households, and income moves in the other direction, from households to businesses. This top half of the model encompasses the product markets.

AN ECONOMY MADE OF PIPES AND TUBES

The circular flow model of economic activity is a simple illustration of the interaction between businesses and households. Households pass money to businesses in exchange for products, and businesses pass their money to households in exchange for labor and other resources. Money thus moves in a circular fashion through the economy.

There are more sophisticated versions of this model in which the influence of taxes, imports, savings, and other factors are included. One such complex version was memorably transformed into an actual physical object in 1949 by the engineer and economist William Phillips (1914–75). Phillips's contraption was a circular network of clear pipes, tubes, and tanks that used colored water to show how money moved through the economy. Water exited the circular flow into sections of the model corresponding to taxes, savings, and the purchases of imports, and water reentered the circle through valves corresponding to exports, government spending, and investment. Today Phillips's seven-foot-tall device can be seen displayed at the Science Museum in London, England.

The money that flows into the hands of businesses is not absorbed or simply stored by businesses, however. In order to continue functioning, businesses must spend money on the factors of production: land (including physical land and any natural resources needed in their operations), labor, and capital (money, buildings, equipment, and other goods). Businesses use the money they obtain in the products market to buy these goods and services from households on the factor markets. In the case of labor, it may be obvious that this is so. One or more members of most households work in order to pay for the things they and their family members need and want. Workers sell their labor to businesses in much the same way that businesses sell products to households. Thus, the money that households contribute to businesses in the form of purchases comes back to households in the form of payment for labor.

Less obviously, households ultimately sell the other factors of production to businesses as well. One of the main ways that households do this is by saving money in banks. When a worker takes a portion of his or her income and puts it in a savings account, the bank pays the worker interest. Meanwhile, the bank lends the worker's income out to businesses that need it in order to buy land or to make purchases of capital, such as factory equipment, trucks, or computers. The businesses must pay the bank interest on the money they borrow. In this situation the bank is no more than an intermediary: the worker is ultimately lending money to the business for a fee. In

other words, the household is selling its money, at a price, to the business.

The circular flow model is an intentional simplification of any actual market economy. The model's validity is limited in several ways. First, the model assumes a straightforward market economy, whereas even the most market-oriented economies, such as that of the United States, are mixed economies. In a mixed economy the government asserts its influence on the economy with the intent of ensuring its stability, the well-being of citizens, or both. It influences the economy by implementing fiscal and monetary policies (fiscal policies regulate taxes and spending, and monetary policies control the amount of money in circulation), which can substantially affect flows of money and goods. Governments also have the power to regulate businesses and to affect the terms of their market interactions with households.

Another limitation in the basic circular flow model is that it does not take international trade into account. Not all products go to households within the economy; some products are exported to other countries, leaving the circular flow. Likewise, businesses from outside the economy sell their products to households within the economy in the form of imports. This means that money leaves the circular flow and goes abroad. The model also does not account for situations in which the levels of supply and demand fluctuate. Prices may be changed for reasons other than the natural functioning of market forces. For example, if consumer tastes shift, levels of demand would change, causing prices to change. This could result in inefficiencies in the economy that interrupt the circular flow.

Finally, the enormously complex financial industry may not be accurately accounted for by the basic version of the circular flow model. While the model assumes that individuals save or invest their money and therefore loan money to businesses on the factor markets, it may not adequately capture the complexity of investment types and of financial institutions in today's world. Another financial industry detail not illustrated by the model is that when members of households deposit money in banks, banks are required by law to set aside a certain percentage of the money in order to have it on hand when people want to make withdrawals. This money does not flow through the economy but is simply in storage.

Recent Trends

The basic two-sector (households and businesses), two-market (products and factors) circular flow model has become a classic illustration of economic activity. It is usually presented in the early pages of introductory economics textbooks. As a simple way of understanding the interaction of businesses and households, it is still considered an effective tool. Economists, however, regularly attempt to fill in missing details and make the circular flow model more precise. Accordingly, there are numerous variations on the basic diagram. One variation retains the two-sector focus but adds a third market, the financial market, to the product and factor markets. Another alternative diagram adds a third sector, government, and attempts to account for taxes in the circular flow. Yet another appends to both these diagrams the foreign sector, yielding a four-sector, three-market model. Still other economists attempt to build circular flow models that account for other factors, such as environmental damage and the monetary costs that it imposes on an economy.

$ Ceteris Paribus

What It Means

Ceteris paribus is a Latin term that translates as "all other things being equal" or "holding all else constant." When analyzing a particular aspect of the economy, it is often necessary to make the ceteris paribus assumption—that is, to hypothesize that all other things besides the factors under consideration will remain constant. Without making this assumption it would frequently be impossible to theorize about the effect of one factor on another.

For example, consider the relationship between demand (the quantity of a good that buyers are willing to buy over a range of prices) and the price of that good. We can predict what will happen when, say, the price of soda in vending machines on a college campus rises from $1 to $2—students will buy fewer cans of soda—but only if we assume that all other factors are constant. There are other factors that could affect demand for soda, such as an increase in student wealth, which may make the price increase have less impact on demand, or unseasonably warm weather, which may make students more likely to buy soda regardless of the price. In order to understand precisely what effect price and demand have on one another, however, we isolate these two factors from all others and temporarily act as though those other factors are, for the moment, constant.

The ceteris paribus assumption offers a way of simplifying reality in order to achieve greater understanding of the relationship under consideration. Once we possess this information (once we can say with confidence that rising prices result in decreased demand for soda), we have a foundation of more certain knowledge than we

The ability to make predictions about economic outcomes depends on the rule of ceteris paribus, which is Latin for "all other things being equal." To understand why assuming ceteris paribus is important, just imagine how you would predict the outcome of this pool shot if you could not assume that the pool table would stay upright, the pool stick would stay straight, and other such basic factors would remain the same. *AP Images.*

CETERIS PARIBUS AND THE SCIENTIFIC METHOD

When economists theorize about what may happen in the economy if a particular change, such as a change in price, occurs, they often can make predictions that apply only in conditions of ceteris paribus (all other things being equal). Rising prices lead to reductions in the quantity demanded (the amount buyers are willing to purchase) if all other factors affecting demand are constant, but it may not lead to less demand if a factor such as the income of buyers increases, making price increases less important. In order to theorize productively, then, economists must set aside those external factors, such as changes in consumer wealth, that are secondary to what they are studying, assuming ceteris paribus temporarily so that they can isolate the relationship between one economic factor and another.

This method of analysis is not unique to the social science of economics. In fact, it is a basic component of the scientific method as applied by biologists, chemists, physicists, and other natural and physical scientists. For example, if a physicist wanted to predict what would happen if a billiards player hit the eight ball with the cue ball at a 70 degree angle, he would have to assume ceteris paribus. By assuming ceteris paribus, the physicist takes for granted changes that are either unlikely or of only secondary importance, such as a change in the laws of gravity, the chance that the eight ball might be picked up by a passer-by, or the possibility that the pool table will collapse before the cue ball reaches the eight ball. As in economics, the ceteris paribus assumption allows scientists to make predictions about important phenomena without being derailed by the endless complexity of the natural and physical worlds.

would have had if we tried to speculate about multiple inconstant factors at once.

When Did It Begin

The British economist Alfred Marshall (1842–1924) is responsible for making the notion of ceteris paribus a central part of economic theory. Marshall's *Principles of Economics* (1890), the dominant English-language economics textbook for decades after its publication, synthesized the existing economic thought of his time and established a method of analysis that is still used today. That method, called partial equilibrium analysis, or comparative statics, was an answer to the difficulty of comprehending an entire, dynamic economy as a whole. Instead of attempting to account for the interrelation of all economic factors at all times, Marshall showed that economists could gain understanding of individual parts of the economy by temporarily isolating them from all other factors and making the ceteris paribus assumption. Partial equilibrium analysis remains an important analytical method among economists today.

More Detailed Information

Partial equilibrium analysis proposes that economists must necessarily simplify the economy in order to understand it. In a developed capitalist country such as the United States, no central authority controls the forces that shape the economy. Instead, hundreds of millions of individual buyers and sellers of goods and services make billions of individual decisions every day, usually with the intent of increasing their own economic well-being. These independent decisions collectively determine what goods and services are produced, how and in what quantities they are produced and distributed, and who benefits from this production and distribution. It is obviously impossible to monitor every individual economic factor or to account for all factors that might affect production and distribution. By isolating one changing economic factor at a time and assuming that all other factors are momentarily constant, however, economists can build simplified, hypothetical models of the economy. These individual models offer insights into specific parts of the economy, and we can assemble these specific parts into a reasonably accurate view of the overall picture.

A model can be a real economy that is simplified in a way that yields useful insights. For example, economists might study a prison economy in which all individuals, including those who do not smoke, use cigarettes as a form of money. Many factors that affect the national economy (for example, international trade, taxes, and the stock market) are not present in the prison economy, but this does not mean that the insights provided by the model are useless. Instead, an economist studying the prison economy would make the ceteris paribus assumption, acknowledging that, all else being constant, his or her theoretical findings hold true in the outside world no less than in the prison.

Basic economic concepts such as supply and demand are also models. When economists say that sellers are more willing to supply products as price increases, at the same time that buyers demand fewer products as price increases, they are offering a simplified picture of the economy in which all extraneous factors have been set aside (by making the ceteris paribus assumption).

The production possibility curve (PPC) is another such model. The PPC, rendered as a graph, is a tool for understanding the tradeoffs made when one good rather than another is produced. For example, an economist might construct a PPC showing how an increase in the production of chicken causes a corresponding decrease in the production of beef, and indicating what the optimal combinations of chicken and beef would be if the economy were operating at full efficiency. While it is true that there are many products other than chicken and beef, and that increases or decreases in the production of any product has wide-ranging effects that go beyond a single competing product, economists can assume ceteris paribus and study chicken and beef in isolation. This yields insights about the mechanics of economic tradeoffs that would not be forthcoming if we did not simplify.

It is important to understand that the ceteris paribus assumption is always temporary. Economists can build a model, study the effect of one factor on another by assuming ceteris paribus, and then relax the ceteris paribus assumption factor by factor. For example, in the case of the campus vending-machine economy, an economist might first speculate about the changes in demand caused by price, ceteris paribus, and then go on to observe how demand might be further changed by increases in student wealth and/or by unseasonable weather.

Recent Trends

Most economic thought is a product of partial equilibrium analysis: the isolation of one economic factor or set of factors from all others using the ceteris paribus assumption, and the building of models that can be supported mathematically. Partial equilibrium and ceteris paribus remain central to the practice of economics, and they probably always will.

In the latter part of the twentieth century, however, a growing number of economists began to return to an approach pioneered in the late nineteenth century: general equilibrium analysis. Rather than isolating one factor from all others, general equilibrium analysis calls for monitoring the changes brought about in all factors when one factor changes. While partial equilibrium analysis requires the assumption that all other factors are constant, general equilibrium analysis attempts to account for the interconnection of all economic factors.

This is a more demanding approach to economic theory than partial equilibrium analysis. Until the 1970s, in fact, general equilibrium analysis was entirely theoretical. Economists could speculate about how changes in one economic factor might send ripples through the economy, but these ripple effects were too complex to lend themselves to the construction of useful models. With the advent of high-powered computers, however, mathematical modeling of entire national economies became possible.

ECONOMIC SYSTEMS AND PHILOSOPHIES

$ Traditional Economic System

What It Means

Despite the extreme variety of human cultures throughout history, from Cro-Magnon cave dwellers to Ancient Egypt to twenty-first century America, there have only been three basic ways to organize economic life (the production, distribution, and consumption of goods and services in a society). One way is to rely on tradition to decide what goods and services will be produced, how

In a traditional economic system, economic decisions are determined according to tradition, and social and economic roles are rigidly defined. The Navajo tribe of the American Southwest, whose economy was founded principally on the cultivation of corn and the production of rugs and other crafts for trade, is a typical example of a traditional economic system. *Sylvain Grandadam Collection/Getty Images.*

they will be produced and distributed, and for whom they will be produced and distributed. Another way is to defer to some central authority figure who directs all members of society to follow his or her orders in regard to these issues. Finally, a society can allow market forces, such as supply (the amount of any good or service that a seller is willing to sell at a given price), demand (the amount of any good or service that buyers are willing to buy at a given price), and the desire for profit to shape its economic life. Of the three forms of economy, the first, called a traditional economic system, has been by far the most common over the course of history.

Societies relying on tradition to shape their economic life existed 10,000 years ago, and they exist today. As far as anthropologists (those who study humans and cultures) and economists know, traditional economic systems have not changed much during that time. The material needs of such communities are typically provided

THE PYGMIES OF CENTRAL AFRICA

Pygmies (peoples of various tribes whose height averages around four and one-half feet) live in several places in Southeast Asia and in larger numbers in Central Africa. An estimated 300,000 Pygmies live in Central Africa. (They refer to themselves by their specific tribes' names, rather than as Pygmies.) This figure includes numerous tribes that roam the rainforests of the region, meeting their economic needs (the production, distribution, and consumption of goods and services) by hunting and gathering and in some cases also by farming.

The Pygmies of Central Africa are believed to have existed in that region for far longer than any other humans, carrying on what may be one of the longest-lasting civilizations in human history. As economic development in the region proceeds, however, the pygmies will almost certainly cease to exist in coherent societies. They will join the developing world because of the the lure of more comfortable lives and the dictates of governments.

One of the major priorities, if not the only priority, of any economic system is to ensure the survival of a society. Though the Pygmies' economic system, based on hunting, gathering, and some farming, cannot likely compete against the threats of the modern world economy, it has certainly proven itself one of the most successful economic systems in history: it has allowed the tribes to survive intact for thousands of years.

for through hunting and gathering or through agriculture. Questions about which members of the community get which portions of what has been killed, gathered, or harvested are solved according to rules derived from the individual society's traditions.

When Did It Begin

There is no way of knowing the details of the earliest traditional economic systems because the activities of the first human societies are beyond the scope of history, but human societies have no doubt sustained themselves in this way since the first human communities appeared on earth. Certainly during prehistoric times most human societies would have organized their economic life in this way. Experts are unsure of exactly why or when human societies began moving away from tradition-based economies and toward the adoption of command economic systems. Many of the best-known early civilizations, such as those in ancient Mesopotamia, Egypt, and Greece, were command economies in which economic decisions were made by rulers. The third form of economic system, the market economy, did not begin to take hold until around the sixteenth century.

Economics as a field of study came into being in the eighteenth century, and it has always primarily focused on market economic systems. Therefore economists have not typically addressed traditional economic systems at great length, studying them primarily as a way of better understanding the characteristics of market economies.

More Detailed Information

The fact that there have only been three basic economic configurations across all cultures since the dawn of humanity suggests that the problems confronting human communities have been remarkably consistent over time. Indeed, all societies must solve the problem of satisfying their members' needs and wants in a way that ensures the survival of the group. To answer this challenge successfully (that is, to survive and achieve the group's goals), a society must organize the actions of its members effectively.

This organization takes place, economically speaking, in two particular areas: production and distribution. Any society must produce the goods and services that its people need, and it must then distribute those goods and services among its people. These processes lead to three clear questions. What will be produced? How will it be produced and distributed? For whom will it be produced and distributed? The answers to these questions tell us what form of economic system a society employs.

In a traditional economic system, the three questions are answered according to tradition. If a primitive society has always migrated to follow deer herds, hunting deer and gathering berries and nuts along the way, it will continue to answer the "what" and "how" of production in this way for as long as the society itself survives. If that society has always distributed half of a given deer to the person who killed it and divided the remaining half equally among the rest of the community, and if it has done so in a ceremony honoring the hunter, then it will probably continue to answer the "how" and "for whom" of distribution in this way. These rules, established by tradition, are enforced by social pressure. The community bestows its approval on those who follow the codes of tradition and shows its disapproval of those who do not.

One of the key features, then, of a traditional economic system is the fact that there is no concept of private property. A hunter may get a larger portion of a deer he has killed, but the community determines this. Tradition compels him to present his gains to the community in the first place rather than allowing him to hoard or sell them. Another key feature of traditional economic systems is that they usually produce and distribute goods at a level that ensures no more than subsistence, or survival. In other words the community only kills enough deer and gathers enough nuts and berries to survive. Is this subsistence condition a result of how difficult it is to produce and distribute food in this way, or is it a conscious choice not to consume more than necessary? Anthropologists have not resolved this question.

Experts agree that, whatever the comfort level of those living in primitive communities, tradition-based systems do not lend themselves to change or economic growth. Social roles are extremely rigid in these societies, so individuals are largely restricted by the circumstances of their birth. Likewise, because the problems of production and distribution will continue to be solved in the same ways they have always been solved in a given primitive community, the quantity of goods and services produced will likely remain unchanged (or it will only change in a way that accommodates a varying number of community members). Such societies do not promote intellectual development, and they do not tend to produce technological advancements.

Traditional economic systems, however, promote community strength more than the two other economic systems do. The well-defined bonds between individuals provide comfort and guidance, and crime is rarely a problem. Additionally, communities that rely on tradition to guide their economic life tend to live in harmony with the environment; this is because they merely subsist off the earth rather than attempting to control or profit from natural resources.

Recent Trends

In most countries in the twenty-first century, traditional economic systems have been replaced by command economic systems, market economic systems, or a combination of the two. There are, however, parts of Africa, Asia, and South America where tradition guides economic life. The people living in these communities are among the poorest in the world, and they lack the basic resources of education, health care, and sanitation that people in developed parts of the world enjoy. Additionally, their ancient ways of life are increasingly threatened by the economic development that surrounds them. As members of primitive communities within developing countries move to towns and villages and become citizens and taxpayers, they might improve their own material living conditions, but they diminish the chances for survival of the societies they leave behind. Likewise, as outsiders increasingly establish trading relationships with primitive communities, the communities themselves tend to become more like the outside world. If the world economy continues to develop according to the patterns of the twentieth and early twenty-first century, traditional economic systems will likely become even rarer, and some of the oldest societies on earth will cease to exist.

BARTER

What It Means

Barter is a system of trading goods and services directly for other goods and services without the use of money. Though barter occurs in the contemporary world, it was a far more essential part of life in early civilizations and in

BARTER IN COLONIAL AMERICA

During the European settlement of North America, barter (the direct exchange of goods and services for other goods and services) was the main form of economic transaction. Native American and European settlers used barter both within their own communities and with each other. Native American trappers bartered with such businesses as the Hudson Bay Company, exchanging their furs for a wide variety of European manufactured goods. Within individual communities, however, forms of barter called gift exchange and noncommercial barter were most prominent. Gift exchange refers to a situation in which individuals and families gave surplus goods and services to other individuals and families, expecting to receive items of similar value in return at a later date. Noncommercial barter is similar, but under this system an individual, rather than giving an item as a gift, might arrange to acquire what he needs (a certain amount of milk, for instance) with the understanding that he will later provide what the trading partner needs (such as a certain amount of cornmeal) with no payment of interest (fees paid to people who make loans) for the delay. It was not until the early nineteenth century that ordinary people in American cities or the countryside used money regularly to satisfy their household needs.

communities throughout history where no standard money system existed. For example, imagine a settler family in early colonial New England that is able to produce all of the food that it needs but that relies on outside sources for important nonfood items, such as shoes. In the absence of any standardized money system, the father of the family might attempt to barter with the village cobbler, offering eggs, milk, and butter in exchange for shoes.

Barter can be simple and effective when it works well, but there are substantial obstacles to bartering efficiently. What if the colonial cobbler did not need eggs, milk, and butter? Or what if he asked for a larger quantity of those items than the farmer wanted to give him? Even if the farmer surmounted these obstacles and got shoes for his family, he would have to face the same uncertainties every time he set out to barter for his family's nonfood needs.

Economists and historians believe that money arose in response to the complexities of barter. Money greatly simplifies transactions. The farmer, for instance, could sell his surplus goods at market and buy shoes with the money he earned. He could do this at his convenience, regardless of whether the cobbler needed milk, eggs, and butter.

When Did It Begin

The circumstances surrounding the beginnings of barter are matters of speculation rather than fact. The theories that have most heavily influenced economists' views on the origins of barter are those of the ancient Greek philosopher Aristotle and the eighteenth-century political economist and philosopher Adam Smith.

In *Politics*, one of the most influential texts on political philosophy in the history of Western civilization, Aristotle argues that barter developed when social groups grew larger than a single household. With the development of communities, trading between different households became desirable because it allowed people to obtain the necessities they lacked and to contribute their surpluses to those who needed them. Aristotle approved of barter for household necessities; he disapproved of the accumulation of wealth, which was made possible by the introduction of money. Wealth served no purpose, in his view, when it went beyond a household's needs.

Smith's view of barter, included in his landmark work *An Inquiry into the Nature and Causes of the Wealth of Nations,* focused on the phenomenon called the division of labor, the process whereby different people concentrate on different forms of work. This process is usually seen as having originated early in the development of civilization.

In any society people ideally focus on the work most suited to them and that they can do most efficiently; this allows for greater overall efficiency. At the same time, in Smith's view, specialization reduces people's self-sufficiency. Once people specialized, they lost the ability to provide for all of their needs within the household, and they had no choice but to barter for what they lacked. The troublesome complications of barter, Smith and Aristotle agreed, led to the development of money.

More Detailed Information

The details of barter vary depending on the community in which it occurs, but most barter transactions share some key characteristics. These characteristics demonstrate the complexity of a barter system compared to transactions in a money-based economy.

First, anyone who wants to barter must find someone who has what he or she needs and who also needs what he or she has to trade. Economists call this a "double coincidence of wants" and is the most serious obstacle to barter. Imagine a community of 40 households in which each household produces a specific commodity. The

When people barter, they exchange one good for another—a quart of milk for a dozen eggs—rather than using money to buy the products they need. Although bartering is rare in the modern world, it still occurs during times of economic instability, as, for example, in this Iraqi market in 1997. *AP Images.*

intricacy of pairing those who need one another's goods or services would be enormous, and it would increase with the size of the community and the number of goods and services available for trade.

A second characteristic of barter is that both parties must agree that the items being offered are of equal value. If you trade primarily in apples, and you want, say, a horse, you and your trading partners must arrive at a suitable value, in apples, for that horse. Bargaining often plays a key role in this process, and successful barter usually requires that one or both sides be flexible in the amount of goods or services they are offering. Sometimes this is not possible. For instance, if you are trading a wagon for a cow, there is no flexibility in the amount of wagon you might offer.

Related to the act of bargaining is another defining attribute of barter: in any instance of barter, both sides simultaneously perform the acts of buying and selling. If you are trading a leather jacket for a bicycle, you are buying a bicycle and selling a leather jacket at the same time. When you buy something like a bicycle, you must look at its age, its condition, its suitability to your purposes and tastes, then make a decision about its value; and when you sell something like a leather coat, you must make equally difficult calculations about its worth, both to you and to the other person. Having to perform both functions at once, while negotiating, makes barter much more complex than a money-based purchase or sale.

Many communities have dealt with these and other difficulties by developing alternatives to a strict barter system. In a system that anthropologists (people who study humanities and cultures) and economists call gift exchange, for example, people with a surplus of any commodity give gifts of that commodity to their neighbors. Their neighbors, in turn, are expected to give something back of equal or greater value at a later date. A farmer might slaughter a cow and have more beef than he can use all at once. He might, therefore, make gifts of the meat to a number of residents in his village, with the expectation that those people will later help him harvest his wheat. People who fail to give as generously as they receive or who don't give gifts at all lose their standing in the community.

Recent Trends

The use of money is almost universal today, so barter is less necessary than it was in the past. Barter remains a useful way to do business informally, however. It is somewhat common for acquaintances to exchange business products or services. For example, a lawyer might provide legal advice to the owner of a sporting-goods store in exchange for a set of golf clubs. A form of barter also has a role in international business, especially when corporations sell very expensive items (such as aircraft) to poor or less-developed nations. In this type of transaction, the buyer nation might pay partly with a good it has

in excess (such as wheat), which the corporation would then itself sell on the world market. Barter also becomes widespread at times of war and economic collapse, when a nation's money loses its value. During an economic crisis in Argentina in 2001–02 in which the country's money (the peso) lost 75 percent of its value, many citizens reverted to barter to satisfy their daily needs.

$ Market Economy

What It Means

A market economy is a system in which people voluntarily exchange goods and services for a price. Businesses and consumers, not the government, decide how much of a good or service, such as ice cream or furniture repair, is produced and purchased. Other terms for market economy are free-market economy and free-enterprise system.

Market economies are called free markets because individuals are free to pursue their economic self-interest,

Existing only in theory, a pure market economy is based on the free exchange of goods and services without any government regulation. In some countries regulation is reduced in Special Economic Zones, such as here in Shenzhen, China. © *Joseph Sohm/Visions of America/Corbis.*

JOHN STUART MILL

"The only freedom which deserves the name is that of pursuing our own good, in our own way, so long as we do not attempt to deprive others of theirs, or impede their efforts to obtain it."

JOHN STUART MILL, *ON LIBERTY*, 1859.

Why He Is Important

John Stuart Mill (1806–73), English philosopher, economist, and moral and political theorist, is widely regarded as one of the most influential thinkers of the nineteenth century. Mill lived during a period of profound and rapid change in England. Before the industrial revolution, the economy had been largely based upon the output of family-run farms, but with the advent of the steam engine, economic production shifted to large-scale mines, mills, and factories. Labor became a commercial, rather than a family, enterprise, and the population became increasingly urbanized. Railroad and shipping infrastructure had vastly expanded the possibilities for international trade.

In their formulations of economic theory, Mill's predecessors, such as Adam Smith, David Ricardo, and Thomas Malthus, had argued for the importance of free trade and the need to tie paper currency to gold as an international standard of value. While policies had been adopted to realize their vision of a laissez-faire (free market) capitalist society and Britain was rapidly becoming a major world power, these advancements did little to remedy social ills or improve the quality of life for average citizens.

In this context, Mill's theoretical endeavors were distinctive in their central concern for human liberty. His writings cover a wide range of political, economic, and philosophical topics but are unified by the belief that liberty is essential for individuals to realize their potential and contribute to a vibrant, ethical, and progressive society.

Life

John Stuart Mill was born in London on May 20, 1806, the eldest of nine children of James and Harriet Burrow Mill. His father was a Scotsman, originally trained as a minister, who had immigrated to England, attempted to make a living as a journalist, and eventually secured a position at the East India Company. A prominent political theorist in his own right, James Mill maintained close friendships with Ricardo and Jeremy Bentham, the acknowledged father of utilitarianism, which is the idea that that people's actions should be guided (and judged) by their intention to produce the maximum of happiness, and the minimum of pain, for the greatest number of people.

The younger Mill never attended school but was educated according to a rigorous program designed by his father. Intentionally shielded from contact with children his own age, he began studying Greek at the age of 3 and Latin at 8. By the time he was 14, he had received a thorough foundation in Greek and Latin classical literature, as well as history, logic, mathematics, and the basic principles of economics. Before the age of 20 Mill had published dozens of articles and reviews on various topics and established himself as a younger colleague among the most prominent intellectuals in England at the time, including Bentham, Ricardo, Malthus, and others. Although he had wanted to pursue a legal career, under pressure from his father Mill took a clerkship at the East India Company in 1823. He remained there for 35 years, eventually becoming the company's chief examiner, as his father had been.

In 1826 Mill was stricken by a severe case of depression, which he attributed to the intensive development of his intellectual life at the expense of his emotional life. During several months of this affliction, he carried on with his work even while he doubted its worth. Mill ultimately overcame his depression, aided in large part by his discovery of the highly emotional romantic poetry of William Wordsworth. In the years that followed Mill continued to explore and embrace the ideas of various English, French, and German thinkers whose emphasis on the primacy of emotional over rational experience marked a philosophical departure from the preceding generation.

In 1830 Mill met Harriet Hardy Taylor, a married woman who would become the most important influence in his life and work. Mill and Taylor maintained an intimate friendship over 20 years and eventually married in 1851, following the death of her first husband. In his *Autobiography* (1873), Mill extolled her prodigious intellect and credited her as the coauthor of many of his most important works. Mill was devastated when his beloved wife died suddenly in

choosing for themselves which goods to buy or sell and how much money they are willing to pay or charge for an item. Ideally free trade between consumers and producers results in the greatest abundance of goods for that society. Market economies depend on what are known as market forces. The level of consumer demand for goods and services is an example of a market force, as is the level of goods and services supplied to consumers.

A pure market economy, which would imply an absence of taxation or any other type of regulation, is possible only in theory. The reality of the market system is that while it allows market forces to influence most of the economic activity, it relies on the intervention of the government for its very existence. The government protects the right to private property, for example, allowing people to own businesses and to seek profit. It operates a court system where laws can be enforced, maintains an army to defend the country, establishes a system of money, and creates other organizations and rules that are needed for markets to function. The interplay between free markets and governments is complex. Political debate often centers on how much the government should be involved in the market system.

When Did It Begin

Aspects of the market economy system have existed in the trading systems of nations for thousands of years, but it

John Stuart Mill believed that human freedom and the moral and spiritual health of society were essential ingredients in a thriving economy. As a member of the British House of Commons, Mill was an outspoken critic of racism and an advocate of women's rights. *London Stereoscopic Company/Hulton Archive/Getty Images.*

1858 while they were traveling in southern France. Thereafter he divided his time between London and Avignon, where he could be close to her grave.

From 1865 to 1868 Mill served in the British House of Commons, where he was known for his unorthodox views, including his vehement opposition to racism and his support of voting rights and equal access to education for women. Following the end of his term

in government, he devoted much of his time to championing the latter cause. Mill died in Avignon on May 8, 1873, and was buried next to his wife.

Work
Instead of formulating new, original ideas of his own, Mill viewed his economic writing as an effort to consolidate and elaborate upon the dominant theories of his time. Published in 1848, his *Principles of Political Economy and some of the applications to Social Philosophy* became the standard economics textbook in England for more than 40 years. Mill generally followed the principles laid down by his predecessors and embraced the premises of laissez-faire capitalism as necessary for personal freedom. Yet he challenged the notion that wages, rent, profits, and the distribution of wealth are governed by immutable laws. He argued that that economic self-interest need not be the only guiding motive for economic decision-making, suggesting that the collective moral and spiritual vitality of the society was a legitimate and desirable benefit, too.

In his economic writing, as elsewhere, Mill was chiefly concerned with promoting the conditions (be they social, political, or economic) that would foster self-development for all members of the society. He recognized that this end would require not just freedom of the market but also political freedom and economic security and opportunity. As stated in his *Autobiography,* the goal of his economic writing was to determine "how to unite the greatest individual liberty of action, with a common ownership in the raw material of the globe, and an equal participation of all in the benefits of combined labour." Mill's major works outside the field of economics include *On Liberty* (1859), *Utilitarianism* (1867) and *The Subjection of Women* (1869).

Legacy
Mill was tremendously influential in his own day and has remained among the foremost philosophers in the Western tradition. He is considered among the great economists of the classical school, whose principles, first outlined by Adam Smith in 1776, dominated economic thought until the late 1800s and remain as the building blocks of all economic theory. Perhaps the most distinguishing feature of Mill's contribution to the field of economics was his abiding concern for how economic institutions, laws, and practices affect the moral, spiritual, and intellectual well-being of the people who live and work within that economic system.

was in the nineteenth century that organized political support for the free market was established and that ideas essential to a free-market economy, such as for-profit enterprises and entrepreneurship, became more familiar. A for-profit enterprise is a business venture that seeks to make a profit, and an entrepreneur is someone with the creative ability required to organize a business in ways that produce profits.

At the same time that ideas about the market economy were taking shape, Karl Marx, a nineteenth-century German scholar, developed a philosophy known as Marxism. Marx argued that the value of a product came from the labor a worker put in it, and thus the profit of a

business (when its revenue exceeded its costs) belonged not to the business owner but to the workers. He described a classless society in which all methods of production were owned in common (by everyone), though initially by the government in a transition phase called socialism. Many of Marx's philosophies were supported in the communist societies of the Soviet Union, China, and other countries during the mid-twentieth century, while the United States, Canada, and Western Europe, for example, built market economic systems. Between the late twentieth and the early twenty-first centuries, most communist countries had found government-led economies to be cumbersome and had chosen to move toward free-market systems. The market economy subsequently became by far the dominant economic model throughout the world.

More Detailed Information

The concepts of supply and demand are central to the idea of a market economy. Demand is defined as the quantity of a product or service that is desired by buyers over a range of prices. For example, a consumer may be willing to purchase two pounds of rice if the price is $.60 per pound. The same consumer may be willing to purchase only one pound of rice if the price is $1.00 per pound. Several factors influence the quantity a consumer is willing to buy of a good. These factors are the price of the good, the consumer's level of income, his or her personal tastes, the price of substitute goods (goods that can be used in place of other goods, in the way that margarine can be used in place of butter), and the price of complementary goods (goods that are normally consumed in combination with another good; when more hot dogs are bought, more hot dog buns are also bought).

Supply is defined as the quantity of a good or service that the producers of the market are able and willing to provide to consumers over a range of prices. For instance, perfume producers in an economy may be willing to sell 1 million ounces of perfume if the price is $50 per ounce, but they would produce substantially more if the price were $100 per ounce. The main factors determining supply are the market price of the good or service, the cost of producing it, and the level of competition.

The relationship between demand and supply has a large impact on the forces that determine the allocation (the planned distribution) of resources. In the theory of a market economy, consumer demand for goods and services and the supply of those goods and services will be in balance, or what is known as equilibrium, such that resources are used (or distributed) in the most efficient way possible. An efficient resource allocation means that goods are produced (or supplied) at a level that effectively meets consumer demand for them.

Market economies exist all over the world, although the government of each country restricts pure free-market practices in different ways. For example, the United States does not allow monopolies, in which one company exclusively controls the production of a service or product. Singapore and Ireland are examples of countries that place fewer restrictions on free-market practices.

A market economy contrasts with what is called a planned economy, one in which a government or other authority determines what and how much will be produced and what prices will be. In a planned economy the government intervenes in the open exchange of goods by doing such things as fixing prices, issuing quotas (limits) on imported goods, and subsidizing (providing financial resources to) industry. The main difference between market economies and planned economies is not the level of government influence but whether government influence is used to restrict the decision-making of private individuals and businesses. For example, if the government of a market economy wants more paper, it collects taxes from taxpayers and then purchases the paper at market prices. If the government of a planned economy wants more paper, it orders paper to be produced by paper companies and then sets the price using a governmental policy, or mandate. In general, socialist economies promote planned economic systems, and capitalist economies promote market economic systems.

Milton Friedman (1912–2006), one of the most influential twentieth-century American economists, was a strong advocate of curbing the role of government in the free market in order to create political and social freedom. Friedman believed that the economic freedom of the individual, which was entwined with the political and social freedom of the individual and the society, could be reached only in a market-oriented economy. Stated another way, countries that restricted economic freedom also tended to restrict the political freedom of their citizens.

Recent Trends

In the 1980s most of the planned economies in the world began moving toward free markets. In 1987 the Soviet Union initiated economic reforms, called perestroika, intended to revive its weak, government-led economy. These reforms introduced elements of market competition and encouraged free expression, but they eventually led to the downfall of the government itself. Beginning in 1978, the People's Republic of China created what was termed a "socialist market economy," which sought to combine the flexibility of a market economy with the political control of its socialist government. Using this system, China opened trade with the outside world, began to allow markets to determine prices, and decreased the state's role in distributing such resources as food. Unlike the reforms in the Soviet Union, the reforms China put in place were successful, and the Chinese economy grew rapidly. The standard of living of most Chinese people also improved dramatically. Many economists believe that the Soviet focus on developing heavy industry, which affects only a small group of businesses, kept its reforms from succeeding. In China the emphasis was on light industry and agriculture, both of which produce goods that are consumed by a large portion of the population.

CLASSICAL ECONOMICS

What It Means

"Classical economics" refers to the ideas of the first wave of modern economists, whose work spanned the late eighteenth century and much of the nineteenth century. The classical period of economic thought began with the publication in 1776 of the Scottish philosopher Adam

THE DISMAL SCIENCE

The field of study that we now call economics has been labeled in numerous ways since its appearance as a coherent system of thought in the late eighteenth century. These different labels have often reflected the attitudes of the labelers.

Adam Smith, generally considered the father of modern economics, called his work "political economy." This term suggested that the most important aspect of the study of economic activity was its relationship to political entities, or states that were in competition with one another.

In about 1870, as the discipline was becoming more popular, more mathematically sophisticated, and less centrally focused on the competing interests of different nations, leading figures in the field, such as Alfred Marshall (1842–1924), began referring to their work simply as "economics."

One earlier label, however, is widely remembered: in the mid-1800s political economy (as it was known at the time) became known as "the dismal science." The term is still used in a derogatory sense today, and most people assume that the term's negative connotation has to do with some of the grim predictions offered by political economists in the mid-1800s. For example, Thomas Malthus had outraged many of his English readers by predicting (wrongly, as it turned out) a future of mass starvation as population growth outpaced the country's capacity to supply food.

In fact, the phrase "the dismal science" has origins that, for different reasons, are perhaps even more disturbing. In the nineteenth century doctrines of racial superiority were common. Political economists such as John Stuart Mill (1803–73) challenged such notions by arguing that institutions, not race, led to some countries being rich and others being poor. The British writer Thomas Carlyle (1795–1881), in an essay denouncing the antislavery movement, called political economy a "dismal science" because it was a leading force in the campaign to abolish slavery. Carlyle believed that a racially based hierarchy was the natural order of things, and he saw that this hierarchy was threatened by the basic assumption in economics that all people are equal.

Smith's *An Inquiry into the Nature and Causes of the Wealth of Nations*, the book whose theories gave rise to the modern study of economics. After Smith the most prominent figures generally included in the category of classical economists are David Ricardo, Thomas Malthus, John Stuart Mill, and Karl Marx.

The classical economists differed on many issues, but together they laid the foundation for all economic study to follow. Smith introduced the idea of analyzing the complicated processes involved in a nation's production of goods and services, and the later classical theorists refined, added to, and reconsidered the picture of economic activity that he had drawn.

When Did It Begin

There was no systematic study of economic activity until after the Middle Ages (the period from about 500 to about 1500), when nation-states in Europe (such as England, France, Spain, and Portugal) began building power through wealth that was often amassed by traders. With the growing role of traders, economies were transitioning from being controlled by the nobility to being run by private individuals (a system that came to be called capitalism). This first phase of capitalism (which spanned the sixteenth through eighteenth centuries) was dominated by an economic theory called mercantilism. The mercantilists believed that a nation's wealth equaled the amount of precious metals, such as gold and silver, that its government possessed. Therefore, the European nations attempted to establish a favorable balance of trade, which meant that they intentionally exported more goods than they imported, thus ensuring that they brought in more gold and silver than they sent to other countries.

Adam Smith (1723–90), writing in Scotland, formulated his book *An Inquiry into the Nature and Causes of the Wealth of Nations* (published in 1776) as an argument against mercantilism. One of his chief goals was to show that a nation's wealth was not simply equal to its stockpiles of precious metals. In Smith's view, everything that a nation produced for sale should be taken into account when judging that nation's wealth. Therefore, he said, it was healthy economic activity, and not gold stockpiling, that governments should worry about promoting.

More Detailed Information

Economic health, in Smith's view, arose naturally from market activity (a market is any place where buyers and sellers come together). Self-interest led businesses to seek profits, which meant that they would naturally want to charge consumers as much as possible for their goods or services, while paying their workers as little as possible. The business owners' desires for profits would be balanced, however, by the self-interest of consumers and workers, who wanted, respectively, to pay as little as possible for goods and services and to be paid as much as possible for their labor. When there were multiple businesses competing for customers as well as for workers, prices fell and wages rose until there was just enough profit to keep a business in operation. Thus, the market itself ensured that the goods and services people wanted were produced with maximum efficiency and at a fair price. Smith called this phenomenon the "invisible hand" that guided capitalism.

Smith revolutionized thinking about capitalism by showing that the public interest (the greatest good for all people in a society) could be promoted at the same time that individuals had no motive other than self-interest. He believed that the government should refrain from intervening in market processes as much as possible and should instead trust the invisible hand to guide the economy.

David Ricardo (1772–1823), writing in England during the early nineteenth century, developed some of his most important theories in response to the idea of government intervention in foreign trade; he specifically objected to Great Britain's Corn Laws, which restricted imports of grain. Ricardo focused on the interaction of capitalists (those who used land for speculative business purposes), laborers, and landlords (those who owned land). The capitalists used some of their profits to pay rent to the landlords and some to pay the laborers their wages. When the government protected the profits of capitalists (in the instance of the Corn Laws, these were tenant farmers) through import restrictions on grain, it meant that more grain needed to be grown within England to feed the population. Because the amount of farmland was limited, it became more sought-after, and landlords were able to charge the farmers higher rents. Meanwhile, Ricardo argued, the laborers' rates of pay were bound to be fixed at subsistence levels (allowing them to pay only for the bare necessities). The landlords therefore were the only ones making increased profits in this scenario, because the capitalists would be paying more rent and would still have to pay the same wages to workers. This would result in a decline in profits for capitalists and possible economic stagnation. Ricardo's view was that, because of this process, economic expansion inevitably led to shrinking profits over time even without harmful trade restrictions.

Thomas Malthus (1766–1834), a friend of Ricardo, dealt extensively with the troubling side of economic activity. He first rose to prominence by theorizing that mass starvation would overtake England in the future as a result of overpopulation. Later he focused on the idea that an economy could collapse if there was a "general glut," a situation in which there were more goods and services produced than people wanted to buy. Ricardo and subsequent economists dismissed this theory, but it came back into prominence in the twentieth century, when Malthus's ideas seemed to be borne out by the Great Depression (the worldwide economic crisis that started in 1929 and lasted through the rest of the following decade).

The German political philosopher Karl Marx (1818–83) and the English philosopher John Stuart Mill (1803–73) both focused on the flaws in capitalism, but they came to very different conclusions. Marx built on Smith's and Ricardo's ideas to argue that capitalists derived their profits by exploiting workers, paying them less than they deserved given the amount of value they contributed to the goods and services that were produced. In Marx's view competition and economic growth would inevitably cause capitalists' profits to shrink, forcing them to exploit workers further. As shrinking profits forced more capitalists out of business, economic power would be concentrated in the hands of a few. Meanwhile, the working class would be larger and more dissatisfied than ever, so that revolution and the downfall of capitalism would become inevitable.

Mill, meanwhile, agreed that capitalism did not result in a fair distribution of rewards, but he did not prophesy the system's collapse. Instead he argued that income could be redistributed without harm coming to the overall economy.

Recent Trends

One idea that united all of the classical theorists was a basic agreement on how the value of a good or service was created. Classical economists tended to view value as the sum of the labor that went into the production of a good or service. Beginning in the late 1800s economists started to reconsider this idea, called the labor theory of value. This reconsideration of value inaugurated a new school of thought called neoclassical economics, which continued, with certain major adjustments, to represent the views of mainstream economists through most of the twentieth century.

The neoclassicists viewed value not simply in terms of the amount of labor required to produce a good or service but also in terms of the amount of satisfaction a product gave the consumer. Consumers were seen as rational decision makers who took into account the satisfaction they would get out of buying one product versus another. The greater amount of satisfaction a product gave per unit of cost, the greater its value to consumers. While this issue marked an advancement over classical economists' ideas, the neoclassical school continued to build on the basic ideas pioneered by the first modern economists.

Classical economic concepts were not, in fact, subjected to wholesale reevaluation until the Great Depression, which seemed to refute many of the assumptions that economists had long made. The ideas of the British economist John Maynard Keynes (1883–1946) departed greatly from classical theory and revolutionized economics in the 1930s and 1940s. In subsequent decades, however, the neoclassicists strove to integrate his ideas with their own. Thus, classical economics lives on.

NEOCLASSICAL ECONOMICS

What It Means

More than a century after its principles were developed, neoclassical economics remains the overwhelmingly dominant theoretical paradigm, or framework, in modern economics. Neoclassical economics uses the principles of supply and demand to explain how prices for goods and services are established, how outputs (the amount of goods and services produced) are determined, and how income is distributed among people who participate in market transactions. As it is used here, the term *market* refers not to one specific store where a person might buy strawberries or light bulbs but rather to any arrangement that allows producers and consumers to exchange goods and services for money.

A competitive free market is one where there is little or no government intervention and producers and consumers interact freely, with the producers vying for a limited number of consumer dollars and the consumers trying to obtain a limited amount of goods and services.

Neoclassical economics emerged in the late nineteenth century and has remained the almost universally accepted framework for modern economic thought. One of the major innovations of neoclassicism, the introduction of mathematical equations to economic models, was strongly championed by William Stanley Jevons (1835–82), pictured here. *The Library of Congress.*

In such a market, the price of a good or service will create a balance between the quantity of goods and services available (the supply) and the quantity of goods and services purchased (the demand). This balance is called economic equilibrium.

Neoclassical economists assume that all the participants in the market (often referred to as economic agents) are trying to obtain the best possible circumstances for themselves in the face of market-imposed constraints. Buyers seek to optimize (or maximize) utility (the satisfaction they receive from the goods and services they buy). Meanwhile, producers seek to maximize their profits (the money they make from the goods and services they sell). Both agents employ the information at their disposal (such as advertisements and product reviews, for consumers, and market research and trend forecasts, for producers) and exercise their rational preferences in their decision-making. Both agents' economic decisions are also governed by the fundamental constraint known as scarcity (the conflict between limited resources and unlimited desires). Consumers may not have enough money to purchase all of the goods they want, or the goods they desire may not be available to them. Producers may have limited access to the resources they need to produce their goods, or they may not have enough customers purchasing their products and services to render the profits they wish to gain. According to the neoclassical model, all these dilemmas are eventually resolved in markets, where consumers and producers respond to fluctuating prices.

This neoclassical framework is often referred to as a metatheory, meaning that its principles stand as the foundation upon which other, more specialized economic theories—for example, the neoclassical theory of production or wealth distribution—are constructed. Indeed for twentieth and twenty-first century economists, the premises of neoclassical economics have been so widely accepted that rejecting them is a little bit like a physicist rejecting the law of gravity.

When Did It Begin

Most economic historians agree that there were three founding fathers of neoclassical economics: William Stanley Jevons (1835–82), author of *The Theory of Political Economy* (1871); Carl Menger (1840–1921), author of *Principles of Economics* (1871); and Léon Walras (1834–1910), author of *Elements of Pure Economics* (1874–77). Working independently of one another in England, Austria, and Switzerland, respectively, these pioneers launched what is commonly referred to as the neoclassical revolution. The movement was called "neoclassical" because it was not a complete departure from the principles of classical economics. This new generation of thinkers agreed with the founders of classical theory—most notably Adam Smith (1723–90)—that markets should be guided by an invisible hand (that is, should be left to develop by themselves) rather than controlled

SURVIVOR

The popular American reality-television program *Survivor* can thank neoclassical economic thought for its success. *Survivor* is based on a decision-making principle outlined in a science called game theory, which, in turn, traces its origins to the principles of neoclassical economics. Each episode of *Survivor* depicts a contest among individuals placed in a remote, primitive location, usually a tropical island with few or no modern comforts. The contestants are often separated into teams, or "tribes," and given a challenge that they must meet together. At the end of each episode, one contestant is voted off the island. The final remaining contestant wins $1,000,000.

In order to survive—that is, to avoid being voted off the island—a contestant often must decide if he or she is better served by helping the group or helping himself or herself. In other words, contestants must decide whether cooperating with others or acting selfishly will increase the likelihood that they will survive. There is no fixed rule: sometimes it is better to be selfish, and other times it is better to cooperate. The best course of action depends on the circumstances. This choice between co-operation and selfishness is at the core of game theory, which studies how individual participants maximize their returns, or earn the best outcomes for themselves. According to the principles of neoclassical economics, optimal market conditions (an economic equilibrium with affordable prices for the widest possible range of consumers and maximized profits for producers) evolve out of a complex combination of cooperative and selfish behaviors among the individuals participating in the market.

economic thought is that it provided economists with scientific methods for conducting economic analysis. Although the classicists were certainly aware of the interplay between supply and demand, it remained a rudimentary, intuitive idea until the late 1800s, when the neoclassicists refined it as a set of system dynamics whose interacting components could be measured, graphed, and used to make specific predictions about the outcomes of various economic situations. Indeed, the neoclassicists used the rhetoric of contemporary physics as a metaphor in their conception of economic law, whereby value (or utility) in economics functioned much like energy, and economic agents functioned like atoms.

In their effort to legitimize economics as a hard science, the neoclassicists also introduced mathematics, especially differential calculus, to solve so-called constrained optimization problems—that is, any situation where an agent's effort to optimize utility is constrained by scarcity, and the answer to the question "What is best?" can be expressed as a numerical value. The process by which the economist solves the problem of what is best (or how to optimize) is called marginal analysis.

According to the utility theory of value, the value of a product must be measured not by its total utility (that is, the satisfaction the consumer derives from the total units of that product he or she buys) but instead by its marginal utility (that is, the additional satisfaction the consumer derives from buying an extra unit of the product). If the marginal utility of buying one more unit is greater than the price of that unit, the consumer is likely to do so. Similarly, a producer's estimation of how much product he or she should produce involves a calculation of the marginal cost versus the marginal benefit (in this case, the added profit he or she stands to earn) of producing one more unit. Marginal analysis defines economic efficiency, or equilibrium, as the point where marginal cost and marginal utility (or benefit) are equal. The emphasis on marginal value was another defining aspect of neoclassicist theory, so much so that the neoclassicist revolution is also widely referred to as the marginalist revolution.

Recent Trends

Since the late twentieth century there has been a growing debate about the role of neoclassical economic principles in the development of a global economy, a process commonly referred to as globalization. Because of globalization, more goods and services are available in more markets throughout the world, and there is a growing economic interdependence among nations, which, some say, has allowed countries such as India and China to emerge as leading economies. Many economists and political leaders maintain that globalization has developed according to the neoclassical economic principles of free trade and marginal utility. In other words, resources have been allocated, prices have been set, and money has been

through government intervention. But Jevons, Menger, and Walras—and later, Alfred Marshall (1842–1924), author of the influential *Principles of Economics* (1890)— disagreed with Smith on the concept of value.

Smith's theory of how the value of a good or service is determined was called the labor theory of value. According to this idea, the value of a given item was a function of all the costs involved in producing the item and putting it on the market. In other words, the final price of a product was dictated solely by what it cost to make and distribute it. Neoclassicists argued that this was simply not true, because prices often fluctuated according to how valuable buyers perceived a given product to be— that is, how much utility, or satisfaction, they expected to derive from buying it. Thus, they conceived the utility theory of value, which stipulates that prices depend on a combination of the costs of production and the utility of the product to potential buyers.

More Detailed Information

Perhaps the most significant aspect of the neoclassical revolution and the reason for its enduring primacy in

distributed in the best possible way and with limited government regulation.

Since 1995 there has been a burgeoning antiglobalization movement, which has two main criticisms of the above view of globalization. First, some in the group argue that the neoclassical principles of free trade and marginal utility that have driven globalization have not created an optimal set of conditions for a wide range of people. Rather, they say, free trade has produced a group of large multinational corporations, such as Microsoft, Wal-Mart Stores, Inc., and Sony, that have profited from employing the world's poorest citizens and paying them low wages. Many people have become rich as a result of globalization, they argue, but the majority of people in the world are still poor, with no hope of improving their circumstances. Second, another group in the antiglobalization movement contends that globalization has in fact not developed according to the principles of free trade and marginal utility. Instead, these critics maintain, leading economic powers such as the United States, Japan, and members of the European Union have steered the process of globalization and controlled prices to their advantage.

SAY'S LAW

What It Means

Say's Law, also known as Say's Law of Markets, refers to an influential economic theory first developed in 1803 by French journalist, businessman, and economist Jean-Baptiste Say. One of the most pressing economic questions of Say's time was whether a capitalist country could experience a crisis such as a depression as a result of overproduction. In other words, might there be a situation in which there were more goods produced (too much supply) than there were people willing and able to buy them (not enough demand)? Say did not believe that this was possible, and the reason he gave, which has since become known as Say's Law, was that supply creates its own demand.

Accepting or rejecting Say's Law, for economists and government policy makers, means taking very different approaches to the economy and government's role in it. If, as Say believed, supply creates demand, then as long as businesses are able to produce their goods and services, the free market should be able to solve any problems that arise. Say's Law generally supports the view that governments should adopt a laissez-faire approach to the economy (that is, governments should not interfere with the workings of the free market). The most significant contradiction to Say's Law is that offered by British economist John Maynard Keynes in 1936. Keynes argued that the economy could experience crises (such as the Great Depression, which began in 1929 and lasted through the better part of the following decade) that market forces were unable to correct. In

these situations government alone had the power to correct the problem, and it did so by stimulating demand rather than supply.

When Did It Begin

Jean-Baptiste Say was born in 1767 in Lyon, France. He was an ardent supporter of the French Revolution, and he worked as an editor (eventually becoming the editor-in-chief) of a newspaper devoted to the revolutionary cause and ideology. Say was likewise known for his writing about the ideas of Adam Smith, whose 1776 book *An Inquiry into the Nature and Causes of the Wealth of Nations* signaled the birth of economics as a field of study. Say put forth his own economic ideas (which owed a great deal to those of Smith) most notably in his 1803 book *A Treatise on Political Economy* (*Traité d'économie politique*). It was in this book that he outlined the notion that became known as Say's Law. Say later became a successful businessman and a respected professor.

More Detailed Information

Capitalist economies are regulated not by a central authority but by multitudes of sellers and buyers of goods and services, each of whom is pursuing his own self-interest. These sellers and buyers come together in markets (most of which used to be physical, but some of which now exist only electronically), and the competing interests of each side (the competing forces of supply and demand) interact to determine prices. The forces of supply, demand, and prices dictate what will be produced, how it will be produced, and who will benefit from that production. In other words, everyone in a capitalist society is dependent on the interaction of these basic market forces.

The economic growth that Europe and North America experienced during Say's lifetime was largely caused by huge increases in production (supply) made possible by new ideas and new technology, such as the steam engine. While these increases in production created an enormous amount of wealth, some writers and thinkers worried that supply might one day outpace demand, creating a general glut of products and precipitating an economic crisis.

Say argued that this could never happen because "products are paid for with products." Since the value of money fluctuates, anyone who sells a product will, in Say's view, want to sell it as quickly as possible and then use the money from the sale to buy something else so as not to be stuck holding money whose value has diminished in the meantime. Therefore, as production grew, so would consumption. Economic depressions, in Say's view, were caused by the temporary overproduction of certain goods. The free market mechanisms of supply, demand, and pricing would naturally even out these isolated gluts.

SAY AND NAPOLEON

In 1799 Napoleon Bonaparte, who had just declared himself France's consul, or ruler, created a *Tribunat,* a government body consisting of 100 distinguished Frenchmen for the nominal purpose of sharing power with the legislature and himself. Jean-Baptiste Say, as one of France's most accomplished economic thinkers, was appointed to the *Tribunat,* but his 1803 book *A Treatise on Political Economy* conflicted with Napoleon's vision for his government. Say advocated laissez-faire government policies (that is, he believed that the government should have little or no role in the economy), while Napoleon planned to continue exerting authoritarian control over the economy and other aspects of life in France. Napoleon ordered Say to rewrite the parts of the *Treatise* that contradicted Napoleonic role, but Say refused and was relieved of his role in the *Tribunat.* Disenchanted with Napoleon, Say left Paris and started a cotton mill, which made him enormously wealthy.

Say returned to Paris in 1812. Napoleon lost power in 1814, and Say published the second volume of his *Treatise.* He lived out the rest of his life in Paris as a distinguished professor of economics.

Say's Law went mainly uncontested through the nineteenth and the early twentieth centuries, but the Great Depression (the severe economic crisis that afflicted North America and Europe beginning in 1929) challenged this and other existing economic theories. In the United States, for instance, roughly one-third of the labor force was unemployed. With no income, people demanded far fewer goods and services. The country was equipped with state-of-the-art factories and production methods, but this equipment was lying dormant for lack of customers.

The British economist John Maynard Keynes offered solutions to the Great Depression in the form of his 1936 book *The General Theory of Employment, Interest, and Money,* which overturned Say's Law along with other foundational ideas in economics. Keynes essentially proposed the reverse of Say's Law, arguing that demand created supply. If people had money to spend, producers would open their factories back up to make products that could be sold. This would mean hiring new workers, who, once employed, would demand yet more goods and services.

Keynes's ideas dictated the process of recovery from the Great Depression. Governments spent money on a wide array of projects and relief programs, moving money out of government coffers and into private hands, spurring demand. The Depression's effects did not fully disappear in the United States until the outbreak of World War II, when huge government spending on war materials created yet more demand and inaugurated a prolonged period of prosperity.

Recent Trends

Say's Law has generally been less influential in the years since the Great Depression than it was before that time. It has, however, been embraced by some recent economists in the United States, notably those who, especially during Ronald Reagan's presidency (1980–88), advocated "supply-side" economic policy. Supply-side economics, in keeping with Say's Law, consists of tax breaks for businesses and other policies intended to spur production, rather than demand. Supply-siders reject the Keynesian notion that demand creates supply.

KEYNESIAN ECONOMICS

What It Means

Keynesian economics is a school of thought based on the ideas of the British economist John Maynard Keynes (1883–1946). It emphasizes a balance between the private sector's freedom to conduct business and the government's role as a stabilizing force in the economy. In Keynesian economics the intervention of government is important to the overall growth of an economy, as well as in pulling an economy out of downturns known as recessions and depressions.

Generally, Keynesian economics advocates using government spending and tax breaks to stimulate the economy when it is in a slump. Likewise, it says that cutting government spending and increasing taxes will help curb inflation (the rising of prices in general, which makes currency, such as the U.S. dollar, worth less) during periods of economic growth. This approach is known as fiscal policy.

The economic policies of industrialized nations (such as the United States) have been greatly influenced by the theories of Keynesian economics. In fact, evidence of Keynesian theory is prevalent in everyday life. For example, when the federal government introduces new tax breaks, it is essentially letting more money remain in the hands of consumers so that they can spend it on goods and services. This increased spending will stimulate the national economy. But if it is too high, consumer spending itself can cause problems for the economy by increasing inflation. Whether the government is acting to rein in an economy that is growing too rapidly or injecting financial life into a slow economy, when it attempts to manipulate overall economic growth through taxes and spending, it is drawing upon Keynesian theories.

Keynesian theory contrasts greatly with classical economics, which emphasizes the idea of laissez-faire, the belief that economies will operate most effectively without government intervention.

When Did It Begin

After World War I ended in 1918, the world economic system did not regain stability as quickly as economists

Arguing that increased government spending can revive a struggling economy, Keynesian economic theory was the dominant school of economics from the 1930s to the 1970s. In 1971 U.S. President Richard Nixon famously said, "We're all Keynesians," though an economic downturn soon afterward would call some basic Keynesian ideas into question. © *Bettmann/Corbis.*

expected it would. Global production of goods and services dropped, and capitalism (the economic system in which production and prices are determined by buyers and sellers interacting freely) came under scrutiny. Some people argued that other economic systems, such as planned economies, worked better. For instance, the Soviet Union embraced socialism, a system inspired by the ideas of Karl Marx in which the government controls the economy.

John Maynard Keynes entered this debate as a supporter of capitalism who nevertheless rejected the laissez-faire approach. In his seminal 1936 work, *The General Theory of Employment, Interest, and Money,* he argued that the national government of a country needed to intervene in the economy, especially when unemployment (joblessness) was chronic. Keynes stated that a government could prevent economic depression by increasing government spending on public works (the construction of such things as highways, bridges, and dams). He explained that such projects would stimulate employment by giving more people jobs, and as a result, national purchasing power would be increased. This, in turn, would lead to more consumer spending, more in-

vestment in business, and new jobs beyond the public-works projects.

Keynesian thinking greatly influenced U.S. economic policy at the beginning of World War II (1939–45). After the war many European countries drew upon Keynesian theories as they developed social-democratic economic models (which try to operate according to ideas of equality and fairness rather than unregulated market forces) to stabilize their damaged economies.

More Detailed Information

Today the field of economics is divided into two main branches: one examining economies from the bottom up (studying how individual decisions add up to larger economic trends), the other looking at them from the top down (studying how large-scale factors affect an economy). Keynes was largely responsible for bringing about the top-down view.

The bottom-up approach is called microeconomics; it is the study of how individuals, households, and firms, for example, make decisions about spending, saving, or investing their limited resources. Microeconomics examines how decisions and behaviors on the part of

THE BRETTON WOODS SYSTEM

British economist John Maynard Keynes (1883–1946) was the leader of the British delegation at the Bretton Woods Conference, which established the first comprehensive system for managing monetary relations among independent nation-states. The conference was held in Bretton Woods, New Hampshire, in July 1944, as the end of World War II (1939–45) approached. Delegates from 44 nations attended in order to plan for postwar economic cooperation. They created the Bretton Woods Agreement, which set up a system of rules, institutions, and procedures to regulate the exchange of international currencies.

The two institutions founded at the conference were the World Bank, designed to provide financial assistance to countries; and the International Monetary Fund, which had the task of overseeing exchange rates and debts between countries. Keynes led and greatly influenced the committee that drafted the plans for the World Bank, and the bank continues to put Keynesian theories into action by making loans to countries in order to stimulate their economic development.

individuals affect the overall supply and demand for goods and services, which, in turn, determine prices.

Macroeconomics is the term used to describe the top-down approach, the study of the overall features and activities of a national economy. Macroeconomic concerns include such broad subjects as employment, inflation, the total size of the economy and how fast it is growing, and overall economic patterns (for example, the cycle of economic growth and then economic slowdown that is an ordinary part of capitalist economies). In Keynesian theory, macro-level, or general, economic trends can outweigh the micro-level decisions and behaviors of individuals. It is for this reason that Keynesians believe that government should intervene to influence these large-scale factors.

Two major indicators of the health of an economy are unemployment (the percentage of the workforce that cannot find jobs) and inflation (the general rising of prices). The first usually indicates a declining economy, and the second is usually a sign of economic growth (because rising prices are a side effect of such growth). Both can spell trouble for an economy if they increase too quickly. Inflation makes the currency worth less (for instance, decades ago a candy bar might have cost 5 cents, but today there is not much that a person could buy for 5 cents). A certain amount of inflation is normal and manageable, but it is problematic when it rises too quickly, causing people to lose purchasing power.

The Keynesian approach stresses the role of demand in an economy. Keynesians hold that low consumer demand for goods and services is the primary cause of un-

employment and that the opposite situation, excessive consumer demand, causes inflation. Therefore, they argue, government has a responsibility to manage the total demand for goods and services, known as aggregate demand, by adjusting how much it spends and how much it taxes its citizens.

Keynesians tend to consider fighting unemployment more important than attempting to overcome inflation. Many Keynesians believe that the problems caused by high levels of inflation are comparatively insignificant. For Keynesians the key to economic stability is to keep the country's employment rate as close to full as possible (primarily by raising government spending but also by lowering taxes and increasing the money supply).

Keynes divided the causes of inflation into two types: cost-push inflation and demand-pull inflation. Cost-push inflation results from the rising cost of what are called inputs, the resources that must be used to produce goods and services. Inputs could be the wages that must be paid to workers or the price of the raw materials for a product or service. In cost-push inflation the increased price of inputs causes an increased cost for companies to produce goods and services. When companies across the economy try to protect their existing profits by raising their own prices, prices overall in the economy rise, thus causing inflation. In this sense, increased costs have pushed the economy into higher inflation.

Demand-pull inflation, as the name suggests, results from an increase in the overall demand for goods and services in an economy. The total amount of goods and services demanded by consumers, businesses, and government, for any number of reasons, goes up, but the total supply of these goods and services in the economy does not rise as quickly. This might happen from a sudden increase in government spending or, in a more complicated example, when a country's currency (such as the dollar) falls in value, thus making its goods and services cheaper to foreign countries and increasing their demand for them. Whatever the cause for the increased overall demand, the result is the same: there is now more money being spent by consumers, businesses, and governments, but the supply of goods and services has not increased by the same amount, so producers are able to increase their prices. Increased demand has thus pulled the economy into higher inflation.

Recent Trends

Keynes's policies were widely accepted in the years following World War II (1939–45). In the 1960s, however, the American economist Milton Friedman (1912–2006) and others began challenging the Keynesian approach. He agreed with the Keynesian idea that government should be involved in stabilizing the economy, but he argued that monetary policy was the only effective way to do so. Monetary policy centers on adjusting the national money supply, and it is carried out by a nation's central bank (which in the United States is the Federal Reserve).

In the 1970s the United States and other countries suffered from both high unemployment and high inflation, two economic problems that did not usually appear at the same time. The phenomenon, which Keynesian economics could not explain, was dubbed "stagflation." These problems stretched into the 1980s, causing many economists to blame excessive government intervention for troubles in the economy. It seemed to validate Friedman's criticisms of Keynesian policies, and his economic theory, called monetarism, gained favor. Supporters of monetary policy point out that it is more efficient because it can be put into action much faster than fiscal policies, which must be reviewed and approved by Congress. Even so, many of Keynes's ideas—such as stimulating a sluggish economy with tax breaks or increased government spending—remained influential in government policy and in political and economic debates.

MONETARIST THEORY

What It Means

Monetarist theory, or monetarism, is an approach to economics that centers on the money supply (the amount of money in circulation, including not just coins and bills but also bank-account balances). The basic idea behind monetarist thinking is that the size of the money supply is more important than any other factor affecting the economy.

In the 1970s governments guided by the then-dominant school of economic thought, Keynesian economics (based on the writings of British economist John Maynard Keynes), were battling high inflation (the rising of prices across the economy that causes money to lose value) and conditions of economic stagnation. Monetarists, led by American economist Milton Friedman, maintained that the Keynesian approach was flawed and that inflation could be brought under control by restraining the growth of the money supply. Under the influence of monetarist theory, the United States' central bank, the Federal Reserve System (commonly called the Fed), was successful at reining in inflation, and in the 1980s economists and government leaders accordingly embraced the school of thought in large numbers. But subsequent changes in the economy seemed to disprove an exclusive focus on the money supply, and the doctrine's influence waned. Although monetarism remained influential into the twenty-first century, it was in a modified form that took other variables besides the money supply into consideration.

When Did It Begin

Monetarist theory arose in reaction to Keynesian theory, the mainstream school of economics in the United States from the 1930s to the 1970s, which was based on the

ideas of the British economist John Maynard Keynes. Keynes had provided a blueprint for recovery from the Great Depression (the severe crisis affecting the world economy in the 1930s), suggesting that governments could stimulate their ailing economies by cutting taxes and spending money, even if they had to go into debt. The money they spent (on public projects and on aid to the poor, the unemployed, and the elderly, for instance) would put money in people's pockets so that they would be able to buy the products they needed and wanted. This increased consumer demand would give companies an incentive to expand their operations and hire new workers, which would increase demand still further. The United States and other countries did, in fact, pursue such policies, and their recovery from the Depression seemed to validate Keynes's theories. Keynesian economics continued to dominate in academia and government in the following decades, as governments generally attempted to promote economic stability through tax and spending policies.

Nobel Prize-winning economist Milton Friedman is considered the founder of monetarist theory. Monetarists believe that government should promote growth and stability of the economy not by how it spends money but by making adjustments to the amount of money in circulation. *George Rose/Getty Images.*

TIGHT MONEY AND LOOSE MONEY

Central banks such as the U.S. Federal Reserve System (or the Fed, as it is commonly called) try to stabilize the economy by making decisions about the size of the money supply, the amount of money (in the form of coins, bills, and bank-account balances) in circulation at any given time. If the Fed expands the money supply, money is said to be loose. This means that interest rates are low, and it is easy for people to borrow money. The Fed might adopt loose money policies in order to stimulate a sluggish economy, since people often borrow money in order to establish or expand businesses and to make large purchases. If the Fed decreases the money supply, money is said to be tight. Tight money policies might be desirable if inflation (the general rising of prices, which causes money to lose value) is threatening to get out of hand. When money is harder to borrow and less plentiful in general, the demand for money theoretically will increase, and it will gain value.

The founder and most prominent proponent of monetarism, American economist Milton Friedman, emerged as an opponent of this approach in the 1950s. Friedman's views were at first seen as extreme, but they began to gain the attention of prominent economists with the publication of *A Monetary History of the United States 1867-1960* (1963). In this book Friedman and coauthor Anna J. Schwartz analyzed the role of the money supply in U.S. history, arguing that it was the most important factor in the country's economic fluctuations. Friedman further believed that Keynesian attempts to fine-tune the economy through tax and spending policy did more harm than good. He believed that governments could play a role in stabilizing the economy but that the only effective tool they had for doing so was monetary policy (control over the money supply). Friedman predicted that Keynesian economic policies could eventually lead to an unprecedented situation in which inflation (the general rising of prices, which causes money to lose value) and unemployment (the percentage of people who want to work but cannot find jobs) could both rise at the same time. When this phenomena, which became known as stagflation (a combination of economic stagnation and inflation), occurred during the 1970s, economists and government leaders turned away from Keynesianism and toward Friedman and monetarist theory.

More Detailed Information

The theoretical basis for monetarism is a mathematical equation known as the equation of exchange: $MV=PQ$. M, in this equation, represents the money supply, and V represents the velocity of money, or the rate at which the basic unit of currency (such as a dollar) changes hands. P stands for the level of prices in the economy, and Q for the quantity of goods and services in the economy. In other words, the left side of the equation accounts for all of the money circulating in the economy and for the speed at which it is circulating, and the right side of the equation accounts for the entire output of the economy (the price of all goods and services multiplied by the quantity of those goods and services).

Monetarists use this equation to argue that as M increases (if V remains constant), then either P or Q will increase. It follows, then, that the size of the money supply has a direct relationship to both prices and production and also to employment, since the number of people who have jobs will vary according to how much companies are producing and how much money they can charge for the items they are producing.

P, or prices, is a particularly important factor, since inflation poses one of the most persistent threats to any economy. Though inflation is a natural part of the economy, if it gets out of hand, the level of wages that people bring in will be insufficient to pay for their needs and wants, and they will be likely to demand higher wages. This can force inflation still higher (since companies will likely compensate for the increased wages they are paying workers by raising the prices of their goods) without solving the basic problem, and the devaluation of money continues.

According to monetarist theory, inflation is always caused by there being too much money in circulation. Money, like other products for sale in the economy, is subject to the forces of supply and demand. When there is too much money in circulation, the demand for money is low, and it loses value. When there is not enough money in circulation, the demand for money is high, and it gains value.

Monetarists believe that if a government's central bank can keep the supply and demand for money balanced, then inflation can be controlled. A central bank could theoretically do this by setting a strict rate of increase in the size of the money supply relative to Gross Domestic Product (GDP), a figure that represents the total value of all the goods and services produced in the economy. In other words, as the amount and value of the products generated by the economy increases, the money supply should increase proportionately. If this happens, then inflation will remain low.

Monetarists argue that whereas the effect of the money supply on the economy is direct and verifiable, the effects of fiscal policy (government spending and tax programs) are much less controllable. Monetary policy can reliably be counted on to have specific economic effects, but fiscal policy is inefficient, and it creates more problems than solutions. Monetarists argued, therefore, that governments should stop trying to manage the economy through fiscal policy and adopt, instead, a strictly monetary approach.

Recent Trends

After the onset of stagflation, which Friedman had predicted, U.S. government leaders turned increasingly to monetarist theory. In 1979 President Jimmy Carter nominated a monetarist, Paul Volcker, as chairman of the Fed, and Volcker made it his mission to battle inflation by decreasing the size of the money supply. Between 1981 and 1983 the reduction in the money supply, coupled with falling oil prices, led to the rate of inflation dropping from 13.5 percent to 3.2 percent. It remained low through the early twenty-first century under Volcker's successor, Alan Greenspan, who was also a proponent of monetarist theory.

Monetarism was most completely embraced during the administration of President Ronald Reagan (1981-89). Changes in the economy during the 1980s seemed to disprove monetarist theory, however. After inflation had been cut so drastically, people were slower to spend money. (When money is losing value quickly due to high inflation, people want to spend it quickly so as to get the maximum value for their dollars; when money maintains its value, this urge is muted.) Therefore, the velocity of money (*V* in the equation of exchange, the speed with which the average dollar changes hands) decreased greatly, diminishing the effects of increasing the money supply. Also, new forms of bank accounts made it harder to calculate the money supply (the money supply consists not just of coins and bills but also of bank-account balances). Together, these developments pointed out the shortcomings in a strict monetarist focus. Nevertheless, the Federal Reserve and other central banks continued, into the twenty-first century, to follow modified forms of monetarism when it came to making decisions about the money supply.

SUPPLY SIDE THEORY

What It Means

Supply side theory is an approach to economics based on the idea that the best way to make the economy grow is to encourage businesses to supply more goods and services for purchase. Supply and demand are the basic forces that shape all economic activity. Supply is the quantity of goods and services that businesses are willing and able to produce at any given time over a range of prices, and demand is the quantity of goods and services that consumers are willing and able to buy at any given time over a range of prices. These forces work in opposition to one another, and prices dictate the level of each of them. For example, if the price of digital cameras is high, then camera companies tend to produce as many digital cameras as possible. Conversely, consumers tend

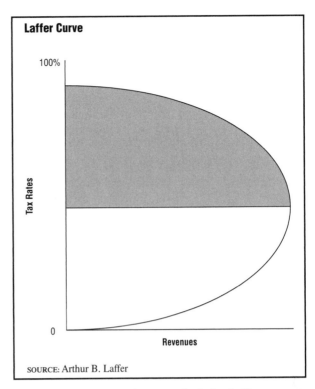

SOURCE: Arthur B. Laffer

The Laffer Curve, named after economist Arthur Laffer, represents the idea that there is a certain tax rate at which the government will receive the most revenue. If the tax rate is lower, the government will collect less money, and the rate is higher, people will be less inclined to work, and there will be less money in the economy to tax. *Illustration by GGS Information Services. Cengage Learning, Gale.*

to buy fewer and fewer digital cameras as prices rise. Prices will therefore rise and fall to accommodate the competing desires of both the buyers and the sellers of digital cameras.

When a government wants to influence economic growth, it can focus on either the demand side or the supply side of the economy. It can use policies focused on spending (social programs, the military, or highways, for instance), taxes (tax increases, tax cuts), and the money supply (the amount of money in circulation) to change the quantities of products people want to buy or the quantities of products companies want to produce.

Supply siders, as those who believe in supply side theory are sometimes called, generally believe that supply creates demand, so they encourage governments to craft policies that will result in increased production. Often this translates into a consistent program of tax cuts, especially cuts in income taxes (the taxes individuals pay on the money they earn each year) and in taxes that affect businesses. The money that individuals and businesses save will, in the view of supply siders, be invested in businesses, which will increase production and cause the economy to grow.

THE LAFFER CURVE

Supply side economics, which argues that the government should encourage production of goods and services by businesses in order to spur economic growth, was triggered by the ideas of Arthur Laffer, an economist who has taught at the University of Chicago, the University of Southern California, and Pepperdine University, in addition to serving as a consultant to businesses and the U.S. government. Laffer's basic contribution to supply side theory was his idea that the government could, by lowering taxes, simultaneously collect more money in taxes and let people keep more of the money they earned. He illustrated this idea with a simple graph called the Laffer Curve, supposedly first drawn on a paper napkin.

The Laffer curve is shaped like a symmetrical hill, with one axis being government revenue (the amount of money the government collects in taxes) and the other axis being the tax rate (the percentage of a person's income the government collects as a tax). When the tax rate is either zero (meaning there is no tax) or 100 percent (a rate at which no one would work, resulting in no income for the government to tax), the government does not collect any revenue. As the tax rate approaches the summit of the curve, tax revenues rise. If the tax rate is too high or too low, the government will lose revenue.

Thus, while many people associate supply side economics with a blind reduction of taxes, in fact true supply side theorists maintain not that all tax cuts are good but that tax cuts up to a certain point may increase tax revenue.

When Did It Begin

In the eighteenth and nineteenth centuries, most economists believed that supply was more important than demand. When supply was high, the economy prospered. Consumer demand was of only secondary importance. The so-called classical economists of these centuries are generally seen as providing the ideological basis for the supply side theory of the late twentieth century.

In between these two eras, governments largely focused on the demand side of the economy. This was a result of the Great Depression, which began in 1929 and lasted through most of the following decade. During the Great Depression people lost their jobs in huge numbers, and factories and businesses of all types closed down in droves. With no jobs people had no money to spend on what they wanted and needed; hence, there was a shortage of demand in the economy. Companies had no incentive to supply products, since there was no one to buy them. The forces of supply and demand had essentially lost their power to regulate the economy.

The British economist John Maynard Keynes argued that government was the only force that could pull the economy out of such a depression and that it could do so by spending money. By spending money the government would move funds out of its own coffers and into the hands of private citizens, who would begin to demand products. Once there was demand for their products, companies would begin to supply those products again, and the economy would eventually recover. The United States and other governments followed Keynes's theories and managed to pull themselves out of the Depression. Accordingly, most governments continued to focus on the demand side of the economy in the decades that followed.

But in the 1970s the United States experienced high inflation (the rising of prices across the economy, which makes money lose its value) as well as high unemployment (large numbers of people wanted jobs but could not find them). Some economists blamed this situation, called stagflation, on Keynesian economic policies, so the stage was set for what became known as the supply side revolution.

More Detailed Information

Keynesian economic policies justified the existence of high tax rates and other forms of government intervention in the economy. These policies were blamed for the struggling economy of the 1970s, and a number of economists and political conservatives began proposing other ideas for economic growth.

One of the most important of these, in the context of supply side theory, was the economist Arthur Laffer. In the late 1970s Laffer put forward the notion that high tax rates did not necessarily result in high tax revenues (the amounts of money actually collected by the government). He argued that cutting taxes could actually result in both higher revenues for the government and higher take-home salaries for individuals. This was because people who got to keep more of the money they earned would have more incentive to work hard. People who work hard produce more goods and services than people who work less hard. The increases in production would lead to increases in demand, and the resulting economic growth would increase the amount of total income for the government to tax.

In addition to tax cuts, supply side theory usually recommends that the government should decrease its regulation of business and provide other incentives for increases in production, such as tax breaks (amounts of money that can be deducted from the taxes owed to the government) for companies that invest in new equipment. Supply siders also often insist on the importance of free trade (the reduction or elimination of restrictions on goods imported from foreign countries) and the free movement of capital (the unhindered ability of money and other resources to move across borders), believing that restrictions on trade or capital movement negatively affect production.

Some of the most dedicated supply siders believe that the money system should be based on the gold standard.

This means that they believe the value of, for instance, a dollar should be linked to the amount of gold that a dollar is worth. While this was once the way that most nations determined the value of their money, that has not been the case in the United States since 1971, when President Richard Nixon ended the nation's reliance on the gold standard, which was hampering the economy. Instead, the value of U.S. money has since been determined by the amount of money in circulation, and the government controls this variable through its central bank, the Federal Reserve System.

Supply side economics was popularized by Ronald Reagan, the U.S. president from 1981 to 1989, who came to office promising to reduce the income tax for all Americans as well as taxes on corporations and investors. Reagan was said to have been strongly influenced by Laffer's notion that the government could collect more taxes by lowering the tax rate. Under Reagan the U.S. Congress cut taxes by 25 percent. Reagan also initiated cuts in spending for education and welfare (various programs that provide aid to the poor and unemployed) and for government agencies such as the Environmental Protection Agency and the Civil Rights Division of the Department of Justice. Reagan simultaneously increased military spending by $1.5 trillion over five years.

Some critics of supply side economics, therefore, argued that the theories promoted by economists such as Laffer were actually smokescreens for conservative ideology. Conservatives had long supported decreases in tax rates without basing their desire for lower taxes on any sound economic theory, and they had likewise long criticized social programs such as welfare as wasteful and had been scornful of environmental and civil rights protections. Likewise, one of the only forms of spending not criticized by Republicans of the time was military spending.

Recent Trends

According to Reagan's supporters, the supply side tax cuts he instituted were largely responsible for the enormous economic growth that the United States experienced, with minimal interruptions, between 1982 and 2000. Critics have argued that Reagan's policies primarily benefited the rich, and that these benefits were often gained at the expense of the poor. Some people agree that Reagan's economic policies are at least partly responsible for the economic prosperity enjoyed by at least some Americans in the 1980s and 1990s, but they argue that Reagan was in fact acting like a follower of Keynes rather than a true supply sider. They point to the fact that he increased government spending even though it meant going into debt. This form of spending, called deficit spending, had been advocated by Keynes.

The legitimacy of supply side theory has never been firmly established or rejected. While in the 1990s and in the early twenty-first century it was out of fashion among mainstream economists, tax policy since the time of Reagan has been greatly tied to supply side notions. Both Republicans and Democrats, since the time of Reagan, have generally supported tax cuts meant to stimulate supply, and the idea that tax cuts lead to economic growth has been accepted as fact by many people across the political spectrum.

RATIONAL EXPECTATION THEORY

What It Means

"Rational expectation theory" refers to an idea in economics that is simple on the surface: people use rationality, past experiences, and all available information to guide their financial decision-making. The implications of the idea are more complex, however. When applied on a macroeconomic level (that is, when considered as a factor in the economy as a whole), rational expectation theory leads to the conclusion that people's current expectations about the economy will themselves influence the future course of the economy.

This idea, though originated in the 1960s, revolutionized economics in the 1970s. At that time government economic policies were largely based on the theories of John Maynard Keynes, who believed that governments could and should make adjustments to the economy using fiscal policy (taxes and government spending) and monetary policy (changes in the money supply). When viewed through the lens of rational expectation theory, however, government attempts to control the economy are bound to be ineffective. This is because individuals, according to the theory, will anticipate the effects of the government's actions and adjust their own decision-making accordingly, nullifying the policies' intended effects. Between the mid-1970s and the mid-1990s, in large part due to rational expectation theory, Keynesian theories about the economy were in decline. New classical economics, heavily reliant on rational expectation theory, became the dominant school of economic thought during that time.

When Did It Begin

Early twentieth-century economists, including Keynes himself (whose landmark work, *The General Theory of Employment, Interest, and Money,* was published in 1936) were aware of the power that people's expectations exerted on the economy. It was not until the early 1960s, though, that this knowledge began to be thoroughly applied to the economy in the form of rational expectation theory. The theory was first outlined by John F. Muth, an economist at Indiana University, in 1961. The economist most associated with the rise to prominence of rational expectation theory is Robert E. Lucas, who taught at Carnegie Mellon University and the University of Chicago. Lucas was responsible for using rational

EFFICIENT MARKETS AND THE RANDOM WALK

Rational expectation theory suggests, among other things, that people are collectively able to predict future economic outcomes with great accuracy. Today, this idea forms the basis of what is known as efficient markets theory, an application of rational expectation theory to the stock market.

Efficient markets theory says that investors seek out all possible information about stocks and stock prices before making purchasing or selling decisions. They buy stocks that they expect to have higher-than-average returns, and they sell stocks that they expect to have lower-than-average returns. These forecasts of future performance become built into the stock price until they in fact *equal* the stock price. In other words, the stock's price is what it should be, and there is nothing that can change this.

Well, almost nothing. In life there will always be occurrences that can never be predicted. According to efficient markets theory, these random events are the only things that can change a stock's price. Stock prices change according to no pattern. Instead, they follow a path that economists call a "random walk."

ces. They watch the price of a given stock in various conditions, and become better able to predict how that stock will perform when those conditions recur. Over time, savvy investors adjust their decisions based on a wealth of past experience. The future tends to grow out of the past in predictable ways, allowing people to make surprisingly accurate collective predictions.

Rational expectation theory thus suggests that economic outcomes will generally be what people predict them to be. Economists who believe in rational expectation theory do not maintain that people always make accurate predictions. They do maintain, however, that the collective predictions of economic decision makers will not be consistently wrong over the long term.

Recent Trends

Keynesian theories urging government fine-tuning of the economy dominated economics from the 1930s until the 1970s. In the 1950s and 1960s "monetarists" such as Milton Friedman argued that Keynesians did not fully account for the effects of the money supply on the economy. Rather than ending the reign of Keynesian economics, this critique resulted in a compromise school of thought known as the neoclassical synthesis. Keynesian theories came under further attack because they failed to account for an unprecedented phenomenon known as stagflation (high prices coupled with high unemployment), which occurred in the 1970s. But it was rational expectation theory, as applied to government intervention in the economy, that provided the most serious critique of Keynesian theory among mainstream economists.

The economist Robert E. Lucas was responsible for challenging Keynesian theories of government intervention using rational expectation theory. He argued that people will always predict the effects of government economic policy before those policies can take effect. Therefore, policies might add "noise" to the economy (that is, activity that is essentially meaningless), but they will not have their intended effect.

During that time Keynes's theories were decreasingly influential among economists. One of the mainstream schools among economists today is known as new classical economics, which applies rational expectations theory to all aspects of the economy.

expectation theory to critique Keynesian notions of government spending.

More Detailed Information

Rational expectation theory arose from considerations of the numerous economic situations in which people's expectations play a role in determining the outcome. The stock market is one such economic situation. If large numbers of investors begin to believe that Wal-Mart stock will lose value in the future, they will be likely to sell their Wal-Mart stock. This causes the price of Wal-Mart stock to fall. In other words, a stock's price is in large part determined by what people expect that stock's price to be in the future.

Similarly, the farming industry is greatly affected by people's expectations. Farmers determine how much corn to plant according to the price they can expect to get when they sell their corn; at the same time, corn prices are determined in part by how much corn farmers decide to plant. On both sides of this situation, with both buyers and sellers of corn, rational expectations influence the economic outcome.

When people base economic decisions on expectations, it is strongly in their interest to build those expectations on sound evidence. The investor who trades stocks based on thorough research into a company's future is more likely to profit from trades than someone who trades based on superstitions. In addition, people tend to build up expertise in predicting future stock pri-

$ Planned Economy

What It Means

A planned economy (also called a command economy) is an economic system in which a government or ruler makes most or all of the important decisions about the production and distribution of goods and services in the society.

In a planned economy the government decides how much of each product to make and where to distribute it. In Cuba, one of the few countries in the world that relies on a planned economy, the government oversees the cultivation of tobacco, as well as the manufacture of cigars, the country's most celebrated product. *AP Images.*

Though there have been countless different kinds of human cultures in history, there have only been three basic economic systems: traditional, planned, and market economies. Traditional economies are those in which production and distribution are governed by inherited ideas and attitudes. In societies based on this form of economic system, people usually hunt and gather to satisfy their needs, as their ancestors before them did, and they distribute the proceeds of their hunting and gathering according to traditional hierarchies or rules. This is the oldest form of economic system, and it has been by far the most common one during the course of human history.

In a market system, by contrast, such forces as supply (the amount of any good or service that a seller is willing to sell over a range of prices), demand (the amount of any good or service that buyers are willing to buy over a range of prices), and prices determine the shape of the economy. Sellers want to supply the largest amount of their products possible at the highest prices possible. When prices are too high, however, buyers generally demand less of any given product, and when prices are low, they generally demand more. Neither buyers nor sellers usually get their way entirely. Prices rise or fall in proportion to

supply and demand, negotiating the opposing desires of buyers and sellers.

In a planned economy central planners (rather than tradition or market forces) decide most matters of production and distribution. This means that they determine what goods and services should be produced and made available (from airplanes to bicycles, medical care to haircuts, houses to paper clips) and in what amounts. Central planners also determine, for example, whether these and other items should be produced by hand or by machine, in what part of the country they should be produced, and how they should be transported from the place they are manufactured to the place they are purchased. Finally, central planners determine who (a ruling party, all of society, certain classes of society, a religious group) should have access to the products and receive the benefits of the economic activity.

When Did It Begin

No one knows exactly why, how, or when planned economies began to supplant traditional economic systems. Traditional economic systems had allowed for subsistence (survival and a minimal level of comfort) and stability, but they did not encourage technological or

PLANNED ECONOMIES IN THE TWENTY-FIRST CENTURY

After the collapse of the Soviet Union in 1991, there remained few planned economies (in which government planners make all or most important economic decisions) in the world. Indeed, the Soviet Union's inability to survive as a nation was largely based on the failure of its economic system. As Russia and the other former Soviet states began adopting market economies (in which individuals own property, and in which such forces as supply, or the amount of any good or service that a seller is willing to sell at a given price, and demand, or the amount of any good or service that buyers are willing to buy at a given price, determine most economic matters) in the 1990s, the world's other large planned economy, China's, likewise began transitioning to a market system.

While all economies are actually a mix of market and planned economic systems, the proportion of those nations that seemed willing to trust central planners over market forces was waning by the beginning of the twenty-first century. Cuba and North Korea were the only well-known, developed countries still largely dependent on planned economic systems.

cultural advances. It was the transition to planned economies that made possible the great early civilizations, such as those of China and Egypt, in about 3000 BC

Though tradition and inheritance continued to exert a significant influence over these societies, strong rulers overpowered traditional forces and created new ways of organizing land, labor, and equipment. Instead of devoting their labor to the vocation that might have been dictated by their birth into a certain segment of society, for instance, many ancient Egyptians were ordered by the pharaohs to spend years of their lives hauling stones and assembling them into pyramids, just as many ancient Chinese men were ordered to direct their efforts toward the building of that country's Great Wall.

Such projects are perhaps the most visible symbols of the changes brought about by planned economic systems, but the reorganization of economic resources under central authority figures in the ancient world had much more extensive effects on human life. Instead of merely subsisting, societies could produce huge amounts of wealth. This wealth, usually held by a single ruler or a small elite portion of society, could be used to change the conditions of life drastically. Planned economic systems made possible the building of great cities, the application of new technologies that improved living conditions, and such cultural advances as written language and artistic achievement. The benefits of the system were typically only enjoyed by the ruling classes of society, however.

More Detailed Information

All human communities throughout history have had to answer the same three economic questions. What will be produced? How will it be produced and distributed? And for whom will it be produced and distributed? The way in which a community responds to these questions determines its economy.

In a planned economy central planners answer the first question (What will be produced?) by first setting targets for public consumption of various products. For example, the government, and not individual consumers, determines how many bicycles the public needs in a given year. The planners must then figure out what quantities of various resources are needed to produce that number of bicycles. Resources required to produce any product include land (in addition to the physical space itself, this term is used to indicate natural resources and other raw materials), labor (human effort), and capital (equipment and other items needed to produce goods and services).

While making these determinations about resources, the planners would additionally need to solve the second of the three basic questions: How will the bicycles be produced? Is it in society's best interest to make low-cost bicycles that will only last a few years or expensive bicycles that will last a lifetime? Numerous other factors also come into play. For instance, the planners might decide to reserve the country's highest-quality steel for military supplies, and they might therefore allot the bicycle industry a combination of cheaper metals and plastics. Planners might decide, further, that modern, efficient bicycle factories are not in the public interest; instead, the goal might be to employ the maximum number of people, even if this means relying on outdated, more labor-intensive methods of manufacturing.

Lastly, the central planners must decide for whom the bicycles will be produced (in this case, how the bicycles will be distributed becomes part of this third question). Will consumers have to line up to buy bicycles, or will certain people be allowed to buy them and not others? Likewise, who will reap the economic rewards of bicycle production? Profits might be given to an elite group in society, they might be divided equally among all members of society, they might be channeled into national defense, or they might be used in any other way that is deemed consistent with that society's goals.

While central planning of an economy gives the society the potential to serve the public interest, the system is a cumbersome one. All of the decisions described above must be made for a multitude of products. At the same time that the details of bicycle production are being outlined by central planners, for example, similar decisions must be made about haircuts, leather jackets, T-bone steaks, apartment buildings, medical care, computers, soap, cars, and ovens, and the list goes on and on.

For this and other reasons even the most strictly planned economies have usually allowed market forces to determine some amount of economic activity. In the area of food production, for instance, a centrally planned economy might relax its control, allowing supply and demand to dictate the production and distribution of wheat, beef, potatoes, and carrots. By the same token even the most market-oriented economies typically yield to some amount of government planning, especially in areas where society's well-being might be most directly threatened, such as in health care and national defense. Thus, all economies are technically mixed (combinations of planned and market economies), but they are generally called either planned or market systems depending on which approach to production and distribution dominates.

Recent Trends

The most prominent planned economy in the twentieth century was that of the U.S.S.R. (Union of Soviet Socialist Republics), also called the Soviet Union. Made up of Russia and other bordering states, the Soviet Union existed from 1922 to 1991, and during this time all of its economic resources were owned and controlled by the government. Many economists applauded Soviet-style central planning during and after the Great Depression (the severe economic crisis that afflicted much of the world in the 1930s) because it allowed the nation to avert the level of suffering experienced in countries with market economic systems. The Soviet economy grew faster than the U.S. economy throughout the 1960s because it was able to mobilize huge amounts of land, labor, and capital for large-scale public projects. By the latter part of the twentieth century, the challenges of planning a modern economy had become insurmountable, however. Soviet planners had to make production and distribution decisions about an ever-growing range of products, the system became clogged and inefficient, and the society's needs and wants went unfulfilled.

By the 1980s Soviet leaders began to admit that there were flaws in the system, and they started allowing market forces to play a greater role in the nation's economy. In a market system countless individuals pursue their own self-interest; these pursuits determine what economic activity goes on. A market economy can process information much more quickly and efficiently than a group of central planners, no matter how skilled. In 1991 the Soviet Union was formally dissolved. Since then the nations making up the former Soviet Union have been fitfully transitioning to market economic systems.

MARXIST ECONOMICS

What It Means

Marxist economics is a branch of economic study based on the writings of Karl Marx (1818–83), a German philosopher, revolutionary, and economist. While largely dismissed by mainstream economists today, Marxist economic ideas have had a great impact on the world since the early twentieth century.

Marx is best known for providing the intellectual foundation for the various socialist ideologies (beliefs in redistributing wealth and property so that individuals share the fruits of the economy more equally than under other political systems) that rose to prominence in Russia, China, and Eastern Europe in the early twentieth century. Marx's popular reputation rests largely on his coauthorship (with Friedrich Engels) of *The Communist Manifesto* (1848), which agitated for a revolutionary overthrow of the capitalist system (the dominant world economic system then and now, in which individuals, rather than the government, own property and are freely allowed to profit from their business ventures).

Many people are unaware, however, that Marx is one of the most important economists in history. His achievement as an economist rests on his thorough critique of capitalism in the three-volume work *Das Kapital*, the first volume of which was published in 1867 and the unfinished second and third volumes of which were published after his death.

In *Das Kapital* Marx outlined the concept of surplus value, which he and his followers considered capitalism's fatal flaw. Essentially Marx argued that workers produce more value, through their labor, than their bosses pay them for and that this excess (or surplus) value is the source of business owners' profits. This was a cornerstone of Marx's belief that capitalism was unsustainable and would ultimately collapse, to be replaced by a system run by and for the working classes.

When Did It Begin

While living in London in the 1850s, having been exiled for political reasons from Germany, France, and Belgium, Marx spent much of his time studying economics at the Reading Room of the British Museum. Intending to critique capitalism using the existing economic theories of Adam Smith and David Ricardo, Marx produced a major work called *A Contribution to the Critique of Political Economy* in 1859 in which he argues that it was not "the consciousness of men that determines their existence, but their social existence that determines their consciousness." The book examines the structures of society (law, politics, art, philosophy, and religion) and maintains that they are all dictated by economic forces. Marx devoted much of his life thereafter to working on *Das Kapital*, an even more ambitious analysis of the capitalist system. Volume 1 of *Das Kapital*, which was published in 1867, introduced the central concepts in Marxist economic theory, the most important of which is the principle of surplus value. Marx was not able to finish *Das Kapital* before his death in 1883, but his friend and colleague Friedrich Engels edited volumes 2 and 3 of the book and had them published in 1885 and 1894, respectively.

KARL MARX

"Let the ruling classes tremble at a communist revolution. The workers have nothing to lose but their chains."

KARL MARX AND FRIEDRICH ENGELS, *THE COMMUNIST MANIFESTO*, 1848.

Why He Is Important

Few individuals have ever had as much influence on world history and thought as Karl Marx (1818–83). A German philosopher, historian, economist, journalist, and revolutionary, Marx was the founder of modern socialism and communism, multifaceted political movements that are motivated by the desire to spread society's fruits more equally among all people than do other political systems. The socialist revolutions that brought into being the Soviet Union and the People's Republic of China were inspired by Marx's writings, and his ideas influenced virtually all of the social sciences during the twentieth century. The root of his influence was his economic critique of capitalism, the economic system characterized by private ownership of property and the unrestrained ability to pursue profit. Marx argued that capitalism rested on the exploitation of the working class and that this exploitation would eventually lead workers to revolt and found new, more equitable societies.

Life

Marx was born in Trier, Germany, on May 5, 1818, the son of a successful lawyer, Heinrich Marx, and his wife Henrietta. Marx's father and social milieu were greatly influenced by the ideas of the Enlightenment, an eighteenth-century social movement that focused on using reason, rather than religion or tradition, as the basis for all authority, and Marx was exposed to early forms of socialist thought by his family's neighbor, the Baron von Westphalen. Marx later married the Baron's daughter Jenny, who was considered Trier's leading beauty at the time the two fell in love.

Marx was educated in Trier before attending the University of Bonn, where he was supposed to study law but in fact spent most of his time socializing. When his father discovered that Karl had run up large debts and had his right eye wounded in a duel, he agreed to pay his son's debts on the condition that he transfer to the University of Berlin. In Berlin Marx studied philosophy, and he took his academic efforts more seriously, falling under the influence of the German philosopher Georg Wilhelm Friedrich Hegel (1770–1831). Marx was especially sensitive to Hegel's idea that the central rule of history was change. Every force in life, according to Hegel, contains its opposite, the seeds of its ultimate destruction. History, then, is

the story of these inseparable, opposing forces continually supplanting one another. Marx, like other "young Hegelians" (as they called themselves), was considered a philosophical radical for discussing such matters as atheism (the idea that there is no God) and communism (the belief in a classless, stateless society in which all property is owned in common).

Prevented from obtaining an academic position by the political controversy surrounding one of his favorite university professors, Marx turned to journalism. His increasing political radicalism caused trouble for the various European newspapers that he edited. In 1848 he and his friend Friedrich Engels wrote *The Communist Manifesto,* which predicted the downfall of capitalism and the rise of communism.

Expelled in turn from France and Belgium for political reasons, Marx and his family eventually settled in London in 1849. Marx continued to earn money by writing newspaper articles, most notably for the *New York Daily Tribune* from 1852 to 1862. He also studied economic theory on his own at the British Museum, and he published his first serious economic work in 1859. It was not until 1867, several years later than he had hoped, that he published the first volume of his masterwork *Das Kapital,* which provided the most thorough and compelling critique of capitalism ever attempted. He never finished the second and third volumes, in part because of his central role in the First International, the London-based organization meant to bring about socialist change. On numerous occasions Marx thought that the overthrow of capitalism he had predicted would be achieved, but he did not live to see this happen.

Though greatly admired in radical circles and feared by world leaders, Marx and his family lived in extreme poverty. His friend and colleague Engels, who inherited and ran a manufacturing business in Manchester, England, was the family's main source of financial support for much of Marx's life. The Marxes' difficult living conditions, miserable enough on their own, also affected the health of their children. Jenny gave birth to one stillborn child, two daughters died in infancy, and the Marxes' only son died at the age of eight. Marx and Jenny, too, suffered from poor health for most of their lives. Despite the overwhelming hardships of his personal life, Marx derived great pleasure from his family and was by all accounts a devoted husband and a doting father to his three surviving daughters. Jenny died of cancer in 1881, and Marx never recovered from her loss. The subsequent loss of one of his adult daughters was

More Detailed Information

Marx's economic theories were rooted in the ideas of Adam Smith and David Ricardo, the two most prominent economists of the late eighteenth and early nineteenth centuries. Smith had developed the idea of a labor theory of value. The labor theory of value holds that the value of any good is produced by the labor that went into its production. A pair of shoes that took 10 hours to make would, according to the labor theory, be more valuable than a pair

of shoes that took 5 hours to make. Ricardo bolstered Smith's labor theory by countering critics who believed that it was subject to too many objections to be valid.

Marx addressed further implications of the labor theory of value, namely the question "If labor produces all value, where do profits and interest (fees paid by people who borrow money) come from?" In other words, why does the economy reward people who do not contribute any labor?

the idea from Hegel that history was pushed along by opposing forces, which in the end would resolve into a new force. For Hegel this process of change, called a dialectic, was formed by opposing ideas emanating from Spirit. For Marx, who believed that life at its core was materialistic, not spiritual, the opposing forces were social and economic classes that confronted each other in class struggle. This class struggle would eventually lead workers to revolt against capitalism, which they would replace first with socialism (a transitional, government-run system that promoted the interests of workers) and then by communism.

Critique of Political Economy was the first book to result from his self-guided study of economics, and *Das Kapital* is a continuation and an expansion of his economic thought. Marx is important not only because he proposed new ideas about how the economy functioned (elaborating on principles outlined by the classical economists Adam Smith and David Ricardo) but also because he was the most successful theorist to use economics to make larger social arguments.

Among Marx's most important insights were the idea that the values and norms of a society are inseparable from that society's economic system, as well as the idea that history is a process of continual evolution that depends on the evolution of economic institutions. Marx believed that capitalism was the last stage of historical evolution prior to the rise of socialism and communism, and that the tensions between the capitalists (business owners) and their exploited workers would bring about society's final evolutionary stage.

Legacy

Marx's influence in his own time was limited. Though he played a major role in socialist politics of his time and was recognized as the founder of modern socialism and communism, it was not until the twentieth century that his ideas truly began to change the world. The Russian Revolution of 1917 was spearheaded by Marxists, and the resulting Soviet Union was based on Marx's ideas as adapted by early Soviet leaders such as Lenin and Stalin. The People's Republic of China was likewise the product of a successful Marxist revolution, which took place in 1949. The conditions behind both the Soviet and Chinese revolutions departed substantially from Marx's predictions and central concerns, however, and both ultimately failed to achieve lasting success. The Soviet Union dissolved in 1991, and China, though still technically communist, has been gradually adopting a capitalist economic system since 1978. Despite the limitations of applying Marxist ideas to politics, Marx's critiques of economics and history have influenced the social sciences as thoroughly as the ideas of any thinker in recent centuries.

Karl Marx (1818–83) was a nineteenth-century German economist, philosopher, and historian. Marx called for the creation of a classless society, where all goods and services were distributed equally. *Henry Guttmann/Hulton Archive/Getty Images.*

said to have further hastened his death. He died on March 14, 1883. Eleven people attended his funeral.

Work

Marx's best-known works are *The Communist Manifesto,* which he cowrote with Engels, and *Das Kapital,* whose second and third volumes were posthumously edited by Engels and published, respectively, in 1885 and 1894. His reputation among economists, philosophers, and other social scientists rests primarily on *Das Kapital* and an earlier economic work, *Critique of Political Economy* (1859).

The manifesto was most important as a piece of propaganda. It was very effective at inciting people to enlist in the revolutionary cause, but it was not intended to be a thorough explication of Marx's ideas. In the brief, fiercely argued text, the authors borrowed

Marx's answer to this question was that workers were paid only as much as they needed to survive and feed their families. Their labor was rewarded at this level, no matter how much value they actually added to the products they made. Imagine a worker in a button factory. The worker might make X dollars worth of buttons, but he might only be paid half of X. Because value is a result, as Adam Smith argued, of the amount of labor that goes into a product, the other half of X (the factory owner's profit)

comes from the surplus value of the worker's labor, or labor for which he was not paid.

Marx believed that this situation was unfair and resulted in an ever-present struggle between the working class and the employing class. This class struggle over surplus value is, in Marx's view, a defining feature of capitalism.

Marx argued, moreover, that competition between business owners always tended to reduce profits and that

Marxist economics is an economic approach based on the ideals of equal distribution of wealth and elimination of class differences. Here members of China's Red Guard Movement rally in support of Marxist principles. *AP Images.*

falling profits would force some owners out of business, sending them into the ranks of the working class. This movement of former employers into the working class would mean that the number of people in the working class would grow, while ownership would be consolidated among fewer and fewer people. Thus, the conditions for the overthrow of capitalism (a large, impoverished working class and a small, unfairly enriched owning class) would emerge from the system itself.

Recent Trends

Marx's theories inspired the Russian Revolution of 1917, which led to the formation of a new communist state, the Soviet Union. V. I. Lenin (who governed the Soviet Union until his death in 1924) and Joseph Stalin (ruled 1924–53) were both committed Marxists, as was Mao Zedong, who in 1949 led the communists to power in China. Although these leaders interpreted Marx in different ways, each of them openly opposed capitalism and, by extension, the United States for much of the twentieth century. Most Americans, as a consequence, unthinkingly dismiss Marx's theories today. The economic failure of both governments (the Soviet Union dissolved in 1991 because of economic crises, and China in 1978 began

adopting capitalist economic policies) has been used as further evidence, among economists as well as ordinary people, that Marx's theories are unsound.

In his writings, however, Marx had focused on highly developed capitalist economies (characterized by private ownership of property and businesses), such as those of England and France. He had predicted that the capitalist system in such countries would break down as a result of struggle between workers and the business owners who exploited them. When Russia and China adopted communist systems, they were not at an advanced stage of capitalism. Russia, for example, was still characterized by a strong aristocracy, an elite class of people who inherited their wealth and that had, until 1861, literally owned those peasants who lived on their land. The class struggle between workers and owners had not yet reached the stage at which Marx predicted crisis would ensue. Because of this many Marxists and socialists around the world worried that the revolution was premature. In fact, the major socialist party in England immediately declared, upon hearing about the revolution, that it was anti-Marxist.

Economists, meanwhile, acknowledge the significance of Marx's critique of capitalism, even though some of his most important theories have not stood the test of time. Most crucially the concept of surplus value lost its validity among economists in the late nineteenth century, when the labor theory of value was no longer accepted as the best explanation for how prices were set. Instead of maintaining that a good's price was determined by the amount of labor that went into its production, economists such as Alfred Marshall convincingly demonstrated that other factors, such as demand (the quantity of a good that buyers are willing to buy at a given price), can have an equally powerful effect on price. Despite the fact that Marxist economic thought lost much of its force due to this development, virtually all economists today acknowledge Marx's importance as a critic of the capitalist system. Prior to Marx, economists primarily concerned themselves with understanding the workings of the economy. Marx showed that it was also important to consider the moral and social dimensions of economic phenomena.

Today there are economists who more openly identify themselves with Marx. They call themselves Marxian economists to distinguish themselves from those who used and abused Marx's theories for political purposes. *Marxian* is intended to suggest that they are following in the wake of Marx's theories without following those theories exactly, as Marxists aspired to do. Marxians draw on a wide range of sources in their examination of capitalism but are united by a tendency to view capitalism in moral terms.

$ Mixed Economic System

What It Means

A mixed economic system combines elements of a planned economy and a market economy. In a planned economy government planners make most of the decisions about the production and distribution of goods and services, while in a market economy such forces as supply (the amount of any good or service that a seller is willing to sell over a range of prices), demand (the amount of any good or service that buyers are willing to buy over a range of prices), and prices make most of these decisions.

In the strictest planned economies the government decides the quantities of all goods to be produced (how much milk and ice cream, how many airplanes and cars, how many computers and telephones). It also determines how these products should be produced and how they should be made available to consumers, given the available materials and labor in the country. The government in such an economic system would also determine which citizens are allowed to buy these products and under what circumstances, and it would be in charge of distributing the proceeds from the sale of these products. All of these economic activities could be tailored to match

the society's goals rather than being determined by uncontrolled forces.

In a strict market economy, by contrast, there would be no government involvement in the production and distribution of goods and services. High prices for any given product (milk, airplanes, computers, and all other items for sale in the economy) would make sellers more eager to supply that item at the same time that buyers would demand it in lesser quantities. Low prices for any given product would reverse these attitudes. By creating a balance between the opposing forces of supply and demand and by sending signals to both sellers and buyers, prices would establish the grounds for making all important economic decisions. Prices would tell sellers what to supply (and in what quantities), and prices would necessitate the most cost-efficient production and distribution methods. The interaction of supply, demand, and prices (rather than a central authority figure) likewise would determine who buys what and who benefits from production and distribution.

Practically speaking, all economies mix qualities from both of these ways of organizing production and distribution. The most famously market-oriented economy in the world, that of the United States, uses central planning to organize production in such areas as national defense, education, and agriculture. Though belief in market forces dominates in the United States and among many economists internationally, other countries in the world have found sustainable combinations of market and planned economic structures that differ greatly from the U.S. model.

When Did It Begin

The earliest human communities employed neither planned nor market economic systems. Instead they relied on tradition to orchestrate the production and distribution of material needs and wants. Traditional economic systems were usually employed by societies dependent on hunting and gathering foods and other necessities that would then be distributed according to inherited rules and hierarchies. Even these relatively pure economic systems, however, might be considered mixed economies, though in a different sense than we use the term today. Instead of a mix between market and planned economies, these societies can be said to have had mixed traditional and planned systems. Rigid traditional hierarchies within a tribe, for instance, might have functioned similarly to a group of central planners organizing the community's hunting and gathering efforts and distributing the produce of these activities in various quantities to different tribal members.

No one knows exactly when true economic planning, as it is known today, emerged from tradition-based systems, but the impressive accomplishments of early civilizations in Egypt, China, and elsewhere were made possible by a high degree of such planning. Pharaohs in

Egypt, for example, forced people away from their traditional occupations and into such endeavors as pyramid building, along with the other, more mundane forms of labor required to build cities. Planned economies overseen by powerful rulers dominated the civilized world through the Middle Ages (which lasted from about 500 to about 1500), but it is unlikely that any of these economic systems relied exclusively on central planners. Marketplaces where merchants and consumers could freely come together to exchange goods and services existed in the earliest planned economies, for instance, and tradition continued to play a major role in organizing society.

Market economies began to overtake planned economies in global importance between the sixteenth and the eighteenth centuries. During this time capitalists (those who owned their own businesses and freely pursued profits) were able to amass money in greater quantities than many aristocrats (those belonging to a small privileged class with inherited wealth), who had depended on central authority figures to ensure their financial well-being. More and more the market system eclipsed central planning as the key to economic development, but even economies that trust market forces most fully,

such as the U.S. economy, have always relied on central planning in some areas.

More Detailed Information

Economic systems are classified as traditional, planned, or market-driven depending on how they answer three basic questions: What will be produced? How will it be produced and distributed? And for whom will it be produced and distributed? In any society either traditions, central planners, or market forces take the lead in answering these questions, with far-reaching results for individuals and societies.

Though people generally speak of economies as falling into one of these three basic categories, in reality all nations have mixed economies. Those nations dependent on traditional economies today (usually poorer, less-developed countries) might adopt more planning or more market-based elements in their attempts to modernize, depending on a variety of cultural and other factors. Developed, wealthier nations might be viewed as occupying specific positions on a spectrum that stretches from a pure planned economy at one extreme to a pure market economy at the other. It is often difficult to decide what point along this spectrum a given nation's

In a mixed economic system the economy is shaped by both market forces and government planning. China, particularly in business centers like Shanghai, has been reducing its dependence on government planning and giving more freedom to private businesses. *Photograph by Wolfgang Kaehler. Reproduced by permission.*

economy occupies, and there is often a lack of consensus about this among the nation's own members.

Many Americans, for example, assume that the United States relies entirely on market forces to determine the size and shape of its economy. In reality the government intervenes significantly (if less than in most developed countries) to answer the what, how, and for whom questions listed above. Like all governments, the U.S. government plans economic activity related to military and other national-defense issues. It also oversees the public educational system and portions of the health-care system (providing health care to elderly and poor people through such programs as Medicare and Medicaid and regulating the pharmaceutical industry through the Food and Drug Administration). These and other government activities are financed with taxes. Though U.S. citizens pay lower taxes than people in most other developed countries, the collection of taxes and the provision of free services in an attempt to meet society's basic goals interfere with market forces. There has been and perhaps always will be debate about what portions of the economy should be influenced by the government and what portions should be left alone. Some Americans believe that the government should play a greater role in economic affairs, while others believe that the United States should move as close as possible to a pure market system.

At the other end of the spectrum, the Soviet Union, which existed from 1922 until 1991, had the best-known example of a planned economy in recent history, and its leaders indeed attempted to plan virtually every aspect of production and distribution. Though central planners were effective at solving production and distribution problems early in the nation's history, modernization throughout the world made economic decision-making more complex, and planners could not gather and process information as effectively as markets could through their pricing systems. Many people view the collapse of the Soviet Union, caused chiefly by the failings of its planned economy, as proof that planned economies do not work.

It is common for people to believe that there is no middle ground between a market economy and a planned economy, but successful economies with a more even mix than the United States exist. One example is Sweden's economy. Most Swedish businesses are privately owned and depend on market forces to decide production and distribution issues (as in the United States), but the government intervenes much more broadly in the economy than the U.S. government does. While Sweden's per capita gross domestic product (the total value of goods and services its economy creates, per person) rivals that of the United States, its taxes are much higher. Approximately 60 percent of all wealth created in Sweden is channeled through the government. This allows the nation to distribute the benefits of its economic activity much more evenly than in the United States and to

PRIVATIZATION

Though the United States has always had a mixed economy (combining a reliance on some amount of government planning with a reliance on such market forces as supply, or the amount of any good or service that a seller is willing to sell at a given price, and demand, the amount of any good or service that buyers are willing to buy at a given price), public opposition to government intervention in the economy began to grow in the 1970s and 1980s. By the 1990s many people both in and out of government took for granted the idea that government performed all tasks less efficiently than private businesses, which were subject to market forces. This conviction resulted in a trend called privatization, or the turning over to private companies of jobs previously performed by government agencies.

Much of the privatization of the 1990s occurred at the city and regional level. Cities, including New York, Los Angeles, and Dallas, began relying on private companies to perform tasks like waste disposal, data processing, and even prison management. But federal agencies were affected by the trend as well. The U.S. Postal Service, for instance, began operating like a private business rather than a branch of government, using income from customers rather than tax revenues to fund its operations.

Privatization is controversial, however. Some argue that it simply represents a giveaway to private companies, which profit from contracts with cities and states without improving on the job done by municipal workers. The trend remained popular into the early twenty-first century, even reaching realms as sensitive to the national interest as war. When the United States went to war against Iraq in 2003, for example, an unprecedented proportion of the war effort was undertaken by private companies.

provide citizens with a wide range of services that a more market-based economy cannot supply. Citizens of Sweden are guaranteed a certain minimum standard of living, and they have access to government assistance in case of emergencies. There is a national health-care system to which all citizens have equal access, parents are allotted much more leave from work to take care of their children than in other countries, and all education up to and including the university level is free.

Recent Trends

Views about the roles that market forces and central planning should play in the U.S. economy shifted periodically during the twentieth century. Bolstered by the economic theories of the British economist John Maynard Keynes (1883–1946), who encouraged government intervention, public sentiment during and after the Great Depression (the severe economic crisis that afflicted market economies in the 1930s, lasting from 1929 until about 1939 in the United States) favored large increases in government planning. The basic idea that the government could and should play a substantial role in assuring the economic well-being of society began to lose influence in the 1970s, when a stagnant U.S. economy was blamed on the very government intervention that had helped the country out of the Great Depression. The 1980s saw Americans, led by conservative economists and politicians, embrace ideologies calling for a more purely market-based economy. Though these views were moderated somewhat in the 1990s, the idea of large-scale government planning remained out of fashion into the early twenty-first century. In general Americans were more likely, during this time, to distrust government planning of economic matters than were the citizens of other wealthy countries.

TRANSITION ECONOMY

What It Means

A transition economy is an economy that is shifting from a planned economy to a free-market economy. A planned, or command, economy is one in which the central government makes all of the decisions regarding how resources such as land, labor, and capital (money and other material assets) are allocated to produce goods and services. In a planned economy the government sets the prices for goods and services, dictates supply (the amount of goods and services produced), and tries to manipulate demand (the amount of goods and services that consumers want to buy) to match supply. This stands in

A transition economy is one based on government planning that is in the process of moving toward a capitalist, free market approach. China's adoption of free-market reforms has increased the presence of foreign companies, including McDonalds, within its borders. © *Reuters/Corbis.*

contrast to a free-market economy, in which supply and demand are not regulated by the government. In a free-market economy, prices are determined by a variety of factors, including what consumers are willing to pay for goods and services and the number of businesses competing for consumer dollars. According to most experts, the transition from a planned economy to a free-market economy takes at least 10 years.

The transition to a free-market economy begins with a three-step process. First, there is a general liberation of all economic processes. Prices that were controlled by the government are freed and left to be set by market activity among suppliers and consumers. Other government-controlled economic factors, such as interest rates (the charge for borrowing money) and exchange rates (rates of converting foreign currency to local currency and vice versa), are also freed. Second, a stabilization program is installed to limit inflation (the general rising of prices), control the national budget, and minimize government debt. Third, the longer process of building the infrastructure of a free-market economy is initiated. This process includes privatization (putting formerly state-run businesses into the hands of individuals and corporations); eliminating the monopoly of a state-run bank and building a private sector based on the extension of credit (that is, making loans available to businesses); and establishing a stock market where individuals can buy and sell shares (partial ownership) in corporations. Another aspect of creating the infrastructure of a free-market economy is limiting government involvement in social programs such as health care and housing.

When Did It Begin

The term *transition economy* is normally applied to the 25 free nations that emerged in Eastern Europe and Central Europe after the fall of Soviet communism in 1991. The Soviet Union (U.S.S.R.) was founded in 1922 in the aftermath of the Russian Revolution of 1917 (in which the monarchy was overthrown and the radical socialist party, the Bolsheviks, ultimately seized power) and the Russian Civil War (1917–20). The U.S.S.R. reached its largest geographic size after World War II (1939–45), when it annexed large portions of Central and Eastern Europe. All of the peoples under Soviet control were forced to adopt a form of communism, an economic and political system in which the economy is under state control. The CPSU (Communist Party of the Soviet Union) controlled production, regulated trade, and set wages throughout the Soviet bloc (those nations under the rule of the Soviet Union).

Although Yugoslavia and Albania broke with the Soviet system in 1948 and 1961, respectively, Soviet domination of Eastern and Central Europe remained firmly intact until the mid-1980s. In 1985 CPSU leader Mikhail Gorbachev (b. 1931) instituted an economic restructuring plan called perestroika, which loosened the

Soviet government's hold on the economy. The reforms initiated under this plan notwithstanding, many historians trace the dissolution of the Soviet Union to the dismantling in 1989 of the Berlin Wall, which had divided the German city of Berlin into East Berlin (occupied by the Soviets) and West Berlin (occupied by Great Britain, France, and the United States) since 1961. Shortly after this event, single-party totalitarian states within the Soviet bloc were replaced by democracies, and private individuals and corporations took control of the factors of production. The Soviet Union officially disbanded in December 1991, when the presidents of Russia, Ukraine, and Belarus signed the Belavezha Accords, which established an international alliance called the Commonwealth of Independent States (CIS).

More Detailed Information

The 25 countries that have been attempting to establish free-market economies since the fall of the Soviet Union include 13 nations in Central and Eastern Europe (Albania, Bosnia and Herzegovina, Croatia, the Czech Republic, Estonia, Hungary, Latvia, Republic of Macedonia, Montenegro, Poland, Romania, Serbia, and Slovakia) and 12 nations in the CIS (Armenia, Azerbaijan, Belarus, Georgia, Kazakhstan, Kyrgyz Republic, Moldova, Russia, Tajikistan, Turkmenistan, Ukraine, and Uzbekistan). There are also transition economies in Asia, Africa, and Latin America. In Asia the transition economies include Cambodia, China, Laos, Mongolia, Thailand, and Vietnam. Transition economies in Africa include Mozambique and Angola, and in Latin America the economies of Brazil and Chile are considered to be transition economies.

In addition to the leaders, entrepreneurs, and laborers in each of these countries, there are three institutions that provide assistance to countries making the shift to a free-market economy. These are the World Bank, the International Monetary Fund (IMF), and the European Bank for Reconstruction and Development (EBRD).

Both the World Bank and the IMF were formally established in December 1945 to help countries rebuild their economies in the aftermath of World War II. Since that time, these two institutions have contributed to the growth of transition economies throughout the world. The World Bank was created to provide low-interest loans to developing countries to help finance education and health care; the building of roads, irrigation systems, and other important infrastructure; and the formation of legal institutions to limit corruption. The World Bank also helps countries establish and maintain environmental regulations to minimize air and water pollution, and it funds efforts to treat people with HIV/AIDS in developing countries. Despite its many successes, the World Bank has been criticized for its policies. Detractors argue that it often tries to create free markets too quickly in

BORIS YELTSIN

On June 12, 1991, months before the fall of the Soviet Union, Boris Yeltsin (1931–2007) became the first popularly elected leader of Russia. As president his stated mission was to establish a free-market capitalist economy to replace the communist system that had been in place for nearly 70 years. Although he assumed power with widespread support, his presidency was a failure, and he left office in 1999 with an approval rating of less than 2 percent. Most historians agree that Yeltsin failed because he tried to implement change too quickly. Calling his plan to transform the economy "shock therapy," he almost immediately removed many of the former regime's price controls and public-assistance programs. Wide-scale deregulation caused hyperinflation (a drastic rise in prices), which increased poverty levels and allowed for the growth of organized-crime rings, which in turn seized control of newly private business enterprises. In the wake of these financial disasters, Yeltsin began ruling like an autocrat, appointing friends and allies to key positions and at one point in 1993 surrounding the Russian White House with tanks. Yeltsin resigned at the end of 1999, and Vladimir Putin (b. 1952) took power.

societies that are not ready for them. What often happens, they maintain, is that larger countries such as the United States and Japan benefit from having new markets for their goods and services, but the people of developing countries remain poor because their initial economic growth is unsustainable.

The IMF's goal is to establish and maintain a global financial system by encouraging free trade among all economies, monitoring currency exchange rates and the balance of payments among nations (that is, tracking the funds each nation pays to and receives from its trade partners), and providing financial assistance to developing countries. In 1995 the IMF began instituting a set of standards that required all member nations to share financial information with each other. The IMF has faced some of the same criticism that the World Bank has, namely that its policies work to the advantage of economic superpowers rather than developing nations. It has also been accused of supporting military dictatorships that were on friendly terms with the United States.

The EBRD was founded in 1991 to help the new democracies in Central Europe and Asia construct their economies. The EBRD has focused its efforts on Central and Eastern European nations that have demonstrated a commitment to democracy. In the past the EBRD has loaned between 5 and 250 million euros for private-sector projects. To ensure the success of its projects, the EBRD has stringent criteria for loan eligibility. Those seeking loans must be able to show that their project will benefit the local economy, help develop the country's private sector, and meet banking and environmental standards. Applicants must also be able to match the funds they seek from the EBRD. In other words, if a corporation requests 10 million euros to begin a project, that corporation must demonstrate that it will be able to commit 10 million euros of its own funds to the project.

Recent Trends

In June 1999 the IMF published a report titled "The Determinants of Growth in Transition Countries," which outlines some of the lessons that the agency had learned about promoting free-market economies in developing countries. It summarizes its findings in five lessons. The first and most important lesson is that stabilizing inflation (the overall rising of prices in an economy) is crucial to the long-term success of any transition economy. Most transition economies experience an initial three- to five-year period of decline because of inflation before undergoing a sustained period of growth. Some amount of price control is therefore necessary during this initial period of decline. The second lesson is that it appears to be impossible to avoid this initial period of economic decline. The third lesson is that there is no formula for economic reform that will guarantee success. Entrepreneurs and politicians learned from the failure of Russian president Boris Yeltsin's abrupt post-Soviet reforms that any transition plan must take into account the particular conditions of the region's economy and that this plan must be subject to modifications as it unfolds.

The fourth and most surprising lesson is that unfavorable initial conditions do not rule out long-term success, because economic reforms can be effective in offsetting these conditions. The report points out that countries such as Latvia, Estonia, and Lithuania, which had seemed the least prepared of the former Soviet bloc countries to sustain free-market economies, achieved significant economic growth after implementing reforms. The fifth lesson is that, even though the governments of these new democracies are giving up control of the economy, they need to maintain strong legal institutions to fight the proliferation of organized crime that often accompanies economic liberation. Many of the new democracies struggled against the rise of criminal organizations that used robbery and extortion to secure and expand their private holdings.

WHAT IS MONEY?

$ Money

What It Means

Over the course of history various items have been used as money. These include shells, stone disks, gold, silver, and government-issued paper bills and metal coins.

Generally speaking, money is anything to which people assign value in order to make it easier to exchange goods and services.

Without money people must rely on bartering (trading goods and services directly for other goods and services). For example, if you were hungry, you might go to a restaurant with several books that you had already read, hoping that the restaurant owner might be willing to accept one or more of the books in exchange for lunch. If she wanted your books, you might be pleased with the simplicity of the barter system. If she did not want your books, you would have to come up with a new plan, and you would still be hungry.

While simple when it works properly, bartering gets extremely complicated when it is the only way of acquiring goods and services. People still barter today (for instance, a tenant might perform repairs on his apartment in place of paying rent to his landlord), but without money many basic transactions would be much more troublesome.

Although paper bills and metal coins serve as the primary form of money in most countries today, often people do not even need actual bank notes or coins to purchase goods and services. For example, money can be exchanged via checks, credit cards, and electronic bank transfers. In these cases nothing real is even exchanged. All that happens is that numbers are changed in computers that keep track of people's bank-account and credit balances. Such technological innovations make it clear that, in the modern world, money is a symbol and not an actual valuable object. Instead, the items (or numbers in computers) that we consider money have value only because we, as a society, have agreed to believe that they are valuable. In reality, money has always been symbolic. Even gold, which was the primary form of money for centuries in Europe, has value only when societies agree that it does. For instance, when Europeans colonized the Americas and Africa, the tribal peoples they encountered typically had no use for gold. The Native Americans and Africans could purchase things with gold only if they chose or were forced to participate in the Europeans' society.

Money stands in for the goods and services that we need or want (such as apples or haircuts) so that we can obtain these things efficiently. By increasing the efficiency of the way people exchange goods and services, money allows for a wide variety of activity that would not be possible otherwise.

When Did It Begin

People in ancient Mesopotamia (a region that lies in present-day Iraq, Syria, and Turkey) may have used money as early as 3000 BC. According to clay tablets found there by modern archaeologists, some of the first forms of money used were silver, grain, and cattle.

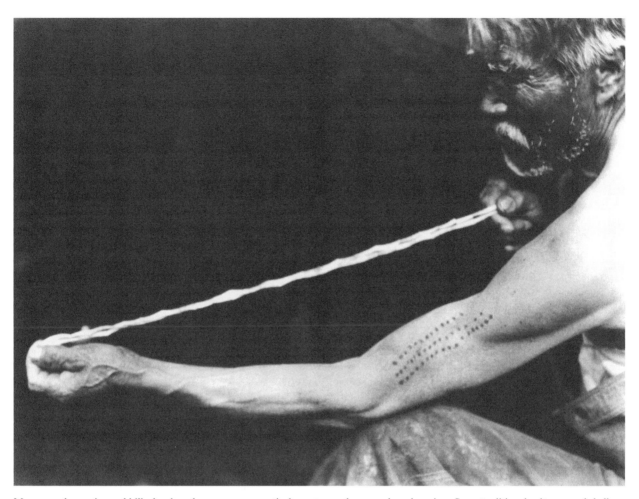

Money, such as coins and bills, has long been an easy, practical way to purchase goods and services. Some traditional cultures used shells as money. *The Library of Congress.*

The first coins made of gold and silver are said to have appeared Lydia (a country that is now part of Turkey) in the seventh century BC. (The Lydian king Croesus, who reigned in the following century, became synonymous with wealth, as in the phrase "as rich as Croesus.") The appearance of coins was a significant step in the evolution of money because it marked the first time that money was given a legal guarantee. Coins in the ancient world, like government-issued bills and coins today, typically bore designs on both sides to show the authority under which they were created. Such designs indicated that the ruler who had issued the coins was guaranteeing their worth.

The ancient Chinese used money as early as the twelfth century BC, and they did so in a fashion similar to that of their contemporaries in the Middle East and the Western world. In China animals, metals, and shells were among the early materials assigned value in economic transactions. In the sixth century BC one form of money was miniature bronze farming hoes marked with the name of the imperial dynasty of the time. Coins appeared in China in about the third century BC.

More Detailed Information

Money evolved in response to the overwhelming complexity of a bartering economy. In this kind of economy buying and selling happen at the same time. Both parties to the trade are simultaneously acquiring and letting go of something, and this requires a complexity of thought that goes beyond what is required to perform either of these tasks alone. The complication of bartering is further enhanced by the fact that, for the trade to occur at all, both parties must want what the other person has to offer.

For instance, imagine that a farmer in a primitive society has a surplus of milk and needs someone to help him rebuild his fireplace. He might take a jug of milk to the stonemason's house and suggest trading the milk for the stonemason's time, building materials, and expertise in constructing fireplaces. The stonemason, however, might believe that the building of a fireplace is worth five jugs of milk. Assuming that the farmer agreed on this trade, he might have to go home, wait for his cow to produce the correct amount of milk, milk his cow, and then hitch up his horse and wagon in order to carry the milk to the stonemason and conclude the deal.

THE VELOCITY OF MONEY

Many ordinary people understand that the amount of money in circulation affects the economy as a whole. For instance, if countries A and B have the same size economy, but A's economy has twice as much money in circulation as country B's economy, then country A has prices that are twice as high.

There is another equally important measure, however, in determining the size and health of an economy: the velocity of money. This is the rate at which money passes from person to person.

Each time a given dollar bill changes hands, for instance, a transaction worth one dollar has occurred. In the case of country A and country B, suppose that, although country A has twice as much money in circulation as country B, the velocity of money in country B is twice that of country A. The total value of all transactions in each country's economy would be the same.

Perhaps after the farmer had left to retrieve the extra milk, the stonemason would find himself wondering if he had calculated the value of his work properly: an entire fireplace, requiring several days of hard work, in exchange for a few jugs of milk? Possibly the stonemason did not balance his roles as seller and buyer properly, and now he must either compromise his dignity by backing out of the deal or feel as though he has been cheated.

Or imagine that the stonemason has a surplus of milk and does not want any more. Perhaps what the stonemason really wants at the moment is a pair of pants and a shirt. He might agree to build the fireplace for the farmer on the condition that the farmer finds him a pair of pants and a shirt. To get the pants and shirt, then, the farmer could take his milk jug to the tailor's house and hope that the tailor is currently in need of milk. But what if the tailor does not need milk or wants to negotiate the amount of milk that must be exchanged for pants and a shirt?

Transactions in a bartering economy have the potential to get infinitely complicated. Money's most basic function, and possibly its most important one, is to provide a medium of exchange, something everyone in a society accepts as payment for goods and services. When they all use the same medium for payment, the farmer can set a price for his milk, the stonemason can set a price for his services, and the tailor can set a price for his shirts and pants. Everyone can sell their products and then buy what they need and want with the proceeds, resulting in huge savings of time and energy for all.

Secondly, money serves the related function of acting as a standard of value, or a "unit of account." When a monetary system of value is established in a society, all goods and services can be characterized according to the amount of money required to buy them. Therefore, al-though the value of money might fluctuate, and although the cost of milk, fireplaces, and pants might vary over time, the farmer, the stonemason, and the tailor can all expect to address one another on a more predictable footing than that provided by a barter economy. Personal preferences and other unforeseen factors play a smaller part in any transaction.

The third function of money is that it allows for stored value. The farmer, the stonemason, and the tailor can all ply their trades in exchange for money, and they can store that money, in the form of coins or bills, for later purchases. This is much less possible in a barter economy, in which objects and services to be exchanged (such as milk, cows, fireplaces, and pants) might be much less convenient to store or less likely to maintain their value over time.

Money's fourth function is that it operates as a standard for deferred payment. In other words, it allows for a common system for borrowing and lending. The farmer, for instance, might be able to buy his fireplace on credit, meaning that the stonemason will let him pay later and will charge him for the cost of the fireplace plus a fee called interest. Meanwhile, the farmer might use the money still in his possession to hire more workers so that his wheat fields can be cultivated. At the same time, the stonemason is able to increase his own wealth through the collection of interest.

Since ancient times all of the various functions of money have been further complicated by inflation (the general rising of prices), which causes money to lose value. Although money is usually a stable way of measuring value, during times of rapid inflation it becomes an ineffective tool. People lose faith in the value of a badly inflated currency, and it stops performing the functions that we require of money.

Recent Trends

Today economies are much more complicated than they used to be. Many more goods and services are bought and sold, and a large amount of this buying and selling is enabled by loans, which are made using not actual money but checking-account balances. Loaned money is literally created by banks. It does not correspond to money that physically exists in the form of bills and coins, but this money is nevertheless crucial to the functioning of the economy. Similarly, people engage in a wide variety of trading in abstract items, such as shares of stock (which represent partial ownership of a corporation) or even different countries' currencies, hoping to amass wealth when the values of these items change. None of this would be possible if money did not perform the four functions described above.

The world's governments thus have a more complex task than their ancient forerunners when it comes to supplying and guaranteeing the value of the money that they create. Most countries have central banks whose job is, essentially, to create money. But this is much more difficult than it sounds, because any change in the money supply has dramatic effects on a nation's economy.

Consider the central bank of the United States, the Federal Reserve System (commonly called the Fed). Before deciding to increase or decrease the supply of dollars in circulation, the Fed monitors key economic factors, such as inflation and unemployment (the number of Americans who are out of work). In general, increasing the amount of money in circulation causes economic growth, while decreasing the money supply slows growth. It usually takes about six months, however, for these increases or decreases to have their intended effect. This means that when the Fed makes decisions, it bases them on predictions of what world economic conditions will be like six months from the present.

Given such complexity, one might wonder whether the original point of money (essentially, to make life simpler than it was in a bartering economy) has been lost. The truth is that, while a person's understanding of money might be dizzyingly complex if he or she works for the Fed, for the average citizen in the twenty-first century it remains largely possible to treat money as the ancient Lydians might have treated it: as a convenience allowing you to get what you want when you want it, with a minimal amount of difficulty.

$ Money Supply

What It Means

The term *money supply* refers to the total amount of money circulating in the economy. There are different ways of measuring the money supply, depending on how money is defined. In the United States three definitions of money are commonly used; they are called M1, M2, and M3.

M1 represents the narrowest view of the money supply. M1 includes only those forms of money that can be used to purchase goods and services immediately without any substantial restrictions. The measure of M1 is determined by calculating the dollar amount of currency (bills and coins issued by the government), traveler's checks, and checking-account balances at a given time.

M2 includes M1 plus most savings accounts, money-market accounts (savings accounts that usually require larger minimum balances and place other restrictions on withdrawal of money, in exchange for higher interest rates), and CDs (certificates of deposit, a form of interest-bearing account that has time restrictions regarding when it can be cashed in) valued at under $100,000.

M3 is the broadest definition of the money supply commonly used in the United States. In addition to all the forms of money included in M2, M3 also measures some larger forms of assets and CDs of over $100,000. M3 provides a figure for all of the money available in an

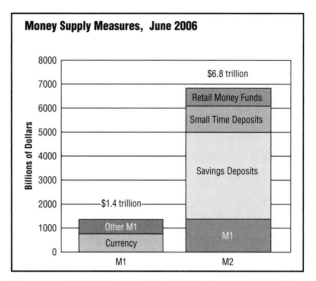

Money supply is all the money in circulation in an economy. One measure of the money supply, M1, refers to the physical currency and checking account deposits immediately available for purchasing goods and services, while another, M2, refers to the sum of M1 plus all the money that is tied up in money market accounts, savings accounts, and other longer term deposits. *Illustration by GGS Information Services. Cengage Learning, Gale.*

economy, though it is possible that a broader definition of money could be devised.

Economists, financial professionals, and government policymakers pay close attention to the size of the money supply in order to understand and make decisions about matters that are important to an economy's health, such as interest rates (the fees charged to borrow money), inflation (the general rising of prices), and economic growth. A country's central bank (such as the U.S. Federal Reserve System) increases or decreases the money supply in order to regulate the economy.

When Did It Begin

For most of European and American history, coins were made of precious metals such as gold and silver, and paper money directly corresponded to an amount of gold or silver for which it could be exchanged. From the 1790s through the early twentieth century, the United States, with some exceptions, tied the value and amount of its money in circulation to the amount of precious metals it possessed. Therefore, the money supply was equivalent to the supply of gold and silver, and regulation of the money supply required ensuring that the country had sufficient amounts of precious metals to back up variations in the amount of money it minted. There was no central authority, however, to monitor the money supply until 1913, when the Federal Reserve System (commonly called the Fed) was created to guard against the failure of banks and ensuing financial panic. Thereafter, the Fed regulated all the other banks in the country and thus had the power to control the money supply directly.

ARE CREDIT CARDS MONEY?

M1, or the narrowest definition of the money supply commonly used in the United States, counts all forms of money that can be exchanged immediately and without restrictions to obtain goods and services. It would seem, then, that credit cards should be included in M1. But they are not. M1 includes currency (bills and coins), traveler's checks, and the balances of checking accounts, but not credit cards.

This is because credit cards are not, strictly speaking, money. For an item to be considered money, it must have three characteristics. First, it must serve as a medium of exchange (that is, it is widely accepted in exchange for goods and services). Second, money serves as a unit of account. This means that it serves as a common measurement for the value of all goods, so that, for instance, we do not have to determine the price of books in terms of computers or the price of computers in terms of apples. Instead, we use money to establish values for all goods and services, and these values can be compared with one another. Third, money serves as a store of value; it has the ability to maintain its value over time.

Credit cards meet the first two criteria, but they do not meet the third. A credit card is a symbol of a short-term loan that the cardholder has arranged with a financial institution; if that institution went out of business, or if the cardholder failed to meet the terms of his or her loan, the credit card would not maintain any value. Additionally, an extension of credit (an increase in a person's borrowing limit) is not the same thing as an addition of the same amount of cash. For instance, $100 in cash has an obvious value that a $100 extension of someone's credit line cannot match. These scenarios indicate that credit cards cannot be considered stores of value.

During the Great Depression (a severe worldwide economic downturn that took place from 1929 through the end of the 1930s), as U.S. paper money lost its value, large numbers of people exchanged their bills for gold or silver. As a result, the country's gold stockpiles dropped considerably, and the government began to impose strict limitations on the ability to exchange money for gold. By the 1960s the connection between U.S. paper currency and precious metals was virtually eliminated, and the nation ceased using silver in the manufacture of its coins. This meant that U.S. dollars had become "fiat money," or money whose value rested entirely on the government's assurance that it was valuable. By this time one of the Fed's primary jobs was to ensure that U.S. money did not lose its value (which can happen because of inflation, or the rising of prices across the economy). The Fed affects inflation and attempts to influence economic growth through monetary policy, or the increasing or decreasing of the money supply.

More Detailed Information

Depending on economic conditions, the Fed may choose to expand or limit the amount of money in circulation. Because the U.S. Treasury Department is actually responsible for printing money and minting coins, the Fed cannot change the amount of money in circulation by simply ordering that money be printed or not printed. Instead it uses various tools for increasing or decreasing the amount of money that banks can lend to individuals and businesses. Banks are able to "create" money through lending; thus, they are responsible for the size of the money supply.

For instance, imagine that Joe Smith deposits $10,000 in his bank. The bank may be required by law to place 10 percent of Joe's deposit (or $1,000) in reserve, to be used if account holders want to withdraw cash from their accounts. The bank can loan the remaining $9,000 to some other individual or business in order to make a profit by charging interest (a fee for the use of the money). Say that Jane Brown borrows $9,000 from the same bank to start a hot-dog-vending business. When she spends the $9,000 to acquire a vending cart and a stock of hot dogs, buns, and condiments from a supplier called Hot Dog World, Hot Dog World will likely deposit that $9,000 in its own bank. Hot Dog World's bank will then set aside the required 10 percent ($900) and then make $8,100 available for a loan.

This process continues, theoretically, until the potential of that original $10,000 has been exhausted. If every bank and every borrower behaved according to the pattern established above, Joe Smith's original $10,000 deposit would ultimately result in an addition of $90,000 to the money supply (using M1 as the definition of the money supply for the sake of this example).

Any given $10,000 does not always result in $90,000. Sometimes a borrower might simply pocket part of his or her loan, and banks do not always lend out the maximum amount that the law allows them to lend. Still, economic theory tells us that when a bank has excess money available to lend, we should expect the money supply to grow by multiples of that available amount. Therefore, when the Fed wants to increase or decrease the money supply, it does so by changing the amount of money banks have available to lend.

Recent Trends

For decades after the Great Depression, U.S. economic policy was built on the ideas of the British economist John Maynard Keynes (1883–1946), who emphasized fiscal policy (taxing and government spending) over monetary policy (controlling the money supply). This approach is thus often called Keynesian economics. But beginning in the 1960s, the American economist Milton Friedman (1912–2006) argued that government mismanagement of the money supply had caused the Depression and that Keynesian fiscal policies were creating further problems for the American economy. When the U.S. economy saw both prices and unemployment rise in the 1970s (an unprecedented phenomena that came to be known as "stagflation" because of the presence of inflation and a stagnant economy), many economists turned to Friedman's views, which had predicted just such an eventuality.

Under President Ronald Reagan (in office 1981–89), Friedman's ideas dominated U.S. economic policy. Chief among them was the idea that a government should not interfere in any part of the economy except the money supply, which was the key to controlling inflation. This idea, called monetarism, continues to influence government leaders and academics, but most economists today focus less exclusively on the money supply in their ideas about how best to regulate the economy.

$ Inflation

What It Means

Inflation is a sustained increase in the average level of prices across the economy. It causes money to lose value over time.

The value of a dollar (or any country's currency) is not constant; it is measured in terms of what it can purchase. During a period of inflation, each dollar in a person's possession decreases in purchasing power. At the beginning of one year, the average American may regularly spend $50 a week on groceries. If prices increase during that year at a rate of 4 percent (this is another way of saying that the inflation rate is 4 percent), he or she would theoretically pay $52 for the same groceries at the beginning of the following year.

As long as inflation is under control, people whose wages or salaries keep pace with the rate of inflation generally have little to worry about. Inflation is more of a concern for those who live on their savings or on fixed incomes (which are set at a certain amount), such as the elderly, but effective retirement planning takes mild inflation into account. Mild inflation, in fact, is generally consistent with healthy economic growth.

Severe inflation, by contrast, is a problem for most individuals, most businesses, and the overall economy. Quality of life can suffer as people lose the power to purchase what they want and need. This is especially true for those on a fixed income. If inflation causes workers to lose purchasing power, they may demand higher wages, but this may cause inflation to spiral even higher, because their employers will have to pass those wage increases on to consumers in the form of higher prices. Out-of-control inflation can cause money to become worthless, or nearly

so, which can lead to the collapse of a nation's economy, as people cannot afford to buy what they need and want and companies lose the incentive to produce anything.

When Did It Begin

Inflation became a persistent concern in the United States and the rest of the developed world in the late twentieth century. People and governments in the nineteenth and early twentieth centuries had been more worried about such phenomena as depressions (periods of severe economic decline). After the Great Depression of the 1930s, during which nearly 25 percent of Americans lost their jobs and the economy ground to a halt, the U.S. government began asserting more power over the economy.

During the middle decades of the twentieth century, the U.S. government primarily used spending programs (which move money out of public coffers and into private hands) and taxes (which move money out of private hands and into public coffers) to regulate the economy. For example, when the economy seemed to be

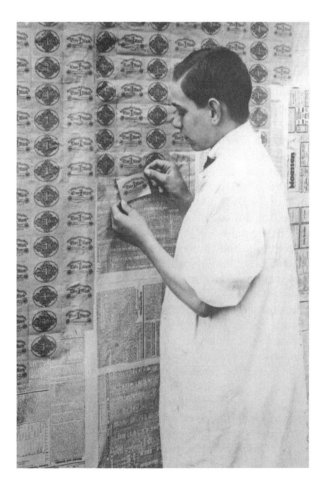

Inflation refers to the average increase in an economy's prices over time. In Germany after World War II, inflation was so high that it was cheaper for this man to paper his wall with Deutsche marks, then the German currency, than to buy a roll of wallpaper to do the job. *Hulton Archive/Getty Images.*

INFLATION OVER THE LONG TERM

If you have ever heard your grandparents tell stories about paying 50 cents for lunch or a few dollars for a fashionable shirt, you may have thought that either they were exaggerating or something horrible had happened in the meantime to make things so expensive. Your grandparents probably were not exaggerating. What happened between then and now was inflation, and although it is a normal, usually unnoticeable part of our daily lives, its effects over the long term can be shocking.

For instance, in the 20-year period from 1987 to 2007, inflation was not particularly high by historic standards. People's wages mostly kept pace with the rising of prices during this time. But the degree to which prices rose—82 percent—may still seem huge. It cost almost twice as much in 2007 to buy the same item you might have bought in 1987. For instance, a nice family car may have cost $20,000 in 1987; in 2007 the same car would have cost $36,400.

stagnating, the government could increase its spending or cut taxes, either of which would increase the amount of money in private versus public (government) possession. More money in citizens' pockets typically leads to more consumer demand for the products that companies make. When companies increase production to meet this demand, the economy grows. Thus, by the middle of the twentieth century, the U.S. government had developed methods for protecting the economy from extreme crises like the Great Depression. But spurring economic growth by increasing demand increased the likelihood that rising prices could become a problem.

At the same time, changed conditions in the private sector made the country more susceptible to inflation. The transition in the United States from a primarily agricultural economy in the nineteenth century to an economy based on industry (manufacturing) and service (the providing of intangible products such as health care, legal assistance, and insurance) in the twentieth century increased the tendency to experience inflation. One reason for this is that inflation tends to be low in agricultural economies; the prices of agricultural crops are more subject to fluctuation, and especially downward movement, than are the prices of manufactured goods or services. Additionally, companies in the nineteenth and early twentieth centuries were generally freer to cut wages in order to keep prices low, thereby preventing inflation, but by the mid-twentieth century workers had won more protection from wage cuts. It was a victory for workers' rights, but it also resulted in the tendency for wages to rise over time and rarely to decline. Increasing wages generally lead to increased prices, or at least the inability to cut prices.

More Detailed Information

Economists disagree about the ultimate causes of inflation, but there are at least three commonly accepted factors. The first is an increase in consumer demand. When there is more demand for goods and services (that is, when people have more money to spend and a greater desire to spend it than there are products available for purchase), producers will naturally be able to set high prices. This can cause inflation across the economy.

Inflation can also occur when the costs of doing business rise. This can be the result of such phenomena as increases in taxes on companies, increases in workers' wages, or increases in the prices of raw materials. Companies will pass these cost increases on to consumers in the form of higher prices. Another possible cause of inflation is an increase in the size of the money supply (the amount of money circulating in the economy).

These factors are often inseparable, with one leading to another. For instance, an increase in the money supply translates into an increase in money per person. When more people have money, there tends to be higher consumer demand for goods and services, which leads to higher prices. And when prices rise, workers are likely to call for higher wages in order to pay their increased costs of living. Companies pass their increased wage costs on to consumers, causing even more inflation.

To measure inflation in one way, governments group together different products that are believed to be representative of the overall economy into what are known as "market baskets." They track the price of these baskets over time in order to observe any changes. The cost of a particular basket today versus the cost of the same basket at a previous point in time yields what is known as a price index. The percentage change in the price index is the inflation rate.

In the United States the most commonly used price index is the Consumer Price Index (CPI). This is calculated using a market basket of consumer goods, such as food, clothing, automobiles, and gasoline. When people in the media make statements such as "inflation rose by 4 percent last year," they are usually referring to the CPI.

Another important price index is the Producer Price Index (PPI). This measures changes in the wholesale prices that producers of goods charge when they sell them to retailers or other intermediaries. Foods, metals, oil, and lumber are among the wholesale products in the PPI market basket. Usually the PPI and the CPI rise together over the long term, but in the short term there can be big differences in their rates of change, because price increases of wholesale goods may take some time to be passed on to consumers. Increases in the PPI are often good predictors of increases in the CPI.

Most people think of rising prices as a negative development, but in fact inflation is desirable within certain limits and when it is balanced by other factors. The increased demand associated with inflation can be positive as long as it is accompanied by similar increases in the production of goods and services. When the economy is growing at a healthy rate, production increases at a rate of 3 to 5 percent a year. An optimal inflation rate of 2 to 3 percent, under these conditions, represents a sustainable balance between production and consumer demand. With inflation and production at these levels, wages can generally keep pace with increases in prices, and businesses can continue to expand at similar rates.

By contrast, falling prices, or deflation, can be a cause for serious concern. When prices fall, businesses make less money, and they are likely to lay off workers. Unemployed workers have less money to spend, so they buy fewer products. This decreased demand for products can lead companies to scale back their operations even further, continuing the downward spiral. Persistent deflation is characteristic of economic depressions.

Recent Trends

Governments today generally try to maintain a balance between economic growth and inflation. Instead of responding to decreasing growth with spending programs meant to spur demand, as was common in the mid-twentieth century, governments today tend to use their control over the money supply to regulate the economy. This is a result of events in the 1970s and 1980s.

In the 1970s inflation in the United States became a serious problem. By 1980 the general level of prices in the nation was rising at a rate of 13 percent annually. At that rate it only takes five years for the cost of living to double. Meanwhile, economic growth was sluggish. Unemployment (the number of workers who could not find jobs) was high, and production was stagnant. This combination of stagnation and inflation, which became known as "stagflation," was unprecedented, and it led many economists to believe that the government's attempt to stabilize the economy by using fiscal policy (tax and spending programs) had failed.

In the 1980s the Federal Reserve, the central bank of the United States, began using its power over the money supply to battle inflation aggressively. By tightly restricting the amount of money in circulation, the Federal Reserve, commonly called the Fed, forced interest rates (the fees paid by people and companies who borrow money) to all-time highs of more than 20 percent. Under such conditions, people and companies are usually very reluctant to borrow money, and a great deal of economic activity is suppressed. These actions thus had the intended effect of cutting inflation, but they also forced the country into recession (a period of economic decline). By 1982 inflation had fallen to approximately half of its 1980 high, but unemployment had risen to its highest levels since the Great Depression.

By the early 1990s inflation had fallen to about 3 percent, and unemployment had returned to normal. By the next decade inflation still had not risen significantly.

Inflation remains, however, one of the primary factors that the Fed, economists, investors, and businesspeople monitor in order to determine how healthy the economy is. One of the Fed's main priorities remains the balancing of economic growth with inflation.

$ Deflation

What It Means

Deflation is a general fall in the prices of goods and services in an economy over an extended period of time. Under conditions of deflation, money gains value relative to all the products that are available for sale in the economy, so buyers can buy more with their money. Deflation is the opposite of inflation, a general rise in prices that causes money to lose value.

Money, whether it is made of gold, stone, paper, or any other material, is only valuable because a society agrees that it has value. There is no actual value in a dollar bill. Americans simply agree that it has a certain value because the U.S. government promises that it does. But the government does not have the power to say exactly how many dollars each individual product in the United States is worth at any given time. The value, in dollars, of each automobile, gallon of milk, doctor visit, and home in the United States is determined by such market forces as supply (the amount of any good or service that a seller is willing to sell at a given price) and demand (the amount of any good or service that buyers are willing to buy at a given price). The value of money shifts in relation to the prices of products over time.

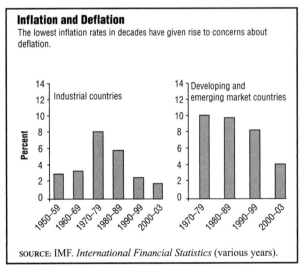

Inflation and Deflation

The lowest inflation rates in decades have given rise to concerns about deflation.

SOURCE: IMF. *International Financial Statistics* (various years).

Deflation, a general fall in prices throughout an economy, is the opposite of inflation, a general rise in prices. With inflation calming in recent decades, policymakers in industrialized countries have worried about the possibility of deflation, which could lead to a downspiraling economy and high unemployment. *Illustration by GGS Information Services. Cengage Learning, Gale.*

DISINFLATION

Deflation (a general decline in prices across the economy) is the opposite of inflation (a general rise in prices across the economy). A third and related term is disinflation, which sounds like a synonym for deflation but is not. Disinflation does not refer to a decline in prices but to a slowing of inflation. If, for example, the rate of inflation is 5 percent one year and 4 percent the following year, the second year would be considered a period of disinflation.

Disinflation is a positive condition for an economy. A small, steady amount of inflation is generally consistent with sustainable economic growth, but inflation that is too high causes problems. Disinflation suggests that inflation is approaching or at healthy levels. It is not desirable, however, for disinflation to go so far as to become deflation. Prolonged deflation is a characteristic of economic crises, such as the Great Depression (the severe financial collapse that afflicted North America and Europe in the 1930s).

On the surface, deflation might seem like a positive economic development. For one, it makes consumers' money more valuable and subsequently gives greater purchasing power to individuals. In the short term, deflation can be particularly advantageous to creditors (people who lend money); the money paid back by debtors (people who borrow money) is suddenly worth more than when the loans originated. On the whole, however, deflation can be extremely harmful to the economy. When prices fall, businesses have a harder time making a profit. As a result, they will be likely to produce less of whatever it is they sell, which means that they will need fewer workers in the production process. Workers who lose their jobs also lose their capacity and willingness to buy products. If job cuts occur on an economy-wide scale, consumer demand for products diminishes. Prices continue to fall as a result of this lack of demand, and companies further restrict production and lay off more workers. Individual debtors are hit even harder by this downward turn, as they must contend not only with layoffs and decreased wages but also with the costs of repaying loans with money that has increased in value. Companies with debts suffer in a similar way, as decreased profits make it harder to repay loans. In this respect, deflation is ultimately bad for creditors as well, as fewer debtors are able to repay their debts. Such a self-perpetuating situation, known as a deflationary spiral, is typical of depressions (severe economic crises) and can take a long time to correct.

When Did It Begin

Deflation, like inflation, is a concern in any money-based economy. Money itself is believed to have been used as early as 3000 BC in ancient Mesopotamia (the region between the Tigris and Euphrates Rivers in an area spanning parts of present-day Iraq, Syria, and Turkey).

The Great Depression (the severe economic crisis that afflicted North America and Europe in the 1930s) is the most prominent example of a deflationary spiral in modern times. During the depression prices fell by about 25 percent in the United States. Accordingly, output (the quantity of goods produced) fell by roughly the same amount, and unemployment (the percentage of people who wanted jobs but could not find them) surpassed 25 percent. Since workers could not afford to buy products, businesses had no incentive to increase output; hence, they did not hire new workers, and the cycle continued.

Government intervention was necessary to spur recovery from the Depression. By spending money on large projects (which required workers) and on direct aid payments to impoverished citizens, the U.S. government increased demand. People with money were able to buy what they needed and wanted, and companies had an incentive to increase production. This required hiring more new workers, which had the effect of further increasing demand.

Since the Great Depression national governments have played an active role in maintaining the value of their currencies. They make decisions about government spending and about the amount of money in circulation with a view toward minimizing the harmful effects of inflation and deflation.

More Detailed Information

The value of money, like the value of products, is affected by the forces of supply and demand. When the money supply (the amount of money in circulation in an economy) is large compared to the supply of goods available for sale in the economy, then inflation can result. There is less demand for money under conditions of inflation than there is for goods. Although prices rise during inflationary times (as businesses, responding to increased consumer demand, try to increase their profits), consumers are nevertheless likely to spend money on items they need and want, since holding onto actual dollar bills is equivalent to losing money because a dollar will continue to lose value for as long as a period of inflation exists. Therefore consumers are likely to spend money on items they need or want, and individuals and businesses are likely to invest money (in bank accounts that collect interest, in the stock market, or in a company expansion, for example) so that their savings grow faster than the rate of inflation. When consumers demand large quantities of goods at the same time that individuals and businesses are eager to invest their money, economic growth is likely to occur. If, however, inflation gets out of hand and prices skyrocket, people cannot make enough money to purchase the goods and services that they need and want.

They might demand higher wages, and if business owners comply, the higher wages will push inflation still higher.

Deflation occurs under inverse conditions. If the supply of products in the economy increases faster than the money supply, then there will be more demand for money than for products. If the value of money continues to increase relative to the value of goods, people will naturally want to hold onto their money in the hope that it will buy more goods in the future than it will today, and prices will fall. In the short term this may not be a problem. Recessions (periods of time during which an economy shrinks instead of grows), which can occur when companies respond to falling prices by cutting back on production, are natural and unavoidable periods in any economy' functioning. Persistent deflation, however, can prolong a recession or increase the intensity of its effects, and a deflationary spiral is a worst-case scenario for any economy. Deflationary spirals are characteristic of severe economic crises, such as the Great Depression.

In today's world modest rates of inflation are considered desirable. The central bank of the United States, the Federal Reserve System (commonly called the Fed), attempts to keep inflation at around 3 percent a year, a level consistent with long-term economic health. It does this by changing the amount of money in circulation. The Fed increases or decreases the amount of money in circulation depending on many factors, including the supply of goods and services at any given time.

The threat of a deflationary spiral is generally seen as more distant than the threat of excess inflation. When the Fed attempts to keep inflation under control by decreasing the amount of money in circulation, however, it must guard against excess deflation.

Recent Trends

In the late twentieth century economists and government leaders worried more about inflation than deflation. Indeed, inflation had been a much bigger problem for the U.S. economy in the 1970s and 1980s, and the government's increased ability to guard against economic crises made a return to depression-style deflation seem unlikely.

Fears of deflation in the world economy were awakened, however, in the 1990s, when Japan (the world's second-largest economy) went into a recession. Together with government mismanagement of the economy, the recession triggered a prolonged period of deflation. The Japanese economy was in and out of recession from 1992 through 2003, and during much of that time, the general level of prices continued to fall. While these economic conditions in Japan never approached the extremity of conditions in countries affected by the Great Depression, many economists and ordinary people were made newly aware of the possible threats posed by a period of deflation. As of 2006 Japan's economy was recovering, but deflation had not been entirely overcome.

$ Stagflation

What It Means

Inflation and unemployment are two powerful forces that are considered to be important signs of whether or not an economy is healthy. They usually happen separately (with the first accompanying a strong economy and the second a stagnant one), but occasionally they occur at the same time. This unusual situation is called stagflation (a term coined by combining "stagnant" and "inflation"), and it is a difficult economic situation to solve, because the usual methods of fixing one problem tend to make the other one worse.

One of the primary indicators of an economy's health is the rate of unemployment, meaning the percentage of the adult workforce that cannot find jobs. Low unemployment figures reflect the fact that businesses are doing well and need employees. When the rate of unemployment goes up (that is, more people lose their jobs), it is usually because economic growth is slowing.

Inflation is a persistent increase in the overall level of consumer prices. As this happens, currency (for instance, the dollar in the United States) loses value. Prices usually rise as a result of high consumer demand for goods and services or excess money in circulation. Thus, inflation is typically considered to be a sign of a strong, expanding economy. Most economists view moderate levels of inflation to be normal if people's income is growing at a similar rate. But when the general level of prices rises too quickly, consumers' purchasing power will fall severely.

Stagflation refers to a period of both high inflation and high unemployment, which usually occur separately. As this graph shows, the U.S. economy suffered from stagflation in the 1970s. *Illustration by George Barille. Cengage Learning, Gale.*

THE 1970S: A DEMANDING DECADE

Part of the reason that the economic slowdown of the 1970s made such an impact was that it represented an abrupt shift from the prosperity of the 1950s and 1960s. The U.S. economy in those decades had been marked by high productivity, growth in wages, and low unemployment rates. In contrast, the 1970s saw not only an increase in inflation (the general rising of prices) and an oil shortage but also other trends that signaled economic crisis. For example, a major migration of the U.S. population out of the cities that had traditionally been economic centers and toward suburbs, especially those in the so-called Sunbelt states of Florida, Texas, Arizona, and California, left many old city centers in decay. Another trend that grew out of economic uncertainty was a steady increase in interest rates, which the Federal Reserve implemented. This made it more expensive for average consumers to borrow the money they needed to make large purchases such as buying a home, which in turn caused even greater economic uncertainty. These, among other trends, made the 1970s one of the toughest decades of the twentieth century for Americans.

Inflation rates usually decline when unemployment rates rise, and vice versa; it is rare for inflation and unemployment to increase simultaneously. Stagflation occurs when the two trends overlap: when the economy moves from a normal period of growth (with low unemployment rates and rising prices) to a period in which people lose jobs but prices continue to inflate rapidly.

When Did It Begin

Most of U.S. economic history has been marked by inflation and unemployment occurring separately. Up until the 1970s unemployment had always been considered a much more serious problem than inflation. Before then prices had generally been stable because consumer demand for goods and services had never grown quickly enough to bring on severe rates of inflation.

Several economic factors came together in the early 1970s to stagnate economic growth. Inflation had been growing quickly since the 1960s. The U.S. government was spending more than it was taking in, creating large national debts (deficits). The high inflation rate caused an increase in interest rates (interest is the fee that people pay when they borrow money from banks or other financial institutions). This made it more expensive to get loans, and business investments suffered as a result. Finally, and most importantly, the Organization of Petroleum Exporting Countries (OPEC), an international body that controlled more than half of the world's oil reserves, imposed a dramatic increase in the price of oil. Because petroleum drove so much of the U.S. economy, this price increase had the effect of raising price levels throughout the economy (that is, it worsened inflation).

By the mid-1970s inflation, which in previous decades had never exceeded 5 percent, had grown to 12 percent; meanwhile the unemployment rate had nearly doubled to 9 percent. This was the first time this economic situation had occurred, causing the creation of the term *stagflation*. It is not certain who coined the word, but it is usually attributed to British politician Iain Macleod (1913–70), who used it in a speech in 1965.

More Detailed Information

When an economy experiences a period of moderate inflation, the usual reaction of businesses is to increase the production of goods and services, because they will then reap the benefits of the higher prices. But if price increases become excessive and result in increased wages for workers, the businesses that employ them react differently: they will produce less and charge higher prices to make up for the higher costs of machinery, natural resources, and wages. Sometimes the government can take steps to curb inflation and unemployment. When even the intervention of government cannot control these two problems, stagflation sets in.

Although unemployment and inflation are often relatively easy to manage, it can be difficult to address both of them at once. For instance, if the government focused on the unemployment problem, it could try to revive the sluggish economy by stimulating the overall level of demand for consumer goods. But increasing demand usually makes prices rise, so this tactic might increase inflation even further. But if the government attempted to slow inflation (which it could do by, for instance, decreasing the lending power of banks, thereby limiting what citizens can spend), unemployment might worsen. The government can only develop policies to solve stagflation when it can identify what is causing it.

When everyone who wishes to work (at the going wage rate for their type of labor) is employed, it is an economic condition known as full employment. Stagflation can be caused by rising inflation occurring before full employment is reached. In this situation, government policy might include providing more vocational training in areas of industry where there is a shortage of skill.

Neoclassical economic theory, which became a favored economic approach in the final decades of the twentieth century, maintains that stagflation is caused partly by the market's failure to allocate goods and services efficiently. One possible solution, in this view, is to use monetary policy (that is, decrease the money supply) to counter inflationary pressures. This is what the Federal Reserve (the central bank of the United States) did in the 1980s. Some economists believe that another solution is to increase taxes on consumption, which encourages saving over spending.

Recent Trends

The Federal Reserve tackled the problem of inflation by reducing the U.S. money supply from 1979 to 1983. By 1983 inflation was back down to normal rates, but as a side effect of slowing down inflation, the economy had gone into a recession. The U.S. government then attempted to revive the economy. It employed fiscal policy in the form of tax cuts and also used monetary policy (specifically, lowering interest rates) in order to increase the money supply; these two actions, coupled with a sharp decline in oil prices, helped to create an economic recovery. For the next two decades the condition of the U.S. economy was strong in comparison to the double-digit inflation and recession of the 1970s.

In 2006 the price of oil rose to almost $80 a barrel at the same time that the Federal Reserve was increasing interest rates. These developments, which seemed similar to what had happened in the early 1970s, led some economists to believe that global stagflation might return. The U.S. economy, however, was not nearly as dependent on oil as it was in the 1960s and 70s. Thus, stagflation did not come about, and oil prices gradually dropped to below $60 per barrel.

$ Debt

What It Means

Debt is money owed by one person, company, or institution to another person, company, or institution. Those who borrow money are called borrowers or debtors, and those who loan money are called lenders or creditors.

In the modern world debt is very common, and it is a central part of the world economy. Borrowers can use loans to finance purchases and projects that they could not otherwise afford, and lenders can generate income by charging interest (a fee for the use of borrowed money) on loans. These activities account for a large portion of the total economic activity in most modern countries. Without debt and the purchases and income it generates, modern economies would be only a fraction of their current size.

Consumers commonly go into debt in order to purchase large items, such as automobiles and homes. Another common form of consumer borrowing is the use of credit cards, which allow individuals to make purchases (of smaller items than homes and cars) and to pay for them at a later point in time. Companies borrow money for a variety of reasons, including to build or purchase new factories and equipment, to hire new workers, to buy inventory and other materials, and to pay for unexpected expenses. Likewise people starting a new business must often borrow money to cover their initial expenses. Governments also routinely borrow money to finance schools, highways, hospitals, and other public projects, and they borrow especially large amounts of money to go to war.

When Did It Begin

The phenomenon of debt dates back to the earliest civilizations. As early as 3000 BC, loans were used to facilitate economic activity in ancient Mesopotamia (which now lies in Iraq, Syria, and Turkey). While creditors charged interest in these early times, this practice was widely condemned by religious figures as diverse as Buddha, Jesus, and Mohammed. Interest collecting and money lending were considered immoral by many prominent spiritual leaders, philosophers, and members of the general public from ancient times through the Middle Ages (which lasted from about 500 to about 1500).

Furthermore, prior to the twentieth century most societies dealt very harshly with debtors. In ancient Greece, Rome, and Israel, among other early civilizations, debtors who could not pay what they owed were sold into slavery, though Israeli custom required the freeing of such slaves every 50 years. The feudal system of the Middle Ages (in which aristocrats, or those belonging to a small privileged class with inherited land and wealth, ruled over all the people who lived on their land) generally treated debtors more leniently. This was true only because all men were required to serve their rulers in the military and could not be spared for the purposes of punishment. As the Middle Ages came to an end and capitalist economies (in which individuals could own property and conduct business with some amount of freedom from feudal or government control) began to develop, harsh treatment again became the norm for debtors. Until the nineteenth century people who could not pay their debts were generally sent to prison.

Even though debtors' prisons were phased out in Europe and the United States in the mid-nineteenth century, most people continued to frown on the practice of going into debt except to purchase the most necessary items. Debt was considered irresponsible and even immoral, an attempt to acquire things one could not afford to buy by honest means. Only essential investments, such as a farmer's purchase of seeds or a company's construction of new factories, were seen as legitimate reasons for borrowing money.

Throughout history governments have borrowed money in order to conduct wars. Only in the aftermath of the Great Depression (the severe financial crisis that afflicted the world economy in the 1930s), however, did government debt during peacetime become routine. National governments found that they could stimulate their ailing economies by spending money (often on public projects and on aid to the unemployed, the poor, and the elderly), and this was seen as beneficial even if the money had to be borrowed. Since that time public opinion of government debt has fluctuated, but governments have continued to borrow money for peacetime needs and with the intent of managing the economy, as well as for the waging of war.

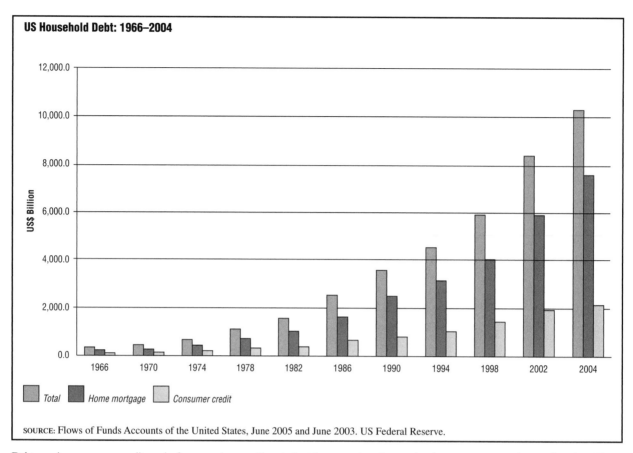

US Household Debt: 1966–2004

Legend: Total · Home mortgage · Consumer credit

SOURCE: Flows of Funds Accounts of the United States, June 2005 and June 2003. US Federal Reserve.

Debt—owing money on credit cards, for example, as well as student, home, and car loans—has become an accepted part of modern life. In recent decades, however, the upsurge in American household debt has worried economic analysts. *Illustration by GGS Information Services. Cengage Learning, Gale.*

More Detailed Information

By the end of the twentieth century, debt had long since been accepted as a natural part of economic life, and borrowing and lending accounted for an enormous part of the economy in all developed countries. It had become common for the amount of debt (including the debts incurred by individuals, companies, and government at the local, state, and national levels) in a developed nation to add up to more than three times the total value of all goods and services produced by the country's economy.

Several conditions are necessary to support an economic system in which debt plays such a big role. First, the members of such a society must be likely to repay what they owe. A credit system in which most people try to avoid payment is unsustainable. Second, there must be a sophisticated legal system that emphasizes the protection of private property. A debt is a loan of one person's or organization's private property to another person or organization; if debts are to be reliably collected, laws must be able to defend creditors' property rights. Third, the society's money must maintain its value. When a country's currency is unstable (that is, when its money tends to lose or gain value erratically as a result of rising or

falling prices), then a creditor cannot count on the value of the money he or she will eventually be repaid.

Most debt is transacted not by borrowers and lenders in direct contact with one another but by intermediaries, such as banks. Banks take in money from depositors and lend it out to borrowers. Depositors are paid interest by the bank for the use of their money, and the bank charges borrowers a somewhat higher rate of interest. The difference between these rates of interest is one of the key sources of any bank's profits.

Debt is often based on created money: figures on paper (or in computer systems) rather than hard cash. Banks do not hand over actual coins and bills to borrowers. Instead, they give borrowers a checkbook with the amount of the loan recorded as a balance (the amount of money available) in a checking account. People can write checks or withdraw money that is subtracted from these balances, but a bank does not have actual currency on hand equal to the full value of all its bank accounts. Banks make loans, instead, in proportion to a small amount of currency that they are required by law to keep on hand. If, for example, Community Bank has $10,000 in currency, it might need to keep only $1,000 in reserve and can lend out the rest. The borrowers then take the money and place it in a bank account, which can then be lent out to other borrowers. This process continues, and the initial $10,000 in currency allows Community Bank to make loans equal to 10 times that much money. Community Bank thus literally creates 90 percent of the money in its accounts out of thin air.

This form of money, which exists only as numbers in banks' computer systems, accounts for much of the total money supply in a country at any given time. In 2006, for instance, there was about $800 billion in physical cash in the United States. If the money supply had been calculated to include not just cash but also checking, savings, and other forms of bank accounts (all of which represent money owed by banks to account holders or by borrowers to banks), however, it would have amounted to more than $7 trillion. Debt, therefore, is one of the chief sources of the nation's money supply. Its importance to the economy can hardly be overstated. Not only does debt fuel business ventures, make possible large purchases, and allow for the construction of highways and the fighting of wars, but it also provides much of the basic material (money) for the entire economy.

Recent Trends

The modern world relies on debt for increased prosperity, but this does not mean that debt does not at the same time threaten prosperity. At the end of the twentieth century and the beginning of the twenty-first century, one form of debt was particularly worrisome to many Americans: credit card debt. Whereas going into debt to buy a house is usually seen as a reasonable way of making a purchase that cannot be made otherwise, credit card debt often results from irresponsible spending on smaller items. In exchange for instant gratification, many Americans sentenced themselves to seemingly never-ending financial burdens and, in some cases, the threat of bankruptcy (an inability to pay debts, which can lead to the seizure of property and other valuable resources).

As of 2007 around 144 million Americans had at least one major credit card, and the average American family had eight different cards. Of the 144 million cardholders only 55 million regularly paid the full balance (the total amount owed) of their credit card bills every month. Nearly 90 million Americans, then, owed not just the amount of their balances to credit card companies but were also paying interest and fees that were often very high. People with poor credit histories (a record of late and missed payments), for instance, might be charged a yearly interest rate of around 30 percent, and the average balance for those who maintained a balance from month to month was estimated at $13,000. Thirty percent interest on a balance of $13,000 would amount to an additional charge of $3,900 a year, not counting additional fees commonly assessed by card companies. Of the 90 million people who habitually failed to pay their monthly

---

THE NATIONAL DEBT

During the early years of the twenty-first century, the U.S. government was in a position not unlike that of a consumer with a maxed-out credit card, in the eyes of many observers. Whereas a booming economy in the late 1990s had led to increased tax revenues that had allowed the federal government to operate at a surplus (that is, the government brought in more money in a year than it spent, so it was in a position to start paying off its existing debt), an economic downturn in 2001 began to erase these surpluses. Soon after taking office in 2001 President George W. Bush enacted tax cuts that diminished government revenues further and increased the size of the federal budget deficit (the difference between the amount of money the government brings in and the amount that it must spend to maintain its operations). He steered further tax cuts through Congress in 2003. Bush also led the United States into two wars during this time, one in Afghanistan (begun in 2001) and one in Iraq (begun in 2003). The combination of decreased tax revenues and massive war expenditures drastically increased the size of the national debt. When Bush took office the federal debt was $5.6 trillion; by 2007 it had increased to approximately $9 trillion.

---

balances, approximately 35 million made only the minimum payment of 2 percent of the total balance each month, which amplified the effect of interest and fees and extended the amount of time they would likely remain in debt.

$ Interest Rate

What It Means

The term *interest rate* is used when discussing credit cards, car and home loans, and other forms of borrowing of money. Represented as a percentage, it refers to the fee the bank, credit card company, or other institution charges to lend money. For example, if you buy an MP3 player for $100 with a credit card, the credit card company pays the bill—in other words, it lends you $100—and charges you interest, or a fee, for that loan.

This fee, known as the interest rate, is a percentage of the amount borrowed. In the example of the MP3 player, the credit card company might charge an interest rate of 15 percent per year. If you paid the bill immediately, you would owe no interest. If you waited a year to pay the bill, you would be charged 15 percent of the $100 loan, or $15, raising the total amount owed to $115.

Charging interest is how banks and other lending institutions make money, and without it they would have no incentive to make loans. Lending money, in turn, is essential for the economy. It allows people to make necessary large purchases, such as cars and homes; to pay for college tuition; and to afford vacations and other desired nonessential purchases. Companies borrow money for a variety of reasons, such as buying manufacturing equipment, that help them start up, grow, and compete with other businesses. Even governments take out loans when they spend more money than they raise with taxes.

Consumers, businesses, and governments all pay an interest rate on their loans. Their desire or even ability to take out a loan will often be determined by the size of the interest rate. If an interest rate is low, such as 5 percent, a loan is much cheaper and much more desirable than if it were 20 percent. For example, when buying a house with a 30-year loan, a person might spend hundreds of thousands of dollars more on interest (over the 30-year period) if the rate were 20 percent as opposed to 5 percent.

Modern economies are greatly influenced by changes in interest rates. Generally speaking, when interest rates fall, three things happen: more loans are made, money from the loans (otherwise not available to people, businesses, and governments) is spent, and thus the economy grows more quickly. When interest rates rise, the reverse happens, and economic growth slows down.

When Did It Begin

The use of interest began thousands of years ago, even before the invention of money. In ancient Mesopotamia (a region in southwestern Asia) people would acquire what they needed through trading (for example, tools for cloth). Loans were often made in silver for large transactions and in grain for smaller ones. Charging interest on these loans met with intense criticism in the ancient world: philosophers and spiritual figures as diverse as Plato, Moses, Buddha, Jesus, and Mohammed condemned the phenomenon as immoral, and prohibitions on "usury," a negative term for the collection of interest, remained widespread as late as the Middle Ages.

In time interest on loans came to be seen as a necessary part of doing business in much of the world, and usury took on a new definition: the charging of exploitative or very high rates of interest. By the Enlightenment (a philosophical movement in the 1700s that emphasized the use of reason over religious and traditional perspectives), economic thinkers focused less on interest collection as a moral issue and increasingly on how interest rates affected the economy.

A notable exception to this historical trend was in the Islamic world, where some Muslims viewed interest as a

Interest refers to the fee charged by a lending institution when issuing a loan. Interest rates change constantly and generally reflect the overall state of the economy. © *MedioImages/Corbis.*

EVERYDAY FINANCE: Economics, Personal Money Management, and Entrepreneurship

form of gambling and a violation of their sacred text, the Koran. Interest, in fact, remains a controversial issue in Islamic countries, and a specialized banking system, called Islamic banking, was developed in the late twentieth century to avoid the religious prohibition on interest. Instead of lending money, a bank would buy the home, car, or other item for the consumer and resell it to the consumer, in installments, at a higher price.

More Detailed Information

There are various ways interest rates are understood. In its simplest form, an interest rate is the percentage of the principal (as the original loan amount is commonly called) charged over a designated period of time, typically a year. In the case of the MP3 player, the interest rate is 15 percent per year.

The real interest rate takes into account the yearly inflation rate (that is, the average percentage increase in the price of all goods and services in the economy). If the average price increase, or inflation, for the year were 3 percent (thus reducing the purchasing power of your money by the same amount), the real interest rate would, in the example, be 15 percent minus 3 percent, as the $115 owed to the credit card company would be worth 3 percent less than when the purchase was made.

Another common term is compound interest. Without compound interest, a $100 loan with a 15 percent interest rate would result in the following amounts due, assuming you made no payments: $115 after the first year, $130 after the second, $145 after the third. In other words, each year the company would charge you 15 percent of the principal. Instead, banks, credit card companies, and other institutions charge compound interest. The first year would be 15 percent of the $100 loan, increasing the amount due to $115; the second year would be 15 percent of $115, boosting the loan amount to $132.25; and for the third year, the amount owed would be $152.09. Each year you would pay interest, or a percentage fee, not only on the principal but also on the interest from the previous year, thus creating "compound" interest. For credit cards, payments are due each month, and the annual interest rate (15 percent in the example) is really a compound interest of 12 monthly interest rates.

Interest rates are also used in such financial services as savings accounts and CDs. CDs, or certificates of deposits, are similar to savings accounts but do not allow any withdrawals for a designated period of time, such as one year. Consumers and businesses open savings accounts and CDs to earn interest on their deposits. If you deposit $100 in a savings account or CD that offers an interest rate of 5 percent, you will have $105 in that account after a year. In this way, consumers and businesses receive interest because they "lend" money to the bank.

THE GREENSPAN EFFECT

The Federal Reserve, the U.S. government's central bank, influences interest rates by increasing or decreasing the supply of American dollars. The Federal Reserve thus has a great impact on the economy, including the stock market, which is sensitive to changes in interest rates.

As chairman of the Federal Reserve from 1988 to 2006, Alan Greenspan (1926—) attained nearly rock-star status among stock-market watchers and commentators. Greenspan shepherded the U.S. economy through two recessions and an overall period of unprecedented growth. Whenever Greenspan made statements about the U.S. economy or the future of interest rates, the stock market responded, sometimes dramatically.

Because of their power, Greenspan's statements were carefully worded and—perhaps intentionally—almost impossible to understand. Indeed, Greenspan joked in a 1988 speech, "I guess I should warn you, if I turn out to be particularly clear, you've probably misunderstood what I said." The Motley Fool, a radio show on National Public Radio, featured a regular game called "What Did the Fed Chief Say?" in which contestants attempted to translate Greenspan's words. Ben Bernanke replaced Greenspan as chairman in 2006.

Bonds, another form of borrowing money, use interest as well. In order to raise money, governments and corporations sell bonds, which are essentially certificates that promise that the government or corporation will repay the price of the bond, plus interest, after a designated amount of time, such as five years. Government bonds are often called securities. The U.S. government, for example, sells securities to pay for the national debt (when the government spends more than it collects in taxes, there is a debt, which the government must pay). Local governments commonly sell bonds to pay for large-scale projects, such as schools, swimming pools, and jails.

The exact interest rate of a loan—5.2 percent or 23.5 percent, for example—is largely determined by the market forces of supply and demand and thus is beyond the control of any individual person or institution, such as a bank. When looking for a home loan, or mortgage, a consumer can go from bank to bank to find the best price, thus encouraging banks to compete with each other in offering the lowest possible interest rates. But because interest pays for a bank's operating costs—and because inflation (rising prices in the economy) reduces the value of money each year—there is a limit to how low an interest rate can be.

Governments, however, have significant influence over interest rates and inflation, notably through their central banks (in the United States, the Federal Reserve), which try to manipulate rates by increasing or reducing the supply of money. Other factors, such as the size of the government's national debt, also have the potential to affect interest rates. When the national debt rises, the government pays for it by borrowing money, in some cases increasing the demand, and thus the price (or interest rate), for the limited supply of money available for loans.

Recent Trends

In the 1990s interest rates in the United States dropped significantly, and as a result, loans became much cheaper for homes, cars, and everyday purchases made with a credit card. For a 30-year home loan, or mortgage (which requires monthly payments for 30 years), the average interest rate fell from almost 10 percent in 1989 to about 5.5 percent in 2003, making it considerably easier to afford a loan. In 1989 you would need to make about $63,000 and have no outstanding debt to afford a $200,000 house using a 30-year mortgage, which required a payment of $1,764 per month. By 2003, because the lower interest rate meant a much smaller monthly payment of $1,148, the salary requirement for the same loan amount dropped to about $40,000.

For consumers, however, the result was mixed. Although it became easier to get a loan for $200,000, the average home price in the United States also rose significantly—from $79,000 in 1989 to $170,000 in 2003 to $213,000 in 2005—largely because lower interest rates allowed consumers to spend more money and because a declining stock market during the same period encouraged people to invest in homes instead, thus increasing the demand for housing. Those who benefited most were people who got their loans before the increase in home prices and who were able to get new and cheaper loans after the interest rates dropped.

THE ECONOMY IN ACTION

$ Economic Growth

What It Means

Economic growth is an increase in the total value of goods and services produced by a country's economic system. The rate of economic growth, which is represented as a percentage, provides a reliable picture of the overall health of a country's economy. For many years the U.S. economy has experienced steadily rising economic growth. On average the rate has been 3 percent a year.

There are several ways to measure economic growth. The most common is to account for the total value of all the goods and services produced within a country, usually in a given year or quarter of a year. This value is known as the gross domestic product, or GDP, and it is a monetary amount represented in the local currency (such as the Mexican peso or the Japanese yen). For example, in 1990 the GDP in the United States was $5.803 billion. For

purposes of comparing the GDPs of different countries, the figures are typically converted to U.S. dollars.

The rate of economic growth for an economy is influenced by several factors. The natural resources (such as coal, steel, and iron) available for manufacturers to use in producing goods play an important role in the efficiency and productivity of the economy. Another factor is the quality of the workforce (the education and skills of the people who are available to work). A country's capital, the resources it possesses for building manufacturing facilities and businesses, also plays a role. Finally, the adoption of technology within the economy can impact its potential for economic growth.

When Did It Begin

The concept of economic growth as a measurement of a country's economic performance has been in existence only since the eighteenth century. Before that, countries typically sought to generate additional money by increasing either their population or the rate at which it taxed its citizens.

During the sixteenth, seventeenth, and eighteenth centuries, colonial empires such as England, France, and Spain developed an economic policy known as mercantilism. In this system, economic growth was measured by calculating the increase in the total amount of gold or silver that the state controlled. To accumulate such precious metals, these empires strove to export more goods than they imported, because exporting (selling to other nations) brought in wealth in the form of gold and silver. The government of each of these nations also sought to increase national wealth by controlling the economic activity within the country. Finally, these countries colonized other areas of the world, because having colonies benefited the home country by supplying materials and labor, thus reducing the home country's dependence on other nations. All of these methods of developing national wealth gradually broke down as the Industrial Revolution of the late eighteenth and early nineteenth centuries made the manufacturing and exchange of goods central to creating wealth.

More Detailed Information

A country can increase its output (the total value of the goods and services it produces) in two ways. The first is to increase the use of its productive capabilities, which means fully using the existing manufacturing resources, the existing technology, industry knowledge, and the entire labor force. This kind of economic growth is relatively easy for a country to achieve and can usually happen in the short term.

The other way for a nation to increase economic growth is to expand its productive capabilities. This entails building new manufacturing facilities, purchasing new technology, and investing in the hiring and training of experienced workers. This sort of investment usually

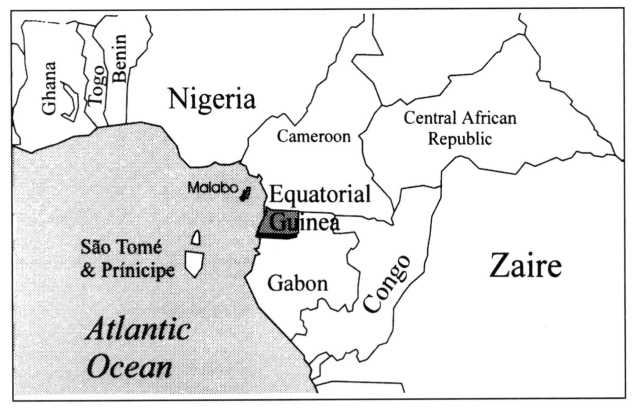

Economic growth is an increase in the value of all goods and services produced in a country. In 2006 the African country Equatorial Guinea, which possessed vast oil reserves, had the world's fastest growth rate of 18.9 percent. *Map by Cartesia Software. Cengage Learning, Gale.*

leads to long-term growth. Over time, all economies that seek to keep growing in the future must have the wealth to invest in expanding existing resources, technology, and expertise.

When a country experiences economic gains in one year, it will help in future years because any efforts it makes to build its economic foundation will broaden the base for more growth. Over many years of accumulated growth, an economy's productive capacity gradually expands, which enables it to continue to grow. Small increases in annual growth rates can, when they accumulate, create dramatic gains in the gross domestic product (GDP).

The GDP, the broadest indicator of a country's economic output, plays an essential role in gauging economic growth. When calculating GDP, economists include the values of several different sources, including consumption (the amount of money all consumers are spending on goods and services), purchases by the government, investment by business, and income from foreign trade (selling to other nations).

The calculation of economic growth must also account for how many people are sharing the total amount of economic output. Therefore, the population size of the country is included in the equation. The "GDP per capita" is the total output divided by the total population. In 2003, for example, the total output of the U.S.

economy was $11 trillion, and the U.S. population was 290 million people. Dividing $11 trillion by $290 million equals $37, 931; this is the GDP per capita for that year. It reflects how much output was potentially available to the average person.

A country can only experience a growth in GDP per capita if its output increase is greater than its population increase. In contrast to the United States, many developing countries (which have economies that are based not on industry but on agriculture or extracting natural resources such as metals or coal) experience slower economic growth and faster population growth. This combination of factors makes it impossible to increase living standards.

Recent Trends

Since the 1950s the American economy has experienced overall growth, but its rate of growth has varied. For example, there have been periods of economic expansion with high growth rates, such as the period between 1976 and 1980. There have also been periods of economic contraction with low growth rates, such as the period between 1980 and 1982. The growth in productivity rose significantly from 1995 to 2000, mainly as a result of a dramatic expansion in information technology, known as the dot-com boom.

PREDICTING ECONOMIC GROWTH

Whether or not the United States will experience future economic growth (increases in the output of goods and services) depends on two factors: the growth rate of the labor force and the growth rate of productivity. The first is a more reliable factor, because long-term growth of the U.S. labor force has remained stable at about 1.1 percent for many years. The growth rate of productivity, however, has been more unpredictable, in part because it depends on several different factors, including:

- Higher skills: increases in the skill level of workers;
- More capital: increases in the money available to invest in new plants, technology, and expertise;
- Technological advances: the development and use of better equipment and products;
- Improved management: better use of available resources in the production of goods and services.

The GDP per capita in the United States has increased since the 1970s, a direct result of the higher productivity of the average worker. The average American worker today produces twice as many goods and services as the average worker in 1970.

Economists have generally thought that saving money and investing in new plants and equipment were the best ways to ensure economic growth. Since the 1980s, however, theories about economic growth have emphasized the idea that new ideas and the spread of knowledge are the primary forces behind economic growth.

$ Business Cycle

What It Means

The U.S. economy has grown tremendously since the eighteenth century. This growth has not, however, been a constant march toward higher levels of production and income; rather, it has been cyclical. Periods of economic expansion are followed by periods of economic contraction (during which the economy slows down, and fewer goods and services are sold), the slowdown reaches its low point, and then expansion begins again. This pattern of expansion and contraction, common to all capitalist economies (economies in which businesses are mostly owned by private individuals, not the government), is called the business cycle.

The term *business cycle* can be used to refer to the overall pattern of fluctuations as well as to an individual period of expansion and contraction. In the second case a business cycle would consist of the period between two economic peaks.

The period between economic peaks can last many years, as with the Great Depression of the 1930s. Since then economic downturns have been less severe. One recession (a milder form of downturn than a depression) in the United States, for instance, officially spanned only March to November 2001.

A contracting economy brings trauma in the form of job losses for ordinary people, but economists generally agree that business cycles are inherent parts of capitalist economies and cannot be prevented. Governments attempt to soften the effects of business cycles by using fiscal policy (decisions about taxes and government spending) and monetary policy (alterations in a country's money supply) to manage the economy and promote stability. Many economists believe that the knowledgeable use of these tools for controlling the economy explains why downturns since the Great Depression have been generally less severe than they were before it.

When Did It Begin

Because business cycles are believed to be a characteristic of all capitalist economies, their existence can probably be dated to the rise of capitalism in Europe during the sixteenth through eighteenth centuries. Capitalism, in which profit-seeking individuals are the main force driving the economy, replaced the feudal system, in which the small number of people who owned land were the possessors of all wealth. Although business cycles may have been one source of economic instability for early capitalists, economists did not begin to understand them in any detail until much later.

In the eighteenth and nineteenth centuries the dominant school of economic thought was classical economics, which grew out of the ideas that Scottish philosopher Adam Smith (1723–90) presented in his 1776 masterwork, *An Inquiry into the Nature and Causes of the Wealth of Nations.* Classical economists believed that free markets (in which businesses are not controlled by the government) regulated themselves and benefited everyone in a society more than alternate systems of organizing business and wealth did. They argued that those economies experiencing difficulties were simply unhealthy. In the late nineteenth century economists began to recognize that all free-market economies fluctuated over time and that these fluctuations were not necessarily signs that the economy was operating wrongly. A detailed understanding of business cycles, however, did not come until the twentieth century.

The American economist Wesley Mitchell (1874–1948) pioneered the measurement and analysis of business cycles as they are understood today. In 1920 he founded the National Bureau of Economic Research (NBER), a nonprofit group devoted to studying business cycles. Mitchell's views were presented most fully in the book *Measuring Business Cycles* (1946), coauthored by economist Arthur Burns (1904–87). Mitchell and Burns

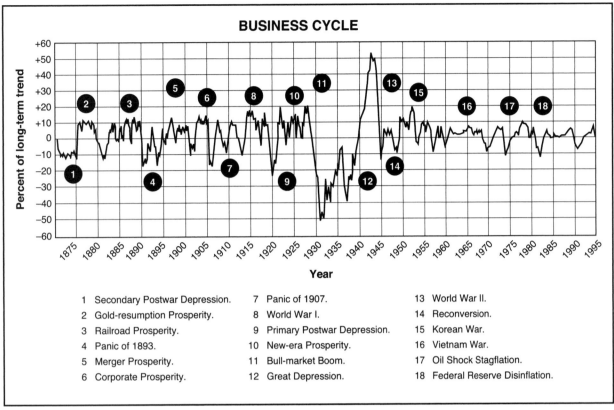

BUSINESS CYCLE

1 Secondary Postwar Depression.	7 Panic of 1907.	13 World War II.
2 Gold-resumption Prosperity.	8 World War I.	14 Reconversion.
3 Railroad Prosperity.	9 Primary Postwar Depression.	15 Korean War.
4 Panic of 1893.	10 New-era Prosperity.	16 Vietnam War.
5 Merger Prosperity.	11 Bull-market Boom.	17 Oil Shock Stagflation.
6 Corporate Prosperity.	12 Great Depression.	18 Federal Reserve Disinflation.

All capitalist economies follow a business cycle of alternating periods of growth and decline. This graph, which charts U.S. business cycles over more than a century, shows the dramatic economic expansion created by World War II (1939–45). *Line graph by George Barille. Cengage Learning, Gale.*

pointed out the ways in which various economic indicators (statistics representing important factors in the economy) moved together to bring about larger economic fluctuations. For instance, output (the total value of goods and services a country produces in a specific period of time) generally moves in combination with prices and the employment rate (which measures how many people have jobs; it is given as a percentage of everyone in a country who wants to work). By looking at these indicators, Burns and Mitchell showed, a government might be able to assess and manage business cycles. The NBER continues to provide the most authoritative word on the measurement of business cycles in the United States. It is extremely influential among government policymakers and within the business community.

More Detailed Information

An individual business cycle (the period between two economic peaks) consists of four phases: peak, recession, trough, and recovery. It is difficult for the NBER or anyone else who studies business cycles to know for certain which phase the economy is currently in or to predict when it will reach the next phase. This is because the actual economy is enormously complex, made up of countless individual transactions whose importance is not always immediately clear. The economy is, however, always in one of the above four phases, and economists keep a close watch on the indicators that are linked to each phase.

The economic indicator that is usually considered the most important one for analyzing business cycles is called gross domestic product (GDP). The GDP is a measure of the monetary value of all the goods and services produced in a country. When GDP is rising, the economy is in an upswing. During a downturn GDP falls, meaning fewer goods and services are being produced. When this happens, fewer workers are needed, so falling GDP is usually accompanied by higher rates of unemployment (the number of people who want to work but do not have jobs). When the economy recovers, more people get jobs, and unemployment rates generally fall. Therefore, employment is also one of the important indicators used to determine what phase of the business cycle an economy is in.

At a peak in the business cycle, GDP is at its highest level since the previous peak. This means that the economy is generating as large an amount of goods and services as it can produce. Businesses are using all of their resources as efficiently as possible, and as many people have jobs as the economy can provide; this level of employment is called full employment. Full employment

SOME CAUSES OF THE BUSINESS CYCLE

Many economists have speculated about the causes of cyclical expansion and contraction. While there is no consensus about which factors are most important, economists generally agree that business cycles result (at least in part) from some of the following factors: variations in investment spending, variations in government spending, variations in the money supply, and politics.

Investment spending refers to businesses spending money on new equipment, research, workers, and other needs. It can have dramatic, unforeseen effects on the economy, yet it is one of the most unpredictable types of economic activity.

Government spending (on social programs, defense, and highways) can also contribute to dramatic fluctuations in the economy, regardless of what is occurring in the private sector. This is especially apparent in times of war, when government spending to make war materials often initiates a period of economic expansion.

The money supply (the amount of money in circulation) has a direct and dramatic effect on the economy as well, and governments control this factor through their central banks (in the United States this is the Federal Reserve System, or the Fed). When the Fed restricts the money supply, interest rates (fees that people pay to borrow money) tend to rise, and the economy slows down. The opposite happens when the Fed increases the amount of money in circulation.

Politics can enter into a government's attempts to affect the economy. Many voters consider the economy the most important issue when voting for a politician. In the lead-up to national elections, therefore, a president will often initiate a tax cut that causes a short-term expansion of the economy. The intent of such an act is to make voters think that the party in power is good for the economy. Just as often this politically triggered business cycle may have to be counteracted after the election, in the interest of promoting long-term economic health, but by that point the desired political effect will have been achieved.

does not mean zero percent unemployment. In the early twenty-first century an unemployment rate of about 4 to 5 percent was seen as full employment.

After the peak in a business cycle comes a period of decline called a recession. Most economic observers consider a recession to be in effect once the GDP has dropped for at least two consecutive quarters (three-month periods into which the economic year is divided). Along with falling GDP, business profits tend to decline, and unemployment rises. During a recession businesses as a whole produce less than they are capable of producing.

The trough is that portion of the cycle when GDP is at its lowest level. Businesses have more unused resources than at any time since the previous trough, and unemployment is usually at its high point. Although recession and trough are two separate phases of the business cycle, the total length of the recession includes both. The economy is not officially out of a recession until it is out of the trough.

After it bottoms out, the economy enters a period of recovery. GDP is rising, businesses are using more of their capabilities, and more people are employed. The economy remains on an upswing, also called an expansion, until it peaks. Then the whole process is repeated.

This sounds like a neat and organized pattern, and the word *cycle* may seem to suggest regularity. In reality, the length of each phase and cycle can vary dramatically. For instance, the recession of 2001 (from peak through trough of the business cycle) officially lasted only eight months. By contrast, the trough during the Great Depression did not come until 1933, four years after the economy's peak in 1929. The intensity of the phases also varies from business cycle to business cycle. During a U.S.

recession that lasted from July 1990 to March 1991, the country's economic output fell by less than 1 percent. During the Great Depression, by contrast, output fell by almost 25 percent.

Recent Trends

The Great Depression radically changed the way governments and economists monitor the economy. Using data such as the information that the NBER provides and analyzes, governments now intervene in the hope of softening the intensity of business-cycle fluctuations. The U.S. government has two tools for influencing the economy. The first is fiscal policy (taxation and spending programs), which the president and Congress are largely responsible for crafting. The U.S. central bank, the Federal Reserve System (commonly called the Fed), is entrusted with the other tool: the crafting of the nation's monetary policy, or control over the money supply.

Today monetary policy is by far the more influential of the two government tools for controlling the economy. The reasons for this are complex, but they include the fact that the other tool, fiscal policy, can be inefficient because it usually takes Congress and the president some time (perhaps years) to approve and enact new measures. By that time the economic situation may have already changed.

The effects of monetary policy on the economy, however, can be dramatic. For instance, the recession of 1981–82 is widely believed to have been initiated by the Federal Reserve. The Fed, concerned about runaway inflation (the general rising of prices) during the 1970s, drastically restricted the money supply. This resulted in very high interest rates (the fees charged by institutions that lend money), which meant that businesses did not take out loans to expand their operations. GDP dropped, unemployment rose, and the economy went into recession. After the recession ended, the economy went into a period of strong growth.

$ Recession

What It Means

A recession is a downturn in the economy. Economists have two ways of identifying when a recession is occurring. According to the most precise definition, a recession is a decline in a country's gross domestic product, or GDP (the total value of all goods and services produced within that country in a specific time period), for two or more successive quarters (in the financial world, each year is commonly broken down into four three-month periods called quarters). For practical purposes, however, most economists agree that a recession is best defined more loosely as an extended period of decreased economic activity marked by the following characteristics: high unemployment rates (a measure of the number of people who want to work but do not have jobs), a decline in the profits made by corporations, and a decrease in the

One of the primary characteristics of a recession, or economic downturn, is increased unemployment. Jobless at Christmastime in Washington, D.C., this man uses an unusual tactic to get people to look at his resume. *AP Images.*

amount of money people are investing in the stock market (a central location, such as the New York Stock Exchange, where people buy stocks, which are shares of ownership in corporations, in order to receive shares in their profits).

Typically recessions can last anywhere from 6 to 18 months. (Before the Great Depression, which lasted from 1929 until about 1938 in the United States, every economic setback was considered a recession. After the Great Depression economists used the word *depression* to characterize a particularly long and severe recession.) During a recession interest rates (the fees that bank customers pay to borrow money) tend to fall. Low interest rates can then offer a way out of the recession. As bank loans become cheaper, more people are likely to apply for mortgages (loans for homes), and more corporations are likely to apply for loans to expand their business. These loans put more money into circulation, stimulating the economy in a way that creates more jobs, more spending, and more corporate profit. Since World War II the average recession in the United States has lasted 11 months.

Economists agree that a recession is a normal and inevitable part of the business cycle, which consists of five stages. The first stage is expansion or growth in the economy, which occurs when more people invest in the stock market and buy homes. During an expansion, unemployment rates go down. The second stage, the high point of the expansion, is called the peak. The peak is followed by the contraction or recession stage. The fourth stage is the low point, or trough, which is followed by the recovery stage, during which the economy begins to regain its strength.

When Did It Begin

The first major downturn in the U.S. economy was called the Panic of 1819 (which lasted from 1819 until 1824). Most economists trace the beginning of this recession all the way back to the War of 1812, a three-year conflict with Great Britain that ended in 1815. Most of the battles took place in the Great Lakes area of the United States (on U.S. soil) and in what are now the provinces of Ontario and Quebec in Canada. In order to finance the war, the American government borrowed money from U.S. banks, which in turn produced more bank notes (money) to help fund the war. More banks opened and produced still more notes, causing a boom (or upturn) in the economy. During the boom investors and families borrowed money to purchase land and to improve farms. Some banks produced false notes to keep up with borrowers' demands.

At the time paper money was backed by silver, which means that a bank note represented a certain amount of silver stored at the bank. Banks realized that they did not have the proper backing for the amount of paper money and loans they were distributing, and they decided to stop producing so many bank notes and issuing credit.

ARTHUR ANDERSON, LLP

Arthur Anderson, LLP, which was based in Chicago and has been renamed Anderson, was dissolved in the aftermath of the Enron Corporation accounting scandal. Before the Enron investigation Arthur Anderson was one of the world's Big Five accounting firms (one of five firms employed to audit, or check the accuracy of the financial records of, publicly traded companies, which are companies that sell shares of ownership to the general public; the other four Big Five firms are PricewaterhouseCoopers, Deloitte Touche Tohmatsu, Ernst & Young, and KPMG). The federal examination of Enron's fiscal activity revealed that representatives of Arthur Anderson knowingly overlooked falsified financial reports that misrepresented Enron's earnings and expenditures.

Since the company's founding in 1913 and through the 1970s, Arthur Anderson had earned a reputation for honesty and integrity. At one time their motto was "Think Straight, Talk Straight," and in the 1970s they were publicly lauded for dropping several major clients because those corporations had prepared dishonest accounting reports. In the 1980s, however, Arthur Anderson began operating as a consulting firm as well as an auditing firm, which means they also began giving financial advice. Performing both these activities presented a conflict of interest: Arthur Anderson advisers were in a position to tell clients how to get around accounting regulations. Soon Arthur Anderson was making more money from consulting than from auditing, and at this time the company's reputation for honesty began to slip.

Investors responded to this contraction by bringing their notes to the bank and attempting to cash them in for silver. Many banks could not honor customers' requests (when too many people demand their money at once, it is called a run on the bank) and were forced to close, further escalating the runs on banks and worsening the recession. Though the crisis struck the entire nation, it was most severe in Philadelphia, where unemployment reached 75 percent. Most economists agree that the Panic of 1819 was a case of a young country's first encounter with the difficult challenges of the business cycle.

More Detailed Information

The terms *recession* and *depression* are the words most commonly used when describing an economic slowdown. Economists do not agree on a precise standard for distinguishing between a recession and a depression, however. In the most general sense they do agree that a depression is a more severe and longer lasting economic decline than a recession, but there is no consensus about exactly when a recession should be considered a depression. A common joke among accountants, economists, and finance professionals is, "A recession is when a friend loses his job. A depression is when you lose your job;" in other words, a person only recognizes the severity of an economic crisis when he or she experiences that crisis directly.

Distinguishing between a recession and a depression may seem like a trivial concern, but the differences between the two types of financial crisis are important for members of a society to recognize. This is so because recovery from an economic decline depends in a large part on consumer confidence. If investors believe in the value of the stocks they are purchasing, they will continue to purchase stocks and thereby keep the economy strong. If, however, any decline in the economy is immediately labeled a depression by the press in newspapers and on the news, investor panic is likely to ensue. Nervous investors often try to unload their stocks. When there is rampant selling and limited buying on the stock market, stock prices fall, and real crisis occurs. In other words, misrepresenting the severity of an economic downturn can cause that decline to intensify.

Some economists claim that the most accurate way to distinguish between a recession and a depression is to examine the actual decline in the GDP during an economic downturn. According to these economists, the country is in a depression when the GDP declines by 10 percent or more. Anything less than a 10-percent decline qualifies as a recession. Using this definition, the United States has not come close to experiencing a depression since the infamous Great Depression. During that period there were actually two separate depressions. In the first, which occurred between 1929 and 1933, the GDP declined by 33 percent. In the second depression, which lasted from 1937 to 1939, the GDP fell by 18 percent. Nothing resembling either of these depressions has happened to the U.S. economy since.

The fiscal disaster that came the closest to being labeled a depression occurred in 1973, when the members of OAPEC (Organization of Arab Petroleum Exporting Countries) refused to ship petroleum to supporters of Israel, a list of nations that included the United States, Japan, and most of the countries in Western Europe. In the United States imports of Arab oil slipped from 1.2 million barrels a day to 19,000 barrels a day. The price of the oil quadrupled, and the cost of gas at the pump rose from $.39 per gallon to $.55 per gallon. As a result of the crisis, the value of stocks on the New York Stock Exchange dropped $97 billion, and the GDP fell by 4.9 percent. Though these certainly qualified as what many people would call hard times, the crisis was a recession rather than a depression.

Though the United States has not experienced a depression since the 1930s, there have been some bad days on the stock market, and at the time people feared that a depression could be coming. One of these days was October 17, 1987, a day commonly referred to as Black Monday. The stock market endured the second-largest one-day drop in its history on that day (September 17,

2001, was the largest), and by the end of October 1987, the U.S. stock market had fallen by 22.6 percent. Other countries, such as Australia, China, and Canada, experienced similar losses that day. Economists do not agree on the causes of the sharp decline, but the crisis was short lived in large part because the media nurtured popular faith in the economy and urged investors not to dump their stocks.

Recent Trends

The recession in the United States that began in 2001 is believed to have had three causes: the widespread failure of dot-com (technology) businesses; the September 11, 2001, terrorist attacks on the World Trade Center and the Pentagon; and two well-publicized cases of large-scale accounting fraud. The widespread failure of technology businesses (what has been called the bursting of the dot-com bubble) began in March 2000, when stock prices for such leading technology firms as Cisco, IBM, and Dell began to fall. Most economists claim that these and other technology companies suffered sizeable losses in the stock market because they borrowed too much start-up money in the mid- and late 1990s and tried to expand the Internet-based sections of their businesses without sufficient planning.

The U.S. stock market also experienced significant losses in the aftermath of the September 11, 2001, terrorist attacks. The New York Stock Exchange, NASDAQ, and the American Stock Exchange closed on the day of the attacks and did not reopen until September 17, 2001. It was longest shutdown of trading in the United States since the Great Depression. When the market reopened, American stocks dropped $1.2 trillion in value in the first week of trading. In addition to the loss of the two World Trade Center towers, many other businesses in lower Manhattan suffered structural damage and the loss of crucial files and records. Shortly after the attacks Enron Corporation, a leading energy company based in Houston, Texas, was charged with accounting fraud. While the press was covering the scandal in November and December 2001, Enron's stock dropped from $90 per share to $.30 per share. Enron filed for bankruptcy in December 2001. The following year WorldCom, a telecommunications company that later became MCI, also declared bankruptcy, largely because of reports that they, too, were guilty of accounting fraud.

$ Great Depression

What It Means

The Great Depression, the most significant economic slowdown in U.S. history, lasted from 1929 until about 1939. A depression is an especially severe and long recession, and a recession is an economic downturn that can be defined in two ways. According to the most precise definition a recession is a decline in a country's gross

BULL AND BEAR MARKETS

A bull market is a market in which the prices of stocks (shares of ownership in corporations) rise faster than the average historical rate of share price increases. A bear market is the opposite: a trend in which stock prices fall at a rate faster than the historical average. In the United States the 1920s were called the Roaring Twenties in part because there was a prolonged bull market. Times were so prosperous that some leading economists of the day went so far as to say that the stock market was invulnerable to a downturn. These predictions proved to be untrue, and the Great Depression (from 1929 until about 1939, resulting in the most significant banking-industry failure in U.S. history) that followed remains the nation's most prolonged bear market.

domestic product (GDP; the total value of all goods and services produced within a country) for two or more successive quarters (in the financial world, each year is commonly broken down into four three-month periods called quarters).

After the Great Depression began in 1929, it quickly spread to Europe and became an international financial crisis. Countries came out of the Depression at different times, but for most nations the crisis lasted well into the 1930s. In the United States more than 9,000 banks closed during the 1930s, depositors lost their savings, and unemployment and homelessness sharply increased. Workers in agriculture, mining and logging, and other industries suffered the greatest losses because international trade sharply declined, and overseas markets for American raw materials and finished goods dried up. The United States began to come out of the Great Depression in 1938 and 1939 at the dawn of World War II.

When Did It Begin

While it is difficult to attribute the Great Depression to a single cause, economists generally point to several critical (and catastrophic) economic developments that occurred during the 1920s and early 1930s. The first major crisis came in the aftermath of World War I, when American farmers, hoping to fulfill global demand for food and other crops following the collapse of agriculture in war-ravaged Europe, began to increase production of major commodities (for example, grain, cotton, and corn). In order to accommodate this dramatic rise in production, many farmers took on large debts to finance additional farming machinery, increased shipping volumes, and other expenses. As production increased, however, farmers soon found themselves with an enormous surplus (a condition where a producer has more goods than can be sold). A rapid decline in agricultural prices resulted in a comparable decline in farming revenues, and many farmers defaulted on their loans (in other words, were

The Great Depression was a period of severe economic hardship that lasted from 1929 to about 1939. This photo shows unemployed workers applying for government benefits during the Great Depression. *The Library of Congress.*

unable to make loan payments) and were subsequently forced into bankruptcy. By 1929 farmers' earnings amounted to only one-third of the national average. In the 1930s severe drought in key U.S. farming states (which became known, collectively, as the Dust Bowl) further devastated U.S. agriculture.

More Detailed Information

Arguably the most infamous event leading to the Great Depression came on October 29, 1929 (a day known in U.S. history as Black Tuesday), when the New York Stock Exchange (the largest organized stock market in the United States) crashed. On that day 16.4 million shares of stock were sold (a single-day record high that was not exceeded for nearly 40 years), and the stock market lost $14 billion. Largely forgotten, however, is the fact that there was a similar crash on the previous Thursday (October 24, 1929), when 12.9 million shares were traded. Heading into the weekend, many newspapers called that day Black Thursday. When trading resumed on

Monday, October 28, investors continued to sell. Though most historians consider Black Tuesday the beginning of the Great Depression, it should be noted that the stock market began to recover in November and December of 1929, recouping almost a third of its losses before the end of the year. This gradual recovery continued until the autumn of 1930, when the market began a steady, long-lasting decline that lasted through most of the 1930s.

According to many economists, the government's failure to act decisively following the stock market crash played a role in making the crisis worse. For one, the Federal Reserve (the central bank of the United States) failed to act when the nation's leading banks began to fail in the early 1930s. Economists such as Milton Friedman (1912-2006) have argued that the Federal Reserve could have averted the disaster by lending money to the failing banks; instead, the collapse of the nation's major banks resulted in the collapse of numerous smaller banks, notably those in rural areas, thereby worsening the crisis. At the same time, the nation's money supply (the amount of money in circulation) dropped by over 30 percent between 1930 and 1931; according to Friedman, the Federal Reserve could have stimulated the economy by making more money available for loans, debt relief, and so on. At the same time, the decision of President Herbert Hoover (1874-1964) not to allow the federal government to take on debt further thwarted the economy's prospects of a swift recovery.

Also thought to be a contributing factor was the Smoot-Hawley Tariff Act, passed by Congress in 1930. A tariff is a tax on foreign goods that is assessed when the goods are imported, or brought, into the country. Tariffs raise the price of imported items and thus encourage local consumers to buy domestically made goods. The Smoot-Hawley act taxed more than 20,000 imported goods at record levels. Some imports received as much as a 60 percent tax. Other countries retaliated, taxing American imports at the same rate. This cycle of events greatly reduced international trade; because the amount of goods imported into and exported from Europe and the United States greatly declined, the Depression worsened. Before the tariff came into being, the unemployment rate in the United States was 9 percent. After the tariff was implemented, unemployment jumped to 16 percent within a year. By 1932 unemployment was at 25 percent.

Recent Trends

After the Great Depression the United States experienced a number of recessions, but all were shorter and less severe. There were also financial crises. For example, on Monday, October 19, 1987, the stock market fell by nearly 23 percent. Losses on this day were greater than those on Black Tuesday of 1929, but unlike in 1929, the market maintained a gradual recovery afterward. The stock market once again plummeted on September 17, 2001, six days after terrorist attacks in New York City and Washington, D.C. That day the stock market recorded its largest single-day loss in history. Common explanations for why the United States has avoided further depressions include the government's willingness to spend money to stimulate the economy during economic downturns and better management by the Federal Reserve of the country's money supply.

$ Industries

What It Means

The term *industry* refers to the production of goods (for instance, automobiles, rugs, and computers) and the sale of services (the transportation of goods, bug extermination, and housecleaning, to name a few). It is often used loosely in conversations about the economy, describing either the sector (subdivision or segment) of the business world to which a company belongs (for instance, General Motors is part of the manufacturing industry) or the primary activity of a business (McDonald's and Burger King are part of what is often called the fast-food industry). In other words, at times economists and others classify businesses broadly; at other times they draw more specific distinctions between industries.

Most economists agree that there are four main sectors of industry. The first is called the primary sector and involves extracting materials from (or drawing resources out of) their natural locations so that they can be transformed into finished products and sold. Agriculture (farming and ranching), mining (digging into the earth to retrieve such materials as coal, iron ore, and silver), and clear-cutting (felling large tracts of trees in forests) are examples of activities in the primary sector of industry. In each case natural resources are used to fashion a product that is later sold. For example, in the agriculture industry cows are milked and the milk is then pasteurized (cleaned of its contaminants) and sold in supermarkets. In the mining industry iron ore is transformed into steel to build machines, and in the lumber industry wood is made into such items as furniture and paper.

The secondary sector of industry consists of businesses that manufacture goods. This sector takes the resources obtained from businesses in the primary sector and makes products for consumers. The automobile and clothing industries are in the secondary sector. The tertiary (third) sector of industry consists of businesses that provide services for consumers. Manufactured goods are sold by companies in the tertiary sector. For example, cars are produced in factories (secondary sector) but sold in auto dealerships (tertiary sector). The auto dealership is providing a service to both the consumer (by displaying and selling cars) and the manufacturer (by offering a location where buyers can purchase the manufacturer's products). The fourth, or quaternary, sector of industry involves research into how companies in the other sectors can improve their methods. For instance, a timber business (primary sector) might employ a team of geologists (quaternary sector) to research the best way to preserve the nutrients in the soil when cutting down trees.

Industries are further broken down by the U.S. government into the Standard Industrial Classification (SIC) and the North American Industry Classification System (NAICS). These two systems place all U.S. and North American businesses into one of many categories and subcategories. For example, using SIC methods, firms producing bagels are SIC major group 20 (food and kindred products), industry group 205 (bakery products), and subgroup 2051 (bread and other bakery products, except cookies and crackers).

When Did It Begin

Agriculture, which first appeared in southwestern Asia in what is today Syria and Iraq, dates back to approximately 9500 BC. It was at this time that the founder crops (the

The term industry refers to any large sector of an economy, such as agriculture, mining, and manufacturing. It can also refer to the production of a particular good, such as airplane manufacturing. © *Jim Sugar/Corbis.*

primary domesticated crops) were first cultivated. The founder crops included wheat, barley, peas, bitter vetch (an ancient legume), lentils, chickpeas, and flax. By 7000 BC agricultural production had spread to Egypt, and by 6000 BC it was developed independently in the Far East, where rice was the staple crop instead of wheat. The Sumerians made significant contributions to the agricultural industry after 3000 BC, creating irrigation systems and domesticating aurochs and mouflon (wild species of cattle and sheep) for meat, hides, and wool. Further developments, such as crop rotation (harvesting different crops in successive seasons on a stretch of land to keep soil fertile and reduce the number of pests), did not appear until the Middle Ages (which lasted from about 500 to about 1500).

The Industrial Revolution in the 1780s brought with it factories, assembly lines, and the large-scale production of goods. Three innovations in the late eighteenth century caused the revolution to gain the strongest foothold in Great Britain. The first, patented by Sir Richard Arkwright (1732–92) in 1769, was the spinning frame (also called a water frame), a water-powered cotton mill that allowed for increased production of textiles (bags, clothing, rugs, and so forth). That same year James Watt (1736–1819) improved the steam engine, making it

significantly more fuel efficient and therefore more widely used in factories. Third, in the 1780s new techniques were developed to extract metals from ore, which allowed for greater production of steel.

More Detailed Information

The four different sectors of industry tend be located in distinct areas of the world. Activities in the primary sector of industry are often conducted in developing countries in Latin America, Africa, and Southeast Asia or in the less economically prosperous areas of developed countries (such as the United States, nations in the European Union, and Japan). For example, the lumber industry extracts large amounts of wood from the Amazon rain forest in Brazil. Within the United States mining businesses were established in West Virginia and Montana, states containing large deposits of natural resources where manufacturing did not flourish. Goods from these areas were transported to the northeastern United States, which had the greatest percentage of the factories. Generally speaking there is more individual wealth (the upper and middle classes are larger) in the manufacturing centers of a country.

During the Industrial Revolution and for much more than a century thereafter, manufacturing (businesses in

BILL BOWERMAN AND THE BEGINNING OF NIKE, INC.

William Jay "Bill" Bowerman (1911–1999) was the head coach of the University of Oregon track team from 1948 to 1972 and the cofounder of what became Nike, Inc., the largest sportswear supplier in the world. Nike was born in 1964 with a handshake agreement between Bowerman and Phil Knight (b. 1938), who had been an accounting major and a distance runner on the University of Oregon track team in the late 1950s. Knight had started a small shoe distribution company called Blue Ribbon Sports, and he was on his way to Japan to begin negotiations with Onitsuka, Inc., to distribute their Tiger running shoes in the United States. Knight agreed to pay Bowerman $500.

Bowerman was included in the deal for two reasons. First, by Knight's own admission, he idolized his former coach. Bowerman had been an Oregon high-school football star and a war hero, and as coach of the University of Oregon track team, he was revered as a legendary motivator. Knight credited Bowerman with instilling in him the discipline necessary to succeed in the business world. Second, Bowerman was obsessed with reducing the weight of running shoes to improve race performance. Knight counted on Bowerman to help maintain high standards of quality control in the expanding business. When first shown the famous Nike "swoosh" logo on the side of a shoe, Bowerman is reported to have said, "Take it off. It weighs too much." In 1971, while eating a waffle breakfast with his wife on their patio, Bowerman came up with his most outlandish idea. As the story goes, after the meal he snuck Barbara's waffle iron out of the kitchen and began burning rubber in it. This experiment resulted in the Waffle Trainer running shoe, which became a leading seller for Nike in 1975. Along with the Air Jordan shoe, Bowerman's innovation is widely regarded as one of the developments that most contributed to Nike's long-term success.

the secondary sector of industry) was conducted in the developed nations of the world. England, for example, used coal extracted from mines in Wales and other resources obtained from places as far away as India and China to operate its factories. In the United States at the turn of the twentieth century, automobile manufacturers such as the Ford Motor Company and General Motors built factories in Michigan, and steel manufacturers ran operations in Pennsylvania. Manufacturing, however, has since shifted to the developing nations of the world. This has occurred because manufacturers can pay workers substantially lower wages to produce goods in developing countries than they can in places such as the United States, England, and Germany. Computers, stereos, automobiles, and clothes are often produced in places such as China, India, and Thailand because factory workers in those areas can be paid a fraction of what those in the United States earn. The practice of relocating businesses to other parts of the world, called offshoring, is the subject of considerable ethical debate. Those opposed to offshoring argue that manufacturers are taking advantage of the labor force in developing countries (paying them badly and subjecting them to harsh working conditions) because those countries do not have institutions, such as labor unions, to protect workers from mistreatment. Defenders of the practice claim that the cost of production is too high in the developed nations of the world and that therefore manufacturers cannot earn profits by building factories in places like the United States.

Businesses in the service industry (the tertiary, or service, sector) are more likely to flourish in fully developed countries and in the major metropolitan centers of the developing world (for instance, in Rio de Janeiro, Brazil; Shanghai, China; and Mumbai [Bombay], India). Most finished products are sold by tertiary sector companies, and fully developed countries have the greatest number of consumers who can afford to buy these products. For example, a large section of the German population can afford automobiles, so there are a significant number of car dealerships there. A smaller percentage of people who live in India can afford cars, so many areas of India lack auto dealerships. In Mumbai, India's most densely populated city, however, a significant number of people can afford cars, and the city therefore has a considerable number of dealerships.

The quaternary sector of industry, the area that consists of research and education, also flourishes in the world's developed countries. As is the case with service industries, research and educational activities require capital (money), which is more plentiful in the developed nations of the world. Though people in developed countries are not more intelligent than people in less developed areas of the world, the developed world has more and often better schools. Consequently students from developing countries often study in the United States and Europe and later seek high-paying jobs in these countries instead of returning home. This trend has been changing in recent years. When manufacturing shifted to places like India and China, those countries acquired more wealth and were therefore able to build more educational institutions. Such places have fast-growing middle classes that are rapidly becoming more self-sufficient. More citizens of these countries are able to purchase the goods that are produced in the United States. Because of this trend, some economists argue that the balance of economic power is shifting from the United States to India and China.

Recent Trends

The most common recent trend in American industry is offshoring: the practice of setting up factories in or sending work and jobs to less wealthy countries in Latin America and Southeast Asia. American companies have had textiles (such articles as clothing, bags, and baskets) and hard goods (durable articles that wear out slowly, such as kitchen and laundry appliances, home furnishings, and sporting equipment) produced overseas for more than 50 years. The technology industry now offshores telephone-based technical support (help fixing problems with computers) to India, where consultants are paid anywhere from 50 to 80 percent less than they would be in the United States. Other corporations, such as banks and airlines, have also set up call centers in India to save money on labor. This means that when a customer in a place like Ohio calls an airline to book a flight to Los Angeles, the customer may secure flight reservations with the help of someone sitting at a desk in Mumbai.

Large corporations are also forming alliances to increase profits. Industry insiders call this partnering. With the continued growth of technology and the expansion of business into global markets, partnering has become a common practice among multinational firms. For example, in June 2005 the company SEVEN, a provider of software for mobile phone operators, partnered with Yahoo! in an agreement that enables Yahoo! clients to access their e-mail accounts from their mobile phones. The telecommunications industry has also grown in China, and large equipment vendors from the United States, France, and Germany, among other places, now seek to partner with local Chinese vendors to reduce operating costs. In the past these large companies would simply have bought out the smaller local companies, but the multinational corporations have since discovered that collaboration is more profitable.

$ Investment

What It Means

In economics the term *investment* refers to purchases that contribute to the overall performance of an economy. This form of investment occurs in all sectors of society and usually involves the participation of individuals, businesses, and governments. When the overall level of investment is high, an economy generally expands, creating greater prosperity for a wider range of the population. When investment is low, the economy generally falters. As such, fluctuations in investment are the primary drivers of the business cycle—the repeated pattern of growth and slowdown that exists in all market economies.

In most cases investment refers to money spent on durable goods. Durable goods are generally defined as products that are designed to be used repeatedly over a relatively long period of time; according to most economists, a product is considered a durable good if it lasts

three years or more. For most people durable goods refer to such material items as television sets, cars, and homes; by purchasing these goods, individuals contribute to the prosperity of the businesses that manufacture the goods, thereby bolstering the economy. Companies typically invest in such durable goods as manufacturing equipment and machinery, while governments invest in infrastructure such as roads, bridges, and dams. The products purchased through this form of investment are often referred to as tangible, or material, assets. Investment can also refer to spending on intangible, or nonmaterial, assets. Intangible assets can include education, skilled labor, or research.

People invest for a variety of reasons. Individuals can invest money in homes in order to improve their quality of life, or they can invest in higher education in order to increase their chances of finding a high-paying job. In both these cases, investment contributes to the overall health of the economy, both through the purchase of durable goods and the potential improvement of the workforce. This type of investment is also known as residential investment. A business will invest in new technologies in order to increase the efficiency of its production process. Government investments in infrastructure contribute to the economy by making it less costly for companies to transport goods. In a sense, all of these various forms of investment work together within an economy, generating economic opportunity, low-priced goods and services, and greater wealth.

When Did It Begin

In certain respects investment has existed since the earliest human civilizations, as ancient societies devoted a portion of their resources to producing and selling goods, building roads and fortifications, and generally contributing to the economic health of the community. Investment in the modern sense, however, did not play a significant role in the economy until the Protestant Reformation of the sixteenth century. According to German sociologist Max Weber (1864-1920), the people who held power in ancient Greece and Rome derived their wealth from land ownership and slave labor. These elite viewed commercial transactions, and working in general, as undignified; at the same time, they feared that large-scale investment would only create a broader base of wealth among the general population, thereby eroding their own power. With the Reformation, however, a new attitude toward commercial activity arose, one based on ideals of hard work (which Weber called the Protestant work ethic), individualism, and economic growth. In order to meet these goals, new business strategies, including investment, began to gain wider acceptance. Weber argued that the emergence of investment as a means of spurring economic expansion represented one of the key factors in the birth of modern capitalism.

Investment sometimes refers to the purchase of financial products, such stocks, bonds, or even gold, with the hope of making money in the future. In the field of economics, investment has a much broader meaning, referring to all expenditures by individuals, businesses, and governments that contribute to the growth of the economy. © *Peter Thorne, Johnson Matthey/Science Photo Library/Photo Researchers, Inc.*

The industrial revolutions of the late eighteenth and early nineteenth centuries witnessed an explosion of investment in both England and the United States, as new technologies accelerated the speed at which goods could be produced. Increased production levels resulted in significantly higher earnings, which led to increased financial investment in commercial activities. Indeed, the entire history of American economic expansion is rooted in the principle of investing in cheaper, more efficient ways of manufacturing goods and services.

More Detailed Information

When businesses consider how to invest their money, they focus on the potential benefits that might result from their investment. Since the goal of all profit-based companies is to earn money, business investments are made with the aim of increasing, or at least maintaining, profit levels. Companies achieve these goals by investing in new machinery, hiring more workers, and funding other expenditures designed to increase their capacity to create more products.

Businesses generally employ two means of funding their investments. In many cases a company will use profits from its existing operations, either to reinvest in its core business (for example, manufacturing tires) or to invest in the creation of a new form of business (such as introducing a line of windshield wipers). A company will also borrow money (a business loan or a line of credit) in order to invest in the expansion of its core operations. Ideally the money earned from the increase in production capacity will be greater than the money invested, thereby earning the company a profit. For example, say a tire manufacturer earns a profit of $200,000 in a given year. The company may want to invest that money in building a second factory, with the ultimate aim of doubling its manufacturing capabilities. If the cost of building a new factory is $1 million, then the company may use its profits for some of the expenditures (buying new equipment or hiring new workers) while taking out a loan to pay the remaining expenses. Once the second factory becomes operational, it will begin to generate income. For the first year or two, the earnings from the second factory might

THE BIG DIG

Investment refers to the money that individuals, companies, and governments spend in order to make an economy grow. Often a government will work with private businesses on projects that are designed both to create economic opportunities and to improve life in the community as a whole. One famous (or, to many observers, infamous) collaboration between government and business was the Big Dig, a massive road, bridge, and tunnel project in Boston, Massachusetts. Originally conceived in the 1970s, the Big Dig was granted federal funding in the 1980s with a budget of $2.8 billion. In the eyes of the planners, the Big Dig would transform the city's downtown area, which was notorious for its traffic congestion and poor roads. As the project progressed, however, the actual building of the new road and tunnel system experienced a series of delays, caused in large part by poor construction, bureaucratic infighting, and corrupt business practices on the part some the project's major contractors. By 2006, the year the project was finally completed, the cost of construction had risen to $14.6 billion, making it the most expensive single highway project in American history.

not offset the costs involved with getting it started, and the company may use all its earnings from that period to pay off its debt. By the third year, however, the company may have paid down its debt considerably and begun earning substantially higher profits than it did before building the second factory.

Government investment also plays an important role in the economic prosperity of private businesses. Government construction projects require the hiring of private businesses, thereby stimulating economic activity. When government invests money in infrastructure, a nation's commercial activities also tend to run more smoothly: good roads and bridges help save transportation time while also reducing wear-and-tear on shipping vehicles, and power stations provide massive amounts of energy to companies throughout the country, enabling them to operate at a high capacity. When government investment in infrastructure declines, as it did during the 1980s, private industry will usually feel the effects.

How money is invested from year to year generally reflects broader trends in politics, the economy, and technology. During periods of increased economic expansion, people invest in commercial activities at a much higher rate, which in turns fuels continued growth. Eventually, however, the economy will inevitably slow down, and investment rates will fall. In this sense investment is regarded by economists to be a cyclical phenomenon.

Recent Trends

Because of the inherently volatile nature of economic activity, investment typically fluctuates over time. A comparison of investment trends in the United States during the 1990s and the early 2000s offers a valuable illustration of how patterns of investing can vary widely. Between 1995 and 2000, business investment in the U.S. rose at a rate of 10 percent per year. In the second half of 2000, however, this trend reversed itself dramatically, as investment dropped nearly 12 percent. Economists attribute this decline to the infamous "dot-com" bust, during which hundreds of computer and information technology firms declared bankruptcy. As a result of this decline in investment, by March 2001 the country had entered into a recession (a period of economic contraction).

$ Employment and Unemployment

What It Means

Employment and unemployment, in common usage, refer to an individual's job status. An employed person is one who has a job; an unemployed person does not have a job. Economists and government officials in the United States take a wider and somewhat different view of employment and unemployment. They consider the number of people who are employed and unemployed versus the entire labor force (the number of people over 16 years of age in the economy who are either working or looking for work). Students, retirees, people who cannot work due to medical conditions, and people who are not looking for work are not considered part of the labor force.

Governments collect and analyze a wide range of data about employment and unemployment. The most commonly discussed piece of data is the unemployment rate. This is determined by dividing the number of people who are unemployed but looking for work by the number of people in the labor force, and then converting this number to a percentage. In actuality no government contacts every person in the labor force when they calculate such figures. Instead, governments base their employment data on small samples of the population. In the United States surveys are conducted and data is released every month.

Employment and unemployment data is closely monitored by the government not only because people who cannot find jobs are likely to suffer physically and emotionally but also because changes in the numbers of employed and unemployed people can have a dramatic effect on the overall economy. Economists generally consider the economy healthy when it produces a growing quantity of goods and services. (The quantity of goods and services that an economy produces during a given time period is called the Gross Domestic Product, or GDP.) If GDP is high, then naturally a large proportion of the labor force will be employed, since it takes more workers to produce more goods and services. Likewise, when the largest possible proportion of the

Employment and unemployment refers to the condition of being with or without work. In this photo, taken during the Great Depression (1929–1939), thousands of unemployed laborers wait to apply for relief jobs subsidized by the federal government   *AP Images.*

labor force is employed, there will be more consumer demand for products, since wages and salaries are the chief source of money for consumer purchases. High unemployment is usually consistent with periods of slower economic growth or recessions, periods during which GDP shrinks.

When Did It Begin

The eighteenth and nineteenth centuries brought the rapid expansion of capitalism (in which individuals are allowed to own property and businesses and pursue profits) and increasing industrialization to Europe and the United States. Large factories drew people away from rural communities and into large urban centers, where working conditions were often extremely demanding and there were no community resources to fall back on in the event of job loss. Economists at this time generally believed that levels of employment would be efficiently regulated by market forces such as supply (the quantity of goods and services that businesses are willing and able to produce at any given time) and demand (the

quantity of goods and services that consumers are willing and able to buy at any given time). Governments did little to regulate their economies even though the suffering of the unemployed was an increasingly visible part of society.

This began to change in the early twentieth century, when most European countries (led by Great Britain in 1911) passed laws providing financial assistance to those who were willing and able to work but could not find jobs. No comparable laws were passed in the United States until the Great Depression, the severe economic crisis afflicting the world economy in the 1930s, when an estimated 25 percent of American workers lost their jobs. Not only was the suffering of the unemployed highly visible during the Depression but the economies of the United States and Europe were paralyzed by the lack of demand resulting from mass unemployment. People who were not being paid wages had no money to spend on goods and services; because there were large numbers of unemployed people, companies had less incentive to make products and hire workers.

HIDDEN UNEMPLOYMENT

Some people believe that government estimates of the number of unemployed people in a nation are inherently inaccurate due to the way unemployment is defined. To be considered unemployed by most governments, a person has to be not only out of work but actively looking for a job. For example, people who have become so discouraged about finding a job that they stop looking for work are not counted as part of the labor force, so they do not turn up in government estimates of the unemployment rate. Another group of people who do not turn up in unemployment estimates are those who have been forced to take early retirement, an option that older workers sometimes choose when they are no longer needed but do not want to be laid off. (Were they to be laid off, they would be numbered among the unemployed.) These uncounted people represent a phenomenon sometimes called "hidden unemployment." Because of hidden unemployment, the possibility exists that a government could be sending a message of optimism about the economy (by declaring that more people are employed than before) at a time when, by contrast, the situation for workers has in fact become more hopeless.

During this period British economist John Maynard Keynes (1883–1946) suggested that market forces might not have the power, under such conditions, to reduce unemployment and bring the economy back into balance. Governments, following Keynes's lead, saw that they could use aid to unemployed people, among other spending programs, not simply as a means of relieving suffering but as a means of spurring economic recovery. By employing out-of-work citizens to undertake public projects, and by giving them direct aid payments, governments increased demand and gave companies the incentive to begin producing goods and services again.

The success in implementing Keynes's ideas led to a significant increase, in the decades following the Depression, in the amount of government involvement in the economy. Governments began closely monitoring their economies, measuring such factors as unemployment and GDP (or, for most of the twentieth century, the Gross National Product, or GNP, which is a similar figure) on a regular basis and attempting to prevent future crises.

More Detailed Information

Though Keynes's influence has waned since the 1970s, governments continue to monitor employment data closely (along with data from other parts of the economy) with the intent of determining the health of the economy. In the United States the Census Bureau gathers information from a sample of households every month to get an estimate of the total number of the employed versus the unemployed. The Bureau of Labor Statistics then analyzes the information and makes it public. Yearly figures are determined by averaging the monthly numbers. While the Bureau of Labor Statistics' analysis breaks employment trends down in many different ways, people in business and in the media pay the most attention to the unemployment rate, since the percentage of the labor force who cannot find jobs is so closely associated with the economy's overall health.

The U.S. government, like the governments of most developed countries, strives to encourage full employment. This is not the same as zero unemployment. Instead, most economists define full employment as the lowest rate of unemployment that the economy, as it is structured at a given time, can support. During the late twentieth and early twenty-first century, estimates of full employment commonly varied from 2 percent to 7 percent of the labor force.

Economists classify unemployment in different ways. One of the most common and useful ways of defining unemployment is according to its cause. Frictional unemployment occurs when people are out of work temporarily as a result of moving to a new job or region. Even when jobs are plentiful and the economy is healthy, some amount of frictional unemployment will exist. An important kind of frictional unemployment is seasonal unemployment, which occurs in industries such as agriculture and the resort industry, where the demand for jobs changes according to the seasons every year. It is normal for workers in these industries to be out of work temporarily while they transition from one season's job to the next.

Structural unemployment, on the other hand, can be a larger problem. It occurs when the demand for labor changes along with the structure of the economy. For example, textile factories might close down in one region, leaving thousands of people out of work, at the same time that there are not enough qualified workers to fill an abundance of computer-programming jobs available in that same region. Structural unemployment can also exist when the labor force is geographically unable to accommodate to changing demand for workers. Layoffs in the computer-programming industry might be occurring in one U.S. state even as the industry in another state cannot find enough programmers. While the labor force can eventually adjust to such changes, both workers and the overall economy often experience painful difficulties during the transitional periods.

Yet another form of unemployment is cyclical unemployment. Cyclical unemployment results from economic downturns such as recessions and depressions. Downturns are a normal part of the business cycle, the pattern of alternating expansion and shrinkage over time that characterizes all economies. Since companies produce fewer goods and services during a downturn, fewer workers are necessary. Governments in developed countries attempt to minimize the difficulties caused by downturns in the business cycle through fiscal policy (changes to tax and spending programs) and monetary policy (changes in the amount of money in circulation), both of which can spur economic expansion. These downturns cannot be eliminated, however, and sometimes they can be severe. The Great Depression is one of the most prominent examples in the modern era of a severe economic downturn. During the Depression, most of the unemployment was cyclical unemployment.

Unemployment can also be classified according to how much control workers have over their job status. Voluntary unemployment is unemployment that occurs as a result of choices made by workers themselves. Most frictional unemployment is generally considered voluntary. Involuntary unemployment occurs when something beyond workers' control forces them to lose their jobs. Structural and cyclical unemployment are forms of involuntary unemployment. In these cases larger economic issues such as changing consumer demand, technological innovation, and the business cycle cause people to lose their jobs through no fault of their own.

Recent Trends

In the late twentieth and early twenty-first centuries, the unemployment rate in the United States remained well below the crisis level of the Depression era. Whereas unemployment during the Depression reached as high as 25 percent, the unemployment rate fell during and after World War II and remained mostly stable in the latter half of the century. The unemployment rate in the United States tended to be between 4 and 6 percent between 1950 and the turn of the twenty-first century with one prominent exception: a period of higher unemployment during the late 1970s and the 1980s. In 1982 unemployment in the United States reached nearly 10 percent.

During this same period inflation (the general rising of prices across the economy) was also extremely high. A normal rate of inflation is 3 percent a year; in 1980 inflation was nearly 14 percent. (This means that prices for most goods increased by 14 percent during that year.) This phenomenon, high unemployment and high inflation occurring together, was unprecedented. Prior to this time most economists believed that when unemployment was high, inflation would be low, and vice versa. The situation, characterized by simultaneous economic stagnation and inflation, was later dubbed "stagflation."

One result of stagflation was that economists and government policy makers changed their approach to encouraging employment. In its attempt to balance concerns about employment with concerns about inflation, the U.S. government had primarily used fiscal policy. But this approach had obviously stopped working in the 1970s, and one of the theories supporting the approach—the constant, direct connection between employment and inflation—was disproved by stagflation. A new school of

economists came to prominence offering a different approach to the economy. This new school, known as monetarism, argued that managing the money supply was the only effective way to fight inflation. Inflation was, in fact, successfully lowered when the government's central bank, the Federal Reserve, forcefully restrained the growth of the money supply in the 1980s. Though this period of inflation fighting had some harsh side effects, the economy regained its balance. In the 1980s, 1990s, and the early years of the new millennium, both inflation and unemployment remained consistently low.

$ Financial Markets

What It Means

"Financial markets" refers, collectively, to the places and systems that bring the buyers and sellers of financial products together. Some of the most important financial products that are bought and sold in the world financial markets include stocks, bonds, currencies, and derivatives.

Stocks, or shares of stock, are portions of company ownership. A company that wants to raise money sells stock to investors, and investors can buy or sell their shares in the stock market. A share of stock typically gains value when a company prospers and loses value when a company struggles. Investors try to predict a company's future performance and buy stocks that will rise in value.

Bonds are portions of government or corporate debt. When a government or company needs to borrow more money than a bank can provide, it may turn to investors. Investors lend money to the government or to a company by purchasing bonds on the bond market, and in exchange they are paid a fixed rate of interest (a fee paid to those who lend money).

Currencies are different forms of money used in different countries. Because the values of all currencies in the world are constantly changing, an investor can use one currency, such as the U.S. dollar, to purchase another currency, such as the Japanese yen. These trades are made on what is called the foreign exchange market. If the Japanese yen then rises in value relative to the dollar, the currency trader makes a profit.

Derivatives are contracts based on or derived from other financial products. For example, an investor can purchase, on the derivatives market, the right to buy a specific stock at a specific price up to a specific date. Such a derivative is commonly called a future or option. If the stock price rises before that date arrives, the derivative rises in value (since the holder of the derivative has the right to purchase that valuable stock at a lower price than that at which it is currently being offered). If the stock price falls, the derivative also loses value. There are many different types of derivatives, but all of them share the common feature of having their value tied to the

Financial markets refer to the systems through which people buy and sell stocks, bonds, currencies, and other financial products. In this photo traders in Japan examine currency exchange rates. *AP Images.*

performance of the financial product from which they are derived.

When Did It Begin

Financial markets can be dated at least to the fifteenth century, when Italian city-states such as Florence and Genoa established the practice of paying interest to those citizens it forced to lend money to their governments. These forced loans had enabled the city-states to defend themselves and to secure the important trade routes that allowed them to prosper financially. With the introduction of interest payments, these loans became the equivalent of today's government bonds, and citizens were allowed to sell them to other citizens.

The world's first organized stock market appeared in Amsterdam in 1602. It was established as a means of buying and selling stock in the Dutch East India Company, a corporation specializing in overseas trade (and the first in the world to issue stock).

As capitalist economies (in which individuals own property and businesses and compete freely against one another for profit) have grown and evolved over the past several hundred years, financial markets have evolved along with them. Financial markets facilitate the raising of capital (money and other resources needed to start or expand a business), one of the keys to large-scale economic growth. Financial markets have increased in number and complexity over time, and they are continually evolving in response to changing economic conditions.

More Detailed Information

Financial markets arose out of the need to bring borrowers and lenders of money together. This remains one of the main reasons that they are vital components of the world economy. There are two basic ways for individuals and institutions to lend and borrow money. One way is to use a bank as an intermediary. When you deposit money in a bank, you are, in reality, lending that money to someone else. The bank pays you interest for the privilege of using your money, and then it lends your money out to a borrower, who must pay interest at a higher rate.

When corporations and governments borrow money, however, often they need much more money than a single bank can provide. Financial markets provide a forum for raising large amounts of capital. When a government needs to pay for a war, for example, it may sell bonds. This allows the government to collect money from thousands of different lenders, including not just individuals but institutions such as banks and companies. A government or company sells bonds directly to investors on what is known as the primary bond market. There is also a secondary bond market, which allows investors to sell bonds among themselves. Trading on both the primary and the secondary markets occurs on what is known as the over-the-counter (OTC) market, a variety of organized networks where dealers sell to buyers using the telephone, fax, or computers.

Similarly, a company that has successfully established a niche selling merchandise on the Internet may see the opportunity to develop a worldwide market for its products and services. By going public (that is, selling stock in the company so that it is no longer a private company but a public one owned by stockholders), a company collects money from people all over the world and can expand much more rapidly than it could by other means. There are many stock exchanges in the world. The largest stock exchanges in the United States are the New York Stock Exchange (NYSE) and the NASDAQ. The NYSE occupies a physical location in New York City, where the buyers and sellers of stocks come together through intermediaries known as brokers. Many NYSE trades are also conducted via computer. The NASDAQ, by contrast, is entirely computerized; there is no physical location where trading occurs. Worldwide there are stock exchanges in many national capitals and large cities. Most of these are computerized as well.

Financial markets benefit lenders as well as borrowers, of course, since few people would willingly lend their money to someone else without the promise of a return on their investment. The different financial markets offer different forms of return. The bond market offers a steady, reliable return in the form of a fixed interest rate. Usually a bond must be held for a specific time period, such as 10 years. During this period the bondholder receives annual or semi-annual interest payments from the bond issuer (the government or company), and at the end of that period the bondholder receives his or her initial investment back. Interest rates vary over time depending on the condition of the overall economy and the riskiness of the company or government issuing the bonds. When interest rates are high, buying bonds is naturally a more popular form of investment than when they are low. On the secondary bond market there are additional possibilities for profit. For example, if you buy a bond in January, and then interest rates fall in February, your bond will gain value in the secondary market, and you may be able to sell it at a profit.

The stock market, on the other hand, offers the possibility for higher returns than the bond market, but it is also a riskier way to invest. Companies' future performance is extremely hard to predict, and the stock market

REGULATION OF FINANCIAL MARKETS

Prior to 1929 financial markets (places and systems for trading stocks, bonds, and other financial products) in the United States and elsewhere were largely trusted to regulate themselves. But irresponsible forms of investing were a primary cause of the U.S. stock market crash in 1929 (a stock market crashes when the overall value of stocks on an exchange drops dramatically, causing widespread financial distress), which was followed by the Great Depression, the severe economic crisis that afflicted the world economy for much of the following decade. In response, the U.S. government passed numerous regulatory laws meant to reassure investors and prevent future abuses. In addition to laws regulating the business practices of banks, Congress passed laws regulating financial markets. Brokers and dealers of stocks and bonds (people who bought and sold stocks on behalf of customers) became legally accountable to their clients, and the Securities and Exchange Commission was established to monitor the trading that occurred on financial markets.

The late twentieth century saw the rise of currency trading, the purchasing of one country's currency (such as the Japanese yen) using another's (such as the U.S. dollar), with the goal of profiting when the purchased currency rises in value. Since these trades went beyond national borders, they were difficult to regulate. Further, a large proportion of the increasingly complex derivatives market (a market for buying and selling financial products whose value is based on other financial products) fell outside the scope of existing federal regulations. The U.S. government, as of the early twenty-first century, has largely chosen not to regulate these financial markets.

is subject to human error. Stocks can gain value quickly because of investor enthusiasm about a company's prospects, but they can lose value just as quickly if the reality of a company's performance does not live up to expectations.

Recent Trends

The foreign exchange market and the derivatives market have become increasingly important financial markets in recent decades. Between 1944 and 1971 the U.S. dollar's value had been measured in the amount of gold it could purchase, and the value of other world currencies was tied to the dollar. Under these conditions currencies were stable relative to one another, so there was no profit to be made from trading one currency for another. The United States abandoned the gold standard in 1971, and by 1973 the value of none of the world currencies was determined by the amount of gold it could purchase. Numerous elements, such as politics and the health of a nation's economy, affect the supply of and demand for its currencies, and the values of currencies change constantly relative to one another. The foreign exchange market is, like the bond market, an informal over-the-counter market consisting of numerous different systems for making trades. It is open 24 hours during weekdays, with major foreign exchange trading centering on the cities of London, New York, Tokyo, and Singapore. The primary traders in currencies include large banks, corporations, the central banks of governments (such as the U.S.'s Federal Reserve System). It is difficult for individuals acting on their own to compete with these institutional traders.

Though derivatives such as futures (also called options) have been around for centuries, the 1970s and 1980s saw the creation of new forms of derivatives, and derivatives trading became an increasingly prominent feature of the world economy in the decades that followed. Derivatives commonly allow investors to "hedge against" risk (that is, to cushion themselves against the blow of any losing risks), and they allow investors to hedge in ways that can sometimes seem exotic. For example, there are derivatives derived from other derivatives, and there are weather derivatives, which enable companies affected by the weather to cushion themselves against the losses they might suffer if temperatures or rainfall runs counter to their business goals.

$ Black Market

What It Means

The black market (also called the underground, unofficial, or shadow economy) refers to an area of economic activity where the buying and selling of goods and services is conducted illegally. Black-market trading occurs for various reasons. Many goods and services are simply illegal to sell; examples include cocaine, assault rifles, prostitution, the body parts of endangered animals, fake passports, and bootlegged (illegally recorded) CDs and DVDs. The general term for such goods is contraband. When people desire goods that they cannot obtain simply by going to a store and purchasing them, they are often willing to pay very high prices to anyone who can provide them. Correspondingly, many merchants and individuals are willing to risk breaking the law in order to earn substantial profits from selling contraband.

There is also black-market trading in legal goods. This arises to avoid certain government regulations, such as when cigarettes and alcohol are smuggled across borders to avoid import taxes (extra fees charged for bringing goods into a country) or when handguns are sold on the black market to avoid laws requiring their licensing and registration.

Another form of government regulation that often leads to black-market trading is rationing. When basic goods, such as meat and sugar, are in short supply (in wartime, for example), the government may place limits on the amount of that good that any individual can buy in order to make sure the supply gets distributed fairly and no one goes hungry. If individuals who want to buy more than the legal limit are willing to pay an extra price for this service, there will be merchants willing to ignore the government's rationing limits to sell the goods for increased profit.

This illegal trade takes place in secret, or in the dark, hence the name "black market." Because black-market trade occurs "off the books," so to speak, it represents a whole sector of a country's economy that cannot accurately be measured.

When Did It Begin

Illegal trading has existed for hundreds of years. In the early seventeenth century, for example, when Dutch and Portuguese traders first brought tea from China to Europe, it was considered a rare and highly desirable luxury. In Britain the government charged merchants a heavy import tax on tea, which made it very expensive to buy. An extensive black market in smuggled tea quickly arose, enabling merchants to avoid the tax and sell more tea at lower prices.

The term *black market* first appeared in print in *The Economist* magazine in 1931 in reference to an unofficial, or "black," market in sterling exchange. Sterling is the word for British money, also called pound sterling. As with other trading, currency exchange (the conversion of one country's currency to another's, such as the conversion of British sterling into U.S. dollars) occurs on the black market in order to avoid government fees and regulations. The term began to be used widely during World War II (1939–45), when strict government rationing was widespread in Europe and illegal trade flourished.

More Detailed Information

Black markets function as they do because of the basic economic principle of supply and demand. Supply refers to the quantity of goods and services that businesses are willing and able to produce at any given time. Demand refers to the quantity of goods and services that consumers are willing and able to buy at any given time. The relationship between supply and demand does much to determine the price of a product. If supply of a product is greater than demand (say 500 concert tickets go on sale for $30 each, but only 150 tickets sell), it means that not enough people are willing to buy it. The theory of supply and demand suggests that, if the concert promoter had charged a lower price, she might have sold more tickets. On the other hand, if supply is lower than demand (say 500 concert tickets go on sale for $30 each, and 750 people line up to buy them), then the principle of supply and demand says that the promoter could have charged a higher price for the tickets.

The black market is a general term for the illegal exchange of goods and services. An example is the illicit traffic in forged passports. *AFP/ Getty Images.*

It is with the latter scenario, when supply is limited, that a black market is likely to arise. Say the first 50 people in line buy 10 tickets each. The tickets are sold out, and 700 people still want to see the concert. The 50 people who bought the tickets would very likely be able to sell them off for more than $30 each. The practice of ticket resale (sometimes called scalping) is considered a black-market activity.

Similarly, by making a product illegal or imposing rations upon it, the government is restricting its supply. When a government imposes import tariffs, its aim is to restrict the supply of foreign goods coming into the country in order to give an advantage to manufacturers of the same product within the country (tariffs may also be a means of raising government revenue). Economists who favor a free-market economy (one in which trade is dictated purely by the law of supply and demand) believe that government interference in the market often causes more harm than good. By restricting the supply of goods, these critics contend, the government effectively assures the rise of a black market and a host of other criminal activities (including, in the drug trade, kidnapping, armed robbery, and murder) that are associated with secretive, high-risk, high-profit trading.

Another problem with driving certain goods into the black market is that, when these goods are sold in secret, there is no one to insure their quality or safety. During the late nineteenth and early twentieth centuries, for example, birth control products were banned in the United States under an antiobscenity law (the Comstock Act of 1873), and a black market arose to supply women with homemade contraceptives. Manufactured by amateurs with no proper oversight, many of these products were defective and even hazardous. While proponents of the Comstock Act believed that birth control products were immoral because they encouraged sexual promiscuity, those who defended women's right to contraception argued that the Comstock Act itself was immoral because it subjected otherwise law-abiding women to the dangers of the black market.

Recent Trends

At the beginning of the twenty-first century, one of the fastest-growing areas of black-market activity was in the computer industry. Before 1998 most computer hacking (the practice of breaking through a computer's security system) was done for sport by curious, but not malicious, individuals. In the next decade, however, there was

WORLDWIDE TRAFFIC IN HUMAN ORGANS

At the turn of the millennium one of the most disturbing trends in black-market (illegal) commerce was the buying and selling of human organs, especially kidneys. With a worldwide shortage of kidneys available for transplants, many people suffering from kidney failure were willing to pay exorbitant prices for the healthy organs that could save their lives. Meanwhile, in Brazil, India, Mozambique, and other developing countries where much of the population lives in extreme poverty, increasing numbers of people were willing to go under the knives of backroom surgeons to sell one of their kidneys for much-needed cash. In China the illegal-transplant trade flourished because prisons were selling organs taken from executed prisoners. Organized smuggling rings around the world reaped tremendous profits from this illegal, unethical, and highly dangerous trade.

rapidly increasing demand for stolen data (such as social security numbers, credit card numbers, corporations' strategic plans, and classified military secrets), and as a result hacking was becoming a highly sophisticated business, delivering substantial profits for organized-crime associations.

HOW THE ECONOMY IS MEASURED

$ Gross Domestic Product

What It Means

Gross domestic product (GDP) is a figure that represents the total value of all goods and services produced in a country in a given time period. More simply, it is a measure of the total size of an economy. In the United States, government economists calculate GDP every quarter (in the financial world, each year is commonly broken down, for purposes of analysis, into four three-month periods called quarters), as well as yearly. GDP is generally considered one of the most important measurements of a country's economic health. Therefore, it is used by government officials as an aid in creating policies, by business leaders in making business decisions, and by economists to improve their understanding of the economy.

In order to avoid counting certain goods (those that are part of other goods) multiple times, GDP measures only what are known as final products, or products that are sold to consumers on the open market. For instance, the plastic used to make a laptop computer might be made in the United States and sold in the United States

to a computer manufacturer, but economists use only the sale of the computer itself when they calculate GDP. If they included the sale of the plastic to the manufacturer as well as the sale of the computer to the consumer, they would be counting the value of the plastic twice.

When Did It Begin

GDP represents both a refinement of and an alternative to a similar measure of economic health called gross national product (GNP). GNP also measures the total value of goods and services produced in a country during a given period of time, but GNP is calculated using a different approach to the U.S. business activity of foreign citizens and to the foreign business activity of U.S. citizens. The statistics yielded by both calculations are typically very similar in countries with developed economies.

The concept of GNP was developed in the 1930s by a Ukrainian-born U.S. economist named Simon Kuznets (1901–85; Kuznets won the Nobel Prize in 1971, in part for work related to the concept of GNP). The U.S. government, reeling from the effects of the Great Depression, was in search of a way of measuring the country's economic problems. Kuznets's idea of calculating the value of only final products provided a sorely needed way of measuring economic health and growth accurately, and it became a standard economic indicator (a statistic that reflects the health of the economy) in countries around the world. In the early 1990s the U.S. government began using GDP rather than GNP in its assessments of economic health, though GNP is still widely applied as well.

More Detailed Information

GDP is generally arrived at by using a formula that adds together the monetary value of products in four different economic categories: consumer spending, investment, government spending, and net exports. Household purchases fall into the category of consumer spending; purchases made by businesses come under the category of investment; government spending refers to purchases made by the government; and purchases of American-made products by citizens of other countries (minus U.S. purchases of imports, which are excluded from the calculation of GDP) make up net exports. Because these four categories include all of the major kinds of purchases of U.S. goods and services, GDP can be thought of as a measure of the total national income.

When the GDP is rising, a national economy is growing. In the United States GDP increases of 3 to 5 percent each year are considered optimal. These figures indicate that the economy is growing at a healthy, sustainable rate (a rate that can be kept up). GDP increases of 2 percent and below are considered sluggish. A recession (a time of economic decline less severe than a depression) is generally defined by the shrinking of the GDP for two straight quarters.

Government officials depend on GDP to judge the rate at which the economy is growing; they use it to determine the future course of economic and other policies. For instance, a U.S. president or Congress might use sluggish GDP figures as a reason to lower taxes, a strategy that is believed to promote economic growth; or a nation's central bank (an agency of the government responsible for overseeing the money supply) might see rapid increases in GDP as a reason to restrain economic growth by raising key interest rates (the fees borrowers pay to institutions that loan money).

Similarly, business executives in a variety of private industries look to GDP as a way of predicting economic activity in the future. An executive trying to decide whether or not to invest in new factories, for example, might be more likely to do so if the rate of overall economic growth (as measured by GDP) is strong. Financial professionals and investors, likewise, might pay close attention to GDP numbers (along with other economic data) when determining whether to buy stocks and bonds at any given moment.

Economists, meanwhile, rely on GDP figures in improving their theories about how economies develop and behave. A record of GDP growth and declines during the past three decades in the United States, for instance, might provide crucial insights into how the national economy has evolved from one based primarily on manufacturing to one increasingly dependent on service industries (forms of business activity dealing with human services rather than physical goods).

Still, while government officials and other analysts may point to a high GDP as evidence of a society's economic vitality, it can sometimes be misleading to equate this particular measure of economic size with a country's or region' overall economic well-being or standard of living. Consider, for example, the economic consequences of one of the biggest environmental disasters in U.S. history. In 1989 the Exxon Valdez oil tanker ran aground in Alaska, dumping more than 11 million gallons of crude oil into pristine Prince William Sound. The spill generated so much spending for cleanup-up efforts (Exxon claimed to have spend more than $2.1 billion on the project during the next few years), media coverage, and law suits that it led directly to a rise in Alaska's GDP. This rise masked the lasting environmental damage to Price William Sound and the crippling of the region's fishing industry, one of its main sources of income. This example points out that while the GDP is a valuable measure of the size of an economy, it does not a describe what is in the economy, nor does it necessarily reflect the quality of life the economy provides. Another limitation of the GDP is that it does not include certain types of economic exchange—for example, the black market (such as drugs, prostitution, and illegal weapons), bartering (goods and services that are traded, not bought or sold), and work done without pay, such as volunteering at

JOBLESS RECOVERY

When the September 11, 2001, terrorist attacks occurred, the United States was already in an economic recession (a period of economic decline), though many people did not know it at the time. Immediately after the attacks, however, when business across the country virtually stopped and the New York Stock Exchange remained closed for four days (the longest such closure since 1933, during the height of the Great Depression), few doubted that the country had plunged into a period of prolonged economic decline. From the perspective of many ordinary citizens, the decline lasted well into the succeeding years.

In the view of economists, however, recession is a time during which GDP shrinks and eventually bottoms out before beginning to rise again. According to a government report issued in July 2003, the recession lasted only from March to November 2001. The country's economy had officially been in recovery, with the gross domestic product, or GDP (the total financial value of all goods and services produced in a country in a given time period), growing slowly though somewhat irregularly in the years since November 2001. Many ordinary people failed to notice the growth, primarily because more people were out of work in 2003 than at any time since 1994. It had taken economists so long to determine the recession's official duration precisely because the high unemployment figures made them doubt that true recovery was underway, even though the GDP was growing. The report's conclusion that the recession had ended almost two years earlier probably did not provide a great deal of comfort to the scores of newly jobless Americans.

the local humane society or even helping a friend move. Conversely, it does not measure positive aspects of a society that have no easily assigned monetary value, such as healthy children, clean water, ecological diversity, and close-knit neighborhoods.

Recent Trends

GDP is likely to remain one of the chief tools economists and government officials use for evaluating economic health both in a given country and in relations between countries. One particularly useful way of comparing the economic health of different nations is by calculating per capita GDP: the measure of income produced by a national economy per citizen (the dollar figure divided by the number of citizens). The reason that the per capita figure is more meaningful than total GDP in some cases is that two countries may have the same GDP, but one of the countries may have a far higher population. In this case per capita GDP differs greatly. For instance, imagine two economies, both with a GDP of $100, but one has 2 citizens and the other has 10 citizens. The first economy would have a per capita GDP of $50, and the second would have a per capita GDP of $10.

Per capita GDP tends to correspond to many other statistics about a country, such as access to medical care, the infant mortality rate (the percentage of infants that die), and life expectancy (the number of years the average person lives). In the United States in 2005, per capita GDP stood at almost $42,000. Per capita GDP in most western European countries was somewhat lower but still comparable. For example, France and Germany both had a per capita GDP of roughly $30,000. The split between such developed economies and developing economies, like those of China and India, is extreme. China and India have larger total GDPs than France or Germany, but in 2005 China's per capita GDP was just under $7,000, and India's was around $3,000. Meanwhile, the per capita GDP of Afghanistan was well below $1,000.

$ Consumption

What It Means

People often think of consumption as the process of using consumer products, which are all the kinds of goods and services that can be purchased. In economics, however, *consumption* is a term used to talk about how much money all consumers are spending on goods and services. It is represented as a number that indicates the total amount of money consumers spend (an amount known as expenditure) in a given time period.

The goods and services that matter in the calculation of consumption are those that are "final" goods and services—things such as food, heating oil, telephone service, electronics, and home appliances. They are called "final" because they are either used up or transformed to such a degree that they cannot be reused or no longer resemble the original good. Purchases of machines, buildings, or factories by businesses are not included in the calculation of consumption because these things are used to produce other goods but are not consumable goods in and of themselves. They are thus referred to as "intermediate products."

Every time people purchase and use goods in order to keep their homes running, transport themselves to school and work, and clothe and feed themselves, they are, as consumers, contributing to the overall spending patterns of the economy. When economists analyze the economy on a macroeconomic (large-scale) level, consumption is of primary interest because it accounts for about two-thirds of all spending in a given time period.

In the field of economics, consumption refers to the amount of money consumers spend on goods and services during a given time period, such as a year. Groceries, along with electricity and shelter, are among the essential items that everyone, regardless of income, must purchase. *Robert Daemmrich/Stone/Getty Images.*

When Did It Begin

As modern capitalist economies have developed over the past few hundred years, they have been grounded in the exchange of goods and services for money. (Capitalism is a system in which business is owned by private individuals and prices are determined through the free interaction of buyers and sellers.) Philosophers and economists, recognizing that spending is one of the basic features of capitalism, have studied the way people spend money and how it affects the economy. For instance, the British philosopher Jeremy Bentham (1748–1832) believed that consumption was motivated solely by the desires and wants of individual consumers. His theories paved the way for other theorists to develop ideas about consumption's fundamental role in economic systems.

In the 1930s the British economist John Maynard Keynes (1883–1946) attempted to find out how the income levels of consumers related to the ways in which they spent their income. According to Keynes, in making a decision about how much to spend, the typical consumer is mainly influenced not so much by the price of goods as by how much income he or she has. Consumers, Keynes said, usually spend most of whatever income they have on goods and services. He called this relationship between consumer income and consumption the "consumption function."

More Detailed Information

Consumption is one of the four kinds of spending that add up to what is known as "aggregate expenditures" (the total amount spent on goods and services in a nation's economy). The three other kinds of expenditures are investment expenditures (spending by the business sector), government spending, and the value of goods exported to other countries. Each of these components represents a stream of spending that contributes to aggregate expenditures, but consumption carries the largest amount. In fact, in the U.S. economy consumer expenditures make up, on average, two-thirds of total spending.

In determining (or predicting) the rate of consumption, a specific part of consumers' income called "disposable income" plays a crucial role. Disposable income is the amount of income consumers are free to use after paying taxes. Consumers can use their disposable income for consumption or save it, thereby not spending it.

The proportion of the total amount of disposable income spent on consumer goods and services is referred to as the average propensity to consume, or APC. To figure out the APC, economists compare the disposable income of a given time period to how much consumers spend during that period. For example, in 2001 the disposable income of U.S. households was $7,469 billion. Of this amount, consumers spent $7,342 billion and saved $127 billion. What this means is that American consumers spent almost all of the money they received in 2001. On average, they spent 98 cents per dollar of in-

come (an APC of 0.98), leaving only 2 cents per dollar for savings.

As this example shows, the United States has an extremely consumer-oriented economy. Some years, in fact, the APC in the United States has been higher than 1.0; this happens when consumers spend more than 100 cents per disposable dollar. In order to do so, they have had to pay for some of their consumption with credit (borrowed money) or with savings from the past. When consumer spending exceeds disposable income, consumer saving is negative. At that point, consumers are said to be "dissaving."

Economists seek to understand consumption so that they can observe trends in consumer behavior and attempt to predict how consumers will use their disposable income. Although it has been proven that consumer spending is linked to income, there are other influences on consumption. One of these is expectations. People who know they will receive money in the form of such things as gifts, bonuses, or raises will start spending more money before they receive their extra money. In this way, expectations can alter spending habits.

Wealth is another influence on spending habits. For example, if an individual can sell some of her stock (portions of ownership in companies) in order to pay for her child's education, her spending is being financed by wealth, not by her current income.

AUTONOMOUS CONSUMPTION

There are many forces that affect consumption (the rate of consumer spending). In recognition of this, the English economist John Maynard Keynes (1883–1946) made a distinction between two different kinds of consumption. One type is affected by the current level of income, and the other is not. Spending that varies according to income is called discretionary consumption—the consumption of items that are not essential for survival, such as vacations and televisions. The type of spending that takes place independent of current income is called autonomous consumption.

Autonomous consumption is a minimum level of consumption that must exist regardless of whether or not the consumer has income. For instance, nearly everyone requires electricity, food, and shelter. The money needed to pay for these expenses is considered to be absolutely necessary for survival and therefore separate (or autonomous) from other expenses. If a consumer were to lose his source of income, he would still need shelter and food. In order to pay these expenses, he would have to use savings or borrow money (often in the form of credit). Expectations, wealth, credit, taxes, and price levels are among the influences that affect the level of autonomous consumption.

A third influence on spending habits is credit. This is money that consumers borrow from banks or other institutions (including stores themselves) in order to purchase goods and services. When a customer uses credit, he or she has to pay the institution a fee called interest, which is usually calculated as a percentage of the loan amount. Some consumers are eligible for higher levels of credit and lower rates of interest than others; others are not eligible for credit at all.

Income taxes and price levels also influence consumer behavior. If the government cuts tax rates, consumers are able to keep and spend more of their earned income. Likewise, if the government raises taxes, disposable income decreases and as a result so does spending. Increases in general price levels reduce the real value of money (because each dollar of income does not go as far as before) and may lead people to cut back on spending.

When economists want to predict the effect of new government programs, it is important for them to know not just the APC but also the MPC, the marginal propensity to consume. This measures the total amount of spending on consumer goods from an increase in disposable income. For example, if the government were to cut taxes on a household by $100 and they spent an additional $80, the MPC would be 0.80. Knowing the MPC helps governments understand how fiscal policy (changes in government spending and taxation) effect the economy as a whole.

Recent Trends

In recent decades businesses have been increasingly competitive in their attempts to convince the individual consumer to spend money. They primarily do so through advertising and marketing, two tools that have become highly developed. Often their strategies involve researching consumers' needs and desires so that they can tailor their marketing and advertisements to a specific type of consumer. For example, many manufacturers and retailers use computer software to match advertisements to the content of private e-mails and the information provided by credit card purchases. Economists have begun to study more closely the effects that marketing has on consumption.

$ Aggregate Demand

What It Means

Aggregate demand is a term used in macroeconomics (the study of the economy as a whole, as opposed to microeconomics, which concerns the individual parts of an economy). It refers to the demand of all buyers in an economy for what are called "final products" (in other words, the willingness and ability of these buyers to purchase the products). Final products are not all the products in the economy. Rather, they are those pro-

ducts, such as bicycles or furniture cleaning, that are sold to their final users (consumers, businesses, and governments). A product, such as plastic, that is purchased by a business to produce another good, such as a comb, is not a final product, but the comb purchased by a consumer is.

The demand for final products is also influenced by price. Because aggregate demand refers to all buyers and all final products in an economy, what influences aggregate demand is not the price of a particular good or service but the average price of all final products in the economy. As buyers have only so much money, the higher the average price for final products, the lower will be the demand (the willingness and ability to purchase the products). The opposite is also true. The lower the average price, the higher will be the demand, as buyers can afford to purchase more.

The definition of aggregate demand, then, is the amount of final products demanded by all buyers in an economy at a given average price. Its complimentary concept, aggregate supply, is the amount of final products the economy's sellers are willing to produce at a given average price. These macroeconomic concepts of aggregate supply and aggregate demand are based on the microeconomic concepts of supply and demand. Supply is the quantity of a good or service that a business is willing to sell at a given price, and demand is the amount of a particular good or service that consumers are willing to buy at a given price.

Aggregate demand is commonly represented using a diagram called an aggregate demand curve (AD curve). The AD curve shows how buyers respond to varying price levels. With price level on the vertical axis and output, or products demanded, on the horizontal axis, the quantity of goods buyers demand forms a downward-sloping curve, moving from right to left, indicating that as the price level falls, buyers want increasing quantities of products. The AD curve, together with the aggregate supply, or AS, curve, is a useful tool for understanding and predicting the behavior of the economy under a variety of different conditions.

When Did It Begin

The British economist John Maynard Keynes first developed the concept of aggregate demand in his landmark book *The General Theory of Employment, Interest, and Money* (1936). Whereas economists previously had analyzed the workings of individual buyers and sellers and the places or systems (called markets) that bring them together, Keynes showed the importance of theorizing about the economy from the top down. By observing and theorizing about the behavior of the total, or aggregate, activity of all those buyers, sellers, and markets, Keynes demonstrated, governments could better manage their national economies. As a result of Keynes's work, economics has since been split into two basic subfields: microeconomics and macroeconomics.

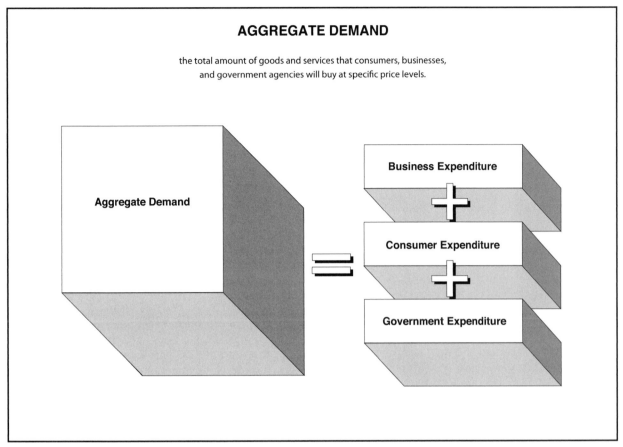

AGGREGATE DEMAND

the total amount of goods and services that consumers, businesses, and government agencies will buy at specific price levels.

Aggregate Demand

=

Business Expenditure

+

Consumer Expenditure

+

Government Expenditure

Aggregate demand refers to the total amount of final goods and services that businesses, individual consumers, and governments are willing and able to buy over a range of prices. Final goods do not include raw materials that go into making products. *Illustration by Smith & Santori. Cengage Learning, Gale.*

Specifically, Keynes outlined the various components that together add up to aggregate demand: consumer demand for household goods and services, business demand for productive equipment and other investments, the demand of government (at the national, state, and local levels) for goods and services, and foreign demand for domestic products minus domestic demand for foreign products (exports minus imports).

More Detailed Information

The components of aggregate demand are the same today as when Keynes first outlined the concept. Taken together, these components represent all of the possible purchases of final products (products sold to their final buyer, rather than products sold in raw or intermediate forms, to be made into other products) in any economy.

Consumer demand for household goods and services makes up one key portion of aggregate demand. This category takes into account all of the purchases that people make for personal, as opposed to business, reasons. Examples include purchases of food, clothing, haircuts, electronics, cars, and movie tickets.

Business spending is another primary component of aggregate demand. Businesses commonly make investments in their equipment and other resources in the hope of increasing profitability. Any finished products companies buy (such as pencils, hardhats, computers, and trucks) therefore contribute to the overall level of aggregate demand. Raw materials and labor costs do not count toward aggregate demand, since they are not considered finished products.

Government spending on finished products is the third main component of aggregate demand. Governments at the local, state, and national level buy a wide variety of goods and services. Examples include buildings to house schools, machinery for building roads, computers for government workers, and missiles for the armed forces. Not all types of government spending contribute to the overall level of aggregate demand. Direct payments of money to the elderly, in the form of Social Security, or to the poor, in the form of welfare, are not directly included in aggregate demand since they do not represent additional output of products. Likewise, the salaries of government workers are not counted toward aggregate demand.

DEMAND AND AGGREGATE DEMAND: WHAT'S THE DIFFERENCE?

Demand is the quantity of a particular good or service that buyers are willing to buy over a range of prices. As prices rise, demand falls, and as prices fall, demand rises. Similarly, aggregate demand is the quantity of all goods and services that all of the various buyers in the economy are willing to buy at a given price level (an average of all prices). As the price level increases, aggregate demand falls, and as the price level falls, aggregate demand rises.

Though demand and aggregate demand are similar, there is a distinction between them. Demand falls because, assuming the price of other goods is constant, buyers will seek out substitutes for an item that seems overpriced. Someone who leaves home to buy a steak might find that the grocery store's price for steak has risen, while the price of chicken has stayed the same. That person may come home with chicken instead of steak.

When considering the economy as a whole, however, it does not matter at all whether chicken or steak is bought in greater quantities. Aggregate demand deals with *all* goods and services in the economy, and it fluctuates according to an average price level meant to represent *all* prices. The overall amount of purchases is what matters. So, though the notion of aggregate demand is based on that of demand, it is important to recognize that the two terms are not interchangeable.

Finally, domestic products exported and sold to foreign individuals, businesses, and governments contribute to the overall level of aggregate demand, at least as long as their quantities outweigh the quantities of goods produced by foreign companies and sold domestically. In other words, the total quantity of imports minus the total quantity of exports is added to the other three components of aggregate demand. Sometimes a country spends more money on imports than exports; in this case the difference would be subtracted from the overall aggregate demand total.

The AD curve indicates the level of aggregate demand at different price levels. At low price levels aggregate demand is high, and vice versa. The resulting curve moves downward from left to right, with price level on the vertical axis and output (goods or services demanded) on the horizontal. There are three explanations for this.

First, there is what is known as the wealth effect. When prices fall consumers' money is suddenly worth more than before. This additional purchasing power (additional wealth) leads to increased demand for economic output.

The second reason for the shape of the AD curve is the interest rate effect, which explains what happens to interest rates at different prices. Interest rates are fees charged to those who borrow money from banks or other lenders.

When prices for products are low, consumers and businesses need less money to make transactions, and they put additional money into bank accounts. In response, banks and other lenders lower their interest rates, and lending activity picks up, allowing individuals and businesses to make large purchases. Thus, demand is stimulated.

Finally, the net exports effect—which deals with the relationship between imports, exports, and prices—helps explain why the AD curve slopes downward. When domestic prices are low, domestic-made goods tend to be a better value than imported goods. Thus, domestic consumers and businesses buy domestic products. Likewise, low prices at home result in low prices for the foreign buyers of exported goods, so export sales increase. Both of these developments result in high levels of aggregate demand at low price levels, which takes the form, when diagrammed, of a downward sloping AD curve.

The AD curve can shift from left to right at any given price level (that is, the whole downward-sloping line is moved over). This represents a change in aggregate demand that is independent of the price level. If the level of aggregate demand increases independently of the price level, the downward-sloping curve would shift to the right. If the level of aggregate demand decreases for some reason other than the price level, the downward-sloping curve would shift to the left. Numerous factors can cause such a shift to occur.

Changes in the expectations of consumers and businesses can cause the AD curve to shift. Consumers base their buying decisions not only on the amount of money they have in the present but on how much money they expect to have in the future. Similarly, companies make decisions about investing in new equipment based on how good they expect business to be in the future. If consumers and businesses are optimistic, aggregate demand can rise even though there has been no change in the price level. This would be represented by a rightward shift of the AD curve. Pessimism on the part of consumers and businesses would likely have the opposite result.

Changes in wealth not related to prices can also cause the AD curve to shift. For example, many consumers in the 1990s were owners of shares of stock (portions of company ownership that can be bought and sold and that gain value when companies prosper). In the mid-to-late 1990s, the stock market boomed, and shares of stock gained value dramatically. In such an environment, with prices for consumer goods remaining steady, an influx of wealth derived from the stock market resulted in increased aggregate demand, which shifted the AD curve rightward. Stock markets sometimes crash without warning, as well, suddenly making shareholders poorer than they were a day or a week earlier. This could cause the AD curve to shift to the left even if the price level for products is unchanged.

Another common cause of shifts in the AD curve is a change in businesses' capital (equipment) needs. If, for example, new computer technologies make it necessary for businesses across the economy to purchase all new office equipment, the AD curve might shift to the right as a result of increased business spending. On the other hand, it is also possible for businesses to fulfill their equipment needs fully; once they have done so, they have no need to continue buying equipment. If this happens across the economy, a leftward shift of the AD curve could result.

Recent Trends

John Maynard Keynes was responsible not only for founding macroeconomics but also for setting the stage for government management of the economy. Keynes showed that governments could effectively manage aggregate demand (shift a country's AD curve to the right or the left) by manipulating tax rates and levels of government spending. Since government spending on final products is itself a component of aggregate demand, changes to this form of spending directly shifts the AD curve. Changes to other types of government spending, such as direct payments to the poor or the elderly, shift the AD curve indirectly by making people more or less wealthy (and thus more or less likely to buy products). Similarly, increasing or decreasing taxes is an indirect way of inducing a shift in the AD curve, since increased taxes result in decreased wealth, and vice versa. The United States and other governments successfully recovered from the Great Depression by implementing Keynes's ideas, and for the next several decades the U.S. government attempted to manage aggregate demand through fiscal policy (changes to tax and spending programs).

By the 1970s many economists had come to believe that managing aggregate demand through fiscal policy was messier and less effective than using monetary policy (changes in the quantity of money circulating in the economy) to influence the economy. When the government increases the size of the money supply, lenders have more money available to make loans, and business investment and consumer spending increase. This shifts the AD curve to the right. Decreasing the quantity of money in circulation sets off a chain reaction in the opposite direction, shifting the AD curve to the left.

Today central banks (those government entities responsible for setting monetary policy, such as the Federal Reserve System in the United States) take the lead in managing the economy. Though some people see this as a repudiation of Keynesian-style management of aggregate demand, others see it as a refinement of and addition to Keynes's ideas about aggregate demand.

$ Aggregate Supply

What It Means

Aggregate supply, along with its complementary concept, *aggregate demand*, is a term used in macroeconomics (the study of the economy as a whole, as opposed to microeconomics, which concerns the individual parts of an economy). It refers to the supply, or quantity, of all "final products" in an economy. Final products are the economy's finished products, such as cars or a loaf of bread, not the raw materials or "intermediate products," such as steel or wheat, that are converted into other products. These finished products might be sold to consumers, businesses, or governments.

Prices also play a role in the concept of aggregate supply. The amount of final goods and services that sellers in an economy are willing and able to produce is influenced by the prices they can charge. In general, the higher the prices, the more sellers will produce. In discussing aggregate supply, economists use the average price for all final goods and services in an economy, not the price of any particular product. Aggregate demand is commonly defined, in fact, as the amount of final products sellers are willing to produce at a given average price.

The macroeconomic concepts of aggregate supply and aggregate demand are based on the microeconomic concepts of supply and demand. Supply is the quantity of a good or service that a business is willing to sell at a given price, and demand is the quantity of a good or service that consumers are willing to buy at a given price. As prices rise, supply increases, and demand decreases. Aggregate supply and aggregate demand follow the same pattern.

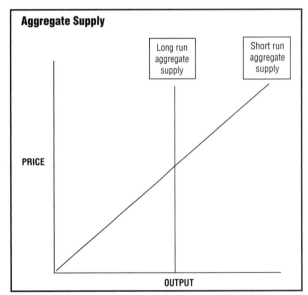

Aggregate supply refers to the total amount of goods and services supplied by sellers in a national economy during a given time period. As shown in this graph, economists believe over the short run aggregate supply increases as prices increase, but over the long run the maximum amount a nation can produce is affected not by price but by its ability to expand its labor force or build new factories. *Illustration by GGS Information Services. Cengage Learning, Gale.*

Aggregate supply is commonly represented using diagrams called aggregate supply, or AS, curves. There are two different AS curves, the short run aggregate supply curve (SRAS curve) and the long run aggregate supply curve (LRAS curve). The short run and the long run refer not to specific time periods, such as one month or one year; rather, they describe undefined time periods, one shorter than the other, during which businesses have different options open to them. In the short run a business can increase profits by making some changes, but it cannot alter other aspects of its operations. In the long run a business can make adjustments to all aspects of its operations.

The two AS curves are shaped differently to reflect different conditions of doing business over time. With price level on the vertical axis and output, or production, on the horizontal axis, the SRAS curve slopes upward from left to right, indicating that in the short run, aggregate supply rises as the price level rises and falls as the price level falls. In other words, businesses produce more when prices are higher. The LRAS curve, by contrast, is vertical, indicating that in the long run, price levels have no effect on aggregate supply. Aggregate supply curves, together with the aggregate demand curves, are useful tools for understanding and predicting the behavior of the economy under a variety of different conditions.

When Did It Begin

The concept of aggregate supply, like that of aggregate demand, came into being as a part of the so-called Keynesian Revolution in economics. This radical reshaping of the field of economics was named after its instigator, the British economist John Maynard Keynes, whose book *The General Theory of Employment, Interest, and Money* (1936) offered solutions to the Great Depression, the severe economic crisis that afflicted the world economy in the 1930s. Keynes showed that the principles of supply and demand could be extended beyond individual markets and applied to the economy as a whole. He introduced the concepts of aggregate supply and aggregate demand, the grand totals of goods supplied and demanded in an entire economy. Likewise, Keynes showed, these grand totals could be observed in relation to average prices across the economy. Viewing the economy in this top-down, big-picture way would, in turn, allow governments to better regulate their economies.

Keynes thus laid the foundations for what we now call macroeconomics and to the division of all economic study into its macro and micro branches. The concepts of aggregate supply and aggregate demand as he outlined them are still at the foundation of all macroeconomic theory.

More Detailed Information

As the price level in the economy rises, so does aggregate supply. This occurs because rising prices mean that the difference between producers' costs (such as the cost of paying wages, the cost of equipment, the cost of land, and the cost of electricity) and producers' revenue (the total value of sales) widens. This difference between cost and revenue is profit. The greater the potential for profit in the economy, the more goods and services sellers will supply.

At any given time some producers' costs are fixed: they are either impossible to alter or unlikely to be altered. For example, employers often enter into contracts with their workers specifying their rate of pay for a period of a year or more. This means that if the price level falls, sellers cannot simply adjust their costs; some of those costs, such as labor, cannot be changed right away. Even if workers are not covered by contracts, employers may be hesitant to reduce wages as soon as the price level drops, because they may fear angering their employees. Likewise, if prices are rising, employers may not leap to adjust wages and salaries upward for fear of making workers believe that they can expect regular pay increases in the future.

The period of time during which some costs are fixed is the short run. The short run could be one day, or it could be two years. During a prolonged period of economic stagnation, for example, employers will renegotiate contracts or cut wages regardless of the effect this has on worker morale. This change would mark the moment when the short run gives way to the long run. The long run begins at the point when fixed costs become flexible. In the long run, all costs are flexible.

The existence of fixed costs in the short run explains the different shapes of the two AS curves. In the short run, as the price level rises but some seller costs remain fixed, sellers will increase supply in response to growing levels of profit. Under opposite conditions, a falling price level would result in diminished profits for sellers, who would respond by cutting back on production. Thus, the SRAS curve is upward sloping, indicating a steady rise in aggregate supply as the price level rises or, in the other direction, a steady decline in aggregate supply as the price level falls.

In the long run, however, since employers can alter all costs, supply is not affected by changes in the price level. If prices fall over the long run, for example, sellers can alter any and all of their costs, including their labor costs, to keep their profit levels constant. Long-run aggregate supply is equal to the potential output of all sellers, which is dependent only on society's resources (such as land and natural resources, the size and characteristics of the labor force, and the amount and variety of equipment available for production). The LRAS curve is, accordingly, a vertical line.

Both the SRAS curve and the LRAS curve can shift (that is, the entire curve moves to the left or the right on the diagram). A shift in the SRAS curve indicates that aggregate supply has either increased or decreased independently of the price level. Shifts occur because there are factors other than the price level that can affect a company's level of profits. When these factors change, the curve shifts to the left (indicating decreased aggregate supply) or to the right (indicating increased aggregate supply).

One development that can cause shifts in the SRAS curve is a change in production costs. For example, when the price of oil increases dramatically because of tensions in the Middle East (where much of the world's oil comes from), the cost of producing goods rises for sellers across the economy, since many industries are highly dependent on oil-based fuels. This development would cut into profits, and if businesses responded by cutting production, the SRAS curve would shift to the left. A decline in the price of oil could trigger the reverse phenomenon: increased profits for sellers, leading to increased production and a rightward shift of the SRAS curve.

Another factor that could result in a shift of the SRAS curve is an unexpected change in wages. Many employers pay workers not only in dollar amounts specified by contracts but also in benefits such as health insurance. If insurance companies raise premiums dramatically from one year to the next, sellers who provide insurance for their employees will absorb this cost and, in turn, possibly cut back on production. This would be represented by a leftward shift of the SRAS curve. A decline in the costs of health insurance could result in a rightward shift of the curve.

Increases or decreases in workers' productivity can also cause the SRAS curve to shift. For example, new computer programs that allow companies to keep accurate tabs on their operations across great geographical distances might speed up production and eliminate costly errors. This would result in lower production costs, which would increase profits and spur companies to increase supply. A rightward shift on the SRAS curve would illustrate this development. Worker productivity could, on the other hand, be hampered by new government regulations requiring increased paperwork. If the paperwork slowed down the production process across the economy, its effect would appear as a leftward shift of the SRAS curve.

The LRAS curve can also shift, in connection with increases or decreases in a society's resources. The potential output of the U.S. economy has grown consistently over the country's history, reflecting a growing and increasingly skilled workforce, technological progress, and other developments that increase potential production. The LRAS curve for the U.S. economy has thus shifted regularly to the right (the rate at which the LRAS curve shifts to the right measures long run economic growth). On the other hand, a country whose population is decimated by a natural disaster or war would experience a dramatic decrease in potential production. This would be represented by a shift of the LRAS to the left.

SUPPLY AND AGGREGATE SUPPLY: WHAT'S THE DIFFERENCE?

Supply is the quantity of a particular good or service that businesses are willing to sell over a range of prices. As the price of an individual product rises, existing businesses increase supply, and new firms enter the industry. If prices were to fall, existing businesses would restrict supply, and some might leave the industry. Similarly, aggregate supply is the quantity of all goods and services that all businesses in the economy are willing to sell at a given price level (an average of all prices). As the price level increases, aggregate supply increases. The reverse holds true when the price level falls.

There is, however, a distinction between supply and aggregate supply. Supply increases when prices rise because, assuming the price of other goods is constant, sellers shift production into the high-priced goods that allow them the largest levels of profit. If the price of chicken doubles while the price of beef stays constant, agricultural producers who generally raise more beef than chicken might increase their supply of chicken. When considering the economy as a whole, it does not matter at all whether people specialize in chicken or beef. Aggregate supply deals with *all* goods and services in the economy, and it fluctuates according to an average price level meant to represent *all* prices. The overall amount of supply is what matters. Though the notion of aggregate supply is based on that of supply, it is important to recognize that the two terms are not interchangeable.

Recent Trends

The study of economics has been directly shaped by the major economic crises of the twentieth century. The Great Depression stumped economists who believed in the self-regulating ability of the market system. In the United States and other countries, up to 25 percent of workers lost their jobs and had no ability to buy the products that the country's numerous state-of-the-art factories could produce. Businesses therefore shuttered their factories or dramatically scaled back production. John Maynard Keynes revolutionized economics by showing that governments could effectively stimulate aggregate demand (the quantity of goods buyers across the economy were willing to buy) by spending money in a variety of ways. Keynes's theories led to recovery from the Depression and were thus adopted as the authoritative word on economic regulation.

In 1979, however, the U.S. economy experienced its most drastic crisis since the Depression because of events that affected aggregate supply rather than aggregate demand. A revolution in Iran, one of the world's largest oil producers, led to oil shortages and fears of further instability in the region, which sent the worldwide price of oil soaring. Since so many businesses are heavily dependent on oil-based fuels, high oil prices meant increased production costs across the economy; this translated into decreased aggregate supply. A Keynesian approach to the crisis—managing aggregate demand—offered no solutions, since demand was not the problem.

As a result, another evolution of economic thought occurred. The 1979–80 crisis helped economists understand that some recessions (periods of economic stagnation) could be caused by demand shocks (as with the Great Depression, a particularly severe recession), while others could be caused by supply shocks.

$ Income

What It Means

Income is the money that individuals and businesses bring in during a given period as a result of work or investments. If, for example, a person is paid $50,000 per year as a computer programmer, she is said to have an annual income of $50,000. If the company that employs her brings in $1 million on top of the expenses it incurs during the year (these expenses would include costs such as office rent, maintenance, equipment purchases, and salaries), its income for that year is $1 million.

Income is either spent, invested, or paid to the government in the form of taxes. The U.S.-based computer programmer in the above example, for instance, might pay $15,000 of her salary to federal, state, and local governments in the form of income tax (a percentage of personal income that is owed to the government, and that varies depending on the size of the income). Money collected through income taxes provides governments with a large share of the expenses they need to operate. Of the $35,000 that remains, the computer programmer will use a large portion to purchase the food, clothing, and shelter that she needs to live. If any money remains after this, she might spend it on movie tickets, a new car, or graduate business courses; or rather, she might invest this leftover income, with the hope of increasing her income further. Whenever she purchases basic necessities or luxuries, she is contributing income to another person or business (a grocer, a landlord, a clothing store, a movie theater, a car dealership, a university). When she invests the money in a bank account that pays interest, or in the stock market, where she buys a portion of company ownership that stands to increase in value if the company succeeds, she increases the income of the bank or company to whom she is contributing her money at the same time that, if all goes well, she increases her own.

Because income drives the overall economy in this way, economists and government agencies pay detailed attention to the incomes of people and businesses, and they classify incomes in a number of different ways that lead to further understanding of how the economy works. One way they classify income is called the gross domestic

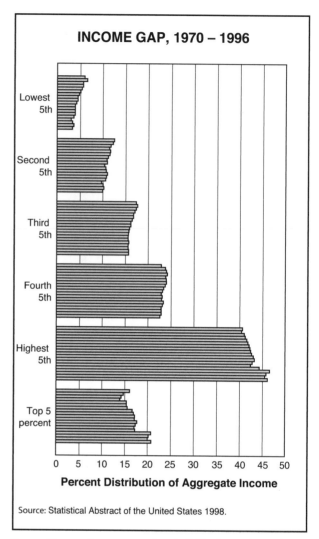

INCOME GAP, 1970 – 1996

Lowest 5th
Second 5th
Third 5th
Fourth 5th
Highest 5th
Top 5 percent

0 5 10 15 20 25 30 35 40 45 50

Percent Distribution of Aggregate Income

Source: Statistical Abstract of the United States 1998.

Personal income is a measure of an individual's earnings, whereas aggregate income is a measure of the total earnings of a country. According to this graph, in 1996 the poorest fifth of the U.S. population made less than 5 percent of the country's income, while the richest fifth made more than 45 percent. *Illustration by George Barille. Cengage Learning, Gale.*

product (GDP). Because spending by one person represents income to another, adding up either side of the transaction should yield the same amount. GDP is either the total amount of spending or the total amount of income generated in the economy over a year, and it represents the total size of the economy.

When Did It Begin

Today in capitalist countries (those nations in which individuals are allowed to own property and businesses and freely seek profit) people and companies are rewarded with incomes in proportion to such qualities as their capacity for hard work, their natural and cultural advantages, their performance on the job, and luck. This was not always the case.

The oldest and most common form of economy (examples of which still exist today in undeveloped countries) is what is known as a traditional economy. In a traditional economy people usually hunt and gather for food, and the proceeds are not kept by individuals but are divided up on the basis of traditional hierarchies. By 3000 BC a new economic model had allowed for the development of some of the great civilizations of the ancient world (for example, Egypt and China). This new form of economy, called a planned or command economy, was one in which a strong central ruler, such as a pharaoh or emperor, organized all wealth and income for his own benefit or the benefit of a small elite group of society. This allowed for more organization of resources like land and labor and, accordingly, a much larger ability to create wealth and undertake the vast projects necessary for the building of large cities and impressive monuments. Such great achievements were, again, enjoyed primarily by only a small portion of society. Ordinary people still had little power to produce incomes that benefited themselves.

This began to change in Europe during the sixteenth through eighteenth centuries, when their planned economies began to move toward capitalism. During this time the European nations that we know today were being formed out of smaller and more numerous preexisting kingdoms. These centralized governments (of France, England, and Germany, for example) needed to raise vast amounts of money in order to compete with one another militarily and politically, and capitalism provided a more efficient means of wealth creation than planned economic systems. Individual freedom did not emerge instantly; ruling elites still controlled a large part of the incomes produced by the capitalist system. Nevertheless, the notion that each individual has the right to work or otherwise produce an income strictly for his or her own benefit is a product of the rise of capitalism.

More Detailed Information

For most individuals income is the amount of money they are paid by their employers, prior to making any tax payments. Other people bring in income by investing money in ways that collect interest (fees paid by people who borrow money) or dividends (profits made in the stock market) or by renting out property. A company's income, by contrast, is not simply the amount of money that it brings in through its normal business activities but the amount of that money that is left over after it has paid its expenses.

Economists classify income in numerous ways for the purposes of analysis. One way of doing so is by determining to what use people put their incomes. The uses to which income can be put include buying goods and services, paying taxes, and making investments. The amount of one's income that is left over after paying income taxes is known as disposable income. The amount

that is left after food, shelter, and clothing have been purchased is what is known as discretionary income. Discretionary income is used to buy goods and services other than these basic necessities.

When trying to understand what is happening at the national level, economists break income down into personal income (that which is acquired by households) and business income (that which is acquired by companies). The combination of these two quantities yields a figure called the national income, or the amount of money brought in by all people and businesses during a given time period.

Another useful way of looking at income is to consider the difference between money, or nominal, income (the value of a person or company's income in actual currency, such as the dollar) and real income (the value of an income in terms of what it can purchase). Money income and real income represent different values chiefly because the prices of goods and services tends to rise over time. Thus, $10 in 1990 bought more than $10 in 2000.

Income is also commonly classified according to its source. Earned income is the wages and salaries that people are paid in exchange for their work. This represents about two-thirds of the U.S. national income. Unearned income makes up the other one-third, and it is derived from interest, rent, business profits, and other sources whose common characteristic is that they all represent money that is received for reasons other than straightforward labor. For example, interest is a fee paid for the use of money; rent is a fee paid for the use of property; and business profit is money that is acquired through combining all of a business's resources to create value.

Yet another important way of evaluating income is to consider how it is distributed, or spread out over a country's population. An economy's health depends not simply on the total amount of income produced in a country but on how it is distributed. If, for example, an increasing amount of income goes to a very small minority in a nation, while the middle class holds a diminishing share of overall wealth and the number of poor people grows, the economy may not thrive over the long term. Economists therefore ask a variety of questions about how the national income is divided up among citizens. How much of a nation's income goes to the rich, the middle classes, and the poor? What is the median individual income in a country (the income figure below which half of the population earn and above which half of the population earn), and how do the various portions of the population measure up against that median? How wide is the gap between the incomes of the rich and the incomes of the other classes in society?

Recent Trends

In 2005 the median income for American households was around $46,000 a year. This means that roughly half of

REDISTRIBUTING INCOME

Some countries redistribute income (the money that people and businesses bring in as a result of work and investments) in order to avoid what they perceive as an unfair distribution of income—when a small portion of society is able to enrich themselves while middle-class and especially poor people suffer. European countries such as Sweden and the Netherlands, for example, tax their citizens' incomes heavily in order to provide a strong safety net for all citizens. This results in substantial aid for poor people and for such services as free health care and education for all citizens. By comparison, the United States engages in much less redistribution of income, providing some benefits to the poor and elderly while being traditionally skeptical of the large-scale redistribution programs (and the high taxes) generally supported by Europeans.

the families in the United States made less than $46,000 and roughly half made more than $46,000. Adjusting for inflation (the general rising of prices that makes money worth increasingly less over time), American household incomes rose gradually but steadily, with some interruptions, between 1967 and 2005. In terms of what the dollar was worth in 2005, a typical American family made about $35,000 in 1967 (in actuality, the income would have been roughly six times smaller, around $6,000; it took about six dollars to buy in 2005 what one dollar could buy in 1967).

The small size of this increase (from $35,000 to $46,000) was at odds with the fact that the American economy as a whole had grown dramatically during that time. Additionally, individuals were making substantially more in 2005 than they had in 1967, and women had entered the workforce in large numbers in the intervening years, which would seem to result in households that would make twice as much as they had in earlier times.

But while the proportion of wives in the workforce more than doubled, the proportion of married couples within the general population declined dramatically at the same time. Around 40 percent of households in the late 1960s consisted of a married couple with children (the highest-earning type of household), but by the late 1990s these families only accounted for about 25 percent of American households. The U.S. population by 2005 consisted of a larger proportion of smaller households with only one income-earner, so most families were not considerably better off than they had been 28 years earlier, even though some families (especially those with two income-earners) were prospering far more than was possible in earlier eras.

$ Consumer Price Index

What It Means

The Consumer Price Index (CPI), one of the most important economic indicators in the United States, measures the change in prices that consumers pay for goods and services from year to year. This figure tracks inflation (a general rise in prices) or deflation (a fall in prices). A large increase in the CPI over a short period of time represents growing inflation, and a drop in the CPI signifies deflation, both of which can be harmful to an individual's finances and a nation's economy. Generally speaking, moderate and steady yearly inflation rates indicate a stable economy. When prices change rapidly, it usually means that the economy is in trouble. Because erratic price shifts can have such a devastating effect on the economy, the U.S. government takes extensive measures to chart, or figure out, the Consumer Price Index.

Consumers pay close attention to this figure as well. Because the CPI dictates the yearly income for many Americans whose wages rise according to the annual cost of living increase, it is one of the most closely scrutinized of all the economic indicators (statistics that reflect the health of the economy). Economists estimate that the CPI affects the earnings of approximately 2 million union workers, the payments to almost 50 million people on social security (federally sponsored financial benefits, including disability income, military veteran's pensions, and public housing assistance), the value of food stamps for 20 million recipients, and the cost of school lunches for more than 25 million children.

When Did It Begin

The United States began charting price changes in 1893. The figures derived from these calculations became increasingly important at the beginning of the twentieth century with the growth of labor unions (workers' organizations that bargain for their members' wages, benefits, and working conditions). Business owners and union leaders relied on this information to negotiate wage increases that were in step with inflation. After World War I (1914–18) U.S. policymakers realized that a more accurate system would be necessary to monitor the staggering fluctuations of the wartime and postwar economies; thus, in 1919 the Bureau of Labor Statistics began calculating the CPI, extending their research back to 1913, the year before the war started.

In the 1930s, when Keynesian economic theory (which calls for government intervention to stabilize the economy) started to displace laissez-faire economics (trade without government control or interference) in the United States, government economists began to rely more heavily on the CPI to establish economic policies, including tax rates. Later, as government efforts to control inflation depended increasingly on monetary policy

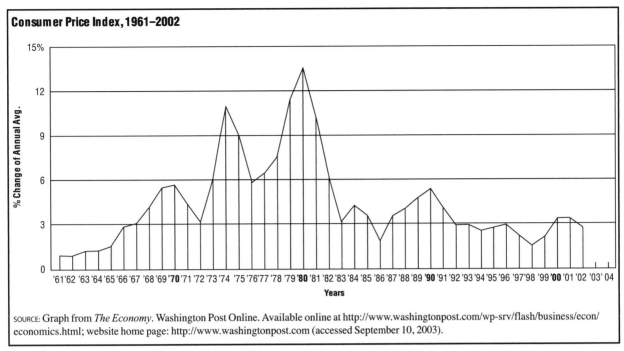

Consumer Price Index, 1961–2002

SOURCE: Graph from *The Economy*. Washington Post Online. Available online at http://www.washingtonpost.com/wp-srv/flash/business/econ/economics.html; website home page: http://www.washingtonpost.com (accessed September 10, 2003).

The Consumer Price Index (CPI) tracks inflation in the economy by measuring the average change in prices of consumer goods and services from one year to the next. As the graph indicates, during the last half of the twentieth century, U.S. inflation soared to its highest point in 1980, during the administration of President Jimmy Carter. *Line graph by GGS Information Services. Cengage Learning, Gale.*

(managing the amount of money in circulation), the CPI was also an important measure. If the CPI indicated that prices were rising too quickly, the Federal Reserve (the U.S. central bank) increased interest rates (fees charged to borrow money) in order to curb spending and bring prices back down to more reasonable levels. In contrast, economic declines and fears of deflation led the Federal Reserve to do the opposite, lower interest rates, in order to encourage consumer spending and, in turn, to bring prices back up. Since its inception, the CPI has remained one of the most reliable indicators of the health of the country's economy.

More Detailed Information

In the United States the CPI is determined by the U.S. Department of Labor's Bureau of Labor Statistics (BLS), which surveys the spending habits of American families and monitors retail prices throughout the country. A team of BLS field representatives visits 24,000 to 29,000 American families per month to conduct interviews and compile data on the items they buy. Participants are also asked to record their purchases in diaries. In addition, the BLS charts the cost of approximately 90,000 goods and services in more than 20,000 retail stores in 85 representative cities. The survey covers most commonly purchased everyday products and services, such as shoes, motor fuel, produce, medical care, washing machines, and automobile repairs. Results are compiled monthly and published the second week of the following month

on the BLS website. For example, the CPI for March 2006 would be posted by April 15, 2006.

Calculating the CPI is more complicated than merely monitoring price changes. To figure out what average Americans spend in a month to meet their daily needs, the BLS separates goods and services into eight categories: food and beverage, housing, apparel, transportation, medical care, recreation, education and communication, and other goods and services. A computer program is then used to compile a fixed set, or "market basket," of representative items drawn from each of the categories.

Each month the BLS publishes the CPI as a percentage increase or decrease of the average cost of the market basket. A typical monthly BLS bulletin might read as follows: "The CPI for American consumers rose 0.2 percent in February 1998. For the 12-month period ending in February, the CPI has increased 1.7 percent." This would mean that the average cost of goods (or cost of living) for Americans is 0.2 percent higher than it was in January and 1.7 percent higher than it was the previous year.

To make this index more meaningful for specific groups of Americans, the BLS publishes numerous CPIs. The two main figures are the CPI-U (Consumer Price Index for All Urban Consumers) and the CPI-W (Consumer Price Index for Urban Wage Earners and Clerical Workers). These two measures divide Americans according to their income, with the CPI-U being the higher of the two income brackets. There is also a

WHAT'S IN THE BASKET?

In order to create the Consumer Price Index (or CPI, a measure of the average increase or decrease in consumer prices), the U.S. Department of Labor's Bureau of Labor Statistics visits thousands of American homes each month, asking questions about their buying habits. The BLS also keeps track of prices in more than 20,000 retail stores. The index itself is calculated from a "basket" of 2,400 consumer goods and services that Americans typically buy. Among transportation items, the BLS tracks prices of new cars, airline tickets, gasoline, and car insurance. Among clothing items, prices of men's shirts and sweaters, women's dresses, and jewelry are monitored. The BLS also takes into account less glamorous expenses, such as water and sewage fees. All these items end up in the market basket. The average percentage change in these prices determines the CPI.

The BLS periodically changes what items are included in the market basket to reflect changes in buying trends. For example, it was not until the 1950s that televisions and frozen foods were included in the market basket because before then the average American did not buy these goods on a regular basis. In the 1990s computer technology was added to the market basket.

separate index for each of the 26 major metropolitan centers and 4 geographic regions in the country. One of the primary weaknesses of the system is that the BLS collects data only in urban areas, and the CPI therefore does not accurately reflect pricing in rural areas. Nevertheless, the CPI is believed to be a reliable economic indicator for 87 percent of the population.

Recent Trends

In the United States the CPI has increased between 1.6 and 3.4 percent per year from 2000 to 2006. The lowest rate of increase (1.6 percent) came between 2001 and 2002. Twice between 1999 and 2006 (from 1999–2000 and from 2004–5) the country saw inflation rise 3.4 percent. During this time costs for medical care increased by about 4 percent per year, while costs associated with housing rose by 2.5–4 percent annually.

The greatest increases in this period were in the cost of motor fuel. For example, from 1999 to 2000 the cost of motor fuel increased 28.4 percent, and from 2004 to 2005 gas prices rose another 22.2 percent. Consumers also paid steadily more for utilities, such as water and electricity, with a 10.6 percent increase from 2004 to 2005 and typical increases ranging between 7.5 and 8.5 percent. A notable exception occurred in 2002, when utility prices dropped by 6.1 percent compared to 2001. There have been only moderate increases in costs for food (about 2.5–3 percent annually), and clothing costs decreased between 2000 and 2006 by about a half percent a year.

$ Producer Price Index

What It Means

The Producer Price Index (PPI) is used to measure the average change in wholesale prices in the United States. Wholesaling refers to the sale of large quantities of goods from a major manufacturer or importer to another industry, commercial organization, professional user, or retailer. Thus, the PPI tracks price change from the perspective of the large seller and distributor. Often the PPI is compared with another important economic indicator, the Consumer Price Index (CPI), which is used to measure the average change in retail prices. Retailing is the sale of smaller quantities of goods, as well as services, to consumers, whether they are individuals or other businesses.

Analysts use the PPI to predict the future condition of the economy. Prices that companies are paying in their transactions with other companies affect the prices that consumers ultimately pay for goods and services. For example, if businesses in the frozen-desserts industry were required to pay higher prices for milk, those businesses would likely charge the consumer more for a gallon of ice cream. Depending on the sector of the economy, increases in the PPI might take as little as a few weeks or as long as a year or more to show up as increases in consumer prices.

Because the prices of supplies vary, businesses and industries use PPI data when negotiating long-term contracts for these supplies. For instance, a bread manufacturer will purchase wheat to make bread and then sell that bread to a supermarket. Over the course of the contract, wheat prices will vary, depending on the quality of the crop and a number of other factors. The bread manufacturer and the representatives from the supermarket will therefore agree to consult the PPI for wheat to adjust the price of the bread throughout the life of the contract. The U.S. government also uses PPI data in formulating long-term economic policies.

When Did It Begin

The origins of the PPI date back to 1891, when a U.S. Senate resolution authorized the Senate Committee on Finance to examine how laws regarding tariffs (taxes on goods imported from other countries) affected the U.S. economy. One of the many things the study sought to discern was the relationship between tariff laws and wholesale prices. Roland P. Falkner, a professor of statistics at the University of Pennsylvania, led the study, which collected data on wholesale prices from 1840 to 1891. In 1900 Falkner updated the report, covering the years 1891 to 1899. Two years later the U.S. Department of Labor (the federal agency responsible for regulating issues pertaining to the U.S. workforce) began publishing the report as the Index of Wholesale Prices. The

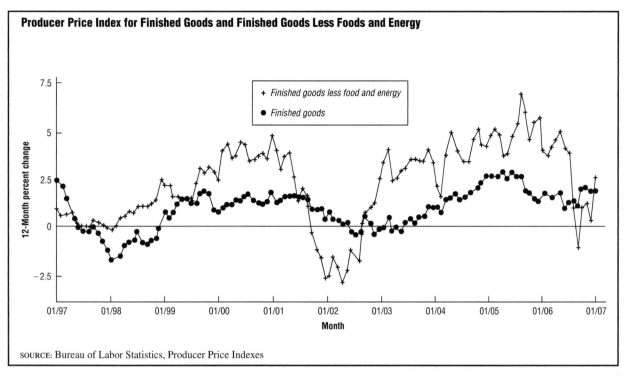

Producer Price Index for Finished Goods and Finished Goods Less Foods and Energy

SOURCE: Bureau of Labor Statistics, Producer Price Indexes

The Producer Price Index, or PPI, measures changes in the price of wholesale goods and services, which are sold from one business to another. Analysts track changes in the PPI, using graphs such as this one, to make predictions about economic trends. *Illustration by GGS Information Services. Cengage Learning, Gale.*

document was published under this title until 1978, when it was renamed the Producer Price Index.

More Detailed Information

The PPI is published monthly by the Bureau of Labor Statistics (BLS), an agency within the U.S. Department of Labor. The BLS is responsible for gathering and analyzing statistics related to the nation's workforce and the economy. In order to calculate the PPI, each month the agency collects price quotations by distributing surveys to producers in the manufacturing, mining, and service industries. Nearly every type of industry is invited to participate in these surveys. Response is voluntary, and the BLS keeps all of the data confidential.

The PPI is divided into three major categories: industry-to-industry sales, commodity-based sales, and stage-of-processing sales. An example of an industry-to-industry sale would be an oil company selling large quantities of gas to an airline. The second category of the PPI, commodity-based sales, charts the prices that manufacturers and wholesalers receive for their finished products. The stage-of-processing PPI measures sales of goods that are going to be treated or transformed into more-refined goods before finally being sold to consumers. For example, a mining company will retrieve iron ore (rocks and minerals that contain iron) from the ground and sell it to a smelting company, which will extract the iron from its ore so that steel can be produced.

A manufacturer will then purchase the steel and fashion its steel products. The sales along this chain of buyers are examples of stage-of-processing sales.

The Bureau of Labor Statistics continually adds pricing statistics for new industries to the PPI in order to ensure that the index reflects buying and selling patterns among all relevant domestic producers and suppliers in an ever-changing economy. For example, in January 2007 the BLS introduced new price indexes for management-consulting services (management consultants provide companies with expert advice on running their businesses) and blood and organ banks. Both are included in the category of industry-to-industry sales.

Recent Trends

The PPI tracks changes in prices for food and energy (coal, natural gas, and crude oil [petroleum]) more closely than prices for other products. In fact, most of the graphs in the monthly document, especially those at the beginning of the report that give a more general overview of the month's price changes, contain separate columns for food and energy products. One wholesale price that significantly affects both the average consumer and the daily operation of large businesses is the price of a barrel of standard crude oil. The price of oil determines how much people pay to put fuel in their cars, and because so many industries and businesses use gasoline in their daily operations, it also has a wide impact on the economy.

GDP DEFLATOR

In economics, inflation refers to an average increase in the price of all goods over a specific period of time. In the United States, two common methods of evaluating inflation include the Producer Price Index (PPI) and the Consumer Price Index (CPI). The PPI measures the costs of producing goods (for example, the price of supplies and raw materials, the costs associated with distributing goods, and other aspects of the production process), while the CPI focuses on changes in the retail prices of goods (in other words, the amount of money a consumer must pay to purchase a product). In addition to the PPI and CPI, economists often use a third means of measuring inflation rates, known as the Gross Domestic Product (GDP) deflator. Gross Domestic Product, or GDP, refers to the value of all products and services created in a nation over a period of time. Like the CPI, the GDP deflator measures changes in retails prices of goods; at the same time, however, the GDP deflator also evaluates changes in the types of goods consumers are buying. In other words, the GDP deflator tracks not only inflation but also the ways that inflation has an impact on consumer spending habits.

Thus, increases in the wholesale price of crude oil raise the cost of airline tickets as well as the costs of the many goods, such as farm produce, that need to be transported by truck. Fluctuations in crude-oil prices can be extreme. In 2003 it was priced at $25 per barrel, but by 2005 that figure had increased to $60 per barrel, and by July 2006 a barrel of crude oil cost $78.40. Although these prices were high, they still did not exceed the records set in 1980, when, factoring in the rate of inflation (the percentage by which prices in general have gone up), crude oil was selling for $90 per barrel.

Rising crude-oil prices had a significant impact on the American automobile industry. Before the price hikes many American consumers purchased large automobiles such as sport-utility vehicles (SUVs) and full-size pickup trucks, which used more gas than smaller cars. In reaction to the higher oil prices, sales of these vehicles began declining in 2005, while sales of hybrid vehicles (those that use gasoline and rechargeable electric batteries) increased. The effects of rising crude-oil prices were also felt in the delivery industry (which includes the companies UPS and FedEx); some delivery companies began adding a fuel surcharge and scaling back the scope of their deliveries.

$ Index of Leading Economic Indicators

What It Means

The Index of Leading Economic Indicators is a system of analysis that evaluates economic data in order to try to forecast future economic trends. An economic indicator, or business indicator, is a statistic expressing the performance level of a specific sector of the economy. By studying economic indicators, economists, business experts, and government officials are able to make informed predictions about whether the economy will be strong or weak in the foreseeable future.

Those indicators that tend to change before the overall economy does are called leading economic indicators, or LEI. Leading indicators are considered the most vital for predicting future economic tendencies. For example, when the average manufacturing workweek (which measures the number of hours per week that the average worker in the manufacturing industry spends at his or her job) goes down, economists can forecast an impending downturn in the manufacturing industry and possibly in the overall economy.

There are 10 principal categories of leading economic indicators. In making determinations about general economic trends, economists study shifts in all 10 categories and then analyze the composite data (that is, the data as a whole). For example, if the average workweek goes down slightly, but all other indicators rise, analysts will conclude that the economy is growing stronger.

The Index of Leading Economic Indicators was created by the Conference Board, a private nonprofit research group based in New York City. It began publishing the index in 1996. The index is announced once a month; it describes shifts in the 10 leading indicators in terms of percentage points, quantities, and dollar amounts, depending on the category. These factors are then combined (using complex statistical methods) into a single composite figure. The way this figure changes from month to month is intended to reflect whether the economy is strengthening or declining.

When Did It Begin

By the mid-1990s commerce officials under President Bill Clinton had begun to search for more accurate measures by which to gauge future economic trends. In 1995 the Bureau of Economic Analysis (BEA), a government agency that releases data about the overall status of the U.S. economy, decided to hire a private firm to oversee the monthly publication and distribution of economic indicators.

After reviewing proposals from a range of private companies, the BEA selected the Conference Board, a research firm based in New York, to assume responsibility for collecting, analyzing, and publishing data concerning various economic indicators.

Between October and December 1995 the monthly reports on economic indicators were released as a joint publication of the Conference Board and the BEA. On January 17, 1996, the Conference Board independently

Economists, business leaders, and governments all use the Index of Leading Economic Indicators to analyze major trends in the economy. One important indicator is the overall strength or weakness of the construction industry. © *Robert Maass/Corbis.*

released the Index of Leading Economic Indicators for the first time.

More Detailed Information

The Index of Leading Economic Indicators tracks changes in 10 categories of economic activity:

The "average manufacturing workweek" indicator measures the average weekly work hours of employees in the manufacturing industry over the course of a given month. This indicator reflects the overall productivity of the manufacturing industry.

The indicator for the "average number of weekly initial claims for unemployment insurance" tracks how many people file for unemployment insurance (the system by which money and benefits are paid to qualified unemployed individuals) over the course of a given month. By analyzing these statistics, experts can determine the overall direction of the job market. For example, a rise in the average weekly initial claims for unemployment insurance will likely reflect an increase in layoffs, a slowdown in hiring, or both.

"Manufacturers' new orders for consumer goods and materials" is an indicator that refers specifically to products used by consumers, such as motor vehicles, electronics, clothing, and groceries. It gauges whether wholesalers and retailers are ordering more or less of such goods than in the preceding month. This indicator reflects increases and decreases in demand for consumer goods.

Another leading indicator tracks manufacturers' new orders for nondefense capital goods, which are products used by manufacturers in the production of consumer goods. ("Nondefense" refers to the fact that goods produced for military use are not included.) When businesses spend money to improve their operations, it is a sign of a strong economy.

The indicator called "vendor performance—slower deliveries diffusion" monitors the speed at which companies receive supplies necessary to manufacture their products. A slowdown in delivery times typically means that there has been an increase in demand for supplies, which in turn reflects an increase in demand for products. In

ECONOMIC INDICATORS: LEADING, COINCIDENT, AND LAGGING

In addition to studying leading economic indicators, economists consider other factors when evaluating the overall state of the economy. There are three types of economic indicators: leading, coincident, and lagging. A leading economic indicator refers to a change in a specific sector of the economy that potentially foreshadows a more general economic shift in the future. Co-incident indicators, such as personal income, occur simultaneously with a business cycle (a period of expansion and contraction that occurs in an economy). A lagging indicator is a statistical measure that follows a more general shift in the economy. For example, a decline in business profits reflects a general slowdown in the overall economy, and it is therefore a lagging indicator of economic activity. Because they always come after significant economic shifts, coincident and lagging indicators have little value as far as predicting the economy's future.

other words, a slowdown in deliveries is a sign of a growing economy.

The building permits indicator reflects the number of residential building permits (permits obtained in order to begin the construction of homes) issued. This statistic measures overall activity in the residential-construction sector, and it usually changes before the other leading indicators do.

Another indicator measures the stock prices of 500 common stocks. Common stocks are those shares in a company or corporation most commonly owned by investors. By measuring the amount of money that people are investing in a range of common stocks, this indicator reflects the attitudes of investors toward the overall economy. It can also reflect changes in interest rates, which are fees that borrowers are charged for loans (the rate is a percentage of the loan amount). When interest rates rise, borrowing decreases, and fewer people invest in stocks.

The money supply, or M2 (designated as such because it is just one of various ways to define the money supply), indicator measures the amount of money available within an economy at a given time. Increases in the money supply result in decreases in interest rates, which tend to encourage consumer spending.

Another indicator, the "interest-rate spread between 10-year Treasury bonds and federal funds," gauges investor confidence in the long-term health of the economy by comparing the relative sizes of long- and short-term interest rates. A large discrepancy between these rates generally indicates that long-term economic growth will be difficult to achieve, while a narrower discrepancy suggests that the economy will become stronger.

The index of consumer expectations measures the attitudes of consumers toward future economic conditions. These statistics are measured by surveys through which analysts ask consumers for their opinions on both personal financial prospects and the prospects of the business community in general. For example, if a large number of consumers respond that they expect to see an improvement in both their financial situation and the overall business climate over the coming year, the index of consumer expectations will be high.

Recent Trends

In 1996, the first year the Index of Leading Economic Indicators was used, the index was listed as 100. This number rose steadily over the latter half of the 1990s, reaching 139 by May 2000. In the summer of 2000, however, the index began to stagnate. The figure remained at 139 through October 2000, and it subsequently began to fall considerably, descending to 111 by May 2003. After 2004, however, the index began to rise again, achieving a level of 138 by December 2006.

$ Standard of Living

What It Means

A standard of living is the level of material comfort, or quality of life, enjoyed by an individual or group. Factors that determine a standard of living include income, physical health, quality of the environment, housing availability, life expectancy, personal safety, and access to education, medical facilities, and social services. In economics standard-of-living measurements are typically used to gauge the level of material comfort attained by entire nations. These evaluations of the overall population do, however, take into consideration the standard of living of the individual (by measuring factors such as average incomes and life expectancies).

Opinions vary widely as to which factors are most important for measuring standards of living. Some experts determine a nation's standard of living by monitoring the per capita income (the average amount of money an individual earns) of the general population, while others measure levels of consumption, or the average amount of goods and services purchased by consumers. Other analysts pay closer attention to factors not directly related to economic forces. For example, some experts examine

Standard of living refers to the level of material comfort that an individual or society enjoys. In this photo taken in 1999, working class Romanians wait for a streetcar in Bucharest while a luxury sedan drives by. *AP Images.*

how government affects standard of living through programs and subsidies (a type of financial assistance) designed to raise the quality of life.

When Did It Begin

Although human beings have probably always pondered questions of material comfort when evaluating the quality of their lives, the modern concept of a standard of living as a measure of a society's health dates to the Enlightenment in Europe. The Enlightenment was a period of intellectual and scientific progress in the seventeenth and eighteenth centuries, during which philosophers and scientists attempted to explain human existence through reason and science instead of religion. Enlightenment thinkers developed the idea that nations could improve the quality of life of most of their citizens by improving government and social institutions so that they functioned according to rational principles.

The notion of an improved quality of life for society in general later informed the American Declaration of Independence (1776), which guaranteed all citizens a right to the "pursuit of happiness." This concept of

happiness was generally understood to mean the freedom to pursue economic prosperity. Indeed, by the 1840s the United States was one of the most economically powerful nations in the world, offering a higher standard of living for the individual than had existed at any other time in history.

More Detailed Information

Determining the standard of living of a nation as a whole is an inexact process. For the sake of simplicity, many economists focus solely on economic factors. One common criterion for measuring standard of living is per capita income (the average amount earned per person). A higher per capita income generally leads to increases in the amount of goods consumers can purchase, increases in access to quality health care, and increases in life expectancy, all of which are important factors in determining an individual's standard of living. By measuring per capita income, these economists reason, one can make an informed estimation of a country's overall standard of living.

In the final analysis, however, using per capita income to gauge a country's standard of living can be

THE UNITED NATIONS' UNIVERSAL DECLARATION OF HUMAN RIGHTS

Economists generally gauge a nation's standard of living (level of material comfort) by measuring that nation's per capita income, or average individual income. In its Universal Declaration of Human Rights, first published in 1948, the United Nations (an organization that seeks to facilitate cooperation among nations, ensure human rights, and pursue social justice) set forth a different notion of standard of living. Article 25 of the declaration states, "Everyone has the right to a standard of living adequate for the health and well-being of himself and of his family, including food, clothing, housing and medical care and necessary social services, and the right to security in the event of unemployment, sickness, disability, widowhood, old age or other lack of livelihood in circumstances beyond his control." This declaration represents the first time an international organization expressed the notion of a standard of living based on humanitarian, rather than purely economic, concerns.

misleading. For one, per capita income does not account for increases in the cost of living (the cost of basic necessities, such as food, clothing, and housing). If a nation's average cost of living increases at a higher rate than its per capita income, then standards of living might in fact be declining because people are spending more to live but not earning enough money to cover these increases. Furthermore, per capita income measurements neglect questions of how income is distributed among a country's citizens. In some instances a nation's per capita income rises because the income of the wealthiest sector of the population has grown at an extremely high rate, while the income of the poorest sector has remained stagnant. In other words, a nation with an increased per capita income may have also reached a higher overall standard of living, but the total number of individuals enjoying an acceptable standard of living may have actually declined.

At the same time, determining standards of living according to per capita income, or any other economic measurement, necessarily ignores other aspects of material comfort that are not determined by economic forces, such as environmental quality. These factors are controlled by government policy rather than the economy, and so they are not reflected in a nation's per capita income.

Recent Trends

Over the course of the twentieth century, the overall standard of living in the United States rose dramatically. This improvement was largely a result of the increase in poor Americans' standard of living, compared to increases in the standard of living of the richest segment of the population. At the beginning of the century, the income gap between the nation's wealthiest and poorest citizens was extreme (the total wealth of the richest 5 percent of Americans was eight times greater than that of the remaining 95 percent of the population); by the 1970s this gap had shrunk considerably (the richest 5 percent had five times the wealth of the bottom 95 percent).

In the 1980s, however, the discrepancy between the standards of living of the wealthiest and the poorest Americans began to grow again. The principle causes of this gap included weaker labor laws (which had traditionally safeguarded the legal rights of workers), relatively large pay increases for those with college degrees, and systematic cuts in government social programs such as welfare (financial assistance to poor Americans) and Medicaid (government-subsidized medical care).

The Individual Parts: Microeconomics

$ Overview: Microeconomics

What It Means

The field of economics is divided into two basic areas of study: macroeconomics and microeconomics (the prefixes *macro* and *micro* are derived from Greek words meaning large and small, respectively). Macroeconomics is the study of whole economies from the top down, with special attention usually paid to large-scale phenomena such as the money supply, unemployment (joblessness), inflation (the general rising of prices), and the economic growth of nations. For instance, the question "What is the effect on the American economy of increasing the amount of money in circulation?" would be very likely to come up in a college class on macroeconomics. Microeconomics, meanwhile, attempts to discover the way that each portion of the economy works; hence it focuses on the decisions of single individuals, business firms, industries, and levels of government. Questions such as "How high can gas prices go before Americans stop buying large automobiles?" are characteristic of microeconomics.

Because an understanding of individual parts of the economy naturally leads to an understanding of the whole economy, there is no clear line indicating where the concerns of microeconomics end and those of macroeconomics begin. Economists use their understanding of microeconomics to help answer macroeconomic questions, and vice versa. While the above question about Americans and gas prices might seem, at first glance, to belong in macroeconomics because it concerns a large group of people and at least two enormous industries, its focus on individual economic decision-making and on specific industries marks it as falling within the domain of microeconomics. This becomes clear if the question is rephrased: "How do individual Americans make decisions regarding high gas prices and large automobiles?" Microeconomic theory provides tools for predicting the behavior of buyers and sellers of gas, automobiles, and every other service and product sold on open markets (a market is any place where buyers and sellers come together to exchange goods and services).

The most basic of these tools, and the foundation for all economic study, are the principles of supply, demand, and pricing. In market economies supply and demand are opposing forces that determine price: a seller's desire to sell as much of a product as he can at the highest possible price competes against a buyer's desire to buy that product at the lowest possible price. The resulting market price represents a balancing of the desires of both sides and makes possible the most efficient allocation of resources for all concerned. When supply and demand interact in a pricing system free from distortion, sellers supply exactly as much of a product as buyers demand.

In the real world numerous complicating factors disturb the simplicity of the model outlined above. Economists apply supply and demand and other basic microeconomic principles to various industries and topics, but they usually have to adjust for various complications.

When Did It Begin

The issue of the decisions made by consumers and business firms has been a preoccupation of all economic thinkers since Adam Smith (1723–90) published *An Inquiry into the Nature and Causes of the Wealth of Nations* (1776), the book credited with establishing economics as a field of study. Smith, a Scottish philosopher, analyzed the interrelationships of supply, demand, and pricing (the concepts at the core of microeconomics), but he emphasized the role of supply in determining prices and quantities of output. The economist most responsible for codifying and popularizing the concepts of supply and demand as they are understood today was Alfred Marshall (1842–1924) of England, whose book *The Principles of Economics* (1890) was a standard textbook in the field up through the 1950s.

The division of economics into macro and micro disciplines came about in the wake of the theories that the British economist John Maynard Keynes (1883–1946)

ALFRED MARSHALL

"Economics has as its purpose firstly to acquire knowledge for its own sake, and secondly to throw light on practical issues. But though we are bound, before entering on any study, to consider carefully what are its uses, we should not plan out our work with direct reference to them."

ALFRED MARSHALL, *PRINCIPLES OF ECONOMICS*, 1890.

Why He Is Important

Alfred Marshall (1842–1924), English economist, was the most prominent figure in world economics from the late nineteenth century until his death. During the Victorian Era (which lasted from 1837–1901) the social, political, and economic fabric of England was transformed by the rapid expansion of large-scale manufacturing and the proliferation of railways. By the turn of the century, the country was approaching the height of its expansion and influence as a world power.

Marshall's work was largely devoted to building upon and refining the foundational ideas of classical economics put forth by Adam Smith, David Ricardo, Thomas Malthus, and John Stuart Mill. Still, Marshall distinguished himself from his predecessors by embracing the discipline not just as a way of analyzing of market functions but also as a unique window into human behavior. For Marshall, economics was to be viewed not as the "science of wealth" (a term coined by the American economist Amasa Walker [1799–1875] about 1866) but as a scientific approach to promoting social welfare.

This shift in perspective is evident in Marshall's most famous work, *Principles of Economics.* Published in 1890, it was hailed as a revolutionary text and institutionalized as the standard textbook on economics in England and the United States for nearly half a century.

Life

Alfred Marshall was born into a middle-class family in London on July 26, 1842. His father, a cashier at the Bank of England, had hoped that his son would become a clergyman in the Anglican church, but Marshall resolved to pursue an academic career. He received his degree in mathematics at St. John's College, Cambridge, and went on to explore his interests in ethics, psychology, and economics. In 1868 he was appointed to a special lectureship in "moral science" (or political economy) at St. John's. In the years that followed Marshall sought to bring mathematical rigor to the discipline and to make political economy a legitimate course of study at Cambridge. He had to leave the university in 1877, however, when his marriage to Mary Paley, a former student, put him in violation of the school's celibacy laws.

That year Marshall became a principal and professor of political economy at the newly founded University College, Bristol. In 1885 he returned to Cambridge as chair of political economy, remaining there until his retirement in 1908, due to health problems. In the latter years of his teaching career, Marshall exerted significant influence upon the development of his most brilliant student, John Maynard Keyes, who went on to become one of the greatest

presented in *The General Theory of Employment, Interest, and Money* (1936). Keynes offered a way of looking at whole economies that focused on the macro subjects listed in his book's title, and he suggested techniques whereby governments could affect economic growth on a large scale. As a result of the widespread influence of Keynes's theories, economists broke from past ideas about employment, interest (fees charged for borrowing money), and money, and they began to solidify the field that came to be called macroeconomics.

No such break from previous theories characterized the simultaneous establishment of microeconomics. Instead, the new label was used to refer to the bottom-up view of the economy made possible by well-established notions such as supply, demand, and pricing.

More Detailed Information

Microeconomic theory focuses on the choices made by individual actors on the economic stage. Choice is necessary because resources are scarce: there is never an unlimited supply of any product or service. The economic decisions that must be made in all societies fall into three basic categories.

1. What goods and services, and how much of each individual good and service, are going to be produced? For instance, how many T-bone steaks, personal computers, insurance policies, action movies, and retirement condominiums should be brought into existence?

2. How will all the various goods and services that consumers want be produced? For example, will a technology company rely on overseas labor for its software programming? Should electricity be generated by burning coal? Are assembly-line workers necessary in the automotive industry, or can most of the required manual labor be mechanized?

3. For whom are all of these goods and services being produced? Who benefits from economic activity, and to what degree? For instance, what should lawyers be paid? Cabdrivers? Schoolteachers? Executives? Housekeepers?

Microeconomics provides tools for analyzing how all of these choices are made. The most fundamental of these tools are the laws of supply and demand. The law of supply states that, as the price of a product rises, sellers

economists of the twentieth century. According to C. P. Sanger, another of Marshall's pupils, the professor regarded his students with affection and respect. He took their questions and ideas seriously and never condescended to them, trusting always their basic decency and intention to use their intellectual skills for the greater good of society. "Above all," Sanger recalled in 1926, "he was never dull." Still, however, Marshall was also widely known for certain shortcomings in his personality. Peter Groenewegen, an acclaimed biographer of Marshall, described him as "often humourless, pedantic, vain, selfish, ungenerous, [and] even egotistical." Even with such liabilities, many of his students, colleagues, and successors, including Milton Friedman, revered him as "incomparably great," both in the extreme diligence of his work and in the depth of his passion for economics.

Marshall worked assiduously until the end of his life, in spite of his continually declining health. He died at Balliol Croft, his home in Cambridge, on July 13, 1924, at the age of 81.

Work

Marshall is considered an important figure in the emergence of the neoclassical school of economics. Announced in the 1870s as "the new economics," the neoclassical school was largely devoted to microeconomics, the study of the economic behavior of individual markets, companies, or households rather than the economy as a whole. Its central premise is that the equilibrium between supply and demand determines almost every important variable in the economy, not only prices and production level but also total production, wages, consumption, saving, and the growth of the national economy.

Marshall devoted particular attention to understanding and measuring the precise interplay between supply and demand. Al-

though the concept of supply and demand was not new in economics, it was Marshall who transformed it from a rough intuitive idea to a scientifically predictable relationship that could be used as a tool to analyze price fluctuations and many other economic phenomena. Marshall's intensive study of supply and demand also led to his discovery of the concept of the "price elasticity of demand," an indication of how sensitive consumers are to changes in price.

Often referred to as the first "modern" economics textbook, Marshall's *Principles of Economics* encapsulates and codifies the principles of the neoclassical school. His other major works were *The Economics of Industry* (1879), written with his wife; *Elements of Economics of Industry* (1892); and *Industry and Trade* (1919).

Legacy

During his lifetime Marshall exerted direct influence over government policies concerning gold and silver, national currency, poverty relief initiatives, taxes, international trade, and other economic matters. At Cambridge in 1903 Marshall finally succeeded in his mission to establish a separate tripos (degree program) for economics (previously economics courses had been taught under the historical and moral sciences triposes), which led the university to become a preeminent center of study for the discipline.

The tools of analysis Marshall developed became the launching point for two generations of British and American economists, who devoted their careers to debating, interpreting, expanding, challenging, and revising the neoclassical doctrine. The enduring importance of his theoretical contributions is evident in the fact that so much of the content of introductory economics courses today is built around Marshall's work.

will be willing to sell more and more of it. The law of demand states that, as the price of a product rises, buyers will be less and less willing to buy it. The competing desires of buyers and sellers, in a market free from distortion, result in what is known as an equilibrium price. At equilibrium the desires of sellers and buyers are balanced, so that supply (the amount of a product produced by sellers) exactly equals demand (the amount of that product desired by buyers).

In a market economy, then, the market itself figures out what will be produced, how it will be produced, and for whom it will be produced. The market does this through the process described above, a process of gauging the opposing desires of the primary decision makers in the economy and encouraging them to make mutually beneficial choices. For instance, it is the combined desires of computer buyers and computer sellers that determine computer prices, and these interrelated forces also dictate virtually every other facet of the computer industry. Supply, demand, and pricing determine how many and what kinds of computers will be produced, the methods according to which computers must be produced, and the rewards that everyone involved in the computer industry stands to gain as a result of this market activity.

Economists use microeconomic analysis to examine real economic situations. They break down real-world market activity according to what they know about supply and demand. Based on past fluctuations of computer-industry supply and demand at various prices, for instance, an economist could offer a prediction about the industry's future. He or she might be able to tell us how many computers will be needed to satisfy demand in the coming months, what processes of production will be required to allow the industry to be profitable, and what kinds of salaries can be expected in the industry. This information would clearly be useful to investors and businesspeople involved in the computer industry. It would also be useful to the national government, which is charged with overseeing the economic well-being of the country.

Analyzing the basic relationships and decisions in the economy according to the laws of supply and demand is, it should be noted, a necessarily limited approach. The supply-and-demand model is an idealized form of market activity, a market free from distortion and inefficiency. Economists can account for some of the distortion and inefficiency that occurs in real markets. In fact, many of the specialized disciplines within microeconomics have arisen out of the study of particular distortions or out of the study of special cases that depart from the basic supply-and-demand model. Microeconomics cannot ever account for every particularity of the market, however. In any sector of the economy on any given day, the number of choices made, and the reasons that each economic actor made them, are dizzying. It would be all but impossible to record every such decision and motivating factor, much less build any coherent theories based on such an exhaustive portrait of an economic sector.

Microeconomics therefore intentionally simplifies market activity for the purposes of clarity and usefulness. Supply-and-demand theory allows economists to propose models, or simplified versions of real-world market activity, which are often rendered as diagrams. Once economists can model the central forces at work in any portion of the economy, they can predict future changes and encourage rational government policies. Because of the simplification necessary to make the leap from the real world to the realm of theory, there is always uncertainty in any economic prediction. Economists at the highest levels of government and academia frequently disagree on questions about the health of various industries or the economy as a whole.

Certain assumptions or simplifications of reality are particularly crucial to microeconomic analysis. One of these assumptions is that both buyers and sellers act rationally in pursuit of maximum gain. For example, each car buyer wants the lowest price possible for the model he or she wants to buy, and each car company wants to sell as many cars it can at the highest prices possible. Another important assumption that is often central to microeconomics is *ceteris paribus* (*ceteris paribus* is Latin for "other things remaining unchanged"), the assumption that everything other than the factor being studied remains constant. For instance, if we were relying on basic supply-and-demand theory to show us what happened when prices across the car industry increased by an average of $1,000 in four months, we might overlook for the moment such factors as consumer taste, assuming for simplicity's sake that no glaring change in taste occurred during those four months.

Recent Trends

Microeconomic analysis is the foundation of most of the more specialized branches of economics today. These branches include labor economics, which applies supply-and-demand theory to employers and employees, and international economics, which considers supply and demand as it relates to trade between nations. Agricultural economics applies microeconomic tools to the study of agricultural products, land, and labor; while the branch called industrial organization and regulation covers such topics as competition (or lack thereof) between firms, the role of trademarks, and all kinds of government regulations of firms. Public finance considers the role that

government intervention (in the form of taxes, laws, and spending programs) plays in markets. The discipline of welfare economics, meanwhile, represents perhaps the most comprehensive use of microeconomic theories among economic subfields. Welfare economics analyzes all forms of economic behavior in an attempt to determine whether market outcomes are beneficial to society as a whole.

SUPPLY AND DEMAND: THE RELATIONSHIP BETWEEN BUSINESSES AND CONSUMERS

$ Market

What It Means

In economics a market is a place or system that allows buyers and sellers of goods and services to interact with one another. Markets used to be specific physical locations. For instance, in the eighteenth century American farmers typically took their harvested goods to market, a site in a town where sellers and buyers gathered to do business. As the world modernized, the meaning of the term *market* expanded. The term still refers to such specific locations (a present-day example would be a flea market or a farmers' market), but in economics it more commonly refers to any geographical region or electronic arrangement in which buyers and sellers interact with one another to establish the same prices for the same items.

In present-day New York City, for example, there is a single market for real estate. The prices of houses and apartments across the city rise and fall together, depending on the collective action of all the buyers and sellers within that market. Though the real-estate market in another American city might be affected by national trends that similarly affect the New York real-estate market, the price of real estate differs dramatically from city to city. By contrast the market for shares of stock (a portion of company ownership that can be bought and sold) in American companies is global. A person in Japan who wants to buy stock in Microsoft will pay the same price as a person in Ohio.

All markets share one central characteristic: they supply a site where sellers and buyers can interact. The simple farmers' markets of the eighteenth century provided a place for the interaction of the forces of supply (the amount of any good or service that a seller is willing to sell at a given price) and demand (the amount of any good or service that buyers are willing to buy at a given price), just as the high-tech stock markets of today do. The competing desires of buyers and sellers, rather than a central authority figure or a government, are responsible for determining the prices of goods and services in any

In economics a market refers to a place or system in which people exchange goods and services. A market can refer to a particular type of commerce, such as the international steel market, or a specific location where products are bought and sold, such as this New York flea market. © *Gail Mooney/Corbis.*

market. Sellers want to make a profit, so the higher the price of any particular product, the more of it the seller tends to produce (the reverse holds true when prices fall). Buyers want to pay as little as possible, so the higher the price of a certain product, the less of it buyers tend to buy (again, the reverse holds true when prices fall). Prices therefore determine how much of any given product is manufactured. Prices also determine how (and how well) something will be produced, as well as the degree to which various people benefit from the economic activity that goes on in the market.

Capitalism, the dominant economic system in the world today, is built on two key pillars: the right of individuals to own private property and the reliance on markets, rather than any central authority, to dictate the production and distribution of goods and services. Markets therefore substantially determine the shape of the contemporary world.

When Did It Begin

Public marketplaces existed prior to the rise of capitalism, which occurred between the sixteenth and the eighteenth centuries in Europe. Before capitalism took hold,

however, much economic activity was directly controlled by ruling authority figures rather than by such market forces as supply and demand. While people bought and sold goods at marketplaces in the ancient and medieval worlds, the prices paid for goods and services were likely to have been set by rulers rather than by the competing interests of buyers and sellers. In such cases economic activity may have been motivated not by a desire for gain but by law. If a ruler demanded, for example, that a farmer grow wheat on his land and sell it for a certain price for the benefit of society, then that farmer had no choice but to engage in that activity and sell for that price.

Many economists agree, however, that public fairs held in medieval Europe were one origin of the market system. A farmer in fifteenth-century England might have been forced to hand over a certain amount of his crop to his aristocratic landlord, but he might also have engaged in the production of profitable sidelines, such as the brewing of beer or the making of cheese. This farmer might then have taken his surplus crop, together with the fruits of these side businesses, to a public fair, where he was free to sell his products to buyers for personal gain.

DO MARKETS FAIL?

Economists generally argue that markets (those places or systems that bring together buyers and sellers of goods and services) organize economic activity as efficiently as it is possible to organize it. There are, however, situations in which markets produce results that are unacceptable to society. In these cases some economists say that market failure has taken place.

One common type of market failure is the creation of a monopoly. When one business succeeds so well that it dominates its industry and can set prices and eliminate competitors, it is said to have a monopoly. Such a business will almost certainly seek to perpetuate its dominance, overriding the market forces (such as supply, or the amount of any good or service that a seller is willing to sell at a given price, and demand, the amount of any good or service that buyers are willing to buy at a given price) that normally regulate economic activity. The result is a loss of efficiency. Resources are used unwisely, products are priced unfairly, and potentially valuable innovations are stifled because of a lack of competition.

Another form of market failure is called an externality. An externality is any side effect of economic activity that is not accounted for by the pricing system. For example, a leather-goods factory that pollutes the river on its property may place a costly burden on society (because people in the area may have to pay higher taxes in order to clean the river and purify their drinking water) without factoring this cost into the price of leather goods. When markets work well, all such costs are accounted for in the price of products. The factory and the people who buy the leather goods, rather than uninvolved citizens, should be paying for the damage done to the river.

The rise of capitalism was caused by a complex set of factors. One of the most important of these factors was the centralization and growth of European nation-states between the sixteenth and the eighteenth centuries. European countries, which had formerly been divided into smaller kingdoms, became more unified during this time, and they competed against one another for power. This rivalry required raising large armies and colonizing land around the world, activities that could not be undertaken without vast amounts of money. Nations could produce more wealth by allowing individuals to own property and pursue a profit in various markets than by keeping ownership and wealth locked up in the hands of a small number of aristocrats (those belonging to a privileged class that lived partly on inherited family money).

More Detailed Information

At the foundation of all markets are the forces of supply and demand. Again, supply is the quantity of any good or service that sellers are willing to sell over a range of prices, and demand is the quantity of any good or service that buyers are willing to buy over a range of prices. The law of supply states that as the price of a good rises, sellers will want to supply more of that good because they want to maximize their profits; and the law of demand states that as the price of a good rises, buyers will want to buy less of that good because they want to keep as much of their money as possible to ensure their well-being. Through trial and error in a market situation, sellers and buyers measure their desires to sell and buy until eventually a price results that is acceptable to both. When this happens, the correct quantities of goods are produced in the most efficient ways, and both sellers and buyers get what they want.

For a concrete example of how markets distribute information and promote efficiency, imagine that an existing automobile company is introducing a new sports car. When the company attempts to calculate a price, it will first determine how much it must charge consumers in order to recover the money it has put into designing, engineering, producing, marketing, and distributing the new model. Beyond this basic level of costs, the company will want to maximize its profits, so it will set the highest price that the car market will bear, which requires keeping in mind the desires of consumers. Those consumers likely to be interested in the new-model sports car will probably not have an unlimited interest in it. If the model is unveiled and the price is generally seen as too high, consumers will look to other sports-car models or refrain from buying a car altogether. If the price is lower than it could be, given consumer demand for the car, the company will not maximize its profits.

Once the car model enters the market, consumers begin communicating to the car company through the amount of purchases they make. If, for instance, sales are disappointing at the first price set by the company, price X, then the market is sending the company a clear message that demand is weak at price X. Based on this information, the company will lower the price by several thousand dollars to price Y. At price Y sales pick up and remain steady over several months. Assuming that price Y still brings in an amount of money well above the car company's production costs, the company now understands how much it can charge, based on consumer demand, at the same time ensuring a satisfactory level of profits.

Further, the company will weigh this information against its own ability to make profits in other ways. For instance, if price Y represents a smaller amount of profit than the company can bring in by selling its economy-car models, then it may want to reduce the number of new sports cars it manufactures and increase the number of economy cars it produces. If the company has 10 different car models, it will use the information on each model transmitted to it via the market to make its future decisions about which models to produce, how many of them to produce, and how to produce them (balancing efficiency and quality).

This basic pattern holds true across the entire economy. Buyers and sellers communicate with one another through prices, and the exchange of information allows each to make the countless individual decisions that add up, every day, to the overall economy. Without markets this same exchange of information would be extremely time-consuming and inefficient, and very little economic activity (by contemporary standards) could take place.

Recent Trends

After the Great Depression (the severe economic crisis that impoverished much of the United States between 1929 and about 1939) people generally had less confidence in markets to regulate the economy and provide for the greater good. In response, the U.S. government began intervening in the economy as a matter of policy, hoping to prevent other dramatic crises in the future. This trend continued into the 1970s, but economic stagnation at that time was blamed on the very government intervention that had previously helped the country out of the Great Depression.

In the 1980s conservative politicians, such as President Ronald Reagan, routinely called for smaller government, the idea being that the smaller the size of the government, the less effect government could have on the economy. The belief that government is often harmful to the economy gained further momentum in the 1990s and the early years of the new century. While there are serious economic arguments to be made for and against government involvement in the economy, many people during this time simply took it on faith that free markets were always preferable to government-managed capitalism.

$ Supply and Demand

What It Means

Markets, the physical or virtual places where buyers and sellers come together, have the capability to determine the most efficient ways of meeting the needs of both the buyers and the sellers of a particular product. To understand how markets do this, it is essential to understand the workings of two independent and competing forces: supply and demand.

Supply refers to the amount of a particular product that sellers are willing or able to sell over a range of prices, and demand refers to the amount of a particular product that buyers are willing or able to buy over a range of prices. The law of supply states that, all other factors being constant, sellers will be willing to sell more and more of a particular product as prices for that product rise. The law of demand states that, all other factors being constant, buyers will purchase less and less of a particular

---

EQUILIBRIUM AND THE INVISIBLE HAND

Although buyers' and sellers' needs seem directly opposed to one another, markets, when functioning properly, allow both sides to satisfy their needs. Sellers try to see how high a price they can ask for their goods without deterring demand, and buyers try to see how little they can pay for a good and still get what they want. Through trial and error, all of the different sellers and buyers of any given product establish a single price at which the needs of both buyers and sellers are balanced. This price is known as the equilibrium price. At equilibrium, the amount of a product that sellers supply will equal the amount of that product that consumers demand.

The ability of a market to satisfy people whose desires fully contradict one another is an example of what the philosopher and political economist Adam Smith (1723–90) called "the invisible hand," or the ability of the free market, in which each individual is pursuing his own economic self-interest, to produce the greatest good for all people.

---

product as prices for that product rise. In the marketplace these two laws compete to determine the price at which any given product will be sold.

As a simple illustration of these principles, imagine that you make handcrafted coffee mugs to sell at a flea market every Saturday. Suppose that you have produced 100 mugs to sell initially, and on the first Saturday you arrive at the market with all of them. You set the sale price of your mugs at $8, but only 10 mugs sell. The next weekend, you slash the price of your mugs to $3, and all 90 of your remaining mugs sell within a few hours. This suggests that at the right price there will be demand for your mugs. You cannot, however, justify continuing to produce them at such a low price. You decide to make another 100 mugs that week and to sell them at $5 apiece the following weekend. It turns out that, at this price, you are able to sell all the mugs during the course of a market day, and you feel that $5 per mug justifies the amount of time and effort required to produce and sell 100 of them each week. The market price of $5 has been established by the opposing forces of supply and demand.

Supply and demand play a similar, if sometimes more complex, role in virtually all financial transactions. Together they form the backbone of all economies and of all economic theory.

When Did It Begin

The forces of supply and demand have no doubt always influenced markets in much the same way that they do today, but it was not until the eighteenth century that philosophers and economic thinkers began to analyze the

---

interrelated workings of supply, demand, and price in detail. Sir James Steuart-Denham (1712–80), the Scottish author of what is considered the first systematic work on economics (*An Inquiry into the Principles of Political Economy*, 1767), was the first to use the phrase "supply and demand" to explain how prices were established.

Another Scottish writer, Adam Smith (1723–90), discussed supply and demand at length in his landmark book *An Inquiry into the Nature and Causes of the Wealth of Nations* (1776), which helped establish and shape the emerging field of economics. But Smith believed that producers based the price of a good on what it cost them to make and bring the good to market and that consumers had little effect on price; this perspective has since been supplanted by the idea of the simultaneous interaction of supply and demand. The French mathematician Antoine-Augustin Cournot (1801–77) helped further the understanding of the interaction between supply, demand, and prices by devising a way of diagramming these forces at work in a market; today such diagrams, called supply and demand curves, are basic tools for economic analysis. Cournot's notion of supply and demand was integrated into the growing body of economic thought and was further refined by the British economist Alfred Marshall (1842–1924), whose *Principles of Economics* (1890) was a standard economics textbook from its publication until the mid-twentieth century. Basic supply-and-demand theory has changed little since Marshall's time.

More Detailed Information

The laws of supply and demand allow us to understand the interaction of supply, demand, and prices for a given product, assuming that all other factors remain constant. These laws tell us that, when prices rise, sellers are willing to sell more of a product while buyers are less willing to buy that product, and that it is the balancing of these forces that determines the price at which the product will be sold. The real world, however, rarely offers economic situations in which all factors except supply, demand, and price are constant. It is important, then, to note the numerous factors other than price that affect both supply and demand.

The chief factors, aside from a product's price, that can determine supply of that product are:

The number of sellers of that same product Variations in the number of sellers of a given product affect supply. For instance, if trade restrictions on beef from foreign countries were relaxed, the supply of beef in the United States would rise as a result of an influx of new, foreign sellers.

New technology that brings changes in production of that product Technological change makes it possible to increase supply drastically and to supply goods at a wider range of possible selling prices. For instance, the introduction of powerful personal computers into virtually every industry in the world has drastically increased the efficiency and cost of producing many goods, allowing for increased supplies of those goods.

The prices of raw materials as well as labor and other investments needed to operate a business If any of these prices drops, producers make higher profits and will want to produce more of a given product; correspondingly, if any of these prices rise, supply will decrease. If, for instance, the price of steel drops, carmakers can produce cars more cheaply and will be likely to increase supply.

Taxes and subsidies All businesses must pay taxes (money charged by the government to fund running the state or country). These ultimately represent an increase in a seller's expenses; therefore, they work like any other increase, such as an increase in raw materials. Governments also give subsidies (financial assistance) to some companies and organizations. Subsidies function in the same way as decreases in production costs, enabling an increase in supply.

Producers' expectations about future events Producers sometimes adjust supply when preparing for future events likely to affect business. If, for instance, farmers expect corn prices to rise in several months' time, they might decrease the current supply in order to have more corn on hand to sell later, at a higher price.

The prices of other goods the producer might be able to bring to market Companies are always balancing the profits they derive from a particular product with the profits they might derive by producing a different product. If a producer decides that he or she can make more money by reducing the supply of one product in favor of increasing the supply of another, that producer is likely to do so.

The chief factors, aside from the price of a given product, that can determine demand for that product are:

The number of buyers Increases or decreases in the potential consumers of a given product affect demand for that product. Take for example, the baby boom generation (those born roughly between 1946 and 1964). It is a much larger generation than preceding generations of Americans, so the demographic shift that will occur as baby boomers age might result in increased demand for condominiums in retirement communities.

Tastes and preferences in the culture at large Based on a variety of often obscure factors, consumers' desires sometimes shift dramatically and affect demand. Wool sweaters might suddenly become horribly unfashionable, reducing the demand for them in a short period of time.

Changes in income When people begin to make more money or fail to make as much money as they did previously, their consumption patterns change. Someone who gets a raise might stop buying frozen dinners and start going out to restaurants, decreasing the demand for one and increasing demand for the other.

Buyers' expectations When buyers themselves sense large-scale changes that might affect the price or availability of particular items, they sometimes adjust their consumption patterns as a means of preparing for the changes. For instance, if prospective homebuyers believe that home-loan rates are going to rise in the future, they might rush to buy homes by borrowing money from a bank at the current, lower interest rate (interest is a fee paid to borrow money; for home loans interest payments can add up to huge amounts over time).

Prices of competing goods or complementary goods Prices of goods that consumers view as alternatives to a given product affect the demand for that product. For instance, if the price of Pepsi dropped significantly, demand for Coke might drop as more soda drinkers choose Pepsi instead. Additionally, the prices of complementary goods (goods that are often bought in combination with, or consumed at the same time as, a certain product) affect demand for a product. A substantial rise in the price of gas, for instance, might decrease the demand for SUVs.

Recent Trends

Although the workings of supply and demand were first outlined by professional thinkers, mathematicians, and economists, almost everyone in the developed world today has an implicit understanding of the laws of supply and demand.

For instance, if you were trying to sell your house for $300,000, and no one made an offer after six months, you would hardly consider attempting to attract new buyers by raising the price. Although you might consult a real estate agent about the fine points, you would have no trouble deciding for yourself that it made sense, after six months in which no demand for your house had surfaced, to lower the price. If you dropped the price to $250,000, you would be doing so because you understood that, at that price, more people would be likely to buy it. This behavior demonstrates a clear understanding of the law of demand, even though you might not recognize it as such.

Similarly, if you were preparing to set up a lawn-mowing service in your town, you might ponder the price per hour that makes the time and effort of mowing lawns seem worthwhile to you. At $15 per hour you might be willing to mow the lawns of as many people as daylight would allow in a given week. At $10 per hour, however, you might only be willing to mow lawns for 20 hours each week, because you know that you could make that

much money per hour as a record-shop clerk, which requires much less physical effort. Although you might contemplate these figures purely in terms of your own comfort and desire for money, you would actually be basing your decision on the law of supply.

One of the reasons that these principles remain so central to economic theory is that they make so much intuitive sense. Although economists at elite universities typically master far more complicated concepts and mathematical operations than those represented by the above examples, virtually all of their work builds on the elegantly simple laws of supply and demand.

$ Elastic and Inelastic Demand

What It Means

The law of demand, one of the most important economic principles, looks at the way consumers react to changes in prices. It indicates that, as the price of a good or service increases, the quantity demanded for that good or service (that is, the desire for or need of it) will usually decrease. In other words, when something becomes more expensive, people will be less willing to buy it. Likewise, as the price of a good or service decreases, consumer demand for that good or service will usually increase (when something becomes cheaper, people will be more willing to buy it).

Just how responsive buyers are to price changes, however, can vary greatly. For instance, if the price of salt were cut, consumers would not be likely to buy more salt, but if the price of airplane tickets were cut, consumers would probably buy more of them. The measurement of the level of responsiveness is called price elasticity of demand. When the consumer reaction to a price change is strong, the demand for that good or service is called elastic (flexible). When there is a smaller reaction, the demand is said to be more inelastic (fixed). In our example, then, the demand for plane tickets would be more elastic than the demand for salt.

When Did It Begin

As capitalist economies (in which private individuals, not the government, own most businesses) have evolved over the centuries, economists have attempted to understand the relationships between supply (the amount that producers want to sell at a given price) and demand (the amount that consumers want to buy at a given price). In 1776 the Scottish philosopher Adam Smith published *The Wealth of Nations*, which served as the basis for what came to be called classical economics. In the book Smith generally assumed that price was determined by the cost of production (the total cost of everything that went into making a certain good) and that the demand for a good would increase when its price decreased and decrease as the price increased.

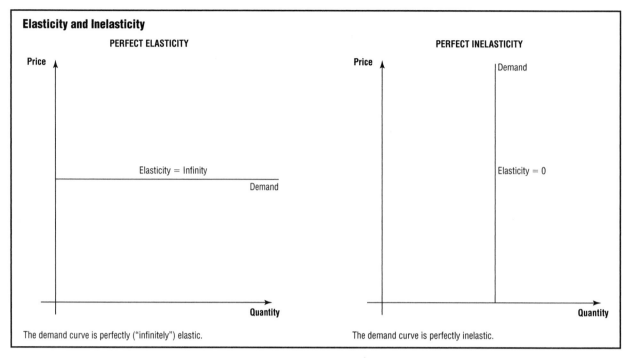

Elastic and inelastic demand measures how much consumer desire for a product is affected by changes in price. As these graphs show, perfect elasticity occurs when even the slightest change in price affects the quantity purchased by consumers, while perfect inelasticity refers to a scenario where customers demand the same quantity of a good no matter how much the price changes. *Illustration by GGS Information Services. Cengage Learning, Gale.*

The idea that the consumer's needs and wants affected the prices of goods and services arose during the late nineteenth century with a new school of thought called marginalism. The marginalists theorized that price, in addition to being set by the cost of production (as classical economics had asserted), is also determined by the level of demand. They believed that the level of demand, in turn, depends upon the amount of consumer satisfaction provided by individual goods and services.

The concept of elasticity of demand was introduced by English economist Alfred Marshall (1842–1924) in his book *Principles of Economics* (1890). He expanded upon the marginalists' ideas about demand, analyzing its varying degrees of responsiveness. Marshall also said that prices are determined by the interaction of supply and demand; he likened these two forces to the blades of a pair of scissors. Modern theories of supply and demand are still based upon this idea. Economists have created models that analyze the point where the amount that producers have available to sell (supply) matches up with the consumer desire for it (demand). This is known as the equilibrium point.

More Detailed Information

Various factors determine the elasticity of demand for goods or services. One such factor is available substitutes.

If one good or service can be consumed or used in place of another (in at least some of its possible uses), it is called a substitute good. Generally, the more substitutes for a particular good or service, the more elastic the demand will be. For example, if the price of beef increased by $1.00 a pound, consumers could replace their beef purchase with poultry, lamb, or pork. This means that beef is an elastic good, because an increase in price will cause a decrease in demand as consumers start buying more poultry, lamb, or pork instead of beef. If the price of meat as a whole were to go up, however, consumers would have fewer products to choose from to replace it in their diets. They would therefore probably not significantly reduce their consumption of livestock. This makes meat a more inelastic product.

Another reason elasticity varies among different goods and services is that some are more essential to consumers. The demand for goods that are necessities, such as food and transportation, is less sensitive to price changes because consumers would continue buying them even if the price increased; these goods are considered inelastic. Goods such as perfume and meals at restaurants, on the other hand, are considered elastic because consumers would be deterred from purchasing them if the cost of buying the product became too high.

Also influential is the proportion of a person's income spent on the good or service. Goods that make up a relatively small share of consumers' budgets tend to be more inelastic than goods for which consumers spend a sizable portion of their incomes. For example, if the price of oranges increased 20 percent, it might not dissuade a consumer from buying oranges. But if the price of a certain model of car increased 20 percent, that same customer, faced with the prospect of spending thousands of extra dollars, would be more likely to reconsider the purchase.

Time can also affect the elasticity of demand. Generally, demand is more inelastic in the short term than it is in the long term. Consumers need time to react to price changes, and the more time they have to react, the more elastic the demand for the good or service. For instance, if the price of gas suddenly doubled, at first most people would continue to buy the same amount of gas because they consider it a necessity. In this case gasoline would be an inelastic commodity. If, however, the price for gas remained high, over the course of time people could reduce their gas consumption by seeking out other options, such as taking commuter trains or buying more fuel-efficient cars. The demand for gas, which started out as inelastic, will have then become more elastic in the long term.

Recent Trends

Beginning in the 1990s sales of personal computers and other electronic products rose dramatically, and competition between companies was intense. Because of the large availability of substitutes, or competing models, demand for electronic products tended to be elastic.

In the market for video game consoles, for example, demand was usually highly elastic when a product was first introduced. Manufacturers had to persuade buyers to choose their new product instead of their competitors'. As a result, some manufacturers resorted to "penetration pricing," which meant that the new console was introduced at a relatively low price with the hope of attracting a large number of buyers. Often the price was set so low (compared to how much each console cost to produce) that the manufacturer did not actually profit from the console sales. For instance, when Sony released its Playstation 3 in 2006, it charged $600, but each console actually cost an estimated $900 or more to manufacture. Like every company in the industry, Sony was counting on making its profits from sales of Playstation 3 software once it had gotten consumers to commit to the system.

Whereas manufacturers tended to underprice their consoles, they typically inflated the prices of the games themselves. This was possible because most gaming software was designed for a specific system; an Xbox owner, for instance, would have no use for a Playstation game. The console owner thus had fewer available substitutes when shopping for games, making the demand

DETERMINING ELASTICITY

To show the degree to which demand (consumers' desire for a particular good or service) reacts to changes in price, economics uses a model called a demand curve. This tracks the quantity of a good or service that consumers want to buy at any given price. The demand curve can be represented on a graph as a line or a curve by plotting the quantity demanded (shown on the horizontal part of the chart) at each price (the vertical part of the chart).

The demand curve is always downward, or negatively, sloping, indicating that when the price of a good or service rises, consumer demand for it decreases. If a small increase in price results in a significant decrease in the quantity demanded, the demand curve will flatten and become more horizontal. The flatness of the curve indicates that the particular good or service is elastic. If the quantity of the good demanded changes little as the price changes significantly, the demand curve is more upright, and the good is considered inelastic.

Elasticity of demand can also be determined by a mathematical equation: elasticity equals percentage change in quantity divided by percentage change in price. If elasticity is greater than or equal to one, the curve is considered to be elastic. If it is less than one, the curve is said to be inelastic. This approach is useful when comparing the elasticity of different products.

for the software more inelastic (less sensitive to price changes).

$ Marginal Utility

What It Means

Marginal utility is a concept used by economists to explain how consumer desire plays a role in determining prices for specific products and services. In economics the term *utility* refers to the amount of satisfaction a consumer receives from a specific good or service. From an economic standpoint, the usefulness of an object has no role in determining its utility; rather, utility is a measure of how much the consumer wants the object.

A consumer's desire for a product usually changes as he or she obtains more of it. For example, while a very thirsty consumer will derive a high level of satisfaction from one bottle of water, he or she will probably gain less satisfaction from a second bottle and even less from a third. Each additional unit thus provides less utility.

The term *marginal utility,* then, is used to describe the amount of satisfaction a consumer receives from each additional unit of a good that he or she acquires. It is called *marginal* because it applies to the margin (or difference) between units. In the case of the thirsty consumer, the water is said to have a declining marginal utility because each additional unit acquired is less

MARGINAL UTILITY AND SCARCITY

The term *marginal utility* refers to the level of satisfaction provided by a single additional unit of a particular product or service. It is a translation of the German word *Grenznutzen* (literally, "border use"), which was coined by the Austrian economist Friedrich Freiherr von Wieser (1851–1926). Wieser's idea of marginal utility arose out of his investigations into the concept of scarcity, or the circumstances under which the resources of a society are limited. According to Wieser, scarcity plays a central role in determining the marginal utility, and therefore the price, of specific goods.

For example, water is absolutely essential to human life, so people derive a great deal of satisfaction (in economic terms, utility) from consuming it. Despite its high utility, however, water is typically not expensive. This is because water is plentiful enough to meet the basic needs of many people, and after those needs are met, additional units will be used for less important uses, such as in car washes and swimming pools. Those units have a far lower marginal utility than the first few units, which sustain life. Wieser argued that it is the marginal utility of the least important use of a good that determines its price. Under these circumstances, therefore, the price of water remains low. If water were suddenly to become scarce, however, people would be driven to hoard it in case of continued shortages. They would skip the car washes and leave swimming pools empty. According to Wieser's theory, in this case the price of water would be high because the least important uses of water would have been eliminated.

desirable than the one before it. A good is considered to have constant marginal utility if the consumer continues to gain a similar amount of satisfaction from each additional unit he or she purchases. In most cases, a product's marginal utility will diminish with additional units, until that product has little to no utility for the consumer.

According to the theory of marginal utility, prices are determined by subjective forces (namely, consumer desire) in addition to objective ones (for example, labor costs). This concept became one of the foundations of the law of supply and demand, the economic principle that explains how prices in a free-market economy are determined.

When Did It Begin

The concept of marginal utility arose in response to what is known as the "diamond-water paradox." This was a dilemma that was first described by Scottish political economist Adam Smith (1723–90) in his landmark study *An Inquiry into the Nature and Causes of the Wealth of Nations* (1776). The diamond-water paradox asks a basic question: Why is water, which is absolutely essential to

human existence, less valuable than diamonds, which have no function in maintaining life?

Smith argued that the price of a certain good was ultimately determined by labor. Producing water required relatively little labor because it was plentiful and therefore easy to acquire; diamonds, on the other hand, demanded a great deal of labor to obtain. In Smith's view, the difference between the amount of labor required to obtain water and the amount required to obtain diamonds explained the difference in price.

Economists in the nineteenth century, however, found Smith's explanation inadequate because it failed to account for the role that consumer desire played in determining a product's price. They believed that a product's utility affected price, but they still found it paradoxical that a product such as water, which has a high level of utility, costs less than diamonds. These economists realized that the paradox could be solved by taking into account the amount of the product that a consumer already possesses. This developed into the theory of marginal utility, which stated that price was determined not by the utility of the first unit of a good (a person with no water and no diamonds would get more satisfaction from a glass of water than a diamond) but by how much consumer desire changed as additional units were acquired.

More Detailed Information

Economists developed the theory of marginal utility to describe the way that the desirability of a particular good changes as a consumer acquires more of that good and therefore to explain why certain goods are more expensive than others.

In the case of water, a consumer's desire for water diminishes as his or her thirst is quenched. The first bottle of water has a significant marginal utility for the thirsty consumer. The second bottle is also desirable if the person is still thirsty, but probably not as desirable as the first bottle; thus, the second bottle has less marginal utility than the first. The third bottle is even less desirable, because at this point the person is not really thirsty; so this bottle's marginal utility is lower than that of the second one. The fourth bottle may bring the consumer no satisfaction at all, because he or she cannot even swallow any more water, and the same with the fifth, sixth, and every additional bottle after that. In this example, each additional bottle has been less desirable than the one before it. With the addition of the fourth bottle of water, the marginal utility has reached zero: the consumer derives no additional satisfaction from that bottle.

On the other hand, while diamonds have no practical use to consumers, their rarity, combined with their beauty and allure, makes them extremely desirable to consumers. This high level of desirability gives them a high marginal utility, meaning that each additional diamond a person acquires continues to provide the same, or nearly the same, level of satisfaction (that is, utility) as the one before it.

Recent Trends

In one respect, the theory of marginal utility rests on a simple premise: that consumers have a clear idea of what they want (in other words, of what objects have utility to them) and make their spending decisions with the aim of maximizing the overall satisfaction they derive from their purchases. The assumption is that, if a consumer spends money on a particular object, it is because he or she has rationally decided that the object has a level of utility greater than or equal to the price of the object.

Over the years, however, a number of economists have disputed the assertion that consumer desire is inherently rational. They argue that consumers often fail to maximize their overall satisfaction because their desire for a good can in fact lead to irrational economic judgments.

The early twenty-first century saw the emergence of a new theory called neuroeconomics, which set out to challenge the notion that economic decisions are made rationally. Neuroeconomics combines neuroscience (the study of the human nervous system), psychology (the study of human thought and behavior), and traditional economics to try to understand how the brain makes economic decisions. Whereas supporters of the marginal utility theory argue that all economic decisions, no matter how unreasonable they might seem, have a rational basis, neuroeconomists assert that certain poor economic decisions are inherently irrational. According to neuroeconomics, it is only by trying to develop a science of irrational consumer behavior that economists can hope to understand the real impetus for certain economic decisions.

$ Economic Shortage

What It Means

An economic shortage occurs when sellers do not make enough of a product to satisfy those who want to buy it at a given price. A common reason for a shortage is that the price of a good is too low: as prices fall, sellers lose the incentive to sell goods because their profits decrease, whereas buyers are increasingly willing to buy products because they save money. In a market economy, in which decisions about selling, buying, and pricing goods are made by businesses and consumers rather than being imposed by governments, economic shortages tend to be eliminated naturally.

If, for example, a clothing company introduces a new line of jeans selling for $25 a pair, and stores immediately sell out of the initial production run of 10,000 pairs, the company, realizing it could make more money, might raise the price of jeans to $35, at which price it would be willing to manufacture 20,000 pairs. If these, too, sell out

immediately, the company will raise the price still higher, and so on, until its willingness to supply jeans matches consumers' willingness to buy them. In this way, market economies avoid economic shortages.

But if the price of jeans were to rise so high that ordinary people could no longer afford them, the government could intervene to keep jeans affordable. It could institute a price ceiling, declaring that no company can charge more than $25 for its jeans. Faced with limited profits, however, the company may be unwilling to manufacture more than 10,000 pairs, even though 50,000 people want to buy them at this price. In this situation the price ceiling has caused an economic shortage, which will continue to exist for as long as the government maintains the ceiling. People may have to wait in line for jeans, buy them on the black market (that is, illegally), or procure them through personal connections. If these problems become too intense, the government may seek to deal with the shortage through rationing. This would entail restricting the distribution of the jeans, perhaps by giving one group of people the right to buy jeans on certain days and another group the right to buy jeans on the remaining days.

Most economists agree that price ceilings are almost always a bad idea, because the problems caused by economic shortages are usually more numerous and troublesome than the problems the price ceilings were supposed to correct.

When Did It Begin

Economic shortages were found most commonly in planned or command economies, in which a central government or other authority sets prices and controls the amounts of goods and services that are produced. The world's earliest civilizations, such as those in ancient Egypt, Greece, Babylon, and China, were characterized by planned economies. While planned economies are good at accomplishing large tasks, such as building the Egyptian pyramids or the Great Wall of China, they are not able to respond effectively to changes in supply (the amount of a good that sellers are willing to provide at a given price) and demand (the amount of a good that buyers are willing to buy at a given price). When demand is greater than supply, an economic shortage exists. In a planned economy fixed prices usually mean that shortages cannot be solved.

In the sixteenth through eighteenth centuries, planned economies began giving way to market economies (in which prices are determined through the interactions of buyers and sellers). Economics as a discipline emerged during the late eighteenth century, when people began to study how a market economy regulates itself. The understanding of supply and demand that economists have today was fully developed by the late nineteenth century, but this understanding did not result in the end of economic shortages. In a market economy

An economic shortage occurs when consumers are willing and able to buy more of a product than is being produced. In 1973, when oil-producing nations cut off their supply of oil to the United States for political reasons, there was a major shortage of gasoline, and people had to wait in long lines to fuel their cars. *AP Images.*

such shortages are solved by market forces (supply and demand tend to adjust until they meet at an equilibrium point). Nevertheless, numerous factors, such as political goals, wars, and the desire to aid the poor, can lead governments to limit prices. Although this almost always results in economic shortages, most ordinary people do not think like economists. Instead, they welcome government intervention that limits prices, because it appears that such policies will simply help people save money.

More Detailed Information

In everyday life, people use the word *shortage* to describe any situation in which a group of people cannot buy what they need. For example, a lack of affordable homes is often called a housing shortage. In economic terms, however, this is not considered a shortage; in any market economy there will always be people who cannot afford certain products. The term *economic shortage* means something more specific; it is a situation in which people who want to buy a product at its current price cannot satisfy that desire. In other words, a shortage results from an imbalance between demand (how much of a product or service consumers want to and are able to buy) and supply (how much of that product or service is actually available for purchase).

In a market economy lowering the price of a good will typically cause an increase in the quantity demanded for that good, because more people can afford to buy it. On the seller's side, lowering the price of a good generally decreases the quantity supplied, because sellers, knowing they will make smaller profits, will be less motivated to supply that good. When the price of a good is too low, a shortage results: buyers want more of the good than sellers are willing to supply at that price.

When markets are functioning properly, economic shortages should be temporary because prices theoretically move toward equilibrium, a point at which supply and demand are balanced. If there is a shortage, the high level of demand will enable sellers to charge more for the good in question, so prices will rise. The higher prices will then motivate sellers to supply more of that good. At the same time, the rising prices will make demand go down. Sellers will continue to increase prices until supply matches demand.

When economic shortages persist, it is usually because a central authority (in today's world, a government) has imposed a price ceiling. A price ceiling is a maximum amount that can be charged for a particular product. During persistent shortages people must wait in line for products or pursue them through extralegal means, such as bribery or smuggling.

For example, in the former Soviet Union, which was founded in the 1920s with the intent of distributing economic benefits equally among its citizens, the government controlled prices and made decisions about how much of a given good to produce, and by what means. As the Soviet economy grew and modernized, it became common for the nation to experience shortages and surpluses (a situation where there is more supply of a good than demand for it). Ordinary citizens often had to wait in lines to acquire such basic necessities as cars, housing, and clothing.

While the United States embraces the market economic system more fully than most other developed countries, it too has used price ceilings throughout its history. During World War I (1914–18) and World War II (1939–45), it was common for consumer demand to outstrip supply. This happened because companies were devoting more of their resources to making war materials and less to making consumer goods. In response consumers rushed to stock up on goods, which caused prices to rise quickly. In order to keep prices from getting out of control, the government adopted price ceilings. Many economists believe, however, that the price ceilings worsened the imbalance between supply and demand, resulting in more severe economic shortages. During the first two World Wars as well as the Korean War (1950–53), the U.S. government had to use rationing to manage the problems caused by economic shortages, restricting the amount of goods people could buy and the frequency with which they could buy them.

If the government allowed prices to go up instead of imposing a ceiling, supply and demand would be more likely to balance one another out. On the demand side, people would find substitute products. For example, in an oil shortage consumers might use more fuel-efficient cars or alternative fuels, which would result in reduced demand for oil. Meanwhile, on the supply side, companies would produce more oil as prices rose, trying to reap the benefits of increased profits. For example, the oil companies in a shortage situation would respond to higher prices by working harder to produce oil, which would result in an increased supply of gasoline. Eventually supply and demand would probably approach equilibrium.

Recent Trends

The most notable economic shortages in recent U.S. history occurred during the 1970s. The first of these took place in 1973, when oil-producing Arab nations cut off the supply of oil to the United States in response to American support of Israel (which was at war with Syria, Egypt, and other Arab countries). The reduced supply of

PRESIDENT CARTER AND THE OIL SHORTAGE

In 1979 political turmoil in the Middle East interrupted the supply of oil to the United States, causing what is called an economic shortage. In other words, there was less oil available than Americans wanted to purchase in the form of gasoline and oil-intensive utilities such as electricity. When demand for a product is higher than the supply of that product, as in this case, the price of the product typically rises, and this happened with gasoline prices in the United States. President Jimmy Carter (in office 1977–81) responded to the increasing price of oil with price ceilings on gas (limits on the price that could be charged for a gallon of gas). In July of that year, he also gave a famous speech in which he asked Americans to turn down their thermostats in order to conserve electricity, and he had solar panels and a wood-burning stove installed in the White House to reduce his own consumption of oil.

Carter lost his bid for reelection in 1980, partly because the oil shortage had damaged the nation's economic climate. His successor, Ronald Reagan (in office 1981–89), had the solar panels and wood-burning stove removed when he moved into the White House.

oil led to skyrocketing gasoline prices in the United States, and President Richard Nixon (in office 1969–74) tried to halt the increases by instituting price ceilings. Economists generally believe that this exacerbated the shortage. Had oil prices been allowed to rise as high as the market dictated, people would have been forced to curtail their gasoline consumption until this restricted amount of demand matched the supply shortage. Likewise, the higher prices rose, the more likely oil companies would have been to supply more gas, thus alleviating the shortage.

In 1979 a crisis in the Middle East again caused an economic shortage. The U.S. oil supply was interrupted by a revolution in Iran that led to the takeover of the country by the religious leader Ayatollah Ruhollah Khomeini (1900–89). The shortage of oil resulted in increasing gas prices and an attempt by the U.S. government to control them through a price ceiling. Again, the price ceiling is believed to have worsened the gasoline shortage.

Since the two oil crises in the 1970s, the U.S. government has generally refrained from using ceilings to control prices that are rising too quickly. Instead, the government's central bank, the Federal Reserve System (often called the Fed), limits the growth of the money supply (the amount of money in circulation) to stop the rise in prices. In general, the less money there is in circulation, the less demand there will be for goods and services, because people have less to spend. Therefore, by cutting back the money supply, the Fed reduces demand, prompting prices to fall. This technique for controlling prices is generally believed to be a better way to manage the economy than the adoption of price controls, which lead to imbalances between supply and demand.

$ Economic Surplus

What It Means

In order to understand the concept of economic surplus, it is important first to define its two component parts: consumer surplus and producer surplus.

A consumer is an individual who purchases products and services. Before making a purchase, a consumer typically decides how much he or she is willing to spend on a particular good. For example, a college student may decide that a compact disk (or CD) is worth no more than $15. If the price of the CD is $18, the college student will not buy it; if, on the other hand, the CD costs $10, the college student will not only purchase it but will also feel as if he got a good deal in the bargain. The difference between the maximum amount the college student would have been willing to spend ($15) and the amount he ended up spending ($10) is $5. In economic terms, this amount is known as consumer surplus.

A producer, on the other hand, is the individual or company that manufactures products and services. When a producer sells a product, it must determine a price for that product. Imagine that the company that makes the CD must spend $5 to manufacture, market (for example, through advertising), and distribute each CD. The CD producer does not want to lose money selling its product, and so $5 is the minimum amount it would be willing to charge for each CD; to sell it for anything less would quickly put the company out of business. Because the CD producer wants to earn a profit, however, it will want to sell the CD for substantially more than $5. Now, a producer would gladly charge $15, $25, or even $100 for a CD if consumers were willing to spend that much (and if there were no competing businesses offering lower cost CDs). Since most consumers would consider those amounts too expensive, however, the CD producer must establish a price that will be attractive to a large number of consumers. If that price is $10, then the CD manufacturer will earn a profit of $5 on each CD. That profit is also known as the producer surplus.

Generally speaking, then, economic surplus refers to the aggregate (in other words, combined) surplus benefit enjoyed by both consumers and producers in an economic transaction. Under ideal conditions, both consumers and producers would enjoy the maximum financial benefit possible from the goods they buy and sell. The point at which a price stabilizes in an economy, so that both consumers and producers receive maximum surplus, is known as the market equilibrium.

When Did It Begin

The modern theory of consumer surplus was first developed by the English economist Alfred Marshall (1842-1924). In his landmark work *Principles of Economics* (1890), Marshall examines the relationship between the utility—in other words, the level of satisfaction—a consumer receives from a particular product and the amount of money that consumer is willing to pay for additional units of that product. To illustrate his theory, Marshall considers a man buying tea. In Marshall's example, the man is willing to pay 20 shillings (and no more) for a pound of tea. When the price of tea is 20 shillings per pound, the man will purchase only one pound of tea. If, however, the price of tea is 14 shillings a pound, then the man will decide to purchase two pounds of tea. Even if 14 shillings represents the maximum amount of money the man is willing to spend on a second pound of tea, he has still derived a "surplus" of satisfaction, in the amount of 6 shillings (that is, the difference between the 20 shillings he would have paid for a pound of tea and the 14 shillings he actually spent) for the first pound of tea.

Looked at another way, if the man is willing to pay 20 shillings for the first pound of tea, and 14 shillings for a second pound, then he is willing to pay a total of 34 shillings for two pounds of tea; in paying only 28 shillings for two pounds of tea, the man enjoys a consumer surplus

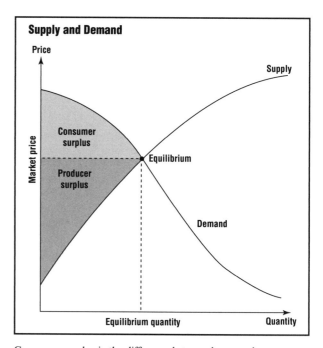

Consumer surplus is the difference between how much consumers are willing to pay for a product and what they actually pay; producer surplus, also known as profit, is the difference between the cost of producing a good and the price of the good. These ideas are combined in the concept of economic surplus, which is used to determine the efficiency of a market and how much consumers and producers are benefiting from it. *Illustration by GGS Information Services. Cengage Learning, Gale.*

of 6 shillings. Marshall then examines what might happen in the event that tea costs only 10 shillings per pound. Following the above framework, if the man purchases two pounds, his consumer surplus will rise to 14 shillings: the amount he is willing to pay (34 shillings) less the amount he actually pays (20 shillings). According to Marshall's theory, this surplus will never decline, even as the man decides to purchase additional pounds of tea. For example, if a third pound of tea is worth 10 shillings to the man, he still enjoys a surplus of 14 shillings if he purchases a third pound of tea: the 44 shillings he would have been willing to pay for three pounds, less the 30 shillings he paid. In a later chapter of *Principles of Economics,* Marshall explores a similar notion of producer surplus, focusing on the amount of value a producer receives by selling a product at a certain price. Taken together, the concepts of consumer and producer surplus form the foundation of what modern economists call welfare economics (a theory of economics that focuses on the general well-being, or welfare, that individuals experience under certain economic conditions).

More Detailed Information

Economic surplus is closely related to the law of supply and demand. Supply refers to the quantity of a given product that producers are able (or willing) to sell over a range of prices, and demand refers to the quantity of a product that consumers are willing to buy over a range of prices. Since producers sell a product in order to earn as much money as possible (that is, to maximize producer surplus), and consumers buy a product with the aim of saving as much money as possible (thereby maximizing consumer surplus), the product's price ultimately plays a key role in determining supply and demand. As the price of a product goes up, fewer consumers are willing to purchase it; in other words, demand decreases. Conversely, higher prices will make it desirable for producers to increase supply of their product. According to this model, producers and consumers are at cross purposes: producers want high prices, and consumers want low prices. In an efficient market these conflicting goals achieve a middle ground, so that the needs of both producers and consumers are satisfied. In other words, if supply and demand are balanced—that is, when a large number of consumers are able to purchase a product at a good price, and producers are able to earn a profit by selling to a large number of consumers—then an economic surplus for both consumers and producers will result. In this way, supply and demand work together to determine, and stabilize, the price of a particular good.

Recent Trends

Unfortunately markets never achieve ideal efficiency. Various outside factors, known as externalities, can disrupt the balance of supply and demand in ways that can

DEADWEIGHT LOSS

Economic surplus is a general term for the monetary gain enjoyed by both producers and consumers in an economic transaction. For producers a surplus occurs when a product is sold for more than the cost of producing it; consumers enjoy a surplus when they are able to purchase a product for less money than they would have been willing to pay for it. Under ideal economic conditions—that is, when an economy is running on maximum efficiency—both consumers and producers will enjoy financial benefits from participating in a transaction. Of course, economic conditions are never ideal, and consumers and producers do not always receive the benefits they should, in theory, receive. In economic terms the cost of economic inefficiency is known as deadweight loss. There are many causes of deadweight loss, among them taxation, government-imposed production limits, and monopolistic pricing (which occur when a producer has no competition and can therefore set an artificially high price for its products).

have a negative impact on economic surplus. In economic terms externalities refer to the effects that an economic activity can have on individuals or groups who do not directly participate in the economic activity. In some cases an externality can be positive, as when a manufacturer opens a new factory, creating jobs and boosting the economy of a specific community in general. In other instances, however, externalities can have a damaging effect on the economy. In recent decades one externality that has exerted a devastating impact on the economy is pollution. In the manufacturing process some degree of pollution is inevitable. Producers must consume fuel in order to operate machinery, which creates air pollution; production also creates waste, which increases the size of landfills and subsequently threatens the ecology of a community or region. In certain respects pollution can undermine the positive effects of an economic surplus by diminishing the overall quality of life of the community. In addition, health problems resulting from pollution can have a direct impact on the economic well-being of a community; for example, lost work time can lead to decreased production while also eroding the purchasing power of the individual consumer who is unable to work to his or her full capacity. In this scenario both consumer and producer surplus are diminished.

$ Income and Substitution Effects

What It Means

The income effect and the substitution effect are distinct but closely related principles in the study of economics. Both effects can be measured when a person's income changes (when he or she begins taking in either more or less money) or when the price of a good changes. According to the principle of the income effect, if a person has more money to spend, that person will purchase more goods. Two factors can cause a person to have more money to spend: he or she can begin taking in more money (from an increase in salary, for instance), or the price of goods that a person normally buys can fall. The latter will allow a consumer to buy more, even though income has not changed. For example, if one Saturday morning a shopper noticed that the price of beef had dropped from $5 per pound to $4.50 per pound, that shopper would likely purchase more beef than he or she normally buys because the price was lower.

The substitution effect is slightly more complicated because it concerns at least two items that are similar in some way and are of equal, or nearly equal, value to the consumer. According to the principle of the substitution effect, if the price of the first item (the one the consumer normally buys) goes up, but the price of second item remains the same, the consumer will be more likely to substitute the second item for the first. To understand the substitution effect, consider a person who eats lunch at the same cafeteria everyday. Normally at this establishment, both ham and turkey sandwiches cost $5. This person likes ham sandwiches as much as he likes turkey sandwiches but nonetheless orders turkey sandwiches more often than he orders ham sandwiches. If the cafeteria were to raise the price of turkey sandwiches to $5.50 per sandwich but keep the price of ham sandwiches the same, this person (assuming that his income remained the same) would likely substitute ham sandwiches for turkey sandwiches.

Income and substitution effects also exert a powerful impact on an economy's labor supply. For example, imagine a person in an office making $10 per hour who is offered two options: to work 20 hours a week, thus earning $200 each week, or 30 hours a week, raising her pay to $300. If she chose the schedule of 20 hours instead of 30 hours, she would lose the possibility of making $100 extra per week. But if her pay were to increase to $15 an hour, her choice between 20 hours and 30 hours per week would look different; with the first she would make $300, and the second, $450. Thus, if she chose to work 20 hours instead of 30 hours per week, she would now lose $150 per week ($450 - $300), not $100. In other words, as her wage rises, the cost of not working more hours increases, and she might be less likely to choose free time over additional pay. As a result, an increase in wages makes some people want to work more hours. A higher wage rate also draws some people who do not work into the labor market (for example, a stay-at-home parent might find it worthwhile to work at a higher wage but will stay home with the children if only low wage jobs are available).

When Did It Begin

The income effect and substitution effects are part of a larger set of ideas known collectively as consumer theory, which was formulated by several economists researching and writing in various countries throughout Europe in the second half of the nineteenth century. Consumer theory attempts to chart buying patterns by studying the relationship between consumer preferences and consumer budget constraints (the combination of goods and services that a consumer can afford, depending on his or her income and the prices of those goods and services).

Manufacturers identified the need to understand consumer buying patterns during the second half of the nineteenth century. By the end of the Industrial Revolution (which began in the 1780s in England and spread to the rest of Europe and the United States during the nineteenth century), there was a dramatic increase in the number of goods available on the market and the number of people who had the money to buy those goods. During this time production costs (the money required to make and distribute a product) also rose steadily; therefore, in order to maximize profit (the money left over from sale of a product after all costs of production have been paid), manufacturers needed to understand how their customers tended to spend their money. Though numerous economists working separately throughout Europe contributed ideas to consumer theory, many contemporary economists agree that London-born economist Alfred Marshall (1842–1924) explained all of these complex ideas best when he published *Principles of Economics* in 1890.

More Detailed Information

The income and substitution effects are based on two related assumptions. Provided there is no change in a consumer's salary or wage (the amount of money he or she earns), these principles assume that, first, if the price of a good rises, a consumer will purchase less of that good; and that, second, if the price of a good falls, a consumer will buy more of that good. After years of charting consumer buying patterns, economists realized that these assumptions only hold true with certain types of goods. Therefore, in order to fully understand the concepts of income and substitution effects, it is necessary to take a closer look at the types of goods that consumers purchase and at how buying patterns change when prices rise and fall. Economists have divided the goods consumers buy into many different categories. The two most important categories for this discussion are normal goods and inferior goods.

A normal good is a commodity that consumers purchase more of when their income increases. It is important to note that income can increase in two ways. First, a person can start earning more money, either by securing a raise (an increase in salary or wages) or by taking a different job that pays more money. The second way people's income can increase is in relation to a drop in the prices of goods and services. In this case people are not actually earning more money, but the value of their money increases, allowing them to buy more goods. Technological equipment (computers, cell phones, iPods) and cosmetics are examples of normal goods. When people have less money to spend (either because of a loss of wages or a rise in prices), they buy fewer normal goods.

An inferior good is one that consumers buy more of when they have less money to spend. When consumers have more money to spend, however, they buy less of the inferior good. Instant noodles and canned goods are two examples of inferior goods. Studies have shown that college students earning little or no money tend to purchase large quantities of instant noodles. After these students graduate and take well-paying jobs, however, they tend to buy fewer boxes of instant noodles and instead purchase other foods, such as fresh fruits and vegetables, butchered meats, and specialty cheeses. Public transportation (buses and subways, which are actually services rather than goods) is also an inferior good. People with little money tend to ride buses and subways more frequently than people with more income. Consumers who use public transportation will often buy their own automobiles or take taxis if their circumstances change and they acquire more money; then they may stop using public transportation altogether.

In the case of a few goods, people may buy more of the commodity when its price increases. This phenomenon is called the Veblen effect after Norwegian-American economist Thorstein Veblin (1857–1929), who studied the buying patterns of newly wealthy Americans at the beginning of the twentieth century. The Veblen effect tends to occur with luxury items, such as fashionable clothes, fine wines, and fancy cars, because these goods give status to their owners. For example, a Lexus is an expensive car, and because it costs so much money, people recognize the owners of these vehicles as successful and important individuals. Many people want to be recognized as successful and important by the rest of society. Consequently, when the price for a Lexus increases, owning one becomes more prestigious, and therefore an increasing number of wealthy people buy these cars. If the cost of a Lexus were to decrease, owning this car would be less prestigious, and fewer wealthy people would purchase them.

Recent Trends

The process of globalization (the development of an increasingly integrated world economy) took hold in the early 1980s, making more goods available in more markets throughout the world. Since then there have been noticeable changes in buying patterns in rural China, one of the areas most affected by this worldwide expansion of the economy. For example, there have been dramatic

"KEEPING UP WITH THE JONESES"

"Keeping up with the Joneses" is a popular phrase in American culture. The phrase refers to the tendency of many Americans to attempt to demonstrate that they are successful by owning the same sorts of commodities (goods) as their successful neighbors. In other words, in a given neighborhood in the United States, a family will try to purchase clothes and cars that match the quality of the neighbors' clothes and cars. Having made such purchases, this family will be recognized as being as successful as the other families in the neighborhood.

The phrase first appeared in 1913 as the title of a comic strip authored by Arthur R. Momand (1886–1987). The strip ran in American newspapers for 28 years. The actual "Joneses" never appeared in the comic strip; they were the neighbors of the family that was the subject of the cartoon. Many cartoon historians believe that Momand took the name for the title of the cartoon from George Frederic and Lucretia Stevens Rhinelander Jones, the wealthy parents of American novelist Edith Wharton (1862–1937).

increases in the purchases of food and appliances in rural China. Before 1980 rural Chinese citizens bought just 30 percent of their food with cash. The rest they either raised themselves or acquired by bartering, or trading, with fellow rural dwellers. By 2003 the rural Chinese were acquiring 82 percent of their food with cash. During this time ownership of refrigerators, which consumers used to store food, rose from 1.2 refrigerators per 100 households to more than 16 refrigerators per 100 households.

The economy changed in rural China because of a series of interrelated factors. First, an increase in industrial production in China brought more opportunities for rural citizens to obtain more lucrative jobs in urban centers away from home. The large number of jobs available in China's cities led to large-scale migration out of rural China. Increased urban populations caused the cities to extend outward, however, bringing the urban centers closer to the countryside. This meant that food-producing farmers found more buyers to purchase their products. These buyers were earning more money in their jobs and also needed to buy food because they were no longer producing it for themselves.

These trends followed the basic ideas of the income and substitution effects. On the one hand, people purchased more goods (in this case, food and refrigerators) with their increased income, thus reflecting the income effect. On the other hand, they substituted the food they raised themselves with food produced by other farmers, as the cost of growing food had become more expensive. More time growing food meant less time working at a job, resulting in an overall increase in real price of their home-grown food.

$ Market Failure

What It Means

Market failure is a term used by economists to describe situations in which markets (the real or virtual places where buyers and sellers come together to do business with one another) fail to serve, or are incapable of serving, the best interests of society.

Most mainstream economists believe that markets offer the best way of organizing economic activity. The market forces that do most of the organizing are supply, demand, and prices. Supply is the quantity of goods that sellers are willing to sell over a range of prices, and demand is the quantity of goods that buyers are willing to buy over a range of prices. Prices rise or fall according to the competing interests of buyers (who want low prices) and sellers (who want high prices). In a free market, where there are many different buyers and many different sellers, prices end up at a level that accommodates both sides to an acceptable degree: buyers get what they want at prices that seem fair to them, and sellers are able to maintain profitable businesses. In addition, the market mechanisms described above encourage sellers to produce the amount and variety of goods and services that society wants and to do so in the most efficient ways possible.

Unfortunately the economy does not always function as smoothly in practice as it does in theory. There are cases in which markets either generate results that harm society or cannot provide the results that society wants. For instance, market activity often produces pollution (dirty air, water, or soil) at levels that are unacceptable to the public. In addition, markets cannot provide for national defense. Every resident of a country needs equal access to national defense, regardless of ability to pay. There is no effective way to generate capable armies and equipment based on supply, demand, and pricing. These are two instances of market failure.

Government intervention can sometimes correct or counteract market failure. Because the market system provides no incentive for companies to stop polluting, the government establishes laws and financial penalties for polluters. Similarly the government assumes exclusive control over matters related to national defense. There is no way to eliminate market failure entirely, however.

When Did It Begin

Until the twentieth century governments in capitalist countries largely stayed out of economic affairs. While there has never been any serious disagreement about governmental intervention in such areas as the defense industry, road-building, or public services (police and fire departments, for example), there was little precedent for governments to correct other forms of market failure prior to the Great Depression, which crippled the economies of North America and Europe in the 1930s.

British economist John Maynard Keynes (1883–1946), writing during the Depression, revolutionized economics by suggesting that the market mechanisms of supply, demand, and pricing could not always be trusted to regulate the economy effectively. Keynes persuaded world leaders that government had to take the lead in correcting the market failures that had caused the Depression. Following Keynes's advice, governments began spending money on public projects and aid programs. The influx of money into the economies of the affected countries helped them recover from the Depression, establishing a precedent for government intervention in the economy.

But in the 1970s Keynes's ideas fell out of favor, especially in the United States. Economic stagnation at

A market failure occurs when an economic system cannot produce by itself what consumers want-for example, national defense or limits on pollution-and the government must step in. Some people have argued that dependence on fossil fuels is a market failure and that the government should invest in solar power and other renewable energy sources. *Ty Allison/Getty Images.*

that time was blamed on the very government intervention that had previously helped the country. As a result, subsequent U.S. government administrations only cautiously stepped in to correct market failures, and a distrust of the government's ability to improve upon the performance of markets began to dominate economics and politics.

More Detailed Information

When a market failure occurs, there is inefficiency in the economy. The case of public goods represents one type of market failure. Public goods include parks, police and firefighting services, military protection, highways, streetlights, and lighthouses, to name a few. Because of the nature of public goods, the market has little incentive to supply them, and governments must step in. Public goods are different from private goods in three key ways that make them unmarketable. First, when one person uses a public good, no one else is prevented from enjoying its use. Hundreds of ships can benefit equally from a lighthouse, just as hundreds of people can benefit equally from a park. By contrast, private goods, such as food or computers, cannot be enjoyed simultaneously by large numbers of people. The second key difference between public and private goods is that public goods cannot be easily denied to any person who wants to use them. There is no effective way to keep any particular ship from using the service provided by a lighthouse. It is relatively easy, however, to deny other people the right to eat food that you have bought for yourself. Third, public goods are beyond the purchasing reach of individuals. Lighthouses cost too much money to build and operate for any single person to bear the financial responsibility for one. Because of these three characteristics, no private business would be able provide a public good and still make a profit, so local and national governments raise money through taxes to supply these public services.

Another common form of market failure occurs when there is a lack of competition among companies in a certain industry. If, for instance, one sneaker company becomes so successful that it is able to buy out its rivals and form a monopoly (when a company gains exclusive control over the market for a particular product or service), or if two leading sneaker companies get together and conspire to raise prices, inefficiency results. Supply, demand, and pricing are then determined artificially rather than through the natural interaction that results from competition. Resources are wasted, with negative effects for the economy as a whole.

Yet another type of market failure is what economists call an externality. An externality is any byproduct of market activity that is not accounted for in the price of the goods produced. For instance, if a company's factory pollutes a town's air while making paper, the townspeople will bear the costs of that pollution (in the form of doctors' bills, cleaning bills, lower real-estate values than in

NONBELIEVERS

The concept of market failure, a situation in which free markets (economic systems in which buyers and sellers come together to do business with one another, free from government intervention) fail to function properly, is subject to interpretation. Different economists apply different standards when determining whether the market has failed. Some economists even deny that market failure is a legitimate concept.

Economists who hold to various forms of libertarian ideals (those based on a belief that government should almost never intervene in economic and social affairs) often argue that there is no such thing as market failure. When problems arise as a result of market activity, libertarians contend, the blame does not lie with the market. In some cases they argue that the problems are inevitable, and in other cases they argue that the cause of the problem is that markets are not free enough to begin with (due to existing government regulation). Government would invariably perform more poorly than markets, according to this view.

In the late 1990s, for example, the software company Microsoft was charged with abusing its monopoly (when one company gains exclusive control over the market for a particular product or service, eliminating its competitors) on software products to push its other products on consumers. Government prosecutors took the company to court and suggested that it be broken up into separate companies. Though monopoly, which results in economic inefficiency because it decreases competition, is generally considered a form of market failure, such libertarians as the famous economist Milton Friedman (1912–2006) argued that Microsoft had not acted wrongly and that the government had no right to intervene. Microsoft settled the court case and was never forced to break up into separate companies.

nearby towns, and so forth), whether or not they purchase the company's paper. For the market to function efficiently, the factory and the purchasers of the paper, and not the townspeople, should be paying for the results of the pollution. Because these costs are not passed on to the paper buyers, they buy paper in larger quantities than they otherwise would, and the factory produces more paper to meet the demand, unhampered by any cut in its profits as a result of having to be responsible for the pollution itself. There are also positive externalities. For example, when a prestigious gourmet grocery store moves into a neighborhood, property values in the area around the store may rise. The homeowners near the grocery store get economic benefits without paying for them.

Market failures can also result from positive externalities. For example, leaving the development of immunizations and vaccines to the workings of a free market will result in too few people getting them. This is because private economic actors usually do not take into account the positive effects on others when they make consumption or production decisions. For instance, a single flu vaccination carries far greater social benefits than private benefits. Because each person who gets a vaccine not only avoids getting the virus himself but also helps to limit the spread of the disease, benefiting countless others. But when deciding whether to get a flu vaccination, individuals usually take their own private benefits into account: they get the shot to avoid contracting the flu, or they do not get it because they think they are not at risk of becoming seriously ill from the virus. Their demand does not accurately reflect the true demand for the product. In determining how much vaccine to supply, vaccine developers likewise fail to take the social benefits into account, because they have no financial motivation to do so. They consider their own private benefits, and therefore the supply of vaccines never meets the demand for them.

Finally, and more controversially, markets may be said to have failed when a certain good or service is more unequally distributed than society believes it should be. In the United States in the first few years of this century, the health care system represented a case of market failure in the eyes of many people, including some economists. Only people with wealth or certain types of jobs could get private health insurance that paid for medical care, even though most people were uncomfortable with the idea of denying health care to people with low-paying jobs and little wealth. Those who saw this situation as an instance of market failure called for government intervention, but many people denied that it was a case of market failure and believed that the government would not improve on the performance of the market system.

Recent Trends

There is no such thing as a perfectly functioning market system. Some amount of inefficiency will be present in the best of times. Mainstream American economists today usually declare, therefore, that market failure exists only when the inefficiency is dramatic and might call for government intervention. This level is reached, in the view of economists, when it seems likely that the government can do a better job of managing the situation than markets are doing. Thus, economists generally believe that whenever the government considers intervening in the economy, it must be shown that the damage the government might inflict on certain people will be less significant than the aid it will be giving to other people.

$ Externality

What It Means

An externality is a side effect of any market activity (an activity related to the buying and selling of goods and services) that either harms or benefits a third party not involved in that particular activity. For instance, a paper mill may pollute the air around its site, but this is not factored into the price of the paper that is ultimately sold. Neither the producer nor the buyer of the paper bears the costs related to the pollution. Instead, the people who live near the paper mill bear these costs, some of which may be economic costs (doctor's bills for lung ailments) and some of which may be difficult to quantify in terms of money (an unpleasant smell that disrupts children's outdoor playtime). Such pollution would be called a negative externality.

Economic activity also frequently results in positive externalities. When one person in a neighborhood renovates her home, for example, she obviously increases the market value of her own property. But she also increases, to some degree, the value of other homes in the neighborhood and the feelings of well-being that neighborhood residents experience because of the improved appearance of the house and area.

Externalities that harm a third party are called negative externalities or third-party costs; externalities that benefit a third party are called positive externalities or third-party benefits. The phrase "spillover effect" is also frequently used interchangeably with "externality," because an externality spills over the boundaries of a buyer-seller transaction to affect uninvolved people.

For economists, both positive and negative externalities represent market inefficiency and are thus potential flaws in the theory, widely accepted in the world of economics, that markets generally achieve maximum economic efficiency. There is no single answer, however, as to how or whether externalities should be addressed.

When Did It Begin

The positive and negative side effects of business activity have no doubt always existed, but negative externalities in particular began increasing exponentially in the nineteenth century as a result of the Industrial Revolution.

The Industrial Revolution was the dramatic shift (made possible by new technologies such as coal-burning steam engines and new techniques for manufacturing textiles and steel) in Western Europe and North America from societies dominated by agriculture and manual labor to societies dominated by mechanized industrial production. In addition to reshaping society at every level, the industrial advances of this time enabled businesses to produce goods on a much larger scale than ever before. The greatly increased production benefited people in countless ways and made possible the development of modern capitalism (a system in which private individuals, not the government, own businesses). It also led, however, to a dramatic increase in negative externalities such as pollution and the depletion of natural resources. These externalities multiplied during the twentieth century, as populations grew and new technologies made possible ever-greater increases in production.

An externality is a by-product of an economic activity that has an impact on people who are not involved in the activity. Some externalities, like the pollution pictured here, have a negative effect on a wide sector of the population. © *Matthias Kulka/zefa/Corbis.*

The British economist Alfred Marshall (1842–1924), author of the most widely used economics textbook of his time, *Principles of Economics* (1890), first theorized that there might be externalities (or external costs) that are not accounted for by the price system. One of Marshall's students at the University of Cambridge, Arthur Pigou (1877–1959), developed Marshall's idea further in his book *The Economics of Welfare* (1920).

More Detailed Information

The fundamental concept of all economic theory is the notion that supply, demand, and prices work together to coordinate economic activity. The law of demand dictates that as the price of a given product rises, consumers become less and less likely to buy that product; and the law of supply dictates that as the price of a product rises, sellers will be willing to sell more and more of that product. In a market, where buyers and sellers freely interact with one another, these opposing laws will result in a balancing of the desires of each side. By trial and error, the price of any product eventually reaches an equilibrium point, a point at which sellers will provide exactly as much

of a given product as buyers want to buy. According to economic theory, such efficiency is most easily produced by markets.

Consider the example of the paper mill again. The paper company and its consumers, according to the laws of supply and demand, would (after a process of trial and error) collectively arrive at the equilibrium price for paper, the price at which the forces of supply and demand are equal. Exactly the amount of paper that consumers require is produced, and exactly the amount of paper that the company is willing to supply is produced. This process represents the most efficient allocation of resources possible, according to supply-and-demand theory.

But in actuality, society at large will have to bear the costs of the pollution (for instance, as medical bills, as loss of property value, and as the natural resource of clean air), so the price that society pays for the paper is actually higher than what the paper company is charging. By failing to take into account the externalities of their transaction, the paper mill and paper consumers have arrived at a false equilibrium price. A correct determination of the equilibrium price would have taken the

GLOBAL WARMING: A GIGANTIC NEGATIVE EXTERNALITY

Regardless of their political affiliation, most economists (along with most scientists) today recognize that there is one giant, looming externality (side effect of market activity) that can be neither solved by markets on their own nor ignored by governments. That externality is global warming, a side effect produced by industries that engage in or encourage the burning of coal, oil, and other fossil fuels. Many industries since the time of the Industrial Revolution (which began in the eighteenth century) share the blame for contributing to global warming, but the primary targets of any government intervention in the future would have to be the auto and oil industries, whose health has always required the burning of ever-greater amounts of oil (in the forms of gasoline and diesel).

The auto and oil industries expanded together in response to consumer demand for greater numbers of automobiles and the freedom to drive them wherever and whenever they wanted. According to economic theory, however, had the externality of global warming been factored into the cost of cars, the price of both oil and cars would have been much higher, and the demand for these goods far lower, than it has historically been. The market has failed to account for an externality that will, according to scientists, have the potential to seriously disrupt not just market economies but entire civilizations.

potential costs of pollution into account, but the pricing system alone cannot do this.

This situation, in which a market has failed to produce maximum efficiency, is called market failure. Economists believe that market failure also occurs when positive externalities are not integrated into the pricing system. In the case of renovating properties, the woman who improves her property increases the value of her neighbors' properties without being directly compensated for this service; although she might have strong motivations for continuing to keep her property in good condition, she would be more likely to do so if the market supplied her with a direct economic incentive. Likewise, her neighbors are less likely to maintain their own houses than they would if they had a clear economic incentive for doing so. The market supplies no reliable mechanisms for encouraging people to maintain their houses' appearance, so there will always be more demand for this activity than there will be residents willing to supply it.

Economists sometimes speak of the presence of externalities in terms of the private cost vs. the social cost of a good. If, for example, you buy a car, the purchase price of your car, together with your gasoline and other maintenance costs, represent the car's private cost. The total cost to society of your car-related purchases, how-

ever, is greater than the price you pay to the dealer and service-station owners. Driving your car results in pollution that can cause health problems for people uninvolved in the purchase of your car, and that contributes to global warming, which scientists and economists expect to impose severe costs on society and the economy. Cars also cause traffic. Traffic imposes costs on the government (such as increases in the size of the police force), and traffic also cuts into the profits of businesses whose delivery drivers and office workers spend time in traffic jams instead of using that time to generate revenue for the company. A more general cost of traffic is that it decreases the well-being of all the individual drivers who endure it. These negative externalities represent real costs to society, even though they can be hard to calculate in dollar amounts. Adding the external costs of your car (the costs of the externalities) to the private cost of your car yields the overall price paid by you and society for your car. This total price is called the social cost.

Arthur Pigou, who pioneered the concept of social vs. private costs, argued that governments should intervene to correct the gap between these costs. In the case of negative externalities, such as pollution, Pigou recommended that the government tax the industries involved. In the case of positive externalities, he recommended that the government subsidize (or pay part of the manufacturing costs of) the industries involved. This would promote social well-being, but it would do so, in theory, by increasing economic efficiency.

Recent Trends

In the case of both negative and positive externalities, part of the reason that market solutions are not readily available is that it is often difficult, if not impossible, to estimate the cost that negative externalities inflict on people and the gains that people enjoy because of positive externalities. The court system today is full of individual citizens demanding payment for the costs (some economic and some harder to quantify) of negative externalities. Likewise, governments often try to correct the market inefficiencies created by externalities; they can do so by taxing activities that generate negative externalities (which increases companies' production costs and therefore theoretically spurs cuts in supply), subsidizing activities that generate positive externalities (money to help cover expenses, which decreases production costs and therefore theoretically spurs increases in supply), and putting in place other laws.

The U.S. government, for instance, regulates pollutants expelled by factories by imposing fines if pollution rises above certain levels. The effectiveness of these regulations is often contested, however. Some of the worst air polluters in the country find it less expensive to pay the fines imposed by the government than to update their equipment and thus cut pollution. Their payments of fines may technically bring about a balancing of supply and demand by factoring in the costs of externalities, but their actions arguably do little to repay the public for the costs they must bear as a result of the pollution.

Meanwhile, some economists question whether government intervention can ever rectify market inefficiency, because government workers are not able to process nearly as much information as can decentralized markets governed by the laws of supply and demand. Further, these economists argue, even the most efficient government involvement results in added costs (of hiring regulators, processing paperwork, and enforcing new rules, for instance) that might ultimately outweigh any balancing out of supply and demand.

$ Economic Rent

What It Means

Most of us think of rent as the cost of borrowing, or using, something (an apartment, a car, a video) for a certain period of time. The concept of economic rent, however, is different and trickier to grasp.

In modern economics the term *economic rent* refers to the financial return on, or income generated by, an asset (in this case, a factor of production, such as a piece of land, a piece of machinery, or a worker) over and above its "next best use." Consider, for example, Donald Brown, a professional football player who earns $1 million dollars per year. Were it not for his rare athletic skills, Brown's next best employment option might be to work as a computer programmer for $100,000 per year. The difference between Brown's most lucrative option (playing professional football) and the next best use of his skills (programming computers) is $900,000. This figure represents the economic rent Brown earns on his athletic ability.

Another contemporary use of economic rent refers to the amount of money, above and beyond the market price (a figure determined by the laws of supply and demand in a freely competitive buying and selling environment), that a supplier can get for his product when competition is restricted. In this scenario the seller, Parvin Tehrani, holds a patent, copyright, trademark, import license, or other government-granted permit that establishes her as the exclusive provider of Sevruga Iranian caviar in the United States. Tehrani's permit enables her to charge $300 per ounce for her caviar, more than twice as much as the same caviar would garner in a competitive marketplace (let's say $120 per ounce). The difference between Tehrani's price and the regular market price is $180; therefore, it is said, $180 is the economic rent she earns by virtue of having the permit.

When Did It Begin

The concept of economic rent was first introduced by David Ricardo (1772-1823), one of the principal founders, along with Adam Smith (1723-1790) and Thomas

Economic rent sometimes refers to the difference in income generated from somebody's job and his or her "next best" employment. For example, if New England Patriot Tom Brady, pictured here, can earn $4 million a year as a quarterback but only $500,000 in his next best job, as a placekick holder, the economic rent he gains from being a quarterback is $3.5 million. *AP Images.*

Malthus (1766-1834), of the classical school of economics. A witness to the radical social and economic transformation of Western Europe during the Industrial Revolution (the widespread adoption of industrial methods of production that began in the late 1700s), Ricardo developed the idea of economic rent in response to changes in agricultural production.

Before the Industrial Revolution, population levels were relatively low and stable. Using only the land that was most fertile, easy to cultivate, and close to markets, farmers could grow enough grain and other crops to sustain the whole society. The Industrial Revolution, however, brought unprecedented population booms, influxes of people to urban centers, and the conversion of centrally located farmland into factory sites. Suddenly it became necessary to begin growing crops on less fertile, more difficult to cultivate, out-lying lands in order to generate enough food. Although the production and transportation costs were higher for crops grown on the inferior land, these crops still garnered the same price at a market as those crops that were grown more cheaply on superior land.

If a bushel of grain sells for $16 at a market, the person who spends only $4 to grow that bushel reaps significantly (3 times) more profit than the person who must spend $12 to grow it (all other factors being equal). Accordingly, Ricardo noted, a tenant farmer would be

COPYRIGHT AND ECONOMIC RENT

In modern terms economic rent may be understood as the amount of money, over and above the free market price, that a person or business can charge for a good or service when they have some way of restricting competition (that is, a way of preventing others from selling that good or service).

In the music industry a copyright identifies a record company (commonly known as a record label) as the only entity permitted to sell a music artist's songs. For example, no company or individual other than Island Records can sell the songs on the U2 compact disc *How to Dismantle an Atomic Bomb*. Anyone other than Island Records who sells the songs on the CD can be sued for copyright infringement. These exclusive rights allow Island Records and other record labels to sell CDs for higher prices than if just anyone were permitted to copy and sell artists' songs.

willing to pay a landowner more money (in this scenario, 3 times more) for use of the superior piece of land. Ricardo used the term *rent* to denote the difference between the fee for use of the superior land and the fee for use of the inferior land, noting, too, that the profits were reaped by the owner of the superior land, not the farmer who worked it.

More Detailed Information

Like the owner of a superior parcel of land, the football player and the caviar merchant earn economic rent by controlling access to something desirable (athletic talent and fine caviar) that is rare or limited in supply. There is an important difference between the two examples, however.

The football player's talent is rare in the same way that intellectual genius is rare; people with such talent are often referred to as gifted. We may assume that the football player has competed intensively against other talented players in order to make it to the top level of his sport. The caviar merchant, on the other hand, is not in possession of uniquely superior caviar, nor has she competed to prove that her caviar is the best; rather, the "gift" she possesses is the special permit that restricts her potential competitors from entering the market. But how did Parvin Tehrani obtain this exclusive government permit? Did she win it in a lottery? Was she the highest bidder in a permit auction? Did she have an inside connection to someone in the government office that awarded the permit? In a situation where there is substantial profit (or economic rent) to be gained from holding such a permit, we can imagine that merchants, manufacturers, and other business entities might go to extreme lengths to acquire this privilege. The effort to obtain exclusive

market power through a permit or other competition-limiting avenue is known as rent-seeking. The rent-seeker tries to establish a competitive advantage by manipulating the economic environment rather than by increasing the quantity or quality of his or her product or otherwise providing any benefit to the consumer (as the profit-seeker aims to do).

Nowadays lobbyists are hired rent-seekers, who petition the government for various kinds of regulations and permits that will favor the corporations or interest groups on whose behalf they work. Notably, one of the lobbyist's main tools of persuasion is to promise campaign contributions to, or threaten to withhold them from, the politicians whose favor they seek. Under extreme circumstances, rent-seeking may even lead to outright bribes and other corrupt or illegal activities.

The concept of rent-seeking was first discussed by Gordon Tullock in an influential paper titled "The Welfare Costs of Tariffs, Monopolies, and Theft," which was published in 1967; the term rent-seeking, however, was coined by another economist, Anne Krueger, in a 1974 paper titled "The Political Economy of the Rent-Seeking Society."

Recent Trends

During a period of profound political, social, and economic transition (even upheaval) when power and influence are up for grabs, many people and organizations become more concerned with brokering deals to secure or advance their own interests than with devoting their resources to activities that are socially or economically valuable to the community. Since the collapse of the Soviet Union in the early 1990s, many economists have turned their attention to studying the rise and impact of rent-seeking behaviors in formerly communist countries. In Russia, although bribery and corruption were well-known facts of life under communism, rent-seeking practices became even more prevalent as the country attempted to establish a market economy.

Rent-seeking behavior in Russia is seen as a significant hindrance to the country's social development and economic growth. It maintains the concentration of power in the hands of a minority elite (the poor, after all, are not in the business of offering bribes), and it undermines legitimate competition and leads to the severe distortion of social and economic priorities.

COMPETITION BETWEEN BUSINESSES

$ Perfect Competition

What It Means

Perfect competition, also known as pure competition, is a theoretical concept describing a type of market structure

Perfect competition is a term used to describe an economy where no individual or company has a competitive advantage over any other person or company. While perfect competition exists only in theory, there are places, including this vegetable market in Freetown, Sierra Leone, that might contain some aspect of it, such as having all sellers offer the same product at the same price. © *Christine Osborne/Corbis.*

(a market is any place or system in which buyers and sellers come together) in which no seller or buyer has more power than another. Perfect competition in an industry would exist if no seller or buyer had the power to alter prices by acting alone.

There are several key characteristics of perfect competition. For one, all businesses engaged in perfect competition must produce the same product or service. In addition, perfect competition requires the participation of a large number of companies, so that all the businesses involved will have a relatively small share of the same market; as a result, no single company will have the advantage of selling to a significantly larger number of customers than any of the others. Companies operating in a state of perfect competition must be "price-takers"—that is, they must be able to change their rates of production and sales without being forced to raise or lower prices on their goods. At the same time, perfect competition would give companies the power of free entry and exit; in other words, companies would have the ability to enter the market (in the hope of earning a profit) or leave the market (in the event their business was not profitable) without incurring the high costs traditionally associated

with market entry and exit. Perfect competition makes it possible for consumers to have all the information they will need (for example, what products are being sold and how much they cost) to make intelligent purchases. Under these conditions, economists argue, no seller or buyer would have the power to alter prices by acting alone.

Sellers and buyers in any market have competing desires that take the form of the forces of supply and demand, respectively. When prices are high, sellers naturally want to supply more of a good and increase their profits, but those same high prices make buyers, who want to maximize their own economic well-being, naturally less likely to buy that good. These opposing desires should balance one another out to determine what is known as an equilibrium price.

This would strictly be the case, however, only under conditions of perfect competition. When a large number of equally powerful sellers are competing with one another to attract buyers, a seller who attempts to inflate his profits by charging higher than the equilibrium price will lose his customers to rivals able to charge a lower price. Prices under conditions of perfect competition tend toward a level that is as low as possible while still allowing companies to pay their operating costs and remain in business. By forcing companies to minimize their costs, perfect competition thus also encourages businesses to produce the maximum feasible amount of any product in the most efficient way.

In reality, however, perfect competition has probably never existed, or only very rarely. Companies often gain competitive advantages over their rivals and are able to influence prices. In some instances, a company is able to take over a particular marketplace, eliminating competition and assuming control over prices, production, and so on; this form of market dominance is known as a monopoly. An oligopoly is similar to a monopoly, in the respect that the market is dominated by a small group, although an oligopoly always involves the participation of at least two separate companies. Some industries also engage in something called monopolistic competition. While the structure of monopolistic competition is similar to that of perfect competition, businesses engaging in monopolistic competition offer slightly different products than their competitors, thereby creating a greater sense of consumer choice; as a result, businesses have greater freedom to raise prices if they perceive a high consumer demand for their particular products. Nevertheless, the idea of perfect competition underlies many basic economic theories, such as the concepts of supply and demand, and it is often seen as the ideal condition of any market system. It is a theoretical simplification that allows economists to speculate about the nature of markets, and it provides a standard against which the competition in actual, real-life markets may be judged.

IMPERFECT COMPETITION

Perfect competition in any market (a market is a place or system bringing buyers and sellers of goods and services together) would exist if there were a large number of companies each providing a nearly identical product and each controlling only a small portion of an industry. Prices under these conditions would be determined not by sellers but according to a compromise between the forces of supply (the quantity of a good that sellers will sell at a given price) and demand (the quantity of a good that buyers will buy at a given price). Perfectly competitive industries do not exist in reality. Instead, the concept lies at one extreme of the spectrum of possible market structures.

At the other end of the spectrum lies the monopoly market structure. A monopoly exists when one company is the only seller of a given product. Monopolies are rare, but they have existed throughout history, and some exist today. Under monopoly conditions the forces of supply and demand lose their power to set prices. The monopolizing company can sell its products for as high a price as it wants. Monopolies tend to set prices at levels that guarantee them larger profits than would be possible under competitive market conditions.

When Did It Begin

Early economists such as Adam Smith and David Ricardo put forward the notion that we now call perfect competition, seeing it as the ideal toward which an economic system should aspire. During the late eighteenth and early nineteenth centuries, when these and other so-called classical economists were writing, government intervention, especially in matters of international trade, was overtly restricting the workings of supply and demand. If the government refrained from tampering with the economy, if buyers and sellers were knowledgeable about the markets in which they participated, and if those markets allowed buyers and sellers to interact freely, early economists believed, then no seller or buyer acting alone should be able to affect the price system.

The practical limitations to this early model of perfect competition were plainly evident by the mid-nineteenth century, as large businesses and combinations of businesses, pursuing profits without any government interference, were able to dominate their industries and structure markets for their own benefit. Trade unions (organizations of workers that were able to appeal more effectively for improved working conditions than individual employees could bring about on their own) also arose during this time, further complicating any hopes that perfect competition might naturally occur. In the late nineteenth and early twentieth century governments began acting to restrain businesses that monopolized their industries and took advantage of workers and con-sumers, partly in an attempt to bring about greater competition in the economy.

Despite the clear evidence that markets in reality were far from perfectly competitive, mainstream economists in the nineteenth and twentieth centuries continued to base most of their theories on ideas of how markets behaved under conditions of perfect competition. The idea maintained its theoretical power partly because it was easier to theorize about markets under conditions of perfect competition than about markets which were imperfect, messy, and unpredictable. But economists continue to study and teach theories about perfectly competitive markets because, despite the fact that these theories rest on a simplified idea of competition, they are able to illuminate many complex economic issues.

More Detailed Information

A perfectly competitive market is one in which no seller or buyer has the ability to affect prices. For this to be the case, the market would have to have several characteristics. In a perfectly competitive market all firms would have to sell an identical product, or products so similar that buyers considered them interchangeable. In reality most companies that compete against one another sell products that are comparable but that have distinct characteristics. For example, in the American sneaker industry, buyers are not choosing between identical products when they buy similarly priced Adidas versus Nike shoes. Some consumers like Adidas shoes, perhaps because they believe them to be of higher quality, perhaps merely because they like the logo or the brand image transmitted by Adidas' advertising campaigns, while others buy Nikes for these or any number of other reasons. Adidas and Nike can exploit these differences in their products and brands to gain market share and raise prices relative to one another, without consumers automatically rushing to buy the other company's shoes.

Additionally, a perfectly competitive market would be characterized by a large number of sellers, none of which controls a large share of the market. This would mean that no single company could affect prices by, for instance, cutting or increasing its production. A company that controls a majority or a substantial share of the market can force prices higher by cutting production (since this would result in a situation in which there is more demand for the product than supply) or can force prices lower by increasing production (so that supply outpaces demand). In a perfectly competitive market, by contrast, a company could triple its output or periodically produce nothing at all, without price or the market's overall volume of transactions being affected.

Conditions of perfect competition would also require that there be complete freedom for companies to enter the industry. If a company in a perfectly competitive market raised prices above the equilibrium level in the hope of inflating its profits, new companies could immediately enter the market and sell the same product at the equilibrium price, forcing the first company either to lower its prices or go out of business. In reality there are often numerous barriers restricting the entry of new companies into markets. For example, a new sneaker company that wanted to compete with Nike or Adidas would have to invest a great deal of money in advertising and marketing in order to build awareness of its brand to rival that of its established competitors. The size and experience of established companies also gives them the ability to buy raw materials and other resources more cheaply than a company that is just launching, making it harder for a start-up company to compete.

Perfect competition also presupposes that every buyer and seller knows the price of every seller's product, so that no seller can get away with charging more than another seller. It also requires that all companies have the same knowledge of and access to technology and any other techniques for improving production. If only one among a dozen sneaker companies discovered a new form of sewing machine that could stitch leather twice as fast at half the cost of the others' machines, it would be able to cut its costs dramatically and gain market share by selling its shoes more cheaply than the others.

There has probably never been a perfectly competitive market. The industry that comes the closest to meeting the requirements of perfect competition in the United States is the agricultural industry. There are, for instance, thousands of wheat farmers selling a nearly identical product, and none of them control a large portion of the overall market for wheat. Wheat farmers have no power to set the price for their product; they must sell their crop for whatever price the market offers them.

Recent Trends

As a company grows it can take advantage of what economists call economies of scale: as the ability to cut costs increases, the larger one's output becomes. For example, imagine a sneaker company, Go!, that sells X pairs of shoes each month. At this level of sales it pays price Y for each pair's worth of raw leather that it buys from its supplier. Once Go! begins selling 10X sneakers, however, its supplier might give it a better deal on each unit of leather, since the supplier's own costs decrease if it can sell a large portion of inventory at once, with minimal money spent on delivery, storage, and marketing. If Go! can buy leather for 1/2X, it will develop an enormous advantage over competitors who cannot sell 10X sneakers. Go! will naturally press this advantage until it gains as much market share as possible.

Economists have long understood that the phenomenon of economies of scale tends to result in industries dominated by one or a handful of gigantic companies. Nevertheless, until roughly the 1970s, most economists still based most of their theories on perfectly competitive markets. Beginning at around that time, however, a number of economists began pioneering ways of studying the messier phenomenon of imperfect competition. Instead of trying to arrive at a simple, general theory for how imperfect competition worked (which was impossible given the complex and irregular nature of imperfect competition), economists instead focused on explaining many different ways it has been observed to work. The exploration of how imperfectly competitive markets function is ongoing today, even as the old models of perfectly competitive markets continue to offer many useful theoretical simplifications.

$ Monopoly

What It Means

A monopoly is a company that is the only seller of a particular product. If Joe's Pest Control is the only exterminator service in a small town, it is a monopoly. At the other end of the spectrum, the energy company Con

When a company has a monopoly, it is able to sell a particular product or service without worrying about competition from other businesses. A famous example in American history is Standard Oil, founded in 1870 by John D. Rockefeller, pictured here, whose company eventually controlled about 90 percent of the U.S. oil industry. *The Library of Congress.*

Edison was, as of 2007, the only supplier of electricity to New York City's approximately eight million residents.

A monopoly is free from the danger of losing customers to competing companies. This means that, without government intervention, a monopoly can set any price it chooses. Usually the company will set prices to guarantee a higher level of profits than it would have generated under competitive conditions. Additionally, it often means that a monopoly can offer products of inferior quality without losing customers.

Under normal conditions monopolies should not be able to survive for long if they charge prices that unduly enlarge their profits. If they do this, competitors can enter the industry and charge lower prices, forcing the monopoly to lower its prices and compete for business. Monopolies are thus very rare. Joe's Pest Control may be a monopoly because the town in which it is located is only big enough to support one such company. Con Edison is a government-granted monopoly. Electricity is difficult to produce affordably in small volumes, so state and city governments often grant utility companies monopoly rights, while closely regulating their business practices.

When Did It Begin

Among the most prominent early monopolies were those granted by the monarchs or other rulers of European nations to companies that participated in international trade. The British East India Company, for example, was granted a charter by Queen Elizabeth I in 1600, making it the sole British company authorized to import goods such as cotton, silk, and tea from India. Similarly, the parliament of the Netherlands in 1602 gave the Dutch East India Company exclusive rights to the Dutch trade with Asian countries.

In the United States the late nineteenth and early twentieth centuries saw the creation of numerous business trusts, a form of company that combined individual business firms under one set of owners with the intent of eliminating competition and creating monopolies. Standard Oil, headed by John D. Rockefeller, was one of the largest trusts. It used unfair practices to put competitors out of business on its way to gaining control of around 90 percent of the U.S. oil industry by 1900. Another prominent trust was U.S. Steel, composed of Andrew Carnegie's enormous Carnegie Steel Company as well as other steel producers. In 1901 U.S. Steel controlled two-thirds of its industry in the United States.

Public and governmental concern about trusts during this era led to federal laws limiting a company's ability to control its industry. The Sherman Antitrust Act of 1890 made it illegal to restrain or monopolize interstate or international trade. In 1911 the act was used to break up Standard Oil into 30 individual companies. The Clayton Antitrust Act of 1914 further restricted unfair business practices that large companies typically used to get rid of their rivals, and the Celler-Kefauver Act of 1950 placed restrictions on mergers (the joining of two separate companies into one larger company). These laws have been, since that time, the basis for judging whether or not a company is operating as a monopoly.

More Detailed Information

The economic argument against monopolies differs from moral arguments against them. Moral objections to monopolies include the fact that they have the ability to charge unfair prices and take advantage of consumers, but economic theory is essentially amoral. According to economists, the problem with monopolies is that they are inefficient.

Prices in the economy are set by the competing forces of supply and demand. Sellers are generally willing to supply more and more goods the higher prices rise, whereas buyers generally buy fewer and fewer goods the higher prices rise. As sellers realize how high they can drive prices without losing too many buyers, they settle on a price that represents a compromise between supply and demand. When there are numerous, equally matched competitors in an industry, prices are naturally kept as low as they can go without eliminating profits. This means that a company must use its resources (land, labor, and equipment) as efficiently as possible, keeping costs low throughout the production and distribution process. Thus, the economy under conditions of healthy competition uses its resources efficiently.

When a business gains complete control over its industry, however, it loses the incentive to keep prices at levels that promote efficiency. Instead, the company will naturally seek to increase its profits and keep them high over the long term. This results in a mismatch between supply and demand. At artificially high prices consumers buy less of the product than they would if market forces set prices. Less is produced, and society as a whole is worse off, because its resources are not being used efficiently.

How does a business become a monopoly? One way, of course, is for a government to grant a company monopoly powers, as occurred in the seventeenth century with European trading companies and as occurs today in the utilities industry, among other industries. In the case of present-day utility companies, government control may prevent a monopoly from gouging consumers, but problems of efficiency are still likely to result from the fact that market forces are not responsible for setting prices. For instance, a power company may put off making costly repairs in order to keep its profits high even as the government restricts the prices it can charge consumers. This could result in blackouts during the energy-intensive summer months. Customers who lose power, in such a situation, do not have the choice to switch to another company.

Companies can also become monopolies by outperforming the competition. A company that produces better briefcases than its competitors, and that is able to sell its cases for lower prices, might eventually drive those competitors out of business simply by being efficient. This is not necessarily a problem, but problems are more likely to arise once the company has achieved its monopoly status. It is at this point that the briefcase maker would have an incentive to raise prices to artificial levels, since there would be no competition capable of under-cutting its prices.

Economists generally believe, however, that such a monopoly will be naturally short-lived. If the briefcase company keeps prices high for an extended period of time, new companies are bound to enter the industry offering prices that more accurately reflect the market forces of supply and demand. This will force the monopolizing company to lower its prices if it wants to compete.

Once a company has a monopoly, though, it might have ways of perpetuating its dominance. It can do so by erecting, sometimes with a government's help, various barriers to entry. One barrier to entry might be a patent. A drug company that develops a cure for a disease will have the sole right to produce and sell that cure; rivals will be kept out of that particular drug market until the patent expires. Another barrier to entry can exist in the form of cost advantages. This refers to an existing company's ability to use its size and experience to buy resources such as raw materials at cheaper prices than would be available to a new firm. A dominant company might also have brand recognition among consumers that will make it hard for new firms to enter the market. For example, Microsoft makes the dominant form of computer operating system (the software that serves as the foundation for all of a computer's operations) in most of the world today. Among the barriers of entry to new competitors is the almost universal consumer recognition of the Microsoft brand name. To compete, a new brand would have to spend huge amounts of money advertising its own name.

Recent Trends

The business trusts of the nineteenth and early twentieth centuries, such as Standard Oil and U.S. Steel, were easily identifiable as monopolies (or near-monopolies) that threatened the public interest, but the laws devised to prevent such trusts from forming do not always apply to today's corporate world.

Mergers of already-gigantic companies such as America Online and Time Warner in 2000 seem, on the surface, little different from the building of trusts in the late nineteenth century. In fact, there are significant differences. Whereas Standard Oil blatantly attempted to create a monopoly, a company such as AOL/Time Warner can assert that its merger allows it to increase economic efficiency by combining various business operations that work better together than separately. Whether or not this is the truth or just a pretext for eliminating competition is difficult to say.

MONOPOLY VERSUS OLIGOPOLY

A monopoly is a business that is the sole seller of a particular good or service. Because it is not subject to competition, a monopoly has unlimited power to raise prices or take short cuts when it comes to the quality of its products. Except in certain cases, most economists argue that monopolies promote inefficiency in the economy and are bad for society as a whole. True monopolies are rare, however.

Opinion is more divided on a more common phenomenon: the oligopoly. An oligopoly exists when a few sellers dominate an industry. An example is the automotive industry in the United States, which consists of just a handful of companies, some domestic and some foreign. Oligopolies can function in such a way as to create some of the same negative effects of monopolies. In an oligopoly consisting of just five firms, it is easy for those firms to agree with one another to raise prices in order to inflate profits. Even if the firms do not collude with one another, the individual decisions of one firm affect the others much more than in an industry with more competitors. If company 1 raises prices, for instance, companies 2, 3, 4, and 5 will immediately understand that, if everyone follows suit, they can all immediately have access to increased profits.

Similarly, few economists would argue against the assertion that Microsoft has monopoly power over the operating-system market, but many economists argue that this is not necessarily a bad thing. In an environment of rapid technological change, the possibility of developing a monopoly gives innovators the incentive to spend the enormous amounts of time and money that are often necessary to come up with good ideas. This is essentially the rationale for patents, which give innovators a temporary monopoly in the production of certain inventions. In the case of Microsoft, many of its ideas were not subject to patents, so the reward of monopoly control over its industry was necessary to spur the innovation that has delivered the company to its current position of dominance.

$ Natural Monopoly

What It Means

In economics a natural monopoly is said to exist when a single business, rather than numerous competing businesses, is the most efficient producer of any good or service. A monopoly exists when a single business is the only seller of a good or service in a market (a market is any place or system allowing buyers and sellers to come together). Monopolies are usually believed to be harmful to society because, in the absence of competition, a

When a single company can produce a product or service more efficiently than competing businesses, it is considered a natural monopoly. Natural monopolies commonly occur in utilities, such as electricity, and in public transportation. © *2006 Kelly A. Quin.*

company can raise prices to ensure itself profits and operate without any concern for efficiency. Some industries, however, are believed to tend naturally toward monopoly conditions because of the costs of doing business.

This has traditionally been true, for example, of public utilities such as electricity. The cost of building plants, transformers, and power lines is enormous, but once these necessary investments have been made, an electric company can sell increasing amounts of electricity without incurring great additional costs. Once a company has made the initial investment, then, it is in a position to provide electricity to an entire market (such as a city or region), and it can spread the costs of its initial investment among this large population. Thus, it can charge a lower price than would multiple competing companies, each of which would have to build its own plant, transformers, and lines and then pass these costs on to a smaller portion of the overall market. Other industries in which some degree of natural monopoly occurs include cable television, phone service, and rail transport.

When Did It Begin

Monopolies have existed throughout history, often as a result of government authorization. For example, the large companies set up in the seventeenth century to facilitate trade between European countries and Asian and African peoples, such as England's British East India Company and the Netherlands' Dutch East India Company, were granted monopoly rights by the rulers of their countries. Other monopolies have arisen independently of government involvement. In the late nineteenth and early twentieth centuries, American industrialists such as John D. Rockefeller (the head of Standard Oil) intentionally set out to monopolize their markets by buying up the competition or forcing rivals out of business through a variety of aggressive tactics. Since this time the U.S. government has generally sought to prevent monopolies from forming or to regulate or dismantle those that have already formed.

The British philosopher and economist John Stuart Mill (1806-73) is generally credited with originating the concept of natural monopolies.

More Detailed Information

Natural monopolies arise because of what are called economies of scale. Simply put, economies of scale are the cost-cutting advantages that companies develop as they expand. Companies that produce an increasing number of goods are able to pay lower prices for raw materials, hire workers to specialize in particular tasks, get more money's worth out of their advertising campaigns, and otherwise increase efficiency and cut costs. This allows companies to multiply their investments in workers and other resources and to grow faster than companies that are not producing a similar quantity of output. Thus, a small company cannot compete in an industry dominated by larger rivals even if it produces a similar product using similar materials and techniques. Economies of scale tend to occur in industries dominated by a handful of large companies, such as petroleum, chemicals, automobile manufacturing, and steel; in some industries, however, they produce natural monopolies.

Natural monopolies result when economies of scale can only be realized at a very high level of production. In the example of the electric industry, the enormous investments required to enter the business mean that it is not profitable to produce electricity until a very large amount can be produced and sold. Beyond this minimum amount, however, electricity production becomes very profitable because of the decreasing costs associated with economies of scale. It happens, often, that this minimum amount is so large as to make it impractical for there to be more than one producer of electricity in one area. If there were two or three producers, they would divide the market among themselves and be unable to sell enough electricity to take advantage of economies of scale.

If electricity markets were divided among numerous competing firms, consumers would presumably have to pay higher prices for electricity than under monopoly conditions. Therefore, it is in society's interest for such industries to function as monopolies. On the other hand, monopolies do not have to worry about competing firms taking away their customers, so they have unlimited power to raise prices and to cut production if these actions allow them more profits.

Governments have traditionally intervened in such industries with the intent of preserving the benefits arising from monopoly conditions without allowing companies to take undue advantage of their monopoly powers. In Europe and much of the world, governments in the twentieth century often assumed total control of public utilities such as electricity, natural gas, telephone service, railroads, subway systems, and airlines, running monopoly companies as public services, subject to pricing and production limits imposed by lawmakers. In the United States the tendency has been to allow private ownership of utilities but to use government at the local, state, and federal level both to support and regulate them, protecting them from competition while limiting changes in prices and production. When a government gives a company or itself exclusive access to an industry, it is known as a government-granted monopoly.

In most cases companies that tend toward becoming natural monopolies stop short of trying to establish an

TO REGULATE OR NOT TO REGULATE?

In economics, a natural monopoly is said to exist when a single company can produce a good more efficiently than numerous competing firms would be able to produce it. A common example has historically been the electricity industry, in which the costs of building plants, transformers, and power lines allow a company to be profitable only if it can control an enormous share of any area's business, usually amounting to an entire city or region. For much of the twentieth century economists generally believed that the existence of such a monopoly was good for society but only so long as the company could be prevented from cutting production or raising prices unfairly. Therefore, natural monopolies in the United States were often supported and regulated by local, state, or federal government agencies.

There have long been numerous objections to government protection and regulation of monopolies. First, critics of government involvement in this area often argue that most so-called natural monopolies are not, in fact, natural but are frequently created when powerful companies, fearing competition, use political influence to gain government protection. Another objection to government regulation is that, even if a monopoly emerges naturally, changes in technology usually create opportunities for new companies to compete. Further, critics sometimes maintain that prices and production levels set by monopolies do not, in reality, differ greatly from those that occur in competitive markets. Finally, there is a widespread conviction that, even in cases where monopolies create inefficiencies in the economy, the involvement of government is likely to exacerbate rather than correct the problem.

outright monopoly, because they do not wish to be the target of antitrust action (legal measures to break up monopoly power) by the federal government. Still, some companies are undaunted by the prospect of regulatory sanctions, including XM and Sirius, the only two satellite radio providers in the United States, which announced in February 2007 that they would to merge (or combine) into a single company.

Recent Trends

Beginning in the mid-1970s, dissatisfaction with the results of government regulation (not only of natural monopolies but of other industries as well, such as banking and finance) led to the trend known as deregulation. In 1978 the U.S. Congress authorized the deregulation of the airline and natural gas industries, opening them to competition, and in 1980 the trucking industry was similarly deregulated. In the 1980s the government likewise forced the breakup of the local and long-distance telephone monopoly AT&T, which had been previously believed to be a natural monopoly, into distinct regional companies providing local services. AT&T continued to provide long-distance service, but other long-distance providers were allowed to compete in this newly privatized industry. In the late 1990s some U.S. states began experimenting with deregulation of the electricity industry. Electricity deregulation consists of allowing numerous companies to compete for the business of consumers using existing power lines.

Deregulation of the trucking industry resulted in the rapid growth of the industry and enormous savings to producers and consumers. Likewise, in the market for long-distance phone service, deregulation resulted in a high level of competition among providers and a 72-percent decrease in consumer prices between 1985 and 1998. The trend has not been an unqualified success, however. In the airline industry deregulation increased the concentration of power in the industry as large airlines took over routes that had previously been protected by government-regulated monopoly rights, and the deregulation of the electricity industry proved a more gradual and complicated process than its proponents originally envisioned.

$ Government-Granted Monopoly

What It Means

A government-granted monopoly is a legal form of monopoly in which the government grants one individual or corporation the right to be the sole provider of a good or service. When a government grants a monopoly, it often regulates the price of the product or service that the firm holding the monopoly may charge its customers. In some cases of government-granted monopolies, the government identifies itself as the sole provider of the good or service. Government-granted monopolies are usually established because they are perceived to be the best option for producers and consumers.

In the United States, for example, AT&T functioned as a government-granted monopoly from 1913 until 1984. The federal government reasoned that Americans needed affordable and reliable telephone service; it also thought that the communications industry could only sustain one producer because operating costs (the telephone poles and lines, the call centers, the research and development, the repairs, and the monthly power bills, to name just a few expenses associated with running the enterprise) were so high. A phone company could only make money if it was large and served numerous customers, so that the average cost of serving each individual customer would be reduced. The best way to ensure that AT&T would have the appropriate customer base was to eliminate the prospect of competition. Prior to the 1990s energy companies in many developing nations operated as government-granted monopolies for the same reason that AT&T enjoyed this privilege for a time in the United States.

When Did It Begin

The British East India Company and the Dutch East India Company were two of the earliest government-granted monopolies. Queen Elizabeth I of Great Britain granted the British East India Company a royal charter on December 31, 1600. The charter gave the organization a 21-year monopoly on all trade between England and the East Indies. The British East India Company acquired considerable authority in India because, over time, the English government bestowed political and military powers on the company so that it could protect England's interests in the colony. The British East India Company had holdings elsewhere in Asia, as well as in Africa. In 1858 England dissolved the British East India Company after a series of uprisings against the company known collectively as the Indian Mutiny.

The Dutch East India Company received its charter in 1602 from the States-General of the Netherlands. Like the British East India Company, the Dutch East India Company was granted a 21-year monopoly on trade in Asia. The first company in the world to publicly trade its stock (offer shares of ownership to private investors), the Dutch East India Company was highly profitable for nearly 150 years before the sugar trade declined and shipments were increasingly lost to pirates at sea and gangs on land. The company was dissolved when it went bankrupt in 1800.

More Detailed Information

One of the sectors in which governments often grant monopolies is public transportation. Robert Fulton (1765–1815), the U.S. engineer who developed the steamship, was granted a monopoly by the state of New York; he was named the sole provider of steamboat transportation for passengers traveling the Hudson River between New York and Albany. Working with partner Robert Livingston (1746–1813), Fulton had launched the first successful steamboat up the River Seine in France on August 9, 1803. Fulton returned to the United States to perfect his invention. In 1807 he launched the *North River Steamboat* (later called the *Clermont*), which became the nation's first commercial steamboat. The first successful trip from New York to Albany left port on August 17, 1807, and arrived two days later. In total the journey lasted 52 hours. The return to New York from Albany took just 36 hours. Commercial operations began on September 4, 1807. The ship left New York every Saturday evening at six. The return run left Albany every Wednesday at eight in the morning.

Fulton's state-granted monopoly was scheduled to last 30 years. Steamboat entrepreneur Thomas Gibbons (1757–1826) challenged the validity of the agreement, however, by hiring Cornelius Vanderbilt (1794–1877) to transport passengers for a cheaper fare. The duo eventually broke Fulton's monopoly in 1824, when the

If the government determines that one company can best provide a particular good or service to consumers, it may grant that company a legal monopoly. Such government-granted monopolies have historically existed for utilities such as electricity and water because of the tremendous infrastructure necessary to supply them. © *Bob Rowan; Progressive Image/Corbis.*

federal government ruled that New York could not regulate commerce in that manner. Following the ruling, steamboat fares dropped almost immediately from seven dollars to three dollars. Even so, in many metropolitan areas today, public transportation on the roads and in the subways is run by companies that have been issued a monopoly. For example, in New York City the Metro Transit Authority operates the city's buses and subways. In Boston, the Massachusetts Bay Transportation Authority provides public transportation.

The United States Postal Service (USPS) also holds a legal monopoly. It is the only agency permitted to put mail in private mailboxes. Until 1979 the USPS was the only agency in the country that delivered letters. That year, however, the post office agreed to exempt extremely urgent letters from the terms of this monopoly. Since that time couriers, such as Federal Express (FedEx) and the United Parcel Service (UPS), have been permitted to deliver letters under certain conditions. Competing providers are required to charge at least three dollars for their services (or twice the rate of the USPS), and they are not permitted to leave letters or packages in private mailboxes. Carriers and citizens are not permitted to send nonurgent materials through agencies other than the

USPS, but this stipulation has proved to be impossible to enforce.

Governments can also grant monopolies in the form of patents, which provide innovators with the exclusive right to make, use, and sell their invention for a specified number of years. In the United States patents are often granted in the pharmaceutical (medicinal drug) industry. The reasoning behind this practice is that the patents will encourage the pharmaceutical companies to invest funds in medical research and the development of new products, as well as in marketing (promoting, selling, and distributing) these products. In exchange for developing new prescription and over-the-counter medications, the patent allows the company to sell them for a period of time without any competition. Whereas the government regulates the prices that the post office charges, however, no such regulation exists for pharmaceutical companies. Free to charge what the market will bear, drug companies have been raising prices at an alarming rate since the mid-1990s. For example, the price for Claritin, a top-selling allergy pill, was raised 13 times before the drug's patent expired. By the first years of the twenty-first century, the average senior citizen was paying $1,500 per year for prescription medications.

PFIZER

Founded in Brooklyn, New York, in 1849, Pfizer has grown into the world's largest research-based pharmaceutical company. The company owes much of its growth to the procurement of patents (which provide the exclusive right to make, use, or sell an invention for a specified number of years before competitors are allowed to make and sell the same thing) from the U.S. government. The equivalent of government-granted monopolies (when a government grants one individual or corporation the right to be the sole provider of a good or service), these patents typically give Pfizer up to 20 years to develop and sell a new drug. In most cases research and development lasts 12 years, leaving Pfizer 8 years to be the exclusive seller of the new drug. A few years into the twenty-first century, Pfizer's best-selling drug was Lipitor, a treatment for high cholesterol that was bringing in more than $10 billion per year in worldwide sales. Pfizer originally held the exclusive rights to sell Lipitor until 2011, when other companies would have been permitted to sell their own versions of the drug. In 2005, however, an India-based company called Ranbaxy brought suit against Pfizer, and a court reduced the term of its patent by 15 months. The decision will cost Pfizer billions in lost sales.

Recent Trends

Since the early 1990s the general trend throughout the developed economies of the world has been away from government ownership of utilities (water, sewage, light, power, and trash collection services) or government-granted monopolies running these businesses. Instead, these services have been privatized, or turned over to private control and ownership. Experts cite two main reasons for this trend. First, government-run companies and companies with no competitors tend to be more inefficient than companies that must compete for a client base. Thus it was widely believed that utility companies could both be more profitable and yield better services if their customers were free to choose among service providers. Secondly, governments throughout the world were increasingly coming under financial strain in the early 1900s, and it was believed that higher returns would be reached if utility services were deregulated. In 1994 $69 billion was raised worldwide from privatization. The following year $62 billion was raised. Australia, Italy, and France experienced the greatest profits.

Privatization of utilities has also become common in the developing countries of the world. Between 1990 and 1997 more than 25 developing economies privatized their natural gas companies. For-profit companies, which began providing natural gas to residential and commercial customers, attracted a large amount of foreign investment, further stimulating growth in the industry. During this time private investors initiated many lucrative projects involving transporting natural gas across international boundaries. The projects included the development of the Yadana gas pipeline from Myanmar to Thailand, the Maghreb gas pipeline from Algeria to Europe, and the Gas-Andes pipeline from Argentina to Chile, all of which would have been less feasible if there had been heavy regulation of the utilities industries in these countries.

$ Monopolistic Competition

What It Means

Monopolistic competition describes a market structure (a market is any place or system in which buyers and sellers of products come together) composed of numerous relatively small businesses, each of which sells similar but not identical products. Each firm has some amount of control over prices and market conditions even though there is a high level of competition among them. Common examples of U.S. businesses subject to conditions of monopolistic competition are clothing stores, restaurants, wine merchants, convenience stores, and other retailers in large cities.

Monopolistic competition combines the features of two opposing theoretical concepts: monopoly and perfect competition. A monopoly exists when a single company is the only seller of a good or service and therefore has the power to raise prices, cut production, or otherwise shape the market for its own benefit. Perfect competition describes a market composed of numerous sellers all offering an identical product, so that none of the sellers has the ability to control prices.

In the real world monopolies are rare, and perfect competition is probably nonexistent. Most industries have the characteristics of monopolistic competition or oligopoly, a market type in which a few large companies dominate and therefore have greater power to control prices and market conditions. There is no precise dividing line between these two most common market structures, but monopolistic competition is closer to perfect competition, and oligopoly is closer to monopoly.

When Did It Begin

Competition has always been the engine of any market system. The most prominent early economists, Adam Smith (1723–91) and David Ricardo (1772–1823), recognized this fact and made it the foundation of their theories. But Smith, Ricardo, and other so-called classical economists believed that, in the absence of government intervention, an economy would naturally gravitate toward conditions of perfect competition.

It had become obvious by the late nineteenth century that this was not necessarily true. Large companies dominated many industries in Europe and the United States, and governments began intervening to regulate and break up monopolies, with the intent of promoting increased competition.

Monopolistic competition refers to a type of market in which relatively small businesses offer similar but distinctive products or services. Examples of such markets include restaurants, clothing retailers, and food stores. *AP Images.*

The first theoretical analysis of monopolistic competition was simultaneously developed by two economists working independently of one another: the British economist Joan Robinson (who introduced the concept in her 1933 book *Economics of Imperfect Competition*) and the American economist Edward Hastings Chamberlin (whose ideas on the subject were published in his *Theory of Monopolistic Competition,* published that same year). While economists recognized that most businesses in the developed world functioned under conditions of monopolistic competition or oligopoly, the concepts were, because of their complexity, difficult to integrate into the framework of existing economic ideas, whereas theories based on perfect competition remained useful despite their limitations. It was not until the 1970s that mainstream economists commonly began addressing markets characterized by monopolistic competition.

More Detailed Information

A market subject to conditions of monopolistic competition has a number of defining characteristics. First, each firm in a monopolistically competitive market is small relative to the overall size of the market. In Chicago, for example, there are thousands of restaurants, each of which has only a small share of the total market. This means that there is a high degree of competition among individual restaurants. No single restaurant has much power to set prices or reduce the number of meals it will serve, since each must be mindful of the other restaurants' prices and production if it wants to remain profitable. By contrast, a firm with a monopoly has complete power to set prices, whereas firms in a perfectly competitive market have no power to set prices.

Additionally, the products in a monopolistically competitive market are close substitutes for one another, rather than identical. This means that each firm has the equivalent of a narrow monopoly. For example, there may be only one restaurant in Chicago that offers meat bought from a specific specialty farm. This restaurant therefore has more ability to charge a higher price for its steaks than it would have if all restaurants got their meat from the same supplier. The restaurant's pricing freedom is, nevertheless, restricted by the likelihood that customers will go to another restaurant and eat similar, cheaper meat if the price of specialty-farm meat rises too high. Product differentiation in monopolistically competitive industries may be a matter of quality (for example, a higher grade of meat), of perception (one restaurant's

MONOPOLISTIC COMPETITION AND ADVERTISING

An industry can be described as monopolistically competitive if most companies are small relative to the overall market (a market is any place or system allowing buyers and sellers to come together), if the products being sold are similar but not identical, and if individual firms have only limited power to change their prices and production levels. Under conditions of monopolistic competition, advertising takes on great importance. Through advertising a company can differentiate its product from the many other similar products in its monopolistically competitive market.

For example, if Jane owns a store in New York City in which she sells her own women's clothing designs, she will be in competition with thousands of other designers, each of whom offers similar products. Jane cannot raise prices on skirts without risking the loss of customers, who can always get similar skirts somewhere else, so she must look elsewhere for increased profits. Jane therefore undertakes an advertising campaign in local magazines, and she is able to create the perception that her skirts are dramatically different from those of the competition. In this way Jane builds a base of loyal customers whose belief in the distinct qualities of Jane's skirts spreads to other consumers. Even though there may not be significant differences between her skirts and those of others, she is able to grow her business more quickly than her competitors thanks to effective advertising.

reputation for high-quality meat), or of subtle differences (one restaurant specializes in skirt steaks, another in filets mignons). In any case, the key factor is that consumers believe products to be different but similar enough to serve as substitutes for one another.

Another characteristic of monopolistically competitive markets is the relative freedom of firms to enter the market. In monopolies there are significant barriers to market entry, such as high start-up costs and government regulations. In perfect competition, on the other hand, there are no barriers to entry; firms can easily enter the market and compete on an equal footing with established companies. In the Chicago restaurant industry, there may not be any significant government barriers to entry, and start-up costs may not be so high as to keep independent businesses out of the market (as would be the case in a monopoly), but some barriers, such as high rent costs and the cost of hiring a chef experienced enough to compete with the many other established restaurants, may exist.

Finally, monopolistic competition requires that buyers have a significant amount of information about all the product and pricing options available to them, and that sellers have a similar amount of information about the production methods and prices of other sellers. The

Chicago restaurant customer must be relatively well-informed about what she can get for her money and where, and the restaurant owner must be relatively well-informed about the options potential customers have. A lack of knowledgeable customers gives companies the ability to pursue a monopoly, since they can increase their profits by raising prices. Similarly, ill-informed restaurant owners will not be able to remain competitive, since they are always at risk of being undercut by the pricing of competitors' food or by cost-cutting innovations being used by rival restaurants. Consumers and sellers under conditions of monopolistic competition, however, do not have the perfect knowledge of the market that they would in a perfectly competitive industry.

Recent Trends

Though Joan Robinson and Edward Hastings Chamberlin introduced theories of monopolistic competition in the 1930s, economists did not immediately integrate these theories into the existing body of economic thought. Instead, mainstream economists continued to build models of the economy (simplified explanations of how the economy works) based on the assumption of perfect competition. These economists persisted with the traditional approach not only because of the difficulty in theorizing about the messier, more complex phenomenon of monopolistic competition but also because the assumption of perfect competition allows them to make a wide range of useful, if limited, predictions. Economics has always required the elimination of certain real-world variables in the interest of crafting useful theories, and this was simply not possible for monopolistically competitive markets.

In the 1970s numerous economists began addressing monopolistic competition in a new way. Rather than try to build universal, simple theories that took into account the many ways in which competition could be imperfect, a new generation of economists satisfied themselves with various useful illustrations of how imperfectly competitive markets worked and with theories about how they might work in various important contexts. New theories of monopolistic competition were applied to international trade (business activity between people and companies in different nations) and economic growth (increases in an economy's productivity), among other economics subfields. This trend continued until the early 1990s, when there was a shift away from speculative theories about monopolistic competition and toward thorough data collection and mathematical analysis of markets.

$ Oligopoly

What It Means

The word *oligopoly* means "few sellers." In an oligopoly a small number of companies control the majority of the output, or the market, for a good or service. The few

An oligopoly is a situation in which a small group of businesses produces most of a good or service. A notable oligopoly in the modern world is the gasoline industry, where several companies control a disproportionately large portion of the market. *Michael Newman/PhotoEdit.*

their prices as well, which would in turn impact Ford. These automakers, like firms in all oligopolies, are able to set their own pricing policies exclusive of market forces (the interaction of supply and demand that affects a market economy).

When Did It Begin

During the Industrial Revolution the production of goods and services and the competition between companies increased, as did the formation of both monopolies and oligopolies. In the 1900s several large companies dominating the U.S. automobile and steel industries were the first oligopolies. These oligopolies attracted the close scrutiny of the U.S. government, and, over time, the U.S. government made some forms of oligopoly illegal under laws known as antitrust laws. The objective of these laws is to encourage greater competition between firms by restricting trade practices that are considered to be unfair. For instance, antitrust laws enforce pricing that is determined by market forces rather than by price setting among a small and controlling group of corporations.

Large corporations have come to dominate the business world in the twentieth century and the early years of the twenty-first century. Many corporations are the result of the merging, or joining, of several smaller companies. Fewer, larger corporations exert much of their power by controlling the supply of a particular good, much as the large automakers and petroleum companies do.

More Detailed Information

There are two basic types of oligopoly. A perfect (or homogeneous) oligopoly is one in which all firms in the industry produce an identical good or service. For example, the oil, milk, coal, copper wire, and cement industries all produce goods that are identical or nearly identical within their respective industries. The breakfast cereal industry is an example of a so-called imperfect oligopoly, or one in which each firm's product has different characteristics but is essentially similar to the others. Imperfect oligopolies are sometimes called heterogeneous or differentiated oligopolies.

An oligopoly may be international, as in the case of automobile manufacturing, in which six automakers from the United States and Japan (General Motors, Ford, Chrysler, Honda, Toyota, and Nissan) control a large majority of U.S. automobile sales. The breakfast cereal oligopoly is a national, U.S. oligopoly. Some daily newspapers in small U.S. cities operate in an oligopoly.

Because there are so few firms in an oligopoly and they operate in highly interactive and interdependent ways, each firm will know the percentage of the total market, called the market share, for the good or service it produces. The decisions of one firm influence and are influenced by the decisions of other firms, so that any alteration in price or percentage of market share on the

companies (which are usually large in size) produce goods that are slightly or somewhat different from each other.

An oligopoly is similar to a monopoly, in which one company alone exerts control over a market. An oligopolistic industry is more concentrated than a competitive industry (that is, a small number of firms operate within the oligopolistic market), but it is less concentrated than a monopoly, in which only one firm dominates the market. A duopoly is an oligopoly in which only two firms control a market.

In an oligopoly there are so few firms that the actions of any one of them will very likely affect the price of the good and therefore have an impact on other firms in the oligopoly. For example, the majority of automobiles in the United States are manufactured by three automakers: Ford, General Motors, and Chrysler. If Ford were to lower its prices, more consumers would buy Fords, and the other two firms would experience a drop in sales. To counteract this, the other firms would most likely cut

PRICE FIXING

Price fixing occurs when two or more competing companies agree to a certain price for a good or service. Although illegal, companies might be tempted to do so in order to keep a price higher than it ordinarily would be and thus to make more money. This arrangement would only work in an oligopoly, where a small number of companies produced most of the product or service.

A famous attempt at price fixing occurred in the United States in 1982, when Robert Crandall, president of American Airlines, called Howard Putnam, president of Braniff Airlines, and suggested they raise their airfares by 20 percent. Unknown to Crandall, Putnum taped the call and handed the evidence over to the government. Crandall was not charged, however, because in the United States it is illegal only to engage in price fixing. Crandall tried to do that but failed.

part of one firm will affect the other firms. Once prices are established by firms in an oligopoly, they tend to remain fixed, since each firm is aware of the consequences for other firms when it makes price and production decisions.

One of the most distinctive traits of oligopolies is the restrictions they place on the entry of firms not established in the oligopoly group, as well as restrictions on the exit of firms already in the group. An outside firm attempting to gain entry into an oligopoly must have money to pay for the high costs of starting up and conducting the research activities necessary to becoming competitive. It also must have resources to advertise and time to build the loyalty of customers. Often the significant financial and technical resources needed to gain entry into an established group of interdependent firms prohibit any other firms from joining.

The collective effort to prevent new firms from joining is a key strategy of oligopolistic competition. Within an oligopoly, firms also devise ways to outmaneuver one another in order to gain a larger portion of market share. For example, while it may be that no single firm in an oligopoly is willing to upset the price equilibrium among all the firms by raising or lowering its prices, a firm might try to distinguish itself from the others by signaling to customers that the quality of its product is superior. One way for a firm to demonstrate confidence in the quality of its product is to offer customers an extended warranty (a type of guarantee). Within an oligopoly, a firm might also vie for a dominant position by concealing from other firms its efforts to innovate in hopes of taking the market by surprise with a new or improved product. Although illegal, some firms in oligopolies have bargained with one another, agreeing to keep prices high or to stay out of each other's most profitable geographical areas. The field of game theory in economics centers around efforts to understand how individual firms engage in strategic competition within an oligopolistic, or interdependent, situation.

Recent Trends

In the last part of the twentieth century and the early years of the twenty-first century the number and power of oligopolies have increased because of corporate globalization, or the growth of transnational companies (companies that operate and invest in many countries around the world). Transnational corporations dominate the global economy, and many of them are parts of oligopolies.

In addition to globalization, increased competition has caused the growth of larger and more powerful corporate concentrations in such industries as food, drug, and agriculture. For example, the world's top 10 seed companies currently control roughly one-third of the seed industry. In the United States oligopolistic industries also include the music-recording industry and the aerospace industry, in which Boeing and Airbus form a duopoly to control the market for large passenger aircraft manufacturing. Within the heavily regulated wireless communications industry, many U.S. states will license only two or three providers of cellular phone services, and these companies form local oligopolies.

When firms in an oligopoly grow intensely competitive with one another, different outcomes will occur. The firms in the group may agree to come together and agree as a group, or collude, to raise prices and restrict production. If the firms involved come to a formal agreement in this way, they are called a cartel.

$ Cartel

What It Means

A cartel is an association of producers that adopts mutually beneficial business practices in order to maximize the profits of all members of the group. Cartels are composed of companies from the same industry, such as the oil or diamond industries, that seek to set specific restraints on the production and sale of their particular product. When forming a cartel, businesses establish fixed prices for their goods, set quotas on production, and regulate the market share (percentage of business deriving from the sales of the product) held by member companies. In agreeing to abide by a set of standard business practices, companies in cartels are able to reduce competition for their product.

In certain respects a cartel resembles a monopoly. A monopoly exists when a single company or business entity controls an entire market (all the selling activity) for a particular product or service. Like cartels, monopolies have little to no competition for their products, and therefore have the power to determine prices, production, and distribution of their products. Unlike

Members of OPEC

A cartel is a business alliance in which various companies or countries work together with the aim of maximizing their profits. The most powerful cartel in the world is OPEC, the Organization of the Petroleum Exporting Countries, which controls most of the world's oil supply and in 2007 included 11 countries: Algeria, Indonesia, Iran, Iraq, Kuwait, Libya, Nigeria, Qatar, Saudi Arabia, United Arab Emirates, and Venezuela. *Illustration by GGS Information Services. Cengage Learning, Gale.*

monopolies, however, cartels always involve more than one company. Some companies belonging to international cartels may also have a monopoly within their own country.

When Did It Begin

One of the first modern cartels, a group of salt-mining companies known as the Neckar Salt Union, was formed in 1828 in the cities of Württemberg and Baden (in what is now Germany). In 1871, following the unification of the various independent German states into a single nation, several new cartels began to emerge. These powerful cartels were predominantly in the natural resource extraction industries, notably oil and coal, and were the driving force behind German industrialization in the late nineteenth century. German cartels later oversaw the manufacture of military supplies during World War I (1914–18).

German corporations also played a pivotal role in the development of the international cartel in the twentieth century, notably in the steel, chemical, and fertilizer industries. Although forbidden to do so by U.S. law, which prohibited participation in cartels on the grounds that their business practices were anticompetitive, a number of

American companies worked closely with German cartels during the 1930s. After it was revealed that German cartels had played a critical role in the Nazi military effort during World War II (1939–45), the United States and Great Britain imposed strict bans on cartel activities in postwar West Germany.

More Detailed Information

Historically there have been two forms of cartel, domestic (operating within a single country) and international. One of the most powerful domestic cartels of the twentieth century was Interessen-Gemeinschaft Farbenindustrie, also known as IG Farben. Formed in 1925, IG Farben consisted of several large chemical and pharmaceutical companies that joined together in order to manufacture and distribute colored dyes. The cartel soon became involved in producing chemicals, and by the late 1920s it had secured a near-total monopoly on chemical production in Germany. During World War II this cartel worked closely with the Nazi government to seize control of chemical plants in countries occupied by Germany, which IG Farben then operated as their own. IG Farben was infamous for the production of Zyklon B, a poison used in the gas chambers at Nazi concentration camps during World War II. After the German defeat in the war,

CARTEL BUSTERS

Cartels, or groups of companies that collaborate on fixing prices and production quotas for their products, are illegal in most countries, including the United States. The U.S. Department of Justice frequently investigates charges of cartel activities in certain industries. One notorious case from the mid-1990s involved companies that manufactured and sold lysine, a popular food additive. With the aid of informants, agents with the Federal Bureau of Investigation (FBI) obtained a series of recorded conversations involving high-ranking executives from several lysine-producing companies, which revealed plans to restrict the global manufacturing of the additive in order to boost prices illegally. These audio recordings later proved instrumental in prosecuting the executives.

a number of executives from IG Farben were tried and convicted for war crimes.

The best-known and most powerful international cartel in modern history is the Organization of the Petroleum Exporting Countries, or OPEC. OPEC was formed in 1960 by Saudi Arabia, Venezuela, Kuwait, Iran, and Iraq as a means of organizing and regulating the production and price of oil. In the ensuing years several other countries joined OPEC, and by the early twenty-first century it consisted of 11 member states, which accounted for 40 percent of the world's oil production.

OPEC's power to control the global economy became apparent in 1973 during the Yom Kippur War, when Syria and Egypt invaded Israel. In retaliation for American and European support of Israel during the conflict, the Arab nations of OPEC conspired to drive up oil prices, imposing an embargo (prohibition) on oil shipments to the United States and doubling the prices of oil sold to Europe. Between October 1973 and January 1974 the price of oil rose from roughly $3 a barrel to $11.75 a barrel. At the same time, the wealth of the OPEC nations vastly increased.

Recent Trends

Cartels are not necessarily limited to legal business enterprises. In the late twentieth century the international drug trade was organized by powerful cartels, many of them located in South America and Mexico. Two of the most infamous drug cartels, both headquartered in Colombia, were the Medellin and Cali cartels. Run by Pablo Escobar (1949–93), the Medellín cartel dominated the cocaine-smuggling business in the 1970s and 1980s, earning more than $60 million a month at its peak. As U.S. and Colombian law-enforcement efforts disrupted the activities of the Medellín cartel during the late 1980s and early 1990s, the rival Cali cartel rose up in its place

and soon gained control of 80 percent of all cocaine smuggled illegally into the United States. Law-enforcement officials captured the leaders of the Cali cartel in the early twenty-first century. By this time, however, the large cartels had made way for more fragmented "baby cartels," which were in many ways more dangerous and difficult to prosecute. In 2004 experts estimated that there were 300 baby cartels in Colombia alone.

$ Game Theory

What It Means

"Game theory" refers to a branch of mathematics used to study real-world situations in which two or more people make choices that affect one another. In such situations, each participant must take the other participant's potential decisions into account in order to make his or her own decisions.

Game theory gets its name from the fact that such competition resembles parlor games such as chess and poker, but its applications are wide-ranging and far from frivolous. Using various models of how people compete against one another, game theorists can offer predictions on a wide range of real-world situations, most notably economic decision-making, including how bidders behave in auctions; cost and profit allocation (how two or more parties involved in the same project decide to divide up the costs and profits of the project); price strategy (how the producers of competing products set their prices relative to one another); the bargaining process in labor negotiations and international trade; and environmental economics, such as how multiple countries agree to share the cost of cleaning up the global pollution their factories emit. Game theory has also been applied to politics, military strategy, international relations, moral philosophy, sociology, biology, and a host of other fields.

When Did It Begin

The originator of game theory was the Hungarian-American mathematician John von Neumann, who first introduced his ideas in a German-language essay (*Zur Theorie der Gesellschaftsspiele*) in 1928. In 1944 Neumann and his Princeton University colleague Oskar Morgenstern wrote a landmark work applying game theory to economics, *Theory of Games and Economic Behavior*. The two mathematicians argued that existing branches of mathematics had been developed for use in the sciences, but that natural processes were very different from economic ones. Whereas nature is disinterested, people involved in economic competition must predict one another's possible decisions, much as in games like chess or poker. They conceived game theory as a new kind of mathematics that could help illuminate the behavior of individual players in the economy.

Game theory refers to the process by which people make decisions by weighing the potential decisions of other people. American mathematician John Forbes Nash, shown here, earned a Nobel Prize for his work in the field of game theory. *AP Images.*

More Detailed Information

Rather than one theory, game theory is actually a body of theories that can be applied to various real-world situations. Different theories usually correspond to different "game" models. For example, there are zero-sum games, in which the players have directly opposing interests and the winner takes all. Chess and poker are zero-sum games, as is, in the real world, competition between two political candidates for one office. These games are easier to understand mathematically than most real-world situations, since there are relatively few outcomes. The early stages of game theory's development largely focused on zero-sum games.

Most real-world situations, however, more closely resemble nonzero-sum games, or mixed-motive games, in which competitors have common interests. Such games break down into cooperative and non-cooperative games, depending on the players' ability to communicate and decide on a common course of action.

For instance, two powerful countries involved in mutual decisions about whether or not to build nuclear weapons are involved in a nonzero-sum game. Arriving at an outcome beneficial to both countries involves weighing their conflicting interests (each wants to be more powerful than the other) with their common interests (neither wants to initiate global destruction). Whether or not the two countries can cooperate with one another (whether their game becomes a cooperative or non-cooperative one) will have an enormous effect on the ultimate outcome.

Game theory provides insights about the decisions that can be made at every stage of such games, whether cooperative or not. This does not mean, of course, that game theorists have all the answers to such complicated real-world situations. It merely means they have tools for understanding them beyond the more straightforward laws of probability, which govern random events.

Recent Trends

One of the most well-known game theorists is the American mathematician John Nash, who in the 1950s began to do pioneering work in game theory. He established important mathematical principles of game theory and proposed what became known as Nash's solution, which explains the interaction of threats and actions involved in two-person nonzero-sum games and offers a cooperative solution to these games. While Nash's solution has limitations, it has been widely employed by decision-makers in the business world in recent decades. In 1994 Nash won the Nobel Prize for his work in game theory. The 2001 movie *A Beautiful Mind* portrays his groundbreaking work in the context

THE PRISONER'S DILEMMA

One of the most famous hypothetical games in game theory, a branch of mathematics used to study real-world situations in which two or more people make choices that affect one another, is called The Prisoner's Dilemma, first proposed by the American mathematician Albert W. Tucker.

Suppose that two suspects are arrested together and charged with bank robbery. They are placed in isolation and separately told that: 1) if both remain silent, they each get one year in prison for concealed weapons violations rather than the bank robbery; 2) if both confess, they get five years in prison for the robbery; 3) if one confesses and the other does not, the confessor goes free and the silent one gets 20 years in prison.

If you were one of these prisoners, would you confess or keep silent? Keeping silent would result in the shortest sentence, but you must rely on your partner to keep silent or else risk being locked up for 20 years. Confessing, meanwhile, would ensure you of a prison term no longer than five years, so self-interest seems to indicate this as the best alternative.

The Prisoner's Dilemma represents a situation in which rational self-interest, as represented by confessing, leaves each player worse off than the apparently irrational decision to trust one another would. This conflict between self-interest and the interest of the group or community lies at the heart of many real-world economic situations.

of the schizophrenia that afflicted him throughout his adult life.

WHAT MOTIVATES BUSINESSES

$ Revenue

What It Means

Revenue is the total quantity of money that a business brings in during a set period of time. Most revenue results from the sale of goods and services. Therefore, revenue is equal to the price times the quantity (in units, weight, or some other measure) of all products sold in the time period under consideration. For example, if a street vendor sells 100 hot dogs in one day at a price of $3 apiece, her business's revenue would be $300 for that day. If a company sells more than one product, the price-times-quantity calculation would be performed for each product, and the resulting totals would be added together.

It is important to distinguish revenue from profit (also called net income). Profit is calculated by subtracting a company's costs from its revenues. If the hot-dog vendor pays $20 a day to rent her cart and $50 a day to

stock it, her costs would equal $70 and her profit $230. Revenue is often referred to as a company's "top line," and profit is often referred to as a company's "bottom line," since these figures appear, respectively, at the top and bottom of income statements (company documents that break down how revenue is transformed into profit).

The goal of any company, from the perspective of economics, is to maximize profits. This depends on making accurate decisions concerning revenue and cost so that the gap between these two amounts—profit—reaches its widest possible range. Likewise, from the investor's point of view, revenue is a crucial ingredient in the health of any business. Investors want to buy stock (shares of company ownership that gain value when the firm prospers) in companies that are healthy and well-positioned for future growth. To measure up to this standard, a company must show steady growth not only in profits but also in revenue.

When Did It Begin

The concept of revenue, along with the corresponding concept of profit, is of central importance in any market economy (a system in which the activity of buyers and sellers acting independently shapes most aspects of economic life). In Europe market economic systems, also called capitalist systems, began supplanting planned economies, in which a ruler or other central authority is responsible for all important economic decisions, in the sixteenth through eighteenth centuries.

In the planned economies that predated market-based capitalism, wealth was generally synonymous with land ownership. Rulers were typically chosen from among an elite group of landowners, and most economic activity was carried out for that group's benefit. Although markets allowing people to buy and sell their goods existed under planned economic systems, the revenue generated by the sale of goods and services was subject to the commands of the ruling elite. The products bought and sold in markets were often what was left over after producers had satisfied their obligations to their rulers.

The rise of market economies gave business owners the right to keep their profits. Of course, with this right came the necessity of managing revenue and costs. Whereas a planned economy may have supported a business enterprise that operated at a loss (in other words, one whose costs exceeded its revenues), the market system provides no such support. Any business that hopes to survive in a market economy must at a minimum bring in enough revenue to pay its costs.

More Detailed Information

Revenue is calculated by multiplying the price of a product by the quantity sold. A company's total revenue grows in different ways as quantity increases, depending on the degree of competition in its market.

In a perfectly competitive market for any product, a business has no control over price. There are numerous small sellers, none of whom is able to affect the selling price. Price is set by the competing forces of supply (the amount sellers are willing to sell at a given price) and demand (the amount buyers are willing to buy at a given price). In this situation, revenue increases at a steady rate as quantity increases.

To illustrate this point, consider an asparagus farmer in a perfectly competitive market. If the price of asparagus is set by the forces of supply and demand at $2 per pound, then it does not matter whether the farmer sells 10 pounds of asparagus or 10,000 pounds of asparagus; he will still be paid the same price per unit. His revenue increases by $2 for each pound he sells, no matter what. Since he cannot change the price, the only way for him to increase revenue is to sell more asparagus.

Revenue increases at different rates under other market conditions. In addition to perfect competition, there are three other basic market forms: monopoly, in which one firm is the only seller of a product; oligopoly,

in which a few firms control the market for a product and have substantial control over prices; and monopolistic competition, in which there are numerous firms that have some amount of control over prices. In these market structures the price for which a product is sold changes with the quantity of the product sold.

For example, imagine a drug company that has a patent on (the legal right to be the only seller of) a new pill that is the only effective treatment for a particular disease. The drug company has a monopoly on its market: there is no other drug available to treat that disease, and no one else can sell the chemical formula that constitutes that drug until the patent expires. Since the company does not have to worry about competitors taking away its customers, it can set any price for the drug it wants. The more it charges for its pills, however, the lower the quantity demanded will be.

This results in changing levels of revenue. Say that at $10 per pill the company attracts no customers; this would result in total revenues of zero. At $7.50 it may be able to sell 200,000 pills, resulting in revenues of $1.5

Revenue is all of the money coming into a business, usually as the result of sales of goods and services. For business managers, such as the woman pictured here, it is one important measure of the health of a company. © *2007/Jupiterimages.*

OTHER FORMS OF REVENUE

In economics and business, the term revenue is used most often in connection with what is called a company's top line: the total amount of money it brings in through sales of goods and services. There are, however, other forms of revenue.

Nonprofit organizations generate revenue, just as for-profit companies do. The revenue of nonprofit groups includes not only the money generated by any product sales they may engage in but also money and other resources received in the form of donations.

Governments generate revenue as well. They do so in a number of ways: by imposing fines on people who violate laws, by selling public lands or the resources (such as minerals or timber) on them, and by selling bonds (shares of government debt), among other methods. But the most important source of government revenue is, of course, taxes paid by businesses and individuals. In the United States the national agency responsible for collecting taxes is named, accordingly, the Internal Revenue Service.

million. If the company lowers its price to $5 per pill, it may be able to sell half a million pills, resulting in revenues of $2.5 million. At a price of $2.50, the drug company may be able to sell a million pills, but notice that the total revenue would be the same as at a price of $5: $2.5 million.

This basic pattern of revenue growth relative to price and quantity would apply to any market in which a seller has some control over prices. When a firm has control over prices, it must lower prices to increase revenue. Revenue in such a market does not increase at a constant rate, however, and it only increases up to a point, after which it will begin to decrease.

When a business makes decisions about how much to produce in order to maximize profits, revenue accounts for half of the information it needs. The other half comes in the form of cost, the sum of its expenses on materials, labor, and other resources that go into producing those goods and services. Cost varies with the quantity of goods produced, so a company must find the level of output that maximizes the difference between costs and revenues.

Recent Trends

Companies that issue stock to investors are literally owned by those shareholders, and they have legal responsibilities toward them. Therefore, public companies, as they are called, periodically report on their financial status. Today, businesses issue what are known as "earnings calls," teleconferences with shareholders, financial analysts, and other interested parties during which the company's recent performance is discussed. The

executives who conduct the earnings calls, along with their audience, typically consider revenue to be as important an indicator of the company's future prospects as profit.

For example, a company whose top line, that is, revenue, is growing steadily might be considered in healthy shape even if its profit or bottom-line growth is flat. This might be because one-time expenses, such as purchases of new equipment, can periodically cut into profits without damaging the company's overall outlook for the future, assuming that revenue growth remains strong. On the other hand, a company could manage to create profit growth by cutting costs even if it generated no top-line growth. This is not as desirable, from the point of view of a shareholder or potential investor, as profit growth that is derived from revenue growth. For a company's stock to remain enticing to investors, that company must show steady top-line as well as bottom-line growth.

$ Profit and Loss

What It Means

In any capitalist society businesses exist to make a profit. Profit, also called net income, is commonly defined as the money left over after all of a business's expenses are paid. If a business's expenses are larger than its revenues (total sales), then the business suffers a loss. To continue operating, a business must operate at least at its break-even point, the point at which revenues equal expenses.

A company's profit or loss is often called its bottom line, because profits are often listed on the last line of income statements, documents that break down, by listing all expenses, how a firm's revenues are transformed into either a profit or a loss. Income statements also commonly list gross profits, a figure that represents revenues minus the cost of producing the goods or services sold. Gross profit does not include overhead costs (ongoing costs required to run the business), payroll costs (payments made to workers in the form of wages, salaries, bonuses, and benefits), taxes (payments made to the government), or interest (payments made to banks or other lenders for the use of borrowed money).

For instance, say that your T-shirt shop brought in a total of $100,000 in sales (revenue) over the course of its first year in operation. If you paid out, from that $100,000, $30,000 to T-shirt wholesalers, $25,000 in wages, $15,000 in rent, $7,500 in taxes, and $2,000 in utilities, your T-shirt shop would have made $70,000 in gross profit (since the only direct expense required to generate sales was the cost of the products themselves). After subtracting your company's remaining expenses, however, net income or profit would be $20,500.

Though business owners and investors think of profit and loss in the terms described above, economists define profits as the amount of money left over after both

Businesses achieve profits when their ventures earn more money than they cost to operate; conversely, businesses incur losses when operations cost more money than they earn. American entrepreneur and television personality Donald Trump, pictured here, has achieved tremendous profits but also suffered significant losses over the course of his career. *AP Images.*

explicit costs and opportunity costs have been taken into account. Explicit costs are all those costs described above (costs required to do business). Opportunity cost is the revenue you give up when you choose one form of business activity over another. The opportunity cost of your T-shirt store might include the salary you gave up at your previous job in order to start your own business, as well as the yearly interest you stopped collecting when you used your savings to start up your T-shirt store. If an economist were to determine your store's profits or losses, he or she would add opportunity costs to explicit costs before subtracting from your revenues.

Say that you were making $45,000 at your previous job as a nurse, and that your savings of $20,000, which you used to start your business, would have brought you a 5 percent yearly return ($1,000 during your T-shirt shop's first year in operation). From the figure of $20,500 (your net income, or profit), the economist

would subtract your implicit costs of $46,000. From the economic point of view, then, your T-shirt store registered a first-year economic loss of $25,500.

Economists define profit in this way because they believe that people make real-world business decisions based not only on concrete figures like explicit costs but also on the less tangible, but very influential, implicit costs that they undertake when they do business. Indeed, as a T-shirt store owner, even if you had never heard of the concept of implicit costs, you would not be likely to forget that you had put $20,000 of your own money into your business nor that you used to be guaranteed $45,000 a year in your nursing days. In deciding whether to renew your lease and stay in business for another year, you would almost certainly take these factors into account.

When Did It Begin

No doubt businesspeople throughout history have always tried to make a profit wherever possible, but in precapitalist systems the profit motive was not the primary engine of economic activity. Many ancient and medieval societies were dominated by monarchs and other nobles who controlled virtually all land and, therefore, all political power and wealth. Workers in such societies practiced their trades as dictated by traditions and the direct commands of these authority figures. Even when there were markets, places where buyers and sellers of various products came together, these seemingly capitalist phenomena were limited to that portion of a farmer or tradesman's produce that was left over after his obligations to authority figures had been fulfilled.

Land was necessary for the acquisition of wealth as well as power in most precapitalist societies. Those who inherited large plots of land were able to use that land to add to their wealth, and others could become wealthy by being given land by a monarch or by being made the ruler of a large amount of land. Julius Caesar, for instance, began to build his power and wealth when he was appointed governor of what is now Spain. Though Caesar and others in similar positions throughout history could amass great wealth simply by claiming it from those who lived in their territories, this was not profit. The more power and land a person could obtain, the more wealth he could obtain essentially by force.

The rise of capitalism in sixteenth- to eighteenth-century Europe dramatically changed this situation, however. Once markets (any place where buyers and sellers come together to do business) became the central way of organizing economic activities, capitalists—or those who conducted business with a view toward profiting—began outstripping aristocratic landowners in both wealth and power. The Industrial Revolution, the drastic change in daily life brought about by new technologies that radically increased the efficiency with which businesses could produce goods and services, cemented

PROFIT MAXIMIZATION AND RATIONAL CHOICE

Economists base many of their theories on the notion that economic decision-makers act rationally in the pursuit of maximum profits for themselves. If this dual assumption (about rationality and profit-maximizing behavior) can be made, then using basic laws such as those of supply and demand (as well as other, more specialized concepts), economists can make predictions about a wide variety of phenomena ranging from the behavior of criminals to the effects of globalization on the computer industry. Those of us who are not economists, however, might wonder whether it is always safe to assume that everyone involved in any sort of economic activity is motivated by a desire for maximum profit, and we might be especially skeptical of the notion that these people act rationally all or most of the time.

Economists are generally aware that these assumptions oversimplify the ways of the world. There are several reasons, however, to take seriously the oversimplified picture of reality that economics offers. First, the assumptions about profit maximization and rational choice allow us to predict human behavior more accurately than most other simplified views of economic activity we might be able to construct. Second, when considering economic phenomena, we are generally considering masses of people, so that general tendencies of behavior are more important than the exceptions to that behavior. Irrationality, when averaged out over a large group of people, may not be as significant a factor in society as we think. And finally, economists often focus not on people randomly selected from a given population but on people—whether they are criminals or the CEOs of computer companies—who have proven themselves effective in their chosen fields. An irrational or insufficiently profit-minded criminal will not remain a criminal for long, just as an irrational or insufficiently profit-minded CEO will not remain a CEO for long.

capitalism as the dominant mode of wealth creation in the eighteenth and nineteenth centuries. Capitalist societies, which could not exist without the motivating forces of profit and loss, have dominated world history since this time. Attempts have been made since the Industrial Revolution to create societies not fueled by the desire of individuals to make profits. The most notable of these is perhaps the Soviet Union, which existed as a socialist state (in which profits are commonly redistributed among the population to serve social goals) from 1922–91. Such societies have so far proven less enduring than their capitalist counterparts.

More Detailed Information

The motivating powers of profit and loss are crucial to the operation of a capitalist system. One of the chief assumptions made by economists is that all economic decision-makers (buyers and sellers at the individual or the group level) are motivated by the desire to maximize profit. Profit maximization involves combining resources in the most efficient ways, so that the difference between revenue and expenses grows to maximum possible levels.

Businesses in competitive industries do not have control over prices. Sellers must compete against one another for buyers, and vice versa. All sellers want the highest possible prices for their goods and services, but they cannot set prices too high because their competitors could undercut them, and they would not be able to find buyers. Likewise, buyers compete with other buyers for the products they want, and this combined force of self-interested individuals keeps prices from falling too low.

With prices thus beyond their control, businesses find as many ways of cutting costs as is possible. As a result, they develop the most efficient possible methods for producing their goods and services. The urge for

profit maximization therefore results in maximum efficiency throughout the economy. Resources such as land, labor, and equipment are combined in ways that allow all of them to contribute the maximum amount of usefulness to society.

The self-interested drive to profit also results in markets that are, according to economists, able to respond more effectively and quickly to the desires of consumers, and to changing circumstances more generally, than are any other systems for organizing production and distribution.

For instance, assume that an economy produces an equal amount of beef and chicken, but that, for whatever reason, a large number of buyers suddenly prefer chicken to beef. All of those chicken buyers will compete against one another for a limited supply of chicken, and this heightened demand will mean that chicken sellers can raise prices. Once chicken farming has become more profitable, more farmers will rush to allocate their resources to the raising of chickens, and fewer to the raising of cattle, which is what that large group of buyers was asking for in the first place. When the supply of chicken begins to equal the demand for chicken, prices will begin to fall.

Thus, according to mainstream economic theory, prices in a competitive market will eventually approach the break-even point, the point at which revenues and expenses balance one another out. This is the minimum level of revenue that a company must obtain in order to stay in business. If prices fall so far that chicken farmers' expenses outweigh their revenues and losses result, farmers will stop producing chicken.

If profit theoretically disappears as competition balances the market forces determining the price of any good over the long term, why do profits exist? Some economists throughout history have theorized that profits exist only because of the behavior of business owners. The economist, philosopher, and revolutionary Karl Marx (1818-83), for example, suggested in his book *Das Kapital* that profits, which should not exist in competitive industries but that, in reality, often do exist, must consist of the capitalist business owner's unfair seizure of wages that rightfully belonged to workers. Though this idea has been very influential over time, economists largely disagree with it because it is based on a theory that the prices of goods are based strictly on the cost of producing them rather than on other factors as well, such as consumer demand.

Mainstream economists, accordingly, have developed a variety of explanations for the existence of profits. Most of these theories hold that profit is the legitimate product of certain attributes of capitalists. Among these attributes is the business owner's willingness to delay his or her gratification. Rather than consuming all of his or her income and resources in the present, the owner of a profitable business firm invests in capital (physical things that add to the productive capacity of his or her business) that will bring in more money in the future.

Another explanation for profit is that it is sometimes a reward for the capitalist's willingness to take risks. Some investments inevitably fail, so anytime a capitalist puts money into a business enterprise, he or she stands to lose it. The riskier a business enterprise is, in general, the more profitable that enterprise must potentially be.

Yet another way that capitalists are said to generate profits is through any combination of innovation, organization, and entrepreneurial ability. Those who have the ability to invent new products or to find new ways of maximizing the difference between revenue and expenses have, in this view, earned the profits that result.

Recent Trends

In addition to the aforementioned three ways in which capitalists are said to generate profits, there are at least two other explanations for the existence of profit in today's world. One of these is market imperfections, or situations in which prices may vary for identical products without good reason. You may buy a pair of shoes online at a price that seems reasonable, only to find later that day that the same pair of shoes costs $10 less at the mall in your town. In this situation the seller of the overpriced shoes has made a profit that cannot be accounted for by market forces. While such imperfections are likely to persist in all market economies, they make up a small portion of total profits in any economy today.

Another undesirable form of profit creation happens when there is a monopoly in any industry. When a single business firm dominates an industry, it has the power to set higher prices than would be possible under conditions of perfect competition and therefore to make profits independently of any value its owners have created. Profits

from monopolies were a larger part of economies in the nineteenth and early twentieth centuries than they are today. Those monopolies that exist in rich societies today tend to have less power than their predecessors because the economy in a rich society is typically based on sales of luxury products and products for which there are many viable substitutes. In the United States, for instance, Major League Baseball has a monopoly on a particular form of entertainment, but if prices for watching games in person or on television were to rise unreasonably, Americans could easily choose to focus on other forms of entertainment.

One monopoly that continues to profit greatly from its status, despite the many forces arrayed against monopoly creation in the present age, is the De Beers diamond monopoly. De Beers controls 80 percent of the world diamond market, and it therefore has the power to set quantities and prices for all diamonds sold in the world, ensuring itself profits that comfortably exceed the natural returns that would be dictated by a competitive market.

$ Long Run versus Short Run

What It Means

In analyzing decisions that businesses make, economists talk about two different time frames: the short run and the long run. These terms do not correspond to literal periods of time, such as two months or two years; instead, they are defined according to the range of options a business has for changing its output, or the final items it produces for sale. In the eyes of economists, a business can change its output by making alterations to inputs, the various ingredients required to produce whatever it is that a given company produces. Inputs (often called the factors of production) include land and natural resources, labor, and capital (equipment needed to do business). The short run is the period during which some inputs are fixed and unchangeable, while others are variable. The long run is the period during which all inputs are variable.

For example, imagine a company, Best Bats, that makes wooden baseball bats. In the short run, Best Bats has fixed as well as variable inputs. One fixed input is the size of its factory and machines. One variable input is the size of its labor force. The quantity of bats the company can produce is constrained by the fixed size of the factory and machines, but within the limits imposed by these fixed inputs, Best Bats does have some flexibility to increase output by increasing the number of its workers or the hours they work.

In the long run, by contrast, all inputs are variable. Best Bats can alter its workforce to meet any variety of business demands, and it can also build new factories and purchase new machinery. Additionally, new bat

When imagining ways to expand its business, a company typically considers both short-run solutions (such as hiring new employees in order to increase production right away) and long-run measures (for example, building a new factory in order to double production capacity in the future). Here a project manager presents various factors involved in short- and long-run business plans. *David De Lossy/Photodisc/Getty Images.*

manufacturers can build factories and enter the market in the long run.

The length of the short run, and the moment at which it gives way to the long run, would be defined by the length of time it takes Best Bats (or a new company) to build the factory and install the new machinery. Accordingly, the duration of the short run differs from industry to industry, company to company, and situation to situation.

When Did It Begin

The concepts of the short run and the long run, as they are understood today, were popularized by the British economist Alfred Marshall (1842–1924), whose *Principles of Economics* was the standard economics textbook for decades after its first publication in 1890. Marshall was one of the first economists to grasp fully the importance of time in the interaction between supply (the quantity of a good that sellers are willing to sell over a range of prices) and demand (the quantity of a good that buyers are willing to buy over a range of prices). Prices are always dependent on supply and demand; these competing forces balance one another out, theoretically,

at an equilibrium price that is acceptable to both sellers and buyers. Marshall's contribution was to point out that the equilibrium price for any good was different depending on the time conditions of the buying and selling. In the short term, a diamond merchant and his customers might bargain over a set number of diamonds (the ones he had with him at that moment), arriving at an equilibrium price based on the fact that the supply was clearly limited. Over the long term, however, the merchant or his employers could open more diamond mines if consumer demand warranted it. This change in the level of supply would change the equilibrium price for diamonds.

More Detailed Information

To understand the variable nature of the time periods represented by the terms short run and long run, consider the contrast between our bat manufacturer, Best Bats, and a hot-dog vendor, Sally. Say that Best Bats produces 5,000 bats a day between the hours of nine o'clock in the morning and five o'clock in the afternoon, utilizing a 10,000 square-foot factory and a workforce of 50 men and women. If Best Bats begins getting orders from sporting goods stores that require it to produce 10,000 bats per day, in the short run it has some options but not others. It cannot satisfy these orders immediately by building a new factory. It might, however, quickly develop the capability to fill these orders if it hires 50 new workers to work a late shift, after the other 50 have gone home. If Best Bats' orders begin to outpace even these increases, its owners might decide to invest in a new factory. A 10,000 square-foot factory might take as long as a year to build. In the case of Best Bats, then, the duration of the short run would be one year, and long run would be any amount of time greater than one year.

Sally, meanwhile, rents her hot-dog cart on a daily basis and then wheels it out into the city streets and tries to sell out of her supply of 500 hot dogs. Say that Sally consistently sells out of her hot dogs after eight hours at her cart, and that she decides she wants to try and sell more hot dogs in a day. She can return to the cart-supplier's warehouse tomorrow with her little sister Sheila in tow, rent out a cart and purchase hot dogs for Sheila to sell, and expand her operation immediately. In this case, the short run lasts less than one day. Long-run changes in inputs are those that require at least one day to take effect.

In the short run businesses are susceptible to the law of diminishing returns. This law states that as additional units of a variable factor (such as labor) is added to a fixed factor (such as capital), productivity will decrease beyond a certain point. For example, if Best Bats tries to increase production of bats not only by adding a night shift of workers but by doubling the number of workers that operate the factory equipment at any given time, the law of diminishing returns may come into play. It may be that the bat factory's machines cannot be efficiently operated by more than 75 people. Once there are more than 75 people on the factory floor, some amount of the workforce is not doing efficient work. People stand around without anything to do because there is no room for them at the machinery. They might even get in the way of those who are otherwise able to do productive work. Best Bats has doubled the amount of money it is spending on the variable input of labor, but it is not doubling its output of bats.

When considering long-run changes to such inputs as capital, a company seeks to take advantage of what economists call economies of scale. As a company produces more and more units of a good, it has numerous opportunities to cut its input costs per unit. Thus, Best Bats might build a new factory that doubles the amount of money it spends on inputs, but it might be able to produce and sell more than double the amount of bats as a result. This is because there are various ways of cutting costs open to large-scale producers that are not available to smaller-scale producers. Economies of scale, as these ways of cutting costs are called, do not inevitably result from expansion, however. It is possible that a business

could make long-run changes to capital and labor that yield a result that is roughly proportionate to its previous level of output. It is also possible that the business's efficiency could suffer as a result of expansion. In this case, a diseconomy of scale would be present.

Recent Trends

The concepts of the short run and the long run have remained constant over time. Companies today make short-run and long-run decisions much in the way that they did in the late nineteenth or early twentieth century. For example, Best Bats' capital inputs (factory size and machinery) would have been fixed in the short run in 2007 no less than in 1907, and its labor inputs would have been similarly variable regardless of the historical context. However, the length of the short run likely would have varied considerably during these periods due to such factors as technology. In 1907 it might have taken three years to build a new factory with the technologies then available, whereas it may only have taken one year in 2007. Likewise, a business would have been able to hire, fire, or otherwise alter its labor inputs in both eras, but in 2007 the company may have been subject to greater government restrictions in this regard, though not to the degree that its labor input had become fixed. Thus, the scope of short- and long-run decisions may change over time, but the basic principles remain the same.

$ Economies of Scale

What It Means

As companies produce larger and larger quantities of goods, they have an increasing ability to cut the cost of producing each individual good. When they are able to

As a company's production increases, the average cost of making the product sometimes decreases. The phenomenon, called economies of scale, has been used by Wal-Mart to become one of the biggest and most successful corporations in the world. *Photograph by Kelly A. Quin. Cengage Learning, Gale.*

do so, they are said to be taking advantage of economies of scale.

Imagine that Jim opens a business, Pies by Jim, that produces cherry and apple pies to sell at wholesale prices to restaurants and at retail prices on his bakery grounds. In the beginning Jim not only bakes the pies, but he also takes orders from restaurants, makes deliveries, personally sells pies over the counter at his bakery, writes advertisements that run in the local newspaper, does the accounting each day, and cleans his bakery and storefront every night. Though Jim's costs are low, since he does not have to pay anyone to do these various jobs, he could in fact be conducting his business in an inefficient way. Say that Jim decides to focus his own energies on the baking. He hires someone to take orders, sell the pies, and make deliveries; he hires a second person to market the pies and do the accounting; and he hires a third person to do the cleaning. It might seem that, with four workers (including Jim), Pies by Jim would naturally produce four times as many pies as before. In fact, it is likely that Jim can oversee the production of more pies than that, due to the increased efficiency that arises when each employee specializes in one set of tasks. Jim has begun to experience the benefits of economies of scale. As his company grows, Jim will likely have other opportunities and methods for using his company's increased output to his advantage.

The principle of economies of scale explains much of the economic growth that occurs at the company, the national, and the international level.

When Did It Begin

In the late eighteenth and early nineteenth centuries, Europe's economy began to be transformed by the advent of new technologies such as the steam engine, machines for spinning and weaving thread for textiles, and coal-burning furnaces for making steel. The use of these technologies allowed business owners to set up factories and greatly increase their output, reaping the benefits of economies of scale and, in the process, dramatically changing the way people lived and worked. The dramatic changes in society resulting from these economic innovations became known as the Industrial Revolution.

The Industrial Revolution continued in the next century and spread fully to the United States. Yet again, new technologies led to increased efficiency and the ability to enjoy economies of scale. The rise of railroads, oceangoing steamships, and telegraphs made long-distance communication and the transport of large volumes of goods possible, so that business could be conducted beyond the regional level. Likewise, the ability to make large number of goods while minimizing costs was enhanced by the invention of electricity, which increased the efficiency of industrial machinery and factories, and by the numerous advances in modern science that led to new, better, and cheaper consumer products. The increases in industrial efficiency available to late-nineteenth and early-twentieth industrialists allowed such figures as John D. Rockefeller (of Standard Oil) and Andrew Carnegie (of U.S. Steel) to conduct business on a previously unimaginable scale and to overwhelm any competitors. Another industrialist who famously took advantage of economies of scale was Henry Ford. By inventing the assembly-line mode of producing automobiles, Ford greatly increased his workers' efficiency and cut the cost per car measurably.

More Detailed Information

Economies of scale come in many forms. One form occurs when a company lowers its input costs (an input is any resource needed to make a good or service). For example, as Pies by Jim expands into a regional powerhouse, opening numerous bakeries and supplying all restaurants in a three-state area with pies, Jim will likely be able to buy the ingredients for his pies more cheaply. This is possible because buying in larger amounts reduces the costs to his suppliers. The supplier from whom he purchases flour, butter, and sugar fills up one truck and delivers it to Jim's three warehouses, rather than to a dozen individual bakeries; this reduces the supplier's fuel costs as well as the costs of employing a driver to make deliveries.

Other economies of scale can result when, because of the increasing size of a company's output, the company gets more use out of particularly expensive inputs. Advertising and management are examples of expensive inputs. Say that Jim paid $1,000 a week to run advertisements in local papers. When Pies by Jim only produced 1,000 pies a week, that amounts to $1 per pie for advertising. Once Pies by Jim's output increases to 10,000 pies per week, Jim is only paying $0.10 per pie for advertising. Thus, Jim keeps more money per pie. The same goes for Jim's managers. Assume that, at an early stage of his expansion, Jim employed a manager to oversee his bakery workers so that he, Jim, could concentrate on refining his recipes. If Jim pays his manager $4,000 per week, Jim gets more mileage out of that manager as his labor force grows. Assuming that the manager can efficiently manage 20 employees, Jim has cut his managerial costs in half by increasing his work force to that level.

A company can also create economies of scale by developing more specialized inputs. For example, say that Jim employs one person to roll out pie crusts, to mold them into pie pans, to fill them, and to apply the top layer of crust. If, as Pies by Jim expands, Jim assigns each of these four jobs to a specific person, pies will get made faster because each person can focus on one task and

master it, rather than waste effort and concentration trying to master a variety of tasks.

Economies of scale may also result from improved organizational strategies. If, for instance, as Jim's workforce expands so that 50 people work behind the scenes making pies at each of his four bakeries, Jim might be able to establish efficient organizational structures. Jim might split the 50 bakers at each site into squads of five workers, each doing the same job, led by a squad leader who has the most seniority and can solve most problems as they arise. The squad leaders, in turn, might answer to a manager who, like 10 other managers, answers to Jim. Such a clear-cut organization of bakers might increase the company's efficiency.

Finally, there are learning inputs that can improve efficiency. As each member of Jim's workforce learns how to do his or her job better and better, the overall cost per pie produced falls.

The above are all examples of internal economies of scale; each was a product of changes within Pies by Jim. There are also external economies of scale, which occur outside a company. For example, if the state government paves back roads connecting the farms of the fruit growers Jim buys from to the highways along which Jim's warehouses are located, the growers might charge Jim less for their fruit, since their delivery costs are reduced. Alternatively, imagine that a jam manufacturer also exists near the towns where Jim does business. As Jim and the jam company both expand their operations, their presence might encourage more farmers to put their land into fruit production. An increase in the supply of fruit will probably lower the costs that both Jim and the jam company pay.

It should be noted that expansion of a business does not always produce lower costs. Sometimes inefficiencies develop when a business expands too quickly or unwisely. For example, Jim may not hire enough managers to oversee his ballooning workforce, with the result that the workers' productivity actually decreases, or Pies by Jim may find that expansion into an ever-growing geographical area eventually produces transportation costs that are so high as to eliminate other cost-cutting methods made possible by the expansion. Such problems are called diseconomies of scale.

Recent Trends

In the pursuit of ever-expanding economies of scale, businesses in the late twentieth and early twenty-first century increasingly began doing business outside the borders of their home countries. This resulted in a phenomenon that became known as globalization, the growing interconnectedness of national economies. While globalization brought increased jobs and economic growth to many parts of the world, it also had many critics. One fear that many people shared was that globalization would lead to a world economy completely

ECONOMIES OF SCALE, OLIGOPOLY, AND MONOPOLY

In some industries the principle of economies of scale (which says that as a company grows and increases its output, its production costs will decrease) naturally produces oligopolies (situations in which a handful of businesses dominates an industry) and monopolies (situations in which a single business dominates an industry).

For example, the automobile industry in the United States is one that naturally tends toward an oligopoly. Because of the steep cost of manufacturing cars, a company can get a healthy return on its investment in materials, labor, and other resources only if it produces a quantity of cars roughly equal to 10 percent of the entire U.S. market. The U.S. auto market could only accommodate, at a maximum, around 10 auto makers.

The electric power industry, by contrast, is one that tends toward a monopoly. A power plant must reach a certain, very large size before electricity production becomes efficient. Beyond that point, the average cost per unit of electricity decreases rapidly. Thus, in many areas the presence of two electric companies would mean that consumers would end up paying more for electricity than under a monopoly.

dominated by a handful of multinational corporations (companies that do business in more than one country). Because of their ability to take advantage of economies of scale on the global level, multinational corporations were during this time making it increasingly difficult for smaller businesses to compete.

A soda company trying to enter the market in virtually any part of the world today would, for example, have to compete against such brands as Coca-Cola and Pepsi. No matter how superior the new company's soda might be, the company would have nowhere near the ability to cut its average costs as Coke and Pepsi have by virtue of their size. Therefore, the new soda would inevitably cost more to manufacture, even if it used the same basic ingredients and was manufactured by a similar method. Until the company grew to the size of its gigantic multinational competitors, it would have a pronounced disadvantage in the marketplace. Most companies inevitably fail to overcome such a disadvantage.

$ Barriers to Entry

What It Means

Barriers to entry include all of the obstacles that discourage and sometimes prevent new companies from entering an area of business. High start-up costs (the money required to open a business) and licensing fees are two of the most effective barriers to entry, especially in

the restaurant business. For instance, the start-up costs to open a dining establishment include the rent (monthly fee) for space in a building, the kitchen equipment, the cost of food and ingredients, and many other fees. After these costs have been met, the restaurant owner is likely to want to offer customers alcoholic beverages. This requires two separate licenses, a wine-and-beer license and a liquor license. In the United States the fees for such documents vary from state to state. All of these impediments benefit existing restaurants by restricting the number of new competitors that can enter the market and lure away customers.

Barriers to entry can also refer to the obstacles an individual faces when seeking employment in a certain trade or occupation. These barriers frequently include educational and licensing requirements. For example, in the United States a person who wants to become a lawyer must graduate from law school and pass a bar examination (a test given by each state, which, if completed successfully, certifies that an individual can practice law in that state). In other fields, such as athletics and the arts, the degree of talent required to make a living is an effective barrier to entry.

When Did It Begin

Political rule by an aristocracy (a small, privileged social class that usually consists of nobility) was one of the earliest and most effective barriers to entry for individuals seeking to rise in society and acquire wealth. Throughout history most aristocracies have been hereditary, meaning that an individual had to be born into this group in order to claim membership. In Western culture the aristocratic or noble class came into being in ancient Greece, where leaders of armies were judged to be the most virtuous, and therefore the best, men in society. They were given authority to make decisions on behalf of the community, a privilege they earned through their deeds. Throughout the Middle Ages (approximately 500 to 1500), as nations were formed in Europe, membership in the aristocracy gradually came to be determined by birth. If an individual was not born into an aristocratic family, that person would not be able to gain entrance into the aristocratic class.

In the Early Middle Ages (from about 500 to 1000), guilds (associations of craftspeople such as blacksmiths or carpenters) began to appear, acting as a new kind of barrier to entry. These organizations were composed of people who were in a lower class than the aristocrats and provided goods and services for them. Guilds had formal systems in place for admitting, training, and ranking members. Individuals entered as apprentices (beginners learning the trade), developed into journeymen (who were trained but still supervised by an expert), and progressed to become master craftsmen. Advancing to this final status required the formal approval of all members of the guild.

Barriers to entry refer to obstacles, such as high start-up costs, that make it difficult for a company to gain entry into a certain business area. It is even more difficult if another firm has a government patent, such as the one in this photo, giving the firm exclusive right to an important technology, process, or good. *AP Images.*

More Detailed Information

In the arena of nationally distributed products and services, two of the most significant barriers to entry are economies of scale and brand recognition (also called brand awareness). The term *economy of scale* refers to the way that, when a business grows, its average production costs usually decrease. As a result, large businesses tend to be less expensive to operate than small businesses. For example, consider the challenges facing a small entrepreneur who wants to manufacture and distribute ice cream in the northeastern region of the United States but who must compete against a national brand-name ice cream company. Suppose the larger business spends $10,000 a day to produce ice cream, and the smaller one will only spend $5,000. The national company is spending twice as much money, but it produces 7,500 gallons of ice cream a day, while the regional company will only produce 2,500 gallons. According to these figures, the larger company spends $1.33 per gallon of ice cream. Meanwhile, the smaller company will spend $2.00 per gallon. Thus, the average cost of producing a gallon of ice cream is significantly lower for the larger company. This allows it to sell its ice cream for less money, making it

difficult for the regional business to lure customers away from the national brand.

The other major barrier is brand recognition, which refers to customer familiarity with a product or a corporation. For example, Coca-Cola and Pepsi have created a high degree of brand awareness. Most American consumers immediately think of these two brands first when they consider purchasing a cola beverage. Any company that wanted to put a new cola on the market would have a difficult time getting prospective customers to think of its product before Coke and Pepsi.

Economists and lawmakers monitor barriers to entry because these market factors affect competition. If barriers to entry are too difficult to overcome, the number of manufacturers for a specific good decreases. This could lead to a situation in which there is only one provider of a good; in such a case the company producing that good is called a monopoly. For example, if Pepsi were the only manufacturer of soft drinks, the company would have a monopoly in this market and would be free to charge as much as it wished for its products. Except in rare cases, monopolies are illegal in the United States. On the other hand, if there are no barriers to entry to a given market,

HOW NETFLIX ENTERED THE DVD-RENTAL MARKET

One way for a new business to attract customers in a competitive market is to conduct sales in a noticeably different manner than rival corporations. In the late 1990s, for instance, the U.S. video-rental market was dominated by Blockbuster and Hollywood Video. At that time it was unlikely that a start-up company could compete with either of these establishments by opening stores that operated on the same business model. Both companies rented movies in a traditional walk-in, over-the-counter format (customers went to the store, selected a video, and paid a rental fee at the counter). They also charged late fees when customers did not return the videos on time. Instead of imitating this model, Netflix, Inc., which began operations in 1998, used the Internet and the United States Postal Service to rent out movies. Customers subscribed to Netflix online at http://www.netflix.com, paid a monthly fee, and received by mail the DVDs they wanted to rent. There were no late fees. Customers mailed the videos back whenever they wished (Netflix provided a self-addressed, stamped envelope), but they would not receive new disks until they returned those that they had borrowed. In 2006 Netflix shipped an average of 1.4 million DVDs a day.

too many producers can enter that market, and the excessive competition will keep prices too low. This will reduce profits, which in turn will limit the amount of money companies can invest in improving their products.

Recent Trends

The technology boom and the rise of the Internet since 1995 have had a series of effects on the barriers to entry in the computer industry. When the Internet and home computers became popular in the mid-1990s, many new types of businesses arose. Three of these were Web-development firms (companies that design and maintain websites for other companies and for individuals), online stores (businesses that sell products over the Internet), and technical support (companies and individuals that help others maintain their computer systems). Early in this period people could open businesses in these fields with little trouble because customers were eager to acquire these products and services but had few standards for judging the quality of what they were receiving. The only things preventing an individual from creating one of these businesses were the start-up costs and the technical knowledge required to provide such services.

More significant barriers to entry in the computer industry have gradually emerged. For instance, with regard to Web development, websites have grown more sophisticated and require not only significant computer programming skills but also expertise in design. The majority of the initial online stores failed, and e-com-

merce soon became a big-business endeavor dominated by large operations such as eBay and Amazon.com. In the field of technical support, a major barrier to entry for individuals is that licensing policies have gotten stricter and more costly.

$ Law of Diminishing Returns

What It Means

The law of diminishing returns, one of the best-known economic ideas, concerns the production of goods or services. In the production of any good or service, there are "inputs" and "output." Inputs are all of those things required to make the good, such as land, labor, machinery, and raw materials. Output is the sum of all the final products that these inputs are able to generate. In a simple farming operation, for instance, the inputs might include four laborers, 100 acres of land, one tractor, one truck, and seeds. Using these inputs, the farm might be able to produce an output of 500 bushels of corn.

The law of diminishing returns addresses what happens when one input in the production process is increased while the others are held steady. If, for instance, the farm in the above example sets out to increase output, it might start hiring new workers. But if all the other inputs stayed the same, there would eventually be a point at which the increases in output, per worker, would begin to diminish. Past that point, the output produced by each worker would be less than the output produced by the smaller number of workers at an earlier stage of the farm's development.

While the law of diminishing returns results in decreased output, it does not necessarily have a bearing on the farm's profitability. In business a profit is the amount of money an individual or company earns through output after accounting for input expenses. For example, if a farmer spends $10,000 a month on production costs (equipment, materials, labor, land-related expenses, and so on) and earns $12,000 a month in crop sales, then the farmer's profit (commonly known as a profit margin) is $2,000 a month—or, $200 per $1,000 spent on operational costs. In this respect, the farm is profitable.

Using the same example, say the farmer hires two additional laborers at an additional cost of $2,000 per month, bringing his total operational expenses to $12,000. If his total monthly earnings increase to $14,300—or, roughly $192 per $1,000 spent—then the farmer has seen diminishing returns on his hiring of two additional workers; however, the farmer has still increased his total profit, from $2,000 to $2,300. In this sense, while the hiring of two additional workers resulted in diminishing returns, it also resulted in greater profits.

When Did It Begin

The first appearances of the concept that we now call the law of diminishing returns can be found in the writings of several early economists, such as those of the eighteenth-

When applied to agriculture, the law of diminishing returns states that if the number of workers on a farm increases and all other factors remain the same, the amount harvested per worker will eventually decline as additional workers are added. In other words, a farm cannot continue to increase output at the same rate simply by hiring new workers. © *James Leynse/Corbis.*

century French statesman, writer, and economist Anne-Robert-Jacques Turgot (1727–81). The concept came to the fore of the work of two of the most important nineteenth-century economists, Thomas Malthus and David Ricardo, both of whom lived and worked in England.

Malthus and Ricardo, writing in the early decades of that century, both worried about England's population relative to the amount of food and other goods that could be produced in the country. Malthus believed that England's population was growing faster than its capacity to produce food and that the end result would be a nightmarish catastrophe. Ricardo did not agree entirely with Malthus's doomsday predictions, but he also noted that increased inputs did not always result in proportional increases in output. Malthus, Ricardo, and economists that came after established the idea that, as population expanded, the output per person would inevitably decline.

More Detailed Information

Diminishing returns begin at the point when the proportion of all the other inputs (land, raw materials, ma-

chinery) falls relative to the input that is changed. There is only so much corn, obviously, that can be grown on 100 acres of land, using one tractor, one truck, and a constant number of seeds. At first, the farmer might find that with only four workers, some of those other inputs (the land, the tractor, the truck, the seeds) were not being fully utilized. Maybe after he increases his workforce to six laborers, he finds that those six people use those inputs more efficiently than the original four did. But he might find that, at eight employees, he has lost efficiency. It might be that with eight bodies on 100 acres, the workers begin to get in one another's way, or they spend too much time waiting around to use the available equipment. At any rate, if the farmer finds that his expanding workforce does not produce a proportional expansion of output, diminishing returns have begun. If the farmer keeps hiring workers, the amount of output per worker will continue to diminish.

The same principle would apply if it were another input being changed. For example, imagine that the farmer keeps his workforce stable at four employees,

RETURNS TO SCALE

The law of diminishing returns states that as one input is increased while all other inputs remain stable, eventually the increases in output will diminish. If you own a button factory, for instance, and you need two people to operate the button-making machine, hiring an additional person will not result in a proportional increase in button output. The third worker might be able to replace workers one and two when they need to take a break, but if she is not able to work just as much as one and two were working beforehand, then you get diminishing returns from employing her.

But what if you buy another button-making machine? Well, naturally, then, you will not be subject to the law of diminishing returns at the same point in your hiring process. You would, in fact, need to hire two more workers, instead of just one, to reach your optimal capacity of workers. If you increase your machinery and your workers in proportion, then you have a good chance of increasing your output by the same proportion. This property of the production process is what economists call a "return to scale."

maintains all the other inputs at their original levels (100 acres, one tractor, and one truck), but increases the number of seeds he plants by one-half. He might initially find that this increases his output proportionately (by one-half), which encourages him to increase the number of seeds yet again. Once he has increased his seed count by double the original amount, however, he might find that his output begins to diminish. If double the amount of seeds only yields one and three-quarters the output he produced initially, then he has reached the point of diminishing returns. If he goes on to add even more seeds, his return per seed will continue to drop.

Recent Trends

One of the reasons that the law of diminishing returns does not necessarily result (as early economists believed it would, in a situation where population increases faster than the world's food production capacity) is the existence of technology. The early economists understated (or did not take into account at all) the effect of new technologies on production. Similarly, the law of diminishing returns assumes a situation in which technology, like all the other inputs, is constant. If the farmer in the above example started using a dramatically effective new fertilizer, for instance, the law of diminishing returns might not take effect at the same point. He might be able to triple output by doubling the number of seeds he plants. With this drastic increase in the food supply, further expansion of the population will be much less problematic.

In countries where new technology is not always readily accessible or implemented, however, the effects of the law of diminishing returns become clear. If production methods remain unchanged for long periods of time, economic stagnation is the norm.

$ Opportunity Costs

What It Means

Every economic decision carries a cost, a price that must be paid in order to acquire or produce anything. Costs can come in terms of money, time, labor, or even the trouble it takes. For instance, nearly every action a person makes uses up money, time, or both; that money or time could have been used for other things that that person values. In economics, cost is often viewed in terms of the opportunity that is given up when a decision is made; this is called opportunity cost. In a simple example, if Maria chooses to go to college full-time, she chooses not to spend that time on working and earning a full-time salary at a job. Therefore, the cost of attending college is not just the money Maria spends on school; it also includes the value of her next-best alternative, the job she has given up to attend college.

The opportunity cost of a choice includes both explicit and implicit costs. The explicit cost is easily identifiable because it is a measurement of the money sacrificed through actual payments for a particular choice. In Maria's case, the explicit cost of going to college is the amount she spends on tuition and books (but not food and clothing, because she would have to purchase those regardless). The explicit costs a business might typically have include a wage paid out to an employee, rent paid for use of a building, and payments for new materials. The explicit, or direct money, cost may only be a part—and sometimes just a small part—of the opportunity cost of a choice.

The implicit cost is the value of anything other than direct payment that is sacrificed. Time is usually the biggest type of implicit cost, because time can often be spent earning money. When Maria chooses to attend college full-time, one implicit cost of that decision is the time she could have spent earning money at a full-time job. Because implicit costs are largely intangible, they can be hard to assess. For a business, use of its facilities and equipment and even the time that the owner spends on the business are all considered implicit costs.

When Did It Begin

The concepts of opportunity cost and explicit and implicit costs developed along with modern forms of business. In the decades after World War II (1939–45), business in the United States grew rapidly. With that growth came a greater understanding of economic profit and the various types of costs that a business takes on in order to achieve profitability.

Additionally, the population increase of the last half-century has meant that all resources, including land and money, have been growing increasingly scarce. The scarcities of resources such as land, money, and time have contributed to greater competition and, for some members of society, have created more wealth. A talented entrepreneur, for example, can earn hundreds of dollars for an hour of work. Therefore, each activity that such a person undertakes carries a high opportunity cost.

Greater population pressure on land in many U.S. cities means that officials making real estate decisions there have to consider opportunity costs carefully. For instance, if a city is choosing between constructing a stadium and a convention center, it needs to determine as fully as possible the costs of giving up either option.

More Detailed Information

With many choices, the largest part of the opportunity cost is the money sacrificed. For instance, if a person spends $18 on a new compact disc, he has to part with $18, which is money he could have spent on something else. Other than this sacrifice, there is little additional cost involved. For other choices, money may be a small part of what is given up. Sometimes there is no money sacrificed. If you decide to spend an hour watering your plants instead of working out at the gym, you have given up time but no money.

Economists tend to attach monetary values to costs that do not involve money, although individuals rarely do. By giving a monetary value to sacrifices, it is easier to understand costs in terms of a number, even if the number is an estimate. This makes it easier to compare the cost of a choice with its benefits, which are often represented in dollars (or whatever the local currency is). The person who chooses to attend college full-time instead of working full-time can develop an estimation of the many explicit costs of her choice (by adding up the payments she makes to go to college). She could also estimate the implicit cost, the amount of income she would be able to make if she were to work full-time instead of attending college. Added together, these explicit and implicit costs would give her the total opportunity cost of a year in college, which is significantly greater than the price of school tuition.

The information gathered from the analysis of costs must be weighed against information about the advantages of attending college. In addition to its substantial cost, a college education has substantial benefits, including financial ones. Over the course of 40 years in the workplace, the average college graduate makes significantly more money and may enjoy greater job security than the average high school graduate. This benefit is easier to quantify than the enjoyment and satisfaction that some students can derive from attending college. Although such benefits might be difficult to measure, they

INTANGIBLE ASSETS

Just as it can be difficult to quantify the implicit costs of working at a particular job (for instance, the amount of happiness an employee would derive from a different job), companies often own assets that are very valuable but are difficult to assess in financial terms. Assets can be tangible or intangible. A tangible asset is a piece of property with a financial value (for instance, a building or a truck), and an intangible asset is valuable property that is not physical in nature. For example, a trademark and a copyright are both considered property that add to the value of a company, but they are intellectual in nature, not material. Another example of an intangible business asset is brand recognition. What is the value of the brand recognition of the Nike "swoosh" logo? It is difficult to say, but the logo is a intangible asset of the Nike Corporation that is critical to its success as a company.

are important factors in analyzing the costs and benefits of attending college.

The same distinctions about opportunity costs and explicit and implicit costs apply to business firms. In business an explicit cost is the money spent on inputs (any resources used in the processes of production, such as new equipment or the wages paid to an employee). Sometimes explicit costs are referred to as outlay costs. Technically speaking, outlay costs are any concrete costs that can be identified in the past, present, or future.

For businesses an implicit cost is the cost of inputs for which there is no direct money payment, such as the time that the business owner spends working. In other words, the implicit costs of a business's decision are the opportunity costs of using the business' self-owned, self-employed resources. The number attached to these costs is the amount of money that those resources could have made in their best alternative use. For example, if the business were trying to determine the implicit cost of its owner's time, it would consider the best possible financial compensation its owner could receive if she was employed elsewhere.

Recent Trends

Operators of business firms today are able to determine costs for virtually all decisions they need to make in the course of running a business. For example, suppose an entrepreneur who owns a business that produces greeting cards brings in $40,000 in total revenue in a year. The owner would carefully consider the other products he might be able to make with the business's available production resources. He estimates that, by producing children's notebooks instead of cards, he could generate $50,000 in a year. Therefore, he is able to recognize that the implicit cost of producing cards is $50,000 and that to continue to do so for another year would mean sacrificing the $10,000 difference.

This example, however, is the simplest possible scenario: the opportunity cost only involves the $10,000 in revenue that the business sacrifices to make cards instead of notebooks. There are usually many more factors involved, making it much more complicated to calculate opportunity costs. For instance, in the above example, card production would probably carry different business expenses than notebook production (perhaps the raw materials for one of the products would cost less). The entrepreneur would have to take these expenses into account. Other factors might include different ways that the business could be cutting its expenses (such as adopting different production techniques and finding ways to pay less business tax) and different ways it could spend the money it usually puts into the business (for instance, by investing some of it). Companies have increasingly been employing business analysts with specific training in determining opportunity costs.

$ Production Possibilities Curve

What It Means

In economics the production possibilities curve (PPC), also called the production possibilities frontier (PPF), is a tool for illustrating the idea of trade-off by showing the maximum quantities of two goods that can be produced at a given time from an existing, finite pool of resources.

The fundamental quality dictating the economy is scarcity: the resources that we as a society draw on to produce goods and services are limited. Most of us probably see scarcity at work in our daily lives. Someone with a weekly salary of $500 understands that the quantity of purchases he can make with that amount of money is limited. He may allocate part of that sum to rent, part to a car payment, part to groceries, and part to entertainment, allocating different amounts of money to different uses in an attempt to create maximum well-being. A business, likewise, is faced with limited resources. A car company is limited in the number and variety of cars it can produce by the amount of land, labor, and capital (equipment and money for doing business) in its possession. The company must make choices based on its limited pool of resources, and it will allocate its resources in a way that will bring the maximum amount of profit. The same goes for the entire economy. An economic system takes limited quantities of resources and assigns them to certain uses as opposed to other uses. Instead of well-being or profit, an economy's goal, in the eyes of economists, is efficiency.

Any time we as individuals, businesses, or a society choose one way of allocating resources over another, we pay what are called opportunity costs. If you buy a movie ticket for $10, the cost to you is not strictly monetary.

You also pay the price of foregoing other enjoyments, such as a hamburger and soda. Similarly, when society chooses to allocate its land, labor, and capital to the production of one type of good (cars, for example), it gives up other possible uses of those resources (the production of computers, for example). An increase in car production may mean a decrease in computer production. The unproduced computers represent the opportunity costs imposed on society by choosing cars.

The production possibilities curve is a visual aid allowing us to understand scarcity, choice, and opportunity cost. We can devise a PPC that will show us the amount by which computer production will decrease as car production decreases, and vice versa. We can graph the tradeoff between any two goods using the PPC. It is important to note, however, that PPCs are used only to

Production Possibility Table

Soap (thousands of bars)	Soda Pop (thousands of bottles)
0	30
10	28
18	24
24	18
28	10
30	0

Production Possibilities Curve

The production possibility curve, or frontier, offers a visual illustration of the various trade-offs a company or an economy must make if it devotes its limited resources to producing two different products. As the production possibility curve for soap and soda pop indicates, an increase in production of one product necessitates a decrease in production of the other. *Illustration by GGS Information Services. Cengage Learning, Gale.*

give us a hypothetical understanding of these economic conditions. PPCs are intentionally simplified illustrations of what happens when one good is produced instead of another. In reality, there are many goods in most economies, and the complexity of the economy as a whole cannot be reduced to the impact of simple tradeoffs. Nevertheless, examining these tradeoffs leads to significant insights about different facets of the economy.

When Did It Begin

The concept that came to be known as the production possibilities curve was first outlined by the Austrian-born American economist Gottfried von Haberler (1900-95). Von Haberler was best known for his writings on international trade, and he first came to prominence with the publication, in 1937, of *The Theory of International Trade*. In this book von Haberler formulated the notion of opportunity cost and showed what happens when different choices are made about what to produce in an economy. He called the visual representation of his ideas the production substitution curve, but today it is known as the production possibilities curve (or frontier).

More Detailed Information

The production possibilities curve, or PPC, shows us the different ways we might balance production of two different products. To make PPC analysis easier to understand, we have to make some simplifying assumptions.

Assume, for example, that we live in a country whose economy produces only two items, cars and computers. The economy might be able to produce cars in the following combinations: 15 cars and 0 computers; 14 cars and 5 dozen computers; 12 cars and 9 dozen computers; 9 cars and 12 dozen computers; 5 cars and 14 dozen computers; 0 cars and 15 dozen computers. By placing cars on the vertical axis and computers on the horizontal axis and then graphing these different combinations of car and computer production, we would create a production possibilities curve for these goods in our economy.

The curve illustrates all of the potential efficient combinations of car and computer production. If the economy produces these goods at a point anywhere on the curve, then the resources necessary to make cars and computers are being used with maximum efficiency. The economy in its current form cannot produce combined numbers of cars and computers that fall outside of the PPC, because there are not sufficient resources to allow production at such levels. The curve thus represents the furthest "frontier" that production may reach. The economy's output of cars and computers might, however, be located at a point inside the curve. This would mean that the economy is not utilizing its resources as efficiently as possible.

The PPC is usually concave rather than straight. This is a result of the law of increasing costs, which says that as more of one product is produced, an increasing amount

AT THE COMPANY LEVEL

The production possibilities curve (PPC) is a graph most commonly employed to show the different quantities of two goods that an economy can produce while using resources most efficiently. The PPC can also be applied to the decisions of a single company. When, for example, a technology company wants to branch out from the production of computers to produce laser printers as well, it could graph the different options for the quantities of each that it could produce, based on its current supply of raw materials, equipment, and labor. Just because a firm is using its resources efficiently, however, does not mean it is using them in the most profitable way possible. Any point along a production possibility curve represents an equally efficient use of resources, but consumers will likely have more specific desires. A company would thus be short-sighted if it relied exclusively on the PPC to determine how many computers and how many printers to manufacture. It must balance its production possibilities with consumer demand.

of the second product is given up. At first, producing five dozen computers requires giving up only one car (car production goes from 15 to 14), but with the production of an additional four dozen computers (for a total of nine dozen), two more cars must be given up. This is another way of saying that the opportunity cost of producing computers grows as we produce more of them. The reason that this happens is that the economy must retrain workers and make changes in how it uses resources. These shifts result in decreased productivity. In a situation in which two very similar products are being measured (such as wooden chairs and wooden tables), the PPC would more closely resemble a straight diagonal line from one axis to the other.

But what if the basic conditions of the economy changed? What if, for instance, new technologies made it cheaper to manufacture computers, while the car industry remained unchanged? If computer productivity doubled, the PPC would shift dramatically to the right. What if new technologies made car-production cheaper, while the computer industry remained unchanged? The PPC would shift dramatically upward. Technology thus allows for an outward expansion of the PPC.

Another way that the PPC for any two goods can shift outward is when resources increase. For example, an influx of immigrants who are willing and able to work in the automotive industry might result in an upward shift on the PPC for our two-product economy.

During times of economic growth, the PPC in a country shifts outward. A PPC can also shift inward if resources are depleted. For example, if our hypothetical country went to war and lost one-third of its labor force, the number of cars and computers the economy would be able to generate afterward would fall, and the curve would move downward and to the left.

Recent Trends

One common use for PPCs today is to illustrate the tradeoff between consumption and investment (or savings) in a society. When people make money, they have two choices about what to do with it, assuming they do not want to hide it under a mattress or in a sock drawer: they can spend it, or they can invest it. Consumer spending, of course, contributes to economic growth, since the money is spent on goods produced by the economy. Spending promotes growth in the short term. To save money, on the other hand, is to invest it in future economic growth. When people put money in the bank, the bank uses it to finance loans that commonly enable businesses to grow. Similarly, when an investor buys shares of stock (portions of company ownership), she is giving that company money that can be used for expansions that will allow it to become more productive in the future. Investing promotes growth over the long term.

Since there is a finite quantity of money to begin with (the money people earn from their jobs and investments), and it can only be allocated in two ways (consumption or investment), the nature of the tradeoff between these two uses of money can be analyzed using a PPC. Consumption and investment would be considered goods that society provides, and the resulting PPC would illustrate the different ways in which these two goods can be combined.

Further, economists can compare the outward movement of PPCs (outward movement indicates economic growth) under conditions when more money is spent, versus conditions when more money is invested. Using PPCs in this way, economists have made the case that weighting the economy more heavily toward investing than consumption will ultimately allow not only for long-term growth but for more rapid growth overall. This is one way to explain why many poor countries have slow economic growth and why many rich countries enjoy high rates of economic growth. The poorest countries have to allocate all their resources and spending to basic consumption, leaving little available for investment. This is a major contributor to low rates of economic growth. Rich countries can afford to save more, have higher rates of investment, and, as a result, grow more rapidly.

But while it is true that the PPC provides a helpful way of visualizing the effects of the tradeoff between savings and investment, these are only two among many factors that fuel the economy. The United States economy grew enormously during the 1990s, for example, even though Americans at that time were notoriously irresponsible spenders, saving a smaller proportion of their incomes than people in any other comparable country.

$ Technology

What It Means

For many people technology refers to advances in the computer sciences and electronics that have produced such things as cell phones, the Internet, and TiVo. While these inventions are all examples of technology, they do not adequately explain the term. *Technology* comes from the Greek root *techne,* which means craft, or the skill and experience in making objects. Thus, any human invention (such as the screwdriver, the wheel, or the ball point pen) that gives people control over their environment is an example of technology.

Because of its capacity to introduce new products and services—while at the same time improving the production, distribution, and exchange of these goods and services—technology has always played an important role in the economy. Technology primarily contributes to the economy by introducing new objects, inventions, or ideas that help a society produce and distribute more goods and, in the process, create a higher standard of living. For example, the development of the assembly line by Henry Ford (1863–1947) at the beginning of the twentieth century made it possible for the United States to produce more cars. This new technology helped improve the American economy by creating more jobs, which meant that more people could buy the cars. Most people agreed that having a car improved one's standard of living. In contemporary society the Internet is an example of a new technology that has expanded the economy. This development created new jobs and made shopping easier for consumers, who can now go online to purchase anything from books to laptop computers.

When Did It Begin

In order for a group of people living in the same area to be considered a civilization (a complex, interactive society), some people in the community must devote themselves to activities other than producing food for themselves. This means that the food-producing members must produce a surplus of food and trade that extra food for the various goods and services that the other members of the civilization provide. For example, a person who makes arrowheads would trade his arrowheads for food and other goods and services he requires for survival. This organized system of trade is an economic system, and such systems require technology. The processes and equipment used to grow and store extra food are examples of required technology. Thus the advancement of technology and the development of economic systems have coincided with each other since the beginning of recorded civilization.

The earliest civilizations existed in the sixth millennium BC in Mesopotamia between the Tigris and Euphrates Rivers in what is now Iraq, Syria, and Turkey. Among the ancient technology discovered there,

Technology, such as computers, the Internet, and cell phones, plays an important role in the expansion of economic activities. Here a telephone company employee secures high-speed fiber optic cable, which uses light, rather than electricity, to transmit communication signals onto a telephone pole. *AP Images.*

archeologists have found evidence of irrigation systems used to grow barley. An irrigation system allows farmers to obtain water for crops from sources other than rainfall, such as a nearby river or underground spring.

More Detailed Information

There are several eras in history during which the world has experienced significant technological advancement and accelerated economic growth. One such era was the Industrial Revolution. The Industrial Revolution began in Great Britain in the eighteenth century (around 1780, most historians agree), and its effects spread throughout the world. The major change during this time was a shift from manual labor (human beings making goods by hand) to mechanized labor (machines producing large quantities of goods quickly). The revolution began in the textile (fabric goods, such as clothes, rugs, and handbags) industry. Before the Industrial Revolution humans would weave, knit, or crochet these fabrics. During and after the revolution, these goods were manufactured by machines, which produced greater quantities of textiles more quickly than humans could. One of the most important

inventions during this time was the steam engine, which used external heat to power machines.

After machines had been successfully deployed in the textile industry, scientists began looking for ways to improve the machines and to use them in other industries. What followed were developments in several other areas, most notably in transportation. Roads were improved. Canals and railways were built. During the Industrial Revolution the first iron railways were constructed in Great Britain, and between the early 1800s and 1830 steam locomotion developed. Thus machine use in factories allowed businesses to produce more goods, and technological developments in transportation gave those businesses the opportunity to move those goods over greater distances to reach more customers. Most people working during the Industrial Revolution toiled under harsh conditions, working long hours for very low pay. The changes in technology and in the economy created a new class of wealthy businessmen, however, ushering in the rise of the middle class (a group of people often holding managerial positions in factories who lived at an economic level between the very rich and the very poor).

R & D

R & D stands for research and development. In the business world this term refers to scientific research that is done for the purpose of improving existing products and services. The R & D department of a company is responsible for discovering new technologies that will help the company improve its economic performance. For example, members of R & D at a cell-phone company might try to develop faster and more efficient ways for people to communicate with cell phones in order to attract larger numbers of new customers. By improving its own products and services, the cell-phone company will motivate its rivals to develop their own new technologies to remain competitive in the cell phone market. Taken as a whole, these competing technological improvements have a positive impact on the economy, as consumers are able to choose from a wide range of superior products. In 2006 companies in the United

After machines had started producing large numbers of goods, manufacturers began to find new ways of using human labor. Before the Industrial Revolution, a single craftsman or a team of workers worked together to build a single product. When they were finished, they would begin work on a second product. In the new mechanized factories, production or assembly lines began to appear. The first successful assembly line was developed by an Englishman named Marc Isambard Brunel (1769–1849), who developed a way to mass-produce rigging blocks, or pulleys, for the Navy in 1801. In the production-line system workers stand beside a conveyor belt that carries a set of products, which are pieced together as they pass the workers. As each product passes a person, that person adds a part to the product. At the end of the line, the product is complete. The assembly-line system was perfected by Henry Ford, whose corporation in 1906 could produce a car every three minutes.

Recent Trends

Since 1994, when the Internet and the World Wide Web became available to large numbers of people, globalization has been the most dominant trend in economics. Globalization is a complex process of standardizing products (of making them similar across the globe) and of selling these products in as many markets as possible throughout the world. For example, in the 1950s there was a greater difference in the snack beverages and the casual footwear people chose across the world. While there are still differences in soft drinks and sneakers in various countries, it is also true that many people throughout the world drink Coca-Cola and wear Nike sneakers. People in London, Tokyo, New York City, Seoul (Korea), Bombay (India), and Beijing (China) share more of the same habits in dress and eating than ever before.

No one person or country has been responsible for this trend toward globalization. Most experts agree that Information Technology (or IT, which includes the Internet and other complex computer networking systems) is most responsible for this unifying process. Because of IT, both money and information can be exchanged more quickly around the world. This rapid exchange has allowed manufacturers to establish factories and advertise their goods in more countries.

$ Consumer Sovereignty

What It Means

For years economists have debated about whether the producers of goods and services or the consumers have greater control of the market. In this discussion the term *market* is not a single place but rather a social arrangement that allows producers to sell goods, services, and information to consumers who pay for these commodities with money. *Consumer sovereignty* is a term used by economists who argue that it is the consumers who rule the market. According to these thinkers, consumers dictate what goods and services are available in the market because they have purchasing power (the money required to buy what is available on the market). Producers respond to consumer buying patterns and make available the goods and services that consumers have shown they will purchase in large quantities. In other words, producers supply goods and services in response to consumer demand.

To examine both sides of this argument in more detail, consider a product such as Coca-Cola, which is popular with American consumers. This beverage is available in quantity at nearly every store in the United States, even at small roadside establishments along unpopulated stretches of American highways. An economist who believes in the principle of consumer sovereignty will argue that so much Coca-Cola is available because, over time, Americans have purchased more Coke than any other soft drink. As consumers have continued to purchase this beverage, the producers have made increasing amounts of it available on the market. Economists who dispute the principle of consumer sovereignty, on the other hand, will argue that many other market forces have worked together to make Coca-Cola the most popular beverage in the United States. These thinkers might point out, for example, that the Coca-Cola Company has had the most money and therefore has been able to supply more of its soft drink than has its competitors. According to this line of thought, consumers have demanded so much Coke over the years because it was most readily available to them.

When Did It Begin

The principle of consumer sovereignty was most avidly discussed in the late nineteenth century, when economists engaged in disputes about the merits of laissez-faire economics (the idea that governments should not make laws that control the buying and selling of goods). In his influential book *Principles of Economics* (1871), Polish economist Carl Menger (1840–1921) took up the idea of consumer sovereignty along with many other topics. Menger wrote that consumers, if left alone, would purchase the goods and services that most benefited them. Consequently, the state of the market (the number and types of goods and services available and the prices of those commodities) would be determined by consumers acting in their own interest. Menger and the economists who shared his views believed that society should be shaped by the principles of consumer sovereignty and laissez-faire economics rather than by a government trying to steer the development of society and the economy.

The concepts of consumer sovereignty and laissez-faire economics emerged when they did because of the impact of the Industrial Revolution, which spanned 1760–1830 in England and spread initially throughout Europe and then to many other parts of the world. During this period machines were first used to mass-produce goods. The vast increase in the number of goods available to consumers significantly changed the structure of society by introducing a middle class (a group of people falling between the wealthy upper class and the lower, or working, class) that gradually acquired more purchasing power. Because society and the economy were changing so quickly, many economists in the late nineteenth century questioned whether governments should intervene to regulate these changes or simply stand aside and let the changes continue unimpeded.

More Detailed Information

Those who disagree with the principle of consumer sovereignty argue that economists are mistaken when they consider the economy only in terms of producers and consumers. These thinkers claim that since the Industrial Revolution the economy has been separated into two entirely different camps: the minority who own and operate businesses and the majority who have to work in those businesses to produce the goods and provide the services that are available on the market. According to this school of thought, the owners control all facets of the economy because they keep most of the profits for themselves and then determine how much the laborers get paid for their work. The amount the laborers earn

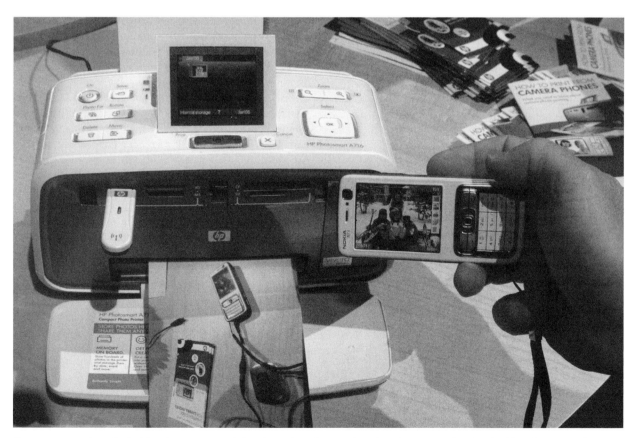

Consumer sovereignty is the idea that consumer desires determine what goods and services are produced and sold in the marketplace. The electronics industry is one in which consumers exert a major influence over new product development *AP Images.*

A CHAMPION OF CONSUMER SOVEREIGNTY

Born in Brooklyn, New York, Milton Friedman (1912-2006) is considered one of the most influential economists of the twentieth century. He won the Nobel Prize in Economics in 1976. In his most famous book, *Free to Choose* (1980), Friedman argues on behalf of consumer sovereignty (the idea that consumers should have greater control than producers over goods and services) and laissez-faire economics (the idea that governments should not make laws that control the buying and selling of goods). He notes several examples of countries whose economies failed because their governments tried to regulate supply and demand. He also notes examples of economies, such as that in Hong Kong, that succeeded because they were allowed to operate more freely. The American nonprofit Public Broadcasting Service (PBS) produced a televised 10-episode adaptation of the book in January 1980. Each episode had two parts. In the first part Friedman appeared by himself as a teacher might before a classroom and shared examples of economic successes and failures throughout history. In the second part he discussed economic issues with prominent owners of businesses and with other economists.

determines how much they can spend on the goods available to them on the market. To make matters worse, when laborers spend their wages on food, clothing, and other items, they are merely giving their money back to that small minority of wealthy people who control the market. Without government regulation, the rich minority will be permitted to maintain unfair control over the lives of the poor.

The opponents of consumer sovereignty assert that one of the most important things a government can do is maintain a certain level of competition among the owners of business, because the working class benefits from this competition. If the government does not regulate the economy, one company in a given business will acquire a monopoly (a situation in which there is only one provider of a good or service). Once this occurs, the company can charge whatever it wishes for its goods and services, with the profits from those sales going directly to the small group of individuals who control the company. Consider the example of the American telephone industry in the mid-twentieth century. By 1940, the Bell System, which was owned by the American Telephone and Telegraph Company (AT&T), controlled almost all aspects of telecommunications in the United States, which meant that it was free to set high prices for its long-distance service. To make long-distance calls, Americans were forced to pay Bell's rates because there was no rival company to keep the pricing schedule in check. However, after a series of antitrust lawsuits (lawsuits which claim that a given

company is stifling economic competition), AT&T was forced to relinquish its control over this aspect of the telecommunications industry in the early 1980s. Shortly afterward, rival companies such as Sprint and MCI began selling long-distance services. These companies had to compete for consumer dollars by offering the consumers better rates.

Unfortunately, government regulation does not always benefit working-class people. For example, in the 1970s many Americans began buying Japanese cars because these vehicles were less expensive than American cars and because they tended to last longer and require fewer repairs. To protect the American automobile industry, the United States government negotiated a trade agreement with Japan that restricted the number of cars that Japan would export to the United States. This agreement allowed the price of American cars to remain high and limited the extent to which American automakers had to improve their products.

Most economists agree that the issue of government regulation is always complex. In the case of the automakers, for example, it could be argued that, by limiting the number of Japanese cars that came into the United States, the government preserved American jobs. Economists who take this position would reason that, if Americans at that time continued purchasing Japanese cars, American automobile companies would have lost money and therefore laid off workers. On the other hand, economists who favor no government intervention would argue that unregulated competition from Japanese products would have forced American automakers to improve their products and that over time both the owners and the workers would have benefited from these improvements. In other words, if consumers had been given more control, or sovereignty, they eventually would have been able to buy better, less expensive cars, and American manufacturers would have sold more of these cars to them. When considering the idea of consumer sovereignty, students need not resolve the dispute. Rather, they should study the question closely to better understand the complex relationship between consumer sovereignty and laissez-faire economics.

Recent Trends

Since World War II (1939–45), governments throughout the world have imposed fewer barriers to international trade. This means that most governments have allowed goods produced in other countries to be sold in their markets. During this time consumers worldwide have had more choices than in any other period in human history. Despite the increased options, however, most economists agree that consumer sovereignty is declining. Although consumers have more products available to them, they do not necessarily have many varieties or brands to choose from. For example, corporations such as Coca-Cola and the footwear company Nike have been expanding into markets throughout the globe and eliminating smaller, local companies who produced the same kinds of goods. In this environment, a relatively small number of large corporations control the consumers' range of choices.

In addition, large corporations tend to spend more money on market research than they do on researching ways to improve their products and services. This means that many corporations are more concerned with convincing buyers that their products are good than with actually making those products better. Because such companies have eliminated much of their competition, they do not need to monitor the quality of their products and services as closely as they once did. Many market analysts agree that what is most discouraging about this recent trend is that corporations are trying to convince consumers that the buyer has more power than ever before. Most commercials suggest that a given product is made especially for the individual consumer watching the ad. This creates the false impression that the corporation exists to please the consumer.

LABOR: THE PEOPLE WORKING IN THE ECONOMY

$ Labor Force

What It Means

A labor force is all the people in a country who are economically active during a given time period. In the United States people older than 16 who are employed, self-employed, in the military, or unemployed but looking for work are considered economically active.

Governments typically monitor the composition of their country's labor force regularly. The Bureau of Labor Statistics (BLS) of the U.S. Department of Labor, for instance, takes stock of the U.S. labor force every month. It does this by conducting a survey of 56,000 randomly chosen households, asking each person over the age of 16 whether he or she is employed or unemployed. To be counted as employed a person must work at least 1 hour for pay each week or 15 hours at unpaid work in a family business each week. To be counted as unemployed a person must have looked for work in the past month. Those people who are older than 16 but are not considered part of the labor force include retirees, full-time students who do not work, people who are disabled or seriously ill, and people who do not work because they stay at home to take care of their children.

When Did It Begin

The concept of a labor force developed in the 1930s, when the U.S. government set out to determine exactly how bad the Great Depression was. The Depression was a severe, worldwide economic crisis that followed the 1929 stock market crash and lasted through most of the 1930s. One of the worst problems facing the United States at this time was widespread unemployment. Government officials understood that huge numbers of people were out of work, but they did not have any established method for calculating the extent of the problem. Simply counting the number of unemployed people and comparing that to the entire U.S. population did not give a clear view of the economic situation, because that method would include the many people (such as children and stay-at-home mothers) who would not have jobs even if the economy were thriving. A more useful method would be to compare the number of unemployed people to the number of people who wanted to work. Using this method of calculation, it turned out that, at the height of the Depression (1932–33), 16 million people (roughly one-third of the entire U.S. labor force) were unemployed.

More Detailed Information

The concept of the labor force represents an attempt to distinguish between types of work that have direct economic consequences and types of work that do not have direct economic consequences. For example, although many stay-at-home parents undoubtedly perform work and are capable of holding their own in the job market, their child-rearing work produces no direct economic result. The same is true of students or volunteer workers, both of whom are typically productive members of society but whose efforts are not economically productive.

There are limitations to the criteria used to judge who is part of the labor force and who is not, however. For instance, in the United States the BLS makes no distinction between part-time and full-time work when it is defining the labor force, nor does it account for those who are underemployed (that is, those who would like to work more hours, or work more productively, than the economy allows them to do). Therefore, despite the fact that the labor force is meant to serve as a major indicator of how the economy is doing at a given time (especially as it relates to unemployment), the numbers may not always tell the full story about current conditions for workers.

Although labor force criteria have remained fairly consistent over time, the composition and size of the labor force has changed dramatically in the United States since the beginning of the twentieth century. This is true of any country with a growing economy.

As an economy develops, its labor force changes in composition and size. Economies are divided into primary, secondary, and tertiary (third-degree) sectors. Agriculture, mining, fishing, and other such industries make up the primary sector of an economy. The secondary sector of an economy includes all industries based on manufacturing and construction (examples include the

THE CRYSTAL BALL

The Bureau of Labor Statistics (BLS) of the U.S. Department of Labor determines the size and composition of the U.S. labor force every month. The BLS derives a wide variety of useful information from these monthly surveys. Sometimes it even uses them to predict the future.

By analyzing economic trends at the beginning of the twenty-first century, the BLS projected that the U.S. labor force would grow dramatically and continue to diversify in the coming decades. Increasing numbers of people of Asian, African, and Hispanic descent were expected to enter the labor force, diminishing the size of the white majority in the labor force. The BLS predicted that the numbers of both men and women would increase but that women would join the labor force in greater numbers than men. Both the youth labor force (those between 16 and 24) and the primary working-age group (those aged 25 to 54) were expected to decline in terms of percentages. This was largely because the number of older workers would increase as the baby boom generation (those born during the spike in the birth rate that occurred after World War II, which ended in 1945) aged.

was partly the result of economic development; when the economy was strongly tied to heavy industry involving manual labor, there were fewer options for women in the workplace. As the economy shifted from the secondary (manufacturing and construction) to the tertiary (service) sector, there were increasing opportunities for women. These increases were also facilitated by technology, which made domestic work less time-consuming. This freed women up to undertake economically rewarding work even when they had substantial domestic responsibilities. But attitudes toward women's domestic roles have changed greatly in America since the early twentieth century, and even since the 1970s. Whereas in 1970 only 40 percent of women with at least one child worked outside of the home, by 2000 some 70 percent did. It became less typical for marriage and childbirth to mark the end of a woman's career, as they often did in the first three-quarters of the twentieth century.

At the same time the proportion of men in the U.S. labor force has dropped. This is not, however, a result of men losing their jobs to women so much as it is a function of changing lifestyles and expectations. More men who once would have begun working at age 16 now stay out of the labor force until after college, and older men retire in much greater numbers than they once did.

clothing, automobile, electronics, telecommunications, tobacco, and home-construction industries). The tertiary sector, meanwhile, consists of those industries that provide services (examples include the insurance, banking, education, film, tourism, transportation, and retail industries). As an economy develops, its focus tends to shift from the primary, to the secondary, and finally to the tertiary sector.

When the economy shifts in this way, so does the labor force. For instance, 38 percent of the American labor force worked in agriculture (part of the primary sector) in 1900. That figure had dropped to 3 percent by 2000. Similarly, in the 1970s the percentage of the American labor force in the secondary sector began to decline dramatically. By the first decade of the twenty-first century, more than 75 percent of the U.S. labor force was working in the tertiary (service) sector.

At the same time the U.S. labor force has grown tremendously. In 1900 the size of the labor force was 27 million. In 1980 it was 108 million. Two decades later it was roughly 150 million. On the one hand, the size and skills of the U.S. labor force have been crucial ingredients in the economy's growth and development; on the other hand, the economy's growth and development have made possible the increases in the size and the changing skills of the labor force.

Recent Trends

One major reason the labor force grew in the late twentieth century was that more women were joining it. This

$ Division of Labor

What It Means

The division of labor (also known as specialization) refers to a method of producing goods or providing services whereby a job is split into separate, distinct tasks or roles. Each task or role is then performed by one person or group of people; the person or group performs only that task or role, specializing in it. If a group of one hundred people were to build a ship without dividing the labor into categories and specializing, they would all work together on the hull (the frame of the ship), the decks, the sleeping quarters, and the sails. If this group were to divide the labor into categories and specialize, one group would build the hull, another the deck, another the sleeping quarters, and the final group would assemble the sails. When the first group finished the hull, they would begin constructing a hull for a second ship. Over time these workers would master all aspects of building the hull, but they would not necessarily be adept at building decks, sleeping quarters, or sails.

Workers often divide labor and specialize when they provide services, as well. For example, companies that offer house-cleaning services often send teams of cleaners to their customers' residences. One of the cleaners vacuums, another washes floors, another dusts, and another cleans bathrooms. When the team is finished, they move to the next client's house. Labor studies have shown that dividing labor and specializing significantly increases efficiency and production. With regard to shipbuilding, it

Division of labor involves separating different aspects of the manufacturing process into distinct, specialized tasks. This image depicts diverse occupations typically associated with seventeenth-century Europe, where the concept of division of labor began to be put to use. © *Mary Evans Picture Library/The Image Works.*

has been shown that workers produce a greater number of ships and the ships are of a higher quality if the workers separate into teams and specialize in one aspect of the job. Likewise, teams of housecleaners do better, faster work when individuals specialize in one aspect of the cleaning process. The division of labor also helps to ensure a high degree of standardization, or consistency, in the process of production and in the quality of the final product. In the case of the shipbuilders, if workers master a specialized role, then the ships are likely to resemble each other. Standardization of products and services is crucial for large businesses looking to build a reputation for high-quality work with their client base.

When Did It Begin

Sir William Petty (1623–87), an English economist and philosopher, was one of the first people to publicize the advantages of specialization. In the 1640s, when he was in his twenties, Petty visited Dutch shipyards. Most manufacturers during that era built ships one at a time, deploying a large group of men on one ship and not beginning another until the previous vessel was completed. The Dutch, however, constructed several ships at once. They assembled teams of workers and made each team responsible for a different area of the ship. Petty noted that this approach produced ships more quickly; it also required less time and money to be spent on training the labor force. Instead of having to master all aspects of

shipbuilding, a worker only had to know how to perform the tasks associated with his area of the ship.

After his stay in the Netherlands, Petty returned to England and began a distinguished career as a surveyor and a writer on such subjects as mathematics, statistics, economics, and philosophy. By the 1660s Petty had a wide readership, and at this time his early observations on the division of labor found a large audience. Throughout the Industrial Revolution, which began in the 1780s in England and spread to the rest of Europe and to the United States during the nineteenth century, manufacturers continually studied ways to get the highest level of productivity out of the labor force. Dividing workers into groups and making each group responsible for one part of a larger project did not become commonplace, however, until the beginning of the twentieth century, when the assembly line was first used in the American automotive industry.

More Detailed Information

Assembly lines in factories that produce large amounts of goods encourage a high degree of specialization. An assembly line is a manufacturing process in which the product being assembled moves on a conveyor belt past workers. As the product moves along the belt, workers add parts to it. For example, in an automobile manufacturing plant a car frame may be placed at the beginning of an assembly line and sent past the workers operating the line. As the car proceeds, workers along the line add parts to the car. One group might put the engine in, the next the radiator, and another group further down might operate a device that places the windshield on the car. The car proceeds to the end of the line until it is fully assembled. Each group of workers specializes in performing one task associated with the building of the car.

Although this approach to manufacturing produces a large number of identical vehicles in a short period of time, there are some drawbacks to the process. The most notable shortcoming is a high degree of worker dissatisfaction. Workers on assembly lines often find the work boring and unchallenging, for example. Because they repeat the same task thousands of times a day and contribute only one small part to the manufacture of the vehicle, these workers often feel no connection to the process. Such workers are not as likely to take pride in the quality of the finished product because they regard their contribution as small and insignificant. Their jobs, they reason, require no particular skill; any properly trained individual could perform the task. This attitude toward the job increases absenteeism (frequent absences) from work. Furthermore, workers trained to do only one aspect of a job have a limited amount of flexibility in the workplace. Their supervisors may deem them capable of performing only that one task. As a result the workers may have a hard time distinguishing themselves and moving to higher positions in the corporation.

FREDERICK WINSLOW TAYLOR

Frederick Winslow Taylor (1856–1915) was one of the leaders of the Efficiency Movement (1890–1932) in American engineering. Taylor argued that workers who are required to perform repetitive tasks will do only the amount of work that goes unpunished, which means that the average laborer will do as little as possible. This approach to the job, of course, minimizes productivity. To alleviate this problem, Taylor argued that companies needed to identify "one best way" to perform each of the tasks associated with building their products. The company should then require workers to perform each task using that particular method. With regard to workers on an assembly line, Taylor suggested that employers should conduct "time and motion" studies to determine how many bodily motions are required to get a task done in the most efficient manner. Though some of his requirements for workers sound exacting, Taylor was also one of the first to argue that workers should be given breaks during their shifts to recover from fatigue.

Another problem with dividing labor into small, particular tasks is that if there is a problem in one part of the process, the entire process stalls. For instance, on an automobile assembly line, if the mechanisms responsible for placing the hood on the car break, the entire line may need to be shut down in order to fix the problem. This means that there will be a drastic reduction in output until the problem is fixed. Such breakdowns cost large corporations millions of dollars in lost revenues.

Despite these problems the division of labor is considered a necessary component of economic progress. If a corporation wants to produce a high volume of goods or serve a large number of clients, that corporation must develop a highly specialized workforce. Even within medium-sized firms the work staff is often divided into specialized groups. For example, in a technology firm of 30 people, workers will be responsible for distinct tasks that contribute to the success of the firm. The staff may include five or six salespeople whose job it is to recruit new clients. There may be two or three graphic designers who design websites, several programmers who write code, and a few individuals who provide technical support. In addition, the firm may ask several employees to monitor internal affairs, such as cash flow and inventory. Within such a company it would be unproductive to require workers to excel in more than one area. Programmers, for example, need to keep up to date with the latest techniques in their field. If these workers were asked to master sales techniques and to do the accounting for the money coming into the firm, their programming skills would lag.

Recent Trends

It has become common for companies in many developed countries (fully modernized countries with a large middle class and a skilled labor force) to have their products made in factories located in poorer countries. Nike sportswear, for example, is produced in factories in Vietnam, Taiwan, and the Dominican Republic, among other places. Companies like Nike produce their goods overseas because operating factories and paying workers is considerably less expensive in developing countries than in highly developed nations. Regulations in these developed countries set minimum standards for pay, safety in the workplace, and treatment of employees, especially those who perform specialized tasks on assembly lines. No such laws exist in many of the world's less prosperous nations. To prevent abuses of worker rights in these parts of the world, the United Nations created the International Labor Organization (ILO) in 1919. Through a series of conventions throughout its history, the ILO has defined proper labor conditions for all workers.

In recent years, however, labor activists (people who try to protect the rights of workers) have noted that along with the rapid growth of the global economy, there has been a marked increase in violations of workers' rights. Specifically, child labor laws and prohibitions against the abuse of workers have been violated more frequently in factories in Central America and Southeast Asia. To reverse this trend, such agencies as the Fair Labor Association (FLA) commission studies to verify reported abuses. The FLA also establishes emergency funds to provide monetary relief for workers in need. For example, in February 2007 Nike announced that it was decreasing its production in the Dominican Republic, forcing a BJ&B factory (the corporation that produced Nike's goods in the Dominican Republic) to announce that it would have to close without giving its workers sufficient notice. According to some estimates, this meant a loss of more than 50,000 jobs. The FLA commissioned a legal report and sent financial aid to the workers. The organization took similar action in December 2006 when the Hermosa Manufacturing plant in El Salvador was closed abruptly.

$ Wages

What It Means

A wage is the payment that a worker or employee receives for his or her labor. A wage is commonly in the form of money, but it can also be in goods. A wage is usually paid for a specified quantity of labor, which most often is measured as a unit of time. For example, it is common for a worker to make a certain dollar amount for each hour, day, or week the worker provides labor to an employer. The wage differs from another form of monetary compensation for work, the salary, which typically is not based on a specified quantity of labor and is usually paid on a weekly, biweekly, or monthly basis.

The term wages refers to the money an employee receives for his or her work. When employees are dissatisfied with their wages, they will sometimes go on strike, or refuse to work. © *Bettmann/Corbis.*

The United States government determines a federal minimum wage, which is the lowest dollar amount per hour of labor that an employer is allowed to pay. In 2007 a new minimum wage law was enacted, which specified that the minimum wage rate of $5.15 per hour in force since 1997 would be raised in three stages, increasing to $5.85 per hour in July 2007 and peaking at $7.25 per hour in mid-2009. An employer may choose to pay a worker the minimum rate or an amount above it. The rate of the wage for a particular job is sometimes the focus of negotiations between a worker and an employer before the job agreement is completed.

The wage rates paid in the United States are determined mainly by market forces, that is, the supply of, and the demand for, goods and services. The economic systems in other countries determine wage rates according to different criteria. In Japan, for example, cultural tradition and social structure influence wage rates more than do market forces. Beginning in the last decades of the twentieth century, some developing countries that for-

merly had provided the developed world with goods and services produced with extremely cheap labor have established minimum wage rates that must be paid to workers.

When Did It Begin

Wages paid as compensation for labor have been in existence for many centuries. When economic systems were more agriculturally based, the wage for farm labor commonly came in the form of a portion of the farm's harvest rather than as money. The oldest definitions of wage encompass more than monetary compensation for work. Even among contemporary economists, the satisfaction that workers may gain from their labor is considered a type of wage.

The federal minimum wage rate in the United States was established in 1938. It was 25 cents per hour at that time, and it provided a higher pay for a large part of the country's workforce. The minimum rate, set by the U.S. Congress, has increased numerous times since then,

WAGES AND THE LAW OF SUPPLY

The economic theory of supply and demand makes use of two basic laws. The law of supply states that, as the price of a product rises, the producer will supply more of the product. The law of demand states that, as the price of a product rises, the consumer will demand less of the product. It is the interaction of these two laws that determines the price of the product and the quantity produced at any given time.

Economists note that labor can also be considered to be a product and wages to be the price of the product. In this case, however, the law of supply may operate in an unusual way. In general, as a worker's wage (the price) increases, he or she is willing to supply a greater number of hours of labor (the product), because the higher wage makes working additional hours more useful and less costly than some other way of spending the time. But when the wage reaches a fairly high level, the worker may find that he or she has less need to work additional hours because of the larger amount of money the worker is making. Hence, as the wage continues to rise, the worker will labor less (that is, produce less of the product) and devote more time to enjoying the additional income.

though typically within a political climate influenced by workers who wanted higher pay and employers who wanted to contain business expenses. In 2007 the federal minimum wage rate was $5.85 per hour, but there were higher minimum wage rates in 20 states, such as Illinois, where it was $7.50 per hour. Unfortunately the prices of goods and services rose between 1938 and 2007 as well. When adjusted for this inflation, the purchasing power (the value of money measured by the items it can buy) of the minimum wage was highest in 1968.

More Detailed Information

Many American workers who are paid hourly wages are members of labor unions, which are legal, formally organized groups of workers who gather to represent their collective views on wages, hours, and working conditions. Wage rates in the United States are sometimes set by a negotiation, known as collective bargaining, between union representatives and company leaders. The Fair Labor Standards Act of 1938, the law that established the first national minimum wage in the United States, also guaranteed time-and-a-half pay (compensation amounting to 50 percent more than the standard wage rate) for overtime (working time above the agreed-upon amount per day, week, or month) in certain jobs.

A living wage in the United States is the wage a full-time worker would need to earn to support a healthy family. In most instances the requirements of a living wage are above those of a minimum wage. Living wages are usually defined by local ordinances (laws of a city or county). Living-wage ordinances cover specific groups of workers, typically those employed by businesses that supply goods or services to city or county governments. The city of Milwaukee, Wisconsin, for example, had a living-wage ordinance in 2007 mandating $6.25 per hour, and the city of Santa Cruz, California, had one mandating $12 per hour.

Employers are sometimes required by federal or state governments to follow a wage rate known as the prevailing wage. This is the hourly wage, including benefits and overtime pay, paid in the largest city in each county of a state to the largest group of workers, laborers, and mechanics. The U.S. Department of Labor and Industries establishes prevailing wages for each trade and occupation (for instance, electricians, ironworkers, or carpenters) that are part of the labor force used to complete public works (construction or engineering projects that a state government puts in place for local communities).

Recent Trends

The wage gap is an indicator used in the United States since the mid-twentieth century to illustrate the difference between women's and men's earnings at a given time. It also has been used to compare earnings of other ethnicities to those of white males, since white males form a group that typically is not subject to sex- or race-based discrimination. The wage gap is expressed as a percentage; for comparing women and men, it is calculated by dividing the median annual earnings for women by that for men. For example, women in 2006 earned 77 percent of what men earned, as they had each year for about a decade previous.

The Equal Pay Act, signed into law in 1963, made it illegal for American employers to pay unequal wages to men and women who hold the same job and do the same work. Nevertheless, a wage gap between male and female workers has persisted.

$ Inequality in the Labor Force: Opportunity versus Outcome

What It Means

Inequality in the labor force can most easily be seen in how much workers are paid. Some individuals, such as business executives and celebrity chefs, receive high salaries for their jobs. Others, for example, employees at fast-food restaurants, receive only the minimum wage (the lowest pay allowable by law). One reason for this type of inequality is simple: the executives and the celebrity chefs provide work that demands highly specialized skills, while the fast-food employees perform very simple tasks requiring minimal education or training. The root causes behind this inequality, however, are complex and difficult to identify.

The reason why some people make more than others is complex, involving differences in talent, education, and family wealth, as well as discrimination, choice of occupation, and luck. This image reflects a fundamental imbalance in the ways that male and female employees are compensated in the modern business world. © *Images.com/Corbis.*

In discussing economic inequality, economists generally adopt one of two approaches. One focuses on the question of equal opportunity. Some people, because of discrimination or lack of education, for example, have fewer opportunities to participate and make money in an economy. Without finishing high school or going to college, it is impossible to enter certain highly skilled and well paying professions, such as law or medicine. The establishment of public education and laws forbidding discrimination on the basis of race and sex were attempts to address long-standing differences in economic opportunity.

A second approach to economic inequality focuses not on access to well paying jobs, for instance, but on the very fact that there are substantial differences in the "outcome," or compensation, for people's work. Although a business executive—because of the willingness of others to pay him a high salary so they can benefit from his rare set of skills—might be able to make one hundred times the salary of his secretary, the question remains whether he should be able to make such a large amount of money. Among people who would say yes are those who believe that free markets (where governments interfere little in the conduct of business) distribute goods and services in the most efficient and fairest way; in this perspective, the business executive receives a salary that corresponds to the value he contributes to the economy. Other people believe the such inequalities in income are not ethical, do not truly reflect the value of each person's effort in the economy, or threaten to undermine political support for free markets; a person with these beliefs might propose a higher rate of taxation for wealthier people (which could then be given to people with less income), government programs that address particular problems among poor people (such as the inability to afford health care), and other laws that would encourage a reduction in income inequality.

Few people, however, support the same salary for every job. If all salaries were the same, there would be little incentive for people to work hard, to be innovative,

BEN & JERRY'S "SEVEN-TO-ONE" POLICY

Famous for making rich, high-quality ice cream with interesting flavors, Ben & Jerry's opened its first store in 1978 in a renovated gas station in Burlington, Vermont. The two founders, Ben Cohen and Jerry Greenfield, had taken a correspondence course in ice-cream making and knew little about running a company. When business began to pick up, they hired a local nightclub owner to help manage the finances. By the early 1980s, as they opened new stores and Ben & Jerry's became a national brand, sales ballooned, rising from $9 million in 1984 to $20 million in 1986. This was all the more surprising because the founders, as Cohen admitted, "were afraid that business exploits its workers and the community."

Reflecting the values of the hippie culture of the 1960s and 1970s, Cohen and Greenfield adopted a "seven-to-one" policy for their employees. No one could earn more than seven times what the lowest-paid worker made. The company also donated 7.5 percent of its pretax earnings to charity. The salary policy remained in force until 1994, when Cohen stepped down as CEO (chief executive officer), and the company had to attract someone new to oversee its operations. Ben & Jerry's subsequently adopted a more vague "salary compression" policy, and in 2000 Unilever, a giant multinational corporation, bought the company for $326 million.

or to train themselves for specialized and difficult jobs. Some degree of income inequality, therefore, is essential to most economic systems.

When Did It Begin

The concepts of equal opportunity and equal outcome trace their roots to the political and social upheavals of the late eighteenth and early nineteenth centuries. Philosophically the American and French revolutions were inspired by principles of freedom and equality; the American Declaration of Independence asserted the right of the colonists to have social and economic freedom, while the French revolutionaries espoused ideals of "liberty, equality, fraternity." In reality, these revolutions failed to provide equal opportunities for all individuals; the rights outlined in the Declaration of Independence were not extended to women or African-American slaves, and the French Revolution failed to create a lasting democratic government in France. Still, the underlying belief in equal opportunity for all men, regardless of origin, class, or economic standing, would serve as the foundation for later efforts to achieve equality for all individuals, regardless of race or gender.

The idea of equal outcome is often associated with the writings of German philosopher and economist Karl Marx (1818-1883). In such works as *The Communist Manifesto* (1848) and *Das Kapital* (1867), Marx outlined a radical vision of a "classless" society based on communist principles of economic cooperation, in which the proletariat (in other words, working class) would control the means of production, and the benefits of this production would be distributed according to the individual needs of the members of the society. While most economists regard Marx's vision of communism to be both politically and economically unworkable, his ideals concerning equity are still influential and are at the core of many modern economic and social welfare programs.

More Detailed Information

Several factors play a role in determining whether or not an individual enjoys economic success. Social forces are often cited as the most important. For example, an individual who grows up in a wealthy family, attends expensive private schools, and receives glowing references from his father's business associates will generally have an enormous advantage over an individual who grows up in a broken home, lives in a poor neighborhood with high crime rates, and attends poorly funded public schools.

In addition to individual economic circumstances, social factors concerning race and gender also play a role in creating conditions of inequality. Racial and sexual discrimination, though illegal, are still pervasive in the American workforce. For example, in 2002 American women still earned only 69 percent, on average, of the money men earned for the same work, despite decades of social reform. At the same time, while the Civil Rights Movement of the 1960s helped create greater economic and political opportunities for African Americans, problems of discrimination (in hiring practices and in compensation) continued to exist in the twenty-first century.

The government can also play a role in creating or reducing economic inequalities. For example, tax breaks for big corporations can make it more difficult for smaller companies to remain competitive, resulting in lower wages, unemployment, and the closing of businesses. At the same time, government refusal to raise the minimum wage can also widen the income gap between the rich and the poor; indeed, many economic thinkers have begun to draw a distinction between a minimum wage, which is the lowest wage allowable by law, and a living wage, which is a wage that is considered adequate to support an individual and his or her family.

Recent Trends

The late twentieth and early twenty-first centuries witnessed a dramatic rise in income inequality in the United States. Economists attribute this shift to a range of causes, from tax policies that favor corporations over individuals to the natural effects of globalization. Some economists have even suggested that this imbalance has resulted from the rapid emergence of new technologies. As demand for workers with technical skills (such as those relating to computers) increased, individuals with a high level of education gained an even greater advantage over people with less formal training. As incomes for these high-technology jobs rose, wages for lower-skilled work dropped. Economists referred to this phenomenon as "skill-biased technical change" (SBTC).

$ Distribution of Income

What It Means

When people say things such as "the rich get richer, and the poor get poorer," they are referring to distribution of income. It describes how all the money (income) earned in a nation is divided among people of various income levels. The most common image used to talk about distribution of income is a pie. If we think of a pie as representing all of the income earned by the people of a certain country, then the sizes of the slices of that pie given to the rich, the poor, and the middle classes represent the distribution of income.

In any capitalist society (in which most businesses are owned by individuals, not the government), the rich tend to get a disproportionately large piece of the economic pie; this is called income inequality. Economists explain this imbalance in terms of the workings of natural market forces, but there are many other factors that contribute to income inequality, and some of them lie beyond the

range of economic explanations. The issues connected with income distribution are among the most controversial in economics, and they are of interest to ordinary citizens as much as to economists and government leaders. Because government has some power to affect the distribution of income in a capitalist society, people's opinions on the issue are often closely related to their political views.

When Did It Begin

Before the rise of capitalism in Europe in the sixteenth to eighteenth centuries, the distribution of wealth was determined primarily by heredity, tradition, and force. People who inherited or ruled large areas of land were able to extract wealth from the people who lived and worked on that land, and those who did not own land could not amass wealth beyond the amounts dictated by the commands and traditions of the landowning classes of society. As capitalism became more widespread, so did the ability of non-landowners to generate more income. Once markets (places where buyers and sellers freely come together to do business) became the primary means of determining the economic structure of society, there ceased to be a centralized authority in charge of dividing up wealth. Market forces (such as the laws of supply and demand) determined who benefited from an economy, and to what degree.

Income distribution in capitalist societies has been a subject of interest since the field of economics was

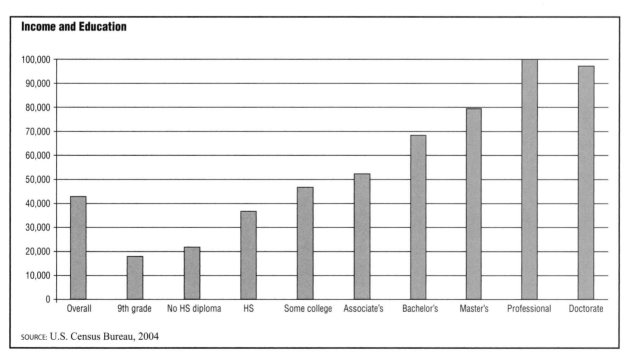

Income and Education

SOURCE: U.S. Census Bureau, 2004

Distribution of income refers to the way in which the earnings of a society are divided up among its members, with some making more and some making less. According to this bar graph by the U.S. Census Bureau, income distribution in the United States is closely correlated with the level of education someone achieves. *Illustration by GGS Information Services. Cengage Learning, Gale.*

THE EIFFEL TOWER MAY BE HIGH

In the 1948 edition of his popular economics textbook, the American economist Paul Samuelson (who won a Nobel Prize in 1970) used a vivid analogy to help people visualize the extremes of income distribution in the United States. He said that if we used children's building blocks to construct a pyramid representing incomes in the United States, with each layer of blocks representing $1,000 in income, the pyramid (its peak representing the highest income) would be taller than the Eiffel Tower in Paris. The vast majority of our incomes, however, would be located less than one yard off the ground.

Some evidence suggests that income disparities at the extremes of U.S. society remained the same until about 1970, after which they greatly increased. Samuelson, in fact, revised his analogy in 2000. He said that most American incomes remained at levels represented by the bottom yard of the pyramid, but the top of the pyramid had now reached the height of Mount Everest.

established in 1776 with the publication of *An Inquiry into the Nature and Causes of the Wealth of Nations* by the Scottish philosopher Adam Smith (1723–90). Smith and other so-called classical economists explained the distribution of wealth as a natural and efficient outgrowth of market forces, but German political philosopher Karl Marx (1818–83) and his followers contended that capitalism unfairly favored owners over workers in any business enterprise. Subsequent examinations of income distribution have been complex and wide-ranging, and debate about the fairness of unequal income distribution has continued.

More Detailed Information

The ways in which income is distributed in a capitalist society is extremely complex, and people's views on it are substantially affected by their political beliefs and other assumptions and interpretations that lie outside the realm of economics.

The basic economic explanation for unequal distribution of income is that individuals are rewarded in proportion to the value they bring to the economic process. Value, in this context, refers to a complicated mixture of intelligence, education, training, health, experience, talent, motivation, and willingness to give up leisure time to engage in economically productive activity. These and other desirable personal attributes make up what economists call an individual's human capital.

As a simple illustration of how human capital affects income, consider a neurosurgeon and a janitor. A neurosurgeon must possess many of the attributes listed above in extremely high degrees. People who have such attributes in abundance are rare. Therefore, neurosurgeons typically command very high salaries. The job requirements of being a janitor, however, are not nearly so rigorous. A person need not offer high measures of human capital to qualify for a janitorial position. Therefore, there will always be a much larger supply of potential janitors than neurosurgeons in the labor market, and janitors accordingly are not able to command nearly as large salaries.

But many other factors affect income distribution. One of the primary factors is luck. For instance, a software programmer who happens to work for a small company that is bought out by the software giant Microsoft Corporation might suddenly see her income rise dramatically, while a programmer with an equal amount of human capital who happens to work for a similar small company sees no equivalent increase in income.

Likewise, deep-rooted societal problems can greatly affect a person's potential earning ability. According to U.S. census estimates, for example, African-American and female heads of households consistently earn less than their white male counterparts. Economists, however, can offer little explanation for these uncomfortable facts. It is left to historians and sociologists (who study human societies) to explain how patterns of discrimination might figure into an individual's earning potential.

At either extreme of the income-distribution spectrum, the role of human capital is complicated by additional factors. For instance, poor people might be poor because they do not have many skills deemed desirable by the market system, but their poverty itself might prevent them from being able to obtain those skills, especially when the educational opportunities available to the poor, the middle class, and the rich are unequal. Also, the poor are often surrounded by other poor people in isolated neighborhoods, so that they do not have many positive role models. This can lead to situations in which insufficiently developed work habits are passed down from generation to generation.

Many of the richest people in the United States and the world, meanwhile, either inherit a portion of their wealth or amass great wealth out of proportion to their abilities and productive capacities. For an example of the second type of wealth creation, imagine a person who invents a new software product and opens a business selling that product. While he is in private business, his profits might be seen as corresponding with his human capital, the value he brings to the economic process. If, however, his business goes public (that is, if shares of it are offered for sale to investors on the stock market), investors may contribute vast amounts of money to the project of selling that software in the belief that the business can become profitable on a large scale. Thus, the individual entrepreneur can suddenly become far richer than he ever could have done through simple business transactions. In this way people such as Microsoft founder Bill Gates go from being college dropouts (albeit a brilliant one, in Gates's case) to being billionaires in a matter of one or two decades.

Some people who are concerned about inequality of income distribution worry, therefore, about noneconomic factors that seem to rig the system for or against various groups. Additionally, those who favor equalizing income distribution to some degree (this could be done by raising taxes on the upper classes) worry about the correlation between wealth and political power. If the rich are able to influence government, they might push for legislation that encourages economic developments that give them a bigger slice of the economic pie.

Those who maintain that income inequality is beneficial to society, however, point out that if incomes were equalized, there would be no incentive for people to act in ways that benefit society as well as the individual. If all occupations paid $20,000, why would anyone engage in the most demanding forms of work? Most people, if given the choice between living in a society in which all jobs paid $20,000 or a society in which one set of jobs paid $10,000 and another, more challenging set of jobs paid $30,000, would choose the second society because it offers the possibility of a better life, even though it also offers increased risk. According to this argument, the incentive of making the higher salary (and being able to live more comfortably) encourages people to be productive. In the society where everyone makes $20,000, no one has an incentive to be productive.

Recent Trends

In 1929 (just before the economic collapse known as the Great Depression), the wealthiest 20 percent of Americans earned more than half (54.4 percent) of the nation's income. Meanwhile, the bottom 20 percent of U.S. families earned only 3.5 percent of the total income. By 1947 the American middle class had grown greatly, and the proportions of income claimed by the top tiers of society had dropped: the wealthiest 20 percent of Americans claimed 43.3 percent of the total income in that year, while the share of the bottom 20 percent had risen to 5.1 percent. The change was most drastic among the very elite: in 1929 the richest 5 percent earned 30 percent of U.S. income, but by 1947 that number had decreased by almost half, to 17.5 percent. The numbers changed only slightly through 1970, and this period is considered to be the heyday of the American middle class.

After 1970, however, the proportion of income claimed by the top 5 percent of society rose again, and at the same time the earnings of families in the lowest 20 percent fell. By 1995 the top 5 percent claimed 20 percent of the nation's income, and the bottom 20 percent claimed 4.4 percent. Between 1973 and 1995 the productivity of the United States increased significantly:

gross domestic product per capita (the average amount of wealth produced annually in the country per person) grew 39 percent. Almost all the income stemming from this increase went to the top 20 percent of the American workforce. During this period the incomes of nonsupervisory workers (those who are not managers or supervisors) fell 14 percent. These trends have caused a renewed debate over the acceptable levels of income inequality.

$ Productivity

What It Means

Productivity is the ratio of output (goods created or services performed) to input (all costs of production, including workers' wages and costs required to run business equipment). Productivity is not merely a measure of the final output from a company. For example, an automobile factory (Factory A) produces 1,000 new cars in an eight-hour workday. Another factory (Factory B) produces only 500 cars in an eight-hour day. To measure each factory's productivity, it is necessary to compare the production of cars (the output) at each factory against workers' wages and the cost to run the assembly line (the input) at each factory. Assume that both factories pay the same cost for using exactly the same equipment and that both factories pay their workers at the same rate. If Factory A required 50 workers to produce 1,000 cars in an eight-hour workday and Factory B required only 20 workers to produce 500 cars in an eight-hour workday, then Factory B would be more productive than Factory A, even though Factory A produced more cars than Factory B.

Productivity is difficult to measure accurately. Most companies measure productivity by weighing the total output against one aspect of the input, usually the total number of labor hours required to produce the final product. The total number of labor hours is the sum of the number of hours worked by each individual involved in the making of the product. For example, if 10 workers each worked eight hours to make a product, then the production required 80 total hours of labor.

Productivity is closely related to another economic concept called efficiency. Whereas productivity is a ratio of the *amount* of the output to the cost of the input, efficiency is a ration of the *value* of the output to the input. A business is considered to be operating at peak, or optimal, efficiency if it produces the greatest number of goods possible at the lowest possible cost.

When Did It Begin

Finding ways to increase productivity has always been important to the long-term success of a business. Maximizing output became even more important after the Industrial Revolution because of the high costs associated with mass producing goods. Securing land and building a

Productivity refers to the total value of goods relative to the costs involved in making them. In 1913 car manufacturer Henry Ford (1863–1947) invented the modern assembly line, which enable him to increase the productivity of his automobile factory dramatically. *The Library of Congress.*

factory, purchasing and installing equipment, paying for fuel for equipment, and paying a labor force is expensive. Given these costs, it is crucial that a factory produce enough goods to make a profit. Thus, not long after the rise of factories came an outpouring of productivity and efficiency studies as well as numerous methods for getting the most possible output from a factory.

One of the best known of these ideas is called Fordism. Named after Henry Ford (1863–1947), the automobile entrepreneur who introduced the concept, the principle of Fordism states that in order to make workers happy (and therefore productive) it is necessary to pay them high enough wages so that they can afford to purchase the merchandise that they are producing. With a large group of his workers eager to buy his cars, Ford had a guaranteed market. This increased the demand for his cars among middle-class Americans, which in turn required his workers to be more productive to meet this demand. The strategy worked. By 1910 the

Ford Motor Company had sold over 10 million Model T Fords. At the time, his employees were the highest paid factory workers in the world. In the aftermath of this success, Fordism was promoted as a model for worker management throughout the United States and Europe. These ideas now form the basis for what is called "efficiency wage" theory, which states that a worker's productivity and efficiency is positively related to the wage he or she is paid. That is, if you pay workers more than the going wage, they will want to make sure they do not lose their job, encouraging them to work harder.

More Detailed Information

Businesses of all sizes, whether they produce thousands of cars a day or cut lawns in a suburban neighborhood, are always trying to maximize worker productivity. One of the best ways to maximize productivity is to create a working environment in which workers are likely to be working at their full potential for most of the time that they work. There are numerous theories about how to maximize worker production, and most economists agree that there is no single way that works best in all situations. Ford's theory of paying high wages to workers is just one of those theories, and, though it worked for Ford, many economists point out that this approach is not always good for small businesses.

Consider the case of a landscaping business that makes most of its profits from cutting lawns. Each day the manager sends two teams of three workers to various clients. If the manager were to pay one team of older workers $10 per hour and the younger team $7 per hour, one might assume that the older, better-paid team would mow more lawns. This would likely be true in the beginning of the season. However, by the middle of the season, the younger team would likely be able to work as fast as the older team. Also, the younger team might work harder because they wanted to make more money. Say, for instance, that the workers on both teams socialize together in off hours and that all the workers spend about the same amount of money. Each of the workers decides that he or she must earn about $200 a week to make ends meet and to have enough money to spend recreationally. This would mean that the younger team would have to cut 29 lawns a week, but the older team would only have to cut 20 lawns (for the sake of this example, each lawn takes one hour to mow). Even though they were paid a better wage, the older team would be less productive than the younger team.

This example highlights two important aspects of productivity. The first is that when dealing with individual workers, individual motivation has a significant impact on productivity. In the above scenario, the younger group was motivated to work harder than the older group because they wanted to earn as much money by the end of the week as the older group had. The second concept is that money does not always motivate workers the way an employer would expect. Sometimes instead of raising the level of productivity, increased wages produce a "productivity gap," or the difference between what a person is capable of producing and what he or she actually produces. In the above example, the older group was capable of mowing at least 29 lawns a week, but they mowed only 20. This productivity gap decreased the business's profits.

Because money does not always motivate workers, employers make many other attempts to maximize workers' productivity. For example, many employers purchase ergonomically sound equipment with the hope that these devices will make their employees more comfortable while doing their jobs. Ergonomics is a science that studies the best way to design products so that workers will maximize their output. For example, an ergonomically sound chair is comfortable and designed in a way that prevents back injury. Thus an office worker who has to spend his or her entire shift sitting down will be

THE 3/2 RULE OF PRODUCTIVITY

According to the 3/2 Rule of Productivity, the more employees that a company has, the less productive each of those employees is. Mathematically, this rule states that if the size of the staff at a company were to be tripled, each individual worker would be half as productive. The 3/2 Rule is not so much a rule as a generalization or a guideline; however, most people who have worked for a growing business agree that individual workers become less productive as a company hires more staff. Various reasons have been offered to account for the decline in productivity. According to some experts, productivity drops because a growing business must add layers of communication and internal bureaucracy to manage the larger staff. Effective communication becomes more difficult when more opportunities for distraction arise. Others belief that as a business grows, it is less likely that all of the employees will share the company's vision and work as hard to achieve the company's goals.

more productive seated in an ergonomically sound chair. This person will not need to take as many breaks to relieve tension in his or her back, nor will he or she be as likely to call into work sick because of back pain from sitting all day. This chair might cost as much as $300 more than other chairs, but it might prove to be a worthwhile expense because workers who use these chairs would generate more revenue. Businesses have taken many other measures to ensure that the work environment makes workers more productive. Scientific studies have shown the temperature at which workers are most productive. A Japanese company even saw increases in worker production when the air in the office was perfumed.

Recent Trends

Immediately after World War II, productivity in most sectors of U.S. industry increased sharply. This trend continued into the early 1970s, at which point there was a significant decline in productivity that lasted until the mid-1990s. Then in 1995 productivity in the United States increased and continued to grow through the turn of the millennium. Some economists attribute the growth in productivity to the growth of the Internet and the introduction of e-commerce (the buying and selling of goods online) in the mid-1990s. Other economists attribute the rapid growth in productivity to an influx of foreign talent into the United States. According to some reports, entrepreneurs from India and China operated 29 percent of the technology firms opened in Silicon Valley (a region of the San Francisco Bay Area) from 1995 through 1998. These leaders were making important contributions to the fastest growing industry in the United States, information technology.

Many talented immigrants joined the U.S. workforce throughout the second half of the 1990s. According to the 2000 census, more than 8 million college-educated, foreign-born people resided in the United States at the turn of the millennium. The United States was host to the largest such population in the world. The United States is also home to more immigrants with doctorate degrees than any other country. Consistent levels of high-skill immigration are crucial to the technology industry because intelligent workers are required in the Research and Development (R&D) departments of technology firms. More intelligence means more innovation, and more innovation translates into greater productivity.

$ Labor Union

What It Means

A labor union is a group of workers who have joined together to negotiate with employers in order to secure better wages and working conditions. Unions originally consisted of male "blue-collar" workers (people who perform manual or physical labor, often for an hourly wage). Since the latter half of the twentieth century, however, more women and "white-collar" workers (people who perform less physically exacting labor, often for a salary rather than an hourly wage) have joined unions. As of 2006, about 12 percent of all workers in the United States belonged to a union.

Labor unions negotiate the terms of their employment through a method called collective bargaining. In this process a representative of the union negotiates with a representative of the employer. The two sides in these negotiations are often referred to as "labor" (the union) and "management" (the employer). By means of collective bargaining, labor attempts to set favorable terms of employment, which include a fair wage, a reasonable amount of hours of work required per week, health insurance, safe working conditions, and an official process for filing grievances or complaints concerning working conditions.

When labor and management agree to a set of working conditions, they sign an official document called a collective bargaining agreement (CBA). When labor and management cannot settle on the terms of the CBA, a work stoppage often occurs. Sometimes workers refuse to report for work until their demands are met. Such an event is called a strike. Other times owners close down operations and do not grant workers the opportunity to do their jobs. This is a called a lockout. When either of these events occurs, negotiations often turn bitter and one side is forced to give in because it cannot bear the financial losses of a work stoppage. No matter how the agreement is achieved, the terms of the CBA apply to all

members of the union. In order to receive the benefits of union membership, members are required to pay union dues (a small portion of a worker's wages that pays for costs associated with the organization and governing of the union).

When Did It Begin

Labor unions first appeared in the late 1700s, shortly after the start of the Industrial Revolution. Large-scale industrialization during the Industrial Revolution in Europe and the United States brought intolerable working conditions: most notably low wages, long hours, and dangerous work environments. Workers, many of whom were women and children, were often required to work from dawn until dusk for only pennies a day. Employees learned that they had to unite to force management to meet their demands.

In the United States, two types of labor unions evolved: craft unions and industrial unions. Craft unions consisted of workers who practiced a specific trade. In 1792 Philadelphia shoemakers organized what many historians believe was the nation's first craft union. Boston carpenters formed a craft union in 1793, as did New York City printers in 1794. An industrial union, on the

Workers form labor unions in order to negotiate with employers over such issues as pay, employee benefits, and workplace safety. One of the most famous labor union figures of the twentieth century was Jimmy Hoffa, shown here with fellow union members, who was leader of the International Brotherhood of Teamsters from 1957 to 1964. *AP Images.*

other hand, consists of a group of employees in the same industry, regardless of the task they perform in that industry. For example, members of the United Steel Workers Union all work in the steel industry, but not all of the members of the union have the same job.

During the late 1830s, industrial unions were nearly eliminated in the United States when the nation suffered an economic crisis, but unions rebounded just prior to the Civil War and grew steadily thereafter through the mid-1950s. The greatest period of growth for American labor unions came between 1933 and 1944. During this time, union membership quadrupled because of President Franklin D. Roosevelt's New Deal legislation, which supported the organizing power of unions, and because of an economic boost that resulted from the impending World War II.

More Detailed Information

The strike is a labor union's greatest weapon when management remains unwilling to meet the union's demands. Although strikes can be effective, they can also cost workers a considerable amount of money in lost wages. Thus, most labor unions use strikes as a last resort after all other measures to reach an agreement have been exhausted. When they do strike, workers gather outside their place of employment and form what is called a picket line. Walking back and forth outside of the job site, strikers typically carry signs protesting their working conditions and describing their demands. Any worker who "crosses the picket line," or reports to work before the strike has been formally resolved, is called a scab.

Workers do not often strike over just one issue. In most strikes, a union prioritizes one or two issues above all other demands. Strikes are therefore identified according to the union's primary demand. In an "economic strike," workers demand higher wages, fewer work hours, or better benefits, such as health care or holiday pay. In an "organization strike," the union seeks official recognition of its status as a labor union from its employers. A "grievance strike" occurs when the labor union finds that management has failed to live up to the terms of an existing CBA. Other types of strikes include the "wildcat strike" and the "sympathy strike." Wildcat strikes are unauthorized by the union. They happen when a faction of disgruntled laborers organizes a work stoppage without the consent of union leadership. Sympathy strikes happen when one group of workers stops reporting for duty on behalf of another group of workers.

Philadelphia, which is likely the birthplace of the nation's first craft union, is also believed to be the location of the first labor strike in the United States. In 1786 a group of printers who were not joined in an official labor union waged a strike. In May 1786 a skilled print craftsman in Philadelphia made $5.83 per week. On the final day of the month, 26 of the printers vowed not to work another day until they were paid $6.00 per week.

JIMMY HOFFA

Because of the circumstances surrounding his mysterious disappearance in 1975, Jimmy Hoffa has remained a compelling figure in American history. Originally a warehouse worker, Hoffa rose through the ranks of the International Brotherhood of Teamsters (one of the largest labor unions in the United States) because of his talent as a brilliant organizer and his ties to organized crime. He served as the union's leader from 1957 through 1964. By 1964 Hoffa had nearly all of the truck drivers in the United States allied under the same collective bargaining agreement. His hope was to extend the agreement to include airlines and other forms of transportation. That same year, however, he was convicted of attempted bribery and sentenced to 15 years in prison. President Richard Nixon commuted his sentence in 1971, stipulating that Hoffa discontinue all union activity. In violation of this restriction, Hoffa was scheduled on July 30, 1975, to meet with mafia leaders at Machus Red Fox, a restaurant just outside of Detroit, Michigan. He was never seen again. It is presumed that on that day he was killed by mafia members.

The strike worked. Not all strikes staged in Philadelphia were as successful, however. For example, when an association of shoemakers called Philadelphia's Society of Journeymen Cordwainers (the word *cordwainer* comes from cordovan, which is a soft leather used to make many types of shoes) went on strike for higher wages in 1806, the Philadelphia Mayor's Court ruled that unions were criminal conspiracies whose aim was to wrongfully injure owners and their businesses. Most states ruled similarly, with one notable exception being the Massachusetts Supreme Court, which stated that labor strikes were not by definition criminal conspiracies.

Some of the most highly publicized strikes in recent history have been staged by professional athletes. For example, major league baseball players went on strike on August 12, 1994, and the dispute was not settled until April 2, 1995. During the strike, all of the playoffs, including the World Series, were cancelled. Up to this point, no professional sports league had cancelled its playoffs because of a work stoppage. Ten years after the baseball strike, the National Hockey League (NHL) lost the entire 2004–05 season and the playoffs due to a lockout staged by the owners.

Recent Trends

Union membership in the United States has steadily declined since the mid-1970s, due in part to a decline in American manufacturing. Consequently, unions have looked to the service industry to acquire new members. In the late-1990s health-care professionals began joining the

Service Employees International Union in unprecedented numbers. After an increase of more than 265,000 new members in 1999, which was the largest growth in 20 years, union membership in the United States began declining once again in first years of the twenty-first century. In 2002 unions lost a total of 280,000 members, slipping to 16.1 million members nationwide.

Though their membership numbers are down, unions remain a considerable force in the United States, especially those associated with the transportation industry. In 1997 union employees at UPS (United Parcel Service) staged what would become the largest strike in the United States in 20 years. UPS acquiesced to nearly all of the union's demands. The company lost an average of $30 million per day during the two-week strike. In 2002 dockworkers at ports throughout the United States went on strike for 10 days, costing shipping companies between $400 and $600 million in losses. In 2003 Broadway musicians in New York City went on strike, causing the theater industry to cancel 18 musicals. During the strike, theaters lost more than $10 million in revenues, and nearby restaurants lost over $50 million in sales, according to some estimates.

$ Labor-Management Relations

What It Means

The term *labor-management relations* refers to interactions between employees, as represented by labor unions, and their employers. Labor unions are organizations of employees in particular industries, companies, or groups of industries or companies, who join together in order to further workers' individual interests.

Unions came into being as a result of the increasing industrialization of Europe and North America in the nineteenth century, which led to enormous increases in the number of people who worked in factories and other facilities for mass production. Unions gained power in the United States after the Great Depression, the severe economic crisis that impoverished many ordinary Americans, and they were most powerful in the mid-twentieth century, when the economy was relatively stable and heavy manufacturing industries such as steel, automotive, and mining were prominent. In the latter part of the twentieth century, however, the U.S. economy began to be dominated by service industries (such as banking, insurance, and health care) whose employees have rarely unionized, and the rapid pace of technological progress eroded the stable relationships between labor and management that had been characteristic of American industry in the past. By the beginning of the twenty-first century, the future of unions in the United States was uncertain.

The range of interactions between unions and employers has varied from adversarial to accommodating at different times and places, depending on a number of factors. Some of the most important of these factors are the government's attitude toward unions, the nature of the industries involved, and the degree of prosperity in society. Negotiation between labor and management has been instrumental, in many cases, in determining such issues as wage and salary levels, working hours, working conditions, hiring procedures, training programs, and benefits such as health insurance and retirement plans. Traditionally, unionized workers have negotiated with their employers based on collective bargaining agreements, which set out the rules according to which union representatives and management must deal with one another. In cases when labor and management cannot come to an agreement, arbitration (resolving of the dispute by a third party) may be necessary. When all else fails, unions sometimes use strikes (a collective refusal of employees to report for work until their demands are met) to force management to yield.

When Did It Begin

The economies of Europe and North America underwent drastic change beginning in the nineteenth century as a result of the increased ability of businesses to produce goods on a mass scale thanks to technological innovations, such as the invention of the steam engine and new techniques for manufacturing textiles and iron. The Industrial Revolution, as this set of economic and cultural changes was called, resulted in a dramatic increase of people employed in factories, mines, and other large-scale operations. Employers no longer had personal relationships with workers, and there were no laws regulating employer-employee relationships. In the nineteenth century it was common for men, women, and children as young as six or eight to work in factories and mines for as long as 16 hours a day. Such intolerable conditions became cause for public concern, and gradually governments began intervening to establish laws regarding employees' treatment of their workers.

Even as labor laws began to be passed regulating working conditions and outlawing such practices as child labor, the right of workers to organize into unions was generally denied in both Europe and the United States. Members of unions such as the American Federation of Labor (AFL), which was established in 1881, were routinely fired or blacklisted (added to lists of people whom employers agreed not to hire), and strikes were suppressed by people paid by management as well as by the government, which frequently contributed federal troops to guard management's interests.

This began to change at the beginning of the twentieth century in Europe, but in the United States the government continued to side with employers until the Great Depression, when public dissatisfaction with economic conditions became extreme. American workers won the right to organize under the National Labor

In labor-management relations, workers and employers negotiate over pay, health care benefits, and other forms of employee compensation. Here unionized hotel workers in San Francisco protest the business practices of their employers. *AP Images.*

Relations Act of 1935, also known as the Wagner Act. In the decades that followed, employers were required to recognize the right of unions to exist, and to address their concerns under collective bargaining agreements.

More Detailed Information

Labor-management relations in the United States have varied greatly since workers first won the legal right to organize. During and after the Great Depression, there was widespread skepticism about allowing business owners to seek profits without any government or other forms of intervention. Unions represented a balancing of the interests of workers with the interests of management, and the American population generally supported the right to organize and engage in collective bargaining. Unions also became an important political force in the 1930s, putting pressure on politicians to pass legislation favorable to workers. Organized labor thus became a very powerful force in national life, and the number of Americans who belonged to unions grew dramatically.

When the United States entered World War II in 1941, labor leaders promised the government that they would not engage in strikes that might hamper the defense industry. After the war, however, unions agitated

for higher wages, and numerous strikes resulted. The tide of public opinion turned partially against unions at this time, and Congress passed a law in 1947, the Taft-Hartley Act, restricting the power of unions. Among other measures, Taft-Hartley made it possible for management to hire non-union workers and to postpone strikes.

Though some amount of anti-union sentiment persisted between the 1940s and 1960s, in general unions remained a very powerful force in American business and politics at this time. Their power was partly a function of the economy's stability. World War II had ended the Depression, and the boom in industry sparked by the need for war materials continued in the decades that followed. America was the world's leading industrial power, and the skills required in the workplace, like the products generated by U.S. industry, changed very little. Workers, in part thanks to unions and their stable relations with management, could count on wages that would allow them to pay for their basic needs, stable long-term employment, and generous health-care and retirement benefits.

In the 1960s and 1970s, though, the United States fell behind other countries in industrial productivity.

LABOR-MANAGEMENT RELATIONS IN PROFESSIONAL SPORTS

At the end of the twentieth century and the beginning of the twenty-first century, perhaps the most visible labor unions (organizations of workers) in the United States were those consisting of players in the various professional sports leagues. All four major team-sports leagues in the United States—Major League Baseball (MLB), the National Basketball Association (NBA), the National Football League (NFL), and the National Hockey League (NHL)—had a history of poor relations between players' unions and team management. In baseball, a strike by the players led to the cancellation of the 1994 World Series. Similarly, the NBA's 1998–99 season was shortened by one-half because of an inability of the players' union and team owners to agree on a collective-bargaining agreement (an agreement regarding the terms for negotiating between players' interests and owners' interests). The NHL's problems were even worse: it was the first major sports league to lose an entire season (2004–05) to a disagreement between labor and management. The NFL narrowly averted similar difficulties when team owners and players agreed to new terms for salaries and the sharing of revenues in 2006.

While these difficulties received a great deal of media coverage, it was generally hard for Americans, whether sports fans or not, to feel a great deal of sympathy for either side, since both players and owners were among the richest people in the world.

Other countries could provide high-quality products at cheaper prices than American companies could, and U.S. businesses had to change their strategies to compete. One of the reasons that other countries had an advantage over the United States when it came to manufacturing was that the higher wages paid to U.S. workers resulted in higher prices for the final manufactured products. As management began trying to cut costs and find new ways of doing business, their relations with labor grew strained. Business owners began reducing wages and trying to increase efficiency through measures that cut into the gains unions had made over the preceding decades.

The 1980s and 1990s saw unions struggle to maintain their strength, as changes in laws pertaining to taxes and international trade made it easier for business owners to move manufacturing facilities to foreign countries where workers could be paid less. These decades also saw

the U.S. economy shift from a focus on manufacturing to a focus on service, that range of industries whose common denominator is that people are employed to interact with other people, rather than to make physical objects. The financial, insurance, health-care, legal, retail, real estate, and utilities industries are included in this designation. Unions had always been strongest in the area of manufacturing, and they had never succeeded in taking hold among service workers. Additionally, unions were not equipped to deal with the rapidly changing realities of American economic life. Service jobs paid unskilled workers less than manufacturing jobs, and management in these industries usually provided little in the way of benefits. Workers could no longer depend on management for long-term employment, health care, or retirement planning. Even though many working Americans were unsatisfied with these realities, unions did not appear to have solutions, since the ground rules of labor-management relations had shifted.

Recent Trends

At the height of union influence in the 1940s, more than one-third of employed Americans were union members. By the early 1980s, this figure had dropped to around 20 percent, and by the early twenty-first century, only about 12 percent of the U.S. labor force was unionized. In addition to the structural changes in the economy described above, unions in the late twentieth and early twenty-first centuries had to grapple with government opposition under conservative Presidents such as Ronald Reagan (1980-1988), George H. W. Bush (1988-1992), and George W. Bush (2000-2008), each of whom consistently took a pro-management stance in economic matters. The most heavily unionized industries, as of 2006, were those dominated by local, state, or federal government entities and therefore not subject to the rapidly changing economic realities that shaped other industries. While only 7 percent of workers in the private (non-government) sector belonged to unions, more than 36 percent of government workers were union members. The most powerful unions in the United States were typically those of public-school teachers, policemen, and firefighters. Unions had been instrumental in shaping the U.S. economy in the twentieth century, but workers at the beginning of the twenty-first century were largely in the position of fending for themselves in their relations with management. It was unclear whether organized labor would be able to answer the challenges facing workers of the future.

How Countries Work Together: International Trade

$ Overview: International Trade

What It Means

International trade is any legal exchange of goods and services between countries. When a business in one country exports goods or services to consumers in another country, it is called international trade. International trade also takes place when consumers in one country import goods and services from a foreign producer.

An import is a product that is purchased from international sources for domestic consumers, and an export is a product that is made by domestic producers and is sold to international buyers. In general, the products a country exports are those it has efficiency in producing. Japan, for example, exports electronics and automobiles because it manufactures those goods more efficiently than many other countries do. A country might also export its natural resources as goods. For example, Saudi Arabia and other Middle Eastern countries with an abundance of domestic oil fields export oil to many countries around the world that do not have rich oil reserves.

International trade is important because it allows national markets to provide a diversity of goods and services to their consumers that they would be unable to provide if they were limited to the production of goods and services within their borders. The result of international trade is that almost any type of good is available on the international market, from resources such as oil, water, and steel to necessities such as food, clothing, and building materials to luxury goods such as diamonds, designer clothing, and limousines. Many services are traded internationally, such as legal, accounting, advertising, banking, and tourism services. Another important result of international trade is that the more manufacturers that participate in an industry, the greater the competition between manufacturers becomes. Greater competition results in more competitive prices, which means that consumers have access to a number of inexpensive products.

When Did It Begin

The beginnings of international trade date back to the ancient world when people first began traveling long distances to exchange goods. The Silk Road, a 5,000-mile long system of interconnected routes, was used by traders and travelers from 200 BC to AD 900 and linked China to Greece and other Mediterranean countries. Initially established to support the transportation of Chinese silks to the west, the Silk Road was also used to export other Chinese goods, such as porcelain, spices, gunpowder, and paper. Over time, the Chinese used the Silk Road to import such goods as cosmetics, silver, and perfume produced by European, Central Asian, Arabian, and African suppliers.

In the mid-sixteenth century a philosophy supporting international trade emerged in England. Known as mercantilism, the theory asserted that gold and silver (the currency of the time) were the basis of a nation's wealth and crucial to healthy and active commercial activity. By exporting goods a country could earn gold and silver, but when it imported goods, it paid for these with gold and silver. According to mercantilism, it is in a country's best interest to export more than it imports, or to maintain what is called a "trade surplus." Since national wealth and prestige hinged on accumulations of gold and silver, those countries with the highest value of exports were the most powerful.

Scottish philosopher and economist Adam Smith (1723–90) criticized mercantilism in his book *An Inquiry into the Nature and Causes of the Wealth of Nations*. Smith asserted that each country differs from others in its ability to produce goods efficiently. For example, the English had the advantage of efficiently manufacturing textiles, while the French had the advantage in producing wine. Smith argued that countries should not attempt to produce goods domestically that can be purchased for a cheaper price internationally. A country benefits, said Smith, by focusing on the goods that it can produce most advantageously and by trading them on the international market. Smith's influential arguments helped shape the

DAVID RICARDO

"To produce the wine in Portugal, might require only the labour of 80 men for one year, and to produce the cloth in the same country, might require the labour of 90 men for the same time. It would therefore be advantageous for her to export wine in exchange for cloth. This exchange might even take place, notwithstanding that the commodity imported by Portugal could be produced there with less labour than in England because it would be advantageous to her rather to employ her capital in the production of wine, for which she would obtain more cloth from England."

DAVID RICARDO, *PRINCIPLES OF POLITICAL ECONOMY AND TAXATION*, 1817.

Why He is Important

David Ricardo (1772–1823), English economist, was one of the most important contributors to modern economic theory. His work marked a departure from economic studies before his, as he was the first economist to systematize his ideas: whereas previous writing about the discipline, including Adam Smith's groundbreaking *Inquiry into the Nature and Causes of the Wealth of Nations,* had employed a narrative style, using anecdotes to illustrate economic ideas, Ricardo approached economics scientifically, presenting his theories with logical proofs, or formulas.

Ricardo's most significant achievement was his discovery of the law of comparative advantage, according to which all countries benefit from trading with one another, even if they could otherwise produce all the products they need domestically. Along with radical changes in the manufacturing and transport of goods brought on by the Industrial Revolution, Ricardo's theory of comparative advantage helped pave the way for an unprecedented expansion of international trade during the nineteenth century.

Life

David Ricardo was born in London, England, on April 19, 1772. The third of 17 children, he came from a family of Sephardic Jews who

had settled in Holland in the early eighteenth century. Ricardo's parents immigrated to England from Holland shortly before his birth. His father was a wealthy merchant banker who had made his fortune trading on the London Stock Exchange. Although Ricardo distinguished himself as a passionate student from an early age, he nonetheless left school at the age of 14 to work for his father at the stock exchange. At 21 Ricardo split with his family and his Jewish faith to marry Abigail Delvalle, a Quaker. Having earned a formidable reputation in London as a gifted young businessman, he was able to establish himself independently as a dealer in government securities.

Ricardo soon became tremendously wealthy in his own right. Indeed, by 1814, when he was in his early forties, he had earned enough money to retire from the business world. He purchased a country estate called Gatcombe Park, in Gloucestershire, and devoted his time to intellectual pursuits, which included not only economics but also literature, mathematics, chemistry, and geology. Ricardo's interest in economics had been sparked more than a decade earlier when, at the age of 28, he had happened to read Smith's *An Inquiry into the Nature and Causes of the Wealth of Nations.* He spent several years developing his own ideas before he began to write articles on contemporary economic issues, such as the Bullionist Controversy, which emerged in the early 1800s over the question of whether or not paper money should be made convertible to gold on demand. Ricardo's writing on the subject, in which he argued that the overly high supply of bank notes in circulation was causing inflation (price increases), led to a lengthy debate in letters with Thomas Malthus, another pioneering economist of the era, with whom he became close friends. During this period his intellectual development was also significantly influenced by friendships with philosopher Jeremy Bentham and philosopher-economist James Mill (father of John Stuart Mill, one of the most influential economic thinkers in history).

Published in 1817, Ricardo's most important work was *Principles of Political Economy and Taxation* (1817), a comprehensive

production and trade of goods and services in developed economies around the world.

More Detailed Information

International trade has many economic benefits. If a country does not have the assets or natural resources to produce a good efficiently, it can trade with another country to acquire that item. For example, Sweden benefits from trading products it can produce efficiently and at low cost, such as iron ore, for products it cannot produce at home, such as grapefruit. When a country is able to produce a particular good efficiently and focuses on the production of that good in order to export it to other countries, it is known as specialization.

When a country is more efficient at producing a particular good than any other country, it is said to have an absolute advantage. The production of any good (the output) requires such resources as labor, materials, money, and land (the input). Countries determine whether or not they have an absolute advantage in the production of a certain good by calculating the units of resources (the sum of inputs) they use to produce that particular good. A country has an absolute advantage in the production of a good when it uses the lowest number of units of resource to produce that good. When Country A specializes in the production of a good that it has an absolute advantage in producing and then trades with Country B for the exchange of another product for which

David Ricardo, a key figure in the classical school of economics, was a wealthy businessman before he retired at the age of 42 to become an economic theorist. The law of comparative advantage, which he devised, remains central to modern trade theory.
© *Bettmann/Corbis*.

theory of the distribution of all products that can be produced by the three economic classes: the landlords who collect rent for their property, the owners of capital who earn profits, and the workers who receive wages for their labor. In his preface to the book, he

wrote that his predecessors and contemporaries had failed to address adequately the topics of rent, profit, and wage.

In 1819 Ricardo purchased a seat (as was then customary) in the British House of Commons, where, owing to his stature as one of the foremost economic thinkers of the era, his opinions on trade and finance were highly valued. Ricardo was 51 years old when he died at his home in Gloucestershire on September 11, 1823.

Work

It is in *Principles of Political Economy and Taxation* that Ricardo outlines the theory of comparative advantage, which suggests that country A is better off specializing in production of the one product it can make most cheaply and efficiently (bicycles, for example) and then trading this product with countries B, C, and D for other goods it needs (such as bread, books, and bells). While this idea might seem reasonable enough, it becomes more difficult to grasp when you consider that even if country A produces bicycles *and* bread more cheaply than country B does, it will be better off (it will have more goods and services available to it) specializing in bicycles and trading with country B for bread, where bread is the specialty. Further, the more bread country B is able to sell, the more bicycles it will be able to buy. In this scenario, even though country A can produce bread more cheaply that country B, the latter economy benefits more from the production and sale of bread; therefore, it has a comparative advantage with bread. Ricardo believed that comparative advantage worked best when there was free trade between countries—that is, when countries exchanged goods and services without import taxes or other government restrictions.

Legacy

Ricardo is widely credited with systematizing the ideas of what came to be called the classical school of economics. Interestingly, Ricardo's ideas have been embraced by people on opposite ends of the economic and political spectrum, from laissez-faire capitalists wanting an economy free from government involvement to socialists, such as Karl Marx, seeking an alternative to capitalism. Simple and elegant in its explanation, Ricardo's law of comparative advantage exerted a profound influence on government trade policy throughout the nineteenth century, and it remains a cornerstone of modern trade theory.

Country B has the absolute advantage, the production of both goods is increased.

At times it is beneficial for two countries to trade one product for another even if a country has the absolute advantage in producing both products. For example, France produces a wide variety of cheese and has an abundant supply of dairy milk. Japan produces a wide variety of televisions and has an extensive electronics manufacturing base. If France wanted to produce televisions, it would have to take substantial resources out of industries it currently has. Likewise, if Japan wanted to manufacture cheese, it would need to take resources out industries, such as electronics, and develop a production process for making cheese. Thus, for France to start making televisions and for Japan to begin making cheese,

both would have to give up something. In economics this trade-off is called an opportunity cost. But even if we suppose that Japan could make both televisions and cheese at a lower cost than France could, it might still make sense for Japan to continue its current production level of televisions and to buy cheese from France. This is because what matters to Japan is how it can most profitably use its limited resources, not whether it can make cheese at a lower cost than France. If Japan makes more money manufacturing televisions than it would in producing cheese (thus making more efficient use of its limited resources), it would be better off making televisions and using some of its profits from television production to buy French cheese. Thus, even though in this example Japan maintains an absolute advantage over

International trade—the buying and selling of goods and services between different countries—expanded significantly in the late twentieth century. Bill Clinton, a prominent advocate of international trade during his presidency (1993–2001) and after, is seen here speaking before the Hong Kong Trade Development Council, an agency whose mission is to increase trading opportunities for Hong Kong-based businesses. *AP Images.*

France in cheese production (as it can produce cheese at less cost than France), France has a comparative advantage over Japan in making cheese, as cheese production benefits France's economy more than it does Japan's.

International trade also allows countries to participate in a global, or worldwide, economy. As more countries participate in the international market, more international investment takes place. When a business invests its money or other resources in business activities outside of its home country, it is known as foreign direct investment (FDI). A business may recognize that labor is cheaper in another country and decide to build a factory there to produce its goods. For example, if a U.S. boat manufacturer builds a manufacturing plant in Thailand, the U.S. company is making a foreign direct investment. Foreign direct investment may also mean that a firm manages a foreign company or invests in a project with a foreign company. If the U.S.-based boat manufacturer buys a company in Thailand, this is also an example of foreign direct investment. With increased foreign investment, nationally based economies can grow more quickly and can more easily become competitors in the global economic market. FDI can also improve employment rates and the growth rate of the gross domestic product

(GDP), a measurement of the market value of all goods and services produced in a country. For most countries, money made through international trade constitutes a significant portion of the country's GDP.

Countries trading on the international market typically try to keep the value of their imports and the value of their exports in equilibrium, or balance. *Balance of trade* is the term used to describe the difference between the value of the goods and services a country imports and the value of the goods and services it exports. When the value of exported goods and services is greater than the value of imported goods and services in a given period, it is called a trade surplus because the balance of trade is positive. When the value of imported goods and services is greater than the value of exported goods and services, it is called a trade deficit because the balance of trade is negative.

Recent Trends

Since the mid-twentieth century, national economic markets have become so integrated with one other that they have begun to function together as one large global market rather than separate economies. Separate economic systems, at one time isolated by geography and poor transportation and communication, have become increasingly less isolated. Barriers to international trade, such as tariffs (taxes) on imports, have been gradually removed. Differences in time zones, languages, government regulations, cultures, and business systems no longer hinder international trade as they once did.

The Internet is one of the major forces causing international trading practices to evolve rapidly. The Internet has greatly eased businesses' ability to import products across borders and make a profit selling them locally. Internet sales of all types of products have driven up the volume and diversity of international trade.

One of the most common ways for countries to encourage open trade is to open what are called free-trade zones. In these zones, such barriers as tariffs and import quotas (government-imposed limits on the quantity of the goods or services that may be imported over a specified period of time) are officially removed and bureaucratic restrictions lifted so that business can practice free trade. Examples of free-trade zones are the Jamaican Free Zone and the Jebel Ali Free Zone, located in Dubai, United Arab Emirates.

BASIC CONCEPTS

$ Exports

What It Means

Exports are any goods and services that are sold to foreign buyers. They are produced or manufactured in the home country and transported legally across borders. The United States exports many goods to other countries, including wheat, corn, soybeans, tobacco, automobiles, and chemicals.

Exports are the opposite of imports, which are goods and services a country purchases from international sources. The exchange of exports and imports is the branch of economics known as international trade. For most countries, international trade—selling exports abroad and buying imports from other countries—makes up a significant portion of the gross domestic product (GDP), the value of all the goods produced within a country in a certain period of time. Thus, the amount that a country exports and imports plays a crucial role in that nation's overall economic health.

When a country has an established trading system, its exports to other countries can make up a significant portion of its manufacturing and production base. The United States is the largest trading country in the world; its exported goods include electrical machinery, software, financial services, appliances, road vehicles, office machines, and cereals; the production of these goods requires many U.S. factories, farms, and manufacturers. The major trading partners of the United States are Canada, Japan, Mexico, and countries in the European Union.

The value of exports is closely tied to the value of imports. In fact, to assess the role of exported goods in a country's economy, it is important to calculate the value of that country's exports in relation to the value of its imports. The value of a country's total exports minus the value of its total imports is called net exports. For example, if in a given year foreign countries buy $500 billion worth of China's exports and Chinese consumers buy $450 billion worth of foreign imports, China's net exports would be positive $50 billion. Net exports are positive when the amount of foreign spending on a home country's goods and services is greater than the home country's spending on foreign goods and services. This is called a trade surplus. When the opposite happens—the amount of foreign spending on a home country's goods and services is less than the home country's spending on foreign goods and services—the home country has a trade deficit. Once the net exports for a country are calculated, it can be used to calculate a country's GDP, which provides a reliable measurement of the size of its economy.

When Did It Begin

The practice of exporting dates back to the ancient world and the first traders who traveled long distances to exchange goods. The Silk Road, a 5,000-mile system of interconnected routes through southern Asia, was used by traders and travelers from 200 BC to 900 AD. It linked China to nations as far west as the Mediterranean Sea. Initially established to support the transportation of Chinese silks from China to the West, the route came to be used for additional Chinese exports, such as porcelain, spices, and eventually gunpowder and paper. Over time, Chinese buyers sought such goods as cosmetics, silver, and perfume and used the Silk Road to import these goods from European, Central Asian, Arabian, and African suppliers.

In the sixteenth and seventeenth centuries the first businesses developed that were designed to produce goods for export to other countries. At first, this type of manufacturing and trading was carried out by the few powers that could control remote resources. For example, the Dutch East India Company, a monopoly that promoted and supported colonialist activities in Asia and Africa (colonialism is when one country controls another country or area), was formed in 1602 and developed its business and trade for almost 200 years, controlling the resources of rubber production in Central Africa.

As competition among colonialist countries intensified, companies' exclusive control over trade dissolved. Countries developed systems of pricing and tariffs (taxes on imported goods and services) to regulate the flow of goods across borders.

Even with government oversight and controls that help regulate trade, the openness of trade between countries has still, at times, been affected by political instability. For example, free trade between European

Exports are products and services that are shipped overseas to be sold to buyers in foreign countries. In this photo assembly-line workers in Egypt prepare raw cotton for export. *AP Images.*

nations was disrupted during the 1930s when the United States, Germany, and other countries erected barriers to trade. These disruptions were believed by many to have been a principal cause of World War II (1939–45). In response, more than 40 countries approved an international economic plan called the Bretton Woods system. It went into effect in 1946 and included institutions and rules that discouraged countries from creating trade barriers. As a result, it contributed to a worldwide postwar economic recovery that lasted until the early 1970s.

More Detailed Information

In 2003 the United States exported $726 billion in goods, including farm products, automobiles, and raw materials such as iron ore and lumber. It also exported $320 billion in services such as financial services and tourism. The United States is the largest exporter of goods and services in the world, but the amount of money it spends on manufacturing and producing its exports is a fraction of the money it spends on the total output of goods and services, or its gross domestic product (GDP). This is because the United States has a large domestic market (goods and services produced in

the United States that are purchased by Americans). Relative to other nations, the United States is self-sufficient in terms of food and resources.

Other nations, by comparison, spend a greater amount of their GDP on the production of goods and services for export. The economy of Ireland, for example, is heavily dependent on foreigners purchasing tourism services. The Southeast Asian country of Myanmar, which is very poor, has few legalized exports and is essentially a closed economy. The Saudi Arabian economy is highly dependent on its oil exports. Countries such as China and India, which are rapidly developing their economies, depend on exports to bring in foreign money, which helps to expand their markets and to increase the incomes of their workers.

Even though the United States is not as heavily dependent on exports as other countries are, in specific industries it does rely heavily on international purchasing of its products. For example, every year 25 to 50 percent of U.S.-produced rice, corn, and wheat are exported to other countries. If consumers from other countries decided to stop buying U.S. agricultural products, it would have a great impact on American farmers. Many large

American corporations sell sizable amounts of their products to foreign buyers. These include the airplane manufacturer Boeing, the farm- and construction-machinery manufacturer Caterpillar, and the computer manufacturer Sun Microsystems. Other exports include movies distributed to other countries and educational services purchased when hundreds of thousands of foreign students attend U.S. universities every year.

Countries do not usually export the same amount that they export. The difference between its exports and imports is known as the trade balance (or balance of trade), and it is calculated by subtracting the value of imports in a given year from the value of exports that year. When a country imports more than it exports in a given time period, it has a negative trade balance, also known as a trade deficit. When the value of exports exceeds the value of imports, it is known as a trade surplus.

Many factors can affect a country's balance of trade, including its advantage in producing certain goods and services. Japan, for example, has an advantage in the production of electronic games, which allows it to export more and hence improve its trade balance. Another factor affecting a country's balance of trade is the standing of its currency relative to the currencies of its trading partners. For instance, if the Japanese yen is weak (less valuable), the goods produced in other countries will be more expensive for Japanese consumers.

One of the ways in which a country may manage and influence its balance of trade is to apply tariffs to the goods it imports from abroad. A tariff (also called an import duty) is a tax charged on goods when they are imported into a country. It is usually levied (charged) as a percentage of the declared value of the good. In order to pay tariffs, foreign manufacturers must increase the price of their goods, which dissuades consumers from buying them. Tariffs thus have the effect of controlling the number of foreign products that can enter the domestic market. They are also a source of revenue for governments.

Another tool that countries use to manage the balance of trade is the quota. If the country wants to regulate the amount of a particular imported good or service, it sets a limit on the quantity of that good or service that can be imported. This is known as an import quota. Import quotas are less commonly applied than tariffs.

Recent Trends

The introduction of the Internet as a communication and marketing tool has resulted in a dramatic increase in the diversity of goods and services that are traded across international borders. The phenomenon known as globalization means, in part, that goods and services manufactured in one country are more available than ever in other countries.

ORGANIZATION OF PETROLEUM EXPORTING COUNTRIES (OPEC)

One of the main influences on political stability today is the reliable flow of petroleum (crude oil) from the major petroleum-producing countries located in the Middle East to the countries outside of that region. Iran, Iraq, Kuwait, and Venezuela, which in 1960 were the major petroleum-producing nations, organized as the Organization of the Petroleum Exporting Countries (OPEC). Their objective was to coordinate the petroleum policies of the member countries. Since 1960 OPEC has become the organization that largely manages the worldwide supply of oil and therefore is able to affect its price in the world market.

In addition to its founding members, the countries belonging to OPEC as of 2007 were Algeria, Indonesia, Libya, Nigeria, Qatar, Saudi Arabia, and the United Arab Emirates. OPEC member nations supply approximately 40 percent of the world's crude oil and 16 percent of its natural gas. In 2003 more than three-quarters of the world's crude oil reserves were in the possession of OPEC nations. Because oil production has grown in recent decades, and areas such as the Gulf of Mexico and the North Sea (the part of the Atlantic Ocean that lies north of Great Britain) have developed petroleum production, OPEC's power has diminished somewhat.

In the globalized economy, jobs themselves have become resources and commodities that countries can choose to export. Many blue-collar and white-collar jobs in industrialized countries have been shifted to developing countries. When jobs are exported, it is called outsourcing or offshoring. In recent decades many U.S. corporations have employed workers in such countries as India and Canada in order to keep down the costs of paying for human resources.

International trade has grown at a much faster rate than the world economy has. The results of the growth in trade have included an overall reduction of tariffs as well as an increase in trade that is allowed without governmental restrictions such as tariffs and quotas. This is known as free trade. A country's support of free trade does not mean that the government relinquishes control; it means that it holds back on regulations so that each nation can produce and market the products that can best compete in the international marketplace.

$ Imports

What It Means

Imports are any foreign-made goods and services that are brought into a country to be sold. The United States imports many different types of goods from other countries, including electronics, automobiles, wine, clothing,

Imports are foreign-made goods and services sold in a country. The United States imports many electronic goods, such as mobile phones, that are produced in China, Japan, and other Asian countries. *AP Images.*

and diamonds. Imports are the opposite of exports, which are the goods and services transported out of a country and sold abroad.

When a country imports foreign goods and services into its markets for domestic consumers to purchase, it can benefit its economy in two important ways. First, it is able to broaden the range of goods and services it offers to its consumers. For example, when the United States imports tires made in the Czech Republic, it provides another choice of tire for American consumers. Second, if the goods or services bought from foreign producers have been manufactured at low costs, the importing country can potentially enable its citizens to pay lower prices for those goods. For instance, if Indonesian clothing factories can make jackets at a lower cost than American factories can, and they are offered to U.S. consumers through clothing retailers, the consumers will have a lower-priced alternative.

When a country chooses to import goods, it also benefits foreign producers because it gives them another market for their products. For example, car manufacturers in Japan make many types of automobiles to be sold in other countries. In 2005 Japan exported more than 5 million vehicles, the total value of which was about 10.5 trillion (about $94 billion).

In any given month the United States imports goods and services from Canada, France, Germany, Mexico, Japan, and other countries. Meanwhile, many countries around the world import goods and services manufactured in the United States. The diversity of goods transported across borders has increased dramatically since the Internet has become a widely used communication and marketing tool. The phenomenon known as globalization means that goods and services produced in one country are increasingly available in other parts of the world.

The branch of economics known as international trade studies the exchange of commercial goods across international boundaries. The amount that a country imports and exports plays a crucial role in the overall economic health of that country. International trade makes up a substantial part of what is known as a country's gross domestic product, or GDP. GDP is a measurement of the market value of all final goods and services produced in a country within a specific time span (typically one year).

When Did It Begin

Importing has taken place since ancient times, when the first long-distance travelers began engaging in trade. An example of an ancient system promoting trade was the Silk Road, a 5,000-mile-long network of interconnected overland routes through southern Asia that was used from 200 BC to 900 AD and connected China with regions west of it (including India, Persia, and the Mediterranean). Traders used the Silk Road to transport Chinese products, such as silks, porcelain, spices, gunpowder, and paper, to the West, and to transport Western products, such as silver, to China.

Importing increased in the sixteenth and seventeenth centuries. At first, importing such goods as valuable raw materials was only an option for a relatively small number of consumers, those who could afford to pay the high costs of shipping. The Dutch East India Company, a Netherlands-based monopoly that was instrumental in colonizing Southeast Asia and Africa, was formed in 1602 and developed its business and trade for almost 200 years. One of the primary goods Dutch East India ships brought to Europe was exotic spices. But as trade expanded and became more competitive, countries such as the Netherlands lost their isolated control over trade. Once they had begun trading more freely with one another, countries developed systems to regulate the flow of goods across borders.

Changes in political and economic stability have affected the openness of trade between countries. For example, the presence of trade barriers that restricted free trade between European nations was widely believed to have been a principal cause of World War II (1939–45). To prevent the recurrence of such problems, an international coalition of more than 40 countries adopted an economic structure called the Bretton Woods system in 1946. In addition to stabilizing rates of currency exchange, it established rules to end trade barriers.

More Detailed Information

When goods and materials arrive at the borders of the country importing them, they must pass through the customs authority in that country. Every country's customs agency oversees the collection of customs taxes, which are sometimes called duties. The customs agency also oversees the flow of animals, people, and goods into the country. If the import (or export) of certain goods is restricted or forbidden, it is the responsibility of the customs authority to enforce the laws and prevent goods from entering the country.

An import duty, often called a tariff, is a tax levied (charged) on certain goods when they are imported into a country. Usually the tariff is a percentage of the declared value of the good. It serves to control the number of foreign products that can enter the domestic market. For example, if the U.S. government puts a 20 percent tariff on imported Peruvian llamas, and $50 million worth of llamas are imported in a year, the customs agency will collect $10 million. Import tariffs are the second-largest source of revenue for the U.S. govern-

---

CAPTIVE IMPORTS

Sometimes automobile companies import vehicles manufactured by another automaker and sell them under their own brand name. This type of import is known as a captive import. The foreign manufacturer may be a subsidiary of the importing company (that is, controlled and owned by it). Captive imports may also be produced in partnership with another company or be purchased from a completely separate entity. For example, in the 1970s the American car company Dodge imported several models that had been manufactured by Mitsubishi in Japan, selling them in the United States as Dodge Colts.

What motivates automobile companies to add captive imports to their lineup of models? Captive imports can sometimes help them increase the competitiveness of their domestic (home-country) brand because it allows them to satisfy a consumer need that they could not feasibly meet if they tried to manufacture the cars domestically. Captive imports are often, but not always, aimed at the lower end of the market, meaning they are less expensive.

Other examples of captive imports in the United States include the Chrysler Crossfire (built by the German manufacturer Karmann), the Geo Storm (manufactured in Japan by Isuzu and sold in the United States by General Motors), and the Saturn Astra (manufactured by Opel, a German subsidiary of General Motors).

---

ment (after income taxes). It collects $20 billion a year in tariff revenue.

The government sets the rate at which tariffs are charged and controls the revenue they generate. If the government determines that it needs to regulate the amount or number of a particular import, it sets a limit on that import; this limit is known as an import quota. Import quotas are generally less popular than tariffs because quotas can be withheld from some importers (while the quota is being met) and enforced on other importers (after the quota has been met). If set at unreasonable levels, both tariffs and import quotas will result in escalations of smuggling. For example, if the tariff on Peruvian llamas is set at 90 percent, then those producing the llamas will be more likely to avoid bringing the animals into the country through the regular customs process and instead use illegal methods.

Balance of trade is the term used to describe the difference between the monetary value of exports and imports in an economy over a measurable period of time. When a country is exporting more than it is importing and the balance of trade is positive, it is known a trade surplus. When a country is importing more than it is exporting and the balance of trade is negative, it is known as a trade deficit.

A country's balance of trade can be influenced by various factors, including the strength or weakness of its currency in relation to those of the countries with which it trades. For example, if the U.S. dollar is weak (meaning it has a lower value compared to other currencies), that weakness makes goods produced in other countries relatively expensive for American consumers. A country's balance of trade is also affected by any advantage the country might have in producing particular goods or services. For example, clothing is often imported from China because Chinese factories can manufacture it at a lower cost. A third factor influencing a country's balance of trade is how well the country's production of goods meets its residents' demand for those goods. If the production level of a particular good or service cannot satisfy the consumer demand for it, the country will import more than it exports and run the likelihood of encountering a trade deficit for that good or service.

Recent Trends

An expansion in the trade of goods and services between nations after World War II (1939–45) built economic connections between nations and increased the level of imports and exports to countries around the globe. The General Agreement on Tariffs and Trade (GATT) was signed in 1948 by 23 nations, including the United States. Its purpose was to encourage trade agreements among member nations that supported the fair treatment of resources (such as labor and the environment); it officially laid out the terms and conditions for open trade. GATT was replaced by the World Trade Organization (WTO) in 1995. One hundred and twenty-five nations were members, governing 90 percent of world trade and laying the foundation for one worldwide system of economics.

As a result of the WTO and other policies, rates of both importing and exporting began accelerating dramatically in the 1990s. This was a result of the trend in the economies around the globe to move away from functioning as distinct national economic markets and toward operating as one huge global market. This trend is known as globalization. Lower trade barriers have enabled the increased interconnectedness and interdependence between markets and countries.

The North American Free Trade Agreement (NAFTA) is an agreement among Canada, the United States, and Mexico that went into effect on January 1, 1994. When NAFTA was passed, it called for the immediate removal of the taxes that had been imposed on half of all U.S. goods shipped to Mexico and Canada. It also laid out a plan for a gradual removal of other tariffs over approximately 14 years. NAFTA caused trade between the United States, Canada, and Mexico to increase dramatically. In fact, trade between the United States and Mexico has doubled since NAFTA went into effect.

$ Absolute Advantage

What It Means

Absolute advantage is a term used in discussions about international trade (the purchasing of goods made in one country by people in another country). When a country can produce any good more cheaply (using fewer resources) than a second country can, the first country is said to have an absolute advantage in regard to that good. If two countries are considering trading with one another, and each of them has an absolute advantage in a different good, then both can be sure of benefiting from free trade in these goods. In free trade goods and services are allowed to flow between countries without restrictions such as quotas (limits on the quantity of imports) and tariffs (taxes on imports).

For example, suppose that France can produce high-quality wine more cheaply than England, and England can produce high-quality beer more cheaply than France. It makes sense for the two countries to trade with one another, because consumers in both countries will get high-quality beer and wine at good prices. At the same time, French winemakers will produce more wealth by specializing in what they do well, and English beer manufacturers will produce more wealth by specializing in what they do well. Both countries will be better off than if they did not trade with one another.

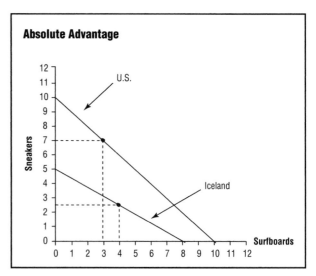

When one country has an absolute advantage over another in producing a product, it means the country can make the good more cheaply than the other, possibly because its workers are more efficient. In this hypothetical graph showing the number of sneakers, surfboards, or some combination of the two an average worker can produce per day, the United States has an absolute advantage over Iceland in producing both products because its workers make both sneakers and surfboards more quickly. *Illustration by GGS Information Services. Cengage Learning, Gale.*

When Did It Begin

Adam Smith (1723–90), the Scottish thinker widely considered the founder of the field of economics, introduced the concept of absolute advantage in his landmark book *An Inquiry into the Nature and Causes of the Wealth of Nations* (1776). Prior to the publication of Smith's book, there was little support, among European countries, for free trade. A doctrine called mercantilism was the prevailing ideology among national leaders. According to this theory, a country should amass wealth by exporting more than it imports and by protecting its own industries from foreign competition (imposing tariffs and quotas on imports was the main way to do this). Smith successfully showed that mercantilist theories were illogical and harmful to the national interest.

Absolute advantage makes intuitive sense to most people. This may be because, if we translate it to the personal level, we can see that we all employ our own version of this principle in our daily lives.

In the contemporary world few of us produce our own food. Instead, we prefer to go to the grocery store and buy bread, meat, and vegetables. We understand that grocery stores can make these items available to us more efficiently than we would be able to produce them personally. If all of us had to grow and process our own wheat and then bake our own bread; feed, tend, and butcher our own cows and chickens; and plant, raise, and harvest our own vegetable crops, we would spend all of our time doing these things.

While such a lifestyle might have its appeal, it does not allow for the creation of wealth. In a modern economy farmers and grocers specialize in food production so that the rest of us can focus on what we do well. A computer programmer can create more economic value for herself and her community by spending as much time as possible writing software, while leaving other jobs, such as food production, in the hands of those who specialize in them.

Absolute advantage, in the arena of free trade, is simply the application of this idea to the level of nations. If a company in another country can provide jeans to American consumers for a lower price than U.S. companies can, it makes no sense, in the eyes of economists, to keep the foreign jeans out of the country and force consumers to go on paying higher prices for domestic jeans (domestic means produced within the country). While U.S. producers of jeans might have to fire employees if most Americans begin buying foreign jeans, ultimately the U.S. economy will be better off, because makers of jeans can focus on other products that cannot be made as efficiently in other countries. For instance, the United States excels in computer software. If more U.S. workers focus on making software than jeans, then the overall economy will produce more wealth than it did when trade in foreign jeans was restricted. At the same time, American consumers will get access to cheap jeans.

Recent Trends

Smith's views regarding absolute advantage have not been seriously contested in the centuries since he first conceived them, but another early economist, David Ricardo (1772–1823) of England, supplemented Smith's idea with the theory of comparative advantage, which justifies free trade in more complex situations. Together, the two theories provide the foundation for the belief, common to most present-day economists, that free trade among nations should be encouraged.

Comparative advantage addresses a situation in which a country has an absolute advantage in more than one area. For example, many Americans in the early twenty-first century worry about the fact that companies in a country such as China can produce virtually any item more cheaply than companies in the United States, because Chinese workers generally get paid far less than their American counterparts. The worry is that this will harm the U.S. economy by leading to American wage cuts and unemployment. But economists who subscribe to the idea of comparative advantage argue that this is not necessarily so.

Consider the hypothetical example of two products, blenders and radios. According to the theory of comparative advantage, even if Chinese companies can produce both items more cheaply than American companies, the Chinese might have a greater advantage in one good than the other, and they would benefit financially by specializing in this good and trading for the other. For instance, say that the Chinese can produce a blender for $10 and a radio for $10, while the Americans can produce a blender for $20 and a radio for $15. China has an absolute advantage in both products, but it has a comparative advantage in blenders. The comparative advantage is calculated according to opportunity cost, the value of the option given up. Whenever a company decides to use its resources to produce one product, it is giving up the chance to make a different product.

Continuing the above example, if a Chinese company spends $10 making 1 blender, it gives up the opportunity to use that $10 to make 1 radio. Meanwhile, if an American company makes 1 blender for $20, it gives up the opportunity to use that $20 to make 1.33 radios. The fact that the Chinese would be giving up less to make blenders than the Americans would (1 radio compared to 1.33 radios) means that China has a comparative advantage in blenders. Using the same reasoning, the Americans have a comparative advantage in radios, because they sacrifice less to make a radio than China does. (To make 1 radio for $10, the Chinese company would be giving up the opportunity to make 1 blender, but if the U.S. company makes 1 radio for $15, it gives up the opportunity to make 0.75 blenders.)

BANANAS AND COFFEE

An absolute advantage exists when one country can produce a certain good more efficiently than another country. In the contemporary world, people may have trouble accepting this notion, because most believe that people in all cultures are equally capable of achieving impressive things. Absolute advantage, however, is not meant as a commentary on the relative worth of different cultures. Instead, it addresses the fact that the realities of climate, geography, and history (among many other factors) affect a country's ability to produce certain goods.

For instance, the United States simply is not a good place to grow bananas or coffee. No matter how hard American farmers might work to grow banana trees or coffee plants, the climate of the mainland United States will never allow them to compete with banana growers in Ecuador, Colombia, Costa Rica, or the Philippines or with coffee growers in East Africa, Latin America, and Southeast Asia.

The key idea of comparative advantage is that it is in the best interests of both countries to maximize their combined production. That production is maximized by specializing and trading can be illustrated by comparing the total amount that could be produced if each country was self-sufficient with the total amount produced if each country focused on its comparative-advantage good and traded for the other good. If Chinese companies spend their available resources (say $1,000 for simplicity's sake) on making both blenders and radios, allotting $500 to each product, they could produce 50 blenders and 50 radios. Meanwhile, if U.S. companies spend their resources (say $2,000; the amount that China spends does not affect the calculation, because each country is weighing its own options) on making both items (suppose it spends $1,000 on each, although it could be any proportion), they could make 50 blenders and 66.67 radios. In this example, the total amount of products made by both countries is 100 blenders and 116.67 radios. But if, spending the same amount of money as above, China focuses on blenders while the United States focuses on radios, and they trade blenders and radios accordingly, then the countries would create a greater total amount of products: 100 blenders (all made by China) and 133.3 radios (all made by the United States). The same amount of resources will have been used to create more goods to sell, and therefore more wealth, than if the countries restricted trade in these items.

$ Comparative Advantage

What It Means

Many economists agree that the theory of comparative advantage is one of the most difficult but important ideas in global economics. Comparative advantage is challenging because at first glance the hypothesis appears to defy simple logic. According to this theory, even if Country A can produce all goods more cheaply than Country B can, both Country A and Country B will maximize their production and economic well-being if they trade with each other.

To understand the basic idea, take the example of a highly skilled heart surgeon. Arguably one of the abilities that makes the surgeon successful in her profession—an unusually high level of manual dexterity—would also make her an excellent typist. Still, while the surgeon could perform both tasks at a high level, it makes more sense for her to allow her office assistant (who has good typing skills) to do all the typing, because surgery offers a greater opportunity for gain (both in terms of how much money the surgeon will earn for performing surgery and in terms of the good it provides to the patients). In other words, the surgeon has a comparative advantage over the office assistant (who has no medical skills at all) in the field of surgery and will therefore keep the office assistant employed to perform the typing duties.

For an example of how comparative advantage applies to an economy, consider the imaginary countries of Freeland and Homeland trading beef and cereal. Freeland can produce both beef and cereal more cheaply than Homeland. While Homeland has some capacity to produce cereal, its geography makes it very difficult to produce beef by raising cattle there.

Because both products are made more cheaply in Freeland, there seems to be no reason that Freeland should buy either beef or cereal from Homeland. This is not necessarily true, however. According to the theory of comparative advantage, if Freeland makes more money from beef than from cereal, the best way for the country to be profitable is to specialize in beef production and purchase cereal from Homeland. By producing less cereal, Freeland can sell more beef and make the largest possible amount of money. Homeland, meanwhile, can specialize in cereal and benefit by having a foreign market for its goods. Homeland's economy will then be stronger, and it will be able to purchase more of Freeland's beef. Because Freeland produces cereal more cheaply than Homeland, Freeland has what is called an absolute advantage in cereal production. But cereal production benefits Homeland's economy more than Freeland's, so Homeland has a comparative advantage in producing cereal.

When Did It Begin

The theory of comparative advantage grew out of the theory of free trade that was developed by the Scottish philosopher Adam Smith (1723–90), which he documented in his influential book *The Wealth of Nations* (1776). Smith reasoned that, if one nation makes a product cheaply, and another nation makes a different

Emphasizing the benefit of international trade for all countries, the theory of comparative advantage has important implications for the global economy. As noted by Nobel Prize-winning economist Paul A. Samuelson, pictured here, it is a theory that, while logically true, is often misunderstood or disbelieved by "important and intelligent" people even after it is explained to them. © *Bettmann/ Corbis.*

product cheaply, then those nations should specialize and trade with each other instead of producing both products for themselves.

The free-trade theory gained acceptance among economists who tested the hypothesis by considering more complicated trade scenarios. In "An Essay on the External Corn Trade" (1815), British economist Robert Torrens (1780–1864) was the first person to argue that a nation should specialize and import certain goods even if it produced all goods more efficiently than its trading partner. He used the examples of England and Poland trading corn and wool. English economist David Ricardo (1772–1823) introduced the theory of comparative advantage in full detail in his book *On the Principles of Political Economy and Taxation* (1817). Ricardo used an example involving the trade of cloth and wine between Great Britain and Portugal. The theory gained credence as a key factor in understanding international trade after John Stuart Mill (1806–73) published *Principles of Political Economy* in 1848.

More Detailed Information

Ricardo's theory of comparative advantage is based on several assumptions and economic terms. The first assumption is that all trading countries must be following the principles of free trade. No country can tax the goods it imports. In an environment of free trade, a country will make more money in the long run through specialization and exchange than by producing as many different goods as possible for its own consumers. This means that if a country can produce cars, meat products, agricultural goods, cloth, and televisions, it should dedicate the majority of its labor force to the production of the single most profitable good and import the others. Specialization maximizes the total world output of goods, which helps economies grow in all trading countries. Notice that Ricardo's model considers only the supply of goods (the amount that producers make) and not the demand (the amount that consumers are willing to buy). It was John Stuart Mill who factored demand into the theory of comparative advantage.

Comparative advantage is dependent upon two other economic concepts: labor productivity and opportunity cost. Labor productivity is the average amount of output per worker that a country can get from its labor force. This output varies depending on the product and the country. For example, in the case of Freeland, labor productivity is greater for beef than it is for cereal. On average, in one hour a worker in Freeland can produce more beef products than cereal. In Homeland a worker can produce more cereal in an hour. Remember that a worker in Freeland can still produce more cereal in one hour than a worker in Homeland can. This brings up the idea of opportunity cost.

Opportunity cost refers to the choices a producer has when making goods. Specifically, the opportunity cost is the value of the item not chosen, that is, the item given up. In Freeland there is a high opportunity cost for choosing to produce cereal instead of beef products. Each worker assigned to produce cereal is making the country less money than the worker producing beef. To maximize profits, Freeland needs to maximize labor productivity. To do this, Freeland needs to have as many workers as possible making beef products. In Homeland, however, there is no opportunity cost for producing cereal instead of beef (because it could not produce beef in any case), and to maximize labor productivity there, Homeland needs to have as many workers as possible producing cereal.

The main criticism of the theory of comparative advantage is that it does not take important factors into account, including the costs of transporting goods and retraining the labor force. In the example of Freeland, the cost of producing beef products will rise if more of those products have to be shipped to other countries. Also, if Freeland decreases its production of cereal, many laborers will have to be retrained to work in the beef industry.

PAUL SAMUELSON

Born May 15, 1915, in Gary, Indiana, Paul Samuelson won the Nobel Prize for Economics in 1970. Samuelson was once asked by the Polish mathematician Stanislaw Ulam (1909–84), who helped develop nuclear weapons as a member of the Manhattan Project, to name one theory in all of the social sciences that was both true and nontrivial. (In academic language, a nontrivial idea is one that can only be understood through careful reasoning and not by using common sense. Ulam's question was a challenging one because nontrivial theories are usually debatable, not definitively true or false.) After taking several years to consider this question, Samuelson wrote to Ulam saying that the theory of comparative advantage was the only idea he could think of that fit Ulam's specifications. Samuelson said that any mathematician could see that the theory of comparative advantage was logically true, but that it was a nontrivial idea because most intelligent people failed to understand it even after it was explained to them.

This may also involve building new factories and moving people to different areas of the country, which may not be cost-effective. Defenders of comparative advantage say that the theory holds up even after these factors are taken into account.

Recent Trends

Some economists think that the idea of comparative advantage is not as relevant as it used to be because of the rise of intra-industry trade (IIT). IIT refers to the exchange of goods within the same industry. For example, in 2000 the European Union exported nearly as many motorized vehicles as it imported. It is estimated that IIT increases by 5 percent each year throughout the world. This means that more and more countries are exporting the same types of goods that they are importing, regardless of the comparative advantage. Therefore, it is argued, these countries are not choosing a specialty based on comparative advantage.

$ Free Trade

What It Means

Free trade in its ideal form refers to a situation in which all countries allow foreign goods and services to flow across national borders without imposing any restrictions, such as quotas (limitations on the amount of certain imported products) or tariffs (special taxes imposed on imported products). Free trade has almost certainly never existed in this form. Economists and politicians often use the term *free trade* when discussing the government's role in international business.

International trade sounds like something that occurs between two nations, but in reality this trading most commonly takes the form of individual business transactions between members of different nations. For instance, anytime someone in the United States buys a watch made in Switzerland or a banana grown in Ecuador, he or she is participating in international trade. There are much more complex forms of international trade, but even in these cases governments primarily play only a regulatory role.

Although many governments support the notion that trade should become increasingly free in the world at large, all nations restrict imports to some degree, usually to protect certain domestic industries (domestic means that the industry is based in the home country). For instance, if the United States wants to protect domestic manufacturers of toothpaste, and if the U.S. government knows that manufacturers in India can produce high-quality toothpaste more cheaply than their American counterparts can, the government might impose a steep tariff on toothpaste originating in India. Indian toothpaste manufacturers, in order to compensate for the money lost to the tariff, must charge a higher price for their product in the United States, and American consumers will be more likely to buy American toothpaste than Indian toothpaste.

Economists today generally argue for increased freedom of international trade (that is, for a reduction, in most cases, of such restrictions as quotas and tariffs), believing that freedom from import restrictions usually benefits all countries that trade with one another. Economists also tend to claim that protecting an industry only postpones the problems that will eventually threaten that industry anyway. This overall relaxation of restrictions on international trade is what is usually meant when free trade is mentioned by the media and in politics.

Ordinary citizens in the United States and abroad are much more divided in their opinions about free trade than are economists, and the issue plays a large role in politics around the world. Because international trade is increasingly important to the economy in many countries today, the political decisions made about free trade have a great impact on individual businesses and workers, even if they do not realize it.

When Did It Begin

International trade has existed for as long as there have been organized states, kingdoms, and nations, but free trade in its ideal form has probably never existed. In fact, it was not until the late eighteenth century that economic thinkers began to take the idea of free trade seriously.

From the sixteenth century through the eighteenth century, European countries laid the groundwork for today's capitalist economic system (in which most businesses are owned by private individuals and not the government) while adhering to trade policies outlined by a theory called mercantilism. Mercantilism argues that a

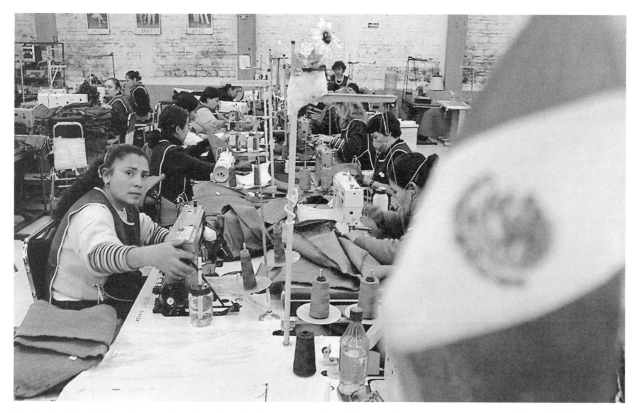

Free trade refers to the exchange of goods and services between countries without restrictions or government regulations. While supporters of free trade argue that it provides economic benefits for all nations, opponents contend that it leads to the exploitation of cheap overseas labor. *AP Images.*

nation's economic strength is crucially tied to its possession of precious metals such as gold and that a country should make sure that it exports more goods than it imports, thereby stockpiling gold and guaranteeing its economic superiority.

It was not until 1776 that the first coherent argument against the mercantilist system emerged. That argument came in the form of the landmark work *An Inquiry into the Nature and Causes of the Wealth of Nations* by political economist and philosopher Adam Smith (1723–90). Among many other influential notions, Smith put forward the idea that a nation's wealth should not be judged by the size of its gold stockpiles but by the goods and services to which the nation's people have access. Smith also believed that the greatest good was achieved when each individual, acting in his own self-interest, was free to compete in the economic marketplace. By the nineteenth century these ideas had opened the door to a freer international exchange of goods and services than had ever been seen before.

More Detailed Information

Economists maintain that the free exchange of goods and services between the members of two countries nearly always benefits both countries in the long run. Because of

differences in climate, geography, and the makeup of their populations (including such factors as skills and education), each country in the world brings different advantages to the global marketplace. If countries are able to trade freely with one another, all are able to benefit from their natural advantages while avoiding wastes of both money and time in the pursuit of business ventures to which they are not suited.

Because of the climate in the United States, for instance, growing bananas would cost more there than in Ecuador, and the bananas might also be inferior to those grown in a more naturally suitable tropical climate. American consumers save money by eating Ecuadorian bananas, and Ecuador enjoys a large U.S. market for its bananas, which it can produce very easily and expertly compared to other nations. Such adeptness in the production of a certain product is called an absolute advantage, one of the key principles economists talk about when explaining the benefits of free trade.

Absolute advantage does not explain all cases in which it may be beneficial for a nation to cease production of certain goods. Economists use a concept called comparative advantage to talk about another primary way in which free international trade naturally distributes the global workload efficiently.

WHEN FREE TRADE MAY NOT BE A GOOD IDEA

———————

Today the consensus of economists is that increased freedom to trade internationally serves the economic interest of all countries, although most also believe that there might always need to be some exceptions to free trade.

For instance, the defense industry in any country will almost certainly be seen to deserve protection from foreign competition. Suppose that a nation's military relied on a neighboring nation's factories for its bullets. If the two nations went to war with each other, the bullet-importing nation would suddenly find itself extremely vulnerable, unable to acquire bullets and unprepared to manufacture them at home.

Another legitimate exception to free trade is infant-industry protection. This involves an industry just beginning to get a foothold in a country. Such an industry, economists acknowledge, might deserve protection from more established foreign competition for a time. As soon as such an industry is mature, however, it should be forced to compete on the international market.

Protecting an infant industry is simpler in theory than in practice. What are the standards for determining that an infant industry is deserving of protection? Once it is protected, how does the government determine when it is ready to compete against the rest of the world? A protected industry will probably not willingly give up its advantage against foreign rivals. For these and other reasons, the infant-industry exception is rarely applied properly in the real world. The industries most likely to be granted government protection, in fact, are hardly infant industries but instead established, declining industries that retain influence with politicians. Many trade restrictions in today's world are traceable to special interests such as these.

To take a hypothetical example, suppose that U.S. workers were slightly better at producing electric fans than Taiwanese workers, but that U.S. workers could produce desk lamps that were many times better and cheaper than those produced by most other countries in the world. In this case, even though the United States can hold its own or better in electric-fan production, it has a comparative advantage in the field of desk-lamp production. Therefore, it would be more productive for the United States to allow the Taiwanese to assume the burden as well as the benefits of the electric-fan industry, while American time and energy are devoted to desk-lamp production. Put another way, the United States would need to give up relatively large amounts of desk lamps to produce a relatively small amount of electric fans. The benefits the United States derived from making desk lamps would be greater than the benefits from continuing to make both electric-fan and desk-lamp production together. Taiwan, meanwhile, would benefit in a more obvious way from acquiring a larger share of the electric-fan industry.

Great Britain offers a useful real-world illustration of the principle of comparative advantage. Great Britain no longer produces enough food to feed its population, but this is not because British farmers are incapable of doing so. It is true, however, that because of its climate, geography, and the nature of its population, Great Britain might never be a world agricultural leader. The British do, however, surpass most other countries in such industries as manufacturing, shipping, and finance, so it makes sense for them to focus on these industries (which represent its comparative advantages) while importing much of their food. Great Britain thus prospers more than it would by continuing to supply its own food, and those countries with comparative advantages in agriculture benefit by having an enlarged market for their farm produce. Every country, even the poorest and least productive ones, enjoy comparative advantage in some good or industry. Trade theory suggests that countries get the greatest benefit by specializing in those goods in which they have a comparative advantage.

In business, as in all areas of life, time and resources are never unlimited. A country, like an individual, must choose how to spend its time and resources most effectively, even if this means giving up a business at which it has excelled in the past. According to its proponents, free trade, by opening up all industries to competition with one another regardless of nationality, would result in ever-increasing degrees of business efficiency.

The reality of the economic changes produced by free international trade often seems messy, however. When confronted with the spectacle of a collapsed industry, individuals and even governments have trouble seeing the benefits of free trade.

For instance, the hundreds of thousands of American steelworkers who lost their jobs in the late twentieth century make a deeper and more vivid impression on most Americans than would any figures supplied by an economist to show why the industry's decline was ultimately a positive development. Likewise, no doubt British farmers of a hundred years ago would be displeased with the country's move away from agricultural production.

Partly for such emotional and cultural reasons, and partly because established industries tend to have great influence over politicians and government officials, all governments protect certain industries. There are also remnants of the mercantilist mindset even today. For instance, the belief that a country should export more than it imports remains widespread more than 200 years after Adam Smith convincingly refuted it.

Recent Trends

In the late twentieth and early twenty-first century, large numbers of people around the world became dissatisfied with their governments' commitment to increasing free trade. These dissatisfied people were most visible to mainstream society when they participated in so-called antiglobalization protests. These protests, often organized to coincide with meetings of powerful international officials committed to increasing free trade, were part of a loosely organized social movement commonly referred to as the antiglobalization movement.

Some antiglobalization critics of free trade believe that free trade empowers corporations at the expense of ordinary citizens, especially citizens of developing countries (also called Third World countries). Other critics of globalization contend that free trade disproportionately favors rich nations such as the United States. They also argue that globalization in effect makes every nation more and more like the United States because many of the world's most powerful corporations (examples include Coca-Cola, Microsoft, and Wal-Mart) have roots in the that country. Still other critics worry about the potential of ever-increasing business efficiency to trump all other concerns, such as cultural values, the health of ecosystems, and personal morality.

Meanwhile, the strongest U.S. opposition to free trade tends to arise regionally, in areas where large numbers of businesses have been shuttered as a result of international competition or the relocation of jobs to countries where labor is cheaper. This form of labor-oriented opposition to free trade continues to influence national politics, even though most economists agree that government intervention to preserve American jobs is not realistic in the long term.

MONEY MOVING BETWEEN COUNTRIES

$ Balance of Payments

What It Means

The balance of payments (sometimes referred to as BOP) is a financial statement that summarizes a country's international economic purchases and sales in a given period of time. It is expressed in financial terms and shows all of the international money movements, called flows, in and out of a country in a certain time period. These money flows can be generated by exported goods, imported goods, international investments, and other sources.

Countries use balance-of-payments accounting to keep track of their payments to other countries as well as their receipts from other countries. In a balance-of-payments account record, any transaction that is the result of a payment to another country is entered as a debit and given a negative sign. Any transaction that is the result of a receipt from another country is entered as a credit and given a positive sign.

THE INTERNATIONAL MONETARY FUND AND BALANCE-OF-PAYMENTS RELIEF

The International Monetary Fund (IMF) is an organization that was founded by representatives of 44 countries at the end of World War II (1939–45) to maintain the stability of the international monetary system. Since 1994 the IMF has grown to include 180 countries, and it has promoted economic growth and sought to sustain high levels of employment within countries. Many nations with developing economies struggle to create healthy balance-of-payments accounts. The IMF lends funds to these countries and provides technical resources and economic training if countries request it. It also uses financial and tax reform and the privatization of public enterprises to address the root causes of balance-of-payments problems and inequities.

The balance of payments is sometimes used, along with other reports and economic indicators, to determine how economically and politically stable a country is. If the balance of payments is negative for a given period, it indicates that more money is flowing out of a country than flowing in. Likewise, if it is positive, it means that more money is flowing in than out.

When Did It Begin

The balance-of-payments accounting system developed with the increase in international trade that began some 500 years ago. In the sixteenth and seventeenth centuries commerce between nations escalated rapidly, enabled by advances in maritime shipping, communications, railway development, and the growth of centralized trading cities. The major trading nations, including England, France, and the United States, built their national wealth and power by exporting more manufactured goods than they imported. This meant that these countries were essentially selling more than they were purchasing, and the practice, known as mercantilism, allowed these and other countries to become enormously wealthy.

A relationship between the merchandise exported out of a country and the merchandise imported into the country is automatically established whenever a country is involved in international trade. This relationship between exports and imports is known as the balance of trade. As the early trading nations discovered, the balance of trade plays a crucial part in determining the balance of payments.

More Detailed Information

Balance-of-payments accounts are made up of two sections, the current account and the financial account (also called the capital account).

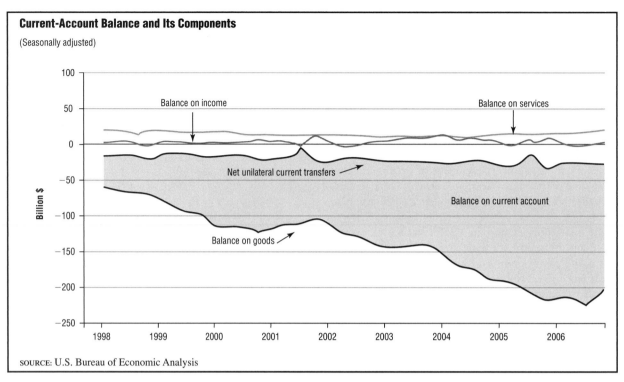

Current-Account Balance and Its Components

(Seasonally adjusted)

SOURCE: U.S. Bureau of Economic Analysis

The balance of payments (BOP) is a financial statement that measures how much money is flowing into and out of a country through trade during a given time period. This graph shows the U.S. balance on goods being negative, meaning the country was spending more to buy goods from other countries (imports) than it was selling goods abroad (exports). *Illustration by GGS Information Services. Cengage Learning, Gale.*

The current account shows the financial transactions of imported and exported goods and services. Automobiles, electronics, and chemicals are examples of merchandise that would be covered in this category. The import or export of services, such as banking, insurance, and other intangible products, would also be registered in the current account. Finally, any income from investments in foreign companies (which is known as investment income) must be registered in the current account. For example, if a U.S. citizen owns a share of a Polish company and receives a dividend payment of $15 (dividends are portions of profit that a company distributes to its investors), the payment appears on the U.S. current account as the receipt of $15 of investment income.

If a country imports more goods, services, and income than it exports, it has what is known as a current-account, or trade, deficit. If the opposite is true, and exports of goods, services, and income exceed those of imports, the country has a current-account surplus. The balance-of-payments accounting for the United States has shown a steady trade deficit in recent years, the result of higher import amounts than export amounts.

The earnings and payments for internationally traded goods and services together make up a country's balance of trade. The amounts registered in the current account are typically the bulk of all of those registered in the balance of payments.

The financial account shows the financial transactions involving the purchase or sale of assets (that is, the transfer of wealth, which includes investments, loans, and currencies). This means that if a foreign company buys stock in a U.S. company, the transaction appears on the U.S. balance of payments as a credit in the financial account, because capital (money) is coming into the United States with the stock purchase. If the U.S. company were to buy stock in the foreign company, capital would flow out of the United States, and the transaction would be registered in the financial account as a debit.

One important piece of economic information illustrated by the balance of payments is the value of a country's total exports and that of its total imports. When the value of a country's total imports is subtracted from the value of its total exports, the result is what is known as net exports. This figure shows how much more money foreign countries spend on a home country's goods and services than the home country spends on foreign goods and services. For example, if, in a given year, other countries purchase $100 billion worth of U.S. exports and Americans purchase $75 billion worth of foreign imports, the net exports would be positive $25 billion.

Recent Trends

Since the late 1950s the United States has increased the amount of money it invests in European corporations. It has also invested in the U.S. military's presence abroad. These factors have contributed to unfavorable balances of payments, meaning that they show deficits instead of surpluses.

In the early 1970s the U.S. government attempted to improve the balance of payments by adjusting the exchange rate of the dollar downward in relation to the currencies of other countries. This action is known as devaluing the dollar, and it results in making the home country's exports relatively less expensive for foreigners and foreign products relatively more expensive for consumers in the home country. Thus, the amount of imports decreased. This potentially could have improved the balance of payments, but oil-producing countries during this time increased the cost of petroleum. Because the United States is dependent on petroleum from these countries, Americans continued to purchase it, which negatively affected the balance of payments and counteracted any benefits resulting from the devaluation of the dollar.

In the early twenty-first century the dollar again experienced a significant decline in value. U.S. exports did see improvement as U.S. products became less expensive to foreign countries. At the same time, some Americans were concerned that the Chinese government had unfairly set the value of its own currency, the yuan, too low, reducing the price, and thus increasing the quantity, of Chinese goods sold in the United States.

$ Trade Surplus and Trade Deficit

What It Means

The balance of trade for a country is the difference between the monetary value of the country's exported products (goods and services) and of its imported products over a certain period of time. If the balance of trade is positive (that is, if the country exports more than it imports), it has a trade surplus. On the other hand, if the balance of trade is negative (if the country imports more than it exports), it has a trade deficit, or trade gap. Because the values of a country's exports and exports are not likely to be exactly the same, most countries operate with a trade imbalance.

Countries trade goods and services with one another because it helps them expand their markets. For instance, when American rice brokers import rice that is grown in Indonesia, the American rice market becomes more diverse, and American consumers who buy rice are provided with more choices. Every country that trades goods and services internationally must manage the inflow and outflow of the products so that the overall economic effects on the country of trading are beneficial. This management is highly complex. A country may have trade surpluses with some countries and trade deficits with others.

WHEN A TRADE DEFICIT CAN BE A GOOD THING

When a country engages in trade with other nations, it deals in two distinct quantities: imports (those products that a country buys, or imports, from another country) and exports (products a country sells to another country). When a nation exports more products than it imports, it has what is called a trade surplus; when imports exceed exports, the country has a trade deficit. From the perspective of monetary gain, a trade surplus seems more desirable than a trade deficit, because it indicates that a nation is earning more money than it is spending. Some economists argue, however, that a trade deficit is not necessarily a disadvantage. Indeed, when a country has a trade deficit, it often means that its domestic economy (that is, its economic activities within its own borders) is growing at a fast rate. An expanding economy results in an increased demand for goods, many of which are imported. During the 1990s—a period widely considered to be one of the most prosperous in American history—the U.S. trade deficit more nearly tripled, from 1.5 percent of Gross Domestic Product (GDP; the value of all goods bought and sold in a country during a specific period) in 1995 to 4.2 percent of GDP in 2000.

The United States trades goods and services with most of the world's other countries, and the flow of products between countries is continually changing. For example, in May 2005 the United States had the greatest trade surpluses with The Netherlands, Hong Kong, Australia, the United Arab Emirates, and Singapore. By January 2006 this top-five list had shifted to Canada, Mexico, China, Japan, and Germany. And by July 2006 the list was made up of Hong Kong, Australia, the United Arab Emirates, The Netherlands, and Panama.

When Did It Begin

Countries and territories have bought and sold each other's products for thousands of years. Although modern theories of trade surpluses and trade deficits have evolved out of sophisticated economies, the basic concepts behind them are old.

An example of an ancient system that promoted trade between distant peoples is the Silk Road, a 5,000-mile-long network of trade routes through southern Asia, the Middle East, and Europe that was used by traders and travelers from 200 BC to the Middle Ages. The Silk Road connected China with civilizations in the West such as Greece and Rome. The route was originally established to carry Chinese silks from China to the West. In addition to silk, Europeans began to rely on the Silk Road for other Asian goods including porcelain, spices, and eventually gunpowder and paper. Over time, Chinese consumers

A country is said to have a trade surplus when the value of its exports is greater than the value of its imports. In Japan automobile exports account for a significant portion of the nation's trade surplus. *AP Images.*

also developed an interest in goods from the West, including cosmetics, silver, and perfume.

Even during ancient times, Chinese goods were heavily exported. Chinese goods have historically been relatively cheap to manufacture and sell abroad, and China has sold more to other countries than it has bought from them, resulting in consistent trade surpluses. During the days of the Silk Road, ancient Rome eagerly bought large amounts of Chinese silk, although China wanted little of Rome's products except glass.

More Detailed Information

Global pricing is one of many factors that affect the movement of products between countries and the surpluses and deficits that countries experience. For example, if the global price of crude oil drops, any country that is exporting oil sees the value of its product go down. The country's trading partners will pay less for the oil, which shifts the balance of trade with them and potentially contributes to a trade deficit in the oil-producing country. Some factors that can shift trade surpluses and deficits are seasonal. Each year the Christmas retail season in the United States, for example, promotes an increase in exports of certain popular products from China and other

countries having strong, low-cost manufacturing bases. Another factor that can alter the balance of trade for a country is a growth in the rate of consumption of domestically produced products. Using more products made at home will reduce the country's reliance on exports and potentially contribute to a trade surplus.

Trade surpluses are not necessarily indicators of a country's strong economic health, and trade deficits are not necessarily indicators of industrial decline. Many economists hold that the freedom of the country's consumers to experience a choice among quality goods and services in the market, the level of an economy's efficiency, and the openness of the country to international trade are more reliable indicators of the prosperity of the country's economy. For example, even though the United States has run a trade deficit with the rest of the world since 1976, its economy has grown steadily. Some economists argue that trade deficits may be a positive sign for a country's economy because they show that foreign investors have confidence in the country. Trade deficits also can indicate growth in domestic consumption because, in a country that is exporting more than it is importing, consumers may be buying goods faster than the country can produce.

China has experienced rapid economic growth in the late twentieth and early twenty-first centuries, and it also has run a trade surplus. A trade surplus can be an indication that a country's economic policies are more supportive of demands from foreign consumers than from the country's own consumers; such policies depress living standards within the country. China has long had a practice of keeping manufacturing costs low for exported goods, and its lowered living standards contribute to its ability to maintain these low costs.

Recent Trends

Globalization is a process involving the merging of economies, governmental policies, political movements, and cultures around the world. Beginning in the last decades of the twentieth century, globalization has had the effect of increasing the interconnectedness of the separate markets of individual countries and accelerating their transformation into a single global market. Goods have come to be traded across borders in greater volume and greater diversity than ever before. In fact, the level of trade between countries (international trade) has grown at a much faster rate than has the world economy. The rampant growth of international trade has resulted in an opening of trading practices and a general reduction in tariffs (taxes placed on imported goods).

One result of the growing global market is an increase in outsourcing, a practice in which companies reduce costs by paying an outside producer to take on a specified portion of work that would otherwise be done internally. When companies outsource to foreign operations, it is called offshoring. Some American computer companies, for example, buy computer components from countries where labor costs are lower than in the United States, thereby reducing their own production expenses. Critics of offshoring claim that the ultimate costs of sending work to a foreign manufacturer are greater than the savings in production costs. For example, in addition to taking jobs away from domestic workers, offshoring can discourage the domestic labor force from developing or maintaining important skills.

$ Foreign Exchange

What It Means

In the field of economics, the term *foreign exchange* is defined as a foreign currency, or money. In more common usage, however, foreign exchange refers to the exchange of the currency of one nation for the currency of another. People who travel in foreign countries must exchange their own currency for the local currency wherever they travel in order to pay for hotels, meals, and other purchases. Most international trade requires foreign exchange, too; without it businesses could not buy or sell goods or services beyond the borders of their own

country. If a large department store chain in the United States wants to buy thousands of televisions made in Japan, the store must pay for the televisions in Japanese currency (yen) rather than in dollars. The U.S. company would contact its bank, which would arrange to purchase yen for the transaction on the foreign exchange market (or FX market) at a certain price, known as an exchange rate. An exchange rate is the expression of one currency in terms of another. When 1 dollar can be traded for 100 Japanese yen, for example, the exchange rate is 100 to 1.

The FX market is the largest financial market in the world, with more than one trillion dollars worth of currency trading hands each day. The market is comprised of a worldwide network of brokers (agents who arrange purchases and sales) and banks concentrated in New York, London, Tokyo, and Singapore that buy and sell currency.

Currency exchange rates constantly change depending on a number of factors, including supply (the quantity of a currency available for sale) and demand (the quantity desired by buyers), as well as a country's

Foreign exchange usually refers to the process by which one nation's currency is converted into another nation's currency. The board in this photo contains a list of currency exchange rates. *AP Images.*

FORT KNOX

From 1933 until 1971, U.S. paper currency was backed by gold; that is, the issuing bank guaranteed that the printed currency could be exchanged at any time for an equal amount of gold held in reserve at the bank. For this to work, the United States had to maintain vast reserves of gold bullion that matched the value of all its circulating cash. One of the main storehouses of the gold reserve was at the United States Bullion Depository near Fort Knox, Kentucky. Fort Knox was an underground vault guarded by many layers of sophisticated, high-level security, including guards, cameras, alarms, fences, and a 24-ton vault door to which no one person had the full combination. Even when American currency was no longer backed by gold, the depository remained stocked with nearly 5,000 tons of gold bullion, and it continued to be used as a secure storage facility for other precious or highly valuable objects in the possession of the U.S. government. During the heyday of the gold reserve, people in the United States often referred to any ultrasecure location or item as being "locked up tighter than Fort Knox."

economic strength, national debt (how much money the country owes to other countries), rate of inflation (the general rise in prices that can cause currency to lose value), and political stability. Thus the countries with the most consistently valuable currencies (the United States, the United Kingdom, the European Union, and Japan) are those with the strongest economies and little political upheaval.

When Did It Begin

Throughout history most trade between countries was conducted with goods rather than with money. For reasons of convenience and portability, gold and silver coins evolved as small, valuable, and easily traded commodities. The coins were made from rare metals whose value was widely accepted. A gold coin minted in one country was worth its weight in gold in any other country.

The eighteenth and nineteenth centuries saw the rise of paper money. So that people would be willing to ascribe value to a mere piece of paper, issuing banks guaranteed that the printed currency could be exchanged at any time for an equal amount of gold (or in some cases, silver) held in reserve at that bank. Most major world currencies came to be backed by gold and silver; the gold and silver had a universal value, and the exchange rate was consistent.

The global importance of foreign exchange markets emerged in 1971, when the United States (and subsequently most other countries) stopped backing currency with gold. With no universal standard for the world's major currencies, each one's value could now float (or

fluctuate) in relation to the others depending on a variety of market forces.

More Detailed Information

The electronically connected network of banks and traders on the foreign exchange market has no central headquarters; its operations are spread across the globe and it functions 24 hours a day. As traders in Tokyo finish their day, their counterparts in London are just getting going; when the London traders go to lunch, the New York traders are beginning; and so on.

The FX market is comprised of four groups: banks, brokers, customers, and central banks. The banks are by far the largest participants. They buy currencies from and sell currencies to each other on behalf of customers or as a form of investment. A bank may make an investment when, for example, through detailed research, it comes to believe that the euro is going to go up in value relative to the dollar. If the bank were to purchase $100 million worth of euros at an exchange rate of 1.3 euros to 1 dollar, the bank would end up with 130 million euros. If the exchange rate between euros and dollars does change in favor of the euro, and 1 euro now equals 1 dollar, the bank may exchange the euros it bought for dollars. It will now have $130 million, including a hefty profit of $30 million. Approximately two-thirds of all FX transactions consist of banks dealing directly with each other, investing or trying to earn profits by trading currencies.

Brokers act as intermediaries between banks. They work with a variety of banks and know which of them are offering the best price on which currencies at any given time. A person or corporation who wishes to speculate in currency (that is, to invest in the hope of making a profit) contacts a broker to find out the best bank to use for the transaction. When investors deal with large sums of money, even a small fluctuation in an exchange rate can generate large profits (or losses). As an intermediary the broker also offers anonymity for the buyer or seller. Brokers earn money by charging a fee for their services.

Customers in the foreign exchange market can range from corporations looking to make large international purchases to people traveling to Mexico and in need of pesos for the trip. Some of the largest international corporations employ their own currency traders on staff for the sole purpose of tracking and trading in currency.

Central banks (such as the Federal Reserve, an independent agency of the U.S. government) act on behalf of their respective governments. Their primary role is to ensure the stability of the national currency. A central bank occasionally exerts its influence in the FX market by either increasing or reducing its country's money supply. This will lower or raise the value of the national currency. Central banks use this tactic to stabilize rapid changes in the value of the nation's currency that can result from both internal factors, such as inflation, or external factors, such as FX market fluctuations.

Variations in supply and demand can also cause changes in the value of a particular currency. When demand for a currency goes up (that is, when more buyers want to purchase it), so does the price of that currency in the market. This is known as appreciation of the currency. Conversely, when there is lower demand for a certain currency, the price of that currency often goes down; this is called depreciation of the currency. Because of the enormous amounts of currency being traded each day, even a fraction of a percent increase or decrease in value can have a significant impact on how much (or how little) a currency is traded.

When the value of the dollar goes up, or appreciates, each dollar will buy a greater amount of foreign currency. This means that the overall price of imported goods, such as televisions and cars, goes down. On the other hand, when the value of the dollar goes down, those same imports become more expensive. The value of any country's currency has a direct impact on the balance of its international trade (the difference in value, over a period of time, between its imports and exports): the number of exports and imports rises or falls depending on the strength or weakness of the currency. Currency values can also affect tourism: for example, if a country's currency becomes too strong, travelers from other countries will not be able to afford to visit that country.

Recent Trends

Since the early part of the twenty-first century, China has had one of the largest and most rapidly expanding economies in the world. The growth has been driven in large part by the vast amount of goods China exports. One of the ways China has kept the demand high for its exported goods around the world is by artificially sustaining its currency at a low, fixed value in the FX market. By undervaluing its currency, China ensures that its exported goods are be affordable. High demand means that China continues to export more and more goods and therefore can build more and more factories and hire more and more workers. Under normal market conditions, as China's economy grew and became more stable, the value of its currency would rise in the marketplace; instead, China's central bank has made sure to keep the exchange rate for the Chinese yuan fixed within a narrow range. Many U.S. manufacturers, unable to compete with China's relatively low wages and lower production costs, have gone out of business. The United States has worked hard to convince China to float its currency in the market. This would inevitably lead to an appreciation, or rise in value, of the Chinese currency.

$ Foreign Direct Investment

What It Means

When a business or firm invests its money or other resources in business activities outside its home country,

---

BILATERAL INVESTMENT TREATIES

When two countries determine that they want to establish favorable market conditions that will allow them to invest resources in one another, they enter into a formal agreement known as a bilateral investment treaty (bilateral means two-sided). This type of treaty establishes the terms and conditions for private investment in one country by companies of the other country. Bilateral investment treaties typically support the fair treatment of the host country's resources, such as labor. They also lay out the provisions for resolving disputes; in the event that the host country violates an investor's rights under the treaty, the investor can rely on an international arbitration (dispute-resolving) system for support.

Bilateral investment treaties promote economic stability, which, in turn, fosters political and social stability. The United States has bilateral investment treaties with dozens of countries. In recent years there has been a dramatic increase in the number of bilateral investment treaties between countries worldwide, which has promoted high levels of foreign direct investment. According to the United Nations, as of January 1, 1997, there were 1,330 bilateral investment treaties worldwide (involving 162 countries), a threefold increase since 1991.

---

it is known as foreign direct investment (FDI). Foreign direct investment typically involves constructing a factory or manufacturing facility in another country or providing equipment or buildings to a company in another country. It can also mean that the firm in the home country manages a foreign company or invests in a project with a foreign company. For example, if a U.S.-based automaker built a manufacturing plant in Indonesia, it would be making a foreign direct investment. The U.S. automaker buying a company in another country would be another example of FDI.

The practice of FDI has many benefits. When a company invests money or resources abroad, it automatically gains access to that country's economic market, which expands its opportunities to sell its products. It also might have access to cheaper production facilities, new technology, or new products that it is unable to get at home; these factors can help increase its efficiency.

The country in which the investment is made, called the host country, also benefits from FDI: it gains new technology, products, and business or manufacturing skills that help to stimulate economic growth. These benefits can improve the country's economic conditions by raising the income levels of workers or developing the country's market for goods and services.

In recent decades the barriers that regulate trade between nations (called international trade) have been gradually reduced, allowing countries to trade goods and

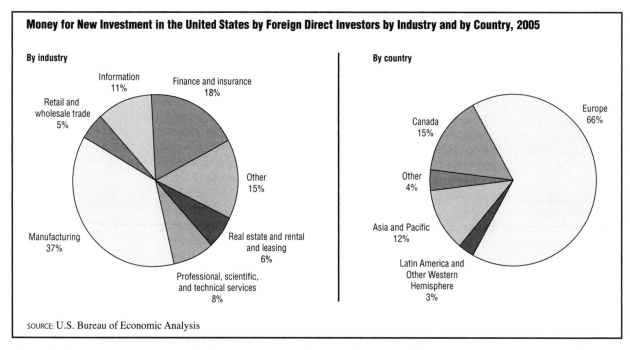

Money for New Investment in the United States by Foreign Direct Investors by Industry and by Country, 2005

By industry

Information 11%
Finance and insurance 18%
Retail and wholesale trade 5%
Other 15%
Manufacturing 37%
Real estate and rental and leasing 6%
Professional, scientific, and technical services 8%

By country

Canada 15%
Europe 66%
Other 4%
Asia and Pacific 12%
Latin America and Other Western Hemisphere 3%

SOURCE: U.S. Bureau of Economic Analysis

When a business in one country buys or builds a factory, opens offices, or otherwise establishes operations in another country, it is called foreign direct investment. According to these pie charts, in 2005 37 percent of foreign direct investment in the United States occurred in the manufacturing industry, and 66 percent came from Europe. *Illustration by GGS Information Services. Cengage Learning, Gale.*

services freely with one another and, as a result, enabling more foreign direct investment to take place. Both increased trade and increased FDI have paved the way for firms all over the world to set up their production facilities at the location that is best for that activity, even if it is in another country. A firm can design a product in one country, manufacture its components in factories located in another country, and assemble the product in yet another country. The product may end up being sold anywhere in the world.

When Did It Begin

The increase in international trade since World War II (1939–45) has laid the groundwork for the worldwide growth of foreign direct investment. Since the 1940s the barriers to international trade, such as high tariffs (taxes) on imported manufactured goods, have been lowered. The General Agreement on Tariffs and Trade (GATT) was a contract signed in 1948 by 23 nations, including the United States, for the purposes of promoting trade agreements among members. GATT and other agreements helped to establish worldwide trade and to increase the ways in which companies invested their resources in foreign locations. For smaller firms, investing internationally provided opportunities to become more actively involved in the global marketplace. Larger firms were able to build entire offices in other countries and integrate deeply into local economies; large companies with many locations worldwide came to be known as multinationals.

In 1995 GATT was succeeded by the World Trade Organization (WTO). By 1999 the volume of world trade had grown to almost 20 times what it had been in 1950, an increase caused in large part by steady growth in foreign direct investment.

More Detailed Information

Companies that want resources such as cheap labor and close proximity to natural resources may need to set up part of their operations in foreign locations in order to obtain those resources. For several decades American, European, and Asian companies have found cheap labor in countries in Southeast Asia and Eastern Europe where the local economies are not developed. Unlike workers in the United States and other developed countries, workers in these countries are generally unorganized (not united to protect their rights and improve their working conditions), which greatly lowers the chance that they will strike (protest by stopping their work) or issue demands for higher wages. For close proximity to natural resources, many companies from the United States and elsewhere have located manufacturing or office buildings in the Middle East and Africa, where there are countries rich in such resources as petroleum, coal, iron ore, and copper.

Accounting firms, advertising firms, and law firms also invest their resources in other countries, typically when they are seeking new clients for their services. A business that does this is said to be broadening its market. For example, a law firm based in New York City that provides legal services to clients of Czech descent might determine that having an office in Prague (the capital of the Czech Republic) would help it gain more Czech clients. If the firm already had clients in Prague, investing in opening an office and hiring Czech lawyers would help sustain the relationships with those clients and also support the local Czech economy by providing jobs for lawyers.

Another reason why firms invest in other countries is to take advantage of what are known as economies of scale and scope. Economy of scale refers to the way that the cost of producing a good goes down when the quantity of the good being produced goes up. Large manufacturing facilities, such as car factories, are generally able to make goods more efficiently than smaller facilities, because the larger facilities can mass-produce goods using assembly lines and automated machinery. For example, if a U.S.-based maker of silicon chips opens a manufacturing plant in the Latin American country of Costa Rica, it can bring its advanced manufacturing technologies and facilities to a place where the real estate is cheaper than in the United States and the cost of paying workers is significantly lower. In addition, the company is taxed at a very low rate by the Costa Rican government, and it receives subsidies (government-supported reductions in price) for electricity and water. These benefits all contribute to lowering the cost of each computer chip that is manufactured in the Costa Rican plant.

Economy of scope is a theory that states that the average cost of production goes down as the number of different types of goods produced goes up. For example, a paper-product company that manufactures a variety of products, from paper plates to paper napkins to note cards, will have facilities that can share the production of different goods, which will reduce the overall cost of producing each good. The costs of making diverse products for one company are cheaper than the costs of producing each one in a separate facility. For example, suppose that a Chinese razor-blade manufacturer has built up a global distribution network for shipping its razors to many different countries. If that company is purchased by a U.S. battery manufacturer, then the battery manufacturer can increase its efficiency by using the distribution network of the razor manufacturer to ship both razors and batteries to other countries. The investment in the Chinese company gives the U.S. company a new advantage.

Recent Trends

Large companies such as Boeing, General Motors, and Ford were among the first to make significant investments in other countries and to become what are now called multinational corporations. Today medium-sized companies are also participating in the trend to invest abroad, which has further increased the amount of cross-border investment. According to the United Nations (an organization that fosters political, legal, and economic cooperation among countries), between 1984 and 1997 the total annual flow of foreign direct investment from all countries increased from $42 billion to $430 billion. This was more than double the rate at which world trade grew during that period.

Between 1991 and 1996 more than 100 countries made 599 changes in laws pertaining to foreign direct investment. The majority of these changes involved loosening the regulations for foreign investment in the home country in order to make it easier for foreign companies to enter their markets. The decrease in regulations improved the ability of countries to trade goods and services across borders. When both trade and investment are open between countries, it is easier for companies to find and develop the best location for production.

INTERNATIONAL TRENDS

$ Globalization

What It Means

Globalization is a term used to describe a general economic trend in which distinct national economic markets become so integrated with each other that they function more as one large global market than as separate economies. Separate economic systems have increasingly become less isolated from each other by barriers to cross-border trade and investment; by distance, time zones, and language; and by differences in government regulations, culture, and business systems. Less isolation means that countries share goods, services, labor, and capital (resources used to generate wealth). Increased trade between nations and investments of resources across borders have also stimulated global activity.

Coca-Cola beverages, Levi's jeans, Nintendo videogame consoles, iPods, and McDonald's hamburgers are examples of goods that have come to be recognized and purchased by consumers all around the world. Their brand-name recognition is one outcome of the phenomenon of globalization. Coca-Cola drinks, like thousands of other products, are not just marketed, sold, and consumed in almost every country; they are also produced in many different locations around the world.

Globalization has two main components: the globalization of markets and the globalization of production. The globalization of markets (in this context the term *market* means a geographic region where goods and services are bought and sold) refers to the way that national markets, which at one time may have been distinct from one another, merge to form one huge global marketplace. The primary force in the development of a globalized market has been the way in which consumers' tastes and preferences have grown similar, even though the consumers may live in different countries. Products such as Nike running shoes and Starbucks coffee have been accepted by consumers globally. The companies that embrace this trend and benefit from it are offering a standardized product worldwide, one that does not vary depending on the location. With the aid of advertising and technology, these products promote a uniform set of consumer tastes and demands.

The globalization of production refers to the tendency among many businesses to use locations all around the world to produce their goods and services. This means that many businesses choose to make goods in foreign locations in order to take advantage of differences in the cost and quality of such things as labor, energy, and land. For example, many U.S.-based manufacturers of retail clothing have determined that they can produce clothing more efficiently by manufacturing it in countries in Southeast Asia, where labor is much cheaper than it is in the United States. By investing resources in locations where production or labor costs are lower, companies can lower their overall costs and, at times, improve the quality of their products.

When Did It Begin

The first time that the world economy showed signs of globalizing was during the period of economic expansion that occurred from 1850 to 1914. Open trade practices, advances in manufacturing, and government-supported communication and transportation allowed the United States, Great Britain, and economically advanced European countries to develop their resources in remote locations and to build consumer interest in goods from other nations. For instance, U.S. companies sold agricultural machinery to farmers in Russia, Australia, and Argentina, boosting the worldwide supply of grain. Transportation of goods and manufactured products was improved by the invention of the steamship and the openings of the Suez and Panama canals. The globalization trend in this period did not affect millions of people worldwide, as it does today, but it did establish interrelationships between separate, nationalized economies.

An expansion in international trade after World War II (1939–45) built further economic connections among countries. In 1948 the United States and 22 other nations signed the General Agreement on Tariffs and Trade (GATT). Its purpose was to encourage trade agreements supporting the fair treatment of resources (such as labor and the environment), and it officially laid out the terms and conditions for open trade. By 1995

Globalization refers to the increasing economic interaction between countries, meaning products made in one country are often sold in another. A visible sign of globalization is the proliferation of American fast-food restaurants, such as Pizza Hut, throughout the world. © 2007 Kelly A. Quin.

some 125 countries had signed onto GATT, and 90 percent of world trade was being conducted according to the agreement's rules. That year GATT was replaced by the World Trade Organization (WTO); the countries that had signed the agreement became the first members of the WTO. At the start of the twenty-first century there were more than 140 WTO member nations.

More Detailed Information

When a company exports goods or services to consumers in another country, it participates in international trade. Since the end of World War II barriers to international trade (such as high taxes on imports of manufactured goods) have declined. This has increasingly enabled businesses to view the world, rather than a single country, as their market.

In addition to reducing trade barriers, many countries have steadily removed restrictions on foreign direct investment (which is when a firm invests money or other resources in business activities outside its home country). The lowering of trade and investment barriers allows firms to base production at the optimal location for that activity and serve the world market from that location. Thus, a company may design a product in one country, produce component parts in three other countries, assemble the product in a fifth country, and then export the product worldwide. Foreign direct investment increased dramatically in the 1980s and 1990s. The major investors have been American, Japanese, and Western European companies investing in Europe, Asia, and the United States.

Lowering trade barriers has not been the only motivating force behind economic globalization; developments in technology have also contributed to the trend. For instance, the rise of the Internet has increased the global consumer awareness of products and trends. Improvements in communications, information processing, and transportation technology have also contributed to the creation of a global community of consumers and businesses.

One of the most significant technological innovations of the last century was the development of the microprocessor, which enabled the growth of fast, cheap computers. The microprocessor has also supported the development of satellite, optical fiber, and wireless technologies, as well as the Internet and the World Wide Web. As the cost of microprocessors has fallen, so have the costs of global communications; this, in turn, has lowered the costs of controlling and coordinating large, global organizations. The World Wide Web has made it much easier for buyers and sellers to find one another, regardless of their location.

Communication networks and media have both contributed to the creation of a worldwide culture. U.S. television networks such as CNN, MTV, and HBO are now viewed in many countries around the world. The media has also become a prime transmitter of culture, resulting in the global marketing of such products as Levi's jeans, which consumers can now purchase as easily in Tokyo or Paris as in San Francisco.

Although economic developments play the largest role in the globalization trend, developments in travel, immigration, technology, communications, and transportation have all contributed significantly to the trend. For example, advances in air transportation since World War I (1914–18) have transformed the movement of freight and passengers around the globe. The world's containership fleet has expanded four times over since 1980, reflecting the growing volume of international trade and the relative ease of moving goods by container (truck-size boxes that are moved between ships, trains, and trucks without needing to be repacked). The transportation costs associated with production have also declined as a result of the use of container shipping.

International businesses are organized in various ways. Some businesses have separate operations in different countries with no centralized headquarters, and others keep a headquarters in one country and have branches in other countries. A transnational or multinational company has separate business units in different countries, and each unit is managed as a business in and of itself, responding to local needs. All companies that work internationally stand to grow, expand their operations, improve their profits, and positively impact the countries in which they work.

Recent Trends

The benefits of globalization for business and economic markets are many, but there are also drawbacks. With higher levels of interdependence between markets, the fact that some countries have had more rapid economic growth than others has at times led to economic and political volatility (unexpected instability). For example, in the 1990s the developing countries in Asia attracted large amounts of investment from developed nations, and the region's economy was growing at an unprecedented rate. For many reasons, an economic crisis started in 1997, many Western investors pulled their money out of the region, and in 1998 the Indonesian dictator Suharto (b. 1921) was forced from power. These events caused business and political leaders to question the expansion of free-market practices and the influences of globalization. In another example, when certain Latin American countries opened their markets to foreign trade and investment, they became so vulnerable to pressures from the global economy that they lost control of their financial policies. Abrupt changes caused by politics, natural disasters, social unrest, and conflicts such as war can have major repercussions for poorer countries.

In general, those who argue against globalization claim that its trends have not resulted in a real increase in open and free trade, and that powerful, multinational

NORTH AMERICAN FREE TRADE AGREEMENT

The North American Free Trade Agreement (NAFTA) is a free-trade agreement among Canada, the United States, and Mexico that went into effect on January 1, 1994. NAFTA eliminated tariffs (import taxes) on half of all U.S. goods shipped to Mexico and Canada. It also established a plan for gradually phasing out other tariffs over approximately 14 years. Since NAFTA was passed, trade between the United States, Canada, and Mexico has increased dramatically. By 2006 trade between the United States and Mexico had doubled since NAFTA went into effect.

NAFTA has been controversial. While NAFTA's decrease in tariffs resulted in increased profits for companies, Canadian and U.S. labor unions opposed the agreement because they feared that lower labor costs in Mexico would draw jobs out of the United States and Canada. Whereas the U.S. government supports U.S. farmers by providing them with subsidies (monetary contributions), Mexican farmers are not subsidized by their government. Many farmers in Mexico have gone out of business because of falling agricultural prices in that country. Forced off their land by bankruptcy and drawn to higher wages in the United States, many former farmers in Mexico have attempted to illegally immigrate to the United States.

NAFTA is one of many examples of regional trade blocs, or groups, that exist around the world. Other regional trade blocs include the European Union (EU), a union of 25 European and Scandinavian member states, and the Caribbean Community and Common Market (CARICOM), a union of 15 independent states and territories in the Caribbean.

corporations do not take the interests of poorer nations, the working class, and the natural environment into account. Globalization, they argue, focuses too much on corporate profit and not enough on the rights and freedoms of individuals.

Those who support open trade and greater economic integration among nations emphasize that free trade leads to lower prices for goods and services, higher employment levels, and more efficient production of goods, because production units (such as factories and manufacturing plants) are located where they are the least expensive to operate. Supporters view globalization as a positive spread of free will and capitalism and therefore of economic freedom.

$ Developed Countries

What It Means

The term *developed countries* is used to designate nations that enjoy high per capita income (average income per citizen), high standards of living (the quality and quantity

of goods and services available in a society), long life expectancy (the average expected life span of a nation's citizens), and other measurements relating to a high quality of life for the individual. Developed countries are also known as First World countries, industrialized nations, advanced economies, and more economically advanced countries.

In addition to their high level of prosperity, all developed countries have several characteristics in common. For one, they are fully industrialized. In other words, developed or industrialized nations are founded on technologically advanced, manufacturing-based economies. Developed countries also share a commitment to free-market economies, or economies based on the law of supply and demand, in which prices are determined by the relationship between the availability of goods (supply) and the desire among consumers for those goods (demand). Some economic experts also regard democratic political institutions, coupled with relatively low levels of political corruption, as essential components of a developed country.

When Did It Begin

The concept of developed countries, as opposed to developing countries (countries characterized by low per capita income, widespread poverty, and an undeveloped economic infrastructure), first emerged during the Cold War (a period of political tension between the United States and the Soviet Union that lasted from the late 1940s until the early 1990s). In 1952 French anthropologist and historian Alfred Sauvy (1898–1990) coined the term *Third World* (in French, *Tiers Monde*) to describe the underprivileged status of the world's impoverished nations. The term soon became synonymous with areas of the globe that were not involved in the ideological conflict between the United States and the Soviet Union. As a rule, these nations were poor, politically unstable, and economically undeveloped; many were former colonies of industrialized nations. As the term *Third World* became popular, people also began using the expressions *First World* to mean the United States and Europe and *Second World* to mean the Soviet Union and its allies. These terms were originally political, used to distinguish the democratic, capitalist (free-market) societies of the West from the communist nations supported by the Soviet Union.

Over time the terms *First*, *Second*, and *Third World* became obsolete. One reason for this was that the dichotomy between the First and Second Worlds ceased to exist after the collapse of the Soviet Union in 1991. Furthermore, the name *Third World* began to be viewed as pejorative because it implied that poorer nations were somehow inferior to First or Second World nations. As these expressions fell out of use, the terms *developed country* and *developing country*, which focused more on economic factors, became more common.

Developed, or industrialized, countries enjoy high levels of economic prosperity. Many of the world's developed countries are in Europe, where some have formed a political alliance called the European Union, or EU. © *Reuters NewMedia Inc./Corbis.*

More Detailed Information

Most developed countries are in the western hemisphere, and they include the United States, Canada, and the nations of Western Europe. Australia and New Zealand, both former British colonies, are also developed countries. Although most Asian countries are not considered developed, a few meet the criteria of developed nations (notably Japan, South Korea, Singapore, and Taiwan), as do the administrative regions of Hong Kong and Macau, both of which are controlled by the People's Republic of China. In the Middle East only Israel is considered a developed country. There are no developed countries in Africa.

Developed countries are generally ranked according to several criteria. One of the most significant is a nation's gross domestic product, or GDP. GDP refers to the value of all goods and services produced in a country over a set period of time. It accounts for the consumption of goods and services, the total monetary value of a nation's investments, total government spending, and the difference between a nation's exports (goods sold to other countries) and imports (goods purchased from other countries). GDP is usually measured on an annual basis.

Although GDP offers a fair gauge of whether or not a nation is developed, there are some exceptions. For example, while the GDP in Saudi Arabia is high, the distribution of wealth is uneven, and many people live in poverty.

Another factor used to determine whether or not a nation is developed is the Human Development Index (HDI). HDI measures the well-being of a nation's citizens (with a particular focus on the welfare of children) according to three categories: standard of living, education and literacy rates, and life expectancy. In 1993 the United Nations, or UN (an international organization dedicated to fostering legal, political, and economic cooperation among various nations), began using HDI ratings to rank countries according to their quality of life. In 2006 Norway ranked the highest, with a rating of 0.965, followed by Iceland (0.960), Australia (0.957), Ireland (0.956), and Sweden (0.950). The United States ranked eighth, with a rating of 0.948. According to economists, developed nations should have an HDI rating of at least 0.8.

Recent Trends

The disintegration of the Soviet Union in the late 1980s and early 1990s caused a major shift in the relationship between the developed countries of Western Europe and the communist republics of Eastern Europe. (Communist countries are governed according to principles of state ownership of property and economic production and the socialization, or sharing, of material and social resources for the use of all citizens.) After breaking free of Soviet influence, a number of former Eastern Bloc countries (a term referring to those Eastern and Central European countries under Soviet political domination) began to implement substantial political and economic reforms. They held democratic elections and launched major industrialization programs in the hope of eventually gaining admittance to the European Union (a confederation of developed democratic nations in Europe originating in the 1950s), commonly known as the EU. For former Eastern Bloc countries membership in the EU was synonymous with achieving "developed nation" status.

By the early twenty-first century a number of Eastern European nations had attained this goal. In 2004 several nations from Eastern and Central Europe, among them the Czech Republic, Hungary, Lithuania, Poland, and Slovenia, earned membership in the European Union, largely because of the stability of their democratic institutions and the overall strengths of their economies. In 2007 Bulgaria and Romania also joined the European Union. While some economists remained cautious about designating these countries as developed, in part because of the relatively recent nature of their industrialization, by the time of their entering the EU they ranked among the

NEWLY INDUSTRIALIZED COUNTRIES

Countries that have not quite attained the status of a developed country (a country with a high average income per citizen along with a high quality of life) but are undergoing a process of rapid economic and technological growth are commonly known as newly industrialized countries, or NICs. Economies in NICs are marked by a shift away from an agricultural economy and toward an industrialized economy (one based on technology and manufacturing). The term *newly industrialized country* originated in the 1970s and was used to denote Asian nations with rapidly growing economies, among them Singapore, Taiwan, and South Korea. They were also known as the "East Asian Tigers." By the end of the twentieth century, all of these countries were regarded as developed. In the early twenty-first century the most prominent NICs were China, Mexico, Brazil, Turkey, and South Africa.

world's most politically stable and economically prosperous nations.

$ Developing Countries

What It Means

Developing countries are nations that have a low per capita income (average annual income per person), a low standard of living (availability of quality goods and services for average citizens), low life expectancy (number of years of the average person's life span), high infant-mortality rates, widespread poverty, and an underdeveloped economy. The economies in developing countries are generally based on agricultural production or natural-resource extraction (for example, oil, coal, or metals) rather than industry (manufacturing). In this sense one of the defining characteristics of a developing country is that it is not industrialized.

Developing countries often have underdeveloped political and judicial systems, inadequate social services, and high levels of government corruption. Until the 1990s many were undermined by rapid population growth, which placed great strain on their food supply and other resources; since that time many of the poorest countries have seen life expectancy and populations fall because of the HIV/AIDS epidemic. In many cases developing countries are former colonies of more powerful developed countries (countries with high per capita incomes, high standards of living, and long life expectancies).

Other names for developing countries include underdeveloped nations, less developed nations, and Third

World countries. Such countries are predominantly found in Asia, Latin and Central America, and Africa.

When Did It Begin

Developing countries were originally known as Third World countries. The designation *Third World* dates to 1952, when the French historian and anthropologist Alfred Sauvy (1898–1990) coined the term to describe economically underdeveloped countries whose needs were largely ignored by the more advanced, powerful nations of the world. The term *Third World* (*Tiers Monde* in French) is derived from *Third Estate,* a French term for portions of the population, generally peasants, who were not members of the First Estate (the aristocracy) or the Second Estate (the clergy).

The term *Third World* quickly became associated with nations that were not aligned with either the United States or the Soviet Union in the Cold War (a period of ideological conflict between the two countries that lasted from the late 1940s to the early 1990s). Subsequently the United States and its allies became known as the First World, while the Soviets and other communist states became known as the Second World.

Over time the term *developing countries* replaced *Third World*; many people had begun to regard the latter as derogatory because it was reminiscent of European colonialism (the practice by which European nations created settlements, or colonies, in poorer countries for the purpose of exploiting the natural resources and labor force of those countries). Toward the end of the twentieth century, however, some political economists also began to question the designation *developing country* because many of the world's so-called developing nations were economically stagnant, demonstrated no signs of becoming industrialized, and had even shown indications of economic decline.

More Detailed Information

In the second half of the twentieth century there emerged several key organizations dedicated to assisting developing countries. One of the most influential of these organizations has been the World Bank Group, an association of five global agencies that fosters economic development in poorer, unindustrialized nations, with the ultimate aim of eradicating world poverty. The first of these agencies, the International Bank for Reconstruction and Development (IBRD), was formed in the years following World War II (1939–45) and was originally dedicated to providing economic assistance to European and Asian countries in the aftermath of the conflict. One of its first loans was intended to help with the postwar reconstruction of France. From the mid-1950s to mid-1960s, other agencies joined with the IBRD to create the World Bank Group.

Over the years the World Bank Group has extended its efforts to include providing aid to developing nations,

Developing nations are generally poor and have economies based on agriculture and natural resource extraction rather than manufacturing. Many people, like the Tanzanian man pictured here, earn a living by selling produce at a local market. *Photograph by Cory Langely. Reproduced by permission.*

particularly in Africa. One way that the World Bank Group has tried to stimulate economic development is by helping developing countries to implement policy reform (that is, modify their government's economic and social policies), with the aim of creating conditions that will enable free-market trading with the world's more prosperous, developed countries. These reforms are often accompanied by large grants and loans that are to be used for improving infrastructure (for example, roads, water supplies, energy generation and distribution, and other aspects of a society that allow it to operate productively and efficiently) and providing educational opportunities for the country's citizens. The World Bank has also played a significant role in providing financial assistance to countries suffering from the epidemic of AIDS (an infectious viral disease that destroys the human immune system and is rampant in developing countries). In the first years of the twenty-first century, the World Bank spent more than $2 billion on programs designed to help eradicate the disease.

In 1990 the Pakistani economist Mahbub ul Haq (1934–98) created the Human Development Index, or HDI, a method of measuring the quality of life of a nation's citizens. The HDI focuses on three factors: life expectancy, literacy rates, and standard of living. In 1993 the United Nations (an international organization intended to foster peace, security, and friendly relations among countries) began using the HDI to gauge economic and living conditions in developing countries worldwide, and it published its findings annually in its Human Development Report. The Human Development Report also provides a periodic analysis of global efforts to fight poverty, hunger, and disease in developing countries. In 2005 the report stated that, while financial assistance had increased since the late 1990s, it was still inadequate to meet the needs of most of the world's most impoverished nations.

Recent Trends

Toward the end of the twentieth century, the rise of globalization (the process by which the economies of different nations become integrated) seemed to offer developing countries new opportunities for economic development. The World Trade Organization (WTO) was created in 1995 in order to facilitate international trade in the increasingly global economy; its goals included reducing trade barriers between nations, promoting fair business practices worldwide, and mediating

THE NON-ALIGNED MOVEMENT

In 1961, in an act of protest against the Cold War, the ideological conflict between the United States and the Soviet Union, a group of developing countries (impoverished nations with low per capita income and low standards of living), led by Yugoslavia, India, Egypt, and Indonesia, formed the Non-Aligned Movement (NAM), an organization dedicated to developing peaceful alliances among Third World (developing) nations. The movement was based on five basic principles: respect for the borders and sovereignty of all nations; policies of nonaggression; equality and cooperation; noninterference in the internal affairs of other nations; and peaceful coexistence (the idea that all nations can peacefully coexist despite ideological differences). By the early twenty-first century there were more than 100 NAM countries, accounting for roughly 55 percent of the world's population.

trade disputes between nations. One of the stated priorities of the WTO was to create economic growth in the world's developing countries by promoting international trade reform and encouraging industrialization in those nations. By 2006 the WTO had more than 150 member nations, the majority of which were developing countries.

In spite of its pledge to help developing nations take advantage of the global economy, the WTO soon became an object of intense criticism. Opponents of the WTO, many of them from developing countries, complained that the organization demonstrated an unfair bias toward the interests of the world's developed nations, particularly the United States and European countries. Critics focused primarily on the fact that the United States and Europe closed their markets to most agricultural products from the poorest countries. In addition, many critics of the WTO also voiced concerns about issues of environmental protection and fair labor practices, arguing that the organization's economic policies actually increased pollution levels and promoted the exploitation of workers in developing nations.

$ International Labor Issues

What It Means

The term *international labor issues* refers to violations of workers' rights that recur consistently throughout the world. Workers' legal rights, which protect them from abuses by employers, vary from country to country. However, Articles 23 and 24 of the United Nations (UN) Universal Declaration of Human Rights (UDHR) describe rights that create a universal standard for proper labor relations.

These articles state the following:

Article 23

Everyone has the right to work, to free choice of employment, to just and favorable conditions of work and to protection against unemployment.

Everyone, without any discrimination, has the right to equal pay for equal work.

Everyone who works has the right to just and favorable remuneration [payment] ensuring for himself and his family an existence worthy of human dignity, and supplemented, if necessary, by other means of social protection.

Everyone has the right to form and to join trade unions for the protection of his interests.

Article 24

Everyone has the right to rest and leisure, including reasonable limitation of working hours and periodic holidays with pay.

The International Labour Organization (ILO) is the agency within the UN that seeks to secure these rights for all workers. During the first decade of the twenty-first century, the ILO's fundamental areas of concern included child labor and forced labor, safety and sanitation in the workplace, discrimination in the workplace, and workers' right to free association (that is, the right to unionize and engage in collective bargaining with employers).

When Did It Begin?

Workers have been demanding fair treatment from their employers for centuries. In 1381 John Ball, Wat Tyler, and Jack Straw led the Peasants' Revolt in England. Although the issue that sparked the uprising was an unpopular tax increase to pay for the Hundred Years' War, the underlying source of the peasants' discontent had to do with their position as serfs in the feudal economy. Barely a notch above slave laborers, serfs were legally bound to the fields of the lords (or landlords) who employed them. Not only were they paid very low wages, but they were also forbidden to look for better work elsewhere. Angry peasants gathered in London, destroyed the property of the wealthy, stormed the Tower of London, and presented their demands to the young King Richard II, who promised to honor their requests. A militia of 7,000 men, however, assassinated the rebellion's leaders, and the peasants' demands were never met.

Coauthored by German philosophers Karl Marx (1818–83) and Friedrich Engels (1820–95), *The Communist Manifesto* (1848) is regarded by many as the most influential call for the unification of workers throughout the world. Written as a summation of the guiding principles of the Communist League, to which both men

The term *international labor issues* refers to the legal rights of workers throughout the world. In 1997 this 12-year-old Palestinian boy, working in a sewing factory, earned less than $1.50 a day, providing the main income for his family. *AP Images.*

belonged, the volume called upon workers, who occupied the lowest class of society, to overthrow the managers (the middle class) and the owners of the factories (the upper class). The ultimate goal of this revolt was to produce a classless society in which wealth was distributed evenly among all people.

At the end of World War I, world leaders agreed that lasting world peace could be maintained only if it was based on social justice. Further, there could be no social justice if large masses of workers were subject to exploitation by wealthy industrialists and entrepreneurs. Widespread unjust treatment of workers, they feared, would create social discontent, which would in turn lead to violence, upheaval, and war. Thus, in the interest of promoting and protecting the rights of workers around the world, the ILO was established under the Treaty of Versailles in June 1919. Later that year at the first international labor conference in Washington, D.C., the agency issued its first six proclamations, which set standards for unemployment, maternity protection, night work for women, minimum age and night work for young persons in industry, and hours of work in industry. Originally part of the League of Nations, the ILO was incorporated into the United Nations in 1945.

More Detailed Information

The most urgent areas of concern in international labor involve child labor, forced labor, and workplace safety. According to ILO statistics published in 2005, 246 million children (1 out of 6 in the world) are involved in child labor, and nearly one-third of these children are younger than 10 years old. Most children work as a matter of economic necessity for themselves and their families.

Although the greatest concentrations of child laborers are found in the Asia-Pacific region and Sub-Saharan Africa, there are millions of children being forced to work in Western industrialized countries and, indeed, all over the world. The overwhelming majority of child laborers work in agriculture, where they are routinely exposed to toxic chemicals and dangerous machinery. Outside the agricultural sector, children also work in factories, in mines and quarries, as domestic servants, as street peddlers, and in the sex trades.

Most children work informally, without legal or regulatory protections, and it is estimated that some 22,000 children die in work-related accidents every year. Moreover, in addition to the physical risks they face, child laborers also suffer from the immediate and long-term

MULTICULTURAL SNEAKERS

Although globalization (economic expansion across international borders) is sometimes criticized as little more than an opportunity for giant multinational corporations to exploit cheap labor in poorer, developing countries, there are instances in which partnerships between these corporations and poor people in other parts of the world undoubtedly benefit both parties.

In one such collaboration, reported in 2006, the Converse shoe company (a division of Nike) hired a group of expert women embroiderers in Huanta, a small village in the Andes Mountains of Peru, to stitch patterns from their ancestral culture onto Converse footwear. The business relationship was said to offer a much-needed financial boost to the area's impoverished rural economy. Converse initially employed 1,000 workers in the village and planned to employ as many as 15,000. The International Labour Organization (ILO; an agency of the United Nations), which helped establish this relationship between the shoe company and the villagers, noted that the program not only helped to alleviate poverty but also contributed to these women's sense of self-worth by demonstrating the value of their technical expertise and engaging them in the development of a product that honored their cultural heritage. The ILO also monitored working conditions in the village to ensure that workers were given appropriate breaks and that they were allowed to talk to each other while they worked.

mental and emotional consequences of being denied an education and a real childhood.

Forced labor represents an overlapping concern, as at least 40 percent of people who are made to work against their will are children; more than 50 percent are women. Described as human trafficking, a form of modern-day slavery, forced labor occurs as the result of fraud, coercion, kidnapping, and other means. In 2005 it was estimated that more than 12 million people on every continent are forced to work against their will; between 600,000 to 800,000 of them are trafficked across international borders, while the rest are enslaved in their own countries.

Although reporting practices vary widely from country to country and reliable statistics are difficult to compile, it is estimated that more than two million people per year die from injuries, exposure to hazardous materials, and communicable diseases acquired at work. Further, for every person who suffers a fatal accident in the workplace, several hundred people suffer injuries that cause them to miss at least three days of work. Data suggests that workplace injury and disease rates are much higher in developing (poorer) countries than in developed (wealthier and more industrialized) countries, even while many injuries and deaths go unreported. Part of the problem is that occupational safety laws either do not

exist or remain unenforced in many parts of the world. Initiatives to improve workplace safety focus on implementation of policies and legislation to compel safety protections, increases in infrastructure and manpower to monitor and inspect working environments, and improvements in recording and reporting practices so that the true nature of the problem can be evaluated and addressed.

Recent Trends

Since the 1990s globalization (economic expansion across borders, facilitated by free trade agreements) has made it increasingly desirable and possible for large corporations in industrialized countries to establish factories and take advantage of lower wages in developing countries. This trend has raised new issues regarding international labor and human rights. Whereas the ILO is seen as a major multilateral advocate for the rights of workers around the world, the World Trade Organization (WTO), which was established in 1995 to promote globalization, is widely regarded by members of the human and labor rights community as an enemy of their cause. Human and labor rights organizations see the WTO as an agency that seeks to protect corporate profits at the expense of human and labor rights. Among the most often cited charges against the WTO are its rulings that it is illegal for a government to ban a product based on the way it is produced, such as with child labor, and that governments cannot ban products from companies who do business with brutal dictatorships, such as Burma.

$ Foreign Worker

What It Means

Foreign or migrant workers are people who travel to another country looking for work. The classification is broad enough to include expert technology workers, language teachers, laborers, and even entertainers. Most often, however, foreign workers take agricultural jobs, such as picking fruit or harvesting crops. These workers tend to send nearly all of their wages back to their families in their home countries. It is estimated that there are 25 million foreign workers throughout the world and approximately 14 million working in the United States. The highest concentrations of migrant workers in the United States work in California, but every state in the Union hosts migrant workers at some point during the calendar year. Other agricultural areas that draw large populations of migrant workers include the cotton fields of Texas and the sugar beet fields of Colorado, Michigan, and Ohio.

Migrant workers are paid low wages and often live together in what are called migrant worker communities. The living conditions in these communities are often substandard, with tight sleeping quarters and a limited amount of running water. When the work is complete, foreign workers either return to their home countries or go to another area or country in search of more work. In this way foreign workers are different from immigrants, who seek permanent residence and citizenship in the countries to which they move.

When Did It Begin

Historians date the emergence of migrant worker communities to the rise of industrialization in the eighteenth and nineteenth centuries in Europe and the United States. The United States and several European countries recruited workers from Africa, India, and South America to work in European and American factories. Industrialized countries tended to draw migrant workers from the countries they had colonized. For example, English industries drew large numbers of migrant workers from India.

One of the first major influxes of foreign workers in United States came from China after the 1848 discovery of gold in California. Gold mining became a major commercial industry, and few Americans were willing to endure the hard physical labor required by commercial mining operations. Peasants in rural China viewed this work as an opportunity to improve their living conditions back home. Thousands sailed from China to the United States planning to return eventually to their native land. They lived together in communities called Chinatowns, and many of them never ended up getting back to China.

More Detailed Information

In a migrant worker situation the country that hosts foreign workers is referred to as the receiving country and the country from which the foreign workers come is called the sending country. Sending nations tend to be rural, with undeveloped economies and not enough jobs for a large group of impoverished citizens. Receiving countries are usually developed nations looking for cheap, unskilled labor. In the past receiving countries have established official programs to attract foreign workers. This happened in the 1960s in Germany, when over a million workers were invited to come from Spain, Italy, and Turkey. The United States and Mexico had a similar arrangement when the United States offered Mexican workers temporary employment during World War II.

Developed nations prefer migrant workers to immigrants for several reasons. First, receiving countries accept migrant workers only when they are old enough to work; the sending country bears all the costs associated with raising children until working age. A second reason is that in most cases foreign workers come to the host country without their families, whereas immigrant workers are more likely to come with dependents. Receiving countries have to provide resources to support nonworking members of immigrant working families, including medical care for the elderly and often state-supported child care for the young. Finally, when foreign workers

CESAR E. CHAVEZ

Cesar E. Chavez was born on March 31, 1927, in Yuma, Arizona. In 1962 Chavez founded the National Farm Workers Association (NFWA), a Latino civil-rights (citizens' rights) group based in California. On September 8, 1965, the NFWA led a strike to protest the low wages and terrible working conditions of migrant grape pickers. Migrant workers include both foreign workers and low-income residents born in rural parts of the United States who move regularly in order to find work. During the strike the NFWA combined with Filipino migrant workers to become the United Farm Workers. The grape strike in California lasted five years and, after the migrant workers received verbal support from members of the United States Senate, the workers were awarded higher wages. The strike gained national attention and was considered a major victory for migrant workers. Cesar Chavez died on April 23, 1993, of natural causes. In 2004 the United States Postal Service issued a postal stamp in his honor.

are too old to work productively, the receiving country may send them back to the sending country rather than bearing any cost for supporting them in old age. Many social critics consider this an unfair system.

Foreign laborers are often forced to work and live in hazardous conditions. After mining, farm work is the second most dangerous occupation in the United States. Exposure to pesticides frequently results in chemical infections of the skin, and prolonged overexposure can cause cancer and death. Overcrowded living situations allow for the easy spread of disease. It is not uncommon for migrant workers to be housed in barns, shacks, or even chicken coops and open fields. According to some reports, an average of 40 percent of migrant farm workers in the United States test positive for tuberculosis, and it is estimated that each year over 24,000 migrant workers are injured in the fields. Another study reported that up to 25 percent of foreign workers suffer from psychiatric disorders and that 20 percent of the females in migrant living communities experience physical or sexual abuse.

Recent Trends

After the attacks of September 11, 2001, on the World Trade Center in New York, many countries increased national security and allowed fewer migrant workers across their borders. Workers from the Middle East have had the most difficulty gaining entrance into other countries, especially the United States. Many social activists argued that while increased security is a logical response to widespread violence, migrant workers and immigrants seeking opportunities for work and safe living conditions were being denied basic human rights. In response to debate on this subject, the United Nations held the International Convention on the Protection of the Rights of All Migrant Workers and Members of Their Families, at which a document requiring all countries to inform migrant workers and immigrants of their rights was drafted. No major Western nation signed the document, however. The countries that signed, such as Egypt, Mexico, and the Philippines, were those whose residents tend to emigrate to other countries in large numbers each year.

Government's Role in the Economy

$ Overview: Government's Role in the Economy

What It Means

Over the course of history some governments have attempted to exercise complete control over economic affairs in the interest of accomplishing social or political goals, and other governments have attempted to stay completely out of economic affairs in the belief that economies work best when they are unregulated. Today the roles that most governments play in their national economies fall somewhere between these two extremes.

Most of the world's largest economies today are capitalist; that is, they are systems allowing individuals and businesses to own property and compete with one another in the pursuit of profits and economic well-being. In a capitalist economy producers and consumers make countless individual decisions that together add up to the bigger economic picture. No central authority dictates what goods and services companies produce or sets prices for those goods and services. Instead, the competing forces of sellers (supply) and buyers (demand) result in prices that ultimately dictate what will be produced, how it will be produced and distributed, and who will enjoy the fruits of this production and distribution.

In the United States more than in most countries, people tend to believe that the economy should be shaped by the competing interests of individual businesses and consumers, rather than by government decrees and plans. It is true that governments at the local, state, and national levels in the United States intervene in economic affairs less than their counterparts in many other countries, but they nevertheless play an important role in, and have the power to monumentally alter, the national economy. While local and state governments can have a significant affect on their economies, at the national level the federal government has far more power to alter the economic landscape.

A government typically plays an important role in promoting economic growth and stability. Building roads and other infrastructure is one way it lays the foundation for a modern economic system. *Photograph by Tom Carroll. Phototake NYC. Reproduced by permission.*

JOHN MAYNARD KEYNES

"Long run is a misleading guide to current affairs. In the long run we are all dead."

JOHN MAYNARD KEYNES, *A TRACT ON MONETARY RE-FORM*, 1923.

Why He Is Important

John Maynard Keynes (1883–1946), English economist, was one of the most influential and revolutionary thinkers of the twentieth century. Published in 1936, his most famous work, *The General Theory of Employment, Interest, and Money,* is considered the foundational text in macroeconomics, the study of the behavior of the economy as a whole.

Keynes's economic predecessors generally took the pessimistic view that certain economic problems, such as unemployment, recession, and depression, were necessary evils of free market capitalism to be endured and certainly not to be meddled with or solved. Keynes, however, was an unfailing optimist who believed life was too short to stand by and wait for the economy to work itself out over the long run.

Keynes's radical notion was that the government had an important role to play in regulating and stabilizing the economy: it could stimulate a lagging economy by investing money in public works, by hiring the unemployed, and by cutting taxes so that the public would have more purchasing power (or money to spend), and business owners would be more inclined to hire new employees; conversely, it could rein in a booming economy (whose side effect is inflation) by cutting spending and increasing taxes. These government interventions in the economy comprise what is called fiscal policy.

Ironically, though Keynes approached economics problems as mathematical rather than social in nature, his theories were instrumental in refiguring the economy as an engine for social change.

Life

John Maynard Keynes was born in Cambridge, England, on June 5, 1883, the son of John Neville and Florence Ada Keynes. His father was a noted Cambridge economist and his mother was active in various social causes and city politics. From an early age Keynes distinguished himself as a brilliant student with a particular gift for mathematics. He attended King's College, Cambridge, receiving his degree in mathematics there in 1905. Keynes stayed on at the college the following year to study economics under Alfred Marshall and Arthur Pigou, both of whom influenced him profoundly.

From 1906–08 Keynes worked as a British civil servant in India. He returned to England thereafter and took an economics lectureship at Cambridge, maintaining his affiliation with the university until 1942. In 1911 he was appointed as editor of the Royal Economic Society's esteemed *Economic Journal,* a position he maintained for more than three decades and through which he help to shape the thinking of an entire generation of economists.

In 1917 Keynes took a leave of absence from Cambridge to work for the British Treasury. Immediately recognized for his extraordinary talents, he was able to rise quickly through the ranks and served as the Treasury's principal representative at the Versailles peace conference that ended World War I in 1918–19. Keynes disagreed strongly with the Allies' punitive measures against Germany at that conference. Upon his return to England he unleashed his complaints in *The Economic Consequences of the Peace* (1919), a short but vehement treatise, which warned that the exorbitant war reparations imposed against Germany would cripple the nation's economy, impoverish its people, and cause grave political instability that would threaten all of Europe. With the rise of Nazism, Keynes's warning proved prophetic; at the end of World War II the Allies understood that helping to rebuild vanquished countries was the only way to secure a lasting peace.

Over the course of his career Keynes served as an economic advisor in a variety of influential posts. In addition to his work in economics, he was also at various times a collector of modern art, a

The U.S. government's role in the economy can be broken down into two basic sets of functions: it attempts to promote economic stability and growth, and it attempts to regulate and control the economy. Its tools for promoting stability and growth are fiscal policy (alterations in tax rates and spending programs) and monetary policy (alterations in the amount of money in circulation). The federal government regulates and controls the economy through numerous laws affecting economic activity. These range from laws enforcing private property rights to laws promoting competition among businesses.

When Did It Begin

Aside from the establishment and enforcement of private property rights, which are essential to any capitalist economy (an economy in which businesses and individuals are allowed to compete freely in the pursuit of their own economic well-being), the U.S. government, like its European counterparts, did little to regulate its economy during the eighteenth century and most of the nineteenth. The federal government's hands-off approach to the economy was in keeping with the views of early economists such as Adam Smith (1723–90), who believed that a government best promoted economic well-being when it stayed out of economic affairs. By the late nineteenth century, however, the inhumane conditions to which the increasingly large working class was subjected in the factories and mines of Europe and America led to increased government regulation of industry.

The first two decades of the twentieth century saw the United States, under Presidents Theodore Roosevelt

member of Virginia Woolf's avant-garde literary circle, the Blooms-bury Group, and a patron of the theater. In 1942 he was made a British lord. Keynes died of a heart attack in Sussex, England, on Easter Sunday, April 21, 1946.

John Maynard Keynes is considered the father of macroeconomics, the study of the economy as a whole. He initiated a radical departure from previous economic thought by suggesting that the government can and should intervene in the economy to keep it stable and robust. © *Bettmann/Corbis.*

Work

The 1919 publication of *The Economic Consequences of the Peace* ignited a storm of controversy and launched its author to international fame. In the decade that followed Keynes published several other texts, including *A Tract on Monetary Reform* (1923), *The End of Laissez-Faire* (1926), and *A Treatise on Money* (1930), which laid the groundwork for his magnum opus, *The General Theory of Employment, Interest, and Money.* Published during the depths of the Great Depression (a severe economic downturn in Europe and the United States during the 1930s), the unorthodox views of *General Theory* not only transformed the language and premises of the study of economics but also led to government policies that altered the lives of much of the population of the industrialized world.

The economic measures Keynes outlined required the government to run a budget deficit, meaning that it was spending more money than it was bringing in. Deficit spending was virtually unheard of when Keynes proposed it in the mid-1930s, but it proved so successful in lifting the United States and much of Western Europe out of the Great Depression that policymakers enthusiastically embraced it for decades thereafter.

Legacy

The impact of *The General Theory of Employment, Interest, and Money* was immediate and far reaching. For the originality of its assertions and the magnitude of its implications, it has earned a place alongside Adam Smith's *The Wealth of Nations* (1776) and Karl Marx's *Das Kapital* (1867) as one of the seminal works in economics.

Keynesian economics came under fire in the 1970s, however, when it could not provide a solution to the problem of stagflation (a combination of high inflation and high unemployment). Since then deficit spending has been questioned as a remedy for economic downturns. Still, while Keynes's theories have been endlessly challenged, revised, and expanded, his basic premise—that the government has a responsibility to implement fiscal policy that will stabilize and promote the vitality of the economy—is almost universally accepted.

(1901–09) and Woodrow Wilson (1913–21), more heavily enforce existing industrial regulations and pass new ones, including laws creating many of the regulatory bodies (such as the Food and Drug Administration, the Federal Trade Commission, and the Interstate Commerce Commission) that still regulate businesses today.

Government involvement in the economy became much more pronounced, however, in the aftermath of the Great Depression, the severe economic crisis that crippled the world economy and left approximately 25 percent of American workers jobless during the 1930s. As part of President Franklin D. Roosevelt's (1933–45) New Deal, a set of government efforts meant to revitalize the economy, the federal government backed large-scale public-works projects that employed out-of-work Americans, and it began making transfer payments (direct financial aid) to citizens through such programs as Social Security, which benefits the elderly and the disabled. Both of these forms of spending had the effect of putting money in people's pockets, which gave businesses an incentive to increase their activity, at the same time that the programs provided much-needed relief to those suffering the effects of unemployment. Additionally, the New Deal included the establishment of important regulatory bodies such as the Securities and Exchange Commission, which oversees the stock market, and the Federal Deposit Insurance Corporation, which insures people who deposit money in banks.

More Detailed Information

The U.S. government influences economic growth and stability through the use of fiscal policy (manipulating tax rates and spending programs) and monetary policy (manipulating the amount of money in circulation). It uses these tools with the intent of steering the economy toward conditions of steady growth, low unemployment, and stable prices.

Fiscal policy consists of alterations to tax rates and spending programs. These alterations are proposed and passed by the U.S. Congress and the president; as such, they are often subject to political priorities as much as economic ones. When the government raises taxes, money moves out of private hands and into government coffers. Thus, people have less money to spend, and they demand lesser quantities of products. Businesses produce less, and the economy slows. When the government cuts taxes, private citizens and businesses have more money to spend and invest, and this tends to spur economic growth. Likewise, government spending (on military equipment, education, scientific research, and transfer payments, for example) moves money out of government coffers and into private hands. This stimulates demand and encourages economic growth. Cuts in government spending have the opposite effect.

Monetary policy consists of alterations in the money supply. The central bank of the United States, the Federal Reserve System (often called the Fed), has the sole power to regulate the money supply, and it operates independently of the president and Congress, focusing on economic rather than political concerns. When more money is in circulation, the economy tends to grow. When the money supply is restricted, the economy tends to slow down. The Fed does not increase the size of the money supply simply by ordering more dollar bills printed. Instead, it primarily uses its influence over banks and other lending institutions to change the size of the money supply.

The money supply includes not simply coins and bills but also the bank-account balances against which people can write checks or make withdrawals. One group of people who possess this form of money is depositors, those who hand over their paychecks and other money to a bank for safe keeping. Banks do not simply store this money, though. They lend it out to borrowers, people and businesses who want to make large purchases, such as purchases of real estate or business equipment. When a bank loans money, the borrower is, like a depositor, given a bank account balance against which he or she can write checks or make withdrawals. By loaning money, then, a bank literally creates money: a borrower is given money to spend, in the form of an account balance, even though no new bills or coins have been minted.

When the Fed wants to increase or decrease the money supply, therefore, it lowers or raises interest rates, the fees that borrowers pay for the use of money. The lower interest rates fall, the more inclined people are to borrow money, and the more money banks put into circulation. The higher interest rates climb, the less inclined borrowers become to pay for the use of money, and the amount of money in circulation falls.

In addition to these active forms of intervention into the economy, the federal government has wide-ranging regulatory responsibilities over private businesses. Traditionally, the government has regulated industries such as utilities, where one company tends to have a monopoly (sole control over the industry) in a given region. The government has often set limits on prices to prevent utility monopolies from raising prices at will. Other industries have historically been subject to price controls. Examples include agricultural producers, trucking, and airlines.

The government has also, since the early twentieth century, sought to prevent monopolies from forming. In general, consumers and the economy as a whole benefit when there is a high level of competition in any industry. To compete with one another for customers, firms must price their goods fairly and produce high-quality products; when a company has a monopoly, on the other hand, it naturally tends to focus solely on assuring its own profits, regardless of the interests of consumers or economic efficiency. If two companies want to merge, but the resulting company threatens to become a monopoly, the government has the power to intervene to prevent the merger. Likewise, if two dominant companies conspire to keep prices artificially high, the government is empowered to intervene.

Social goals, such as consumer health and environmental protection, also serve as the basis for a substantial amount of government regulation. Government agencies monitor companies' environmental impact, the safety of food and drug supplies, and workplace conditions.

Recent Trends

Having discovered during the Depression that fiscal policy could be effective at creating demand and stimulating the economy, the U.S. government primarily used fiscal policy to manage the economy and bring it through recessions (periods of slow economic growth typically accompanied by increased unemployment) in the following decades. Focusing so intently on lessening the impact of recessions (and on preventing depressions), the government perhaps paid less attention to inflation (the rising of prices across the economy) than was warranted. Out-of-control inflation in the 1970s threatened to dislocate the economy as badly as any recession, especially since it corresponded, as had never been the case before, with high unemployment.

Fiscal policies could do nothing to turn the tide of these problems, and economists began paying more attention to the effects of managing the money supply. Inflation was brought under control through a severe reduction of the money supply (which threw the country into recession in 1982), and has never since been a serious problem. Monetary policy, accordingly, has replaced fiscal policy as the government's primary tool for shaping the economy.

The latter part of the twentieth century also saw a wave of deregulation. The relatively tight control that the government had exerted on the utility, transportation, and other industries was relaxed. This was partly due to concerns that government regulation prevented companies from responding to market forces in a way that would force them to innovate and remain efficient. It was partly due to the appearance of new technologies in industries like communications, which allowed new companies to compete in fields such as telecommunications that had once tended naturally toward monopoly conditions.

More controversial was the tendency of the U.S. government, under conservative presidents such as Ronald Reagan, whose term ran from 1981 to 1989, George H. W. Bush, who served from 1989 to 1993, and George W. Bush, 2001–09, to pursue the relaxation of regulation that had been proposed for social reasons. The Reagan and George W. Bush administrations were particularly aggressive at trying to eliminate environmental, workplace, and consumer protections.

BASIC RESPONSIBILITIES

$ Private Property and Property Rights

What It Means

One of the most basic conditions necessary for a capitalist economic system (in which people are allowed to pursue profit and in which market forces such as supply and demand dictate most of the system's features) is the existence of private property and clear property rights.

Property is anything that can be owned; it can be tangible (land, house, car, computer, shoes, carrots) or intangible (a bank-account balance, an investment such as a share of stock in a company, the patent on an invention). Private property is property that is owned by an individual or group of individuals (such as a company or corporation), rather than by the government or society at large. The legal systems of all nations have rules regarding the ownership of property and answering questions regarding who is entitled to use, profit from, sell, and otherwise take advantage of the various things that people can own. These rules amount to a system of property rights, which define the extent to which any given country supports private ownership of property.

Property laws are meant to establish peaceful means of competing for property. Instead of killing one another to take possession of land or shares of stock, people who live in a nation with clear and enforceable property rights can compete for these items in a market setting. This means that forces such as supply and demand set prices, and ownership can be transferred from one person to one another in exchange for money.

In a system without private property, the risks and rewards of economic activity diminish. For example, if a tire company is owned by the government, the head of that company has little incentive to push for efficiency and high quality, because he does not get to claim the profits from the tire making. By contrast, a system that promotes private ownership of property encourages economic efficiency. The owner of a tire company risks poverty if his products do not sell and he has to shut his company down, and he stands to enrich himself if he can sell a large number of tires at a high rate of profit. These pressures will theoretically spur him to organize his business and manufacture tires in the most efficient way possible, and to ensure that the final product is of good quality.

When Did It Begin

One of the earliest thinkers to deal with the notion that we now call private property was the ancient Greek philosopher Aristotle. In his work *Politics*, Aristotle pointed out the tendency of people not to respect or maintain property that was public. Likewise, he noted, when people are required to share equally both the burdens and rewards of property ownership, there is a high likelihood that they will become displeased over disparities in workloads and rewards. While humans came into conflict over many issues, Aristotle observed, they were especially likely to do so over issues arising from common ownership of property.

Western systems of property rights evolved from classical Roman law as it was established in the years 1 through 250 AD. The Romans defined a concept called *dominium*, or *proprietas* (ownership), which acknowledged the current possessor of a thing to have certain rights, powers, and privileges to do what he wanted with that thing. Current notions of property rights are further based on laws created in England at the end of the twelfth century. During this time the feudal lords who owned estates began granting tenants (people who farmed or used a certain portion of an estate but were not the ultimate owners) certain rights over the land that they were allowed to use. Previously lords could dictate tenants' rights as they pleased, but the laws that evolved during this period essentially limited the lord's control to the collecting of rent payments. Some experts believe that this bestowing of rights on individual tenants, rather than only on aristocrats, paved the way for the modern legal approach toward property rights, in which these powers are one of the individual's basic rights.

Still, tenants on aristocrats' land in medieval England did not have rights equal to those of their lords, and property rights were not absolute. It was not uncommon for a king or queen (in England or anywhere else in the Middle Ages) to strip people of their possessions if they

Private property is anything owned by an individual or group of individuals, not the government. The owner of private land is legally entitled to restrict access to his or her property and to put up fences and "No Trespassing" signs *AP Images*.

were perceived as a threat to the monarchy. Private property as we know it today (for example, land that could be freely bought, sold, and rented) did not come into being until around the sixteenth century. With the rise of capitalism in the sixteenth through eighteenth centuries, and with the great expansion of capitalism in the nineteenth and twentieth centuries, clearly defined property rights increasingly became a priority in the Western world.

More Detailed Information

Private property is commonly divided, by law, into different types. One of the most important distinctions is between real and personal property. Real property is land and those things permanently attached to the land, such as buildings. Personal property includes all objects that can be moved. In other words, a person's house and yard are considered real property and are subject to certain laws, while everything he or she owns that is not attached to the house or yard is considered personal property and is subject to different, but related, laws.

An owner's private-property rights consist of three basic elements: the exclusive right to choose how prop-

erty will be used, the exclusive right to any benefits derived from property, and the right to exchange property with someone else on terms that are mutually agreeable to the two parties.

In a society that entitled owners to complete private-property rights, an owner of a building would have the right to decide whether to live in that building herself, rent it out to others, renovate it, or tear it down. If she chose to rent it out, she alone would have the right to benefit (that is, to collect rent payments). And if she wanted to sell it for the highest price the real estate market would support, or to give it away to a homeless person, she would have the legal right to conduct these exchanges of her property.

Complete private-property rights do not, however, actually exist in the modern world. National, state, and local governments commonly restrict property rights to some extent. They do so for a variety of reasons, including political traditions and beliefs, the desire to promote the well-being of a community, and the need to combat social problems.

In the realm of real property, most governments (including the U.S. federal government and many state and local governments) increasingly imposed restrictions during the twentieth century. For example, private-property rights are restricted in some cities in the form of rent controls, which prevents owners of certain buildings from demanding whatever rent prices the market will allow. Instead, rent controls limit the amount of rent some landlords can charge, with the intent of preserving affordable housing options when prices rise. Likewise, there are numerous zoning requirements that specify the uses to which certain properties might be put. For instance, cities and towns of all sizes often restrict commercial uses of property to certain streets in order to preserve a residential feel in other parts of town. Zoning codes often specify what kinds of buildings can be constructed in various areas, the quality level of the materials to be used, and the methods according to which structures must be built.

Land and buildings are one of the most regulated forms of property, but they are hardly the only things that fall under the laws concerning property rights. Almost all tangible items can be private property and are subject to government protections and regulation. For example, you have the exclusive right to use, benefit from, and exchange a car once you have purchased it, although these rights are subject to specific laws (requiring registration, licensing, and insurance, among other things) meant to promote public safety. Some tangible things, such as rivers and the air, cannot be owned, but the owner of land adjacent to them might have certain rights to and responsibilities for them. The government might intervene, for instance, if a landowner pollutes a river or the air near his property.

Many intangible things can be owned as well. Some of the most important of these relate to money. Bank-account balances, for example, are not physical objects. They are numerical quantities that exist in computers. Yet it is very important that your right to ownership of these numbers be protected and regulated. If the bank could simply delete your balance at any time or give it away to someone a bank director liked better than you, the banking system obviously could not survive. Similarly, there are highly detailed laws concerning the buying and selling of stock in companies. A stock is nothing more than a contract between an investor and a company, according to which the investor is said to own a portion of the company that may be bought and sold. A stock is, in itself, worth nothing, but the contract that it represents can be worth a great deal. Stocks can dramatically increase or decrease in value (generally increasing in value when a company thrives and decreasing in value when a company struggles), enriching or impoverishing the people who own them. The government therefore takes an active role in regulating and enforcing the property rights of stockholders.

Another form of intangible private property recognized by many governments is intellectual property. If a

SOCIALISM

The political doctrine of socialism can take many forms, but all of them are based on some amount of opposition to the concept of private property. Socialists have generally promoted the creation of an economic system that prioritizes the well-being of all members of the community over the right of individuals to own property and create wealth for themselves. Some socialists, as well as communists, have advocated for complete government ownership of all private property, while others, such as social democrats, have argued for selective government control that modifies the negative effects of capitalism (an economic system that champions the individual's right to make a profit).

The collapse of the Soviet Union in 1989 resulted in large part from the failure of its state-owned and state-run economic system. Social democracies in countries such as Sweden and Norway were, by contrast, better positioned to adapt to the realities of modern economic life at the end of the twentieth century and the beginning of the twenty-first. These countries were characterized, at that time, by stable and strong economies that provided high levels of social benefits (such as universal health care and low costs of living) through selective government control of property and the economy.

person writes a novel, for instance, she has certain rights regarding other people's ability to reproduce, quote from, or make that novel into a movie. When someone buys a physical copy of the novel, they do not own the ideas and words that appear on the page; the author and publisher do.

Recent Trends

One controversial form of government restriction of property rights in the United States is eminent domain. Eminent domain is the doctrine allowing the government to seize an individual's private property for public use. The government must pay a fair price for the property, but the individual does not have the option to maintain ownership. The construction of highways, for instance, has often necessitated that the government seize land through which the roadway passes.

Beginning in 1954, however, the definition of "public use" was expanded as a result of the Supreme Court's ruling in the case *Berman v. Parker*. In this case, the Supreme Court upheld the District of Columbia's attempt to demolish a neighborhood consisting of some blighted (neglected or abandoned) and some non-blighted homes, for the purpose of letting someone else build a shopping center on the site. "Public use" was interpreted to include the public benefit that would arise from eliminating blighted properties, even though the property was being taken from private individuals and given to other private individuals.

Since that time the U.S. courts have consistently allowed for a further broadening of the definition of public use. In New London, Connecticut, the owners of 115 properties were forced to sell their land and homes to the local government so that a complex consisting of a hotel and conference center, a state park, and new residences could be built. The city claimed that the economic growth that would be generated by the project outweighed the individuals' property rights, but 15 of the owners refused to sell, and 9 eventually took their legal concerns to the Supreme Court. In 2005 the Supreme Court ruled in *Kelo v. City of New London* that the government could seize land for the purposes of promoting economic development even if property was not blighted.

This case sparked increasing public awareness of the possible abuses of eminent domain. Critics of the decision felt that it empowered wealthy real estate developers at the expense of private citizens and especially the poor. Many states, in response to such concerns, moved to pass legislation limiting the use of eminent-domain powers.

$ Creation of Public Goods

What It Means

In order for a good (a product or a service) to be a public good, two conditions must be met. First, the good must be nonrival. This means that if one individual uses the product or service, the supply available to other users is not diminished, so there is no rivalry or competition for the good. In this sense air is a public good because one individual who breathes air does not significantly reduce the amount of air available to other individuals. The light from a lighthouse is also a nonrival public good. If one sea captain uses the light to sail into port, that captain does not diminish the amount of light available to another captain who may also need the light; the two captains are not rivals or competitors for the light. Second, the good must be nonexcludable. This means that once the good is produced or the service is created, the manufacturer cannot prevent anyone from using it. A fireworks show is an example of a nonexcludable service. The organization setting off the fireworks cannot prevent people from looking up at the sky to witness the show. Police and firefighting forces, as well as the national defense, are considered nonexcludable public goods.

The opposite of a public good is a private good. Such goods are exhaustible, and therefore consumers compete for them. For example, once a can of soup or a piece of cake is consumed, less of that good is available to others. Also, it is possible for the manufacturer of a private good to exclude people from its use. With private goods anyone unwilling or unable to pay the asking price is excluded from using the good.

When Did It Begin

The lighthouse is one of the most frequently mentioned examples of a public good. These towerlike structures send light out to sea to help ship captains navigate at night. Lighthouses can send a number of different signals. Their light can warn a captain of a dangerous coastline, mark the entry point of a harbor, or indicate a shoal (a dangerously shallow area of water). The earliest lighthouses sent their signals by fire and later with kerosene lamps. These lamps were replaced by a system of rotating lenses that cast beams out to sea at a series of angles. Lighthouse keepers were required to wind a clockwork mechanism to set the system in motion. By the turn of the twentieth century, these systems were automated, and lighthouse keepers gradually became obsolete. Though at one time lighthouses were a crucial part of safe sea travel, only about 1,500 operational lighthouses exist today. One of the oldest and most famous lighthouses was the Lighthouse of Alexandria, which was built in the third century BC. Standing more than 400 feet high on the island of Pharos off the coast of Alexandria, Egypt, this structure lasted for over a thousand years and was for many centuries the tallest man-made building in the world.

More Detailed Information

Economic theorists often argue that there is no such thing as a pure public good, that no good or service is entirely nonrival and nonexcludable. They believe that even air and drinking water, both of which appear to be pure public goods, fail to meet the definition of a pure public good. It is possible, for example, to exclude or limit people's access to clean air. This frequently happens in large cities, where people from the lower classes reside in smoggier, more polluted neighborhoods, and wealthier people enjoy the cleaner air of the suburbs. Though the government cannot legally prevent a poor person from breathing clean suburban air, poor people who do not own automobiles may have limited access to the suburbs. With regard to drinking water, there is competition for this resource. While drinking from a stream does not significantly diminish the amount of water in the stream available to others, there is a limited supply of bottled drinking water. When one person buys a bottle of water at the supermarket, there is one less bottle available to other buyers. In many of the world's cities, bottled water is the only safe water to drink, and it is not made equally available to all citizens.

One example of a public good that is not considered a pure public good is the World Wide Web. In many ways (but not all) a website is nonrival and nonexcludable. First, a website is nonrival in that if one person examines it, that person's visit to the site does prevent others from looking at it. In other words one visitor does not use the site up and leave less of it for the next visitor. In fact, a nearly unlimited number of people can examine a website at the same time. If there is merchandise for sale on the website, however, those goods are considered private goods, not public goods. For instance, if a person visits Amazon.com and buys a book, there is one less book available to rival shoppers. Thus, the goods on Amazon.com are exhaustible, but the website itself is not. Many websites are nonexcludable. This means that the people who own and operate the site have no control over who visits it. Many websites require a password, however, and those that do are excluding visitors from examining their content.

Private businesses that seek profits have little incentive to create public goods because of what is called the free-rider problem. This term refers to the tendency of consumers to obtain goods and services for free if given the chance. Fireworks displays provide a clear illustration of the free-rider problem. A consumer is unlikely to pay a five-dollar admission fee to stand in a fenced-off area of a field to watch the show if it is possible to stand on the other side of the fence and still witness the pyrotechnics. The people who watch without paying admission are free riders. Two other arenas in which the free-rider problem exists are law enforcement and the construction and maintenance of roads. No private business could provide the protection of the law to those who could pay and not to those who couldn't, nor could a business prevent people from using roads unless they paid. For this reason local and national governments take responsibility for providing these public services, raising the money for them through taxes.

Recent Trends

Since the inception of the Internet in the mid-1990s, many people have used it to provide for the public good. Groups of people have worked together to post information and other resources on websites so that web users can access these items for free. In a process known as commons-based peer production, volunteers working separately contribute portions of a larger project to a review board, which examines the material and then posts appropriate submissions on the Internet. There it is made available to anyone who visits the website. These collaborative efforts have been responsible for posting computer software programming code, scientific data, reviews of new books and movies, and library reference materials, among other things, on the World Wide Web for public use. The book reviews available on Amazon.com are an example of commons-based peer production. Anyone who visits Amazon.com can review one of the books for sale there. Online shoppers can then read the reviews posted below the book and determine whether or not they wish to purchase the book. ClickWorkers is a website sponsored by NASA (the National Aeronautics and Space Administration) that asks volunteers to analyze data collected on space missions. Participants do not need to be trained scientists. Their work helps scientists

---

NATIONAL PUBLIC RADIO

Created in 1970, following the passage of the Public Broadcasting Act of 1967, National Public Radio (NPR) became the first nationwide, noncommercial radio network in the United States. It has more than 800 member stations in all 50 states. NPR's mission is to provide high-quality news, cultural, scientific, business, and entertainment programming to the American public. The network acquires funding from government grants, corporate underwriting, and listener donations. Because of its diverse funding platform, NPR is not as dependent on revenue from corporate sponsors as regular commercial radio stations are on revenue from business advertising. The network's relative independence from corporate influence has contributed to its reputation as one of the most trusted news sources in the United States.

NPR is a prime example of a public good because it is nonrival (meaning that one person's enjoyment of the radio does not in any way diminish the supply of radio available to others) and nonexcludable (meaning that the radio stations that produce the programming cannot prevent anyone with a radio, or within earshot of a radio, from listening).

---

review and classify such data as pictures taken of Mars's topography.

PROBLEM OF FREE RIDERS

What It Means

The problem of free riders is an economic dilemma that emerges in situations involving what economists call public goods. A public good is a product or service that, in being made available to one person, can be freely enjoyed by others. People cannot be easily prevented from using the good, and one person's use of the good does not diminish its usefulness to other people. For example, if Jane's neighborhood association pools money to build new sidewalks, everyone in the neighborhood will benefit equally. Jane's enjoyment of the sidewalks does not prohibit her neighbors' enjoyment of the sidewalks in the way that her use of a car prevents her neighbor from using that particular car.

If, however, Jane suspects that the project will still go ahead even without her contribution to the neighborhood association's pool of money, she may decide not to pay her share because she knows that she will still get the benefits of the new, smooth sidewalks anyway. Jane has chosen, in this situation, to be what is known as a free rider. If a large proportion of her neighbors made the same calculation that Jane made and chose not to pay their share, the new sidewalks might not get built.

Certain goods and services, such as parks and the national defense, are considered public goods because everyone can benefit from them, and no one can be excluded. In order to prevent free riders—people, for example, who would be kept safe by national defense but who would not want to pay for it—governments force people to fund public goods with taxes. *AP Images.*

In situations involving public goods, economists, governments, and other interested parties must address the problem of free riders: that is, they must consider ways of discouraging free-riding, of guarding against its negative effects, or both.

When Did It Begin

Thinkers in a wide variety of contexts have, throughout the history of civilization, addressed the problems arising from public goods. Some scholars suggest that the logic behind free-riding is embodied by the arguments of Glaucon, a character in Plato's *Republic* (c. 360 BC; Plato, who lived from approximately 428 to 348 BC, was an important ancient Greek philosopher, and one of his best-known works is *The Republic*, which concerns the form that a model society should take). Glaucon suggests that people have no reason to obey laws if they can be certain that they will not be caught or, if caught, that they will not be punished.

The founder of economics, Scottish philosopher Adam Smith (1723–90), wrote at length in his land-mark work *An Inquiry into the Nature and Causes of the Wealth of Nations* (1776) about the public benefits that arise when individuals independently pursue their own self-interest. His treatment of this topic suggests an understanding of the concept of public goods, but Smith saw the positive effects of the phenomenon more clearly than the potential problems. Smith's friend and contemporary, the Scottish philosopher David Hume (1711–76), had an earlier and more thorough grasp of what we now call the free-rider problem. In *A Treatise of Human Nature* (1739–40), Hume noted that, though two neighbors might agree to share the burden of draining a meadow they own together, trying to get a thousand people to agree on any common project and on their share of the burden would be all but impossible.

Since that time the problem of the free rider has been a fixture in popular notions of human nature. Economists and other social scientists only began analyzing the problem in detail in the latter part of the twentieth century, however, after the publication of *The Logic of Collective Action* (1965) by American economist Mancur Olson (1932–98). Olson dealt thoroughly with what motivates individuals in the realm of collective action and public goods, and his theories have inspired detailed study of the conflicts between private drives and public goals in the decades since.

More Detailed Information

The problem of free riders emerges in many situations involving public goods, but it becomes a bigger problem, generally, as the number of people who share in the use of a particular good grows. The phenomenon of neighbors cooperating to fix sidewalks or otherwise improve their common living conditions is a fairly common one in today's world. The frequent success of these projects probably results from the fact that a relatively small number of people are usually involved. When a small group of people band together to solve some problem, each individual's participation is often vital to the success of the project.

If the sidewalk project in Jane's neighborhood involves five square blocks' worth of houses, Jane may understand that the project will not go forward if she does not pay her share. If she wants the benefit of sidewalks, then she has an incentive to pay her share. If the sidewalk project encompasses twenty square blocks of houses, however, Jane may feel that her participation is less vital and that she may as well save her money and enjoy the new sidewalks without contributing.

Voting in national elections is commonly influenced by the problem of free riders. Jane's political beliefs may be strong, and she may want a certain candidate to be elected president of the United States, but she may feel that the large number of votes cast means that one measly vote cannot possibly have any effect on the ultimate outcome. Jane chooses to avoid the effort of taking time off work to go to the polls, trusting others to cast their votes for her candidate and bring about the outcome that she wants; or she may not vote because she doesn't believe her vote can help her candidate win. If a large number of people feel as Jane does, the results of the elections will not reflect the desires of the voters.

Another factor that can encourage people to free ride is if the difficulty or expense of the burden they are being asked to share seems too great. For instance, if Jane's neighbors want to fix the sidewalks on their own and they ask Jane to contribute 20 hours of heavy labor in addition to money for materials, she would be much more likely to free ride than if she only had to contribute a small amount of money and no labor. Because of this phenomenon efforts encouraging people to vote often address the ease of voting. Polling places frequently open early and stay open late to enhance the convenience of voting, and there are no registration or other fees required to vote.

Solutions to free-rider problems are often devised by governments. National defense is a classic example of a public good that would flounder under the free-rider problem if the government did not step in. It is a public

---

PRIVATE SOLUTIONS TO THE PROBLEM OF FREE RIDERS

The problem of free riders is a dilemma that results when one person enjoys the benefits of a public good (a product or service that is enjoyed by the public at large) without contributing his or her fair share to the purchase or creation of that good. While in some cases, such as national defense (a public good that cannot be trusted to voluntary contributions from individual citizens), the government steps in to minimize the negative effects of free-riding, some economists argue that solutions to the free-rider problem can often be accomplished within the realm of private business.

For example, public lakes are often polluted, but individual users of a public lake have no economic incentive to contribute their own effort and money to keeping that lake clean. A private owner of a lake, however, could charge fees for entrance to the lake's beaches and boat ramps, set limits on how many people are allowed to use and thus impact the lake's environment, and put the proceeds toward keeping the lake clean.

---

good in that no one can be prevented from enjoying it and in that one person's enjoyment of it does not prevent another person's enjoyment of it. The amount of money and effort required to protect a nation from invasion and turmoil is immense, however. An effective national defense simply would not result from the self-interested actions of private individuals, so the government collects taxes and undertakes the burden of defending the nation's people independently of individual attitudes toward the problem.

Recent Trends

In the early twenty-first century one of the public goods most susceptible to the problem of free riders is the health of the natural environment. Although most people accept that such threats as global warming and air pollution are serious issues and cannot be ignored, individual Americans are generally unwilling to do their part to bring about such desired public goods as clean air and reduced carbon emissions (carbon emissions, which contribute to global warming, are the pollutants that result from burning fossil fuels, such as coal and oil). Jane may be worried about global warming, but she may not be willing to change her lifestyle to help decrease it (by taking public transportation to work and by minimizing her plane travel and use of air conditioning, for instance) because she believes that she alone can do little to solve the problem. Meanwhile, many other people are making the same calculation as Jane, and the problem continues to grow. Addressing global warming requires vast changes in the habits of typical Americans, and most economists agree that only government has the power to solve the problem of free riders under these circumstances.

$ Fiscal Policy

What It Means

Two of the main ways that a government influences its nation's economy are fiscal policy and monetary policy. Fiscal policy consists of a country's taxation and spending programs. In the United States these are developed and implemented by the legislative and executive branches of government (Congress and the president). Monetary policy, meanwhile, is a government's effort to affect the country's money supply (the quantity of money circulating in the economy), and it is crafted and carried out by a nation's central bank (in the United States the central bank is called the Federal Reserve System).

The two tools used in fiscal policy, taxing and spending, represent opposite directions of money movement. When the government collects taxes from citizens, money is transferred from the public to the central government. This can help combat inflation (the general rising of prices), which weakens an economy. When the government spends money (for example, on Social Security payments, highway construction, or weapons for national defense), money moves from the government back into the public sphere. This can stimulate a sluggish economy by encouraging people to spend money.

Fiscal policy can therefore be either expansionary or contractionary. Expansionary fiscal policy increases the amount of economic activity and is accomplished by increasing government spending, lowering taxes, or by a combination of both. Contractionary fiscal policy decreases the amount of money held by private citizens, and it is accomplished by cutting government spending or raising taxes or by a combination of both.

When Did It Begin

National governments have always engaged in taxing and spending, but it was not until the rise of Keynesian economics during the Great Depression (the worldwide economic decline that occurred in the 1930s) that governments began using fiscal policy to spur changes in their economies. Keynesian economics is a theory named after the British economist John Maynard Keynes (1883–1946). In his 1936 book *The General Theory of Employment, Interest, and Money,* Keynes said that a government could use expansionary or contractionary fiscal policy to alter the level of aggregate demand (the total demand for all goods and services in an economy). Adjusting demand, Keynes believed, was the best way to solve problems in an economy. During the Depression, for example, one-third of the labor force was out of work.

Because American consumers had little money to spend, there was little demand for the goods that U.S. factories could produce. Keynes argued that governments could alleviate an economic crisis of this kind by creating consumer demand through government spending. Once the government transferred money to the citizens, people would demand more goods and services, businesses would raise output, and the economy could get back on its feet.

The United States' recovery from the Depression seemed to validate the Keynesian approach to fiscal policy. The increased spending that was part of President Franklin D. Roosevelt's New Deal programs in the 1930s produced marked improvements in the U.S. economy. Full recovery from the Depression came with World War II (1939–45), when dramatically increased government spending on defense led to an economic boom. In the 1950s and 1960s the United States had a long period of postwar prosperity, and at the same time Keynesian demand-side ideology (so called because it focuses on raising demand) was the dominant economic theory.

More Detailed Information

Fiscal policy, whether it is expansionary or contractionary, can be divided into discretionary and nondiscretionary forms.

Discretionary fiscal policy involves purposefully altering taxation and spending programs in order to change aggregate demand and regulate the economy. The spending increases undertaken by the Roosevelt administration to combat the effects of the Depression were examples of discretionary fiscal policy; they were put in place to achieve a specific economic result. Likewise, when a president or Congressional representative argues that taxes should be cut in order to stimulate the economy, he or she is attempting to use discretionary fiscal policy.

Both of these examples, moreover, represent expansionary fiscal policy undertaken to combat a sluggish economy. But discretionary fiscal policy can also be contractionary, or employed to battle inflation (the general rising of prices that can be brought on by vigorous economic growth). If, for instance, a president's economic advisers believed that inflation was getting out of hand, the president could either reduce government spending or raise taxes, either of which would decrease aggregate demand (by transferring wealth out of the public's hands and into the government's bank account) and rein in the economy.

Nondiscretionary forms of fiscal policy, commonly called automatic stabilizers, are tools of fiscal policy that work to stabilize the economy without any changes in taxation or spending levels. The established spending programs that provide citizens with unemployment and welfare benefits, for example, are automatic stabilizers.

When the economy is struggling, more people file for these forms of government aid, and the payments these people receive help to diminish the effects of unemployment on the overall economy. When the economy picks back up again and people find jobs, government spending on these programs automatically falls. Taxes also work as automatic stabilizers. Under good economic conditions, jobs are created, people are more universally employed, and wages rise. As a result, the government collects more income tax from citizens, offsetting the economic growth and protecting against inflation. The reverse holds true for a stagnant economy.

Recent Trends

The Keynesian approach to fiscal policy has always been controversial, and although it dominated economic thought and government from the 1940s through the 1970s, it was partially blamed for the 1970s phenomenon known as stagflation, when both unemployment and inflation rose. Inflation usually occurs during times of economic expansion; the term *stagflation* was coined to describe the unusual situation of inflation occurring during a stagnant economic period. Ronald Reagan, elected president in 1980, ushered in an economic approach known as supply-side economics. Unlike the Keynesian idea of regulating aggregate demand and thereby controlling the economy, supply-side economics holds that the government should play no role in affecting demand. Instead, supply-siders contend, increasing aggregate supply (the total amount of goods and services produced by businesses in the economy) encourages simultaneous growth in an economy's output, full employment, and low prices.

The most common tool of supply-siders, however, is tax cuts, which is also a Keynesian tool for managing aggregate demand. The two opposing economic viewpoints interpret tax cuts differently, however. In the supply-side view, tax cuts are noteworthy not for the effect they have on demand but rather because they motivate people to work and invest their money. An increase in income, according to the supply-side theory, encourages workers to put in more hours and take less time off. More work done by more people produces more goods and services (in other words, it causes an increase in aggregate supply). Workers will have more income to deposit in their bank accounts, which leads to increases in the number of loans banks can make to people who want to start or expand their businesses, which in turn leads to further increases in supply.

Supply-side tax cuts also often target businesses directly. For instance, the Reagan administration instituted tax credits (amounts of money that can be subtracted from one's total tax payment) for businesses that invested in new equipment, new facilities, or increased research. The intended result was increased capacity to produce goods and services.

THE BUDGET

A government's approach toward taxation and spending is its fiscal policy, and the actions it takes in the realm of fiscal policy can be seen in the federal budget, the documentation of the government's revenues and expenditures. Since the start of the twentieth century the character of the U.S. budget has changed several times.

For much of its history, the United States has run a budget deficit. In other words, the government usually spends more money than it takes in. Until about 1970 deficits corresponded roughly to wartime (when the government increased defense spending dramatically) and economic downturns (when the government collected fewer taxes), and times of peace and economic expansion brought budget surpluses (that is, the government took in more money than it spent). Between 1970 and 1997, however, even though the United States was primarily at peace, the budget deficit ballooned whether the economy was expanding or not, reaching $290 billion in 1997. During the economic boom of the 1990s, this situation was reversed: in 1998 the U.S. budget ran a surplus for the first time since 1969. That first year's surplus ($69 billion) grew to $125 billion in 1999 and $236 billion in 2000. But this was to be the last surplus year for some time. The economic downturn of 2001–02, spending on the wars in Afghanistan and Iraq, and a series of tax cuts instituted by President George W. Bush worked together to bring the federal budget deficit back to record heights. In 2005 the estimated budget deficit was $319 billion.

$ Government Spending

What It Means

Government spending represents an enormous part of any modern economy. In 2006, for example, the U.S. government spent 36 percent of the country's gross domestic product, or GDP (the monetary value of all the products and services that are bought and sold in an economy over the course of a year). Although a third of the economy might seem like a lot, other governments that year spent a much higher percentage of their country's GDP. In Germany the percentage was 47 percent, and in Sweden it was 56.7 percent. Spending per GDP tends to be lower in developing, or poorer, countries.

All governments, regardless of size, must spend money in order to operate. Much of their money goes toward social programs, national defense, infrastructure, and other expenditures that contribute to the general well-being of its citizens. Because government spending is so large, its effect on the economy is profound. By spending money, the government makes important decisions about what products and services are provided

All governments spend money to pay for their services, from national defense to financial assistance for needy families. Government spending, for example, funded the computers here in the Alameda High School library in California. *AP Images.*

in the economy and who benefits from these products and services.

In the United States more than half of government spending is at the national level, with the remainder done by state and local governments. The largest expense for state and local governments is typically education, followed by welfare (partially funded by the national government), highways, healthcare and hospitals, public safety (police, fire departments, jails, and prisons) transportation (roads, highways, and airports), sewer systems, and parks and recreation. Some expenses are large, such as funding a public university, and other are comparatively tiny, such as a fireworks display on the Fourth of July.

A third of all U.S. government spending at the national level goes toward taking care of the elderly. This is done through two programs: Social Security, which provides income to people generally over the age of 65, and Medicare, which reimburses the cost of much of their healthcare. National defense represents another fifth of the national government's budget. Other large expenses at the national level are "income security" (for example, welfare and public pension benefits), Medicaid (healthcare for people with low incomes), and interest owed on the national debt (the government borrows money when it does not collect enough revenue through taxes, and it

has to pay interest, or a fee, on that debt). Smaller but important expenditures include funding regulatory agencies, such as the Securities and Exchange Commission (which monitors financial markets), the Environmental Protection Agency (which addresses such environmental problems as pollution), and the Consumer Product Safety Commission (which tries to protect consumers against safety risks in consumer products).

Governments finance their spending largely through taxes. Whether it is a tax on income, property, or the sale of a product, the end result is the same: governments require citizens to send them money to pay for their spending. Although everyone benefits from some aspect of government spending, the government does not have the same competitive pressure to restrain costs that businesses do, and concerns about wasteful government spending are common.

When Did It Begin

Government spending is as old as the formation of government itself. The Code of Ur-Nammu, which is believed to have been written sometime between 2100 and 2050 BC in Mesopotamia (now in modern-day Iraq), is the oldest-known collection of laws. In the prologue carved onto the tablet, King Ur-Nammu of Ur (a city in southern Mesopotamia) invokes all of the deities that ruled the city before him and notes how one of those gods established a spending budget for the city's temple, which was regarded as a part of the city's governing body. After noting how many sheep and how much butter the members of the temple are permitted to barter (exchange), Ur-Nammu goes on to explain the units and subunits of the civilization's exchange system.

As is the case with any modern government, the United States has operated on a budget since its foundation. Throughout most of its history, the country has maintained a high level of debt, which means that more often than not the U.S. government spends more money than it takes in. For example, by 1791 the national debt was reported to be almost $75.5 million. The debt grew for most of the early 1800s before it was eliminated in 1835, only to grow back up to $65 million by the start of the Civil War (1861–65). During the war the debt soared, eclipsing the $1 billion mark in 1863 and climbing all the way to $2.7 billion the following year. The debt grew steadily throughout the remainder of the century and climbed rapidly again during World War I (1914–18).

More Detailed Information

In the United States when the members of Congress draft the yearly budget, they separate expenditures into two categories: mandatory spending, which accounts for two-thirds of the U.S. budget, and discretionary spending, which accounts for the remaining third. Mandatory spending refers to the money that Congress is obligated by law to set aside each year for programs such as Social Security, Medicare, Medicaid, and national defense. Discretionary spending refers to the money that the government allocates on a yearly basis to other projects. For example, each year the government spends different amounts of money on intelligence (the FBI and CIA, for example) and highway repair. No laws commit the government to allocate a predetermined amount of funds for these projects; instead, members of Congress must appropriate the money (in other words, assign it to specific purposes) during the legislative session.

Recent Trends

One area of government spending that has risen dramatically in the early twenty-first century has been the funding of national security. Since the terrorist attacks on New York City on September 11, 2001, federal spending on the global "war on terror" has gone up significantly each year. Between 2003 and 2006 the rise in spending on the wars in Afghanistan and Iraq was particularly striking. In 2003 the federal government spent more than $70 billion on these overseas conflicts; after a slight decline in 2004, the figure rose to more than $100 billion in 2005 and nearly $120 billion in 2006. By the summer of

BIG GOVERNMENT?

A common complaint of many Americans in the late twentieth and early twenty-first century was that the U.S. government had gotten too big. An oversized government was believed to be hampering the performance of businesses, and many political candidates campaigned for constant reductions in the size of government.

While the size of state and local governments did in fact grow substantially in the latter part of the twentieth century, most complaints and political campaign promises were directed at the federal government, which grew only modestly in these years. Measuring the size of government by the number of people it employs, the federal government grew only slightly between 1960 and 1990: from 2.4 million employees to 3 million employees. During that same time, the U.S. population grew from around 179 million to around 248 million. Partly as a result of repeated calls to reduce the size of government, the federal workforce declined substantially between 1990 and 2007. As of 2007 there were fewer than 2 million government employees, even as the national population had increased to more than 300 million.

2007, a government report indicated that the projected cost of the wars would ultimately exceed $1 trillion.

MULTIPLIER EFFECT

What It Means

In an economy the multiplier effect occurs when government spending spurs an expansion in economic activity, which in turn promotes further spending by consumers and private businesses. In one sense government spending is designed to provide society with things it needs, such as highways, bridges, schools, and financial assistance programs for the poor. At the same time, government spending also creates jobs by hiring private businesses to undertake various government-funded construction projects. These businesses must hire workers, who use a portion of their earnings to pay for various goods and services. In turn, the companies that produce these goods and services experience an increase in their business, which prompts them to hire new workers. These workers spend their wages on other goods and services, and so on. In other words, when government spending leads to widespread increases in consumer spending, the impact on the economy is known as the multiplier effect.

When Did It Begin

The concept of the multiplier effect was first introduced by British economist John Maynard Keynes (1883–1946). In the years following World War I, Keynes developed an economic theory that emphasized a balance

BURIED MONEY

In general terms the multiplier effect refers to the notion that government spending has the power to promote further spending by businesses and consumers, thereby helping an economy grow. The concept of the multiplier effect was first introduced by British economist John Maynard Keynes (1883-1946) in his 1936 work *The General Theory of Employment, Interest, and Money*. According to Keynes, the way that the government spends money does not ultimately matter, so long as it stimulates additional spending within the economy. To illustrate this point, Keynes used a unique analogy. He described a scenario in which the government buries old bank notes in an abandoned mine. In Keynes's view companies interested in earning a profit would be willing to invest resources (purchasing equipment and hiring workers) in order to retrieve the bank notes. In this way the buried money would stimulate economic activity.

between the private sector's freedom to conduct business and government's role as a stabilizing force in the economy. (The private sector is that part of the economy not controlled by the government.) Keynes believed that government intervention in the economic process, particularly in the form of spending programs, was sometimes the best method of ensuring economic growth and stability. In order to illustrate the role of government spending in economic expansion, Keynes developed the idea of the multiplier effect, which he outlined in detail in his 1936 book *The General Theory of Employment, Interest, and Money*.

The "Keynesian multiplier" was the term economists first used to denote the multiplier effect. The term described the effect on the demand for goods and services of any increase in spending coming from outside of business production, including increased government spending. Ultimately government spending goes to people who use it to purchase goods and services. More spending means that more workers are needed to produce goods, so employment levels rise and wages and consumer spending increase, which provide the economy with needed stimulus. Economists who support Keynesian theories believe that it is the government's role to correct the economy's irregularities.

More Detailed Information

Many economists consider government spending to be an effective means of stimulating growth during periods of economic stagnation. Most of the time, an economy is driven by private investment—that is, by the money that individuals, companies, and other entities pay to businesses in order to help them grow. When private investment decreases, however, companies are unable to

expand, and the overall economy ceases to grow; in some cases the economy may actually decrease in size. Confronted with a lack of private investment, a government might try to prevent economic contraction through its own spending. While the government typically spends its money differently than private investors, devoting funds to government-related projects rather than investing them directly in private businesses, the end results of the spending can be similar. So long as the government spending prompts an increase in aggregate demand (the term for overall demand for goods and services within an economy), then the economy will see increased spending on goods and services. In principle, then, the multiplier effect has the potential to create a cycle of growth, in which spending spurs economic activity, which leads to continued spending, and so on.

For example, imagine that the government decides to spend $10 million on a new bridge. The government will hire a private construction company, which will use the $10 million to purchase equipment and hire workers. In this arrangement two companies have enjoyed an increase in revenue: the construction company, as well as the company that sells the equipment. Now, imagine that the company that manufactures the equipment saves 10 percent of its earnings while investing the other 90 percent in expanding its production capacity. At the same time, assume that the construction workers on the bridge project spend 90 percent of their earnings on food, clothing, electronic equipment, and leisure activities. If 10 percent of the original $10 million goes into savings, then $9 million is being spent on materials and new workers (in the case of the equipment manufacturer) and consumer goods (in the case of the workers). This $9 million has been distributed to a wide range of businesses and individuals. If all of these businesses and workers adhere to the same formula (saving 10 percent of their earnings while spending 90 percent), then they will eventually be putting $8.1 million back into the economy. The businesses and workers who receive the $8.1 million will eventually spend $7.29 million. The growth created by the government's initial $10 million expenditure, in other words, multiplies throughout the economy.

In light of this scenario, the growth in consumer spending caused by the multiplier effect depends to a large degree on the average rate of savings among businesses and consumers. In Keynesian economics the proportion of earnings that an individual is willing to spend is known as the marginal propensity to consume (MPC). If consumers feel uncertain about the economy, they might be more inclined to save 50 percent of their earnings rather than 10 percent. This high level of saving would have a dramatic effect on consumer spending, which would subsequently slow overall growth in the economy. For this reason economists often discuss the multiplier

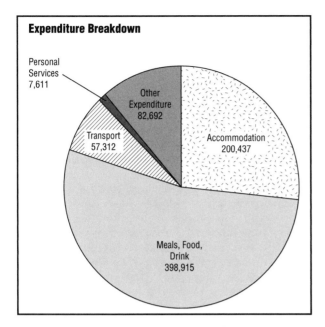

Expenditure Breakdown

Personal Services 7,611

Other Expenditure 82,692

Transport 57,312

Accommodation 200,437

Meals, Food, Drink 398,915

When government spending creates a ripple of business and consumer spending that stimulates the economy, it is known as a multiplier effect. If, for example, a city government decided to fund major new acquisitions for its art museum, which brought an influx of tourists to the city, the multiplier effect of the initial expenditure might be seen in restaurant, hotel, transportation, and other spending, as this pie chart indicates. *Illustration by GGS Information Services. Cengage Learning, Gale.*

effect in terms of a ratio between consumption and savings.

Recent Trends

Although economic growth in the United States had already begun to slow by the beginning of the twenty-first century, the terrorist attacks of September 11, 2001, made matters dramatically worse. The stock market (where shares in companies are bought and sold) was suspended for several days, global trade was disrupted, and a number of businesses (notably in the airline industry) were forced into bankruptcy. In the final months of 2001, consumer spending slowed considerably.

Not long after the terrorist attacks, President George W. Bush and the U.S. Congress decided to implement several new government spending measures, nearly half of which were designated for military and national security purposes. In 2002 and 2003 federal spending grew at an average rate of 7.6 percent, more than double the average rate of spending between 1993 and 2001, when it rose only 3.4 percent a year. Although this rise in government spending prompted harsh criticism from a number of fiscal conservatives (who are generally opposed to high levels of federal spending), many economists believed that the increased funding helped salvage the economy during an otherwise uncertain period. These economists argued that, by bolstering the defense and security industries, the

government prompted a cycle of spending that helped contribute to continued economic growth.

GOVERNMENT FAILURE

What It Means

When the government intervenes in the economy and the end result is to make the economy less efficient or to create new problems, economists say that "government failure" has occurred. Economists generally believe that markets, those real or virtual places where buyers and sellers come together to do business freely with one another, provide the best way of organizing economic life. Prices dictate how much of a product a seller will be willing to supply and how much of that product buyers will demand. When there is competition among both buyers and sellers, the market ensures that the correct quantities of the product are produced by the most efficient methods.

There are some situations, however, in which markets fail to produce the results that society wants. For instance, markets cannot be relied upon to provide for national defense. The government must intervene to make sure that the right amounts of military equipment and training are produced, and to make sure that its military forces can respond effectively in case of threats from other countries.

The government's role in the economy is not always so clear-cut, though. Government leaders may genuinely want to improve social and economic conditions, but even with the best intentions inefficiency is sometimes unavoidable. In other cases government policies are simply ill-considered, or they are manipulated by interested parties, with the end result of increasing inefficiency and other problems.

When Did It Begin

Economists of the eighteenth and nineteenth centuries tended to argue that markets were almost always more efficient than governments, and that governments should not interfere with the forces of supply, demand, and prices. But the Great Depression, the severe economic crisis that affected North America and Europe in the 1930s, presented society with problems that markets did not seem able to solve. In response to these problems, British economist John Maynard Keynes suggested new economic theories justifying the government's intimate involvement in the economy.

From the 1930s to the 1970s, the U.S. government generally followed Keynes's theories, attempting to intervene in situations where the market did not perform effectively. But during the 1970s the country's economy grew stagnant, and many economists began blaming the government. Bad government policies, it was believed, had interfered with the efficient functioning of markets. Since that time the U.S. government has reduced its role

IMPERFECT INFORMATION

When self-interested buyers and sellers of products come together freely to do business, and the end result is economic inefficiency or other problems, economists say that market failure has occurred. When the government attempts to assume responsibility for some aspect of the economy, and the end result is economic inefficiency or other problems, economists say that government failure has occurred. One reason for both types of failure is very simple: it is difficult for anyone—whether a businessperson, a consumer, or a government official—to know and understand all relevant information before making decisions.

You may spend weeks amassing information about different cars before purchasing a new automobile, but you probably would not put this much effort into deciding which brand of toothbrush to buy. Instead, your purchase might be based on some combination of your friends' opinions about toothbrush brands, information from half-remembered television commercials, and momentary impulses regarding color and shape of the brush. You do not know whether it

makes sense to pay $3.00 as opposed to $1.50 for the toothbrush you have chosen, and you do not care, because the amount is negligible to you. But when hundreds of millions of other Americans treat toothbrush purchases in the same way, a significant amount of distortion can creep into the economy.

Similarly, the government may act on public opinion when it makes economic policies, but there are shortcomings in this approach. For one, the process of electing leaders is an imperfect means of communicating the public will. A politician may get elected based partly on her support for high tariffs on foreign cars and partly on her opposition to an ongoing war. She may implement both policies even though a majority of voters cared only about the war. Additionally, even if a majority of voters support tariffs on imported cars, their support may be based on bad information. In this case, the imperfect information that citizens have is magnified and turned into a government policy. In such situations, the possibilities for economic inefficiency are numerous.

---

in the economy considerably, primarily due to the widespread belief that government intervention usually fails to increase efficiency.

More Detailed Information

Government involvement in the economy takes many forms, so there are many different types of government failure. Generally, economists use cost-benefit analysis to determine whether or not government failure has occurred. According to this standard, government failure results when government action causes more harm than good.

Governments frequently interfere in the pricing system in some industries, and this can result in a significant change in the quantity supplied and quantity demanded of a product. For example, the government might provide subsidies to corn farmers, giving them money that makes it easier for them to produce corn at a profit. While this benefits corn farmers and even consumers of corn (by keeping corn prices low), these benefits come at the expense of taxpayers, who provide the government with the money that it passes on to the corn industry.

Subsidies are not always ill-advised, however. For instance, when one person gets vaccinated against a disease, the entire population benefits because the overall risk of disease drops. By subsidizing the prices of vaccines, the government makes the individual better off, while also benefiting large numbers of other people.

On the other hand, government funding of products that most people see as obviously useful, like new roads, can result in economic inefficiency that harms society. When taxpayers fund the construction of roads in national forests that make it easier for logging companies to

extract lumber from forests, taxpayers have essentially subsidized the logging industry. If cutting trees costs less money, then the industry is likely to cut more of them than it should.

Other types of government policies can have large-scale, but less obvious, effects on the economy. When the government borrows money to pay for its expenses, it can create a greater demand for money across the economy, which leads to higher interest rates (the fees charged to all people who borrow money). When interest rates are high, companies are less likely to take out loans that will allow them to expand, buy new equipment, or open for business in the first place. These activities, forms of what economists call business investment, make up one of the key elements in a country's economic well-being. When business investment is crowded out by higher interest rates caused by government borrowing, government failure has occurred.

Additionally, the U.S. Congress may pass laws that affect the economy without prioritizing whether or not the end result will increase efficiency. The steel industry, for example, might pressure the government into placing high tariffs (taxes paid on imported goods) on foreign steel. By making foreign steel more expensive, Congress essentially encourages domestic steelmakers to increase its production of a good that can be more easily and efficiently produced elsewhere.

Recent Trends

During the 1990s and into the first decade of the twenty-first century, the longstanding practice of the government giving subsidies (or support payments) to farmers was a

Many people viewed the U.S. government's inadequate response in 2005 to the flooding and other devastation caused by Hurricane Katrina in New Orleans as a significant failure. The term government failure, however, has a different meaning in the field of economics and is used when government action leads to economic inefficiency or other problems. *AP Images.*

source of significant political and public debate in both the United States and in Europe.

Agricultural subsidies have a number of effects. First, the money acts as an income supplement for farmers whose crops (and therefore yearly earnings) are vulnerable to fluctuations due to changes in the weather and other uncontrollable circumstances. Farm subsidies also guarantee a price floor (lowest possible price at which it will be sold) for each crop. Suppose, for example, that the subsidy for soybeans is $1.19 per bushel and the price floor is set at $5.26 per bushel; by adding those two numbers, that would effectively guarantee a farmer $6.45 a bushel. If the market price of soybeans were to dip down to $5.16 per bushel, then the government would offset that price by giving a total subsidy (or price support) of $1.29 ($6.45 - $5.16) per bushel. Again, one of the primary concerns with these subsidies (which totaled $21 billion in 2005) is that they are paid for by taxpayers. Further, while U.S. farm subsidies originated during the 1930s as a way to keep small family farmers afloat and protect the national food supply during the financial crisis of the Great Depression, the makeup of the American agricultural industry has changed significantly since then. Nowadays many of the farmers who receive subsidies are wealthy owners of massive industrial farms.

Farm subsidies also have the effect of encouraging overproduction. According to the law of supply and de-

mand, market prices fall as a result of declining demand, and producers respond accordingly by reducing their supply. When subsidies guarantee crop prices, however, farmers have no incentive to cut back their production. The result is a glut of harvested crops, which are sold on the international market at very low prices. Although it can be argued that the low prices are good for poor people in developing countries, the problem is that farmers in those countries, who cannot compete with international prices, are often forced out of business.

Because government farm subsidies interfere with market pricing and lead to a more inefficient allocation of goods and resources than the market would otherwise dictate, they are often used as an example of government failure. Arguments against this idea often focus on the need to provide stability in the agricultural industry and on the desire to help those farmers who are not rich and at risk of going out of business. Some people are also concerned that if the United States eliminated farm subsidies and did not produce enough food to feed itself, it would be vulnerable—in the event of a worldwide political change or crisis—to food shortages.

ECONOMIC DEVELOPMENT

What It Means

Economic development refers to the transformation of a simple, low-income national economy into a more sophisticated one in which citizens' incomes rise. The term *economic development* is often used, in everyday conversation, as a synonym for "economic growth," but economists draw a clear distinction between the two. Whereas economic growth refers to a simple increase in the quantity of goods and services produced in an economy, economic development describes a wide range of interconnected, qualitative changes at the structural level of the economy. The process of economic development involves changes in economic inputs (the resources, such as land, raw materials, equipment, and labor, that are used to produce goods and services), in the technologies used to combine these inputs in the production process, and in economic outputs (the final products produced by the economy).

Undeveloped economies tend to be predominantly agricultural, consisting of workers who act directly on the natural world with only minimal help from tools and technology. Development usually proceeds as businesses accumulate capital (equipment and machines that aid in production, as well as the skills that workers acquire through education and training). New equipment allows workers to increase their efficiency and to produce larger quantities of goods, and new labor skills develop in combination with the use of the new equipment, changing the nature of the labor force. Incomes rise, and people who have more money to spend begin demanding more and different products. The economy adapts to

Economic development refers to attempts to transform a basic, low-income economy into a more complex and productive one. Economic development requires investment in a country's basic infrastructure, which includes the construction of roads and airports. *AP Images.*

these new tastes, spurring the growth of new industries. Over time, as these structural changes occur, the economy shifts away from agriculture and into industrial production, and it begins to be considered a developed, rather than a developing, economy.

When Did It Begin

The economic development of Western Europe began roughly in the sixteenth century and proceeded gradually over the course of several centuries. Industrialization increased rapidly there in the early nineteenth century, and the latter part of that century saw the expansion and development of the economies of Eastern Europe, Australia, New Zealand, South Africa, Canada, and the United States. Russia's economic development came primarily in the twentieth century.

Economic development became a more pressing concern when, after World War II, the colonial era (during which European countries and Japan conquered

and ruled over foreign lands in Asia, Africa, and elsewhere) came to an end. Once ruling governments withdrew from their colonies, new countries were established, and most of these countries had undeveloped economies. Questions about how best to encourage economic development in these poor countries have been a central concern of many economists and government leaders since that time.

More Detailed Information

The most common measure that economists use to judge a country's economic development is gross domestic product (GDP) per capita. Gross domestic product is a calculation of the monetary value of all goods and services produced by a nation's economy, and GDP per capita is an estimate of each citizen's share of GDP. Economists determine GDP per capita by dividing GDP by the size of a country's population. According to their GDP per capita, countries are commonly classified as less-developed countries (often referred to as LDCs), developing countries, or developed countries. Among developed countries, those that have developed only recently are classified as newly industrialized countries (NICs).

GDP per capita does not, however, fully capture the degree to which a country has developed. For instance, the economies of the oil-producing island nation of Bahrain and the newly industrialized country South Korea both grew rapidly in the latter part of the twentieth century, and today the two countries boast similar GDPs per capita (of roughly $20,000 in 2007), but most of Bahrain's wealth is produced by a single industry—oil—and the nation's citizens do not fully participate in this industry. Instead, multinational corporations headquartered primarily in the United States and Europe locate their own employees in Bahrain to conduct the process of finding, extracting, and bringing the oil to consumers, most of whom, again, live in the United States, Europe, and other developed nations. Though the oil industry generates income for Bahrain's government and its people, the economy has not otherwise industrialized or transformed at the structural level, so that the fortunes of the oil industry and the fortunes of the country's economy are essentially inseparable. South Korea, by contrast, has both grown and shifted from an agricultural to an industrial economy. Workers have increasingly left rural areas and moved into cities to find the new jobs produced by a developing economy, and the economy as a whole is on a solid footing in a way that Bahrain's is not. The incomes of South Korea's citizens are growing, and there is real potential for them to keep growing. A broad range of the population shares in the benefits produced by economic development.

South Korea is not the only country to have developed a solid economy since the mid-twentieth century. Other success stories include the economies of Taiwan, Singapore, and Hong Kong, all of which are today considered NICs. At the other end of the spectrum, however, are the many countries of Asia, Africa, and Latin America that have failed to develop significantly since gaining independence from their colonial rulers. The question of how to spur development in such countries is one upon which more than profits and business opportunities depend. Since economic development usually corresponds with increases in quality of life (for example, better health care, education, and public services), the lives and futures of billions of people are at stake.

Though economic opinion is divided about strategies for development, most people agree that two basic ingredients often necessary for a country to transform its economy are the accumulation of capital and access to modern science and technology.

In the decades immediately following World War II, capital accumulation was believed to be the fundamental, if not the only, ingredient necessary for economic development. Capital can be broken down into non-human

DEVELOPMENT ORGANIZATIONS

Today there are three important international organizations committed to promoting economic development (the transformation of a simple, stagnant economy into a complex, dynamic one) in poor countries. These are the World Bank, the International Monetary Fund (IMF), and the World Trade Organization (WTO). Each organization consists of representatives from countries all over the world, and each addresses a particular set of challenges in the world economy. The World Bank focuses on loaning money to less-developed and developing countries (allowing them to accumulate the machines, buildings, and other equipment necessary for economic development), the IMF focuses on stabilizing national currencies (stable currencies are a precondition for economic development), and the WTO focuses on breaking down barriers to trade between nations (these barriers primarily consist of taxes and limits on imported goods, restrictions which are believed by many economists to hinder economic development). All three of these organizations are controversial, however, because of the dominance of the United States in their operations. Supporters of the World Bank, the IMF, and the WTO believe that they are instrumental in improving living standards for people all over the world. Critics believe that they are imposing models for economic development that primarily benefit the United States and other powerful countries.

and human capital. Non-human capital includes buildings, machines, equipment, and other materials that allow for increased productivity. Human capital consists of the education and specialized training of individuals that allows companies to increase their productivity. Development strategies for LDCs during the 1950s and 1960s usually called for massive injections of foreign aid (money contributions) and investment that would allow for the accumulation of capital. It was believed that economic development would proceed naturally from this starting point. This did not turn out to be the case in many countries, however. While capital accumulation is no longer considered the supreme determinant of economic development, it is generally agreed that, if a country does not reinvest a significant portion of its income in capital, it cannot continue to develop over the long term.

Capital was not the sole or even the primary driver of the enormous and rapid development of the U.S. economy in the late nineteenth and the twentieth century. Many economists point to technology as the key ingredient in U.S. development. Indeed, the growth and structural change of the U.S. economy would have been inconceivable without the monumental advances in modern science made during that time. As the laws of physics, chemistry, and biology (among other fields) were applied to the production of goods and services, countless new economic possibilities emerged. While LDCs today have access to the discoveries of the past, they do not always have the capability to convert this knowledge into product innovations that will allow for economic growth and change.

Economists agree, moreover, that government policies are one of the most important factors influencing an economy's course. Political stability is, naturally, one of the necessary preconditions for industrialization. Until the population and businesses in a country can be sure that they can safely pursue their economic goals, development is not possible. But stability alone is not enough. If a government does not actively promote economic development, then it will likely hinder industrialization. This occurred in Cuba in the mid-to-late-twentieth century, where the country's socialist leader Fidel Castro promoted social goals over economic goals. This also often occurs in societies ruled by an elite group that benefits from a lack of economic development. European nations typically governed their colonies with the intent of benefiting the businesses and citizens of the ruling country, making no serious effort at economic development that would have benefited their colonies' native populations.

Recent Trends

Among developing nations at the end of the twentieth century and the beginning of the twenty-first, China and India stood out in the minds of most economists and business analysts. Both countries are enormous in both geographic size and population, and the economies of both were growing at a torrid pace in the 1990s and in the early years of the new millennium. Experts commonly predicted that the countries would, within a few decades, surpass in size all national economies in the world except that of the United States.

China and India were following very different paths toward development, however. China excelled at heavy industrial production, which it bolstered with good infrastructure (roads, ports, and utilities) and large amounts of foreign investment. India, meanwhile, specialized in products and services less reliant on tangible assets, such as software, biotechnology, and advertising. China, as a socialist country (a country in which social goals centrally influence economic policy), exerted much greater government control over businesses and investors. Though government participation in the economy had allowed for the large capital investments necessary for heavy industrial production and for the effective infrastructure that supported those producers, some economists wondered whether government control of the economy might ultimately hinder China's growth. India's government, on the other hand, had since the 1990s taken an essentially hands-off approach to the economy. This had allowed for growth comparable to China's even in the absence of

infrastructure and without significant amounts of foreign investment.

Which one of the two courses would ultimately prove the most fruitful strategy for economic development was a matter of debate in the early twenty-first century. Few people, on the other hand, doubted that China and India would continue to develop, or that both would eventually rival the top economies in the world.

SUSTAINABLE DEVELOPMENT

What It Means

Sustainable development is a term used by business leaders, environmentalists, human-rights groups, economists, and others in discussions about the future direction of the world economy. While economic growth in any nation brings jobs and improvements in quality of life, it also exacts a toll on the environment and natural resources. If the earth's resources are being used up faster than nature can replenish them, or if economic activity permanently causes large-scale damage to the natural world, there may eventually be a time when the earth will no longer be able to support economic growth or even sustain human life. The explosive growth in the world's population in recent times (from 1.65 billion in 1900 to 6.45 billion in 2000) makes the need to find ways of protecting the environment for future generations especially pressing.

The negative results of economic growth inevitably emerge when the desire for profit and wealth alone are allowed to determine the shape that development will take. Advocates of sustainable development call for a shifting of priorities. They want to promote economic growth in order to alleviate poverty and improve the quality of life for all people, but they want to do so while protecting the environment and conserving natural resources for future generations.

Sustainable development as a concept is still being defined. It requires rethinking the entire course of civilization. It involves people in all fields of study, and it requires sacrifices on the part of consumers as well as businesses, individuals as well as societies. The guiding principle is that, in economic matters, we should take into account not simply our own needs or even simply the needs of all the world's citizens, but also the needs of future generations.

When Did It Begin

The United Nations (UN), the international organization devoted to promoting global peace, economic well-being, cooperation, and stability, has taken a lead role, since the 1960s, in pressing the need for economic development that reduces the damage done to the environment. A combination of world conferences and UN commissions in the 1970s and 1980s eventually culminated in a 1987 report called *Our Common Future,* issued

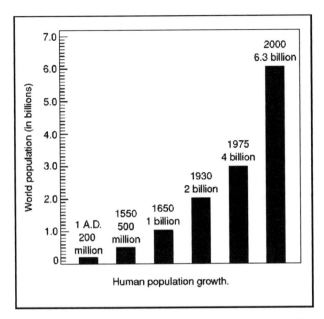

Human population growth.

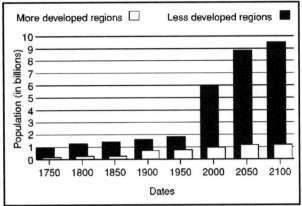

A comparison of population growth in less developed and more developed regions, 1750-2100.

Contrasting the growth (exponential for less developed).

Sustainable development is the idea of balancing the demands of future economic growth with the need to preserve the environment. As this chart shows, the world population is increasing rapidly, making discussions of sustainable development more important than ever. *Line drawing by Hans. Electronic Illustrations Group/Cengage Learning, Gale.*

by the UN's World Commission on the Environment and Development. The report asserted that environmental crises were inseparable from economic crises, and that such problems transcended local, regional, and national borders. *Our Common Future* introduced the concept of sustainable development, which it defined as economic growth that "meets the needs of the present without compromising the ability of future generations to meet their own needs."

More Detailed Information

Traditionally, economic development has proceeded without regard for the environment. An American timber company in the early twentieth century had little incentive to approach forests as anything but a source of potential profits, especially since the supply of trees in the United States seemed so vast. As the U.S. population has grown, however, and the consumption of products made of wood has grown along with it, deforestation on a massive scale has become a concern. Similarly, the U.S. automotive and oil industries grew in response to a growing population that increasingly demanded cars and affordable fuel. These industries have traditionally promoted ever-greater consumption of their products, without regard for the environmental effects of driving. Not only does car exhaust degrade the air quality in densely populated areas, but it greatly contributes to global warming.

These are two of many examples of the environmental damage commonly caused by economic growth. Environmental degradation leads to numerous problems in the short term, such as the extinction of animal and plant species, health problems among humans, and conflict between people fighting over dwindling resources. These problems can seriously diminish the quality of life in a community. If environmental degradation is allowed to persist over the long term, moreover, eventually a location might become uninhabitable. If, for example, a community's water supply becomes undrinkable, the soil becomes saturated with chemical or radioactive waste, and/or the air becomes so polluted as to regularly cause life-threatening sicknesses, that community will no longer support human life.

Global warming, meanwhile, presents a challenge to the long-term survival of humans everywhere. Rising temperatures caused by carbon emissions (the burning of fossil fuels such as oil and coal by automobiles, airplanes, power plants, and a wide variety of industrial machinery) may, according to scientists, eventually become so severe and create so many complications (rising sea levels, increased weather volatility, and droughts, for instance) that large portions of the earth could become uninhabitable.

If a region or nation becomes uninhabitable, there will be no economic activity there. Likewise, a global crisis caused by climate change would drastically affect the world economy. Obviously, then, economic development cannot be separated from environmental health.

Sustainable development advocates do not want to promote the health of the environment over all other factors. For example, a total eradication of industries that use fossil fuels would cripple the world economy so badly as to threaten human life in some places. Sustainable development calls, instead, for a reduction of fossil-fuel

ECOTOURISM

Sustainable development (economic growth that minimizes the harm done to the environment) can be difficult to achieve in practice. One notable concrete form that the desire for sustainable development has taken in recent years is the creation of the ecological tourism (or ecotourism) industry. Ecotourism often involves traveling to wilderness areas and engaging in activities, such as hiking and studying local plant and animal life, that do not negatively impact the natural world, while also staying in hotels or other lodgings that strive to minimize their waste and consumption of energy and natural resources. Meanwhile, of course, the tourist contributes money to the local economy, leading to an increase in jobs and quality of life for the people who live there. In countries such as Costa Rica, Ecuador, Kenya, and Madagascar, ecotourism is one of the most important industries in the national economy.

burning in an attempt to reduce the harm done by global warming, without inflicting great harm on existing populations. One way of doing this might be not only to implement new technologies but to help people change their consumption habits.

Recent Trends

Sustainable development became a very popular concept in the 1980s and 1990s, and many governments and organizations proclaimed their desire to promote economic growth that minimized environmental side effects. But in practice, bringing about changes in economic standards and a society's behavior can be very complicated. If, for example, a timber company sets sustainable economic goals in cooperation with the local community where it is located, how exactly will it decide on its priorities? It might be possible to cull trees from a given forest forever without decimating the forest, but not without forcing a particular species of bird into extinction. Does selective harvesting of timber represent sustainable development even if the bird species becomes extinct? Disagreements over the definition of sustainable development, which changes depending on the individual situation, often come into play when there is not an easy solution to correcting environmental damage.

In the United States in particular, there was also, in the early twenty-first century, considerable resistance to the general concept of sustainable development, especially among conservatives in the administration of President George W. Bush. Bush, along with his advisers and supporters, commonly dismissed concerns about global warming and environmental degradation, openly favoring the interests of the coal, oil, and other industries over both the short- and long-term health of the natural world.

TRANSFER PAYMENT

What It Means

A transfer payment is money or other aid that is given by a government without any good or service in return. The government simply transfers money, for example, from its tax revenue to an individual or business. In the United States federal, state, and local governments all make transfer payments. The three major types of transfer payment at the federal level are social insurance programs, welfare, and business subsidies.

Social insurance programs provide benefits to people regardless of their income level. Examples include Social Security payments to retired workers, unemployment payments to workers who cannot find jobs, and Medicare, a form of free health insurance that benefits the elderly.

Welfare programs provide benefits to the poorest members of society. Examples include direct payments under the Temporary Assistance for Needy Families (TANF) program, credit that can be used to purchase food under the food stamps program, and Medicaid, a form of free health insurance.

Farms are an important target of business subsidies. There are two main types of farm subsidies. Export subsidies are payments to encourage farmers to sell their crops abroad. Domestic subsidies have a variety of purposes: to promote the cultivation of certain crops; to support farmers who are not able to make a profit because of declining prices or increasing costs; to reward farmers who use sustainable, or environmentally friendly, growing practices; or to offset the economic consequences of drought, sudden frost, or other weather-related problems that result in abnormally low crop yield.

Some transfer payments are made as direct cash payments, while others are "in-kind" payments, or payments made in the form of specific goods or services. In either case, transfer payments are a means of redistributing income. The government takes in money via taxes from those who have the capacity to earn it and transfers this money to those who do not. While a substantial amount of transfer payments benefit the poor, many beneficiaries of social insurance programs are middle-class Americans. Social Security and Medicare, for instance, account for far more government spending on transfer payments than any other program. Also, a significant portion of U.S. government farm subsidies are received by the owner-operators of large, successful commercial farms. At the end of the twentieth century, transfer payments represented 44 percent of spending at all levels of government in the United States.

When Did It Begin

Transfer payments in their various forms were not implemented in the United States until the 1930s, although their antecedents in Europe date back much

Transfer payments refer to money, such as aid to the elderly, that a government gives without receiving anything in return. This photo shows John J. Callahan, acting commissioner of the Social Security Administration under President Bill Clinton (1993–2001). *AP Images.*

further. In England at the outset of the seventeenth century, Queen Elizabeth I initiated Poor Laws, which used tax revenues to establish orphanages, hospitals, housing, and other forms of aid for those in need. These laws are considered as precursors to modern welfare systems. At the end of the seventeenth century, the English government also instituted a form of agricultural subsidy by offering so-called bounties to grain farmers as incentives to export their crops. Much like modern-day export subsidies, these bounties enabled farmers to sell grain abroad at a lower price than they would otherwise need to command in order to cover their costs of production. At the same time, the bounties led to an increase in the domestic price of grain. As such, the English people not only shouldered not only the burden of funding the bounties through the taxes they paid but were also faced with paying higher prices for their own food.

Social insurance programs did not take root until the nineteenth century. At this time the Industrial Revolution

(the change from a primarily agricultural economy to an industrial one, made possible by new technologies such as the steam engine) was changing the fabric of society in Europe and the United States; it greatly increased the number of people who worked for wages while diminishing the traditional interdependence between employers and workers. One result was an increased level of risk for the worker. Employers who had no personal responsibility toward their employees could, for example, adjust their workforce depending on economic conditions, cutting jobs in order to maintain profitability regardless of the impact that this would have on individuals or society. This instability led governments in Europe, beginning with Germany in the 1880s, to pass social insurance laws.

It was not until the Great Depression, the severe economic crisis of the 1930s during which roughly 25 percent of U.S. workers lost their jobs, that the federal government began providing transfer payments and other forms of financial aid to those who needed it. One

BUSINESS TRANSFER PAYMENTS

The term *transfer payments* commonly refers to payments made by the government to individuals without any corresponding exchange of goods or services. For example, welfare payments to poor people are transfer payments since the recipients do not earn the money they are paid through work or the sale of products.

Sometimes, though much more rarely, businesses also make transfer payments. For example, a business makes transfer payments when it provides money for college scholarships or for donations to charity.

A less desirable form of business transfer payment is unpaid debt. When customers buy products on credit and never pay their bills, economists say that the business has made a transfer payment. If, for instance, Jane buys 10 outfits from Top Notch Clothing using her Top Notch store credit card and then, the following month, comes down with a serious illness that forces her to quit work and declare bankruptcy, Top Notch Clothing will be left with nothing to show for the 10 outfits that Jane took home with her. For all practical purposes, the company gave away the clothes.

of the centerpieces of President Franklin D. Roosevelt's New Deal, the sweeping series of laws meant to spur recovery from the Depression, was the Social Security Act of 1935, which provided for payments to retired workers, as well as to those who were willing but unable to find work. The Social Security Act also introduced the transfer payments and other forms of aid that would become known as the welfare system. Another key piece of New Deal legislation was the Agricultural Adjustment Act (AAA) of 1933, which offered subsidies to farmers to decrease their crop production by leaving some fields unplanted—the idea being that a reduction of crop surplus would increase the value of the crops, which would restore farmers' economic stability. In addition to aiding struggling farmers directly, the AAA was intended to ensure the viability of rural communities and protect the nation's food supply.

More Detailed Information

Transfer payments represent activity that goes against the grain of the capitalist system. Capitalism is characterized by the right of individuals to own property and pursue profits freely. The economy is controlled not by the government but by the independent actions of countless buyers and sellers acting in their own self-interest. The desires of buyers and sellers, as expressed in markets (the places and systems bringing buyers and sellers together), determine what will be produced and in what numbers,

how it will be produced and distributed, and who will benefit from all economic activity.

While market-based capitalism is unsurpassed at matching buyers and sellers of products and at producing a wide variety of products in the most efficient ways possible, some economists and other social scientists argue that markets often fail to provide benefits that society would like them to provide. One of these benefits is a reduction of economic inequality. Markets reward those who have economic resources and have the ability to use them effectively, but they have no way of providing for those who are not capable of competing in the economy. Welfare programs are thus sometimes justified as a means of correcting this failure.

One prominent economic argument for social insurance programs also focuses on market failures. If, for example, workers were required to purchase insurance that would provide them with income in case they lost their jobs, companies selling such insurance might suspect that the people buying the insurance are those members of society most likely to lose their jobs. Thus, in order to remain profitable, such firms would have to charge unreasonably high rates or decline to offer coverage. Market forces acting alone fail, according to this view, to produce an outcome that society wants, so government must step in to offer unemployment insurance.

One common justification for Social Security benefits is that many individuals, caught up in the demands of everyday economic life, do not have an adequate awareness of the need to save for retirement. In the absence of government aid, society would have to be content with letting some of its elderly members suffer in extreme poverty after retirement. Most people in the United States find such a scenario unacceptable.

Farm subsidies, too, are expressly intended to insulate both producers and consumers from the vagaries of market forces: without this protection, it has long been argued, farmers would suffer from declining prices in years of production surplus, while consumers would suffer from price hikes in years of production shortage. With the benefit of subsidies, on the other hand, farmers can maintain robust production without the consequence of lower prices, while consumers are assured of having an abundant food supply at reasonable prices.

In spite of these justifications, transfer payments are subject to serious and sometimes passionate criticism. Much of the criticism stems from the fact that the money and in-kind benefits people get as a result of transfer payments are essentially gifts rather than payments made in exchange for labor or products. Because of this, some critics argue, transfer payments have adverse effects on individuals' economic decision-making. For example, if a poor person is guaranteed of getting money and food regardless of whether he does any work, then he has no incentive to work. Similarly, some economists argue that Social Security payments create a disincentive to save for retirement. During the active years of a worker's career, these economists argue, one would naturally be compelled to save for the future if there were no alternative sources of income in old age. Since people know they can count on Social Security to supply them with some income, they save less than they would naturally. The same argument is often raised against farm subsidies—that these transfer payments prop up inefficient producers, effectively removing any incentive for them to improve their production efficiency while fostering farmers—dependence on government handouts.

Recent Trends

The end of the twentieth century and the beginning of the twenty-first century saw major political debates about the future of transfer payments in the United States. After decades of criticism from political conservatives, the welfare system was overhauled by President Bill Clinton, a Democrat, in 1996. Seeking to address the disincentive to work that welfare benefits supposedly created, Clinton's reforms restricted welfare recipients to a maximum lifetime limit of five years' worth of aid and made the amount of benefits a family could receive contingent upon the parents' active participation in the job market.

Meanwhile, many economists and government leaders voiced serious concerns about the future of Social Security and Medicare, the two largest transfer payment programs. The aging of the "baby boom" generation (those who were born in the two decades following the end of World War II in 1945) was expected to present enormous challenges to the programs. The members of the baby boomer generation were far more numerous than any previous generation, and they were expected to live much longer due to advances in health care and medical technology. Many experts worried that there would not be enough money in these programs' coffers to make transfer payments in such quantities over so many years. Reform of Social Security and Medicare proved complicated, however, and the issues surrounding these programs were expected to remain a contentious political issue well into the twenty-first century.

Also during this period U.S. farm subsidies came under increased scrutiny, and many politicians, analysts, and members of the public called for their abolishment. Opposition to the subsidies centered on the idea that farm policy was outdated: the U.S. agricultural industry of the twenty-first century bore little resemblance to its predecessor of the 1930s, particularly since the small family farms that had originally been the focus of AAA protection had largely been swallowed up by commercial mega-farms. In 2005, when nearly half of the nation's agricultural output was concentrated among the top 10 producers, transfer payments to such highly profitable businesses were widely derided as a form of corporate welfare.

WELFARE

What It Means

In most countries people who cannot provide for themselves have access to government programs that help them obtain housing, medical care, food, and financial assistance. These various forms of public assistance fall into one of two categories, social insurance or welfare. "Social insurance" refers to programs that provide assistance to people regardless of their income levels. "Welfare," by contrast, refers to various types of assistance targeted strictly at the needy. Government distributions for social insurance and welfare are called transfer payments. Transfer payments, which also include farm subsidies, for example, are funds the government transfers from tax revenue to the individuals and families to whom it has pledged assistance, without requiring goods, services, or other compensation in return.

Different countries take different approaches to social insurance and welfare. European countries tend to have much more expansive social insurance and welfare programs than countries in the rest of the world, including the United States. The United States has a comparatively small social insurance system, focused mainly on aiding the elderly and the disabled, but its social insurance programs are still much larger than its welfare programs. Welfare in the United States, which centers on Medicaid (medical care), the Food Stamp program (food allowances), and cash aid programs, became subject to widespread criticism beginning in the 1970s and is especially unpopular among political conservatives. After reductions in spending during the 1980s, the U.S. welfare system was significantly overhauled in 1996. Welfare since then has focused on urging the poor to find jobs by limiting their benefits and by tying the remaining benefits to participation in the job market.

When Did It Begin

Modern notions of welfare grew out of England's Poor Laws, established by Queen Elizabeth in 1601. The Poor Laws were a series of laws providing for the needs of the poor, children, and the sick. Instead of relying on churches, charities, private citizens, and professional organizations to care for those in need, the Poor Laws required local governments to use tax revenues to start orphanages, hospitals, and poorhouses (free housing for the poor), as well as to fund other forms of relief. Growing criticism of the Poor Laws, much of it centering on those able-bodied people who lived off of government aid rather than getting jobs, led them to be revised in 1834.

Traditions favoring individualism and self-reliance led the United States to lag behind most countries in the establishing of social insurance and welfare programs in the early stages of its nationhood. Few resources were forthcoming for the poor prior to the Great Depression, the severe economic crisis that gripped the United States

Welfare, a form of government assistance, is given to people who do not have the money for food, shelter, and other essential items. Here children in Brooklyn, New York, play while their mothers fill out welfare application forms. *Stephen Ferry/Getty Images.*

and most other developed countries beginning in 1929. As much as 40 percent of the U.S. population is estimated to have fallen into poverty during the Great Depression. The country's economic problems necessitated government intervention.

President Franklin D. Roosevelt introduced sweeping legislation intended to combat the Great Depression. The Social Security Act of 1935 created not only the old-age benefits that today go by the name Social Security but also many of the other types of aid that would eventually grow into the welfare system. President Lyndon B. Johnson expanded the welfare system substantially in 1960, during his so-called War on Poverty.

More Detailed Information

Welfare in the United States varies from state to state. The federal government often supplies the bulk of the funds for the programs in each state, with the state supplying additional funds and controlling the administration of the programs. Welfare assistance is normally awarded only to those living below the poverty line, a standard established by the federal government. The poverty line shifts according to family size, and it changes each year to

account for inflation (the rising of prices that causes money to decrease in value over time). In 2004, for instance, an individual making around $9,600 a year fell below the poverty line; for a family of four, the poverty line was set at around $19,300 in income.

Most welfare assistance in the United States takes the form of Medicaid, Food Stamps, or direct cash payments under a program called Temporary Assistance to Needy Families (TANF). Medicaid provides free health care to poor people. The federal government supplies the state with grants to fund Medicaid, but the states supply additional funds according to their own policy goals. The states administer and set eligibility requirements individually, so that the program differs substantially from state to state.

The Food Stamp program, which provides assistance with food purchases, also varies from state to state. The program got its name because recipients originally received actual stamps that could be used to purchase food. Today those households that qualify for assistance receive credit cards with values that vary according to the family's size, income, and individual needs. The credit cards can be used only for food purchases and only at grocery stores that have agreed to accept them as payment.

TANF replaced a program called Aid for Families with Dependent Children (AFDC) as a result of President Bill Clinton's 1996 welfare reform initiative. Like AFDC, TANF primarily helps single mothers via cash payments. Under AFDC the federal government required states to pay benefits to all families whose income fell below a certain level. TANF, by contrast, allows the states to decide how to determine whether people are eligible for cash assistance or not. TANF is also much more focused on urging welfare recipients to find work than was AFDC. If a recipient of cash aid does not get a job within two years of being on the program, benefits are reduced. Most families are limited to a maximum of five years' lifetime assistance under TANF.

There are other forms of welfare as well. These include programs geared mainly to the elderly and disabled, programs providing assistance for paying energy bills, public housing programs, programs promoting nutritional well-being for the poor, and, increasingly, tax breaks for the poor.

Recent Trends

Welfare programs in all Western countries grew steadily in the decades following World War II, but beginning in the 1970s, public figures and ordinary citizens began to become more skeptical about the usefulness and expense of welfare. This was especially true in the United States during the presidency of Ronald Reagan (1981–89), who was an outspoken critic of welfare. Notions of welfare recipients as freeloaders living off the labor of honest working people became common, and many people blamed the welfare system not just for hampering the economy but for various of the country's supposed cultural ills, including the breakdown of family and community values. Reagan implemented policies calling for reductions in welfare spending in favor of tax cuts intended to stimulate the economy. These often went mainly to wealthy people and to corporations.

Reagan's successor, George H.W. Bush (1989–93), largely extended the Reagan approach to welfare. It was only under Bill Clinton (1993–2001), however, that substantial reform had the political backing to become a reality. TANF, which his administration enacted, answered many of the criticisms of the welfare system by forcing aid recipients to look for jobs and by making benefits temporary rather than permanent.

Since 1996 the number of people receiving welfare benefits has declined substantially, and there has been a corresponding increase of single mothers in the workplace. This has raised other issues, however. Those who leave the welfare system often qualify only for menial, low-paying jobs. With no way of paying for child care and no health-care coverage through their employers, single mothers sometimes find that their problems multiply once they leave the welfare system.

EARNED INCOME TAX CREDIT

Today the largest form of assistance to low-income Americans comes not through the welfare system but through the tax code, via what is called the Earned Income Tax Credit (EITC). The EITC reduces and in some cases eliminates the income taxes that the working poor pay in the United States. It is meant to act in the same way that an actual cash subsidy would, providing those in need with additional spending money by allowing them to keep more of their earnings. Enacted in 1975, the EITC has been expanded four times since then, owing to its popularity among both Republicans and Democrats in Congress.

While very popular compared to other forms of welfare, the EITC, it should be noted, provides assistance to employed people, who in many cases are living above the poverty line rather than below it. The poorest people in the United States, therefore, derive few benefits from this form of assistance.

While welfare remains politically unpopular, social insurance programs have retained the broad support of most Americans. Social Security, which provides cash payments to disabled workers as well as to workers who have reached old age, and Medicare, which provides health care benefits for retired people, represent a far larger share of the national income than assistance to the poor ever has. Though the economic demands of these programs are much greater than those posed by welfare, they generally do not attract anywhere near the same level of criticism.

FOREIGN AID

What It Means

Nations, international organizations, and private groups each provide various forms of assistance, called foreign aid, to countries in need. Foreign aid commonly takes the form of money, food, military equipment, advice, or training.

Foreign aid came into being in the eighteenth century, but both the amount and global importance of such assistance increased dramatically after World War II. The main reason for the increase was the Cold War, the period between 1945 and 1991 during which the United States and the Soviet Union opposed one another and competed to influence other countries. Both the United States and the Soviet Union hoped to enlist the sympathies of other countries by providing them with assistance or by withholding assistance if they showed too much sympathy for the other side.

With the end of the Cold War foreign aid declined, but it remains an important feature of international politics. As in the Cold War, most governments still provide assistance to other governments mainly for political reasons. This does not mean that foreign aid does not benefit countries who receive it, however. It is a key part of the fight against global poverty, and it has helped to alleviate suffering in poor countries.

Nevertheless foreign aid has its critics. Some of these critics argue that the self-interest of donor countries usually wins out over the needs of poorer countries. Other critics within donor countries often believe that foreign aid is wasteful, making up a large part of their national budget while being subject to irresponsible use in recipient countries. In fact, all donor governments spend less than one percent of their national income (the amount of money generated in a country per year) on foreign aid.

When Did It Begin

The modern concept of foreign aid dates to the eighteenth century, when Prussia (present-day Germany) gave assistance to its military allies to promote its own political interests. In the nineteenth and twentieth centuries, European countries aided their colonies (foreign lands that they had claimed as their own), usually with the intent of making those colonies more economically beneficial to themselves in the long run.

After World War II several international bodies were created that would shape the giving of foreign aid over the following decades. These include the World Bank and the International Monetary Fund (IMF), which aim to facilitate economic development and the spread of capitalism in poorer countries, and the United Nations, which aims to promote international cooperation in a wide range of areas. These groups have, since their founding, distributed large amounts of aid while helping to pinpoint the needs and qualifications of recipient countries and judging whether the aid they receive is successful in achieving its aims.

While European countries such as the United Kingdom and France still spent much of their foreign aid after World War II on their colonies and former colonies, great increases in foreign aid came as a result of the Cold War between the United States and the Soviet Union. Both countries, together with their allies, used foreign aid as a way of enlisting new allies and extending their ideological influence. Countries deemed strategically necessary were the targets of both countries' aid programs, and countries that received aid were subject to the withholding of that aid if they did not behave in the way that the donor country desired. Japan, meanwhile, was the largest donor of foreign aid in Asia. Its efforts to assist other countries at first took the form of reparations (money paid to other countries as punishment for the harm it had done them in World War II) and grew into a large program that encouraged economic development in the region.

More Detailed Information

Governments aid other governments and the people of foreign nations for a variety of reasons, most of which tend to have a political dimension. Foreign aid may be exchanged for the right to establish military bases in the recipient country or to prevent a recipient country from becoming sympathetic to a rival government. It might be used to encourage cooperation in fighting terrorism. Countries that do not have high status in international organizations might improve their standing by committing money and resources to aiding countries in need. Foreign aid is sometimes used as a way of creating a market for the donor country's products; for instance, a donor might require a recipient to use a gift of money to purchase food produced by the donor country's farmers.

There are also instances of foreign aid where politics and self-interest are less central. In countries plagued by famine, civil war, disease, or natural disasters, foreign aid sometimes arrives without substantial political strings attached. For example, many countries contributed foreign aid to those affected by the Indian Ocean tsunami in 2004, and efforts to combat HIV/AIDS in Africa rely heavily on aid from individual countries, international organizations, and other groups. In such cases donor governments do not obtain any obvious strategic or other advantages, but foreign aid of this kind, in addition to alleviating suffering, does tend to serve the purpose of

---

Economic Aid

Rank	Countries	Amount
# 1	Luxembourg:	$496.56 per capita
# 2	Denmark:	$390.78 per capita
# 3	Norway:	$303.63 per capita
# 4	Netherlands:	$242.55 per capita
# 5	Sweden:	$188.54 per capita
# 6	United Kingdom:	$176.54 per capita
# 7	France:	$165.91 per capita
# 8	Finland:	$162.58 per capita
# 9	Ireland:	$149.43 per capita
#10	Switzerland:	$146.20 per capita
#11	Belgium:	$103.29 per capita
#12	Austria:	$ 83.12 per capita
#13	Canada:	$ 78.55 per capita
#14	Japan:	$ 69.82 per capita
#15	Germany:	$ 67.94 per capita
#16	Australia:	$ 44.12 per capita
#17	Spain:	$ 32.92 per capita
#18	Portugal:	$ 25.55 per capita
#19	United States:	$ 23.12 per capita
#20	Iceland:	$ 22.38 per capita
#21	Italy:	$ 17.20 per capita
#22	Korea, South:	$ 15.23 per capita
Weighted average:		**$136.64 per capita**

SOURCE: CIA World Factbook.

Foreign aid is economic assistance that one country gives to another. Although the United States has been the world's largest provider of foreign aid since World War II, it ranks nineteenth in per capita foreign aid, which divides the total amount given by the number of people in the country. *Illustration by GGS Information Services. Cengage Learning, Gale.*

making the donor country look good in the eyes of the world. Most of the time, however, foreign aid may serve several of the above purposes at once, so it is not always easy to determine which motives are most important to the donor country.

Foreign aid might consist of money delivered in the form of grants (sums of money for specific purposes with no requirement that they be repaid), loans, or trade arrangements that, by allowing the recipient country to sell its products in the donor country, increase wealth in the recipient country. In countries experiencing crises, packages of food and clothing for private citizens might be the form that foreign aid takes. Foreign aid to a strategic partner might involve donating military equipment such as guns and vehicles. After the Soviet Union fell in 1991, Russia and the other former Soviet states received a great deal of expert assistance in the project of transitioning from communism to capitalism.

The most common kind of foreign aid is that given directly from one country to another, called bilateral aid. About one-fourth of all foreign aid, meanwhile, is distributed through international groups such as the United Nations, the World Bank, and the IMF. This is called multilateral aid. Multilateral aid is especially important in the realms of economic development and disaster relief. Those groups that provide multilateral aid refuse to furnish countries with military assistance.

There are also numerous aid groups not tied to any government, such as the Red Cross, which provides what is known as private aid. Increasingly, as well, private investment (the foreign business ventures of companies based in wealthy countries), together with payments sent by migrant workers to their distant families, has outweighed the money sent via the traditional foreign aid channels. Though these forms of wealth transfer cannot really be called foreign aid, they often function in much the same way.

Recent Trends

Since World War II the United States has been the world's largest provider of foreign aid. During the Cold War much of its foreign aid went to anticommunist countries and governments. After the Soviet Union collapsed in 1991, the focus of U.S. aid shifted. Instead of fighting communism, which no longer threatened its standing in the world, the United States has shifted to an agenda of promoting democracy and capitalism. Its efforts are aided by those of the World Bank and the IMF, both of which are committed to spreading capitalism. In their dealings with the United States as well as these international groups, developing countries are often required to enact economic and government reforms as a condition of the aid they receive.

Foreign aid, perhaps owing to the complex motives that give rise to it, is sometimes criticized. Critics speaking on behalf of the recipients of foreign aid claim that

TOP DONOR AND RECIPIENT NATIONS

The top five donors of foreign aid (money and other assistance given to countries in need), as of 2004, were the United States, Japan, France, the United Kingdom, and Germany, in that order. The United States, however, gave more than twice the amount that the second-largest donor, Japan, gave to foreign countries. Japan, France, the United Kingdom, and Germany each gave similar amounts of foreign aid.

The top recipients of foreign aid in 2004 were Iraq, Afghanistan, Vietnam, Ethiopia, and Congo. As with the top donors, there was disparity at the top of the list of recipients. Iraq received more than twice as much aid as Afghanistan, while Afghanistan and the other three top recipients claimed roughly similar amounts of aid.

In 2004 the United States, responsible for much of the aid to Iraq and Afghanistan, was, of course, engaged in wars in both of those places. War spending, however, is not considered foreign aid. Of the total amount of money the United States spent in both of those countries, the amount categorized as foreign aid was that portion aimed at helping those countries rebuild from the devastation of war, even as both wars were ongoing.

powerful countries use foreign aid as a tool for serving their own interests, and nothing more. Much foreign aid given to poor countries through the IMF and the World Bank, for example, has worsened economic conditions by forcing large amounts of debt on those countries and leaving them vulnerable to global competition. While capitalist reforms have helped wealthy countries achieve their own goals, the countries supposedly being aided have reaped few benefits.

Other critics focus more squarely on the United States, disapproving of the sometimes obvious political motives that lie behind some of the government's aid programs. For instance, after the September 11, 2001, attacks on the World Trade Center in New York City, the United States began increasing aid to countries that agreed to help it fight terrorism, even if those countries were ruled by undemocratic governments known to violate human rights.

Additionally, some people inside the United States criticize foreign aid as wasteful and burdensome to the nation's taxpayers. These critics, knowing that the United States is the world's largest supplier of foreign aid, assume that this means the United States spends a disproportionate amount of its income on other countries. In fact, the United States spends a smaller proportion of its national income (less than 0.2 percent) on foreign aid than most other Western countries. Even Sweden, one of the most generous of countries by this form of measurement, spends less than 0.8 percent of its national income on foreign aid.

$ Monetary Policy

What It Means

The size of the money supply (the amount of money in circulation) is one of the most powerful influences on an economy. In general, when more money is circulating in an economy, there is more demand for goods and services, so businesses produce more, and more people have jobs. By contrast, when the money supply shrinks, there is less demand for goods and services, businesses restrict their activities, and fewer people have jobs. Monetary policy is the government practice of adjusting the money supply in order to bring about a change in the economy.

In developed, capitalist economies (in which businesses are generally owned by private individuals rather than the government), there are central banks that regulate the banking industry and oversee the country's money supply. For instance, the United States' central bank, the Federal Reserve System (often called the Fed),

keeps watch over the U.S. economy and makes adjustments to the money supply in the hope of reaching certain economic goals. These goals usually include making sure there are enough jobs for people who want them, guarding against inflation (the general rising of prices), minimizing the damage caused by cycles of economic boom and bust, and otherwise promoting the long-term health of the economy.

Monetary policy does not adjust the money supply by changing the amount of currency (government-issued bills and coins) in circulation. Much of a country's money supply is actually paperless money created by bank loans. When banks loan money to consumers and businesses, they pump far more money into the economy than actually exists in the form of currency. This money takes the form of balances in individual checking and other bank accounts.

When Did It Begin

Prior to the Great Depression (a decline in the world economy that began in 1929 and lasted through much of the following decade), countries did not have well-defined economic policies. The so-called classical

Monetary policy refers to the ways in which a government modifies a nation's money supply (the total amount of money that is in circulation at a given time) in order to spark economic changes. In the United States, the Federal Reserve Board (headquartered in the Federal Reserve Building in Washington, D.C., above) is responsible for all major decisions relating to monetary policy. *AP Images.*

economists, who at the time dominated economic thought in capitalist countries, believed that economies regulated themselves through market forces (such as supply and demand) and should remain free from government intervention. In capitalist countries there was actually some amount of regulation by the government; in the United States, for instance, the Federal Reserve System had been established in 1913 in response to financial panics that caused many banks to fail. But individual banks still had more control over the money supply than the government did. The problems facing the economy during the Depression, however, could not be solved by market forces. Roughly one-third of the American labor force was out of work and so did not have any wages to spend on goods and services (in economic terms, there was a drop in demand). As a result, companies had no incentive to produce goods and services, which (to complete the circle) meant that they could not hire new workers. The U.S. economy was in a deep hole, and classical economic principles offered no ideas for how to get out of it.

Against this backdrop the British economist John Maynard Keynes (1883–1946) published *The General Theory of Employment, Interest, and Money* (1936), which revolutionized the study of economics as well as the relationship between government and the economy. Among other ideas, Keynes argued that the government could compensate for the loss of demand (the desire to purchase goods and services) that characterized the Depression (and that characterized milder forms of economic downturn, called recessions). He said that governments could do this by spending money on public works projects (such as building roads and dams) and by providing relief payments to people who were out of work. Additionally, governments could use tax policy to affect demand: when the government reduces the amount of money that people pay in taxes, people can spend more of their money on goods and services. The reverse can be expected to happen when governments raise taxes. This use of government spending and taxes to regulate the economy is called fiscal policy.

Keynes also suggested that governments could adjust the money supply to manage demand in the economy, thus laying the groundwork for the Fed's more active role in the economy in the years after World War II (which ended in 1945). For decades after the Depression, Keynes's ideas dominated economic thought. U.S. presidents and Congressional leaders attempted to steer the economy through difficulties using fiscal policy, while the Fed attempted to control inflation and unemployment through monetary policy.

More Detailed Information

To understand the Fed's (or any central bank's) monetary policy, it is necessary to understand the basics of the banking system.

FISCAL VS. MONETARY POLICY TODAY

Fiscal policy and monetary policy are the U.S. government's tools for controlling the economy. Fiscal policy involves taxation and government spending programs, and monetary policy involves changing the country's money supply. But since the 1970s the use of fiscal policy to affect the economy has become more controversial and complicated. This is partly because government intervention has been blamed for inflation (the general rising of prices), partly because of the long time lags associated with getting bills passed through the Senate and House of Representatives, and partly because the enormous size of typical U.S. budget deficits (the imbalance created when the country spends more money than it takes in) makes fiscal policy harder to craft.

The Federal Reserve System (often called the Fed), as the politically independent architect of monetary policy, has increasingly become the main government force in the economy. In fact, many people believe that the Fed and its chairman are as powerful as any government institution in the United States, including the president and Congress. The Fed's chairman can affect the entire U.S. economy simply by stating his or her views about current conditions.

Banks take in money from some customers (called depositors) and lend it out to other customers. People who borrow money from a bank pay interest (a fee for the use of that money), and this interest is the chief source of profits for most banks. Banks therefore typically want to make as many loans as possible at any given time. If they loaned all the deposited money out, however, depositors might worry that they would not be able to get their money back in cash. To give the public confidence in the banking system, every time a bank receives a deposit from a customer, it must set aside a portion of that money and keep it in the bank's reserves. In the United States the Fed decides what the size of that portion will be. Because very few depositors will ask for the majority of their money in cash at any given time, the Fed only requires banks to set aside a small fraction of those deposits. The excess can be loaned out to other customers.

For instance, imagine for simplicity's sake that the Fed currently requires banks to set aside 10 percent of all deposits before making loans. If you deposited $10,000 in your bank, then your bank would have to set aside $1,000 of that money to make sure that it can meet depositors' needs. It could then lend the remaining $9,000 of your account balance to someone who wanted it and who qualified for a loan.

The effect this has on the money supply is tremendous. Notice that the bank has turned your initial deposit of $10,000 into $19,000. This is possible because your $10,000 exists only on paper, as a bank balance. You have full use of your bank balance, and anytime you take money out of your account, you will put it to work in the economy. If you write a $500 check to your landlord, she will deposit that check in her bank account, and her bank will set aside a portion of that money for its reserves and lend out the rest. Meanwhile, the person who borrowed $9,000 from your bank will similarly use that money to pay for goods and services. The businesses that sell these goods and services will then deposit their profits in their own banks, which will use those deposits to finance more loans.

Anytime a bank can add to its reserves, it can (and probably will) make more loans. When a bank makes loans, it increases the country's money supply. Therefore, the Fed changes the money supply by changing the amount of money banks have in reserve. It has three tools for affecting reserve amounts.

First, the Fed can simply change reserve requirements. If, as in the above example, current Fed requirements specify that 10 percent of deposits must be set aside, and the Fed wants to restrict the money supply, it might instruct banks to begin setting aside 12 percent of deposits. Because that extra 2 percent represents money that must be kept in reserve rather than loaned out and thereby allowed to multiply, this would have an immediate and drastic effect on the money supply. Conversely, lowering reserve requirements to 8 percent would cause an enormous increase in the amount of money circulating through the banking system. Because the effects of changing reserve requirements are so broad, the Fed does not use this monetary policy tool very often.

The Fed's second monetary policy tool is to change an interest rate called the discount rate. The Fed provides banks with a special service called the discount window. The discount window is not literally a window but rather an outlet for borrowing money. If a bank suddenly found that it did not have enough money to meet the minimum reserve requirements, it could use the Fed's discount window to cover its shortfall. Just as an individual pays a fee called interest to borrow from a bank, so does a bank when it borrows from the Fed. If the interest rate charged at the discount window is high, banks are not very likely to borrow money from the Fed in this way. If the interest rate charged at the discount window is low, banks are more likely to borrow and, by extension, make loans. In reality, many banks worry that borrowing from the discount window will signal to the Fed that they are having financial difficulties; therefore, most banks choose to borrow money from each other to cover reserve shortfalls.

The third tool the Fed uses is open-market operations. This is the process of buying or selling government securities (low-risk, government-backed investments in the form of Treasury bills, Treasury notes, and Treasury bonds) on the open market. In other words, the Fed acts just like any other investor in the financial markets,

contacting a dealer of securities to purchase or sell its securities, depending on how it wants to affect the money supply. If the Fed buys securities, it injects money into the economy, because money is coming out of the government's own checking account and being placed in the bank accounts of securities dealers, where it will multiply according to the loan process outlined above. If the government sells securities, however, securities dealers write checks to the Fed, which means that the money represented by those checks leaves the commercial banking system, diminishing the money supply. Open-market operations are by far the Fed's most commonly used monetary policy tool today.

Recent Trends

Starting in the 1990s there was a great deal of media coverage of the Fed's actions in regard to interest rates, but few people understand what the Fed really does or what interest rates newscasters are talking about when they mention the Fed.

While the Fed controls the discount rate directly, the discount rate is not the most important interest rate to the wider economy. As noted above, banks usually borrow from one another when they are short on reserves. The interest rate at which they borrow this money is called the federal funds rate. Because this represents one of the main ways, other than deposits, that banks get their money in today's economy, changes in the federal funds rate have a large effect on the money supply.

Therefore, while the Fed's tools for monetary policy do not strictly include the ability to set the federal funds rate, in actuality it does so by announcing its goals for that rate. If the Fed's chairman says that he would like to see the federal funds rate drop by 0.5 percent, the federal funds rate will drop by 0.5 percent. This happens because the Fed backs up its target for the federal funds rate with open-market operations that change the money supply. When more money is in circulation, banks charge less for the use of borrowed money. If the Fed wants a drop of 0.5 percent, then, it increases the money supply by buying enough government securities to bring about that amount of fluctuation.

All other interest rates in the economy tend to be based on the federal funds rate. For instance, the prime interest rate (the rate banks use to determine how much interest to charge people who take out home or business loans), is usually about 3 percentage points higher than the federal funds rate.

BANK RESERVES

What It Means

The money that a bank keeps on hand, either in its own vaults or in an account with a central bank, is referred to as the bank's reserves. Not all the money that is deposited in a bank stays there. When an individual deposits money

Bank reserves are the money that a bank keeps available for cash withdrawals at any given time. After the Great Depression, when widespread bank failures incited panic among account holders, the federal government instituted new laws stipulating that all banks must have reserves of at least 10 percent of their total assets. *AP Images.*

in a bank, the bank uses most of that money to make loans, and the bank charges interest (a fee people must pay to borrow money) on those loans. Because interest payments account for much of a bank's profits, it is natural for them to want to loan out as much of the money deposited with them as possible. They must balance this desire for profit, however, with the demands of depositors (bank account holders); that is, when depositors want to withdraw money from their accounts, the bank must have the money on hand to give them.

To ensure the stability of the banking system, most countries today require banks to keep a certain amount of money in reserve at all times. Usually this amount of money, called required reserves, is defined as a percentage of the amount of money that the bank takes in through deposits. For instance, say that the U.S. government requires banks to maintain reserves equal to 10 percent of their deposits. If a bank takes in $1,000,000 in deposits, it

would be obliged to keep $100,000 in its vaults or in its account with the central bank of the United States (called the Federal Reserve System, or the Fed, an independent agency of the U.S. government). Any money beyond this required amount is called excess reserves and can be used to make loans.

Required reserves represent money that is simply being stored, whereas loans represent money that is being used to generate more money. When banks loan money, the people and businesses that borrow it are able to make a wide range of purchases they could not otherwise make, and the economy grows. Therefore, the proportion of money that banks are required to set aside as reserves has a dramatic effect on the overall economy.

When Did It Begin

During the medieval period in Europe (about 500–1500 AD), gold was the dominant form of money. Gold is heavy

HOW BANKS RELY ON TRUST

The success of the fractional-reserve banking system, in which banks keep cash on hand equal to only a fraction of the deposits they take in, depends on the assumption that only a fraction of a bank's customers will ever want to withdraw their money at any given moment. If all of the depositors (those who have deposited money) of any modern bank showed up at the same time demanding their money, the bank would not be able to pay them, and it would have to shut down. Such an event is known as a bank run.

A large proportion of any country's money exists only on paper; banks keep track of customers' deposit and withdrawal amounts and send out regular statements that show their account balances (the amount of money they have in each of their bank accounts). For the public to remain comfortable with the invisible nature of most wealth, they must trust that the banking system will always be able to deliver money when they want it. If this trust is damaged (historically this has happened in times of war and ex-treme economic turmoil), people panic, thinking that their bank balances will become meaningless figures in an account book. Large numbers of people try to withdraw their money, and bank reserves are not large enough to cover the value of all deposits at once. During most bank runs wealth simply disappears. Banks close down, and depositors lose their money. The effects on individuals and the economy are catastrophic.

The Federal Reserve System (also called the Fed), the central bank of the United States, was created as an independent agency of the U.S. government in 1913 in response to numerous early-twentieth-century bank runs. By centralizing banking procedures and establishing reserve requirements and other banking guidelines, the Fed has drastically limited the likelihood of future bank runs. U.S. bank deposits are also insured (guaranteed against loss) by the federal government, eliminating the possibility that depositors will lose all of their money in the event of a bank's failure.

and cumbersome to move, and in many communities goldsmiths (who, because they worked with gold, were capable of judging its purity, weighing it accurately, and storing it) became the keepers of gold. An individual would take his gold to the goldsmith's place of business for safe-keeping, and the goldsmith would give him a receipt stating how much gold he had deposited. Over time people recognized that the goldsmith's receipts themselves had value, because they were stand-ins for the amount of gold indicated. Rather than retrieve gold in order to make everyday purchases, people began using the goldsmiths' receipts as money.

At some point it became clear to goldsmiths that there was rarely a situation in which a majority of depositors wanted their gold at the same time. Instead, people preferred to use the much more convenient receipts, confident that these could be exchanged for gold whenever necessary. The goldsmiths, realizing that they could generate more profits for themselves by making loans, began to issue receipts to people who wanted to borrow money. In this way they were creating more money than actually existed in the form of gold. They made loans in proportion to the amount of gold they had in reserve, balancing their desire for profit against the need to be prepared when depositors showed up wishing to make withdrawals.

These goldsmiths created the concept of fractional-reserve banking (when banks reserve, or set aside, only a small portion of their deposits and loan or invest the rest in order to make a profit), the cornerstone of the modern banking system. The gold reserves of medieval Europe were the predecessors of what we now call bank reserves.

More Detailed Information

The modern banking system is directly descended from the system created by medieval European goldsmiths, with government-issued bills and coins replacing gold in the scenario described above. Banks today issue far more money (by giving loans in the form of checks and checking accounts rather than in cash) than actually exists in the form of government-issued bills and coins.

This money-creating function of banks is not only essential to the business success of the banks themselves, but it is also the foundation of all economic activity in capitalist countries (countries in which businesses are owned largely by private individuals, not the government). If the money supply (the amount of money circulating in a country's economy) were limited strictly to bills and coins, modern economies would be far smaller and less dynamic than they are. This is because the creation of money does not stop with each individual loan.

Consider the following simplified illustration of how fractional-reserve banking works. John Doe deposits $10,000 in cash at Bank A. Bank A, wanting to make as much profit as possible, sets aside only the amount of money required by law. Assuming for simplicity's sake that the government currently requires banks to reserve 10 percent of their deposits, Bank A would reserve $1,000 and then look for a loan applicant.

At this point Jane Smith walks through the doors of Bank A and applies for a $9,000 loan to start a pizza parlor. Bank A gives her a checking account that has a balance (a credit) of $9,000, along with a book of checks, and Jane begins shopping for equipment and supplies. Say that Jane is able to get all of her start-up needs taken care of at Pizza Suppliers, Inc., and she writes them a $9,000 check. Pizza Suppliers, Inc. will deposit Jane's check at Bank B, where the business has an account.

Bank B, after setting aside 10 percent ($900) of this deposit amount, will loan out the remaining $8,100. This loan will generate more check writing, more bank deposits, and more loans. It will create more and more money that previously did not exist, until the money-creating potential of John Doe's original $10,000 is exhausted.

Because bank deposits have, in this way, tremendous ripple effects, changes in the amount of bank reserves required by law have a powerful influence on the economy. Increases in the required reserve amount mean more money taken out of circulation at every stage of the process outlined above. Decreases in bank reserve requirements, however, represent additional money created at every stage.

Recent Trends

The money supply is one of the financial factors that most influences a country's economy. When more money is in circulation, interest rates tend to fall, loaning activity increases, and the economy expands. When the money supply decreases, interest rates tend to rise, fewer people take out loans, and the economy contracts.

Today the Federal Reserve System attempts to regulate the U.S. economy by changing the quantity of money in circulation at any given time. The Fed does this not by ordering changes in the amount of money minted by the government but instead by influencing banks' lending activities. Banks create money when they make loans, and they can make loans in proportion to the size of their cash reserves. When the Fed wants to influence banks to create more or less money, it uses certain tactics that change the levels of required bank reserves nationwide.

$ Economic Legislation

What It Means

Most governments in the world today regulate the affairs of private businesses with the intent of protecting consumers, small businesses, and the overall health of their economies. This regulation is based on a variety of economic legislation, or laws concerning the economy, passed primarily since the late nineteenth century.

In the United States, governments at the local, state, and federal level all make and enforce laws concerning the economy. Policies toward businesses differ considerably from city to city and state to state, but the federal government has historically taken the lead in crafting the most important pieces of economic legislation. Specifically, the U.S. government has established important ground rules for businesses relating to competition in the

marketplace, the protection of ideas and inventions, the rights of workers, trade with people and companies located in other nations, and the environment, among other areas. The federal government also sometimes intervenes in cases of economic crisis, or when the side effects of economic activity cause problems for society.

When Did It Begin

Government involvement in the economy predates the rise of capitalism, the economic system that came into being in the sixteenth to eighteenth centuries and that is built on private ownership of property and the free competition of buyers and sellers in markets (the places or systems that bring buyers and sellers together). Some forms of economic legislation that existed in the ancient and medieval worlds still exist today. In ancient Egypt, Babylon, and Greece, for example, rulers established maximum prices for such necessities as grain, ensuring that they would remain affordable. Though most economists frown on these policies today, as recently as the 1970s price controls on oil were a major part of U.S. economic policy, and many politicians continue to call on the government to set maximum prices for oil, prescription drugs, and other products. Additionally, intellectual property law, which protects creative ideas as embodied in such forms as books and inventions, dates back to the 1400s, when printing presses first allowed writers to reproduce their works and sell them in large quantities. Intellectual property law today is still developing and being redefined in response to such technologies as the Internet, which have revolutionized the distribution of creative ideas as radically as did the printing press in its day. Likewise, protectionism (the use of high taxes or limits on imports, which protect domestic industries from foreign competition) was almost universally practiced in the pre-capitalist world, and the practice persists today despite the general consensus of economists that it is a bad idea.

Other forms of economic legislation were slow in developing, in part because of the strong arguments of early economists such as the Scottish philosopher Adam Smith (1723–90). Smith believed that market-based capitalism was self-regulating and worked best when government stayed completely out of economic affairs. Thus, as capitalism gained steam in the eighteenth and nineteenth centuries, governments took what is known as a laissez-faire approach to the economy: they left businesses free to pursue profits in almost any way they wanted. By the early nineteenth century, in England and other parts of Europe, this had begun to result in miserable working conditions, workdays of 14 or 16 hours, and the widespread employment of children as young as six or eight years old. The first labor laws were passed in early nineteenth-century England in response to public concern for workers.

Economic legislation can be any law that the government passes to regulate business activities in the interest of economic and social well-being. In many countries legislation is used to curtail deforestation and other instances where businesses exploit the environment irresponsibly for profit. *JLM Visuals. Reproduced by permission.*

The United States generally lagged behind Europe in the realm of economic legislation, in part because the laissez-faire approach to the economy was (and still is) part of the nation's identity. By the end of the nineteenth century, however, the rise of trusts (large numbers of companies united under one common owner) that dominated entire national markets, such as the oil and steel industries, posed obvious threats to consumers and small businesses and led to major pieces of antitrust legislation. But it was not until the Great Depression of the 1930s, during which business activity ground to a halt and roughly 25 percent of American workers lost their jobs, that the U.S. government began to intervene in the economy on the scale that it does today. The Depression seemed to many Americans evidence that capitalism could not work properly without government regulation. President Franklin D. Roosevelt's New Deal programs (wide-ranging legislation meant to spur recovery from the Depression) included new regulations of the banking and financial industries, supported workers' rights to form unions, set a minimum wage and a maximum workday length, and in numerous other ways asserted the government's authority and responsibility to oversee the economic life of the nation.

More Detailed Information

Some of the most important pieces of economic legislation in the United States concern a handful of basic subjects: competition between businesses, which is regulated according to a variety of antitrust legislation; intellectual property rights, which are established by copyrights, patents, and trademarks; labor laws, some of which are federal and some of which vary from state to state; trade policy, which pits the desire for protectionism against the desire for global economic development and unity; price controls, minimum and maximum prices for certain products; and externalities, the side effects of economic activity to which government often must respond for the well-being of society.

Antitrust legislation arises out of the theory that the market for any product functions best when there are a large number of sellers competing for consumers' business. When this is the case, no business is able to raise prices in order to inflate profits, because other businesses would be positioned to lure the first business's customers away by offering lower prices. Likewise, companies tend to produce enough goods to satisfy consumer demand, and they tend to produce high-quality goods to avoid losing customers. By contrast, when one firm is the only seller of a good (this situation is called a monopoly), it can raise prices, cut production, and offer inferior goods without risking failure. Though true monopolies are rare, the U.S. government has, since the late nineteenth century, sought to promote competition by preventing monopolies from forming or by dismantling monopolies and near-monopolies into separate entities.

Intellectual property laws are meant to protect the intangible products of the creative mind. Three basic forms of intellectual-property protections are available in the United States: copyrights, patents, and trademarks. Copyrights protect the works of artists, writers, composers, moviemakers, and others who produce original creative content. Patents protect the rights of those who invent new products, technologies, or processes for making products. Trademarks protect those who come up with original names, symbols, or other elements that are used to identify a brand or organization in the marketplace. Each of these forms of protection allows the individuals responsible for creative ideas to reap the benefits of originating those ideas. In the absence of intellectual property rights, the originator of an idea would have no more right to profit from it than anyone else. Theoretically this would result in a diminished amount of creative effort across society.

Labor laws arose in response to the widespread mistreatment of workers in the eighteenth, nineteenth, and early twentieth centuries. Some of the most important labor laws outline the responsibilities that employers have to their employees (and vice versa), provide standards for workplace safety, and prevent or punish discrimination (on the basis of race, religion, sex, color, and national origin) in hiring and on the job. Another major focus of labor laws at the state and national levels is the accommodation of labor unions, organized groups of employees empowered to uphold workers' interests and bargain with employers for improvements in working conditions. Prior to the Great Depression the U.S. government generally sided with employers in refusing to negotiate with organized labor unions.

Protectionism has always been a fact of life in the realm of international trade. Since World War I the United States has generally followed a policy of reducing tariffs (taxes on imports) and quotas (limits on the number of imports), but some protectionist trade restrictions still exist. Economists generally argue that protectionism reduces economic efficiency and does more harm than good in the long run, but the U.S. government continues to protect certain industries for various reasons, ranging from national security to the lobbying of special-interest groups.

Price controls, likewise, are an old, global phenomenon about which economists generally have little good to say. Although Americans may feel cheated when, for instance, gas prices rise to record highs at the same time that oil company profits are at record highs, economists

U.S. STEEL TARIFFS

Among the various kinds of economic legislation a government can impose are tariffs, or import taxes, which protect a country's domestic industries from foreign competitors.

Although U.S. President George W. Bush was generally known to side with antiprotectionist advocates of free trade, he nonetheless passed a controversial tariff in March 2002 to protect the imperiled American steel industry. In the years preceding the tariff, thousands of U.S. steel workers had lost their jobs because American steel manufacturers were unable to compete with steel products being produced more cheaply abroad. Bush described the short-term import taxes, which ranged between 8 and 30 percent on various steel products, as "temporary safeguards" designed to give American steelmakers time to revamp their businesses in order to return to free competition in the global market.

The planned three-year tariff was applauded by labor unions and the politically powerful domestic steel lobby. It was lifted prematurely at the end of 2003, however, because of overwhelming dissent and threats of retaliatory tariffs from the European Union, as well as a WTO (World Trade Organization) ruling that the tariffs represented an illegal barrier to free trade.

argue that putting a ceiling on oil prices will infallibly result in an imbalance between supply and demand. With their profits limited, oil companies will produce less gas than Americans want, and shortages of gas will result.

Finally, the government makes laws concerning side effects of economic activity, known as externalities. Externalities either harm or benefit third parties not involved in the transaction at issue. For example, a positive externality would be present when one person in a neighborhood pays to have her house renovated, and property values on the whole block rise. Government is often more concerned, however, with negative externalities. For example, a paper manufacturer pollutes the air around its factory, resulting in a diminishment of the quality of life, and possibly even medical problems, for those who live nearby. Governments therefore set standards for pollution, monitor companies' compliance with the standards, and fine those who violate the standards.

Recent Trends

Attitudes toward government involvement in the economy are often subject to political beliefs. In the United States today, conservatives and liberals tend to disagree about the need for economic legislation and its enforcement. Conservatives typically believe that the economy works best, and produces the best results for society, when the government imposes minimal restrictions on it. Liberals, on the other hand, typically have less faith in an unregulated economy, and believe that the government should intervene in some economic matters in order to produce socially beneficial results.

Economic legislation in the United States has, since the beginning of the twentieth century, come in waves depending on which political party is in power. The largest wave of legislation came under Democratic president Roosevelt in the wake of the Depression, and government involvement in the economy generally grew from that time until the 1970s. There was a substantial backlash to government regulation under Republican president Ronald Reagan, who encouraged some government agencies to slack off in their enforcement of existing economic legislation. President Bill Clinton's administration reversed this trend somewhat during his eight years in office, but he was significantly hampered in this for six of those years by a Republican-controlled Congress. His successor, Republican George W. Bush, encountered no such opposition for the first six years of his tenure as president, and he followed Reagan's example of combating what he saw as excessive regulation of the economy.

ANTITRUST LEGISLATION

What It Means

Antitrust legislation refers to a set of laws meant to protect consumers and society by ensuring that businesses do not unfairly dominate their individual industries. Businesses are driven by the incentive for profit, so it is natural for them to want to reduce the success of competitors who cut into these profits. If a business becomes a monopoly (the only producer of a particular good or service that people need), however, its power over consumers is unlimited: it can raise prices as much as it wants, and it can make goods of as poor or as high quality as it wants.

In other cases of unfair domination, two or more prominent business firms in one industry might enter into agreements with one another that similarly harm the public interest. One form of such an agreement is a merger, the legal joining of different business firms. Not all mergers result in harm to the public interest, but if the merging businesses are sufficiently large, they can function similarly to a monopoly. Another way that two or more business firms might trample on the rights of competitors and consumers is by price-fixing (illegal agreements to keep prices at levels that will ensure profitability). Price-fixing is never in the best interest of anyone but the businesses involved in the agreement.

Both the U.S. government and state governments in the United States have laws in place, commonly known as antitrust legislation, to guard against these sorts of abuses. National antitrust legislation first came into being in the late 1800s. The law passed at that time has been supplemented by other laws and updates over the intervening decades as businesses, in their desire for profits, have found new ways of eliminating competition.

When Did It Begin

The late nineteenth century was a time of great transformation for the U.S. economy. Such businessmen as John D. Rockefeller (1839–1937; a founder of Standard Oil Company) and Andrew Carnegie (1835–1919; a founder of U.S. Steel Corporation) presided over an era of enormous industrial growth and dominated their respective industries, conducting business on an unprecedented scale and amassing previously unimaginable fortunes. These men were perceived, however, as using force and manipulation to dominate their industries unfairly, and their critics accused them of being robber barons who would stoop to any unethical act for the sake of profit. Rockefeller intimidated competing oil companies until they went out of business. He then bought up the remaining oil companies, which were thereafter ruled by a single organization (called a trust). Standard Oil was one of the most notorious trusts of its day. Public opposition to such behavior sparked the Sherman Antitrust Act of 1890. The Sherman Act outlawed any "contract, combination or conspiracy in restraint of trade or commerce" and made it illegal to build or try to build a monopoly in any industry.

The U.S. government used the Sherman Act to break up numerous trusts in the following decades, but the lack of specificity in the new law meant that businesses could find other ways to reduce competition. Congress therefore passed the 1914 Clayton Antitrust Act, which specifically outlined a number of anticompetitive practices that would now be illegal. Mergers that reduced competition were among the newly outlawed business practices. Other provisions of the Clayton Act concerned manufacturers and dealers of certain goods who conspire together to squeeze out other manufacturers and dealers of those same goods. The Federal Trade Commission Act, also passed in 1914, established the Federal Trade Commission (FCC), the government organization that has been chiefly responsible for monitoring anticompetitive behavior among businesses since that time. The rules against mergers were tightened further in 1950 when Congress passed the Celler-Kefauver Act.

More Detailed Information

A capitalist economy (one in which firms are owned by private individuals rather than the government) functions best when a high level of competition exists. When there are many producers of, say, automobile tires, and they are all competing for the money of a large number of consumers, tires get produced more efficiently, and prices are driven as low as they can go without making the tire business unprofitable. Those tire makers that master their business under these conditions will prosper while giving consumers what they need and want at a reasonable price.

Suppose, however, that one tire maker, Super Tires, were to win out over all the others by delivering a

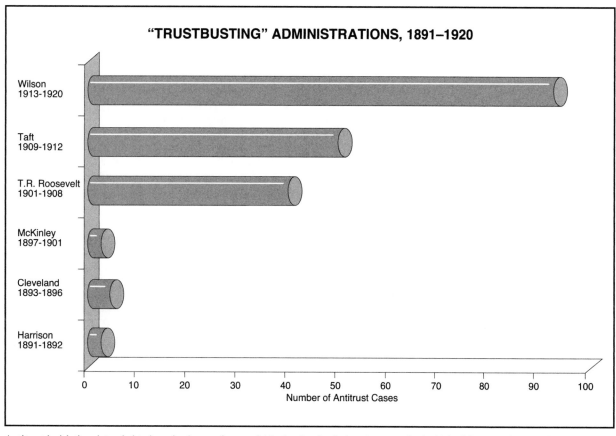

"TRUSTBUSTING" ADMINISTRATIONS, 1891–1920

Wilson 1913-1920	
Taft 1909-1912	
T.R. Roosevelt 1901-1908	
McKinley 1897-1901	
Cleveland 1893-1896	
Harrison 1891-1892	

0   10   20   30   40   50   60   70   80   90   100

Number of Antitrust Cases

Antitrust legislation, intended to keep businesses from unfairly dominating industries, arose in the United States at the end of the nineteenth century in response to aggressive consolidations of power by such companies as Standard Oil and U.S. Steel. Antitrust cases rose dramatically during the administration of President Woodrow Wilson, when antitrust legislation was strengthened. *Illustration by Smith & Santori. Cengage Learning, Gale.*

superior product at a reasonable cost. As Super Tires grew, its owners would naturally want to find ways of ensuring that it continued to grow as quickly as possible for as long as possible. One way of pursuing this goal might be to buy up the competition, purchasing all the tire-producing businesses that threaten its dominance. Free from competition, Super Tires would then have a monopoly over the tire industry. At this point it could charge virtually any price it wanted, and it could provide tires of whatever quality it wanted, because consumers would have no other place to buy their tires, and they would not be able to operate their vehicles without tires. To further reduce the possibility of competition, Super Tires would be able to cut prices long enough to make it impossible for smaller firms to compete, forcing them to lose money and eventually close. Once such competitors had left the industry, Super Tires could simply raise prices again to make up for any losses it incurred while pushing its smaller competitors out of business.

Suppose, alternately, that Super Tires and a competitor, Maximum Tires, were equals at the top of the tire

industry. Suppose both of them had an equal interest in staying at the top of the industry, but neither had enough of an advantage over the other to push it out of business or to purchase it outright. The two companies might agree, in these circumstances, to merge into one company with twice the potential for profits (or more). Alternately, if they controlled enough of the tire industry together so that no smaller firms could threaten them, they might agree to fix their prices at a level that would unfairly benefit both of them. These actions, called mergers and price-fixing, respectively, have the potential to reduce the choices and power of consumers as much as a monopoly does.

In the real world anticompetitive actions can be more complicated than this, and they can be harder for the public and the government to fight. It can also be difficult to tell when a company's dominance has reached a level that does, in fact, harm the public interest. Opponents of antitrust legislation often argue that large-scale businesses are necessary to produce goods at the low prices that consumers are accustomed to paying and that enormous resources are necessary to finance

THE CASE OF MICROSOFT

The computer software company Microsoft has what most people consider a monopoly (being the only producer of a particular good or service that people need) over the software industry, but it has largely escaped the fate of many monopolies before it. Whereas the U.S. government has used antitrust legislation (laws that protect consumers and society by ensuring that businesses do not unfairly dominate their individual industries) to break up numerous twentieth-century monopolies deemed harmful to the public interest into smaller firms, Microsoft has been consistently able to rebuff charges that it is detrimental to consumers or the economy. It has argued that its dominant status serves the public interest because it uses its profits to promote innovation.

In 1998, however, Microsoft was taken to court by the U.S. Justice Department for using its monopoly power in the area of operating systems (the computer program that serves as the foundation for all other programs you install later) to drive competition out of other areas of the software industry. Microsoft's Windows operating system had for years come preinstalled on new compu-

ters, but Microsoft had recently begun giving away its Internet navigation program, Internet Explorer, for free along with Windows. In fact, if consumers removed Internet Explorer from the so-called "bundle" of software that came with new computers, Windows would operate more slowly. This fact discouraged anyone from using the competition's program, Netscape Navigator. Many people saw Microsoft's actions as an unfair use of monopoly power to leapfrog past an already established competitor, Netscape, whose Navigator program was the leader in this portion of the software industry at that time.

Though a federal judge found Microsoft guilty of abusing its monopoly and ordered it, in 2000, to split into two separate companies, an appeals court judge overturned this ruling on the grounds that the presiding judge of the original case had spoken to the media while preparing to make his decision. Related legal issues led to a 2002 settlement between Microsoft and the federal government that did not significantly impair Microsoft's business practices.

---

technological breakthroughs and other difficult tasks in the modern business world.

Recent Trends

Antitrust laws have always been controversial, perhaps never more so than in the early years of the twenty-first century. The business climate of this time was characterized by two trends that, in the context of antitrust legislation, seemed to be at odds with one another. On the one hand there was an increasingly global economy in which businesses were forced to compete with their counterparts all over the world rather than just with their domestic counterparts. This would seem, by the logic of capitalism, to be in the best interest of consumers and the public. On the other hand multinational corporations (business firms that operate in many countries) dominated world business more than ever before. These giant business firms were often large enough to eclipse smaller competitors not just in their countries of origin but in any country in which they chose to do business. If the trend of corporate dominance over global business were to continue, it could (theoretically and according to some) have the effect of reducing the power of consumers worldwide.

In this business climate there was no consensus about antitrust legislation. Some people felt that multinational corporations needed reining in, while others felt that increased antitrust efforts would do nothing but reduce economic efficiency. Whether or not the global economy would be best served by an increase or a decrease in antitrust efforts remained an open question among economists and policymakers.

INTELLECTUAL PROPERTY

What It Means

In most developed countries legal protections exist to ensure that people cannot use other people' ideas for personal profit. For instance, it is illegal to burn and sell DVD copies of a movie made by someone else; to duplicate another person's soap-dispenser design and start manufacturing dispensers to sell to fast-food chains; and to open a new clothing store named the Gap when a successful international chain is already using that name. The ideas behind the movie, the soap dispenser, and the brand name of the clothing chain have value once they have been made into real products (once the movie has been filmed, the soap dispenser constructed, and the store built and named). The people who came up with those ideas have the legal right to make sure that no one else can make money from their ideas without permission. These abstract products of the creative mind are known as intellectual property, and they are protected by their own specialized laws, which vary from country to country.

In the United States there are three main forms of legal protection for intellectual property: copyrights, patents, and trademarks. Copyrights apply to the works of artists, writers, composers, and other people who make original contributions to culture. Patents apply to new inventions and technologies. Trademarks apply to names, words, symbols, or other elements used to identify a particular brand or organization.

While intellectual property rights seem designed to reward the creators of valuable ideas for their labor, the primary purpose of these laws is actually to benefit society

Intellectual property refers to books, films, or other creative works that are owned by a particular individual or company. This photo shows Chinese officials destroying bootlegged CDs and videos confiscated by the government. *AP Images.*

as a whole. It is in society's interest that people write books, make music, invent new technologies, and start companies that provide goods and services that people need or want. Legal protections for intellectual property are meant to stimulate creativity for the public benefit. The financial benefits to individual creators are a by-product of the laws.

When Did It Begin

The notion of intellectual property first became important after the invention of the printing press in the 1400s. Prior to this time books were both written and copied (in very limited supplies) by hand. There were few opportunities to exploit a writer's ideas for profit, so there was little need for the originator of a creative work to be concerned about questions of ownership regarding that work.

Once numerous copies of a book could be printed quickly, people completely unconnected with the writer's labor could make a profit: a popular book could be reprinted and sold by anyone with a printing press. When this happened, the author of the work, the editor, and the publisher saw their own chances to profit from that work

diminish. With no guarantee that they could make a living from their work, there was little reason for them to undertake such work in the future.

In the fifteenth century European rulers responded to this threat to creative work by offering early forms of copyright protections, usually on a case-by-case basis (which enabled these rulers to not only to support writers and publishers but also to suppress certain kinds of work). For instance, popes and rulers of some Italian city-states granted the privilege of printing certain works to individual printers, hoping to encourage the production of books considered vital to the community. In sixteenth-century England, Queen Elizabeth granted monopoly rights (the legal right to be the exclusive seller of a certain product or group of products) to individual printers. The first true copyright law offering broad protection to the creative work of a wide range of individuals was the Statute of Anne, enacted by the British Parliament in 1710. U.S. copyright and patent laws were passed in 1790, soon after the nation's birth.

More Detailed Information

Each of the forms of intellectual property law (copyrights, patents, and trademarks) has its own areas of application and characteristics. Copyrights give writers and artists the sole right to reproduce, distribute, display, perform, or otherwise circulate their work; they also have the right to prepare works derived from or based on that original work. Some of the types of creative work protected by copyrights in the United States are novels, poems, nonfiction writing of all kinds, musical compositions, musical recordings, movies, TV programs, paintings, architectural works, toys, maps, and computer programs. To be copyrighted, the intellectual property must appear in some fixed form. In other words, your idea for the plot of the Great American Novel cannot be copyrighted. Someone who hears your idea and then writes the novel is not in violation of the law. You must actually put the words on paper in order to claim copyright protection. It is not necessary to request copyright protection from the government; once the original work is fixed in some physical form, the copyright automatically exists. For optimal protection, however, it is advisable to register original work. Copyrights generally last until 70 years after the creator's death. After this time, the work enters the public domain, which means that anyone is entitled to use it for his or her own purposes.

Inventions are protected by the U.S. government through patents. A patent is a document issued by the government. It gives the inventor (or other entity holding the patent, such as a business or corporation) the right to prevent other people from reproducing, distributing, or otherwise using that invention in the United States. The U.S. definition of the word *invention* includes machines, manufactured products, processes (for

WHAT ABOUT THE REST OF THE WORLD?

Intellectual property refers to the ownership of ideas; intellectual property laws protect the rights of people who come up with original ideas and put them to good use. Copyrights (for artistic works), patents (for inventions), and trademarks (for the names and logos of organizations) that protect the various kinds of intellectual property in the United States, however, do not apply to people who might use that intellectual property in other countries. Does this mean that if you invented a new type of cell phone in the United States, someone in another country could copy that phone exactly and sell it there? Not really. It is true that if you did not investigate intellectual property laws in other countries, you might be vulnerable to this kind of threat. Most countries, however, have laws similar to those in the United States, so you would simply need to know how to obtain your intellectual property rights in any of the countries where you might do business in the future. While the laws regulating intellectual property differ from country to country, increasing efforts are being made to harmonize them. Some treaties between countries have made it possible to register for intellectual property rights in more than one nation at a time.

In some cases the incompatibility between different countries' notions of intellectual property has caused considerable tension. For instance, U.S. companies that produce software, recorded enter-tainment, and pharmaceuticals have found it extremely difficult to protect their intellectual property in China because the country has relatively few laws governing that area. According to some estimates, in China 95 percent of the DVDs and CDs sold, 90 percent of all software used, and 70 percent of software installed on the government's computers was pirated in 2006. Despite making numerous promises to crack down on piracy, China was slow to do so. Many experts believed that it would not work to protect intellectual property until its own industries were threatened by the problem. But few such products were even made in China, precisely because the lack of protections took away any financial incentive to produce creative work.

Microsoft, which had unsuccessfully waged a 10-year battle with Chinese companies that illegally copied and sold its Windows operating system software, came up with its own solution in 2003. Abandoning its attempts to sue Chinese companies, it instead focused on gaining a long-term foothold in China by opening a dialogue with the Chinese government, founding a research center in Beijing, and drastically reducing its prices in China. Microsoft CEO Bill Gates described the strategy as "an institution-to-institution relationship, where we've really found a win-win way of doing things together that will generate a substantial part of Microsoft's growth in the next decade."

instance, a new way of manufacturing doorknobs), and compositions of matter (a new clothing fiber, for example). An invention can be entirely original or it can be an improvement or variation on an already existing invention. In any case it must have some useful purpose to qualify for a patent. Patents are valid for 17 years from the date the government issues them to an inventor.

A trademark protects any word, symbol, logo, design, name, picture, sound, device, or combination of any of these things used to distinguish one organization from all others. Some trademarks are considered stronger than others and are therefore accorded a greater degree of protection under the law. Strong trademarks are those that have no other recognizable meaning. For instance, the photography company Kodak has a strong trademark on its name, because the name has no other meaning in the English language. Weak trademarks are those that use a common word or description of a product, rather than a truly unique name or other identifier. For example, a brand of soft drink called Fizzy Cola would not receive the same degree of protection as the more strongly protected Pepsi Cola. A business or other organization can claim trademark protections as soon as it begins using a trademark, but the degree of protection provided by the law is strengthened, as with copyrights, if an organization registers its trademark with the govern-ment. Unlike copyrights and patents, trademarks never expire.

Recent Trends

The popularity of the Internet and advances in high-speed computer technology have introduced new issues and debates in the field of intellectual property law. For example, existing copyright laws had to be expanded when MP3 file-sharing technologies were invented. Because songs can be so easily copied and exchanged using technology, they can be extremely difficult to protect. MP3s have changed the way the music industry attempts to profit from the intellectual property of musicians. Intellectual property law is thus being transformed. Once considered a relatively unexciting, specialized niche in the legal world, it is now an issue of vital interest to both lawyers and ordinary citizens.

There is considerable debate about the future of intellectual property. On one side people assert that relaxing or even eliminating copyright, patent, and trademark protections would increase the exchange of knowledge and technology. On the other side of the debate, people cite the same argument as the early proponents of copyright laws: that creative work is encouraged when creative people can be assured they will be able to profit from their ideas.

LABOR LAWS

What It Means

As workers and wage earners, people in most countries are supported by a diverse body of labor laws. These laws vary from country to country (and in the United States there are variations from state to state), but they generally cover such areas as the obligations a worker and employer have to one another, the safety of the work environment, unfair discrimination in hiring and on the job, and the ability of workers to organize with one another into unions that can represent their interests more forcefully than would be possible if they had to make strictly individual appeals to their employers.

This was not always the case. When the first large factories came into being in Europe and the United States as a result of the Industrial Revolution (the dramatic social, cultural, and economic change that began in the early 1800s, chiefly as a result of the introduction of new technologies such as the steam engine), most governments took a hands-off approach to their economies. The mechanization of many industries, such as mining and the manufacturing of textiles and iron, gave business owners the opportunity to produce goods and, accordingly, profit at a much greater rate than their counterparts in

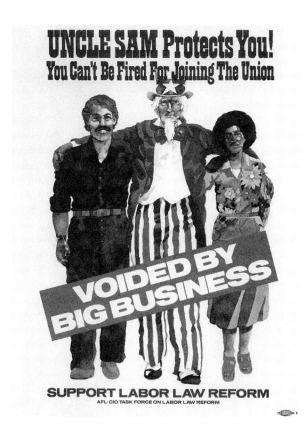

Labor laws are government regulations designed to safeguard the rights of workers. As this poster suggests, labor unions and large companies often hold different positions on the subject of labor laws. *The Library of Congress.*

prior ages, and they naturally pursued this wealth by whatever means necessary. Without any government oversight, factories and mining companies compelled men, women, and children to work unlimited hours (sometimes as many as 16 hours a day) at dangerous jobs for as little pay as possible. Meanwhile, the size of the working class grew tremendously because of the growth of industry, so more and more people were affected by employer-employee issues.

Labor laws grew out of public concerns for workers' health and welfare. One of the basic principles justifying the need for labor laws is that the worker is by definition the weaker party in the employment relationship. Governments have typically tried to level the playing field between employers and laborers and to allow workers to do so themselves through the creation of unions. The progress of such laws has been fitful, however, as public views about the roles of employers and labor tends to shift according to political trends. The United States was slower than European countries to introduce labor laws, and it has traditionally been less active in promoting the interests of workers than other modernized countries.

When Did It Begin

The labor laws of today are an outgrowth of the Industrial Revolution. Though many factors contributed to the Industrial Revolution, some of the most important were the introduction of new technologies concerning textile manufacturing, advances in manufacturing iron, and the invention of the steam engine, which allowed for the mechanization of many industries and great advances in transportation.

Prior to the Industrial Revolution, it was common for manual laborers and their employers to have strong personal obligations to one another and to the communities in which they lived. But the rise of factories in which goods were manufactured on a large scale resulted in huge increases in the number of people who worked for wages. The increased size of the working class and the impersonality of factory employment changed the nature of the relationship between employers and workers. Laws became necessary to protect workers from the abuses of employers interested in the enormous profits to be had thanks to mass production.

The first significant labor law to emerge from these societal changes, dealing with the treatment of child laborers in textile mills, was passed in England in 1802. The first half of the nineteenth century saw England expand on the legal protections of workers, while similar measures were taken by other European countries. Though England had made labor unions legal in 1825, unions were not allowed to press their employers for better wages and working hours.

In the American colonies of the late eighteenth century, laws had been passed that limited a worker's rights and that legalized slavery and other forms of forced

CHILD LABOR

The Industrial Revolution, the drastic change in society tied to the mechanization of numerous industries, led to a vastly enlarged workforce as well as a general population boom. At the beginning of the nineteenth century, factory jobs paid better than agricultural jobs, so factory workers were healthier and better fed, and they had more and healthier babies than people in the preindustrialized world. There was an abundance of children in European and industrialized American cities, and there was little access to education for the working classes. Children were often expected to hold jobs to help their families survive. From an employer's point of view, child labor was attractive because children could be paid less than adults but made to do similar amounts of work.

It was common for children in England, for example, to begin working in textile factories or mines by the age of six or eight, and to work up to 14 or 16 hours a day. Children of the time reported being beaten if they were late or if they fell behind in their work, and in many cases they were given little or no time to eat even though they might be on the job through the hours of breakfast, lunch, and dinner.

Some of the first labor laws (laws regulating employer-employee relationships) passed pertained to child labor, but it was not until the mid-nineteenth century that child labor began to be outlawed in Europe. Some industries in Europe and the United States continued to employ child labor into the twentieth century.

labor. The nineteenth century brought slaves and servants some protections from the cruelty of masters and employers, but slavery persisted until the Emancipation Proclamation was issued in 1863, during the Civil War. Legislation had been passed in 1840 limiting the length of the workday to ten hours for employees of the federal government, but further reduction of the legal workday was suppressed. Unions were typically considered a conspiracy against the public well-being, and U.S. and state courts often allowed the prosecution of union leaders and members if they went on strike to demand better pay or treatment.

It was not until the Great Depression, the severe economic crisis in the 1930s, that the U.S. government began to pass comprehensive legislation protecting workers' rights. At this time, millions of Americans lost their jobs and fell into poverty, and popular sentiment against big business was pronounced.

More Detailed Information

In the United States as elsewhere, the competing interests of employers (who want to minimize labor costs and ensure that they make profits) and workers (who want to maximize their own well-being) are always subject to politics. Generally speaking, conservatives in the United States tend to favor a hands-off approach to the economy in the belief that market forces such as supply, demand, and prices will provide all the necessary regulation, including regulation of employer and labor relations. At the same time liberals tend to be skeptical about the wisdom of relying solely on market forces to determine economic outcomes, believing that a lack of government regulation favors the rich and powerful at the expense of the ordinary worker. Labor laws were first broadly adopted during the Great Depression amid widespread disenchantment with a hands-off approach to the economy. But as the state of the economy and popular attitudes about the government's role in these matters has fluctuated over time, so has the approach to enacting and enforcing labor laws.

Several pieces of legislation passed under President Franklin D. Roosevelt during the Depression provided the foundation for the labor laws of today. The National Labor Relations Act of 1935, also known as the Wagner Act, gave workers the right to organize in unions so that they might more effectively request improvements in working conditions, pay, and other matters. The Social Security Act, passed that same year and known primarily for its creation of benefits for the elderly, also established benefits for the unemployed, easing the dangers posed by job loss. Workers' right to a minimum wage and to extra pay for overtime hours was first established by the Fair Labor Standards Act of 1938 (though the provisions of this law applied only to workers involved in interstate commerce, or business ventures that required the crossing of state lines).

After World War II there was a spirit of reaction against the prewar gains made by workers and labor unions, partly because of the perceived involvement of communists (those supporting the overthrow of capitalism and the establishment of a government controlled by workers) in the labor movement. The Taft-Hartley Act of 1947 restricted the rights of unions and gave the U.S. president the power to temporarily call off strikes if they affected national security. Under Taft-Hartley union leaders were required to sign legal documents verifying that they did not belong to the Communist party.

The political climate of the United States was more progressive in the 1960s, and workers benefited from this along with members of minority groups, women, and other historically oppressed groups. In 1962 the Work Hours Act made the eight-hour workday and the 40-hour workweek standard. Workers required to work more than eight hours a day or 40 hours a week became entitled to time-and-a-half pay (150 percent of the normal hourly wage they were paid) during those extra hours. The Civil Rights Movement's goals of creating equality among people of different races also applied to labor law. As part of the Civil Rights Act of 1964, discrimination against prospective or current employees because of race, sex, national origin, color, or religion was made illegal. Finally, the Occupational Safety and Health Act of 1970 regulated safety in the workplace, establishing a government agency (the Occupational Safety and Health Administration, or OSHA) to conduct inspections and take action against employers who violated national laws.

These laws today serve as the framework for regulating the interests of employers and workers across the United States, but there is also an abundance of state labor laws that pick up where these basic principles leave off. Some states provide greater protection to workers than that which is embodied in federal laws, while some states do little beyond what the federal government requires. Likewise, courts at the state and federal levels constantly expand, trim, and refine the labor laws that are in effect at any given time.

Recent Trends

Antiunion sentiment became pronounced in the United States in the 1980s and early 1990s under the politically conservative presidencies of Ronald Reagan and his successor, George H. W. Bush. Reagan in particular sought to reduce the role of government in the economy. This meant not only cutting taxes but also minimizing the budgets of many federal agencies, including those charged with investigating workplace safety and fairness issues. At the same time, the Reagan and Bush administrations sought to get rid of some restrictions on employers, using the rationale that such government intervention needlessly interfered with industry and gave businesses in less-regulated parts of the world a competitive advantage over U.S. companies.

The 1990s did bring some legal victories for labor and unions. A U.S. Supreme Court decision in 1990 made it more difficult for employers to hire nonunion workers and to file bankruptcy in order to dodge the obligation to pay pensions they had promised to older workers. Likewise, 1990 saw the passage of the Americans with Disabilities Act, part of which was devoted to preventing discrimination against the disabled in the workplace, and in 1993 Congress passed the Family and Medical Leave Act, which entitled workers to 12 weeks off from work per year to take care of their own or their family members' medical concerns.

The size and influence of unions in the United States diminished greatly between the 1980s and the beginning of the twenty-first century. In 1983 more than 20 percent of U.S. workers belonged to unions. By 2006 only 12 percent of workers did. The bulk of unionized workers were, at this time, those who worked in the public sector for various government branches and agencies. More than 36 percent of government workers belonged to unions, whereas only around 7 percent of people employed in the private sector were union members. Public-school teachers, police officers, and firefighters had some of the highest rates of union membership in the United States.

MINIMUM WAGE

What It Means

The minimum wage is the lowest monetary amount that employees are permitted to pay their workers. More than 90 percent of the world's nations have minimum wage laws. In the United States the laws always represent the minimum wage in dollars per hour, but in other places it may be represented as a certain amount of money per day or per month. Retail outlets, restaurants, hotels, and cleaning agencies are the types of companies in the United States that are most likely to employ workers at minimum wage. Approximately one-third of the 11 million American workers earning minimum wage are between the ages of 16 and 19.

Since its inception in the United States, the minimum wage has been raised several times. Beginning at $.25 per hour in 1938, the minimum wage did not rise until 1950, when it climbed to $.75 per hour. The rate went up again in 1956 to $1.00, and by 1968 it was $1.60. The figure rose steadily through the 1970s, reaching $2.30 per hour in 1976. At the beginning of the 1980s, minimum wage topped $3.00, and by 1995 it was up to $4.25. Set at $5.15 in 1997, the national minimum remained the same for 10 years before legislation calling for a two-dollar-per-hour increase was passed by Congress in 2007.

There is much debate about minimum wage laws, both about what the minimum figure should be and about whether or not these laws actually benefit low-wage earners. Those in favor of minimum wage laws see the matter as a question of social justice. All workers, these people claim, have a right to earn enough money to provide for their own basic needs of food, clothing, and shelter. Furthermore, it is necessary that government, mandate a certain wage because, left to themselves, some private employers would not pay their workers enough to live on properly. People who argue against minimum wage laws believe that such laws raise unemployment. They reason that if employers are required to pay more to each individual employee, there will be fewer total jobs available.

When Did It Begin

The first national minimum wage laws were passed in 1896 in New Zealand. That same year a minimum wage law was established in Victoria, Australia. The Australian legislation did not set a national minimum, however; rather, the law was an amendment to the Australian government's Factories Act calling for a wages board to set a minimum wage for the six industries that paid the lowest wages in the country. The wages board was originally created as a four-year experiment but was

Minimum wage refers to the lowest wage businesses can pay their employees under the law. In this photo from August 20, 1996, President Bill Clinton signs a bill raising the minimum wage in the United States from $4.25 an hour to $5.15 an hour. *AP Images.*

renewed in 1900 and then made permanent in 1904, by which time the minimum wage statute applied to more than 150 industries.

By 1910 in the United States, the minimum wage was a controversial political issue. The state of Massachusetts issued a document setting a noncompulsory minimum wage for women and children in 1912, but employers in Massachusetts were not legally required to honor the recommendation. The public debate continued, and by 1920, 13 states had minimum wage laws. These laws were often short-lived, however, because at the time, whenever a minimum wage case came before the U.S. Supreme Court, the law was overruled on the grounds that such statutes interfered with private employers' rights to negotiate wages with their employees. In 1933 the National Industrial Recovery Act included a measure that set the first national minimum wage at $.25 an hour, which was equivalent to about $3.25 in today's dollars. This law was overturned by the Supreme Court in 1935, but in 1938 the Fair Labor Standards Act reset the national minimum wage at $.25

an hour. Since that time the United States has maintained a national minimum wage, and the figure has been raised sporadically to account for price increases.

More Detailed Information

The rate of minimum wage pay at any given time is often a deceptive figure because the dollar amount per hour or per month is not an accurate reflection of a worker's buying power. For example, minimum wage earners had considerably more buying power in the United States in 1968 than they do now. In fact, in the history of American wage laws, the minimum wage had its strongest purchasing value in 1968, when it was just $1.60 an hour. In that year $1.60 was the equivalent of $9.25 in 2005 dollars. Even though the minimum wage had risen fairly steadily since its inception, the purchasing power of the minimum wage figure had declined more than 30 percent by 2007. This meant that minimum wage earners were able to afford fewer and fewer things. Their wages may have gone up but at a slower rate than the prices of things they needed to buy.

Sometimes raising the minimum wage does not achieve the desired effect. The price of goods and services tends to increase with increases in minimum wage, so that necessities, as well as workers' leisure time, cost more money. Wage improvements may also decrease the number of hours available to each worker because employers are often less willing to pay for labor at higher prices; therefore when the minimum wage goes up, there tend to be fewer full-time low-wage jobs available. In addition, each hour spent not working costs idle workers in lost revenues. For example, if the minimum wage is $3 per hour, then each hour during the workday during which workers are idle costs them $3 in unearned revenue. If the minimum wage goes up to $3.50, workers lose $3.50 per hour when they are forced to stay home because an employer has cut back their hours.

Comparisons between the U.S. and Other Countries

Many countries in the world have more generous minimum wage laws than the United States. For example, in France and Ireland the respective minimum wages of 8.27 and 8.30 Euros per hour equal about $10.80 per hour in U. S. currency. Likewise, in the U.K. the minimum wage of 5.15 pounds per hour (approximately $10 per hour in U.S. dollars) is almost twice the rate in the United States. These countries also monitor the relationship between the minimum wage and the cost of living more closely than the United States does. In France, the minimum wage is updated every year, sometimes at a rate higher than the rate of inflation (the rise in prices of goods and services). In 2004 inflation in France registered at 2 percent, but the minimum wage went up by 5 percent. As of 2007 Ireland and England were set to raise wages to a figure amounting to more than $11 per hour in American dollars.

American minimum wage figures compare favorably to those in other parts of the world, however. For instance, in Brazil workers earn a minimum of only $165 per month. In Russia they earn a little more than $40 per month, and in Pakistan the minimum wage is about the equivalent of $66 per month. The People's Republic of China has a more complex minimum wage structure. Full-time workers earn a monthly minimum wage, while part-time workers earn an hourly minimum wage. Furthermore some provinces are permitted to set their own minimum wages, with workers in these areas sometimes earning as little as $.25 per day. While minimum wage figures in the developing world are certainly low compared to those in the United States and Europe, it must also be remembered that the economies in these areas are significantly different than those in the fully industrialized nations. Still, people earning such low wages are living in dire poverty. Of all the nations in the world, minimum wages in Japan, which vary according to industry and region, most closely resemble American figures. In most areas and occupations in Japan, the minimum wage

amounts to between $40 and $45 per day, roughly what an American worker makes in eight hours at $5.15 per hour, the U.S. minimum wage from 1997 until it changed to $5.85 in July 2007.

Debate over Minimum Wage

Minimum wage legislation has long been a subject of intense debate. Those who favor the minimum wage and believe it should be raised, at least in accordance with the rising cost of living, maintain that decent pay is a matter of social justice: all workers have a right to earn enough money to provide for their own basic needs of food, clothing, and shelter; as such, proponents argue, a minimum wage must be legislated because private employers cannot be depended upon to uphold such standards voluntarily. For employers, increased labor costs will be offset by happier, more productive employees and lower employee turnover (which means lower hiring and training costs). Proponents of minimum wage increases also suggest that higher wages will be good for the economy as a whole. Minimum wage earners will have more spending power and better access to bank loans and credit, both of which will stimulate the economy. They will also be more able to pay for health care and less likely to depend on government welfare programs, both of which will reduce the burden they might otherwise place on the economy.

Those who oppose the minimum wage and increases to it, on the other hand, invoke basic economic "common sense," as well as the law of supply and demand, to support their contention that government interference in the bargaining process between workers and employers does more harm than good to low-wage earners and the economy as a whole. At the heart of this argument is the idea that an increase in the minimum wage amounts to an artificial price increase in labor. This overvaluation will necessarily drive down demand for labor; that is, it will lead to increased unemployment. For employers a mandatory wage increase amounts to an increase in the cost of production without any promise of an increase in output; workers will suddenly be paid more but will not necessarily work harder or more efficiently (indeed, one of the premises of this argument is that worker productivity will be unaffected by a wage increase). In order to offset the cost increase of paying each worker more, employers will not be able to hire as many workers, or they will need to fill their lowest positions with more productive workers. Other cost-containing alternatives include replacing employees with machines and outsourcing the work to cheaper labor overseas. In any of these scenarios, the logic goes, those who will lose their jobs or be unable to find work are the least skilled workers with the fewest employment options to begin with.

Another way for employers to offset the wage increase is to cut back on other benefits they extend to their employees, such as paid sick days, health benefits, shift meals (a common benefit of restaurant work), or other workplace amenities, all of which amount to zero gain

NICKEL AND DIMED

In 2002 American journalist Barbara Ehrenreich published *Nickel and Dimed: On (Not) Getting By in America*. The book documents her attempt to make ends meet by working at minimum and low-wage jobs in Florida, Maine, and Minnesota. (The minimum wage is the lowest amount of money that employees are permitted to pay their workers per hour.) Ehrenreich, who for more than 20 years has published articles in such leading American publications as *Time* magazine and the *New York Times* newspaper, began this project because she wanted to verify her hypothesis that Americans working low-wage jobs were not making enough money to support themselves and enjoy decent lives. She defined a decent life as having enough money for food, clothing, transportation, health care, rent on a modest apartment, and a minimum amount of entertainment. To conduct this experiment, she left her comfortable upper-middle-class life and moved to Florida with a small amount of start-up money. After finding full-time work in a diner, Ehrenreich soon discovered that she needed another job just to meet her monthly expenses. The same thing happened in Maine, where she worked as a house cleaner, and in Minnesota, where she worked at Wal-Mart.

for employees. Increases in labor costs might also result in higher prices for the goods and services the employees produce. Such prices would increase the cost of living for everyone in the economy.

Recent Trends

In the United States one debate about low-paying employment is focused on the disparity between the minimum wage and a proper living wage, which is the amount of money one needs to make in a 40-hour work week to meet basic expenses and to experience some recreation. In early 2007 many economists and activists believed that national minimum wage laws did not provide enough for workers to achieve an acceptable standard of living.

Individual states are permitted to set minimum wage laws at figures higher than the federal standard, and, as of 2007, 29 states had done so in an effort to bring the minimum wage closer to the living wage of the area. For example, California, New York, and Florida have set their state minimum wage higher than the $5.85 per hour federal standard. Within some states, there are cities and counties that have set the minimum wage higher than the rest of the state. One example is Sante Fe, New Mexico, where the minimum wage is at a national high of $9.50 per hour, while the rest of the state abides by the federal minimum.

Another trend in individual states is to tie the minimum wage to inflation. This means that the minimum

wage is reset every year to match the rise in the cost of living. As of 2006 six states had set adjustable minimum wage laws so that low-wage earners could continue to meet expenses as prices rose.

PROTECTIONISM

What It Means

Protectionism refers to any action taken by a government to protect domestic (its own country's) industries from foreign competition. For example, a government may impose a tariff, or a tax on goods imported from other countries, to make sure that those goods do not sell for less money than goods manufactured domestically. Consider the case of a country that has built its economy on selling domestically produced cars to its citizens. Prices of these cars range from $15,000 to $35,000. If a foreign manufacturer were to sell cars of similar quality in this country for $12,000 to $30,000, many of consumers would choose the imported vehicles. Eventually profits for the domestic auto company would decrease and workers would lose their jobs. To prevent this from happening, the nation producing the more expensive cars might tax the imported cars to raise prices and ensure that consumers kept buying domestic cars.

Other methods for protecting domestic industries include restrictive quotas (limits on the number of each imported item), government subsidies (financial support) of domestic manufacturers, and tax cuts for domestic producers. Restrictive quotas operate in much the same way tariffs do. Going back to the example above, the threatened nation might drive up prices on foreign cars by only importing a limited number of these vehicles. Prices would rise if the demand for these cars exceeded the supply. Tax cuts and subsidies allow domestic producers to sell cars more cheaply by reducing their operating costs. Manufacturers can then pass that savings to the customer and sell cars as cheaply as the foreign competition.

When Did It Begin

Protectionism was the norm until the late eighteenth century because most economists believed that a nation's wealth depended on maintaining a balance of trade that was in its own favor. In other words a nation needed to export more goods than it imported. Often this could only be accomplished through protectionist tactics. In 1776, however, Adam Smith (1723–90) argued in his book *Wealth of Nations* that free trade rather than protectionism was the best way to prosperity. Smith believed that unimpeded market forces and trends, or what he called an invisible hand, could best guide a nation's economy.

From 1789 through 1913, the United States favored protectionist policies. The country's first tariff was established with the Tariff Act of 1789, which taxed all

When a government takes measures to protect domestic businesses from foreign competition, it is said to be engaging in protectionism. In 2001 China imposed a 100 percent tariff, or import tax, on Toyotas and other Japanese cars, a drastic move that was intended to bring Japanese car imports to a standstill. *Photograph by Susan D. Rock.*

imports at a rate of between 5 and 15 percent. After the War of 1812, American nationalists began calling for higher tariffs, especially on British iron and textile (fabric products) goods. The government responded with the Tariff of 1828, which taxed imports at as much as 50 percent. This tariff met with strong opposition in the South because it left Southerners little choice but to buy goods produced in the North. Through the Civil War and beyond, protectionism continued to be the trend in the United States until 1914, when World War I significantly changed trade patterns and reduced tariffs.

More Detailed Information

Protectionism has been one of the most hotly debated issues throughout the history of the United States. Advocates of protectionism tend to offer two lines of reasoning to defend their position. The first argument has been called the infant industry argument. According to this view a young country, such as the United States was in 1789, needs a period of time to develop industries and train a workforce before it can withstand foreign competition. Guided by this thinking, Alexander Hamilton (1755–1804), who was the first secretary of the treasury

in the United States, proposed a 10 percent tariff on all imported goods. This figure rose steadily throughout the 1800s.

The idea was that protection would create a stable home market for all goods produced in the United States. Farmers would not have to sell their goods abroad, which involved relying on fluctuating international markets, and manufacturers would likewise earn steady profits for the goods they produced and sold in the United States. Small American merchants who sold both finished products and agricultural goods in their stores would also prosper. Though high tariffs initially led to economic growth, they also split the country along regional lines, with the North favoring protection and the South favoring free trade. Along with slavery the tariff issue is considered a leading cause of the Civil War. Other countries that have successfully built strong economies following the infant industry argument are South Korea and Taiwan.

The second argument in favor of protectionism is called the geopolitical argument. Proponents of this idea claim that a country cannot be economically stable without a strong military. In order to win a war, this reasoning goes, a nation must be able to produce the

THE SMOOT-HAWLEY TARIFF

Many economists argue that the U.S. Smoot-Hawley Tariff Act of 1930 was a contributing cause of the Great Depression, which lasted from 1929 to 1939 and is considered the most significant economic slowdown in U.S. history. A tariff is a tax on goods imported from other countries. The Depression began on October 24–29, 1929, when the value of stocks (units that denote partial ownership in a company) plummeted at the New York Stock Exchange. Afterward the stock market recovered. Signed into law on June 17, 1930, the Smoot-Hawley Tariff Act began a gradual reversal of this recovery, many economists contend. Intended to protect American manufacturers and farmers by encouraging consumers to buy domestic-made and grown products, the tariff taxed more than 20,000 imported goods at record levels, with some imports receiving as much as a 60 percent tax. Other countries retaliated, taxing American imports at the same rate, and international trade declined. The stock market began to slide again in 1931 and reached bottom in 1932.

food and munitions it needs to sustain itself during the conflict. In order to be able to produce these goods, a country must encourage the producers and build a dependable home market. This means that protectionist measures must keep the cost of imported goods high so that citizens purchase domestic products. Some people who hold this view take the argument one step further and claim that a strong domestic market unifies the nation because consumers are all buying the same products. Protectionism, they claim, develops patriotism. Unlike the infant industry argument, which advocates protection only until a country builds its economy, the geopolitical argument calls for continued protectionist policies.

The opposite of protectionism is free trade, a policy in which international commerce is unimpeded by tariffs or any other measures that discourage trade. Many economists agree that free trade is ultimately better than protectionism for both consumers and producers because free trade increases the worldwide output of goods. Proponents of free trade argue that there are more goods available because a free-trade environment allows countries involved in trade to specialize and thus to develop an abundance of a given product. For example, Country A could specialize in manufacturing cars, and Country B could focus on producing fabric. Country A would have an excess of cars but a shortage of fabric. Country B would have an excess of fabric but would need cars. The two countries could then trade with each other with no need to levy tariffs on the imports. Countries that engage in trade arrangements similar to the one in this example sign official documents called free-trade agreements in

which they pledge not to impose tariffs on each other. Many argue that free-trade privileges developed countries, however, in that it ensures that industrialized powers will have overseas markets for their goods.

Recent Trends

Since World War I the United States has been committed to a policy of reduced tariffs and free trade. A notable exception occurred in the late 1970s when an influx of reliable, fuel-efficient Japanese cars threatened the American auto industry. The auto workers union petitioned the government for protection. Instead of imposing a high tariff, the United States received an agreement from Japan to limit the number of cars exported to the United States. This strategy did not prove to be helpful, however. In order to maintain trade revenue (or income), Japan increased the quality and value of the cars they sold in the United States. This challenged American control of its domestic luxury-car market. Under Ronald Reagan (1911–2004) and George H. W. Bush (b. 1924) the United States returned to the policy of free trade, most notably with the Canada–U.S Free Trade Agreement of 1987, which was designed to increase cross-border trade over a 10-year period. In 1994 the North American Free Trade Agreement (NAFTA), which included Mexico and Canada, supplanted the 1987 agreement.

With the fall of communism in the late 1980s, low tariffs have become the norm in global economics as well. During this time China's economy has experienced significant growth. One factor that spurred its growth was China's inclusion in the World Trade Organization in 2000 at the urging of President Clinton. Not only was China admitted, but it was also granted most-favored-nation trading status (now called normal trade relations, or NTR). Since then the United States has become China's largest market for overseas goods, which consist primarily of electrical appliances and advanced technology, such as data processors and sound equipment.

FREE TRADE ZONE

What It Means

A free trade zone (called a foreign trade zone in the United States) is a part of a country where goods from foreign nations are not subject to normal export and import laws. All nations impose some restrictions on imported products. The most common types of restrictions are tariffs (taxes on imports) and quotas (limits on the number of imports). Historically, nations have imposed these restrictions in order to protect their domestic industries. When, for example, cars made in Germany are shipped to the United States, they are subject to taxes that have the end result of making them more expensive to U.S. consumers than domestic cars. Given the choice between domestic and German cars, Americans will be

A free trade zone is an area of a country or territory where individuals and companies can buy and sell goods without being subject to normal government regulation, such as taxes or quotas. Pictured here is Katunayaka, a free trade zone outside of Colombo, Sri Lanka. © *Howard Davies/Corbis.*

more likely to buy domestic cars if they cost substantially less.

Products may, however, be shipped to free trade zones within a country without being subject to tariffs, quotas, or other restrictions. Free trade zones are usually near seaports, airports, or at national borders. While in a free trade zone, products may be assembled, repackaged, refinished, and in many cases even manufactured. Products cannot, however, be sold to consumers in a free trade zone. When products leave the free trade zone and make their way to consumers, normal tariffs and quotas are enforced.

When Did It Begin

Predecessors to what we now call free trade zones existed at the time of the ancient Roman Empire, if not earlier. When traders from foreign lands entered the Empire's borders, the government offered them a space where they could be free from mistreatment. When the shipping trade between European countries grew in the late Middle Ages, many port cities in Europe became the equivalent of today's free trade zones, allowing foreign ships to dock so that they could assemble, repack, and manufacture their goods before bringing them to con-

sumers. The number of such ports grew in sixteenth–eighteenth century Europe with the rise of mercantilism, an economic ideology according to which individual countries sought to gain financial advantages over their trading partners.

The American version of free trade zones, which the government refers to as foreign trade zones, came into being in 1934 with the passage of the Foreign Trade Zones Act. This act set up the country's first free trade zone in New York City. By the early twenty-first century there were more than 200 free trade zones in the United States.

More Detailed Information

The basic function of a free trade zone is to facilitate international trade. When goods are shipped to a free trade zone, the seller of those goods has more flexibility to conduct business and the potential to cut costs. For example, an importer of fabrics in Los Angeles might want to store a shipment of her wares and display them to prospective customers before going through the formalities of and incurring the costs associated with the import process. She might therefore choose to leave the goods at a free trade zone near Los Angeles for several months.

Once the importer has lined up customers and prepared to distribute the fabrics, she can move the goods out of the free trade zone and into the hands of those customers, paying any relevant taxes at that time.

Another advantage of free trade zones is that they facilitate the quicker movement of goods across borders. A ship stopping in Copenhagen, Denmark, for example, can unload its cargo and take on a new load without sorting through the bureaucratic tangle of laws that apply to all the various goods it is transporting.

The ability to manufacture and manipulate goods inside a free trade zone also offers advantages for businesses, as well as for the regional economy surrounding the zone. For example, an imported watch might be subject to tariffs in many countries, but the assorted metals out of which that watch is built may not be taxed in their raw form. A U.S. watch company could, then, theoretically set up a manufacturing facility within a U.S. free trade zone in order to get access to cheap foreign metals instead of paying for high-priced metals originating in the United States. The company could hire local employees to build the watches, and then when the watches are sent to retail outlets in the United States, the watches would be treated as an import subject to tariffs. Paying these tariffs might be cheaper than using U.S. materials, with the end result that the company can produce lower-priced watches that sell in greater numbers. At the same time, the local economy around the free trade zone benefits from the jobs provided by the watch maker.

Free trade zones are also intended to allow developing countries to join the global economy. Global corporations often find it fruitful to set up factories in free trade zones located in poor countries. The corporations benefit from the low cost of labor in those areas, and the local economy grows as a result of new jobs. Free trade zones frequently entice global corporations to set up shop by providing them with generous tax breaks. The resulting lower costs of manufacturing more than compensate for the tariffs that will ultimately have to be paid when the goods reach their final destination.

Recent Trends

Since the middle of the twentieth century, the tendency in international trade has been toward globalization, the increasing economic unity of all countries in the world. Proponents of globalization believe that it will bring about peace, unity, and higher standards of living. A large hurdle to globalization is the existence of tariffs, quotas, and other trade restrictions, and powerful groups such as the World Trade Organization (WTO) are committed to the ongoing reduction of barriers to international trade.

The number of free trade zones grew immensely at the end of the twentieth century and the beginning of the twenty-first century. This trend was particularly marked in developing countries, who competed with one another

NIKE AND FREE TRADE ZONES

Free trade zones are areas within individual countries where the ordinary taxes and restrictions on imported goods do not apply. A company can unload, assemble, display, manipulate, and even manufacture its goods within a free trade zone (though it cannot sell them there), no matter the goods' origins, without paying import taxes or submitting to government intervention. Those taxes must be paid and all relevant paperwork completed when the goods are finally made available to consumers, either in the country where the free trade zone is located or elsewhere, but the benefits of manufacturing goods in free trade zones often outweigh these taxes.

Increasingly, multinational corporations have been able to cut costs by locating their manufacturing facilities inside free trade zones located within poor and developing countries, where they can pay much lower wages than they would be forced to pay in the more developed nations of North America and Europe. One of the most heavily criticized of these companies is Nike, Inc., famous for its sneakers and its swoosh logo. Critics of Nike, such as the journalist Naomi Klein and the documentary filmmaker Michael Moore, claim that Nike subjects workers to miserable conditions reminiscent of forced-labor camps. While conducting business in this fashion during the 1990s and the early part of the twenty-first century, Nike's annual revenues more than doubled.

to attract foreign businesses to their free trade zones. But free trade zones, like globalism in general, were subject to intense criticism. Some people argued that free trade zones empowered corporations and corrupt governments at the expense of the poor individuals in developing countries.

PRICE CEILINGS AND PRICE FLOORS

What It Means

Throughout history, governments have attempted to control prices through the use of price ceilings and price floors. A price ceiling is a maximum price that the seller of any good or service may charge. For example, if the U.S. government declared that no street vendor could charge more than $2 for a hot dog, a price ceiling would be in effect. A price floor, by contrast, is a minimum price that the seller may charge. If the government declared that hot dogs could not be sold for any less than $5, a price floor would be in effect. While price ceilings and price floors can be necessary in certain situations, most economists strongly disapprove of them because they interrupt the natural processes by which the economy regulates itself.

If the market for hot dogs is functioning properly and freely (a market is any place or system that brings

When the government institutes a price ceiling or a price floor, it sets the maximum or minimum price, respectively, at which a certain good can be sold. The black beans, rice, and plantains shown here, which represent the most traditional and commonly eaten foods in Cuba, are all subject to price controls by the Cuban government. *David Bishop/Food Pix/Jupiterimages.*

buyers and sellers together to make exchanges), rising prices for hot dogs will encourage vendors to supply more hot dogs to buyers in the hope of maximizing their profits. These same rising prices, however, discourage more and more consumers from buying hot dogs, because consumers want to maximize their own economic well-being. Vendors must therefore balance their desire to maximize profits with what they know about consumer demand for hot dogs at various prices. The competing interests of sellers and buyers (in other words, of supply and demand) efficiently regulate the number of hot dogs produced and sold. Vendors show up to work with the correct number of hot dogs, and vendors and consumers both get what they want with a minimum of waste and inefficiency.

A price ceiling for hot dogs would reduce the supply of hot dogs, because the potential profit to be made on the sale of each hot dog would be diminished. At the same time, the lowered price of hot dogs would make more people willing and able to buy hot dogs. This imbalance between supply and demand (supply is falling while demand is rising) would likely lead to a shortage of hot dogs. On the other hand, a price floor would artificially raise the price of hot dogs, thereby encouraging vendors to supply more than consumers would be willing

and able to buy. Supply will have risen while demand falls, a situation that is likely to lead to a surplus of hot dogs.

When Did It Begin

Price ceilings and floors have probably existed for as long as there have been organized governments. Ancient Hebraic law, as reflected in the Old Testament, forbade the collection of interest, a fee charged to someone who borrows money. Islamic law has had a similar rule for much of that religion's history. Because interest can be thought of as the price that people pay for borrowed money, a prohibition on interest is a price ceiling, one that is set at zero.

In ancient Egypt, Babylon, and Greece, the government set prices for grains and other farm produce, sometimes enforcing these price controls with the threat of the death penalty. A crisis occurred in Rome under the emperor Diocletian (245–316 AD) when, in the year 284, he created inflation (rising prices) by coining too much money. (More money in circulation results in more purchasing power per person and by extension increased demand for products, which forces up prices). In an attempt to stop the out-of-control rising of prices, Diocletian imposed price ceilings. Farmers and other suppliers of goods, unable to get reasonable prices, stopped bringing their products to market, and many people starved as a result.

More recently price controls have been common in times of war, when out-of-control inflation can be a problem. During World War I (1914–18), World War II (1939–45), and the Korean War (1950–53), for example, the U.S. government attempted to control inflation through price ceilings. High inflation in the early 1970s led to the much rarer phenomenon, under President Richard Nixon (in office 1969–74), of price controls on consumer products during peacetime.

More Detailed Information

Despite the consensus of economists on the generally negative impact of price controls, periods of economic difficulty and the needs of particular groups of people have often made specific forms of price ceilings and floors appealing to many. In New York City, for example, the local government in some cases imposes a price ceiling on rent, known as rent control. Rent control is intended to ensure that affordable housing remains available to people who cannot pay the extremely high prices that landlords in the city often ask for apartments. Without rent control poor and middle-class people would, in many cases, be unable to live in New York.

Most economists maintain, however, that rent control creates an imbalance between the supply and demand for housing in the city. Because prices are kept artificially low, demand increases while supply declines. People rush to find rent-controlled apartments, while landlords have little incentive to build new housing if their potential for

LINES AT THE PUMP

In 1973 oil-producing Arab countries cut off oil supplies to the United States in response to American support of Israel during the Yom Kippur War, a conflict between Israel and neighboring Arab nations. This resulted in a massive decrease in the supply of gasoline in the United States, and gas prices accordingly began to skyrocket. President Richard Nixon tried to control gas prices by instituting price ceilings (limits on the maximum price per gallon of gas), a presumably welcome development for most consumers.

The prices ceilings, however, kept prices artificially low, and as a result consumers demanded more gas than was physically available. Artificially low prices also eliminated the motivation for high profits that might have encouraged the oil companies to increase production of oil from non-Arab countries. As a result, there was no mechanism for correcting the gasoline shortage. According to economists, the shortage was worse than it would have been without the price ceiling on gas, and it persisted for longer than it would have if market forces had been allowed to set prices. Consumers had to wait in extremely long lines to get gas, and ultimately their demand for gas had to be restrained through rationing. People whose car license plates ended with an even number could only buy gas on even-numbered days of the month, and people whose plates ended with an odd number could only buy gas on odd-numbered days.

wages). According to economists, the minimum wage actually increases the number of unskilled workers who want jobs but cannot find them.

Recent Trends

In the early years of the twenty-first century, many Americans were calling for various price controls, although most of them probably did not think of it in these terms. There was a widespread belief that two industries in particular, the oil industry and the pharmaceutical industry, were taking advantage of consumers by pricing their goods unfairly. Although Americans had long been accustomed to gas prices that were lower than those in other countries because of lower taxes on fuel, rising prices during this time were a serious economic blow to many U.S. households. At the same time, the corporations that drilled and refined oil, bringing it to consumers in the United States, were making record amounts of profit. A substantial portion of the country's population believed that the government should intervene to make gas more affordable, even though nearly every economist disapproved of the idea.

Similarly, prescription-drug prices were increasingly high during this time, even as the pharmaceutical companies that developed and sold these drugs were among the most profitable of all businesses. As a result, calls for government limits on drug prices were common.

Although some politicians used these issues to gain the support of disgruntled voters, the likelihood that the federal government would impose price ceilings on these items was minimal. Since the 1970s the U.S. government has not seriously ventured into the arena of price controls for consumer goods.

HOW GOVERNMENTS RAISE MONEY

$ Taxes

What It Means

A tax is a fee that a government imposes, or levies, on a type of economic activity. For example, a tax can be imposed on the sale of a product or on the income that a business or person earns. The value of property is often taxed. Taxes are mandatory, meaning you have no choice but to pay them. Governments impose taxes in order to fund their expenses, which range from national defense to health-care for the elderly to maintenance of a city park.

The amount a government taxes is not random. A government must first determine what its essential needs are. It must pay for the costs of running itself (its buildings, as well as its workers, whether these be street cleaners or judges), and it must pay for the services the country views as vital (most people, for example, would consider police and fire departments essential). Other

profits is limited. A shortage of housing results. Additionally, rent control is believed to result in deterioration in the quality of housing. Because people are unlikely to move out of an apartment whose rent is artificially low, landlords do not have to make repairs or conduct routine maintenance to keep their apartments occupied.

An example of an existing price floor that has widespread public support in the United States is the federal minimum wage. If we think of labor as a good that a worker sells to a company, the minimum wage represents a price floor mandating that the price of labor cannot drop below a certain amount ($5.85 an hour as of 2007). The intent of this price floor is to create economic benefits for the poor, a vulnerable group of people for whom most voters have sympathy. If the government did not set price floors for wages, supporters argue, unskilled workers (people who lack special training or education) would have no guarantee of being able to pay for their basic necessities.

As with rent control, however, many economists oppose the minimum wage because of its effect on the balance between supply and demand. Theoretically, the minimum wage increases the supply of workers (because more people want the jobs) at the same time that it decreases businesses' demand for these workers (because they are less willing to employ people at the higher

In order to pay for their expenses, governments impose taxes, or fees, on individuals and businesses. In this 1985 photo former U.S. president Ronald Reagan holds a giant version of a standard income tax form; the black circle represents Reagan's desire to cut taxes. *AP Images.*

expenses might be more discretionary, or dependent upon individual judgment. A national government's decision to purchase more warplanes or a local government's decision to upgrade the municipal swimming pool might be met with approval by some citizens and not others. Ultimately taxing and spending decisions are determined in the political sphere, such as city councils or national assemblies, where representatives of the government make choices about the use of limited sources of tax revenue. A challenge faced by most governments is that people generally like the benefits of government spending—'they might enjoy a nicer pool for the community, or they might want the government to inspect meat and poultry for potential health hazards'—but they often do not like paying the taxes required to provide these services.

In addition to paying for expenses, taxes are used to achieve certain social and economic goals. For example, a government might want to redistribute wealth, taking money from high-income individuals and giving it to people who cannot support themselves, such as the disabled, the mentally ill, or people who have lost a job. Governments sometimes try to influence the behavior of individuals and businesses through taxes. A government might reduce taxes on businesses that invest in alternative energy sources, or it might tax goods, such as cigarettes and alcohol, to encourage people to consume less of them. Some organizations, such as charities, are often exempt from taxation in order to support their activities. Tax policies are important not only because they pay for services and influence behavior but because they ultimately decide who will have control over a large part of

FREE HUMMERS FROM THE GOVERNMENT?

Although everyone benefits from government spending in one way or another, most people do not like to pay taxes, and trying to avoid taxes is a behavior as old as civilization itself. It sometimes leads to unexpected outcomes.

What a business earns is the difference between its costs, or expenses, and its revenue. In other words, what it makes is not the $200,000 in revenue from its products, for example, but the difference between that and its costs, say $150,000, which would be $50,000. It is business income that the government taxes.

In 1984 U.S. tax law was changed to prevent what many people considered a tax abuse. Businesses were buying luxury cars and deducting the cost of these vehicles from their earnings. This meant that the government was actually paying for a significant part of the cost of these luxury items. Because the government wanted to help small business owners, such as farmers and ranchers, buy trucks for legitimate business reasons, it continued to allow a deduction of up to $25,000 but only on vehicles that weighed more than 6,000 pounds.

In 2003 that deduction was increased to $100,000. At the same time, there had been a significant change in car-buying habits. Sports Utility Vehicles, or SUVs, which were built on a truck platform, had become popular, and because they were heavy, they qualified for the tax break. Suddenly businesses began taking advantage of the tax law as they had in the early 1980s, and car dealerships began advertising that one could buy a Hummer (one of the largest SUVs) for free. In truth, Hummers—which, in addition to being expensive, had bad gas mileage and, being trucks, were allowed to emit more pollution than ordinary cars—were not really free. But depending on your income and other factors, as much as a third of the vehicle's cost would be paid by the government.

an economy's resources. This, in turn, has an enormous effect on the functioning of the economy.

When Did It Begin

Because governments cannot exist without taxes, the system of taxation has existed since ancient times. As in countries today, governments in the past devised numerous ways to collect money for their expenses. In ancient Egypt the government for some time taxed cooking oil, and to assure that citizens were not trying to avoid the tax, inspectors went from home to home to verify people were using sufficient amounts of the taxed oil. The Roman Empire over the years tried several types of taxes, including an inheritance tax (a tax on money inherited from someone who has died), a sales tax, and taxes on imports (goods sold to another country) and imports (goods purchased from another country). Governments

sometimes chose tax methods because they were the easiest way to raise money given the circumstances of their countries and economies.

In the twentieth century the United States and many Western European countries experienced a substantial increase in tax rates. Governments began to take a more active role in trying to solve issues of poverty and income insecurity, and government spending came to be seen as a tool for stabilizing and stimulating an economy, especially when it was in a downturn. Also costly were two world wars (in 1914-18 and 1939-45) and the Cold War (after World War II, when the United States and the Soviet Union, each considering the other an enemy, spent vast amounts of money on their militaries). To pay for these added expenses, governments needed more money. For that they raised tax rates and invented new taxes. The tax burden in the United States went from about 6 percent of total income in 1900 to 34 percent in 2000.

More Detailed Information

In the United States people are taxed at the national, state, and local level. Therefore, people with the same income and spending habits might pay a different amount of tax per year depending on where they lived. They might also receive a different set of government benefits.

Everyone in the United States is subject to the same national tax laws, but that does not mean it is simple. The U.S. tax code, which explains the tax system of the national government, is more than 3 million words long. Because of the complexity of the tax code, many individuals and businesses employ accountants not only to ensure that are paying the correct amount but also to avoid paying too much. The national government makes the most money on its income tax, which is an annual tax on a person's income; it is progressive, meaning the more a person makes, the higher the tax rate, or percentage fee, on the income. Other important taxes include the payroll tax for Social Security (12.4 percent of one's income, which goes largely to financing monthly payments to the elderly); corporate, or business, taxes; and excise taxes (which are taxes on a particular type of good, such as gasoline).

Although many states also have an income tax, the most important tax at the state level is usually the sales tax (as high as 7 percent in some states). Local governments—cities and counties, for example—rely heavily on the property tax, which is an annual tax on the value of a property, such as a house, land, and commercial property.

Recent Trends

Economists and political leaders have long argued over the various methods of taxation, as well as the effects of the total tax burden on the economy. In the United States, with the election of Ronald Reagan (1981–89), the national government reduced the highest tax rate on income from 70 percent to 50 percent and later to just 28 percent. By

2001 the highest rate was back up to 35 percent. Although these changes seem substantial, tax revisions in the 1980s and 1990s were complicated. Some taxes were reduced, but others were increased, meaning that the burden of taxation shifted from one part of the population to another. Whatever true reductions in the overall tax burden that did exist had an unpleasant side effect. Because the government did not make corresponding cuts in government expenditures, the government began spending much more than it was receiving in taxes, increasing the government's already sizable national debt.

Arguments over tax policy often centered on how taxes influenced economic efficiency and on different ideas of fairness. Some people believed a progressive income tax, in which wealthier people people paid a higher tax rate than others, was fair because some poor and even middle-class people had barely enough money to get by. Others argued that taxing people at different rates was unjust, punishing wealthy people for succeeding in the economy, and that it led to various tax-avoidance behaviors that were harmful to the economy. Arguments were also fierce over the sales tax. Some people believed it was unfair because it was regressive—that is, because wealthy people tend to spend only a part of their income and to place the rest in savings or investments (which are not subject to the sales tax), wealthy people pay a smaller percentage of their income on sales taxes than other people. Those that defended the sales tax argued that it is a simple, less invasive form of taxation (the government does not have to collect information on the personal income of its citizens) and that the sales tax, because it applies only to purchases, encourages people to save, which has both social and economic benefits.

$ Income Tax

What It Means

An income tax is a portion of an individual's or business's earnings that is collected by the government. The income tax is charged, or levied, as a percentage, and it applies to any money an individual or business has earned over the course of a year. The tax levied on the income of companies is called a corporate tax. In the United States both the federal government and most state governments collect income taxes.

The Internal Revenue Service (IRS) is the federal agency in the United States that collects income taxes. The U.S. Congress determines the tax rate, which is the percentage used to calculate a person's or business's tax. This rate varies with the level of income; in general, the more income an earner (whether business or person) generates, the higher the tax rate.

The form used to file, or submit, income taxes with the IRS and state governments is called a tax return.

An income tax is a percentage fee on a person's income that must be paid to the government. Filing income taxes can be a complicated, time-consuming process. © *Nell Redmond/ZUMA/ Corbis.*

There are many different types of returns, among them Form 1040 (which individuals use) and Form 1120 (which corporations use). Income tax returns for most taxpayers are due each year on April 15.

The income tax on individual earners is the primary source of the funds for the U.S. federal government. In developed countries such as the United States, income tax, especially the tax on individuals' income, has historically been the main way the government redistributes wealth among the population.

When Did It Begin

The first income tax was put into effect in Britain in 1798 by Prime Minister William Pitt the Younger (1759–1806). Britain was fighting in the Napoleonic Wars (1793–1815), and the revenue collected through the income tax helped to pay for the military and its equipment. The first federal income tax in the United States, imposed in 1862, was also created to raise funds to support a war effort, the Civil War (1861–65). The rate of tax was adjusted according to how much an individual had earned. For yearly incomes ranging from $600 to

FORM 1040

The standard IRS form that individuals use to file their annual income tax return is Form 1040. It has 11 attachments, called schedules. Depending on the specific income characteristics of the taxpayer, any of the schedules may need to be filed along with Form 1040. For example, if the taxpayer has collected income from self-employment, he or she would need to report that income as well as related expenses using Schedule C.

Any individual U.S. income taxpayer can use Form 1040, but there are two variations on the form that may be used when a person's tax situation is relatively simple. If an individual is not itemizing any deductions (listing each expense that will be exempt from taxes), does not own a business, and has taxable income lower than a certain amount (as of 2006 it was $50,000), he or she may use Form 1040A. Form 1040EZ is even simpler. To be eligible to use the 1040EZ, the taxpayer's income must be under a certain amount ($50,000 as of 2006), and he or she must not have earned interest income (money earned on savings accounts) over a certain amount ($400 as of 2006).

$10,000, the tax rate was 3 percent, and for incomes over $10,000, the rate was higher. In 1862 President Lincoln (1809–65) also established the Internal Revenue Service, the agency responsible for collecting taxes and enforcing tax laws.

Although the income tax helped the U.S. government sporadically for many years after it was introduced, Congress did not impose a permanent income tax until 1913. That year Congress passed the Sixteenth Amendment, a revenue law that authorized the government to tax the incomes of individuals and corporations.

More Detailed Information

Tax returns are the forms taxpayers use to report to the government how much income they earned during the previous year and the amount of tax they owe. Form 1040 is the standard U.S. individual tax return; forms 1040EZ and 1040A are forms with slight variations. Taxpayers also report their deductions and credits on tax returns. Deductions are expenses that are subtracted from the amount of income that is taxed; credits are directly subtracted from the amount of tax that is owed. There are many kinds of deductions and credits, and the rules about them are complex; expenses that are commonly deducted by individuals include charitable donations, educational expenses, and interest payments on home loans (interest is a fee charged for borrowing money). Companies may also take a wide variety of deductions, mostly for expenses related to running the business.

Two federal forms, Form W-2 and Form 1099, report how much money an employer or other payer (such as a client for whom the taxpayer worked) paid to a taxpayer over the course of the year. Employers and clients send copies of these forms to both the IRS and the employee (or payee), thus ensuring that taxpayers correctly report their income.

In the United States individuals and corporations are required to file income taxes at the federal and state levels. The tax systems of each state frequently vary. For example, the tax rates differ from state to state, and each state has its own rules about deductions and credits. Furthermore, the following states do not require individuals to pay any taxes on income: Alaska, Florida, Nevada, New Hampshire, South Dakota, Tennessee, Texas, Washington, and Wyoming.

There are various types of income taxes, and a federal or state government may apply different types of taxation for different types of income. Two of the most commonly imposed kinds of taxes are the progressive tax and the proportional tax.

A progressive tax imposes a larger percentage of tax on high-income earners than it does on low-income earners. In other words, the tax rate increases as the amount earned increases. When the government applies this type of tax, earners with more income pay a higher percentage of that income in tax than those with less income pay. For example, the first $10,000 in earnings may be taxed at 10 percent, the next $10,000 at 15 percent, and any income over $20,000 at 20 percent. The federal income tax system in the United States is a progressive tax system.

A proportional tax, sometimes known as a flat tax or flat-rate tax, is a tax where the proportion of tax paid relative to income does not change as income changes. It takes the same percentage of income from everyone, regardless of how much or how little an individual earns. For example, low-income taxpayers would pay 7 percent, middle-income taxpayers would pay 7 percent, and high-income taxpayers would pay 7 percent. The result of a proportional tax is that the burden, or obligation, of the tax is applied as much on the poor as it is on the wealthy. Proportional taxes are most widely imposed in Eastern European countries, and proposals for them in the United States, Canada, and other advanced economies have inspired controversy.

The opposite of a progressive tax is a regressive tax, which in effect requires people with lower incomes to pay a larger proportion of their income than people with higher incomes. For instance, for a person with $20, a tax of $2 amounts to 10 percent of that person's money; but for a person with $10, the same tax amounts to 20 percent of their money. Sales taxes are often called regressive because they impact low earners much more than the wealthy. Income taxes are usually not regressive.

Recent Trends

In 1986 President Ronald Reagan (served 1981–89) signed into law the Tax Reform Act of 1986, which lowered the top tax rate on individual income from 50 percent to 28 percent. The act was one of the country's most extreme tax reforms since the introduction of the income tax in 1913. Its passage set a precedent for U.S. presidents after Reagan to authorize tax laws that would further decrease individual income tax rates.

A key feature of the Reagan administration's conservative economic policies was the belief that lowering income tax rates would increase the gross domestic product (GDP), the market value of all the goods and services produced in the country in a given year. Increased growth of the GDP would, in turn, provide more revenue for the federal government because it would be able to collect tax revenues on the excess economic growth. While the country did experience relatively high rates of GDP growth, the corresponding rise in the tax base did not compensate for the reduced tax rates. Tax revenues grew at a slower rate than government expenditures, and large government deficits resulted. As a result, in the 1990s the top tax rate in the United States rose to 39.6 percent, reducing somewhat in 2001 to 35 percent.

Income tax cuts are controversial. Whenever the federal government cuts income tax rates, it must either reduce its spending on government services, such as social welfare, education, and health programs, or go into debt. Those taxpayers in the lowest income brackets are typically the people most in need of such government services. Therefore, income tax cuts are frequently criticized by those who believe that reductions in government services typically decrease the overall well-being of the country's citizens. Another consequence of reducing income taxes is that it limits the government's ability to redistribute income among the taxpaying public. Redistributing income means collecting more from the wealthy to benefit society as a whole. Critics of income tax cuts argue that, when the government does not redistribute income, economic disparities and inequalities in society are likely to increase.

$ Sales Tax

What It Means

As the name suggests, the sales tax is a fee charged by the government on the sale of a good or service, such as a car, a meal at a restaurant, the repair of a bicycle, or a soda. A sales tax is usually a percentage, such as 5 percent, of the price of the good or service. For example, if it cost $100 to buy new wheels for your bicycle and the sales tax were 5 percent, the sales tax of that sale would be 5 percent of $100, or $5. The store that sold the wheels would send the $5 to the government. Large corporations, banks, and other businesses also pay a sales tax when making a purchase.

THE VALUE-ADDED TAX

A sales tax commonly used in Europe is the value-added tax, or VAT, which is charged to businesses. The idea behind the tax is more complicated than a typical sales tax, which is usually a percentage fee, such as 5 percent, added to the price of a good or service. It is called a valued-added tax because the tax is based on the "value," or price, the business adds to the product it makes.

Consider a coffee store that roasts, blends, packages, and sells coffee. With a conventional sales tax, the store would charge a price for its coffee and add to that price the amount of the sales tax. With the VAT the store first adds up the taxes it has paid on the supplies and services it has purchased, such as coffee beans. It then calculates how much tax it has charged on the coffee it has sold. If, for example, the VAT were 20 percent and the store spent $100,000 on supplies and services, it would pay $20,000 in taxes. If store then sold $150,000 worth of coffee it roasted, blended, packed, and sold, it would collect the 20 percent VAT on the $150,000 sales, or $30,000. The amount the store owed the government would be the difference between the taxes paid and the taxes collected, in this case $10,000.

The VAT was conceived by Maurice Lauré, a French tax administrator, in 1954. It has since been an important tax in Europe, as well as in India, Mexico, New Zealand, and many other counties. The tax rate is usually between 15 and 25 percent.

All governments—national, state, and local—need to charge taxes in order to support themselves, to provide essential services, and to ensure the safety, health, and well-being of their residents. Police officers, hospitals, roads, schools, and clean tap water are among the many services funded by sales taxes. Other examples include the salaries of government officials, the maintenance of historic sites and state forests, government programs aimed at promoting new businesses, and aid to low-income, elderly, and disabled residents.

In the United States the national government does not charge a general sales tax—that is, a percentage charge on all consumer purchases—receiving its money from other sources, such as the income tax (which is based on the amount a person earns each year). It does, however, have a sales tax on particular items, such as gasoline, tobacco, and airline tickets. In 2007, for example, the U.S. government charged 18.4 cents on each gallon of gas purchased. Taxes on particular items are called excise taxes.

By contrast, most state governments and some local governments (counties and cities) charge a general sales tax. In 2007 the sales tax was 7 percent in Mississippi and 4 percent in Wyoming. In order to help low-income

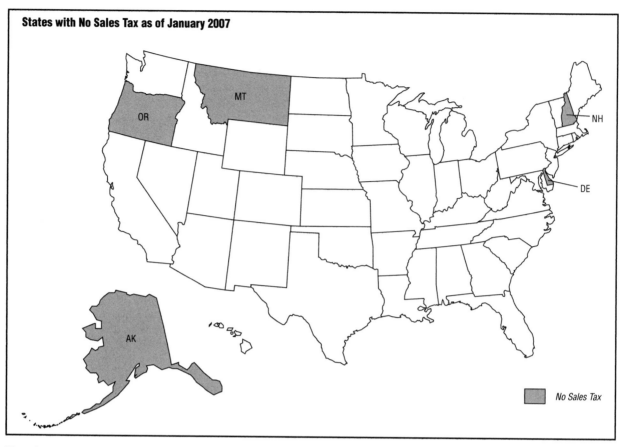

States with No Sales Tax as of January 2007

No Sales Tax

The sales tax, a percentage fee that is added to the price of goods and services, is an important source of revenue for U.S. states. As of 2007 only five states in the country did not charge a sales tax. *Illustration by GGS Information Services. Cengage Learning, Gale.*

residents, some state and local governments do not tax essential items, such as food, prescription medicine, and clothing.

When Did It Begin

Early sales taxes in the United States were excise taxes, directed at particular products, such as liquor. During the War of 1812, fought against Great Britain, the United States needed to raise money quickly for military expenses. It introduced a tax on watches, jewelry, gold, silverware, and other expensive items. After the war the tax was abolished.

States, too, charged excise taxes. In 1919 the state of Oregon began taxing gasoline, which had become an important fuel for the newly popular automobile. Excise taxes, however, because they were limited to particular goods, did not produce as much money as a general sales tax.

In 1921 West Virginia was the first state to adopt a general sales tax. At that time, states received most of their money from taxing property, such as houses, land, and office buildings. During the 1930s, however, other states followed West Virginia's example and replaced their property taxes with sales taxes. Sales taxes not only

provided more money than property taxes but they were easier to collect. By 1971, 45 states and the District of Columbia imposed some form of sales tax.

More Detailed Information

Each state in the United States has the freedom to establish its own system of sales taxes. For example, the sales tax in Massachusetts is 5 percent, while the state sales tax in Mississippi is 7 percent. Sales taxes, like taxes on property and income, are crucial sources of revenue for state governments. Many state governments get half of their income from sales taxes. A few states— Alaska, Florida, Nevada, South Dakota, Texas, Washington, and Wyoming—rely almost entirely on sales taxes for revenue because they do not impose an income tax. In contrast, Alaska, Delaware, Montana, New Hampshire, and Oregon do not collect a general sales tax at all; they raise money by other methods, such as income and property taxes. The states that have the highest sales taxes are California (7.25 percent), Mississippi (7.0 percent), Newo Jersey (7.0 percent), Tennessee (7.0 percent), Rhode Island (7.0 percent), Minnesota (6.5 percent), Nevada (6.5 percent), and Washington (6.5 percent).

Sales taxes are sometimes imposed by local governments, such as cities, counties, and independent public-service agencies, such as those that provide train and bus services. As a result, a consumer might have to pay several sales taxes on a single purchase. For example, if you were to buy a camera in Chicago, you would be charged a 5 percent state sales tax, a 2.25 percent city sales tax, a 0.75 percent county sales tax, and a 1 percent "transportation authority" tax, which would result in a total sales tax of 9 percent.

In general, city governments make more money from property taxes than from sales taxes, and state governments make more money from sales taxes than from any other type of tax. Together, property and sales taxes make up the bulk of income for city and state governments.

Sales taxes are sometimes called "regressive" taxes, meaning over the course of a year a poor person would pay a larger share of his income on sales taxes than a rich person would. In other words, although a sales tax might treat each purchase equally—charging, for example, 4 percent of the total price, regardless of the purchase—it would not treat each consumer equally. That is because people with lower incomes have to spend most of the money they make (on food, rent, utilities, transportation, and other basic items) in order to support themselves. Therefore, much of their income is charged a sales tax. In contrast, wealthier people tend to make much more than they need to support themselves and can more easily save money. The amount a person saves is not charged a sales tax.

In a state that charged a 4 percent sales tax, the effect of that tax could be much different for a low-income person than for someone with a much higher salary. If a person earned $160,000 a year and spent $40,000 of it on goods and services, he would pay $1,600, or 4 percent of $40,000, in sales taxes. This tax of $1,600 would be just 1 percent of his income of $160,000. Compare this to a person making just $12,000 a year who spent $8,000 on goods and services. He would pay $360 in sales taxes, or 3 percent of his $12,000 salary. Because the sales tax tends to have a much stronger impact on lower income residents, some states make certain essential goods (such as food and prescription drugs) and services (such as gas and water for the home) exempt from sales taxes.

Recent Trends

Although some people view the sales tax as regressive and unfair, others believe it has many advantages. It is easy to collect, for example, and because the sales tax applies only to purchases, it encourages people to save money. The U.S. government has periodically considered a federal sales tax, one that would be imposed on retail sales throughout the country. Some have argued that the federal government should replace all income taxes, on businesses and individuals, with a national sales tax.

Many of the proposals for the national sales tax are complex and try to lessen the effect on low-income residents. In some plans the government would provide a sum of money, paid in monthly installments and based on the number of individuals living in the household, to each taxpayer. Some proposals have suggested a federal sales tax of between 15 and 23 percent.

$ Excise Tax

What It Means

An excise tax is a fee charged by the government on specific goods or services that are purchased by some, but not all, consumers. Like a sales tax, an excise tax is collected by the seller when the goods are sold to a customer. Liquor, cigarettes, and luxury cars are examples of goods that have an excise tax.

An excise tax can be a percentage of the price of the good or service. For example, if the government charges a 7.5 percent excise tax on the fare of a domestic airplane ticket, and a plane ticket costs $300, the excise tax of that sale would be $22.50 (7.5 percent of $300). An excise tax can also be charged as a fixed dollar amount. The U.S. federal government's excise tax on hard liquor, $13.50 per gallon (as of 2007), is such a tax. Cigarettes also carry a federal excise tax (39 cents per pack in 2007). Individual states and counties may also charge excise taxes on the same goods. For example, the state of Ohio charged a $1.25 excise tax per pack of cigarettes in 2007. Therefore, for a pack of cigarettes a consumer in Ohio would pay both federal and state excise taxes, a total of $1.64, in addition to the retail price of the pack. In every case, the store or company that sells the good collects the tax and sends it to the government.

In addition to telephone service, cigarettes, and hard liquor, the federal government taxes gasoline, airline tickets, and a variety of other goods and services. These excise taxes increase the total price of the goods, sometimes substantially. They are often designed to discourage producers from making them and consumers from buying them (for instance, increasing the price of cigarettes is an effort to reduce smoking, thereby protecting the public's health). In many cases an excise tax is also used to raise revenue for a specific purpose linked to the good being taxed (for example, revenues from cigarette taxes might fund cancer research). Excise taxes are one of the primary ways the U.S. government collects money.

When Did It Begin

Holland and England, the first countries to impose excise taxes, began doing so in the seventeenth century. When these European nations established colonies in America, they collected excise taxes from American colonists on particular products, such as liquor. The first time the independent nation of the United States imposed a federal

HAWAII'S GENERAL EXCISE TAX

An unusual state excise tax is collected by the government of Hawaii. Instead of imposing a sales tax on consumers, the state charges what is known as a General Excise Tax, or GET, on all business activity. The tax rate of the GET is 4 percent, and it is collected at every level of business. For example, the tax is charged when a fabric supplier sells fabric to a suit manufacturer, again when the suit manufacturer sells the suit to a suit wholesaler, again when the suit wholesaler sells the suit to a clothing retailer, and once more when the customer purchases the suit from the retailer. In the end the tax will have effectively added about 16 percent to the price of the suit, money that will go to the Hawaiian state government. Hawaii raises almost half of its revenue through the GET.

excise tax was in 1791, but so many citizens and legislators opposed the tax that it was abolished in 1802.

Throughout its history the U.S. government has imposed excise taxes when it has needed to raise money for military expenses during wartime. The taxes were usually repealed or removed after the wars ended. During the War of 1812, fought against Great Britain, the United States introduced a tax on watches, jewelry, gold, silverware, and other expensive items. The excise tax imposed during the Civil War (1861–65) was on all manufactured goods. This tax raised a great deal of income. The Spanish-American War, fought against Spain in 1898, was funded by excise taxes on, among other things, petroleum and sugar products. In order to raise the funds it needed to support the military during World War II (1939–45), the U.S. government imposed excise taxes on furs, jewelry, and leather. Excise taxes on liquor and cigarettes have provided constant sources of funding for the government, even during peacetime.

More Detailed Information

The federal government collects several different types of taxes from citizens. Even though the money it gets from excise taxes makes up only about 10 percent of its total revenue, it is still one of the most important sources of funding. The main sources of income for the government are excise taxes, income taxes (which are levied on the earnings that individuals and businesses make), and Social Security taxes (taxes paid by working citizens to fund the federal retirement-benefits program).

A wide range of motor fuels carry a federal tax. In addition to gasoline, fuels such as diesel, boat fuel, and fuel for airplanes (called aviation fuel) are in this category, as are kerosene and liquefied natural gas. As of 2007, the amount of the federal tax on motor fuel was 18.4 cents

per gallon. Some states charge additional taxes on gasoline and other motor fuels. For example, in 2007 Pennsylvania was charging a tax of 2 cents per gallon on motor fuel. The posted price for gasoline includes both the state and the federal taxes. If a buyer of gasoline in Pennsylvania were to see a price of $2.56 per gallon of unleaded gasoline posted on a sign at a gasoline station, $2.56 per gallon would be the exact price he would pay per gallon of fuel, because it would include the federal and state taxes (totaling 20.4 cents per gallon). The state and federal governments use the tax on motor fuel, which is among the most important excise taxes, to pay for highways, roads, and public transportation systems.

Excise taxes are usually imposed on goods, but the government also collects excise taxes on what it refers to as "activities," specific actions that involve a transfer of money. A major example is gambling. Where gambling is legal, as it is in many states and cities, the operators of casinos pay a wager tax on gambling (the rate was 0.25 percent in 2007). This means that they must pay a portion (0.25 percent) of the amount they earn from the gamblers in their casino to the federal government. They collect the amount of this charge from their customers. State lotteries also pay the gambling tax to the federal government. Whenever a customer purchases a lottery ticket, the tax of 0.25 percent is included in the total amount he or she pays for the ticket.

Federal taxes on cigarettes, alcohol, and gambling are sometimes referred to as "sin taxes" because the government uses them to increase the prices of potentially harmful goods and activities and, in theory, discourage customers from purchasing them.

The money the government needs to pay for parks and recreation comes, in part, from a tax on the sale of bows and arrows and fishing equipment. An example of this tax would be a sale of three lures, a fishing rod, and a fishing reel, which together cost $40. With an excise tax of 10 percent on the sale, the final total would be $40 plus $4 tax, or $44.00.

Recent Trends

Excise taxes that the government imposes during wartime are usually abolished when the war ends and the government's need for the funds ceases. At the time of the Spanish-American War of 1898, Congress wanted to focus its collection of taxes on the wealthiest Americans. Telephone service was a luxury at the time, so affluent citizens were charged a 3 percent tax on every phone bill. After the war ended, the tax remained in existence, and over the following decades most American individuals and businesses began to use telephone service. The federal government brought in billions of dollars of income from the tax.

Many federal legislators and corporations sought to have the tax repealed, and several federal courts declared the tax illegal, but it was not until 2006 that the U.S.

An excise tax is a fee the government imposes on certain goods and services. On some goods, such as cigarettes, excise taxes are intended not only to raise money but also to discourage the use of the product. © *1998. Custom Medical Stock Photo, Inc. Reproduced by permission.*

Department of the Treasury eliminated the tax and began to issue refunds for telephone tax payments made by individuals and businesses since 2003.

$ Property Tax

What It Means

A property tax is a fee charged by the government on the value of privately owned property, such as land, houses and other buildings, and machinery. A property tax is usually charged as a percentage of the value of the property. The use of the property also determines how much tax is owed. For example, if a building is used for residential purposes (that is, for people to live in), it will be taxed at a different rate than if it is used for commercial (business) purposes. Property owners must pay taxes whether or not they actually use the property and regardless of whether the property generates income for them (as a privately owned business such as a store might).

People usually pay property taxes to the city, county, school district, or local government where they live. In the United States the state governments make up the guidelines under which local governments can impose property taxes, and the 50 states have different rules about what property is required to be taxed.

Local governments use the funds they gather from property taxes to create budgets for roads, public schools, public libraries, snow removal, policing, fire protection, hospitals, and other public services provided at the local level. In the United States property taxes are the core source of funding for education. Approximately 50 percent of revenue for public schools comes from property taxes.

Some property taxes are paid annually, and some are paid in two, three, and four installments throughout the year. The due date for a property tax depends on the location in which it is levied, or imposed.

When Did It Begin

The first property taxes were based on the amount of property (usually defined by the amount of land) that an individual owned. Centuries ago human societies were largely agrarian, meaning that property ownership and wealth were tied to land, particularly land used for farming. Later, such things as farmhouses, livestock, and machinery were taxed. Because these forms of property were directly linked to the amount of income an owner

ASSESSING REAL PROPERTY

The method used to assess the value of real property (land and buildings) depends on the type of property being assessed. Most residential real estate is appraised using the market comparison (also called sales comparison) method, in which the assessor compares sales of similar properties to provide an estimate. A second approach is the cost (or replacement) method, where an assessor uses the current prices for materials and labor to estimate how much it would cost to replace a given structure. This assessment is appropriate when dealing with a new or specialized property, or when there are no meaningful sales of comparable properties. An assessor employs another approach, called the income method, for property that is used to make money, such as apartments, stores, warehouses, shopping centers, and office buildings. In determining the value of the property, the assessor considers such things as the business taxes, the amount of income the property generates, and the business's operating expenses.

generated, the tax was a reasonable way to collect funds for local government.

The modern property tax is rooted in the medieval feudal systems of Britain and other European countries, in which people (called vassals) were allowed to occupy land in exchange for allegiance to the lord who owned it. In the fourteenth and fifteenth centuries the British tax assessors (the public officials who establish the value of property for the purpose of determining the amount of tax due) estimated the taxpayer's ability to pay based on whether or not he or she owned property. The tax collected was given to the king or landlord.

In the United States the development of property taxes was closely related to the economic and political conditions of the frontier. Property taxes in small, growing towns and communities were one of the most reliable ways for local governments to collect income.

More Detailed Information

In the United States property taxes are usually based on the value of the property. This kind of tax is known as an "ad valorem" tax. The term comes from *ad valentiam*, a Latin phrase meaning "to the value."

The amount of property tax that a local government imposes can be determined either by the full value of the property or a certain percentage of the full value. This means that 100 percent of the value of a piece of property can be taxed, or a smaller percentage, such as 50 percent, can be taxed. The percentage of the value of the property that is taxed is known as the assessment ratio. If the tax rate is 2 percent, the assessment ratio 50 percent, and the assessed value of the property $100,000, then the prop-

erty tax due would be $1,000 ($100,000 times 2 percent times 50 percent).

There are two basic categories of property: real and personal. In general, real property is land and anything that is permanently attached to land (such as buildings or wells). Typical examples of real property are homes, apartments, offices, and the land on which such buildings stand. Personal property is any property that is not real property. In most cases personal property is movable and does not hold its value as long as real property. Examples of personal property include vehicles, farm equipment, jewelry, household goods, and stocks and bonds (financial investments).

All real and personal property is subject to taxation unless it is tax-exempt, meaning it is released from the tax obligation. A building used for religious or charitable purposes would most likely be exempt from taxation. Housing for low-income residents or veterans might also be completely or partially exempt. State and local governments use exemptions to encourage certain types of development or to help attract new businesses.

Property usually changes in value over time. In order to determine the accurate amount of property tax, therefore, the property's value needs to be periodically appraised. An appraisal, completed by an impartial expert who is not invested in buying or selling the property, gives an approximation of its value. When the property changes in value, so does the appraised value.

One factor that can change property value, particularly real estate value, is the economy of the surrounding area. For example, the introduction of expensive homes in an area can positively affect the value of nearby property, as can an increased demand for housing. Likewise, a poor local economy, slow economic growth, and low demand for houses in a particular area can depress property values.

Recent Trends

In many places the money collected from property taxes often goes directly toward the local school system, allowing a wealthier district where homes are worth more to fund its schools with a lower tax rate than the one a poorer district would have to set in order to bring in the same amount of money for each student's education. Some states rely more heavily on property tax than others, but tax rates have increased nationwide since the 1990s.

In the late 1990s the rate at which income levels grew in the United States was higher than the rate at which property taxes grew. In 2000, however, the stock market experienced a downturn (meaning that people's investments in companies began to lose value), and a recession (economic decline) followed. After that, housing prices started to soar, even though personal income levels grew only moderately. As a result, revenues from property taxes increased faster than any other major tax source, including income and sales taxes. Many

Property taxes are fees imposed by the government on the value of property, such as homes and land. In this photo citizens of New York protest a proposed 25 percent hike in local property taxes. © *Najlah Feanny/Corbis.*

economists suggested that the U.S. economy was being strongly supported by a "housing bubble," meaning that real estate was assessed at higher than actual values. If this bubble were to burst, the result could be significant for school districts that rely heavily on property taxes.

If property values fall, local governments, and specifically school districts, might react in one or more ways. They might raise property taxes in order to bring in the necessary revenue. They also might cut spending on schools or request funds from the state or federal government.

$ Estate Tax and Inheritance Tax

What It Means

The property that people accumulate during their lives is often something they wish to leave to their children, grandchildren, or other relatives at the time of their death. The accumulated property—a house, land, money, or other wealth—is known as the person's estate. In the

United States, if the value of an estate reaches a certain amount, the government charges a tax on the right to transfer the property to descendants. This tax is the estate tax. It is charged as a percentage of the total value of all the property owned by the deceased person.

The U.S. federal government imposes the estate tax on an entire estate before it is distributed to those people inheriting it and regardless of how it is distributed. A different federal tax, called the inheritance tax, is a tax on the portion of an estate an individual receives, when and if he or she chooses to take on its ownership. It is charged after portions of the estate are transferred to each heir (a person who inherits the property of a deceased person). The inheritance tax is calculated as a percentage of the amount that the heir receives.

In addition to the federal-level estate tax, 24 U.S. states impose estate or inheritance taxes, and these state-level taxes bring in a total of approximately $4.5 billion a year. States use most of this money to pay for education, health care, and public safety.

When Did It Begin

In the United States the federal government has imposed either inheritance or estate taxes for many years. During both the Civil War (1861–65) and the Spanish-American War (1898), the inheritance tax was one of the ways the government raised money to pay for military expenses. The states individually developed inheritance taxes; in 1826 Pennsylvania became the first state to impose a state-level inheritance tax.

In 1916, when the U.S. government faced the high costs of engaging in World War I (1914–18), Congress needed to find the money to pay for waging the war. It recognized that the tax system at the time, which relied heavily on a consumption tax (a type of sales tax), put the most financial burden on the citizens least able to pay it (because for the wealthy it would seem a negligible amount, but for the poor it would be a more significant portion of their income). Congress believed that the larger portion of the revenue that the government needed should come from those with more income and inherited wealth. Because an estate tax would be easier to collect than an inheritance tax, and because many states already imposed inheritance taxes, Congress instituted an estate tax. Various changes have been made to the federal estate tax since then, but the principals of it have remained the same.

More Detailed Information

Estate taxes can seem complex, but in fact the way they are generally calculated is similar to the way personal income taxes are calculated every year. As with income tax, certain deductions and credits apply, reducing the amount of tax that will ultimately be owed. A deduction is an amount subtracted from the value of the estate (and is therefore not taxed), and a credit is an amount directly

THE GIFT TAX

In the United States the estate tax is closely related to a tax known as the gift tax, which is designed to prevent people from avoiding inheritance and estate taxes by giving away property before death. Estate taxes are imposed on property or asset transfers made upon a person's death, and gift taxes are imposed on property or asset transfers made during an individual's lifetime. The two taxes are paid separately, but federal estate-tax laws are integrated with federal gift-tax laws to make it more difficult for individuals to shield large estates from taxation. The gift tax applies to the transfer by gift of any property, including money or income from property. It is the giver's responsibility to pay the gift tax.

An annual $12,000 exclusion means that a person can give up to $12,000 each to any number of people every year, and none of the gifts will be taxable. If a gift in any year is larger than $12,000, any money beyond that is considered taxable. Gifts are further sheltered from taxation, however, by the lifetime gift shelter, which is $1 million. This means that a person is not taxed on gifts until the amount they give over the course of their lifetime reaches $1 million. The annual excluded gifts do not count toward the $1 million limit. The government keeps track of lifetime gifts by requiring that the giver file an gift-tax return every year.

subtracted from the tax owed. After the deductions are taken from the total amount of the estate, the tax is figured as a percentage of the remaining amount. Any credits are then subtracted from the tax.

Allowable deductions from a taxable estate include funeral expenses, debts owed at the time of death, and the costs of settling the estate. In addition, if the deceased person leaves property to governmental, charitable, scientific, educational, or veteran's organizations, the value of that property may also be deducted from the value of the estate (in other words, it is not taxed). When a deceased person has owned property jointly with a husband or wife, or has inherited property from a husband or wife, that property is not subject to an estate or inheritance tax. This is referred to as the marital deduction.

Knowing that their estates will be heavily taxed by the government leads many people to give some or all of their estates to nonprofit or charitable organizations, both at death and during their lifetime. In effect, the estate tax encourages charitable donations because they significantly reduce the tax on large estates.

As of 2007 the first $2 million of an entire estate was exempt from taxation (that is, not taxed), and this amount (called an exemption) was scheduled to increase to $3.5 million in 2009. Estates over this amount were taxed 45 percent. An estate with a value under this amount was not subject to the estate tax.

Inheritance taxes are the responsibility of the heir (who is called the beneficiary). Determining how much inheritance tax must be paid on a certain estate or part of an estate depends on the date of death of the person leaving the estate to heirs and the relationship of the heir to the deceased person. If the heir is a distant relative or friend, the tax rate is much higher than if he or she is a close family relative, such as a child, grandchild, or sibling. For example, as of 2007 the state of Pennsylvania, for dates of death on or after June 1, 2000, charged a 4.5 percent tax on transfers of property to direct descendents (sons, daughters, and grandchildren), a 12 percent tax on transfers to siblings (sisters and brothers), and a 15 percent tax on transfers to other heirs, such as nieces, nephews, other extended family members, and friends. Consider a Pennsylvania estate valued at $50 million that was divided so that a son was to receive half of it, a sister was to receive a quarter of it, and a nephew was to receive a quarter of it. If there were no exemptions or deductions, the state of Pennsylvania would charge inheritance taxes of $1,125,000 (4.5 percent of $25 million) to the son, $1.5 million to the sister (12 percent of $12.5 million), and $1,875,000 (15 percent of $12.5 million) to the nephew.

Recent Trends

In 2001 Congress passed the Economic Growth and Tax Relief Reconciliation Act, a law that significantly impacts the federal estate tax. As a result of this law, the federal government began to reduce the estate-tax rate in 2002. The rate dropped from 55 percent to 50 percent in 2002, and then by 1 percentage point each year until it reached 45 percent in 2007. Finally, the federal estate tax would be eliminated entirely in 2010.

The Economic Growth and Tax Relief Reconciliation Act also substantially increased the amount that individuals could pass to their heirs without having federal estate taxes imposed on it. The exemption for 2002 was $1 million, and it was set to increase gradually to $3.5 million in 2009. The full repeal (official cancellation) of the estate-tax law would take effect in 2010. The law, however, contained a "sunset" provision, which means that the estate-tax laws in effect before 2001 would be reinstated in 2011 if Congress did not pass an additional law calling for an entirely new estate-tax plan.

$ Business Tax

What It Means

A business tax is just what it sounds like, a tax that the government requires a business to pay. Just as the governments of cities, states, and countries require individuals to pay taxes on the income they earn each year (income taxes), they may also tax businesses and corporations every year. Businesses must pay taxes on such things as sales of goods and services, personal property, and the income they earn.

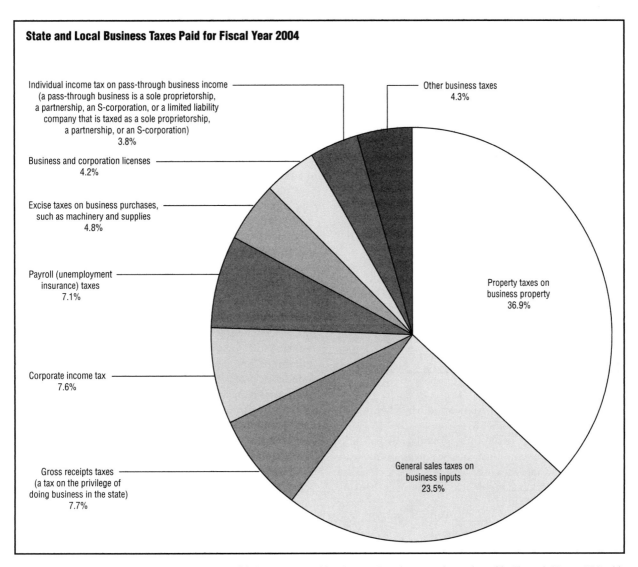

State and Local Business Taxes Paid for Fiscal Year 2004

Individual income tax on pass-through business income
(a pass-through business is a sole proprietorship,
a partnership, an S-corporation, or a limited liability
company that is taxed as a sole proprietorship,
a partnership, or an S-corporation)
3.8%

Business and corporation licenses
4.2%

Excise taxes on business purchases,
such as machinery and supplies
4.8%

Payroll (unemployment
insurance) taxes
7.1%

Corporate income tax
7.6%

Gross receipts taxes
(a tax on the privilege of
doing business in the state)
7.7%

Other business taxes
4.3%

Property taxes on
business property
36.9%

General sales taxes on
business inputs
23.5%

In the United States businesses pay various types of federal, state, and local taxes. Based on a study conducted by Ernst & Young LLP, this pie chart illustrates the breakdown of total state and local taxes paid by American businesses in 2004. *Illustration by GGS Information Services. Cengage Learning, Gale.*

Businesses are taxed by both the federal and, in most cases, state governments. There are several different types of businesses, and in the United States each type is required to pay different kinds of taxes, depending on the state where it conducts business. Forty-four states have some version of either a corporate or a business income tax, which is based on a company's earnings. The rate of tax applied depends on the level of profit a company has for that year and on the state in which it operates. Six states have a tax on gross receipts, which is the total value of all the goods and services sold by a business during the tax year. The taxes that corporations must pay on their income differ from those that a small business partnership must pay.

When Did It Begin

Some of the earliest taxes on businesses were put in place during the fifteenth, sixteenth, and seventeenth centuries. At this time, an economic theory known as mercantilism was established; it held that the growth and prosperity of individual nation-states depended on the strength of their economies. Governments assumed greater control of industry and trade because they needed to pay for armaments and troops to fight wars.

For the young American colonies during this period, the outcome of mercantilism was that the British monarchs heavily controlled businesses in the colonies and often imposed high taxes on them. Even after the independent colonial government was established in 1789, businesses were heavily taxed so that the government

TAX HAVENS

Throughout the world there are politically independent areas that have low or no income tax rates and few financial regulations; some also have laws that protect the secrecy of financial dealings. They have been widely used by individuals and businesses that want to avoid paying income taxes. It was estimated, for instance, that in 2003 American corporations transferred $75 billion in profits to tax havens; if this had been taxed properly, the U.S. government would have collected $10 to $20 billion.

Tax havens, many of which are islands, are often referred to as offshore jurisdictions. Some are countries. Examples include Andorra, Liberia, Liechtenstein, Monaco, Mauritius, Seychelles, and Bahrain. Many are territories or commonwealths that do not have to conform to the banking or taxation rules of any nation. These include Bermuda, the Cayman Islands, the U.S. Virgin Islands, the Marshall Islands, and the Channel Islands. At the start of the twenty-first century, these jurisdictions were facing international pressure to make financial transactions more transparent and to curb illegal activities such as money laundering.

could pay off the debts it had incurred while fighting the Revolutionary War (1775–83).

Another period of business growth and expanded government intervention in business was in the early 1900s, a period known as the Progressive Era. The U.S. government developed regulations for railroads, banking, and utilities. The first U.S. law imposing a federal corporate income tax was passed in 1909 in order to raise money for a growing federal government; the tax rate was 1 percent.

More Detailed Information

There are two components of any business tax. The first is the base, which consists of the elements of a business's activity that are being taxed, such as its income or employees. The second is the rate, which is the numerical percentage that is applied to the tax base. The rate multiplied by the base equals the business tax liability, or amount owed to the government. Thus, if the tax rate of 1.8 percent is applied to business income in a particular state, and one business earns $10,000 in a given month, its tax liability for business income that month would be 1.8 percent of $10,000, or $180.

Each state has different components to the way it defines a tax base. The gross receipts of a business are often taxed. These are the total receipts of a business for the goods it sells or the services it renders during the tax year. A business's assets are also commonly taxed, by both state and federal governments. Assets may include cash, investments (such as real estate loans or loans to company shareholders), and physical property (including buildings

and business equipment). States also commonly tax business income, which is any profit the business or corporation receives from the activity of its business.

Both state and federal governments may collect a corporate tax. States levy taxes on the profits made by the corporations based in that state as well as corporations that do business in the state but may be based elsewhere. The rate of corporate tax usually varies according to the level of profit. Federal corporate tax rates can be substantial (the top tax rate in 2004 was 38 percent), but the amount the U.S. government earns from this source is relatively small compared to what it earns from individual income taxes and Social Security taxes (Social Security is a federal program that provides financial benefits to senior citizens, veterans, and the disabled; it is funded by a tax paid by all individuals who earn income).

When a business hires and pays employees, it is then subject to employment taxes. Social Security and Medicare taxes (Medicare is a federal health insurance program for senior citizens), and federal unemployment tax (called FUTA because it was established by the Federal Unemployment Tax Act) all fall into the category of employment tax. Employees pay part of the Social Security and Medicare taxes themselves (typically by having the employer take the amount out of each paycheck and send it to the government), and the employer pays a matching amount. Employers pay the entire FUTA tax. This money goes to the state programs that provide unemployment compensation to workers who lose their jobs.

Businesses and corporations often owe large percentages of their earnings to the government to pay various taxes. It is common for businesses to look for ways to reduce their tax liability (the amount of tax they owe). When a business organizes itself with the intent of reducing the amount of taxes it owes on its earnings, it is said to be seeking a tax shelter. The government allows some methods of avoiding or reducing tax liability. For example, a company may establish a retirement plan called a 401(k), in which the employee invests a portion of each paycheck in the stock market; the company subtracts the money from the paycheck, makes a matching contribution, and deposits both in the employee's account. The money invested is not subject to income taxes until the employee retires. The government promotes 401(k) plans and others like them because long-term investments typically benefit the economy.

Recent Trends

As companies have grown larger and more financially powerful over the past century, the issue of corporate tax reporting (the way in which corporations report their financial information to state and federal tax agencies) has come to the fore. When corporations want to avoid paying large percentages of their profits in taxes, they generally seek to hide some of their profits from the government. This is known as tax evasion.

Perhaps the most notorious story of tax evasion and illegal corporate tax reporting is that of Enron, an energy company located in Houston, Texas, that was one of the world's fastest-growing companies in the late 1990s. Enron reported record-breaking profits to shareholders (people who had invested their money in the company), but reported low earnings to the tax agencies. One of the ways Enron created the myth of strong corporate performance was by setting up more than 800 fake subsidiaries in tax-haven countries, which served to hide the company's true financial status and also to evade taxes further. Through fraudulent accounting and other schemes, it managed to avoid paying any taxes at all for four of the five years before its demise.

In 2001 Enron was exposed for having lied about its financial success. The accounting firm that managed and reported its finances, Arthur Andersen, was also implicated in the scandal because it had destroyed vital documents related to Enron. When Enron filed for bankruptcy in December 2001, its crash resulted in the loss of millions of dollars of investor money. Since then, numerous other corporations have been investigated for their accounting and tax-reporting methods, and many politicians and watchdog groups have called for corporate tax reform.

WHO OVERSEES THE ECONOMY: GOVERNMENT ORGANIZATIONS

💲 Bureau of Economic Analysis

What It Means

The Bureau of Economic Analysis (BEA) is a division within the U.S. Department of Commerce (DOC), the agency responsible for fostering the nation's economic growth and technological advancement by promoting the health and vitality of domestic (U.S.) businesses and international trade. The BEA is one of two main bureaus (the other is the Bureau of the Census) in the DOC's Economics and Statistics Administration, which uses the information provided by these two bureaus to advise the president, the DOC, and other government agencies on economic matters.

The BEA's mission is to collect, analyze, and publish certain economic statistics that help the government, businesses, and the American public chart and understand the performance of the U.S. economy and its position in the global economy. (Statistics are numerical facts. The study of statistics is the science of turning these numerical facts into useful information.)

The BEA presents statistics about the American economy in the form of two-column accounting reports called NIPA (national income and product accounts)

The Bureau of Economic Analysis (BEA) is a U.S. government agency whose mission is to collect, analyze, interpret, and publish data about the performance of the U.S. economy. In the 1930s Russian-born economist Simon Kuznets, shown above, developed the NIPA (national income and product accounts) tables, which are the BEA's primary tools for measuring economic trends in the United States. *AFP/Getty Images.*

tables. One column shows the amount and breakdown of the various types of production in the economy; the other column shows the amount of income that is earned in the course of production and how it is distributed among the U.S. population. According to the double-entry system, a use (or expenditure) recorded in one column is accounted for as a source (or receipt) in the other column. Thus the sum totals in the right and left columns should be roughly equal. The NIPA tables are used to trace the flow of money in and out of the major sectors of the national economy.

When Did It Begin

Before the Great Depression (a severe, worldwide economic crisis that lasted from 1929 to about 1939), data about the performance of the American economy was fragmentary at best. When the U.S. government was suddenly faced with responding to, and trying to lift the country out of, the Depression, this information gap was exposed, and economists recognized the need for a comprehensive measure of national income and output.

The DOC commissioned Simon Kuznets (1901–85), an economist at the National Bureau of Economic Research, to develop the set of national economic accounts known today as NIPAs. Kuznets's report outlining the original set of accounts was presented to Congress in 1937. The NIPA tables have been refined and expanded since that time. The DOC and many prominent economists regard the development of the NIPA tables as the one of the greatest economic achievements of the twentieth century.

OFF THE BOOKS

The central purpose of the Bureau of Economic Analysis is to determine the GDP (gross domestic product, a measure of the size of the economy) of the United States. GDP is considered the most accurate available gauge of the health of the American economy, but it fails to account for all of the economic activity that occurs in the black market. The black market includes not only trade in illegal drugs, prostitution, weapons, fake identification cards, and stolen goods, but also all money that changes hands "off the books" in an economy, including informal cash payments to babysitters, housekeepers, mechanics, and other service providers, goods sold at garage sales, and many other transactions. Although the covert nature of the black market makes it impossible to measure with much accuracy, economists estimate that the black market in the United States accounts for about 10 percent of the country's GDP.

The predecessor of the BEA was the Office of Business Economics, which was established in 1945 as a division of the Bureau of Foreign and Domestic Commerce (a predecessor of the DOC). In 1972 the DOC reorganized its principal statistical agencies, and the Office of Business Economics was renamed the Bureau of Economic Analysis.

More Detailed Information

The most closely watched economic account published by the BEA is gross domestic product (GDP), the total dollar value of all goods and services produced within the country during the year. Simply put, GDP reflects the size of the economy. An increase in GDP from one year to the next reflects an economy that is expanding, while a decrease suggests that the economy may be contracting (shrinking).

GDP is calculated by adding together the following figures: consumption (private consumer spending for goods and services, including things such as groceries, televisions, and medical care); government spending (from military defense to employee wages to office supplies); investment (not the kind of investment that involves purchases of stocks and bonds, but rather businesses' investments in their own means of production, such as computer software or new factory equipment); and the nation's net exports (total exports minus total imports).

Another main account produced by the BEA is gross domestic income (GDI), a measure of the total of incomes earned in the process of the nation's annual production. In addition to GDP, GDI, and other national accounts, the bureau also collects data that focuses on specific industries and their relationships to one another, international trade and investment, and economic growth (or decline) in specific regions of the United States. In all, the BEA publishes some 130 NIPA tables.

Recent Trends

Prior to 1991 the size of the U.S. economy was measured as gross national product (GNP). GDP differs slightly from GNP in terms of how the country's productivity is measured. GNP counts the total production of all of the country's citizens and firms, whether the production occurs in the United States or in a foreign country. GDP counts only the production that occurs within U.S. borders by either foreign or domestic firms and workers.

As it entered the twenty-first century, the BEA was focused on harnessing technological advances to create coordinated electronic data collection systems that would greatly improve the accuracy, efficiency, and timeliness of its statistical accounts.

$ Bureau of Labor Statistics

What It Means

The Bureau of Labor Statistics (BLS) is a division of the U.S. Department of Labor (the federal agency responsible for regulating issues relating to the U.S. workforce, including occupational safety, wage and work-hours standards, and unemployment-insurance benefits). The purpose of the BLS is to collect, process, analyze, and publish a broad range of statistics (numerical facts) related to the ever-changing conditions of the national workforce and the economy.

The BLS answers various questions related to jobs in the United States. For instance, what percentage of American workers had access to paid vacations (or child care or health insurance) at their jobs last month? How did consumer spending vary according to age, race, region, and income level last year? What industry had the most job-related fatalities last year?

Reports published by the BLS serve as vital source of information for the U.S. Congress, other federal agencies, state and local governments, businesses, labor unions, and individual U.S. citizens. The agency's findings can be influential, and sometimes decisive, in the development of public policy (legislation, courses of action, and funding priorities determined by the government). The primary publication of the BLS is *Monthly Labor Review*. Other BLS reports include *Consumer Price Index*, *Employment and Earnings*, *Current Wage Developments*, *Producer Prices and Price Indexes*, and *Occupational Outlook Quarterly*.

The BLS is an independent, impartial agency; it is not involved in the Department of Labor's policymaking or enforcement activities.

When Did It Begin

The origins of the Bureau of Labor Statistics date back to 1884, when Congress established the Bureau of Labor within the U.S. Department of the Interior. The Bureau of Labor was renamed the Department of Labor (DOL)

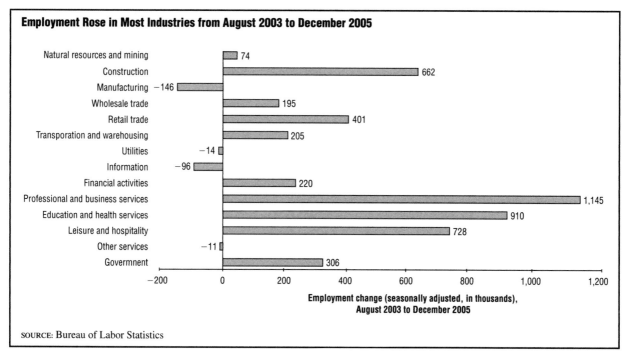

Employment Rose in Most Industries from August 2003 to December 2005

Industry	Value
Natural resources and mining	74
Construction	662
Manufacturing	−146
Wholesale trade	195
Retail trade	401
Transporation and warehousing	205
Utilities	−14
Information	−96
Financial activities	220
Professional and business services	1,145
Education and health services	910
Leisure and hospitality	728
Other services	−11
Govermnent	306

Employment change (seasonally adjusted, in thousands),
August 2003 to December 2005

SOURCE: Bureau of Labor Statistics

The Bureau of Labor Statistics (BLS) is a U.S. government agency responsible for collecting information related to the composition and conditions of the national workforce. According to this BLS graph, "professional and business services" was the industry with the most pronounced employment growth, while "manufacturing" experienced the greatest decline in employment, between August 2003 and December 2005. *Illustration by GGS Information Services. Cengage Learning, Gale.*

in 1913 and became a separate department of the executive branch; the head of the DOL, the secretary of labor, is a member of the U.S. president's cabinet (group of advisers).

While the makeup and responsibilities of the DOL changed several times over the course of the twentieth century (for example, the Children's Bureau, which deals with child-welfare issues, was contained within the DOL until 1945, when it was transferred to the Federal Security Agency), the BLS has been an essential agency of the DOL throughout the department's history. Over the decades the statistical research conducted by the BLS has both responded to and influenced major changes in the makeup of American labor, such as the dramatic increase in the number of women in the workforce.

More Detailed Information

The Bureau of Labor Statistics has its national headquarters in Washington, D.C., and maintains several regional offices throughout the country. The head of the agency is a commissioner who is selected by the president and approved by the Senate. Employees of the BLS include economists, statisticians, computer analysts, administrative specialists, and other professionals.

The BLS gathers its information from business groups (such as national and regional chambers of commerce, the National Restaurant Association, and the National Association of Manufacturers) and labor groups (such as the United Auto Workers Union, United Food and Commercial Workers, and other trade unions) throughout the country. These groups offer information voluntarily, with the understanding that it will be kept confidential and used only for statistical purposes.

The BLS organizes its data collection into several different categories:

Employment and unemployment: The bureau provides basic monthly figures on national employment and unemployment (unemployment refers to the number of people who want to work but cannot find jobs). It also breaks down the composition of the American workforce according to sex, age, race or ethnicity, region, and industry.

Prices and living conditions: One of the main figures that that the BLS calculates is the consumer price index (CPI), which measures the change (usually an increase) in costs of a fixed sampling of products and services that Americans pay for on a day-to-day basis, such as groceries, clothing, gasoline, prescription drugs, movie tickets, school tuition, Internet service, and haircuts. The BLS also calculates the producer price index (PPI), which measures the change in cost of materials used to make the products Americans consume. Both indexes are published monthly. The CPI and the PPI are essential tools for

EMPLOYMENT OUTLOOK

Young people who are choosing their career paths may be interested in the employment-outlook projections published by the Bureau of Labor Statistics (a government agency that collects information about the American workforce and economy). These reports show which American industries are growing (and likely to produce the most new jobs), and which are in decline. According to the BLS's report *Employment Outlook 2000–2010*, the two fastest-growing and most lucrative job markets in the U.S. economy would be in the computer-technology sector and the healthcare sector.

measuring inflation (the ongoing increase in prices of goods and services in an economy).

Compensation and working conditions: The BLS conducts comprehensive studies of employee wages and benefits in different occupations, industries, and regions of the country. It also collects data about injuries and illnesses related to the workplace, which is important for improving safety and hygiene standards in factories, restaurants, and countless other businesses.

Productivity and technology: The BLS measures the productivity (or output) of workers in various sectors of the economy, such as business and manufacturing. It also measures the productivity of specific industries within these sectors.

Employment projections: The data the BLS collects in this category shows which areas of the economy are growing and need new workers and which areas are oversaturated (full). This information is used by businesses, educators, and young people choosing careers.

International programs: The BLS also collects statistics on wages, productivity, and pricing in foreign countries, as a point of comparison for U.S. statistics.

Recent Trends

The BLS's data collection continues to change and adapt in accordance with changes in the character of the U.S. workforce and shifting trends in U.S. industries. For example, with the passage of the 1990 Americans with Disabilities Act (which prohibits workplace discrimination against people with disabilities), the BLS broadened its effort to gather statistical information on disabled workers. Also, technological advancements and changes in lifestyle have produced significant changes in the structure of the American economy. With the emergence of new occupations (such as "Web architect") and industries (including cellular telephones and warehouse superstores), the BLS has had to update its industry-classification system.

$ Consumer Product Safety Commission

What It Means

The Consumer Product Safety Commission (CPSC) is an independent agency of the U.S. government whose mission is to protect the American public from unreasonable or significant risks of injury or death associated with more than 15,000 types of consumer products, including toys, strollers, bicycles, electrical appliances, clothing, furniture, and household chemicals. The agency was established in 1972 with the passage of the Consumer Product Safety Act. The CPSC's jurisdiction does not include certain products, such as guns, cosmetics, pesticides, and cars; these and various other products are regulated by the Bureau of Alcohol, Tobacco, Firearms, and Explosives; the Food and Drug Administration; the Department of Agriculture; the Department of Transportation; and other government agencies.

One of the CPSC's main functions is to establish product-safety standards to serve as a guide for manufacturers, importers, distributors, and retailers. Some of these standards are merely voluntary (recommended), while others are mandatory (required). The CPSC also issues product recalls. A recall is a public request for consumers to return a product that has been found to be unsafe or defective, such as a toy that causes choking in a child or an appliance that poses a serious fire hazard. Companies are required to report discoveries of defects and safety hazards associated with their products to the CPSC. The commission also places bans on hazardous materials, such as paint containing lead (a toxic metal found to cause brain damage, especially in children).

In addition to these regulatory functions, the CPSC also conducts research to identify potential product hazards, and it plays a major role in informing and educating the public about product safety.

When Did It Begin

Issues surrounding consumer rights and public safety gained widespread national attention in the United States during the late 1960s and early 1970s, largely as a result of the political activism of Ralph Nader (b. 1934). Now recognized as the country's foremost consumer advocate, Nader first made a name for himself in 1965 with the publication of *Unsafe at Any Speed*, a best-selling book that exposed serious safety risks associated with the Chevrolet Corvair and led directly to the passage of national auto-safety standards. In 1969 Nader stirred up further controversy with a small team of law students known as Nader's Raiders, who published a harsh, embarrassing critique of the FTC (Federal Trade Commission), another government agency responsible for protecting consumer rights.

During this period Nader played an important role in creating public demand for corporate responsibility,

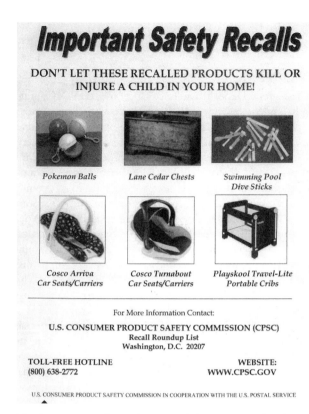

Important Safety Recalls

DON'T LET THESE RECALLED PRODUCTS KILL OR INJURE A CHILD IN YOUR HOME!

Pokemon Balls *Lane Cedar Chests* *Swimming Pool Dive Sticks*

Cosco Arriva Car Seats/Carriers *Cosco Turnabout Car Seats/Carriers* *Playskool Travel-Lite Portable Cribs*

For More Information Contact:

U.S. CONSUMER PRODUCT SAFETY COMMISSION (CPSC)
Recall Roundup List
Washington, D.C. 20207

TOLL-FREE HOTLINE
(800) 638-2772

WEBSITE:
WWW.CPSC.GOV

U.S. CONSUMER PRODUCT SAFETY COMMISSION IN COOPERATION WITH THE U.S. POSTAL SERVICE

The Consumer Product Safety Commission, or CPSC, is a federal regulatory agency responsible for monitoring and guaranteeing the safety of consumer products sold in the United States. When the CPSC determines a particular good to be unsafe, it typically issues warnings to the public and orders manufacturers to recall the defective products from the market. *AP Images.*

which led President Nixon to establish the EPA (Environmental Protection Agency) in 1970 and the CPSC in 1972. The CPSC reached its height during the Carter administration (1977–81), when its staff numbered nearly 978 people. The agency's resources were drastically reduced during the Reagan administration (1981–89), however, and since then it has been staffed by less than 500 employees.

More Detailed Information

The CPSC is run by a team of commissioners who are appointed by the U.S. president and confirmed by the Senate. One commissioner is selected to serve as chairman. Although the agency was intended to operate with a team of five commissioners, since the late 1980s Congress has only given it enough funding for three. The CPSC has headquarters in Bethesda, Maryland (a suburb of Washington, D.C.), and numerous field offices throughout the country.

The CPSC takes various actions to accomplish its mission of protecting the public from hazardous products.

- It develops voluntary safety standards by cooperating with members of particular industries (for instance,

the mattress industry or the toy industry) to identify potential risks and figure out how to make a product safer. This cooperative effort is believed to be effective because the industry knows its products best and is able to contribute its technical expertise to the discussions. The CPSC only imposes mandatory standards when it becomes clear that voluntary standards are being ignored or are otherwise ineffective. For example, during the 1970s the CPSC developed a voluntary agreement with candle manufacturers to stop putting lead in candlewicks. Although the voluntary standard seemed to be effective for some years, a study conducted in 1999 discovered that a small percentage of candlewicks still contained lead. In 2003, then, the CPSC imposed a mandatory ban on manufacturing, importing, or selling candles with lead wicks.

- The commission may enforce mandatory standards by suing violators in federal court (often working with the Department of Justice); if convicted, violators can be forced to pay civil or criminal penalties. The CPSC may also take legal action against companies that fail to report safety hazards discovered in their products.

- The CPSC issues recalls on hazardous consumer products, often in cooperation with the manufacturer. (Usually the manufacturer is eager to recall the product voluntarily in order to show its customers that it values their safety and considers the hazard in question to be an unusual accident.) When a consumer returns a recalled product, he or she may receive a repair, a replacement product, or a refund. Hundreds of products are recalled every year. Over the course of the CPSC's history, it has issued more than a thousand recalls, resulting in more than 17 billion individual product units being removed from store shelves. The CPSC places a special emphasis on identifying and recalling potentially dangerous toys and children's products.

- In addition to reports from companies themselves, the CPSC obtains information about unsafe products directly from consumers via its toll-free telephone hotline and a claim form on its website. Another of the CPSC's primary tools for obtaining information about safety hazards is the National Electronic Injury Surveillance System (NEISS), which compiles data on consumer-product-related injuries in U.S. hospital emergency rooms and enables the commission to make statistical injury estimates.

- Beyond the Consumer Product Safety Act, the CPSC also enforces regulations provided by the Flammable Fabrics Act (originally passed in 1953), the Refrigerator Safety Act (originally passed in 1956), the Federal Hazardous Substances Act (originally passed in 1960), and the Poison Prevention

HISTORIC STROLLER RECALL

In its effort to protect the American public from injuries associated with consumer products, in 2001 the Consumer Product Safety Commission (CPSC) announced the recall (a request for the return of a product to the manufacturer) of 650,000 baby strollers produced by Ohio-based manufacturer Century Products Company. It was found that the defective stroller collapsed, or the car seat carrier unexpectedly detached, while in use, posing a serious risk of injury to the infant or young child inside. At the time of the voluntary recall, Century had received 681 reports of incidents, including 250 injuries, related to this problem. It was one of the largest recalls in recent history.

Packaging Act (originally passed in 1970). These acts have been variously amended over time.

Recent Trends

When Congress passed the Child Safety Protection Act in 1994, it was considered a major breakthrough for the CPSC. Specifically aimed at preventing choking (the leading cause of toy-related deaths), this legislation requires toy manufacturers to place warning labels on toys containing small parts, such as balls, marbles, and other choking hazards. The label must specify that the toy is not intended for use by children under the age of three. Another key provision of the Child Safety Protection Act was the establishment of a bicycle-helmet safety standard. The standards call for adequate protection of the head and the presence of chin straps strong enough to keep the helmet on a rider's head even in a crash, collision, or fall. According to some estimates, bicycle helmets decrease the risk of head and brain injuries by 85 percent.

In the first few years of the twenty-first century, the CPSC was also concerned with a growing rise in the number of injuries and fatalities associated with all-terrain vehicles, or ATVs. It was estimated that 740 people died in accidents associated with ATVs in 2003. In 2004 U.S. hospital emergency rooms treated approximately 136,100 injuries associated with the vehicles. About a third of all ATV accident victims were under 16 years old. In the late 1980s the CPSC had negotiated certain safety improvements and implemented a mandatory "consent decree" (a legally enforced agreement) with major ATV manufacturers, but the decree expired in 1997, and safety standards became voluntary. In September 2006 the CPSC launched a major campaign to improve ATV safety. It promoted public awareness of the vehicles' safety issues and encouraged riders to attend training courses and adopt recommended safety precautions. The campaign also proposed instituting a new set of mandatory safety standards.

$ Federal Deposit Insurance Corporation

What It Means

The Federal Deposit Insurance Corporation (FDIC) is an independent agency of the U.S. government whose mission is to maintain and strengthen public confidence in the American financial system. The agency does this by insuring (guaranteeing) deposits in banks and thrift institutions (which include savings banks, savings and loan associations, and credit unions) for up to $100,000 per depositor in case of the institution's failure. A bank or thrift institution is said to fail when it becomes insolvent, meaning that the value of its liabilities (the money it owes) is greater than the value of its assets (the money and other items of value it has). For instance, if all the depositors at a bank tried to withdraw their money on the same day, the bank would not be able to cover those withdrawals, and a failure would occur. If the bank is a member of the FDIC, however, then every depositor is guaranteed to receive his or her money back (up to $100,000).

The FDIC is not funded by Congress. It raises the funds to insure deposits by charging premiums (insurance fees) to each of its membership institutions. The premiums are calculated according to the amount of deposit insurance each institution requires. The FDIC also derives funds from its investments in U.S. Treasury securities (loans to the government that pay interest). In 2007 the FDIC insurance fund totaled more than $49 billion, and the agency insured more than $3 trillion worth of deposits in U.S. financial institutions.

In addition to its function as an insurer, the FDIC also conducts research and analysis to identify and monitor banking activities and economic conditions that may pose risks to deposit insurance funds. The FDIC also takes various measures to help banks avoid failure and to limit the impact of bank failures on the economy as a whole. In each of these ways the FDIC plays a critical role in stabilizing the U.S. economy.

When Did It Begin

The FDIC was created under the Glass-Steagall Deposit Insurance Act of 1933 in response to the most severe banking crisis in U.S. history. Between the time of the stock market crash of 1929 (at the onset of the Great Depression, which lasted until about 1939) and the inauguration of President Franklin Delano Roosevelt on March 4, 1933, 9,000 banks failed in the United States, resulting in the loss of $1.3 billion in deposits. The establishment of the FDIC was part of a broader effort to prevent such a financial collapse from happening again and to restore public confidence in the banking system. The initial capital (funds) required to start the corporation was supplied by the U.S. Treasury and the 12 Federal Reserve banks (the Federal Reserve is the central banking

Created in 1933, the Federal Deposit Insurance Corporation, or FDIC, is a U.S. government agency that insures bank deposits up to $100,000. This photo shows a transaction at a North Carolina bank in 1940. *The Library of Congress.*

system in the United States, an independent agency of the U.S. government established in 1913).

Under the leadership of Walter Cummings (1879–1967), who served as chairman during the FDIC's initial organization, the agency conducted a massive effort to evaluate the solvency of individual U.S. banks. By the time FDIC insurance went into effect on January 1, 1934, 13,201 banks were insured or approved for insurance, representing 90 percent of all commercial banks (banks that have traditionally focused on short-term accounts and issuing business loans) and 36 percent of all mutual savings banks (a type of thrift; thrifts began by specializing in handling long-term savings deposits and issuing home loans). Under the Temporary Federal Deposit Insurance Fund (which remained in effect for the first year and a half), individual depositors were insured for a maximum of $2,500. When the permanent fund was inaugurated under the Banking Act of 1935 (effective July 1 of that year), the maximum deposit insurance was raised to $5,000.

From the outset of the FDIC's operation, public confidence in the banking system was dramatically improved. During 1934 total deposits in commercial banks increased by about $7.2 billion dollars, or 22 percent, which represented about a 50 percent recuperation of the deposits that had been lost during the preceding three years.

More Detailed Information

The FDIC is headquartered in Washington, D.C., with 12 regional offices and numerous field offices around the country. The agency is run by a three-person board of directors consisting of the Comptroller of the Currency (the presidentially appointed head of the Office of the Comptroller of the Currency, a bureau within the U.S. Treasury Department) and two other directors who are appointed by the president and approved by the Senate. Most of the FDIC's more than 5,000 employees are bank examiners (people who evaluate the solvency of banks).

FDIC insurance covers many kinds of accounts: checking accounts; savings accounts; money market deposit accounts (also known as MMDAs; these are savings accounts that allow the account holder to write a limited number of checks per month); money market accounts (high-interest savings accounts, not to be confused with money market funds); certificates of deposit (also known as CDs; these are deposits that earn high rates of interest but cannot be touched for a preset amount of time); and outstanding cashier's checks (a customer may purchase a cashier's check at a bank in a specific amount in order to

THE END OF BANK RUNS

A bank run occurs when account holders at a certain bank begin to fear that the bank will become insolvent (the equivalent in banking of going out of business). These account holders all rush to the bank at once to withdraw their money before it is lost in the bank's collapse. Even a healthy, stable bank does not keep all of the money its account holders deposit on hand in a vault, however; the bulk of this money is used to issue loans and make investments. When nervous account holders are unable to withdraw their money immediately, it sets off a panic that has ripple effects throughout the economy.

Bank runs were common after the stock market crash of 1929, when public confidence in the American banking system was at an all-time low. The Federal Deposit Insurance Corporation (FDIC) was created in 1934 to restore public confidence in the banking system by insuring each account holder's deposits up to a certain level. Thus, if a bank becomes insolvent, the FDIC will repay each account holder his or her money. Because average account holders no longer have to worry about a bank losing their hard-earned money, the FDIC has effectively ended the phenomenon of bank runs.

make a payment to a specific third party; an outstanding cashier's check is one that has been purchased but not redeemed), interest checks, and any other negotiable instrument (a written order to pay) that is drawn on the accounts of the insured bank.

There are many financial items the FDIC does not cover, even if those items are purchased through or held by an insured institution. Noninsured items include various kinds of investments in corporations or in the federal government (such as stocks, bonds, money market funds, mutual funds, and U.S Treasury securities) and the contents of safe-deposit boxes (boxes kept in a bank vault in which customers can store valuables). Also, the FDIC does not cover insurance policies, financial losses that arise from theft or fraud (banks are insured against these eventualities by private companies), or losses because of bank errors in an individual's account (there are other procedures for pursuing compensation for this).

In order to have its deposits covered (insured) by the FDIC, every bank or other financial institution must maintain certain standards of financial stability. A bank's stability is a measurement of its reserves and its liquidity. Reserves are the amount of money the bank sets aside (and does not loan or invest) in order to meet the daily cash withdrawals of its customers. Liquidity is the amount of assets a bank can convert into cash in a relatively short period of time without losing substantial value (to liquidate an asset is to sell it; stocks, or shares of ownership in corporations, are considered more liquid than property, because they can be sold

more quickly). An optimally stable institution is described as well capitalized, which means that it has a relatively high ratio of capital (money it has on hand) to risk-based assets (investments that have value, generate money, or both but that are not as secure as, or are riskier than, money in hand). Based on its analysis, the FDIC classifies banks in the following categories:

Well capitalized: 10 percent or higher ratio of capital to risk-based assets

Adequately capitalized: 8 percent or higher ratio

Undercapitalized: less than 8 percent ratio

Significantly undercapitalized: less than 6 percent ratio

Critically undercapitalized: less than 2 percent ratio

If a bank becomes undercapitalized, the FDIC takes certain measures to prevent the bank from failing. First, the agency issues a warning advising the bank to take corrective actions to improve its capital ratio. If necessary the FDIC may impose certain corrective actions, such as changing the bank's management, loaning the bank money, buying off some of its assets, or even facilitating a merger (whereby the unstable bank is unified with or absorbed by a stronger bank). If a bank sinks to the level known as critically undercapitalized, the FDIC declares it insolvent.

Recent Trends

Federal deposit insurance faced its first major challenge in the late 1980s, during what became known as the Savings and Loan Crisis. Beginning in 1934 savings and loan associations (also known as S&Ls) were insured and overseen by the Federal Savings and Loan Insurance Corporation (FSLIC), a parallel institution to the FDIC. In the late 1980s various circumstances (including poor management, risky investments, widespread fraud, changing economic conditions, and incompetent government supervision) combined to set off a massive wave of savings and loan institution failures, which led to the insolvency of the FSLIC and ultimately the wholesale collapse of the savings and loan industry.

In response to this disastrous and scandalous episode in U.S. financial history, Congress passed the Financial Institutions Recovery, Reform and Enforcement Act of 1989 (FIRREA), which reorganized the FDIC into two units: the Bank Insurance Fund (BIF) continued to insure banking institutions (as the FDIC had traditionally done); while the Savings Association Insurance Fund (SAIF) was created to insure savings and loan deposits, replacing the FSLIC, which was abolished. With the passage of FIRREA, the financial burden of alleviating the crisis was also shifted to U.S. taxpayers, who ended up paying more than $100 billion to steady the savings and loan industry.

In 2005 Congress passed the FDI Reform Act, which consolidated the BIF and the SAIF into a single insurance fund called the Deposit Insurance Fund (DIF). The FDI Reform Act also increased the maximum amount of federal deposit insurance on retirement accounts from $100,000 to $250,000 and broadened the FDIC's ability to increase insurance maximums on regular bank accounts in the future.

$ Federal Open Market Committee

What It Means

The Federal Open Market Committee (FOMC) is a committee within the central bank of the United States, the Federal Reserve System (commonly called the Fed). The Fed is responsible for regulating the U.S. money supply (the amount of money in circulation at any given time), and the FOMC is responsible for making the most important decisions about the money supply.

Changes in the money supply have a profound effect on the overall economy. When the money supply increases, the economy tends to grow, and prices tend to rise. When the money supply decreases, the economy tends to stop growing, and prices tend to fall. Economic growth is generally desirable, but if it gets out of control, prices may rise too quickly and undermine the value of the dollar, causing a wide range of economic problems. When the economy is growing quickly, then, the Fed may try to keep this growth in check by decreasing the money supply. Alternately, during times of economic stagnation, the Fed may increase the money supply in the hope of stimulating growth. Though it is normal for the economy to go through periods of slow growth, the Fed tries to minimize the hardship caused to businesses and individuals during these downturns.

The FOMC, which consists of 12 of the Fed's most important leaders, meets eight times a year in Washington, D.C., to decide whether or not the money supply should be increased, decreased, or kept constant, depending on economic conditions at the time. The FOMC's means of controlling the money supply is the manipulation of a basic interest rate (interest is a fee charged to those who borrow money) that affects the entire economy.

When Did It Begin

The Federal Reserve System was created in 1913 to regulate the U.S. banking system. The Fed is composed

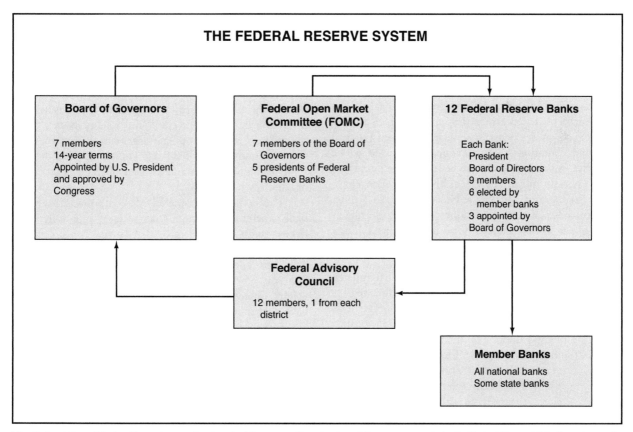

THE FEDERAL RESERVE SYSTEM

Board of Governors

7 members
14-year terms
Appointed by U.S. President
and approved by
Congress

Federal Open Market Committee (FOMC)

7 members of the Board of Governors
5 presidents of Federal Reserve Banks

12 Federal Reserve Banks

Each Bank:
President
Board of Directors
9 members
6 elected by
member banks
3 appointed by
Board of Governors

Federal Advisory Council

12 members, 1 from each district

Member Banks

All national banks
Some state banks

The Federal Open Market Committee makes key decisions regarding the size of the money supply in the United States. This chart shows the position of the Federal Open Market Committee within the overall structure of the Federal Reserve, the U.S. central bank. *Illustration by George Barille. Cengage Learning, Gale.*

THE BOARD OF GOVERNORS

The central bank of the United States, the Federal Reserve System (or the Fed), is responsible for regulating the amount of money circulating in the country's economy at any given time. Within the Fed the Federal Open Market Committee (FOMC), a committee of 12 Fed leaders, makes the most important decisions regarding the money supply. In reality, however, the Board of Governors of the Federal Reserve System, a group of seven financial experts who oversee the Fed, dictate most important decisions within the FOMC as well as in other Fed matters. The seven Board members each have a seat on the 12-person FOMC, giving them a majority voice in the FOMC's decisions.

Board members are appointed by the U.S. President for terms of 14 years, allowing them to operate free from political pressures and changes in public opinion. Among the seven appointees, the President selects one to be a chairman and another to be vice-chairman. The terms for chairmen and vice-chairmen are four years. The chairman of the Fed's Board of Governors, commonly called the Fed Chairman, is by far the most visible representative of the Fed. One of the longest-serving and most widely recognized Fed Chairmen ever was Alan Greenspan, who served as Chair from 1987 to 2006.

not only of the central leadership in Washington but of 12 regional banks, each of which is identified by the city in which it is headquartered. The cities are New York, Boston, Philadelphia, Richmond, Cleveland, Atlanta, Chicago, St. Louis, Minneapolis, Kansas City, Dallas, and San Francisco. At the time of its creation, the Fed was intended to be a decentralized system in which the regional banks made their own policies based on regional economic conditions. This arrangement proved to be ineffective as the U.S. economy became more integrated across regions, and in the 1920s the Fed began eliminating the regional policy differences in favor of a more standardized approach to the money supply. A forerunner to the FOMC was organized on an informal basis during this time by Benjamin Strong, head of the Federal Reserve Bank of New York.

The Great Depression (the severe crisis that afflicted the world economy in the 1930s) led to further regulation and centralization of the U.S. economy, meant to prevent future crises. The Banking Act of 1935, pushed through Congress under President Franklin D. Roosevelt, restructured the Fed and formalized the FOMC's role as a central player in the crafting of monetary policy (government actions affecting the money supply).

More Detailed Information

The FOMC meets eight times a year in Washington, D.C., to review current economic conditions and come to an agreement about the appropriate measures to be taken in regard to the money supply. Of the 12 FOMC members, the seven members of the Board of Governors of the Federal Reserve System (the Fed's governing body) form the majority contingent and therefore have the power to enforce their will. The president of the Federal Reserve Bank of New York is also a member of the FOMC, since New York City is the nation's financial capital. The final four seats on the FOMC are split among the remaining eleven regional heads. The Federal Reserve Banks of Boston, Philadelphia, and Richmond share one voting membership; those of Cleveland and Chicago share another; Atlanta, St. Louis, and Dallas another; and Minneapolis, Kansas City, and San Francisco another.

The FOMC regulates the money supply primarily by affecting the interest rates that banks charge to borrowers. The money supply consists not simply of the bills and coins minted by the government but also of bank-account balances. When you deposit a paycheck in the bank, you own a quantity of money even though you do not physically possess currency; your money exists simply as a number within a bank's computer system. Likewise, when banks loan money to individuals and companies, they do not hand over the money in cash; they give borrowers an account balance. In other words, when banks lend money, they increase the U.S. money supply simply by changing some figures in their computer systems. But banks are not free to create unlimited amounts of money. Their lending behavior is subject to the direct influence of the Fed.

The Fed requires banks to keep a small proportion of its overall balances on hand (or in an account with the Fed) in the form of hard currency. This is to ensure that banks will be able to give account-holders money when they want to withdraw it. The larger a bank's reserves are, the more money it can lend out. Therefore, when the Fed wants to regulate the money supply, it changes the levels of bank reserves.

The Fed, through the FOMC, imposes changes on bank reserves by changing an interest rate called the federal funds rate: the price that banks charge one another to borrow money. Banks generally borrow money from one another in order to maintain their required reserves. When the federal funds rate is low, banks are able to obtain reserves for a low price. Therefore, banks have a greater ability to make loans, and this results in lower interest rates for the individuals and businesses who borrow money from them. Individuals borrow money from banks to make large purchases. This stimulates the economy, of course, but it is the borrowing of businesses that has the power to trigger exponential economic growth.

Businesses commonly borrow money to start or expand their operations. A business may invest this money in equipment that will bring long-term profits, it may use the money to hire new workers, or it may use the money to fund research into new technology. In other words, businesses put the dollars they borrow to work in a variety of ways, so that every dollar borrowed is ultimately multiplied many times over throughout the economy.

Though it has other ways of changing interest rates and altering the money supply, the Fed, through the FOMC, primarily relies on open market operations: the buying or selling of government securities (a security is a form of investment, such as a bond, which can be assigned value and exchanged among investors). When the Fed sells government bonds, they take in money from the buyer and give out a piece of paper (the bond) that the buyer cannot spend. Because the Fed holds onto the money, the amount of money in bank reserves decreases, and the federal funds rate rises. When the Fed buys government bonds, they credit the seller's bank account, the amount of money in bank reserves increases, and the federal funds rate falls.

Because of the ripple effects caused by changing interest rates, the FOMC changes the federal funds rate with the intent of adjusting a wide range of economic variables in addition to the money supply. Chief among these variables are employment levels and prices. The Fed's overall goal is a healthy level of economic growth. Growth of around 3 to 5 percent per year is usually considered healthy.

Recent Trends

Prior to 1994 the FOMC did not inform the public about the actions it meant to take regarding the federal funds rate and the money supply. Economists would study changes in interest rates and open market operations to determine the Fed's stance on the federal funds rate and then relay the news to the general public. In 1994 the FOMC began issuing news releases at meetings that resulted in a change in the federal funds rate, and in 1999 it began issuing a statement about each of its eight yearly meetings.

Since the mid-1990s, the announcement of the FOMC's eight yearly decisions about the federal funds rate has become one of the most anticipated events in the financial world. Because the federal funds rate has such a broad effect on the economy, investors in the stock market (the stock market is a system for buying shares of company ownership; these shares gain value when companies grow and prosper, and lose value when companies struggle) often alter their behavior significantly in response to rate changes. When the federal funds rate is lowered, the stock market tends to gain value immediately as people rush to buy stocks in anticipation of future economic growth. When the rate is raised, investors tend to sell off shares of stock in anticipation of an economic downturn.

$ Food and Drug Administration

What It Means

The Food and Drug Administration (FDA) is an agency within the U.S. Department of Health and Human Services that is responsible for protecting public health. By enforcing various laws and regulations, the agency guarantees the safety and effectiveness of foods, human and veterinary drugs, biological products (such as vaccines, blood products, and gene therapy), cosmetics, and products that emit radiation (including X-ray equipment, cellular phones, and microwave ovens). The agency may regulate products and substances by banning them completely, limiting their distribution, or placing restrictions on the way they can be marketed (or advertised). The FDA also strives to promote public health by funding scientific research and providing Americans with the accurate, science-based information they need to make important medical and dietary decisions.

In 2006 it was estimated that the agency oversaw the production and distribution of $1 trillion worth of goods per year, an operation that cost approximately $3 per taxpayer.

When Did It Begin

The FDA was created in 1906, when President Theodore Roosevelt (1858–1919) signed into law the Pure Food and Drug Act. Fraudulent (fake or ineffective) drugs and impure foods had long been a problem in the American

The U.S. Food and Drug Administration, or FDA, is a government agency charged with ensuring that all food, drug, and other products intended for human consumption conform to certain standards before they become available to consumers. At times FDA health standards have been controversial. *AP Images.*

TWENTY-FIRST-CENTURY MUCKRAKING

Published in 1906, Upton Sinclair's *The Jungle*, a heavy-hitting exposé of rampant greed and unsanitary conditions in the meatpacking industry, was a landmark in muckraking (or investigative journalism) that led to significant reforms in the industry and the establishment of the Food and Drug Administration (FDA), a federal agency responsible for enforcing health and safety standards for food and drugs. Nearly a century later, *Fast Food Nation* (2001) by Eric Schlosser (b. 1959) was considered a new landmark in muckraking. It examined the destructive impact of the fast-food industry on public health in the United States and the failure of the FDA to prevent it. The book sold millions of copies and launched a new wave of public outcry over corporate America's abuse of its own customers.

marketplace, but in the late nineteenth century there was a marked rise in the prevalence of such misrepresented and adulterated (or tainted) goods. For example, many mothers unknowingly gave their sick children morphine, and grocers often simply deodorized rotten eggs. Such goods posed a threat to public safety, and legitimate manufacturers also feared that their own businesses would be ruined by a widespread loss of consumer confidence.

Before the FDA was created, such matters were addressed by the Division of Chemistry (later renamed the Bureau of Chemistry), which President Lincoln had established in 1862 as a part of the U.S. Department of Agriculture. While the division could investigate and conduct scientific studies into adulterated food and drug products, however, it did not have the authority to set and enforce rules (which in the U.S. government is called regulatory power).

A number of factors contributed to the establishment of the FDA as a regulatory agency in 1906. With the appointment of chemist Harvey Washington Wiley (1844–1930) as head of the Division of Chemistry in 1883, the government began to take a more aggressive role in identifying and studying the chemical additives and preservatives contained in food and drugs. Published between 1887 and 1902, Wiley's 10-part study *Foods and Food Adulterants* generated considerable public outcry as well as demand for a federal law to prohibit the use of dangerous adulterants in, and the inaccurate branding of, food and drugs. Public concern was further inflamed by the muckrakers, investigative journalists who exposed the deceitful practices and appalling sanitary conditions of certain American businesses. Two landmark publications that led to the passage of the Pure Food and Drug Act (also known as the Wiley Act) were "The Great American Fraud," a series of articles by Samuel Hopkins Adams

(1871–1958) analyzing some of the country's most popular medicines, which appeared in *Collier's* magazine in 1905; and *The Jungle* (1906) by Upton Sinclair (1878–1968), a shocking portrait of a Chicago meatpacking plant.

The next major milestone in FDA history was the passage of the Federal Food, Drug, and Cosmetic Act in 1938. For several years Congress had been under pressure to make important modifications and updates to the Pure Food and Drug Act of 1906. Still, it was not until a medical disaster occurred in 1937 (wherein an untested antibiotic called Elixir Sulfanilamide resulted in the deaths of more than 100 people, mostly children) that the legislature was forced to act. Although it has been updated and amended considerably over the last several decades, the 1938 law still forms the foundation of the FDA's jurisdiction and duties.

More Detailed Information

The FDA is headed by a commissioner, who is appointed by the president and confirmed by Congress. The agency is composed of five major centers: the Center for Drug Evaluation and Research (CDER), the Center for Biologics Evaluation and Research (CBER), the Center for Devices and Radiological Health (CDRH), the Center for Food Safety and Applied Nutrition (CFSAN), and the Center for Veterinary Medicine (CVM). The FDA as a whole is staffed by about 9,000 employees who work in and around Washington, D.C., as well as in field offices throughout the country.

The FDA's activities fall into five major categories. The first of these is new product review, the process by which the agency tests the safety and effectiveness of a new product before it is approved for sale. This review is conducted for new human drugs and biological products (also known as biologics), complex medical devices, food and color additives, infant formulas, and animal drugs. Second, the FDA is responsible for monitoring these products after they reach the market (become available for sale), to make sure that they continue to be safely manufactured and transported and that no new health risks arise.

Third, the FDA establishes regulations and safety standards to guide manufacturers in the requirements for maintaining product safety and keeping citizens and the health-care community accurately informed. It requires that manufacturers provide truthful and informative labels on packaging for foods, over-the-counter medicines, dietary supplements, and other products, so that consumers can see the ingredients of a product, understand safe dosages, and have ready access to any other information they might need for safe and effective use of the product. The agency also works with foreign governments to make sure that products imported into the United States meet the FDA's safety standards.

A fourth area of FDA activity is scientific research, which is conducted by the agency's biologists, chemists, physicians, biomedical engineers, pharmacologists, veterinarians, toxicologists, and other specialists. Their findings are used as the basis for the FDA's regulatory actions, to establish safety standards, to weigh the risks associated with potential "breakthrough" drugs (new products that may change the way certain diseases are treated), and to inform and educate the public. Although the FDA does not develop new products itself, its scientific findings certainly influence the advancements of the food, drug, medical, cosmetic, and veterinary industries.

Finally, the FDA engages in various enforcement activities. For example, in cases where one batch of a product turns out to be defective because of a manufacturing error, or unforeseen side effects are discovered in a product that was thought to be safe, the FDA may take one or more of the following measures. It may ask the manufacturer to recall the product (a recall is a public request for consumers to return a product that has been found to be contaminated, defective, or otherwise unsafe); it may officially withdraw approval (of a drug, for example); it may require changes to the product's labeling; and it may issue warnings to doctors or other health-care professionals. If necessary, the FDA can also take legal action against those who deliberately violate the law.

Recent Trends

At the turn of the millennium, technological advances in food production, pharmaceuticals, genetic engineering, and other areas were occurring at a rapid pace. As a result, the FDA faced major challenges in protecting public health and safety. The agency was also concerned about developing preventative and response mechanisms for potential sudden health crises, which might include the spread of a dangerous foodborne illness like E. coli bacteria, the emergence of strains of antibiotic-resistant bacteria, and acts of biological terrorism that would introduce deadly agents such as anthrax or smallpox into the population. The continued growth of international commerce also presented new challenges for the FDA, requiring the agency to place a new emphasis on monitoring imports and cooperating with foreign regulators.

$ Federal Reserve System

What It Means

All modern capitalist nations have central banks. In the United States the central bank is called the Federal Reserve System, or the Fed; it is an independent agency of the U.S. government. Most large banks in the United States belong to the Federal Reserve System. That is, they have accounts with the Fed that are almost exactly like the accounts individual people have with their banks. Member banks deposit checks and maintain a balance (an

amount of money) with the Fed. But even those banks that are not Fed members must obey the banking rules set by the Fed, which regulates the entire industry. The Fed also serves as a bank for the U.S. government itself and oversees the circulation of hard currency (paper bills and coins). The Fed's most important and complicated duty, however, is the setting of U.S. monetary policy: the Fed decides whether, when, and how to change the money supply (the amount of money circulating in the U.S. economy).

The size of the money supply affects all facets of the economy, and it has a direct link to inflation (the general rising of prices), which can cause a nation's money to lose its value. The Fed monitors the economy and makes decisions about whether the U.S. money supply should be increased, decreased, or left alone. When it decides to change the size of the money supply, it does so by influencing banks and their ability to make loans.

When Did It Begin

The Federal Reserve System was created by the Federal Reserve Act of 1913, which was introduced in order to strengthen the U.S. banking system. Prior to 1913 individual banks made their own decisions about how much hard currency to keep on hand (in reserve) in case depositors (bank account holders) wanted to withdraw some or all of their account balances in cash. The banks made the rest of the money people deposited with them available for loan, charging interest (fees imposed for the use of borrowed money) in order to make profits. But the amounts of money that banks reserve and loan out directly determine how much money is circulating in the economy; thus uncertainty about reserve levels and other banking issues leaves the economy vulnerable to

The Federal Reserve System, the central bank of the United States, oversees the amount of money circulating in the economy. Alan Greenspan, pictured here, served as chairman of the Federal Reserve Board from 1987 to 2006 and helped steer the U.S. economy through several financial crises. *AP Images.*

THE CHAIRMAN

The public face of the Federal Reserve System is its chairman, who gives testimony before Congress and otherwise takes responsibility for U.S. monetary policy. For more than 18 years (1987–2006), that person was Alan Greenspan (b. 1926), who became a household name during his tenure. Greenspan's celebrity was partly owing to the favorable economic climate of those times (the 1990s saw the biggest economic boom in U.S. history), but he was also popular for announcing the Fed's decisions to the public and taking a more visible role in the public eye than his predecessors had. Greenspan was succeeded on February 1, 2006, by Ben Bernanke (b. 1953). Before becoming chairman, Bernanke served on the Fed's board of governors. He had also been an economics professor at Stanford and Princeton Universities and the chairman of President George W. Bush's Council of Economic Advisors.

economic catastrophe of all kinds, including bank failures, or bank runs, when people lose faith in the system, and everyone demands their money at once (money that the banks do not have on hand). Numerous bank failures led to what became known as the panic of 1907, an economic crisis during which the stock market slumped, millions of bank account holders lost their savings, and many other banks and business firms closed down. By centralizing and stabilizing the banking system with the Federal Reserve Act, the U.S. government was able to take direct control over the money supply, one of the most important factors in the overall health of the economy.

More Detailed Information

The Fed's most important function is the regulation of the country's money supply. The Fed does not, however, simply order new dollar bills printed or pull old dollar bills out of the flow when it wants to change the amount of money in circulation. Instead, the Fed controls the money supply by setting rules for and influencing the practices of banks. To understand how this happens, it is first necessary to understand the way the banking system works.

All modern economies are driven by a fractional-reserve banking system, which means that at any given time banks possess hard currency amounting to only a fraction of the money that has been deposited by account holders. Fractional banking makes a great deal of economic activity possible that would be impossible if everyone needed cash for all purchases. In fact, fractional banking creates money that would not otherwise exist.

For instance, assume that Jane Doe deposits $10,000 in Bank X. Bank X will want to loan most of that money out so that it can collect interest and make a profit. Say

that Bank X puts $1,000 of Jane's total $10,000 in reserve and loans the remaining $9,000 to John Smith, who wants to open a coffee shop. Bank X will give John Smith a checkbook tied to a checking account with his $9,000 in it, and he will use his Bank X checks to pay Big Time Coffee Distributing, Inc. for $9,000 worth of tables, chairs, coffee makers, and coffee. Big Time will deposit John Smith's $9,000 worth of checks at its own bank, Bank Y; then Bank Y will set aside $900 while making the remainder ($8,100) available for loans. Say that Mary Brown shows up at Bank Y asking for $8,100 to open a sandwich shop. The process described above will continue as Mary Brown writes checks that are deposited in yet another bank, and so on, through other individuals and banks, until the original $10,000 is used up. At that point there will be far more than $10,000 in circulation.

Though it would be more complicated in reality, the above scenario describes the process by which banks literally create money. The Fed can, therefore, expand or restrict the money supply by influencing this process. It has three basic methods for doing so.

First, the Fed can simply change the percentage of deposits banks are required to keep in reserve. The above example assumes banks are required to reserve 10 percent of all deposits. If Bank X had been required to keep 15 percent of Jane Doe's deposit in reserve ($1,500), it would have been able to lend only $8,500 to John Smith, and this would have reduced the amount of money ultimately created by the chain of borrowers, businesses, and lenders involved. Likewise, if Bank X had to set aside only 5 percent of Jane's deposit ($500), the amount of money created would be increased. Although the Fed has the ability to modify the reserve requirement to affect lending behavior, in practice it rarely, if ever, makes use of this policy tool.

The Fed's second means of influencing the money supply is to change the interest rate it charges member banks to borrow money (this interest rate is called the discount rate). For instance, if Jane Doe had not made a $10,000 deposit, Bank X could still make a $9,000 loan to John Smith by borrowing enough money from the Fed to cover its reserve requirements (which would be $1,000 if the required reserve rate were 10 percent). If the Fed was currently charging a low price for this borrowed money (a low discount rate), Bank X would be likely to borrow from the Fed and, in turn, loan money to John Smith. If, however, the Fed was charging a high discount rate, Bank X might simply turn John Smith's loan application down. By raising its discount rate, the Fed would have reduced the amount of money created by Bank X.

Finally, the Fed influences the money supply by engaging in what are called open-market operations: the buying or selling of government securities, such as treasury bills, treasury notes, and treasury bonds (different investment opportunities offered by the government, on which the government pays interest, and whose value the government guarantees). When the Fed buys government securities, it essentially injects money into the banking system, because it is buying the securities from individual dealers who deposit the Fed's checks in banks like Bank X. When the Fed sells government securities, it essentially takes money out of the banking system, because then individual dealers write checks that are payable to the Fed, and the money is withdrawn from the individuals' accounts at their own banks. This decreases the deposit totals of banks like Bank X.

Recent Trends

Today the media commonly reports on Fed announcements regarding interest rates, but few people correctly understand these reports. To decipher them, it would be necessary to understand the different types of interest rates (the discount rate, the federal funds rate, and the prime interest rate) that most crucially affect the economy and to understand the Fed's relationship to each.

The Fed is responsible for setting the discount rate, or the rate it charges on loans that it makes to banks who want to borrow money. While this rate can affect the money supply, it is not usually the most influential interest rate in the bigger economic picture. When banks want to increase their reserves, they usually borrow from one another rather than from the Fed.

The rate that banks charge one another for loans is called the federal funds rate. While the Fed does not directly set the federal funds rate, it makes announcements publicizing what it thinks that rate should be; then it can enforce that target rate by using open-market operations to change the money supply. If the Fed decreases the money supply by selling government securities, interest rates tend to rise. If the Fed increases the money supply by buying government securities, interest rates tend to fall. Because banks commonly borrow money from one another to cover shortfalls in their reserves, the federal funds rate has a direct effect on the rates that banks charge consumers and businesses who take out loans.

The rate that individual banks charge consumers and businesses is based on what is called the prime interest rate. The prime rate is the standard interest rate set by major banks. It serves as a baseline to which individual banks add percentage points (raising the interest rate slightly), depending on the circumstances surrounding individual loans. Adding percentage points ensures that the bank covers its costs and makes a profit. In principle the prime rate depends on market forces such as supply and demand; in practice, however, it is closely tied to the federal funds rate. Today the prime interest rate is generally about 3 percentage points higher than the federal funds rate.

Therefore, while TV newscasters are not technically accurate when they say, for example, "The Fed lowered interest rates today," practically speaking the Fed does have the power to change all of the economy's key interest rates.

$ Federal Trade Commission

What It Means

The Federal Trade Commission (or FTC) is an independent agency of the U.S. government. Its purpose is to guard against business practices that interfere with competition in the marketplace and to protect American consumers from various kinds of fraud and deception. A free-market economy, such as the American economy, is founded on the idea that if companies are forced to compete with one another for consumer dollars, they will have to offer goods and services of the highest possible quality for the lowest possible prices, both of which are good for the consumer. Competition between companies also benefits the consumer by making a wide variety of choices available in the market.

Anticompetitive business practices are those in which a company or companies gain an unfair advantage in the market, making it difficult or impossible for other companies to compete with them. As a result, the dominant company may be able to profit without providing the best product or the best prices, because the consumer can no longer choose a better option. Some examples of business practices that can be anticompetitive include: price fixing, in which two or more companies conspire to set prices as they please, so that market forces no longer work; tie-in sales, in which two products are sold in a bundle, so that the consumer cannot buy one without the other; exclusive dealership agreements, in which a retailer or wholesaler is required to buy from a certain supplier or manufacturer; interlocking corporate directorships, in which one individual serves as director of two or more companies that are supposed to compete with each other; and mergers or acquisitions, in which two or more companies join together (or consolidate), becoming substantially more powerful than any of their competitors. When one company gains exclusive control over the market for a particular product or service (meaning that it has eliminated its competitors), it is called a monopoly.

Consumer fraud or deception can be any form of cheating in which a company falsely represents itself or its product, enticing consumers to pay for something they do not receive. In cases of false advertising, for example, a consumer may pay for an expensive product that promises a "miracle cure" for baldness—only to find that his hair continues to fall out. Other common forms of fraud include telemarketing (making sales over the telephone) scams, such as when a consumer agrees to divulge personal financial information (like a credit card number) over the phone in exchange for a fantastic prize that does not actually exist. In addition to cheating consumers out of their money, such frauds may also make consumers less confident about buying things, even from lawful businesses, in

The Federal Trade Commission, or FTC, is a government agency responsible for safeguarding fair competition in the U.S. economy. In the late 1960s activist Ralph Nader, pictured far left, organized a group of law students to investigate corruption at the FTC, leading to drastic reform of the agency in the 1970s. © *Bettmann/Corbis.*

the future. If consumers lose faith in the market and stop spending their money, the whole economy suffers.

The FTC's job is to enforce laws prohibiting consumer fraud and business practices that severely limit competition, to investigate cases where these laws may have been violated, and, when appropriate, to bring these cases to federal court. The FTC also seeks to prevent fraud and anticompetitive practices by educating consumers and businesses about what these issues mean and how to identify and avoid them.

When Did It Begin

In the 1880s and 1890s the American marketplace saw a wave of corporate mergers in which it was common for five or more companies to consolidate to form a business "trust." Known today as a cartel, this kind of trust is a business that seeks to create a monopoly in the market. The widespread rise of these trusts in such industries as railroads, oil, coal, steel, sugar, tobacco, and meatpacking touched off a period of intense national debate over the

issue of fair competition in business. On one hand consolidated businesses could run more efficiently and thus compete more effectively in the international marketplace. On the other hand these giant companies ruled the domestic market; smaller companies could no longer compete, and consumers were at the mercy of the big companies' prices. Free and fair competition, and the right of average citizens to build their own small businesses, were seen as core American values that needed to be protected.

Passed in 1890, the Sherman Antitrust Act formed the foundation of antitrust legislation, enabling Presidents Theodore Roosevelt (1858–1919) and William Howard Taft (1857–1930), successively, to sue and enforce the breakup of dozens of trusts. Perhaps the most notorious of these trusts was Standard Oil Company, owned by John D. Rockefeller (1839–1937). In 1911 the Supreme Court ruled that Standard Oil must be broken up into 36 smaller companies that would compete with one another.

But the Sherman Act failed to define anticompetitive practices in specific terms, and without an independent agency to investigate possible antitrust cases, the law was difficult to enforce. Upon winning the election of 1912, Woodrow Wilson (1856–1924) made antitrust reform central to his New Freedom Program. In 1914 Congress passed both the Federal Trade Commission Act, which established the FTC, and the Clayton Antitrust Act, which outlawed specific business practices that substantially lessened competition, such as those described above.

The FTC Act has been amended numerous times since its passage. Two key amendments were the Wheeler-Lea Amendment of 1938, which prohibited false advertising of foods, drugs, cosmetics, and therapeutic devices; and the Magnuson-Moss Warranty Act of 1975, which protects consumers against misleading warranty practices (a warranty is a guarantee offered by the seller or manufacturer of a product, promising repair if the product breaks within a certain time after purchase).

More Detailed Information

The Federal Trade Commission is run by a bipartisan (including both Republicans and Democrats) body of five commissioners, each of whom is nominated by the president and confirmed by the Senate for a seven-year term. One of these commissioners is chosen by the president to act as chairman. The bulk of the FTC's work is carried out by three bureaus: the Bureau of Consumer Protection, the Bureau of Competition, and the Bureau of Economics.

The Bureau of Consumer Protection (BCP) is dedicated to protecting consumers against unfair or deceptive business practices, including false advertising, telemarketing fraud, insurance scams, and privacy violations. Consumers may file complaints directly with the BCP if they feel they have been victimized by these or other unfair practices. In 2004 an FTC survey found that the most frequently reported types of consumer fraud were advance-fee loan scams, in which consumers paid upfront fees for "guaranteed" loans or credit cards that they never received; instances in which consumers were billed for buyers' club memberships or publication subscriptions they did not order; and scams involving fake offers of credit card insurance (a safety net in case you are unable to make your credit card payments because of job loss or other life events). The BCP investigates such complaints and may bring actions to federal court. In some consumer protection matters the FTC may work in conjunction with the U.S. Department of Justice. In addition to general enforcement of laws and regulations, the BCP also promotes consumer and business education.

The Bureau of Competition (BOC) is the antitrust division of the FTC. Its mission is to protect healthy competition in the marketplace so that consumers have access to a broad array of products and services at the

NADER'S RAIDERS

Consumer advocate Ralph Nader (b. 1934) initiated a radical shakeup of the Federal Trade Commission (FTC; a federal agency responsible for protecting the interests of American consumers) in 1968 when he assembled a volunteer task force of seven law students to investigate the commission. Young, idealistic, and resourceful, "Nader's Raiders," as they came to be known, gained access to inside information about the agency and documented its failings at length. In January 1969 they issued a scathing report of the FTC, calling it "fat with cronyism" and a complacent bureaucracy that did little to shield consumers from commercial fraud and deception. Widely publicized, the report led to important reforms that revitalized the FTC. As a result, the 1970s marked the beginning of a new era of concern for consumer rights and protection.

lowest possible prices. To accomplish this the BOC investigates possible violations of antitrust law and, when necessary, takes rule breakers to federal court. The BOC shares responsibility for enforcing antitrust laws with the Antitrust Division of the Department of Justice (DOJ). One of the most best-known antitrust cases of the late twentieth century involved allegations against software giant Microsoft of anticompetitive practices. The central question of the case, which began as an FTC investigation in 1991 and was eventually taken to trial by the DOJ in 1998, was whether Microsoft's monopoly in the PC operating system market was the result of illegally blocking competition or of simply earning market dominance through superior innovation and competition. Although the DOJ and Microsoft reached a proposed settlement in 2001, controversy continued over Microsoft's practices. In addition to its enforcement capacity, the bureau also conducts research and develops policy on competition issues.

The Bureau of Economics is in charge of evaluating how the FTC's actions and other government regulations affect the economy. It also studies various market processes (such as changes in prices or employment levels) as they relate to competition and consumer protection. This bureau's analyses may influence the FTC's decisions in consumer protection and antitrust cases; it may also affect proposed legislation by Congress. For example, when gas prices soared in 2006, Congress asked the Bureau of Economics to comment on proposed legislation against price gouging (the practice of setting unfairly high prices during a supply shortage). After conducting extensive investigations, the Bureau recommended against the legislation. As with the FTC's other main bureaus the Bureau of Economics' ultimate goal is to ensure healthy competition and ample consumer choice in the American marketplace.

Recent Trends

One of the most successful FTC measures in recent decades is the Do-Not-Call Registry, a free national service designed to help consumers limit the number of unwanted phone calls they receive from telemarketers. The registry is the result of the Do-Not-Call Implementation Act of 2003 (based on the 1994 Telemarketing and Consumer Fraud and Abuse Prevention Act), which is jointly enforced by the FTC and the FCC (the Federal Communications Commission, which regulates interstate and international communications by radio, television, wire, satellite, and cable). Once a consumer has submitted his or her phone number to the Do-Not-Call Registry, most telemarketers are required to delete that number from their call lists.

With the rapid rise of internet commerce in the late twentieth and early twenty-first centuries, the FTC faces a vast new realm of consumer protection issues. Not only have scam artists found countless ways to swindle consumers over the Internet, but also consumers have become increasingly vulnerable to privacy violations and identity theft. The FTC has begun to investigate many of these issues and is making a major effort to educate consumers about the dangers of the Internet by publishing information about invasive spyware programs, spam, identity theft, kids' privacy, online auctions and shopping, electronic banking, and other topics. The FTC is also involved in various efforts to protect and promote fair competition in e-commerce (business conducted over the Internet). As Internet applications continue to multiply and change, the challenge of regulating the virtual world remains significant.

$ Internal Revenue Service

What It Means

The Internal Revenue Service (IRS) is the largest bureau within the U.S. Department of the Treasury. Headquartered in Washington, D.C., the agency is responsible for assessing and collecting most types of taxes owed by individual citizens and businesses. The term *internal revenue* refers to government income from domestic sources (that is, internal to the nation), as opposed to income from foreign (external) sources, such as fees imposed on foreign merchants who sell their goods in the United States. The government uses the tax money it

The Internal Revenue Service, or IRS, oversees the collection of federal taxes in the United States. Each year it processes millions of tax returns from individuals and businesses. *AP Images.*

collects to fund the nation's military defense, space exploration, maintenance of national highways and other public facilities, law enforcement, and public services, such as libraries and education.

Each year individual taxpayers must file their annual returns, or a request for an extension, by April 15, while corporations must file their returns (or extension requests) by March 15. In 2003 it was estimated that the IRS received more than 130 million personal income tax returns and almost 6 million corporate income tax returns, amounting to trillions of dollars in tax revenue.

In addition to collecting taxes, the agency is also responsible for enforcing tax laws, distributing the forms and guidelines citizens need to file their tax returns, and providing information and support to make it easier for people to understand and obey tax regulations.

When Did It Begin

The origins of the IRS go back to the American Civil War (1861–65). Needing to generate funding to cover war expenses, President Lincoln and Congress initiated a federal income tax by passing the Revenue Act of 1862. The act also established a federal agency, the Bureau of Internal Revenue, and the head office of the Commissioner of Internal Revenue to oversee tax collection. Ten years later the income tax was repealed. Although Congress attempted to reinstate an income tax in 1894, the Supreme Court ruled it unconstitutional a year later.

Income taxes did not become a permanent fixture of American life until 1913, when the Sixteenth Amendment to the Constitution was ratified, authorizing Congress to enact an income tax. In 1953 the bureau was renamed the Internal Revenue Service in an effort to emphasize its obligation to "serve" the American public.

More Detailed Information

The most common kind of tax that the IRS collects is personal income tax, which is figured as a percentage of the money an individual earns from employment and investments. This percentage is calculated according to a progressive tax scale, meaning that the more you earn, the higher a percentage you pay. For example, if an individual earns $20,000 per year, he or she pays a smaller percentage of that income in taxes than a person who earns $200,000 per year. Taxes are also applied to corporate income, the money earned by a business. While personal income tax is calculated according to the total money earned, however, corporate tax is based on a business's net income, or the difference between the total amount of money it took in and the amount of money it spent to run the business. Individuals and corporations are required by law to report all of their income to the IRS.

WILLIE NELSON AND THE IRS

Many Americans resent paying taxes to the Internal Revenue Service (IRS), the government agency responsible for collecting most taxes. Every year thousands of Americans engage in some form of tax evasion (hiding or failing to disclose money a person has earned, won, inherited, or otherwise received, in order to avoid paying taxes on it). One of the most infamous cases of tax evasion involved the country-music singer Willie Nelson (b. 1933). In 1990 the IRS ordered Nelson to pay $16.7 million in unpaid taxes. When the musician was unable to pay the debt, the agency seized and sold his ranch and other assets. With millions of dollars of tax debt still outstanding, Nelson recorded an album titled *The IRS Tapes: Who'll Buy My Memories?* (1991) and sent his profits from the album directly to the agency. Ultimately the IRS agreed to settle the debt when it had collected $12.6 million from Nelson.

The Internal Revenue Service collects several other kinds of taxes. For instance, employers and employees pay Social Security tax to fund Social Security programs, which provide financial benefits to groups such as retirees and the disabled. Estate taxes are collected when people inherit property that exceeds a certain value. An excise tax is a special tax on certain goods and activities, such as gasoline and air travel; and gift tax is applied to the giver, not the recipient, of certain gifts. The Bureau of Alcohol, Tobacco, Firearms, and Explosives (not the IRS) is responsible for collecting taxes associated with the sale of the products mentioned in its name.

The IRS is authorized to enforce tax laws by various methods. The most common of these is a civil audit. If the agency considers an individual or corporate tax return to be questionable, it may conduct an audit, or examination, of the return to verify its accuracy. In order to make this assessment, it often requests to see the financial records on which the return was based. During an audit the burden of proof is on the taxpayer, not the IRS. This means that, if the taxpayer cannot back up his or her tax calculations with the appropriate documentation, the IRS may conclude that the return is inaccurate. If underpayment of taxes is judged to be accidental, the agency requires the taxpayer to pay the amount still owed. If, however, the IRS concludes that inaccuracies in the return were intentional (a federal offense), the taxpayer may be subject to jail time, significant fines, or both. In many cases, if a person is either unwilling or unable to pay a tax debt owed to the IRS, the agency may collect the debt by seizing the person's property and selling it at auction.

The IRS audits a small fraction of all taxpayers. In 1997, for instance, it audited about 1.66 million individuals (less than 2 percent of taxpayers). Nevertheless, the unhappy prospect of being audited at any time is regarded as an effective means of encouraging people to obey tax laws voluntarily. In addition to its use of these civil audits, the IRS also conducts criminal investigations into cases of suspected tax fraud, money laundering, narcotics-related financial crimes, and other violations of tax laws.

Recent Trends

The public image of the IRS was seriously tarnished in 1989, when Congress held hearings to investigate charges of corruption and misconduct on the part of top IRS officials. By 1997 the situation had only worsened, and the agency was featured on the cover of *Newsweek* magazine with a headline describing it as "a rogue organization wielding its awesome power under a cloak of secrecy." That year another round of congressional hearings was held, at which IRS employees and angry taxpayers testified to the agency's poor service, managerial incompetence, cruelty toward customers, and other problems.

Substantial changes in the IRS were implemented by businessman Charles O. Rossotti (b. 1941), who served as commissioner of the agency from 1997 to 2002. Rossotti placed an unprecedented emphasis on customer service, coining a fresh mission statement for the IRS: "Provide America's taxpayers top-quality service by helping them understand and meet their tax responsibilities and by applying the law with integrity and fairness for all." Rossotti's efforts received a boost from the Restructuring and Reform Act of 1998, which also contained the Taxpayer Bill of Rights 3 (a modification and expansion of a previous document). Indeed, by the turn of the millennium, many media sources had begun to refer to the transformed agency as a "kinder, gentler IRS."

$ Securities and Exchange Commission

What It Means

The Securities and Exchange Commission, commonly referred to as the SEC, is an official governmental body of the United States that monitors securities markets and protects investors by providing thorough, up-to-date, and accurate information about securities and the companies that issue securities. Securities are financial holdings such as stocks and bonds; people invest their money in securities in order to make money. In the case of stocks, the investor is purchasing a part of a company and can thus receive part of the profits the company makes; with bonds, people lend money to a government or company and get to collect a fee when the loan is paid back. Examples of securities markets include the New York Stock Exchange and NASDAQ, both of which are places

where stocks are bought and sold, or "traded," as investors often say.

Investing in securities is a financial risk. If a person buys $100 worth of stock, the value of that stock could drop substantially the following day. Therefore, investors need information about companies in order to deal in the stock market. All public companies (companies whose shares can be traded on the stock market) are required to make pertinent financial information available to investors by filing that information with the SEC. The SEC then posts the information so that investors can review it and make well-informed decisions about buying, selling, and holding their securities.

When Did It Begin

Prior to 1933 the sale of securities in the United States was governed by state laws, but the stock market crash of 1929 (when the value of investments suddenly and sharply declined) demonstrated that the states could not adequately govern the sale of securities. In order to restore investors' confidence, the federal government began monitoring and regulating the sale of securities. The Securities Act of 1933 was the first federal legislation regulating the sale of securities in the United States. This act required that investors have financial information available to them before purchasing securities. The act also

The Securities and Exchange Commission, or SEC, is a government body that provides information to the public about companies that sell securities, such as stocks. An SEC investigation of accounting fraud at the manufacturing firm Tyco International led to the 2005 conviction of the company's chief executive officer, Dennis Kozlowski, pictured here. *AP Images.*

stipulated that any deceit or misrepresentation accompanying the sale of a security was a federal offense. The Securities and Exchange Commission was established the following year, under the Securities Exchange Act of 1934; it was charged with enforcing the provisions of the Securities Act of 1933.

More Detailed Information

The SEC consists of five commissioners, each of whom is appointed by the president and approved by the Senate. Also with Senate approval, the president names one of the commissioners chairman of the SEC. A commissioner's term is five years, and the terms are staggered so that each year a commissioner steps down and a new one is appointed. Regulations stipulate that no more than three commissioners may belong to the same political party. In addition to its headquarters, which are located in Washington, D.C., the SEC has 11 regional and district offices and more than 3,000 employees.

The SEC is composed of four main divisions: Corporation Finance, Market Regulation, Investment Management, and Enforcement. Corporation Finance makes sure that public corporations disclose all relevant financial information to investors. This division also charts corporate activities such as mergers (the combination of two or more companies) and acquisitions (when one company overtakes or absorbs another company). The Market Regulation division oversees the New York Stock Exchange, NASDAQ, and other securities markets as well as the brokerage firms (companies acting as agents, facilitating trades between buyers and sellers on the stock market) that operate in these markets. The Investment Management division monitors mutual funds (investment companies that buy diverse groups of securities for clients).

Finally, the Enforcement division works with the other branches of the SEC to investigate violations of securities laws. The SEC administers seven laws: the Securities Act of 1933, the Securities Exchange Act of 1934, the Public Utility Holding Company Act of 1935, the Trust Indenture Act of 1939, the Investment Company Act of 1940, the Investment Advisers Act of 1940, and the Sarbanes-Oxley Act of 2002. To enforce these laws, the SEC requires that all public companies submit quarterly (once every three months) and annual (end-of-year) reports summarizing the financial state of the company. In addition to charts and numbers, these companies must also provide a narrative, or written, account of their financial dealings and an outline of their future plans. These reports are posted on EDGAR, the SEC's online database.

Recent Trends

In the first few years of the twenty-first century, there were several high-profile cases of insider trading (the illegal practice of using privileged information to make

EDGAR

EDGAR is an acronym that stands for Electronic Data Gathering, Analysis, and Retrieval. This is the Security and Exchange Commission's automated online system that collects, validates, indexes, and then posts important financial information about companies so that people can make sound investments. As of May 6, 1996, all public companies were required to register their forms online using the EDGAR system. Investors can review this information by visiting the website of the Security and Exchange Commission. The Canadian equivalent to EDGAR is called SEDAR.

investment decisions) and accounting fraud (a company distorting its financial records), which reduced investor confidence in the stock market. To restore fairness and investor confidence, the U.S. government sought to strengthen the power of the SEC. One of the measures taken to accomplish this goal was the Sarbanes-Oxley Act of 2002. This act established the Public Company Accounting Oversight Board (PCAOB) to ensure that firms hired to do the accounting for public companies kept accurate financial records. In 2004 the SEC announced that it would post all comment letters (queries sent by the commission seeking clarification about a company's financial records) on its website so that investors would know which companies were drawing the attention of the SEC.

$ Group of Eight

What It Means

The Group of Eight, or G8, is an organization that consists of eight of the world's largest industrialized democratic nations and that is dedicated to discussing major political and economic issues. It is an offshoot of the G6 (later known as the G7), an organization formed in 1975 to address issues relating to the global economy. When the G6 was founded, its member nations were the United States, Japan, the United Kingdom, France, Italy, and West Germany (now Germany); Canada joined a year later, at which point the group became the G7. Russia began participating in the meetings in 1994; in 1997 the organization shifted its focus from economic to political matters and became known as the Group of Eight. Because Russia is not as economically powerful as other G8 members, it does not participate in the group's economic meetings, which the original G7 members continue to hold on an annual basis.

Although the Group of Eight has emerged as one of the most influential political associations in the world, its structure remains relatively informal, and it is not officially

THE G8 PLUS OTHER NATIONS

The Group of Eight, or G8, is a group of eight major industrialized democracies that meets annually to discuss important political and economic issues. Its member nations are the United States, Russia, France, Germany, the United Kingdom, Italy, Japan, and Canada. In addition to holding the annual summit of these eight nations, the G8 frequently meets with other nations to address specific regional concerns. The most prominent of these annual meetings, the "G8 plus five," originated in 2005, bringing together the G8 and five of the world's most important developing nations to discuss economic policies. These five nations are the People's Republic of China, India, Brazil, South Africa, and Mexico.

recognized as an international organization (as groups such as the World Bank and the United Nations are). The bulk of the G8's agenda is addressed during an annual meeting of the heads of the member nations' governments. In preparation for this event (called a summit), representatives from each country hold a series of meetings to set the agenda and discuss other relevant issues.

In 2006 the G8 nations accounted for 70 percent of the world's total gross domestic product (GDP), which is the value of all goods and services produced over a set period of time.

When Did It Begin

The Group of Eight evolved from a smaller group that was founded in 1973. That year U.S. Treasury Secretary George P. Shultz (b. 1920) invited representatives from the governments of Germany, the United Kingdom, and France to participate in a meeting to discuss international economic policy. Because the meeting occurred in the White House Library, this group of nations became known as the Library Group.

In 1975, in order to continue discussions of these economic issues, French president Valéry Giscard d'Estaing (b. 1926) invited the leaders of the world's six most prosperous democratic nations to attend a summit. On this occasion the group agreed to begin meeting annually, with each representative assuming the role of president on a rotating basis. Participants at the first meeting were the United States, France, West Germany, Japan, Italy, and the United Kingdom. Canada joined the group the following year, and in 1977 the head of the European Economic Community also participated. By this time the group had become known as the Group of Seven, or G7.

In 1994 Russia began meeting with the G7 nations to discuss political concerns of vital interest to the world's

most powerful nations. These meetings came to be referred to as the P8, or Political Eight; the group was also known, informally, as the "G7 plus one." When Russia officially joined the group in 1997, the G7 became known as the Group of Eight, or G8. Although the G8 began focusing solely on political matters, representatives of the G7 nations continued to meet annually to address economic issues.

More Detailed Information

The G8 is predominantly concerned with political and economic issues that affect the international community as a whole. Major issues since the 1990s have included global law-enforcement initiatives, environmental quality, health issues, and other matters that affect international relations.

As the G8 entered the twenty-first century, it had to confront new issues and new threats. Chief among these was international terrorism. In order to combat the proliferation of terrorist organizations worldwide, the G8 began to seek new ways of promoting international cooperation. At its 2005 summit meeting the group devised a plan to create an international database of terrorist activities through which the member nations could pool information concerning specific terror plots, prominent terrorist leaders, and other vital data. In a somber coincidence, on July 7, the second day of that year's G8 meetings, terrorists bombed the London subway system, killing more than 50 people.

By the early twenty-first century other nations had begun to show interest in participating in the organization. Spain, which had one of the fastest-growing economies in the world during this period, began to lobby for inclusion in the group in 2006.

Recent Trends

When the original Group of Seven formed in 1976, Russia still belonged to the Soviet Union, a confederation of socialist states that extended from Eastern Europe to the Pacific coast of Asia. One of the world's two dominant superpowers (along with the United States), the Soviet Union had a tense relationship with the leading democratic countries from the 1950s to the early 1990s, a period usually referred to as the Cold War. After the breakup of the Soviet Union in 1991, however, the newly democratic Russian state began to participate informally in talks with G7 nations, eventually joining the group to form the G8. After the election of Vladimir Putin (b. 1952) to the office of Russian president in 1999, however, relations between Russia and the other nations once again cooled, as political leaders began to fear that the conservative Putin would scale back some of Russia's democratic reforms. By 2005 politicians in the United States, notably Senator Joseph Lieberman (b. 1942) of Connecticut and Senator John McCain (b. 1936) of Arizona, began to insist that Russia be suspended from

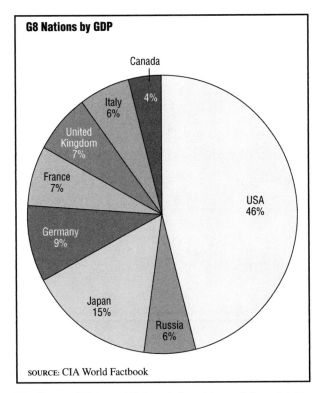

G8 Nations by GDP

Canada 4%

Italy 6%

United Kingdom 7%

France 7%

Germany 9%

Japan 15%

Russia 6%

USA 46%

SOURCE: CIA World Factbook

The Group of Eight, or G8, is an influential association of eight industrialized countries, whose leaders meet annually to discuss economic and political issues. According to this pie chart, the United States earns nearly half of the combined GDP, or gross domestic product, of the G8 countries. *Illustration by GGS Information Services. Cengage Learning, Gale.*

the G8 for what they perceived as Putin's repressive political policies.

$ International Monetary Fund

What It Means

The International Monetary Fund (IMF) is an organization of nations that helps shape economic policies related to international trade, debt, and the exchange of money among participating countries. With a membership of over 180 nations, the IMF has three principal goals: to evaluate world economic trends, to provide financial assistance to poor countries, and to promote commerce between all nations.

Economic activity does not stop at national borders. Consumers in most nations buy goods and services imported from abroad, and businesses often sell their goods and services beyond the borders of their home countries. A wide variety of other transactions, including purchases made by foreign tourists, loans from an institution in one country to people in other countries, and the business activity of corporations that operate in many countries, occur across borders as well. Transactions with

foreign countries have a great impact on individual national economies, so all countries keep track of them.

The record of the financial transactions between people in one country and people in foreign countries is called that country's balance of payments. For a country's currency (the form of money used within national borders, such as dollars in the United States) to remain stable, its balance of payments must be in good order. A country's currency might become devalued (worth less) compared to other currencies if the money leaving its borders outweighs the money coming in. If this situation (called a balance-of-payments deficit) goes too far, that country might experience severe economic problems.

The International Monetary Fund was established in 1944 to help stabilize currencies. Member countries contribute their own currency to the IMF and are therefore entitled to borrow from the fund when they experience difficulties with their balance of payments. These loans help nations stabilize their currencies and, hopefully, their economies. The IMF also provides assistance to countries that need help with their exchange policy (their rules about determining the value of their currency compared to that of other currencies).

When Did It Begin

Anticipating the end of World War II (1939–45), representatives of 44 countries met at Bretton Woods, New Hampshire, in July 1944 to discuss economic recovery and other important postwar financial affairs. The results of this meeting, called the United Nations Monetary and Financial Conference, included the establishment of the organization that became known as the World Bank, as well as the creation of the IMF. These organizations were (and still are) meant to tackle two related aspects of global economic affairs. The World Bank makes loans and provides other assistance to countries in need, with the intent of helping them expand and stabilize their economies. The IMF pursues the same basic goals by helping countries keep their currencies stable.

Initially the IMF promoted stable currencies by regulating exchange rates, or the amount of any currency that can be exchanged for any other currency. The standard that the IMF used for establishing exchange rates was the U.S. dollar. All countries were allowed to declare how many dollars their own currencies were worth, and the exchange rates that any country imposed could only vary within strict limits thereafter. The U.S. dollar itself was expressed in terms of its value in gold and was backed up by the country's gold reserves (gold had for centuries been used as one of the most universal and reliable standards for monetary value, and the United States was the only member country with enough gold to support the arrangement). This method of currency exchange required that the United States be willing to sell gold at a specific, fixed dollar value that set the standard

The International Monetary Fund, or IMF, is an organization of nations dedicated to promoting international trade throughout the world. In 2004 former Spanish Economy Minister Rodrigo Rato, pictured here, was appointed director of the IMF. *AFP/Getty Images.*

for the dollar and, by extension, all of the other currencies. In 1971, with its gold reserves shrinking, it decided to stop providing its gold for sale in this way, and countries began establishing their own exchange rates.

More Detailed Information

The IMF is a specialized agency of the United Nations (an organization that promotes peaceful international relations), but in practice it operates independently of its parent organization. More than 180 countries are members of the IMF, and each is represented by a governor. The governors do not have equal voting rights in matters of IMF policy, however. Voting is weighted according to how much money the member government contributes to the IMF. The day-to-day decisions of the IMF are made by an executive board that is dominated by eight of the world's wealthiest countries: the United States, the United Kingdom, Japan, China, France, Germany, Russia, and Saudi Arabia.

All members of the IMF contribute a quota, or an amount of money calculated according to the country's wealth. The richer a country is, the larger its required quota. The United States, for example, has contributed roughly 18 percent of the IMF's pool of quotas. Once a country has contributed its quota, it is entitled to borrow up to that same amount if it needs to correct deficits in its balance of payments (which occur when there is more money leaving the country than coming in). The size of a

country's quota also determines the amount of voting power it has on the board of governors. The United States, the United Kingdom, Japan, Canada, Germany, France, and Italy together control approximately half of the votes on the board of governors.

When a country experiences a deficit in its balance of payments and its currency becomes devalued, it would be likely, without the IMF's intervention, to engage in defensive behavior that might be harmful to other economies. A country in such a crisis, for instance, might try to reduce its balance-of-payments deficit by restricting the imports of goods from other countries (in an effort to keep its own money inside the country) or by setting the exchange rates for its own currency at levels that could do economic harm to other countries.

The IMF wants to prevent countries from behaving in this way, so it allows members to borrow money from the pool of quotas to restore their balances of payment. Member countries can usually borrow up to 25 percent of their quota amount without being subject to many restrictions. As a country borrows more than this amount, however, it becomes increasingly subject to IMF regulation. This usually means that the IMF will force the country, as a condition of the loan, to save money by taking often-difficult economic steps, such as increasing taxes or cutting funds for domestic programs (health care and education, for instance). The IMF requires countries to take such steps with the goal of helping them correct their balance-of-payments deficits and pave the way for long-term economic health.

The IMF also provides technical assistance to countries experiencing currency and balance-of-payments problems. Most of this assistance is free of charge.

Recent Trends

In the 1970s, having lost its authority to set exchange rates, the IMF began focusing greater attention on the economic needs of the world's developing countries. A developing country is a nation with basic modes of economic production and a relatively low per capita (in other words, per person) income. Some economists have argued that IMF policies during the 1980s and 1990s helped build strong global economies in a number of Asian nations. Over this period countries such as China, Thailand, South Korea, Indonesia, and numerous others witnessed annual growth rates of approximately 10 percent in their gross domestic products, or GDPs (the value of all goods and services produced in a particular nation over a given time).

Along with the World Bank and the World Trade Organization, whose aim is to reduce global trade barriers (such as fees or limits on the goods and services that can move across borders), the IMF is today one of the leading forces in the trend called globalization. Globalization refers broadly to the increasing mobility of money, labor, equipment, and other economic resources across national borders. The rise of globalization has created greater demand for economic policies oriented toward promoting international trade. The IMF has played an important role in promoting globalization through the introduction of debt relief (in other words, assistance with the repayment of debts) for developing countries. In 1996 the IMF established the Heavily Indebted Poor Countries Initiative (HIPC), a program aimed at offering debt relief to developing countries. By alleviating the financial burdens associated with high levels of debt, the HIPC is designed to help poorer countries build the foundations of solid, stable economies. At the same time, the IMF has provided consulting and educational programs geared toward teaching poor countries to manage their economies more effectively.

The IMF also played a central role in helping Asian economies recover from the financial crisis of 1997, when currency and stock values in dozens of Asian countries fell suddenly and dramatically. To counter the resulting economic instability, the IMF provided large-scale debt relief, while also helping nations devise sounder financial policies to prevent future disasters. While some economists applauded IMF efforts in the wake of the crisis, many opponents of the IMF argued that the economic downturn was the result of IMF policies in the first place; according to these critics, the economic growth in Asia during the 1980s and 1990s was too rapid to be sustained, largely because of IMF failures to create the

SUPPORT FOR THE IMF

The International Monetary Fund (IMF), which lends money to countries that are experiencing difficulties related to their currency (their national form of money, such as the dollar or the peso), inspires a great deal of controversy. The IMF's critics, however, tend to be residents of creditor countries (those nations that primarily lend money to, rather than borrow money from, the IMF). Among the residents of some borrowing countries, the IMF gets relatively high marks.

Countries in Asia and Africa, for instance, generally depend more on the IMF than countries in Europe and the Americas. In a survey conducted in 2002 by the Pew Research Center, 60 percent of Asians expressed approval of the IMF, as did 70 percent of Africans. Critics point out, however, that this approval might be related to the fact that textbooks and the media in those regions often paint a flattering picture of the IMF's activities.

infrastructures necessary to support these growing economies.

Another criticism of the IMF has to do with the regulations it sometimes imposes on countries that borrow money. While economic conditions are unique in every country, the IMF tends to impose the same kinds of restrictions on all struggling nations. According to critics, this blanket approach is especially hard on the poorest member countries, whose level of suffering increases as a result of IMF regulations, without any corresponding increase in economic growth.

$ Trade Bloc

What It Means

A trade bloc is a group of nations that has reached a set of special agreements regarding their economic relationships with each other. The agreements generally focus on the relaxation or elimination of trade barriers, which are laws that limit the amount of business done across two countries' borders. The most common types of trade barriers are tariffs (taxes on imports) and quotas (limits on the quantities of various imports).

Trade blocs can take different forms. The most enduring and successful trade bloc, as of the early twenty-first century, was the one binding 27 European countries under the European Union (EU). The EU, whose roots lay in attempts to reunify Europe after World War II, was more than just a trade agreement. It brought about wide-ranging economic, political, and social organization among its member countries, including the establishment of a common currency and many other unifying features usually imposed only by national governments. The United States, Canada, and Mexico established another

A trade bloc is a group of countries, usually within the same region of the globe, that make an agreement to trade goods and services freely among one another. Pictured here are representatives of the South American trade bloc Mercosur, which includes full members Brazil, Argentina, Paraguay, and Uruguay and associate members Bolivia, Chile, Colombia, Ecuador, and Peru. *Al Burafi/AFP/Getty Images.*

of the world's most significant trading blocs with the North American Free Trade Agreement (NAFTA) in 1992. Though NAFTA, by reducing most trade barriers between these three countries, had important and controversial economic consequences, it was not intended to erase national economic boundaries to the degree that the EU did, nor did it actively promote the elimination of social and political boundaries.

The creation of trade blocs generally results in benefits to consumers, as high-quality goods and services can be produced at lower prices than they could with trade barriers in place. Effective trade blocs also tend to create stable political relations between countries and to increase total employment and income levels in all participating countries, at least over the long term.

These benefits come at a cost, however. Inevitably some industries and companies eliminate large numbers of jobs in one member country in order to take advantage of cheaper labor in another member country. This can cause great pain to workers and communities. Likewise, trade blocs, by increasing the freedom of companies

motivated only by profit, often threaten poorer member countries' traditional ways of life and the environment.

When Did It Begin

One of the earliest examples of what we now call a trade bloc was the Zollverein (German for "customs union") enacted by most parts of the German Confederation, a group of nineteenth-century kingdoms consisting of the present-day countries of Germany, Austria, the Czech Republic, Luxembourg, and parts of other surrounding nations. The Zollverein eliminated trade barriers between member territories while raising tariffs that applied to countries outside the union, as many trade blocs do today.

Today's most significant trade bloc, the EU, began life as an attempt to resolve the differences between European nations after World War II. In 1951 France, West Germany, Belgium, the Netherlands, Italy, and Luxembourg entered into a trade agreement establishing the European Coal and Steel Community (ECSC). This union eliminated trade barriers that applied to these essential economic materials, and it served as the basis for future expansions of the trade bloc, which was, for much of the late twentieth century, known as the European Community (EC). The more comprehensive unification plan embodied by the EU was officially enacted in 1993.

NAFTA was modeled on the EC, which had played a key role in helping European countries recover from World War II and rebuild their economies. The United States and Canada entered into a trade agreement in 1988, and NAFTA brought Mexico into the trade bloc in 1992. The reduction of trade barriers under NAFTA went into effect in 1994.

More Detailed Information

A belief in the beneficial effects of free trade is the foundation for trade blocs such as the EU and NAFTA. The early economists Adam Smith (1723–90) and David Ricardo (1772–1823) were the first thinkers to outline the case for free trade convincingly, and the arguments in favor of free trade have changed little since that time. Essentially, free trade proponents argue that tariffs, quotas, and other trade barriers decrease economic efficiency and overall wealth in all affected countries.

When, for example, banana growers in Ecuador can supply better bananas at a lower price than banana growers in the United States, the United States should allow Ecuadorian bananas to be sold without restraint. Instead of growing bananas, U.S. farmers will concentrate on those crops more suited to the soil and climate of their region. Ecuador has what economists call an "absolute advantage" over the United States when it comes to banana production.

But even when U.S. businesses can produce a particular good as well and as cheaply as businesses in another country, it may be in the nation's interest to allow foreign companies to assume both the benefits and the burden of supplying that good to U.S. consumers. Perhaps, for instance, U.S. companies and Japanese companies are both capable of delivering high-quality, low-cost steak knives to U.S. consumers. At the same time, however, U.S. companies might be much more capable than Japanese companies of delivering high-quality, low-cost butter knives to U.S. consumers. In this case, U.S. companies would be better off allowing Japanese steak-knife companies to dominate the consumer market, because the United States could ultimately create more wealth by focusing on butter-knife production. In this situation, economists would say that the United States has a "comparative advantage" in butter-knife production.

Despite the widespread acceptance among economists of the doctrines of absolute advantage and comparative advantage, most nations have only selectively pursued policies of free international trade. If a U.S. policy of free international trade led to the collapse of the American steak-knife industry, for example, the spectacle

FREE EUROPE

Trade blocs usually involve the elimination, among member countries, of barriers to trade such as taxes and limitations on goods and services that move across national borders. This is the case, for instance, with the North American Free Trade Agreement (NAFTA), which binds the United States, Mexico, and Canada together economically. But in the case of the world's largest and most successful trade bloc, the European Union (EU), the elimination of national borders goes much further. Not only are there no restrictions on the movement of goods and services across EU borders, there are almost no restrictions on the movement of people. Whereas a U.S. citizen's residency in Canada or Mexico is subject to government regulation, citizens of any EU country can, with a few exceptions, live, work, travel, and invest anywhere within the EU without a passport or any legal restrictions.

of thousands of out-of-work steak-knife manufacturers would be hard to justify using economic theories. Towns and regions can become economically depressed for decades when a key industry ceases to operate there. Another reason that free trade has only gradually become acceptable to national governments is that large, powerful industries often have a great deal of influence on politicians. Many trade barriers are kept in place for this reason.

Regional trade blocs represent a compromise between totally free trade and total protectionism of a country's industries. In the case of the EU, moreover, economic cooperation has allowed for the accumulation of world power. EU countries trade freely with one another, allowing each country to concentrate on what it does best, but the EU as a whole generally taxes imports from non-EU countries at high levels to protect European industries. The result is the creation of a single, powerful economy. Though individual European countries cannot begin to compete economically with the much larger United States, the EU as a whole rivals and by some measures outperforms the U.S. economy.

Recent Trends

Since NAFTA took effect in 1994, the industrial landscape of the United States has changed significantly. Many companies in the automotive and clothing industries, for example, have moved their manufacturing facilities to Mexico, where workers can be paid much less than in the United States. This has resulted in a large-scale loss of American jobs at the same time that it has allowed those companies to increase their profits. While other parts of the U.S. economy have boomed since the mid-1990s, towns that have lost large automobile or textile factories have largely failed to prosper. Economists can outline theories about why the United States as a whole is better off because of NAFTA, but it is difficult to prove that economic gains in other parts of the economy were caused by, or can make up for, the painful losses in the auto or clothing industries.

The economic unification of European countries was less controversial at the turn of the millennium than the union between the United States, Canada, and Mexico. With decades of successful cooperation behind them, many EU countries in 1999 adopted a common currency, the euro, and ceased using individual national currencies. EU membership is seen as very desirable economically, and the number of member states has grown dramatically. In 2004 alone, the EU accepted ten new member countries. By 2007, the number of member countries stood at 27.

Political unity has proven more complicated, however. In 2004 the heads of EU member governments drafted a constitution establishing a common framework of laws for all member countries, but in 2005 the citizens of both France and the Netherlands voted against adopting it, preventing the legal document from going into effect.

$ World Trade Organization

What It Means

The World Trade Organization (WTO) is an institution composed of more than 150 countries, the purpose of which is to monitor international trade and promote increasingly free (unregulated) trade between countries.

Historically, many countries have taken competitive stances toward one another in terms of exporting and importing goods and services. For instance, a country that wants to protect its steel industry from foreign competition might set limits (called quotas) on imports of foreign steel, or it might charge high fees (called tariffs) to the companies that bring steel into the country. The WTO seeks to end or minimize such practices in the interest of making possible the freer movement of goods and services across borders, which many economists believe is in the best interest, over time, of all countries. With this goal in mind, the WTO sets standards for international trade, monitors member nations' trading practices, and helps countries resolve their trade disputes with one another.

Together with the International Monetary Fund (IMF) and the World Bank, the World Trade Organization is a leading force in the movement called globalization. Globalization refers to the increasing ease with which companies conduct business across national borders. Globalization has many proponents, who often view the trend not only as economically beneficial but also as a stabilizing force responsible for higher standards of living worldwide. There are, however, many who object to the negative side of globalization. Some critics argue that it tends to disrupt local communities and damage the en-

vironment; another criticism is that it empowers multinational corporations at the expense of small businesses and the rights of individuals. Starting in the 1990s meetings of the WTO provided a focal point for protestors against globalization.

When Did It Begin

The WTO was officially established in 1995 as a successor to the General Agreement on Tariffs and Trade (GATT). GATT had been created in 1947 to promote free trade, which was seen as one of the best ways of spurring recovery from World War II (1939–45) and of ensuring international stability thereafter. Although GATT was initially intended to be merely a temporary treaty to be replaced by a trade group called the International Trade Organization, for complex reasons this replacement never happened, and GATT evolved into the global trade organization that would eventually become the WTO. Over the course of its 47-year history, GATT was highly effective at promoting increasingly liberalized (free from rules and regulations) trade between countries.

A revision of GATT in 1994 became the cornerstone of the WTO. The new organization added components to the established GATT provisions, including an increased emphasis on protecting intellectual property (creative work such as patented inventions and copyrighted publications), new rules for solving disputes between countries, and procedures for judging how well the member countries were living up to the standards set by the WTO. One other key difference between the WTO and GATT is that GATT exclusively governed goods (physical objects that are sold), whereas the WTO covers trade practices regarding services (tasks requiring human attention) as well.

More Detailed Information

The WTO sets rules for member countries and monitors their trading activities to make sure that they are abiding by these rules. The rules all have the goal of promoting free trade between nations. In the WTO's view, free trade not only provides for the economic welfare of all countries but also reduces global political tensions. In the interest of promoting these larger goals, WTO rules have several more specific functions.

First, WTO rules emphasize nondiscrimination. The barriers between nations cannot be dissolved if countries engage in double standards by charging some countries higher tariffs than others or otherwise distinguishing between trading partners. For truly free trade, all countries must treat each other equally, accepting goods from one country as readily as another. This ideal also extends to a country's domestic companies (domestic means that it operates within that country). Free trade is hampered when a WTO member nation shows favoritism to its domestic business firms at the expense of foreign competitors. The WTO helps national governments resist the

The World Trade Organization, or WTO, is a global institution dedicated to promoting free trade between nations. Although its goal is to promote fairness in international commerce, some people, including these protesters in Hong Kong, contend that the organization serves multinational corporations at the expense of average citizens. *AP Images.*

temptation to give in to special-interest groups, such as the lobbyists (representatives who try to influence politicians) of a particular industry that wants greater protection from foreign competitors.

Additionally, WTO rules are intended to promote transparency (complete openness) in trade activities. If a government has secret trade priorities, then it necessarily cannot be trading freely. This requirement has the added benefit of encouraging better government. In less developed countries and countries whose economies were in the past centrally planned by the government (as opposed to being run by private individuals, which is the case with capitalist economies such as the United States'), the WTO's rules provide an effective tool for protecting against secretive government maneuvers.

Another goal of the WTO rules is to promote predictability in international trade. Economies flourish when conditions are predictable, and they experience problems in times of unpredictability. Stable economies allow for stable countries.

WTO rules furthermore require that trade disputes be settled by the organization so that countries do not resort to retaliation or other forms of conflict. This promotes international stability.

In reality, few countries perfectly abide by WTO rules. While the organization is able to pressure countries to change their behavior when they violate WTO principles, exceptions to the rules exist. One of the most noticeable of these is that countries are still allowed, in some cases, to favor certain trading partners over others. Even in light of such exceptions, the WTO sees itself as helping to prevent the more extreme problems that might arise from economic competition and unpredictability.

Recent Trends

The WTO is one of the three organizations responsible for regulating the economic interaction of national governments with one another. The other two organizations are the International Monetary Fund, which oversees issues having to do with currency and debt, and the World Bank, which makes loans and provides other forms of assistance to developing countries. These three associations together are responsible for promoting

THE YES MEN

Today many people associate the World Trade Organization (WTO) more with the protests it has sparked than with any concrete actions it has taken. Among the various activist groups opposed to the WTO, the Yes Men stand out for their boldness.

In 1999 the Yes Men, a group of political activists who go by aliases, set up a fake website parodying the WTO's website. When visitors, believing the Yes Men's site to be the true WTO site, sent e-mails to invite representatives of the WTO to speak at various high-profile events, the Yes Men eagerly accepted the invitations.

At a conference in Salzburg, Austria, the Yes Men, disguised as WTO officials, mocked what they saw as the organization's harmful effect on democracy by suggesting that countries sell votes to the highest bidder. On the TV channel CNBC Europe, the Yes Men pretended to be WTO officials and proposed that companies should be able to pay for the right to make people suffer, a satirical way of pointing out the human-rights abuses that they believed the WTO allowed to occur. Further, at a conference of accountants in Australia, the Yes Men declared that, because of its numerous mistakes, the WTO was going to shut itself down and reopen as an organization dedicated to helping the poor rather than helping corporations. The intent of this prank was to suggest that the WTO was in truth dedicated to doing the exact opposite: helping corporations at the expense of the poor.

globalization, a phenomenon that became increasingly visible in most of the world starting in the 1990s.

Globalization makes it easier for goods, services, labor, money, equipment, and ideas to move easily from nation to nation. Businesses benefit greatly when, for example, they can reduce their costs by moving a factory from the United States or Europe, where workers must be paid high wages, to a country where workers make only a fraction of U.S. and European wages. Economists typically argue that the free movement of resources and money increases worldwide economic efficiency, which they see as a desirable outcome. Likewise, globalization has helped strengthen the economies of many poor countries and raise the standard of living for many people.

Many people, however, believe that globalization's chief beneficiaries are multinational corporations, large companies that do business freely around the world thanks in part to the trade liberalization encouraged by the WTO. These corporations have increased their influence in much of the world, making it harder for small businesses to compete and for unskilled workers to protect their interests. Critics of globalization also often contend that free trade takes a great toll on the environment because it allows corporations to pursue their economic interests freely without regard for any other priorities.

One of the largest demonstrations staged by anti-globalization forces occurred in 1999, outside of a WTO meeting in Seattle, Washington. It was estimated that 50,000 protestors participated in the Seattle protests. Since then WTO meetings have been a common object of large antiglobalization protests.

$ World Bank

What It Means

The World Bank Group, commonly called the World Bank, is an international organization that helps poor and developing countries build their economies. It makes loans to these countries and provides financial assistance and supervision, with the overall goal of reducing poverty through the promotion of free-market capitalism (an economic system in which private individuals own most businesses and the economy operates with little government interference).

The World Bank is related to the United Nations (an organization of countries that promotes friendly international relations, peace, and security), but it is not directly accountable to it. As with the United Nations (UN), the World Bank consists of member countries, and each has some voting power in the organization. Most countries in the world belong to the World Bank, but it is dominated by the wealthiest countries.

There are two main components of the World Bank, the International Bank for Reconstruction and Development (IBRD) and the International Development Association (IDA). The first focuses on helping middle-income countries, primarily through loans, and the second focuses on helping the world's poorest countries through no-interest loans (interest is a fee charged for borrowing money) and other forms of assistance.

While the World Bank is the largest source of financial assistance for the developing world, it is also one of the main forces (along with the International Monetary Fund and the World Trade Organization) responsible for shaping global economic priorities. It is sometimes criticized for serving the interests of the United States and other powerful countries rather than the interests of the countries it is supposed to be helping.

When Did It Begin

The World Bank was established in 1944, during the United Nations Monetary and Financial Conference at Bretton Woods, New Hampshire. This conference, commonly called the Bretton Woods Conference, was a meeting of 44 representatives of different states or governments that took place as World War II (1939–45) was winding down. The purpose of the meeting was to discuss solutions to the financial problems that the world would face once the war had concluded. In addition to deciding on the establishment of what would become the World Bank, the Bretton Woods talks led to the

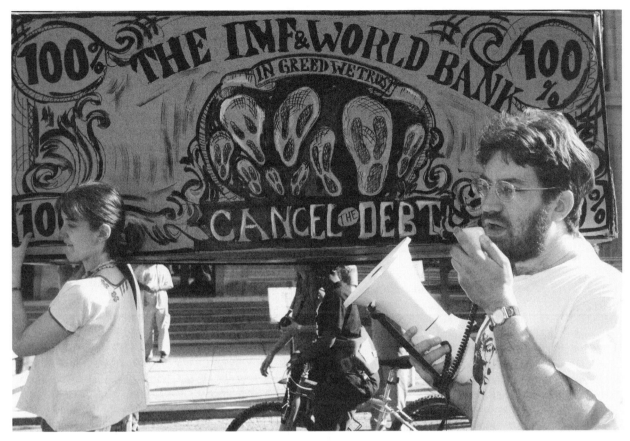

The World Bank is a global organization dedicated to promoting economic growth in developing, nonindustrialized nations. Critics argue that it prioritizes the needs of wealthy countries. *Alex Wong/Getty Images.*

formation of the International Monetary Fund, which oversees exchange rates (how much one country's currency is worth compared to that of other countries) and debts between different countries, among other financial matters. Together the World Bank and the International Monetary Fund are often called the Bretton Woods Institutions, or BWIs.

In its early years the World Bank was primarily focused on helping Western European countries rebuild after the devastation of the war. In the 1950s it began to focus more on the needs of developing countries. Initially it helped with constructing important public systems such as roads, dams, airports, and water and sewage systems. In subsequent decades the World Bank became more concerned with sustainable development (that is, promoting economic development that creates businesses, institutions, and infrastructure that allow for both long-term economic growth and a healthy natural environment) and with reducing the enormous income gap between rich and poor countries.

More Detailed Information

The World Bank generates money for its projects in three main ways: through contributions of capital (money and

other resources) from member countries, by collecting interest on the loans it makes, and by selling government-issued securities on various world financial markets. (When people buy such securities, they are loaning their money to the government, which guarantees to pay back the original amount plus interest.) It uses this money to make loans, give grants, and provide various types of consultation and assistance to developing countries. In its capacity as a lender to poor countries, it often has the power to make its loans conditional, requiring that the country make specific governmental changes that promote free-market capitalism.

The World Bank's two main components are the International Bank for Reconstruction and Development (IBRD) and the International Development Association (IDA). The IBRD offers loans to countries that qualify for credit (which means they have the means to pay back loans). These are nations of middle-income levels rather than the poorest of the world's countries. The IDA is responsible for helping the poorest countries, which would not otherwise qualify for loans. Countries served by the IDA often have access to no-interest loans and assistance in the areas of education, health care, and development of infrastructure (large-scale public projects

IN DEFENSE OF THE WORLD BANK

While the World Bank is often criticized for imposing a Western, U.S.-centered economic agenda on the rest of the world, its defenders point out that it is perhaps the world's most respected financial institution. Further, they argue, no country is forced to borrow money from the World Bank, and countries that receive financial assistance from the World Bank would in many cases be unable to procure money in any other way. World Bank loans are usually offered at below-normal interest rates (fees charged by money lenders), and some World Bank assistance takes the form of grants, which do not have to be repaid.

such as roads and dams) and communications capabilities.

The World Bank Group includes three other agencies: one that helps businesses in developing countries, another that provides guarantees for the investors who contribute money to the World Bank, and a third that helps settle disagreements between investors and the countries to which they lend money.

There are more than 180 member countries of the World Bank, and each country is represented equally in the organization's governing body, the board of governors. The governing body does not dictate the majority of the World Bank's policies, however. This is done by 24 executive directors, who are appointed according to global influence. The United States, the United Kingdom, Germany, France, and Japan are each represented by one executive director, while other countries are grouped together into regions, each of which is represented by an executive director. The president of the World Bank, furthermore, has always been a U.S. citizen (often a former official of the U.S. government), and the organization's headquarters are in Washington, D.C.

Additionally, while some votes are held in which all member countries have an equal say, many of the important votes about World Bank policy are conducted in proportion to each country's financial contribution to the organization. In this arena the United States outstrips all other member countries by a wide margin. At the beginning of the twenty-first century, the United States controlled more than double the votes of the second most influential country, Japan, and it held enough voting power to block most major decisions on its own. Because poor countries, which receive most of the aid, do not contribute much financially to the World Bank's operations, they have little influence over its policies.

World Bank staff members in many developing countries work closely with government advisers to shape policy (plans and procedures for achieving certain goals) and make other financial decisions. The World Bank also has ties with the various financial markets in the world, and it serves as a liaison between organizations in developed and developing countries.

Recent Trends

Some analysts claim that the World Bank is partially responsible for economic stagnation in much of the developing world. In the 1980s difficult world-economic conditions made many poor countries unable to repay the loans made to them by the World Bank. In an attempt to create economic growth and make these countries solvent (which means having enough money to pay back debts), the World Bank forced the countries' governments to enact spending limits and cuts, including cuts in the areas of education and health care. The World Bank also typically forced these countries to adopt free-market mechanisms such as the deregulation of the financial industry (that is, cutting down on government regulation of business), the transfer of government-controlled businesses into private hands, and the discontinuation of price controls (limits on the prices of certain goods). Often conditions worsened as a result of these measures.

Similarly, after the collapse of the Soviet Union in 1991, the World Bank played a major role in helping Central and Eastern Europe with the transition from communism (in which the government controls the economy) to capitalism (in which private individuals own most businesses). In many cases the World Bank forced state-run industries to close, but when this happened, unemployment rose dramatically. The World Bank's free-market reforms increased inflation and reduced the quality of life in several of these countries.

Further Reading

HOW THE ECONOMY WORKS

BOOKS

Bryce, Robert. *Pipe Dreams: Greed, Ego, and the Death of Enron.* Oxford: PublicAffairs, 2002.

Buchholz, Todd G. *New Ideas from Dead Economists: An Introduction to Modern Economic Thought.* 2nd rev. ed. New York: Plume, 2007.

Calavita, Kitty, Henry N. Pontell, and Robert Tillman. *Big Money Crime: Fraud and Politics in the Savings and Loan Crisis.* Berkeley: University of California Press, 1997.

Canterbery, E. Ray. *Alan Greenspan: The Oracle behind the Curtain.* Hackensack, N.J.: World Scientific, 2006.

Case, James H. *Competition: The Birth of a New Science.* New York: Hill & Wang, 2007.

Chancellor, Edward. *Devil Take the Hindmost: A History of Financial Speculation.* New York: Farrar, Straus, and Giroux, 1999.

Coyle, Diane. *The Soulful Science: What Economists Really Do and Why It Matters.* Princeton, N.J.: Princeton University Press, 2007.

D'Amato, Paul. *The Meaning of Marxism.* Chicago: Haymarket Books, 2006.

Ebenstein, Lanny. *Milton Friedman: A Biography.* New York: Palgrave Macmillan, 2007.

Fishman, Charles. *The Wal-Mart Effect: How the World's Most Powerful Company Really Works—and How It's Transforming the American Economy.* New York: Penguin Press, 2006.

Friedman, Benjamin M. *The Moral Consequences of Economic Growth.* New York: Knopf, 2005.

Friedman. Thomas L. *The World Is Flat: A Brief History of the Twenty-First Century.* New York: Farrar, Straus, and Giroux, 2005.

Green, James. *Death in the Haymarket: A Story of Chicago, the First Labor Movement, and the Bombing That Divided Gilded Age America.* New York: Pantheon Books, 2006.

Greenspan, Alan. *The Age of Turbulence: Adventures in a New World.* New York: Penguin Press, 2007.

Harford, Tim. *The Undercover Economist: Exposing Why the Rich Are Rich, the Poor Are Poor—and Why You Can Never Buy a Decent Used Car!* Oxford: Oxford University Press, 2006.

Horowitz, Daniel. *Anxieties of Affluence: Critiques of American Consumer Culture, 1939–1979.* Amherst: University of Massachusetts Press, 2004.

Kay, John Anderson. *Culture and Prosperity: The Truth about Markets—Why Some Nations Are Rich but Most Remain Poor.* New York: HarperBusiness, 2004.

Kynge, James. *China Shakes the World: A Titan's Rise and Troubled Future—and the Challenge for America.* Boston: Houghton Mifflin, 2006.

Levy, David M. *How the Dismal Science Got Its Name: Classical Economics and the Ur-Text of Racial Politics.* Ann Arbor: University of Michigan Press, 2001.

Lowenstein, Roger. *Origins of the Crash: The Great Bubble and Its Undoing.* New York: Penguin Books, 2004.

Maugeri, Leonardo. *The Age of Oil: The Mythology, History, and Future of the World's Most Controversial Resource.* Westport, Conn.: Praeger Publishers, 2006.

McMillan, John. *Reinventing the Bazaar: A Natural History of Markets.* New York: Norton, 2002.

Rivoli, Pietra. *The Travels of a T-Shirt in the Global Economy: An Economist Examines the Markets, Power, and Politics of World Trade.* Hoboken, N.J.: John Wiley & Sons, 2005.

Rose, Mike. *The Mind at Work: Valuing the Intelligence of the American Worker.* New York: Viking, 2004.

Sachs, Jeffrey D. *The End of Poverty: Economic Possibilities for Our Time.* New York: Penguin Books, 2006.

Samuelson, Paul A., and William A. Barnett, eds. *Inside the Economist's Mind: Conversations with Eminent Economists.* Oxford: Blackwell, 2007.

Scheidel, Walter, and Sitta Von Reden. *The Ancient Economy.* New York: Routledge, 2002.

Schlosser, Eric. *Reefer Madness: Sex, Drugs, and Cheap Labor in the American Black Market.* Boston: Houghton Mifflin, 2003.

Shlaes, Amity. *The Forgotten Man: A New History of the Great Depression.* New York: HarperCollins Publishers, 2007.

Skidelsky, Robert. *John Maynard Keynes, 1883–1946: Economist, Philosopher, Statesman.* New York: Penguin Books, 2003.

Skousen, Mark. *The Big Three in Economics: Adam Smith, Karl Marx, and John Maynard Keynes.* Armonk, N.Y.: M.E. Sharpe, 2007.

Stalcup, Brenda, ed. *Turning Points in World History— The Industrial Revolution.* San Diego: Greenhaven Press, 2002.

Watson, Bruce. *Bread and Roses: Mills, Migrants, and the Struggle for the American Dream.* New York: Viking, 2005.

Wheelan, Charles J. *Naked Economics: Undressing the Dismal Science.* New York: Norton, 2002.

PERIODICALS

Hardy, Quentin. "Hope and Profit in Africa." *Forbes* (June 18, 2007).

"India on Fire: India's Economy." *The Economist* (February 3, 2007).

"Outsourcing: Old Assumptions Are Being Challenged as the Outsourcing Industry Matures." *The Economist* (July 26, 2007).

Prestowitz, Clyde. "The World Is Tilted: The Popular Idea that America Is One Step Smarter and More Sophisticated than Its Rivals Is a Dangerous Myth, and a Threat to the Global Economy." *Newsweek* (November 28, 2005): p. 16.

"Secrets, Lies, and Sweatshops: American Importers Have Long Answered Criticism of Conditions at their Chinese Suppliers with Labor Rules and Inspections. But Many Factories Have Just Gotten Better at Concealing Abuses." *Business Week* (November 27, 2006).

WEBSITES

Economic Policy Institute. <http://www.epinet.org> (accessed November 9, 2007).

History of Economic Thought Website. <http://cepa. newschool.edu/het> (accessed November 9, 2007).

Peterson Institute for International Economics. <http://www.iie.com> (accessed November 9, 2007).

Public Citizen. <http://www.citizen.org> (accessed November 9, 2007).

World Economic Forum. <http://www.weforum.org/ en/index.htm> (accessed November 9, 2007).

PERSONAL MONEY MANAGEMENT

BOOKS

Alford, Ron. *Car Insurance Secrets: The Stuff You Need to Keep You in the Driver's Seat.* Queens, N.Y.: The Plan, 2002.

Altman, Nancy J. *The Battle for Social Security: From FDR's Vision to Bush's Gamble.* Hoboken, N.J.: J. Wiley, 2005.

Davis, Kristin. *Financing College: How Much You'll Really Have to Pay and How to Get the Money.* 3rd ed. Washington, D.C.: Kiplinger Books, 2007.

Ehrenreich, Barbara. *Nickeled and Dimed: On (Not) Getting By in America.* New York: Metropolitan Books, 2001.

Ellenbogen, Michael. *The Insider's Guide to Saving Money.* Victoria, Canada: Trafford Publishing, 2005.

Fives, Theresa, and Holly Popowski. *Getting through College without Going Broke: A Crash Course on Finding Money for College and Making It Last.* New York: Prentice Hall Press, 2005.

Fowles, Debby. *1000 Best Smart Money Secrets for Students.* Naperville, Ill.: Sourcebooks, 2005.

Gary, Tracy. *Inspired Philanthropy: Your Step-by-Step Guide to Creating a Giving Plan and Leaving a Legacy.* 3rd ed. San Francisco: Jossey-Bass, 2008.

Harris, Nancy, and Helen Kothran, eds. *Does the United States Need a National Health Insurance Policy?* Detroit: Greenhaven Press, 2006.

Hock, Dee. *One from Many: Visa and the Rise of the Chaordic Organization.* San Francisco: Berrett-Koehler, 2005.

Jones, Brian T. *Getting Started: The Financial Guide for a Younger Generation.* Potomac, Md.: Larstan Publishing, 2006.

Karger, Howard Jacob. *Shortchanged: Life and Debt in the Fringe Economy.* San Francisco: Berrett-Koehler, 2005.

Modu, Emmanuel, and Andrea Walker. *Mad Cash: A First Timer's Guide to Investing $30 to $3,000.* New York: Penguin Books, 2003.

Newlin, Kate. *Shopportunity: How to Be a Retail Revolutionary.* New York: Collins, 2006.

Orman, Suze. *The Money Book for the Young, Fabulous & Broke.* New York: Riverhead Books, 2005.

Schor, Juliet B. *Born to Buy: The Commercialized Child and the New Consumer Culture.* New York: Scribner, 2005.

Shipler, David K. *The Working Poor: Forgotten in America.* New York: Vintage Books, 2005.

Silver, Don. *High School Money Book.* Los Angeles: Adams-Hall Publishing, 2007.

Weiner, Erik J. *What Goes Up: The Uncensored History of Modern Wall Street as Told by the Bankers, Brokers, CEOs, and Scoundrels Who Made It Happen.* New York: Little, Brown and Co., 2005.

Yancey, Richard. *Confessions of a Tax Collector: One Man's Tour of Duty Inside the IRS.* New York: HarperCollins, 2004.

PERIODICALS

Conlin, Michelle, with Jessi Hempel. "Unmarried America: Say Good-bye to the Traditional Family. Here's How the New Demographics Will Change Business and Society." *Business Week* (October 20, 2003): p. 106.

Der Hovanesian, Mara. "Nightmare Mortgages." *Business Week* (September 11, 2006): p. 70.

Grow, Brian, and Keith Epstein. "The Poverty Business: Inside U.S. Companies' Audacious Drive to Extract More Profits from the Nation's Working Poor." *Business Week* (May 21, 2007): p. 56.

Ordoñez, Jennifer. "Baby Needs a New Pair of Shoes." *Newsweek* (May 14, 2007): p. 50.

Walczak, Lee, and Richard S. Dunham. "'I Want My Safety Net.'" *Business Week* (May 16, 2005): p. 24.

WEBSITES

GoodPayer: Education for Financial Wellness. <http://www.goodpayer.com> (accessed November 9, 2007).

Practical Money Skills for Life. <http://www.practicalmoneyskills.com/english/index.php> (accessed November 9, 2007).

SmartMoney. <http://www.smartmoney.com> (accessed November 9, 2007).

360 Degrees of Financial Literacy. <http://www.360financialliteracy.org> (accessed November 9, 2007).

Young Money. "A leading national money, business and lifestyle magazine written primarily by student journalists." <http://www.youngmoney.com> (accessed November 9, 2007).

ENTREPRENEURSHIP
BOOKS

Adamson, Allen P. *BrandSimple: How the Best Brands Keep It Simple and Succeed.* New York: Palgrave Macmillan, 2006.

Battelle, John. *The Search: How Google and Its Rivals Rewrote the Rules of Business and Transformed Our Culture.* New York: Portfolio, 2005.

Baumol, William J., Robert E. Litan, and Carl J. Schramm. *Good Capitalism, Bad Capitalism, and the Economics of Growth and Prosperity.* New Haven, Conn.: Yale University Press, 2007.

Buchholz, Todd G. *New Ideas from Dead CEOs: Lasting Lessons from the Corner Office.* New York: Collins, 2007.

Cantando, Mary, with Laurie Zuckerman. *Nine Lives: Stories of Women Business Owners Landing on Their Feet.* Raleigh, N.C.: Cantando & Associates, 2003.

Capparell, Stephanie. *The Real Pepsi Challenge: The Inspirational Story of Breaking the Color Barrier in American Business.* New York: Free Press, 2007.

Cobbs, Price M., and Judith L. Turnock. *Cracking the Corporate Code: The Revealing Success Stories of 32 African-American Executives.* New York: American Management Association, 2003.

Conley, Chip, and Eric Friedenwald-Fishman. *Marketing That Matters: 10 Practices to Profit Your Business and Change the World.* San Francisco: Berrett-Koehler, 2006.

Drachman, Virginia G. *Enterprising Women: 250 Years of American Business.* Chapel Hill: University of North Carolina Press, 2002.

Esty, Daniel C., and Andrew S. Winston. *Green to Gold: How Smart Companies Use Environmental Strategy to Innovate, Create Value, and Build Competitive Advantage.* New Haven, Conn.: Yale University Press, 2006.

Evans, Harold, with Gail Buckland and David Lefer. *They Made America: From the Steam Engine to the Search Engine: Two Centuries of Innovators.* New York: Little, Brown and Co., 2004.

Gloor, Peter A., and Scott Cooper. *Coolhunting: Chasing Down the Next Big Thing.* New York: AMACOM, 2007.

Hughes, Mark. *Buzzmarketing: Get People to Talk About Your Stuff.* New York: Portfolio, 2005.

Koehn, Nancy F. *Brand New: How Entrepreneurs Earned Consumers' Trust from Wedgwood to Dell.* Boston: Harvard Business School Press, 2001.

Krass, Peter. *Carnegie.* New Jersey: John Wiley and Sons, 2003.

McCraw, Thomas H. *Prophet of Innovation: Joseph Schumpeter and Creative Destruction.* Cambridge, Mass.: Belknap Press of Harvard University Press, 2007.

Morris, Charles R. *The Tycoons: How Andrew Carnegie, John D. Rockefeller, Jay Gould, and J. P. Morgan Invented the American Supereconomy.* New York: H. Holt and Co., 2005.

Newton, Lisa H. *Permission to Steal: Revealing the Roots of Corporate Scandal.* Malden, Mass.; Oxford: Blackwell Publishing, 2006.

O'Loughlin, James. *The Real Warren Buffet: Managing Capital, Leading People.* London: Nicholas Brealey Publishing, 2003.

Parker, Ciarán. *The Thinkers 50: The World's Most Influential Business Writers and Leaders.* Westport, Conn.: Praeger Publishers, 2006.

Ridgway, Nicole. *The Running of the Bulls: Inside the Cutthroat Race from Wharton to Wall Street.* New York: Gotham Books, 2006.

Savitz, Andrew W., and Karl Weber. *The Triple Bottom Line: How Today's Best-Run Companies Are Achieving Economic, Social and Environmental Success—and How You Can Too.* San Francisco: Jossey-Bass, 2006.

Schiffman, Stephan. *The Young Entrepreneur's Guide to Business Terms.* New York: Franklin Watts, 2003.

Tapscott, Don, and Anthony D. Williams. *Wikinomics: How Mass Collaboration Changes Everything.* New York: Portfolio, 2006.

Watson, Joe. *Without Excuses: Unleash the Power of Diversity to Build Your Business.* New York: St. Martin's Press, 2006.

Zygmont, Jeffrey. *Microchip: An Idea, Its Genesis, and the Revolution It Created.* Cambridge, Mass.: Perseus, 2003.

PERIODICALS

"The Battle for Brainpower." *The Economist* (October 5, 2006).

Byrnes, Nanette. "Secrets of the Male Shopper." *Business Week* (September 4, 2006): p. 44.

Frauenheim, Ed. "Your Co-Worker, Your Teacher: Collaborative Technology Speeds Peer-Peer Learning." *Workforce Management* (January 29, 2007): p. 19.

Grow, Brian. "Hispanic Nation." *Business Week* (March 15, 2004): p. 58.

McGregor, Jena. "How Failure Breeds Success." *Business Week* (July 10, 2006).

WEBSITES

AllBusiness. <http://www.allbusiness.com> (accessed November 9, 2007).

Entrepreneur Magazine. <http://www.entrepreneur.com/> (accessed November 9, 2007).

Franchising.com. <http://www.franchising.com> (accessed November 9, 2007).

Idea Cafe. <http://www.businessownersideacafe.com> (accessed November 9, 2007).

Startup Journal. <http://www.startupjournal.com/> (accessed November 9, 2007).

Index

Italic type indicates volume numbers. Illustrations are marked by (ill.)